THE SACRED BOOKS OF THE EAST

F. MAX MULLER (ED.)

LIST OF THE 50 VOLUMES

1. Upanishads.
2. Sacred Laws of Aryas.
3. Texts of Confucianism.
4. Zend-Avesta.
5. Pahlavi Texts.
6. Qur'an.
7. Institutes of Vishnu.
8. Bhagavadgita, & c.
9. Qur'an.
10. (i) Dhammapada.
10. (ii) Sutta-Nipata.
11. Buddhist Suttas.
12. Satapatha-Brahmana.
13. Vinaya Texts.
14. Sacred Laws of Aryas.
15. Upanishads.
16. Texts of Confucianism.
17. Vinaya Texts.
18. Pahlavi Texts.
19. Fo-sho-hing-tsanking.
20. Vinaya Texts.
21. Saddharma Pundarika.
22. Gaina-Sutras.
23. Zend-Avesta.
24. Pahlavi Texts.
25. Laws of Manu.
26. Satapatha-Brahmana.
27. Texts of Confucianism (Li Ki).
28. Texts of Confucianism (Li Ki).
29. Grihya-Sutras.
30 Grihya-Sutras.
31. Zend-Avesta.
32. Vedic Hymns.
33. Minor Law-Books.
34. Vedanta-Sutras.
35. Milinda.
36. Milinda.
37. Pahlavi Texts.
38. Vedanta-Sutras.
39. Texts of Taoism
40. Texts of Taoism
41. Satapatha-Brahmana
42. Atharva-veda.
43. Satapatha-Brahmana.
44. Satapatha-Brahmana.
45. Gaina-Sutras.
46. Vedic Hymns.
47. Pahlavi Texts.
48. Vedanta-Sutras.
49. (i) Buddhakarita.
49. (ii) Mahayana Texts.
50. A General Index

The Sacred Books of the East Vol. 34

THE VEDANTA-SUTRAS

Edited by

F. MAX MULLER

with the Commentary by

SANKARAKARYA

Translated by

GEORGE THIBAUT

PART-I

GYAN

Published by

Gyan Publishing House
5, Ansari Road
Daryaganj, New Delhi-110002
Phone: 011-47034999, 9811692060
E-mail: books@gyanbooks.com

Distribution Network
gyanbooks.com
India, USA, Canada, UK, Australia, France

ISBN : 978-81-212-2981-4 (Set)
ISBN : 978-81-212-2743-8 (HB)
First Published, 1890

2nd Impression 2021

Printed at: Gyan Press, Delhi.

The Sacred Books of the East Vol. 34

The Vedanta-Sutras, Part-I
Edited by: F. Max Muller, Translated by: George Thibaut

THE

SACRED BOOKS OF THE EAST

TRANSLATED

BY VARIOUS ORIENTAL SCHOLARS

AND EDITED BY

F. MAX MÜLLER

VOL. XXXIV

Oxford

AT THE CLARENDON PRESS

1890

THE

VEDÂNTA-SÛTRAS

WITH THE COMMENTARY BY

*S*AṄKARÂ*K*ÂRYA

TRANSLATED BY

GEORGE THIBAUT

PART I

Oxford

AT THE CLARENDON PRESS

1890

CONTENTS.

INTRODUCTION.

TO the sacred literature of the Brahmans, in the strict sense of the term, i. e. to the Veda, there belongs a certain number of complementary works without whose assistance the student is, according to Hindu notions, unable to do more than commit the sacred texts to memory. In the first place all Vedic texts must, in order to be understood, be read together with running commentaries such as Sâya*n*a's commentaries on the Sa*m*hitâs and Brâhma*n*as, and the Bhâshyas ascribed to *S*ankara on the chief Upanishads. But these commentaries do not by themselves conduce to a full comprehension of the contents of the sacred texts, since they confine themselves to explaining the meaning of each detached passage without investigating its relation to other passages, and the whole of which they form part; considerations of the latter kind are at any rate introduced occasionally only. The task of taking a comprehensive view of the contents of the Vedic writings as a whole, of systematising what they present in an unsystematical form, of showing the mutual co-ordination or subordination of single passages and sections, and of reconciling contradictions—which, according to the view of the orthodox commentators, can be apparent only—is allotted to a separate *s*âstra or body of doctrine which is termed Mîmâ*m*sâ, i. e. the investigation or enquiry *κατ' ἐξοχήν*, viz. the enquiry into the connected meaning of the sacred texts.

Of this Mîmâ*m*sâ two branches have to be distinguished, the so-called earlier (pûrva) Mîmâ*m*sâ, and the later (uttara) Mîmâ*m*sâ. The former undertakes to systematise the karmakâ*nd*a, i. e. that entire portion of the Veda which is concerned with action, pre-eminently sacrificial action, and which comprises the Sa*m*hitâs and the Brâhma*n*as exclusive of the Âra*n*yaka portions; the latter performs the same service with regard to the so-called *gñ*ânakâ*nd*a, i. e. that part of the Vedic writings which includes the Âra*n*yaka portions of the Brâhma*n*as, and a number of detached treatises called Upanishads. Its subject is not action but knowledge, viz. the knowledge of Brahman.

At what period these two *s*âstras first assumed a definite form, we are unable to ascertain. Discussions of the nature of those which constitute the subject-matter of the Pûrva Mîmâ*m*sâ must have arisen at a very early period, and the word Mîmâ*m*sâ itself together with its derivatives is already employed in the Brâhma*n*as to denote the doubts and discussions connected with certain contested points of ritual. The want of a body of definite rules prescribing how to act, i. e. how to perform the various sacrifices in full accordance with the teaching of the Veda, was indeed an urgent one, because it was an altogether practical want, continually pressing itself on the adhvaryus engaged in ritualistic duties. And the task of establishing such rules was moreover a comparatively limited and feasible one; for the members of a certain Vedic *s*âkhâ or school had to do no more than to digest thoroughly their own brâhma*n*a and sa*m*hitâ, without being under any obligation of reconciling with the teaching of their own books the occasionally conflicting rules implied in the texts of other *s*âkhâs. It was assumed that action, as being something which depends on the will and choice of man, admits of alternatives, so that a certain sacrifice may be performed in different ways by members of different Vedic schools, or even by the followers of one and the same *s*âkhâ.

The Uttara Mîmâ*m*sâ-*s*âstra may be supposed to have originated considerably later than the Pûrva Mîmâ*m*sâ. In the first place, the texts with which it is concerned doubtless constitute the latest branch of Vedic literature. And in the second place, the subject-matter of those texts did not call for a systematical treatment with equal urgency, as it was in no way connected with practice; the mental attitude of the authors of the Upanishads, who in their lucubrations on Brahman and the soul aim at nothing less than at definiteness and coherence, may have perpetuated itself through many generations without any great inconvenience resulting therefrom.

But in the long run two causes must have acted with ever-increasing force, to give an impulse to the systematic working up of the teaching of the Upanishads also. The followers of the different Vedic *s*âkhâs no doubt recognised already at an early period the truth that, while conflicting statements regarding the details of a sacrifice can be got over by the assumption of a vikalpa, i. e. an optional proceeding, it is not so with regard to such topics as the nature of Brahman, the relation to it of the human soul, the origin of the physical universe, and the like. Concerning them, one opinion only can be the true one, and it therefore becomes absolutely incumbent on those, who look on the whole body of the Upanishads as revealed truth, to demonstrate that their teaching forms a consistent whole free from all contradictions. In addition there supervened the external motive that, while the karmakâ*nd*a of the Veda concerned only the higher castes of brahmanically constituted society, on which it enjoins certain sacrificial performances connected with certain rewards, the *gñ*ânakâ*nd*a, as propounding a certain theory of the world, towards which any reflecting person inside or outside the pale of the orthodox community could not but take up a definite position, must soon have become the object of criticism on the part of those who held different views on religious and philosophic things, and hence stood in need of systematic defence.

At present there exists a vast literature connected with the two branches of the Mîmâ*m*sâ. We have, on the one hand, all those works which constitute the Pûrva Mîmâ*m*sâ-*s*âstra—or as it is often, shortly but not accurately, termed, the Mîmâ*m*sâ-*s*âstra—and, on the other hand, all those works which are commonly comprised under the name Vedânta-*s*âstra. At the head of this extensive literature there stand two collections of Sûtras (i. e. short aphorisms constituting in their totality a complete body of doctrine upon some subject), whose reputed authors are *G*aimini and Bâdarâya*n*a. There can, however, be no doubt that the composition of those two collections of Sûtras was preceded by a long series of preparatory literary efforts of which they merely represent the highly condensed outcome. This is rendered probable by the analogy of other *s*âstras, as well as by the exhaustive thoroughness with which the Sûtras perform their task of systematising the teaching of the Veda, and is further proved by the frequent references which the Sûtras make to the views of earlier teachers. If we consider merely the preserved monuments of Indian literature, the Sûtras (of the two Mîmâ*m*sâs as well as of other *s*âstras) mark the beginning; if we, however, take into account what once existed, although it is at present irretrievably lost, we observe that they occupy a strictly central position, summarising, on the one hand, a series of early literary essays extending over many generations, and forming, on the other hand, the head spring of an ever broadening activity of commentators as well as virtually independent writers, which reaches down to our days, and may yet have some future before itself.

The general scope of the two Mîmâ*m*sâ-sûtras and their relation to the Veda have been indicated in what precedes. A difference of some importance between the two has, however, to be noted in this connexion. The systematisation of the karmakâ*nd*a of the Veda led to the elaboration of two classes of works, viz. the Kalpa-sûtras on the one hand, and the Pûrva Mîmâ*m*sâ-sûtras on the other hand. The former give nothing but a description as concise as possible of the sacrifices enjoined in the Brâhma*n*as; while the latter discuss and establish the general principles which the author of a Kalpa-sûtra has to follow, if he wishes to render his rules strictly conformable to the teaching of the Veda. The *gñ*ânakâ*nd*a of the Veda, on the other hand, is systematised in a single work, viz. the Uttara Mîmâ*m*sâ or Vedânta-sûtras, which combine the two tasks of concisely stating the teaching of the Veda, and of argumentatively establishing the special interpretation of the Veda adopted in the Sûtras. This difference may be accounted for by two reasons. In the first place, the contents of the karmakâ*nd*a, as being of an entirely practical nature, called for summaries such as the Kalpa-sûtras, from which all burdensome discussions of method are excluded; while there was no similar reason for the separation of the two topics in the case of the purely theoretical science of Brahman. And, in the second place, the Vedânta-sûtras throughout presuppose the Pûrva Mîmâ*m*sâ-sûtras, and may therefore dispense with the discussion of general principles and methods already established in the latter.

The time at which the two Mîmâ*m*sâ-sûtras were composed we are at present unable to fix with any certainty; a few remarks on the subject will, however, be made later on. Their outward form is that common to all the so-called Sûtras which aims at condensing a given body of doctrine in a number of concise aphoristic sentences, and often even mere detached words in lieu of sentences. Besides the Mîmâ*m*sâ-sûtras this literary form is common to the fundamental works on the other philosophic systems, on the Vedic sacrifices, on domestic ceremonies, on sacred law, on grammar, and on metres. The two Mîmâ*m*sâ-sûtras occupy, however, an altogether exceptional position in point of style. All Sûtras aim at conciseness; that is clearly the reason to which this whole species of literary composition owes its existence. This their aim they reach by the rigid exclusion of all words which can possibly be spared, by the careful avoidance of all unnecessary repetitions, and, as in the case of the grammatical Sûtras, by the employment of an arbitrarily coined terminology which substitutes single syllables for entire words or combination of words. At the same time the manifest intention of the Sûtra writers is to express themselves with as much clearness as the conciseness affected by them admits of. The aphorisms are indeed often concise to excess, but not otherwise intrinsically obscure, the manifest care of the writers being to retain what is essential in a given phrase, and to sacrifice only what can be supplied, although perhaps not without difficulty, and an irksome strain of memory and reflection. Hence the possibility of understanding without a commentary a very considerable portion at any rate of the ordinary Sûtras. Altogether different is the case of the two Mîmâ*m*sâ-sûtras. There scarcely one single Sûtra is intelligible without a commentary. The most essential words are habitually dispensed with; nothing is, for instance, more common than the simple omission of the subject or predicate of a sentence. And when here and there a Sûtra occurs whose words construe without anything having to be supplied, the phraseology is so eminently vague and obscure that without the help derived from a commentary we should be unable to make out to what subject the Sûtra refers. When undertaking to translate either of the Mîmâ*m*sâ-sûtras we therefore depend altogether on commentaries; and hence the question arises which of the numerous commentaries extant is to be accepted as a guide to their right understanding.

The commentary here selected for translation, together with Bâdarâya*n*a's Sûtras[1] (to which we shall henceforth confine our attention to the exclusion of *G*aimini's Pûrva Mîmâ*m*sâ-sûtras), is the one composed by the celebrated theologian *S*aṅkara or, as he is commonly called, *S*aṅkarâ-*k*ârya. There are obvious reasons for this selection. In the first place, the *S*aṅkara-bhâshya represents the so-called orthodox side of Brahmanical theology which strictly upholds the Brahman or highest Self of the Upanishads as something different from, and in fact immensely superior to, the divine beings such as Vish*n*u or *S*iva, which, for many centuries, have been the chief objects of popular worship in India. In the second place, the doctrine advocated by *S*aṅkara is, from a purely philosophical point of view and apart from all theological considerations, the most important and interesting one which has arisen on Indian soil; neither those forms of the Vedânta which diverge from the view represented by *S*aṅkara nor any of the non-Vedântic systems can be compared with the so-called orthodox Vedânta in boldness, depth, and subtlety of speculation. In the third place, *S*aṅkara's bhâshya is, as far as we know, the oldest of the extant commentaries, and relative antiquity is at any rate one of the circumstances which have to be

[1] The Sûtras in which the *gñ*ânakâ*nd*a of the Veda is systematised go by various names, being called either Vedânta-sûtras, or Uttara Mîmâ*m*sâ-sûtras, or Brahma-sûtras, or *S*ârîraka Mîmâ*m*sâ-sûtras.

taken into account, although, it must be admitted, too much weight may easily be attached to it. The *S*aṅkara-bhâshya further is the authority most generally deferred to in India as to the right understanding of the Vedânta-sûtras, and ever since *S*aṅkara's time the majority of the best thinkers of India have been men belonging to his school. If in addition to all this we take into consideration the intrinsic merits of *S*aṅkara's work which, as a piece of philosophical argumentation and theological apologetics, undoubtedly occupies a high rank, the preference here given to it will be easily understood.

But to the European—or, generally, modern—translator of the Vedânta-sûtras with *S*aṅkara's commentary another question will of course suggest itself at once, viz. whether or not *S*aṅkara's explanations faithfully render the intended meaning of the author of the Sûtras. To the Indian Pa*nd*it of *S*aṅkara's school this question has become an indifferent one, or, to state the case more accurately, he objects to its being raised, as he looks on *S*aṅkara's authority as standing above doubt and dispute. When pressed to make good his position he will, moreover, most probably not enter into any detailed comparison of *S*aṅkara's comments with the text of Bâdarâya*n*a's Sûtras, but will rather endeavour to show on speculative grounds that *S*aṅkara's philosophical view is the only true one, whence it of course follows that it accurately represents the meaning of Bâdarâya*n*a, who himself must necessarily be assumed to have taught the true doctrine. But on the modern investigator, who neither can consider himself bound by the authority of a name however great, nor is likely to look to any Indian system of thought for the satisfaction of his speculative wants, it is clearly incumbent not to acquiesce from the outset in the interpretations given of the Vedânta-sûtras—and the Upanishads—by *S*aṅkara and his school, but to submit them, as far as that can be done, to a critical investigation.

This is a task which would have to be undertaken even if *S*aṅkara's views as to the true meaning of the Sûtras and Upanishads had never been called into doubt on Indian soil, although in that case it could perhaps hardly be entered upon with much hope of success; but it becomes much more urgent, and at the same time more feasible, when we meet in India itself with systems claiming to be Vedântic and based on interpretations of the Sûtras and Upanishads more or less differing from those of *S*ankara. The claims of those systems to be in the possession of the right understanding of the fundamental authorities of the Vedânta must at any rate be examined, even if we should finally be compelled to reject them.

It appears that already at a very early period the Vedânta-sûtras had come to be looked upon as an authoritative work, not to be neglected by any who wished to affiliate their own doctrines to the Veda. At present, at any rate, there are very few Hindu sects not interested in showing that their distinctive tenets are countenanced by Bâdarâya*n*a's teaching. Owing to this the commentaries on the Sûtras have in the course of time become very numerous, and it is at present impossible to give a full and accurate enumeration even of those actually existing, much less of those referred to and quoted. Mr. Fitz-Edward Hall, in his Bibliographical Index, mentions fourteen commentaries, copies of which had been inspected by himself. Some among these (as, for instance, Râmânu*g*a's Vedânta-sâra, No. XXXV) are indeed not commentaries in the strict sense of the word, but rather systematic expositions of the doctrine supposed to be propounded in the Sûtras; but, on the other hand, there are in existence several true commentaries which had not been accessible to Fitz-Edward Hall. It would hardly be practical—and certainly not feasible in this place—to submit all the existing bhâshyas to a critical enquiry at once. All we can do here is to single out one or a few of the more important ones, and to compare their interpretations with those given by *S*ankara, and with the text of the Sûtras themselves.

The bhâshya, which in this connexion is the first to press itself upon our attention, is the one composed by the famous Vaish*n*ava theologian and philosopher Râmânu*g*a, who is supposed to have lived in the twelfth century. The Râmânu*g*a or, as it is often called, the *S*rî-bhâshya appears to be the oldest commentary extant next to *S*aṅkara's. It is further to be noted that the sect of the Râmânu*g*as occupies a pre-eminent position among the Vaish*n*ava sects which themselves, in their totality, may claim to be considered the most important among all Hindu sects. The intrinsic value of the *S*rî-bhâshya moreover is—as every student acquainted with it will be ready to acknowledge—a very high one; it strikes one throughout as a very solid performance due to a writer of extensive learning and great power of argumentation, and in its polemic parts, directed chiefly against the school of *S*aṅkara, it not unfrequently deserves to be called brilliant even. And in addition to all this it shows evident traces of being not the mere outcome of Râmânu*g*a's individual views, but of resting on an old and weighty tradition.

This latter point is clearly of the greatest importance. If it could be demonstrated or even rendered probable only that the oldest bhâshya which we possess, i. e. the *S*aṅkâra-bhâshya, represents an uninterrupted and uniform tradition bridging over the interval between Bâdarâya*n*a, the reputed author of the Sûtras, and *S*aṅkara; and if, on the other hand, it could be shown that the more modern bhâshyas are not supported by old tradition, but are nothing more than bold attempts of clever sectarians to force an old work of generally recognised authority into the service of their individual tenets; there would certainly be no reason for us to raise the question whether the later bhâshyas can help us in making out the true meaning of the Sûtras. All we should have to do in that case would be to accept *S*aṅkara's interpretations as they stand, or at the utmost to attempt to make out, if at all possible, by a careful comparison of *S*aṅkara's bhâshya with the text of the Sûtras, whether the former in all cases faithfully represents the purport of the latter.

In the most recent book of note which at all enters into the question as to how far we have to accept *S*aṅkara as a guide to the right understanding of the Sûtras (Mr. A. Gough's Philosophy of the Upanishads) the view is maintained (pp. 239 ff.) that *S*aṅkara is the generally recognised expositor of true Vedânta doctrine, that that doctrine was handed down by an unbroken series of teachers intervening between him and the Sûtrakâra, and that there existed from the beginning only one Vedânta doctrine, agreeing in all essential points with the doctrine known to us from *S*ankara's writings. Mr. Gough undertakes to prove this view, firstly, by a comparison of *S*ankara's system with the teaching of the Upanishads themselves; and, secondly, by a comparison of the purport of the Sûtras—as far as that can be made out independently of the commentaries—with the interpretations given of them by *S*ankara. To both these points we shall revert later on. Meanwhile, I only wish to remark concerning the former point that, even if we could show with certainty that all the Upanishads propound one and the same doctrine, there yet remains the undeniable fact of our being confronted by a considerable number of essentially differing theories, all of which claim to be founded on the Upanishads. And with regard to the latter point I have to say for the present that, as long as we have only *S*ankara's bhâshya before us, we are naturally inclined to find in the Sûtras—which, taken by themselves, are for the greater part unintelligible—the meaning which *S*ankara ascribes to them; while a reference to other bhâshyas may not impossibly change our views at once.—Meanwhile, we will consider the question as to the unbroken uniformity of Vedântic tradition from another point of view, viz. by enquiring whether or not the Sûtras themselves, and the *S*ankara-bhâshya, furnish any indications of there having existed already at an early time essentially different Vedântic systems or lines of Vedântic speculation.

Beginning with the Sûtras, we find that they supply ample evidence to the effect that already at a very early time, viz. the period antecedent to the final composition of the Vedânta-sûtras in their present shape, there had arisen among the chief doctors of the Vedânta differences of opinion, bearing not only upon minor points of doctrine, but affecting the most essential parts of the system. In addition to Bâdarâya*n*a himself, the reputed author of the

Sûtras, the latter quote opinions ascribed to the following teachers: Âtreya, Âsmarathya, Au*d*ulomi, Kârsh*n*â*g*ini, Kâ*s*ak*ri*tsna, *G*aimini, Bâdari. Among the passages where diverging views of those teachers are recorded and contrasted three are of particular importance. Firstly, a passage in the fourth pâda of the fourth adhyâya (Sûtras 5–7), where the opinions of various teachers concerning the characteristics of the released soul are given, and where the important discrepancy is noted that, according to Au*d*ulomi, its only characteristic is thought (*k*aitanya), while *G*aimini maintains that it possesses a number of exalted qualities, and Bâdarâya*n*a declares himself in favour of a combination of those two views.—The second passage occurs in the third pâda of the fourth adhyâya (Sûtras 7–14), where *G*aimini maintains that the soul of him who possesses the lower knowledge of Brahman goes after death to the highest Brahman, while Bâdari—whose opinion is endorsed by *S*aṅkara—teaches that it repairs to the lower Brahman only.—Finally, the third and most important passage is met with in the fourth pâda of the first adhyâya (Sûtras 20–22), where the question is discussed why in a certain passage of the B*ri*hadâra*n*yaka Brahman is referred to in terms which are strictly applicable to the individual soul only. In connexion therewith the Sûtras quote the views of three ancient teachers about the relation in which the individual soul stands to Brahman. According to Â*s*marathya (if we accept the interpretation of his view given by *S*aṅkara and *S*aṅkara's commentators) the soul stands to Brahman in the bhedâbheda relation, i.e. it is neither absolutely different nor absolutely non-different from it, as sparks are from fire. Au*d*ulomi, on the other hand, teaches that the soul is altogether different from Brahman up to the time when obtaining final release it is merged in it; and Kâ*s*ak*ri*tsna finally upholds the doctrine that the soul is absolutely non-different from Brahman, which in some way or other presents itself as the individual soul.

That the ancient teachers, the ripest outcome of whose speculations and discussions is embodied in the Vedânta-sûtras, disagreed among themselves on points of vital importance is sufficiently proved by the three passages quoted. The one quoted last is specially significant as showing that recognised authorities—deemed worthy of being quoted in the Sûtras—denied that doctrine on which the whole system of *S*ankara hinges, viz. the doctrine of the absolute identity of the individual soul with Brahman.

Turning next to the *S*ankara-bhâshya itself, we there also meet with indications that the Vedântins were divided among themselves on important points of dogma. These indications are indeed not numerous: *S*ankara does not on the whole impress one as an author particularly anxious to strengthen his own case by appeals to ancient authorities, a peculiarity of his which later writers of hostile tendencies have not failed to remark and criticise. But yet more than once *S*ankara also refers to the opinion of 'another,' viz., commentator of the Sûtras, and in several places *S*ankara's commentators explain that the 'other' meant is the V*ri*ttikâra (about whom more will be said shortly). Those references as a rule concern minor points of exegesis, and hence throw little or no light on important differences of dogma; but there are two remarks of *S*ankara's at any rate which are of interest in this connexion. The one is made with reference to Sûtras 7–14 of the third pâda of the fourth adhyâya; 'some,' he says there, 'declare those Sûtras, which I look upon as setting forth the siddhânta view, to state merely the pûrvapaksha;' a difference of opinion which, as we have seen above, affects the important question as to the ultimate fate of those who have not reached the knowledge of the highest Brahman.—And under I, 3, 19 *S*ankara, after having explained at length that the individual soul as such cannot claim any reality, but is real only in so far as it is identical with Brahman, adds the following words, 'apare tu vâdina*h* pâramârthikam eva *g*aiva*m* rûpam iti manyante asmadîyâ*s k*a ke*k*it,' i. e. 'other theorisers again, and among them some of ours, are of opinion that the individual soul as such is real.' The term 'ours,' here made use of, can denote only the Aupanishadas or Vedântins, and it thus appears that *S*ankara himself was willing to class under the same category himself and philosophers who—as in later times the Râmânu*g*as and others—looked upon the individual soul as not due to the fictitious limitations of Mâyâ, but as real in itself; whatever may be the relation in which they considered it to stand to the highest Self.

From what precedes it follows that the Vedântins of the school to which *S*ankara himself belonged acknowledged the existence of Vedântic teaching of a type essentially different from their own. We must now proceed to enquire whether the Râmânu*g*a system, which likewise claims to be Vedânta, and to be founded on the Vedânta-sûtras, has any title to be considered an ancient system and the heir of a respectable tradition.

It appears that Râmânu*g*a claims—and by Hindu writers is generally admitted—to follow in his bhâshya the authority of Bodhâyana, who had composed a v*ri*tti on the Sûtras. Thus we read in the beginning of the *S*rî-bhâshya (Pa*nd*it, New Series, VII, p. 163), 'Bhagavad-bodhâyana-k*ri*tâ*m* vistîr*n*âm brahmasûtra-v*ri*tti*m* pûrvâ*k*âryâ*h* sa*mk*ikshipus tanmatânusâre*n*a sûtrâksharâ*n*i vyâkhyâsyante.' Whether the Bodhâyana to whom that v*ri*tti is ascribed is to be identified with the author of the Kalpa-sûtra, and other works, cannot at present be decided. But that an ancient v*ri*tti on the Sûtras connected with Bodhâyana's name actually existed, there is not any reason to doubt. Short quotations from it are met with in a few places of the *S*rî-bhâshya, and, as we have seen above, *S*ankara's commentators state that their author's polemical remarks are directed against the V*ri*ttikâra. In addition to Bodhâyana, Râmânu*g*a appeals to quite a series of ancient teachers—pûrvâ*k*âryâs—who carried on the true tradition as to the teaching of the Vedânta and the meaning of the Sûtras. In the Vedârthasangraha —a work composed by Râmânu*g*a himself—we meet in one place with the enumeration of the following authorities: Bodhâyana, *T*anka, Drami*d*a, Guhadeva, Kapardin, Bharu*k*i, and quotations from the writings of some of these are not unfrequent in the Vedârthasangraha, as well as the *S*rî-bhâshya. The author most frequently quoted is Dramida[1], who composed the Dramida-bhâshya; he is sometimes referred to as the bhâshyakâra. Another writer repeatedly quoted as the vâkyakâra is, I am told[2], to be identified with the *T*aṅka mentioned above. I refrain from inserting in this place the information concerning the relative age of these writers which may be derived from the oral tradition of the Râmânu*g*a sect. From another source, however, we receive an intimation that Dramidâ*k*ârya or Dravidâ*k*ârya preceded *S*aṅkara in point of time. In his *t*îkâ on *S*aṅkara's bhâshya to the *K*hândogya Upanishad III, 10, 4, Ânandagiri remarks that the attempt made by his author to reconcile the cosmological views of the Upanishad with the teaching of Sm*ri*ti on the same point is a reproduction of the analogous attempt made by the Dravidâ*k*ârya.

It thus appears that that special interpretation of the Vedânta-sûtras with which the *S*rî-bhâshya makes us acquainted is not due to innovating views on the part of Râmânu*g*a, but had authoritative representatives already at a period anterior to that of *S*aṅkara. This latter point, moreover, receives additional confirmation from the relation in which the so-called Râmânu*g*a sect stands to earlier sects. What the exact position of Râmânu*g*a was, and of what nature were the reforms that rendered him so prominent as to give his name to a new sect, is not exactly known at present; at the same time it is generally acknowledged that the Râmânu*g*as are closely connected with the so-called Bhâgavatas or Pâ*ñk*arâtras, who are known to have existed already at a very early time. This latter point is proved by evidence of various kinds; for our present purpose it suffices to point to the fact that, according to the interpretation of the most authoritative commentators, the last

[1] The name of this writer is sometimes given as Dramida, sometimes as Dravida. In the opinion of Pa*nd*it Râma Mi*s*ra *S*âstrin of the Benares College—himself a Râmânu*g*a and thoroughly conversant with the books and traditions of his sect—the form 'Dramida' is the correct one.

[2] Viz. by Pa*nd*it Râma Mi*s*ra *S*âstrin. As the Pa*nd*it intends himself to publish all the traditional information he possesses concerning the history of the Bhâgavatas and Râmânu*g*as, I limit myself in the text to stating the most relevant results of my study of the *S*rî-bhâshya and the Vedârthasaṅgraha.

Sûtras of the second pâda of the second adhyâya (Vedânta-sûtras) refer to a distinctive tenet of the Bhâgavatas—which tenet forms part of the Râmânuga system also—viz. that the highest being manifests itself in a fourfold form (vyûha) as Vâsudeva, Saṅkarsha*n*a, Pradyumna, Aniruddha, those four forms being identical with the highest Self, the individual soul, the internal organ (manas), and the principle of egoity (ahaṅkâra). Whether those Sûtras embody an approval of the tenet referred to, as Râmânuga maintains, or are meant to impugn it, as *S*aṅkara thinks; so much is certain that in the opinion of the best commentators the Bhâgavatas, the direct forerunners of the Râmânugas, are mentioned in the Sûtras themselves, and hence must not only have existed, but even reached a considerable degree of importance at the time when the Sûtras were composed. And considering the general agreement of the systems of the earlier Bhâgavatas and the later Râmânugas, we have a full right to suppose that the two sects were at one also in their mode of interpreting the Vedânta-sûtras.

The preceding considerations suffice, I am inclined to think, to show that it will by no means be wasted labour to enquire how Râmânuga interprets the Sûtras, and wherein he differs from *S*aṅkara. This in fact seems clearly to be the first step we have to take, if we wish to make an attempt at least of advancing beyond the interpretations of scholiasts to the meaning of the Sûtras themselves. A full and exhaustive comparison of the views of the two commentators would indeed far exceed the limits of the space which can here be devoted to that task, and will, moreover, be made with greater ease and advantage when the complete Sanskrit text of the *S*rî-bhâshya has been printed, and thus made available for general reference. But meanwhile it is possible, and—as said before—even urged upon a translator of the Sûtras to compare the interpretations, given by the two bhâshyakâras, of those Sûtras, which, more than others, touch on the essential points of the Vedânta system [1]. This

[1] Owing to the importance of the *S*aṅkara-bhâshya as the fundamental work of the most influential Hindu school of philosophy, the number of topics which might be discussed in the introduction to its translation is considerable. But

will best be done in connexion with a succinct but full review of the topics discussed in the adhikara*n*as of the Vedânta-sûtras, according to *S*aṅkara; a review which—apart from the side-glances at Râmânu*g*a's comments—will be useful as a guide through the Sûtras and the *S*aṅkara-bhâshya. Before, however, entering on that task, I think it advisable to insert short sketches of the philosophical systems of *S*aṅkara as well as of Râmânu*g*a, which may be referred to when, later on, discrepancies between the two commentators will be noted. In these sketches I shall confine myself to the leading features, and not enter into any details. Of *S*aṅkara's system we possess as it is more than one trustworthy exposition; it may suffice to refer to Deussen's System of the Vedânta, in which the details of the entire system, as far as they can be learned from the Sûtra-bhâshya, are represented fully and faithfully, and to Gough's Philosophy of the Upanishads which, principally in its second chapter, gives a lucid sketch of the *S*âṅkara Vedânta, founded on the Sûtra-bhâshya, the Upanishad bhâshyas, and some later writers belonging to *S*aṅkara's school. With regard to Râmânu*g*a's philosophy our chief source was, hitherto, the Râmânu*g*a chapter in the Sarvadar*s*a*n*asa*m*graha; the short sketch about to be given is founded altogether on the *S*rî-bhâshya itself.

What in *S*aṅkara's opinion the Upanishads teach, is shortly as follows.—Whatever is, is in reality one; there truly exists only one universal being called Brahman or Paramâtman, the highest Self. This being is of an absolutely homogeneous nature; it is pure 'Being,' or, which comes to the same, pure intelligence or thought (*k*aitanya,

the limitation of the space at our disposal necessitates a selection, and it can hardly be doubted that, among the possible tasks of a translator, that of ascertaining how far the teaching of *S*aṅkara agrees with that of Bâdarâya*n*a, and, further, how far either of them represents the true doctrine of the Upanishads, is the one first to be taken in hand.—Some other topics, such as a detailed account of *S*aṅkara's teaching according to the bhâshya, an enquiry as to the books and authors quoted by *S*aṅkara, &c., have, moreover, been treated not long ago in a very thorough fashion by Dr. Deussen in his 'System des Vedânta.'

*g*ñâna). Intelligence or thought is not to be predicated of Brahman as its attribute, but constitutes its substance; Brahman is not a thinking being, but thought itself. It is absolutely destitute of qualities; whatever qualities or attributes are conceivable, can only be denied of it.—But, if nothing exists but one absolutely simple being, whence the appearance of the world by which we see ourselves surrounded, and in which we ourselves exist as individual beings?—Brahman, the answer runs, is associated with a certain power called Mâyâ or avidyâ to which the appearance of this entire world is due. This power cannot be called 'being' (sat), for 'being' is only Brahman; nor can it be called 'non-being' (asat) in the strict sense, for it at any rate produces the appearance of this world. It is in fact a principle of illusion; the undefinable cause owing to which there seems to exist a material world comprehending distinct individual existences. Being associated with this principle of illusion, Brahman is enabled to project the appearance of the world, in the same way as a magician is enabled by his incomprehensible magical power to produce illusory appearances of animate and inanimate beings. Mâyâ thus constitutes the upâdâna, the material cause of the world; or —if we wish to call attention to the circumstance that Mâyâ belongs to Brahman as a *s*akti—we may say that the material cause of the world is Brahman in so far as it is associated with Mâyâ. In this latter quality Brahman is more properly called Î*s*vara, the Lord.

Mâyâ, under the guidance of the Lord, modifies itself by a progressive evolution into all the individual existences (bheda), distinguished by special names and forms, of which the world consists; from it there spring in due succession the different material elements and the whole bodily apparatus belonging to sentient beings. In all those apparently individual forms of existence the one indivisible Brahman is present, but, owing to the particular adjuncts into which Mâyâ has specialised itself, it appears to be broken up—it is broken up, as it were—into a multiplicity of intellectual or sentient principles, the so-called *g*îvas (individual or personal souls). What is real in each *g*îva is only the universal Brahman itself; the whole aggregate of individualising bodily organs and mental functions, which in our ordinary experience separate and distinguish one *g*îva from another, is the offspring of Mâyâ and as such unreal.

The phenomenal world or world of ordinary experience (vyavahâra) thus consists of a number of individual souls engaged in specific cognitions, volitions, and so on, and of the external material objects with which those cognitions and volitions are concerned. Neither the specific cognitions nor their objects are real in the true sense of the word, for both are altogether due to Mâyâ. But at the same time we have to reject the idealistic doctrine of certain Bauddha schools according to which nothing whatever truly exists, but certain trains of cognitional acts or ideas to which no external objects correspond; for external things, although not real in the strict sense of the word, enjoy at any rate as much reality as the specific cognitional acts whose objects they are.

The non-enlightened soul is unable to look through and beyond Mâyâ, which, like a veil, hides from it its true nature. Instead of recognising itself to be Brahman, it blindly identifies itself with its adjuncts (upâdhi), the fictitious offspring of Mâyâ, and thus looks for its true Self in the body, the sense organs, and the internal organ (manas), i.e. the organ of specific cognition. The soul, which in reality is pure intelligence, non-active, infinite, thus becomes limited in extent, as it were, limited in knowledge and power, an agent and enjoyer. Through its actions it burdens itself with merit and demerit, the consequences of which it has to bear or enjoy in series of future embodied existences, the Lord—as a retributor and dispenser—allotting to each soul that form of embodiment to which it is entitled by its previous actions. At the end of each of the great world periods called kalpas the Lord retracts the whole world, i.e. the whole material world is dissolved and merged into non-distinct Mâyâ, while the individual souls, free for the time from actual connexion with upâdhis, lie in deep slumber as it were. But as the consequences of their former deeds are not yet exhausted, they have again to enter on embodied existence as soon as the Lord sends forth a new material world, and the old round of birth, action, death begins anew to last to all eternity as it has lasted from all eternity.

The means of escaping from this endless sa*m*sâra, the way out of which can never be found by the non-enlightened soul, are furnished by the Veda. The karmakâ*nd*a indeed, whose purport it is to enjoin certain actions, cannot lead to final release; for even the most meritorious works necessarily lead to new forms of embodied existence. And in the *gñ*ânakâ*nd*a of the Veda also two different parts have to be distinguished, viz., firstly, those chapters and passages which treat of Brahman in so far as related to the world, and hence characterised by various attributes, i.e. of Î*s*vara or the lower Brahman; and, secondly, those texts which set forth the nature of the highest Brahman transcending all qualities, and the fundamental identity of the individual soul with that highest Brahman. Devout meditation on Brahman as suggested by passages of the former kind does not directly lead to final emancipation; the pious worshipper passes on his death into the world of the lower Brahman only, where he continues to exist as a distinct individual soul—although in the enjoyment of great power and knowledge—until at last he reaches the highest knowledge, and, through it, final release.—That student of the Veda, on the other hand, whose soul has been enlightened by the texts embodying the higher knowledge of Brahman, whom passages such as the great saying, 'That art thou,' have taught that there is no difference between his true Self and the highest Self, obtains at the moment of death immediate final release, i.e. he withdraws altogether from the influence of Mâyâ, and asserts himself in his true nature, which is nothing else but the absolute highest Brahman.

Thus *S*ankara.—According to Râmânu*g*a, on the other hand, the teaching of the Upanishads has to be summarised as follows.—There exists only one all-embracing being called Brahman or the highest Self or the Lord. This being is not destitute of attributes, but rather endowed with all imaginable auspicious qualities. It is not 'intelligence,'—as *S*aṅkara maintains,—but intelligence is its chief attribute. The Lord is all-pervading, all-powerful, all-knowing, all-merciful; his nature is fundamentally antagonistic to all evil. He contains within himself whatever exists. While, according to *S*aṅkara, the only reality is to be found in the non-qualified homogeneous highest Brahman which can only be defined as pure 'Being' or pure thought, all plurality being a mere illusion; Brahman—according to Râmânu*g*a's view—comprises within itself distinct elements of plurality which all of them lay claim to absolute reality of one and the same kind. Whatever is presented to us by ordinary experience, viz. matter in all its various modifications and the individual souls of different classes and degrees, are essential real constituents of Brahman's nature. Matter and souls (a*k*it and *k*it) constitute, according to Râmânu*g*a's terminology, the body of the Lord; they stand to him in the same relation of entire dependence and subserviency in which the matter forming an animal or vegetable body stands to its soul or animating principle. The Lord pervades and rules all things which exist—material or immaterial—as their antaryâmin; the fundamental text for this special Râmânu*g*a tenet—which in the writings of the sect is quoted again and again—is the so-called antaryâmin brâhma*n*a (B*ri*. Up. III, 7) which says, that within all elements, all sense organs, and, lastly, within all individual souls, there abides an inward ruler whose body those elements, sense-organs, and individual souls constitute.—Matter and souls as forming the body of the Lord are also called modes of him (prakâra). They are to be looked upon as his effects, but they have enjoyed the kind of individual existence which is theirs from all eternity, and will never be entirely resolved into Brahman. They, however, exist in two different, periodically alternating, conditions. At some times they exist in a subtle state in which they do not possess those qualities by which they are ordinarily known, and there is then no distinction of individual name and form. Matter in that state is unevolved (avyakta); the individual souls are not joined to material bodies, and their intelligence is in a state of contraction, non-manifestation (sankoka). This is the pralaya state which recurs at the end of each kalpa, and Brahman is then said to be in its causal condition (kâranâvasthâ). To that state all those scriptural passages refer which speak of Brahman or the Self as being in the beginning one only, without a second. Brahman then is indeed not absolutely one, for it contains within itself matter and souls in a germinal condition; but as in that condition they are so subtle as not to allow of individual distinctions being made, they are not counted as something second in addition to Brahman.—When the pralaya state comes to an end, creation takes place owing to an act of volition on the Lord's part. Primary unevolved matter then passes over into its other condition; it becomes gross and thus acquires all those sensible attributes, visibility, tangibility, and so on, which are known from ordinary experience. At the same time the souls enter into connexion with material bodies corresponding to the degree of merit or demerit acquired by them in previous forms of existence; their intelligence at the same time undergoes a certain expansion (vikâsa). The Lord, together with matter in its gross state and the 'expanded' souls, is Brahman in the condition of an effect (kâryâvasthâ). Cause and effect are thus at the bottom the same; for the effect is nothing but the cause which has undergone a certain change (parinâma). Hence the cause being known, the effect is known likewise.

Owing to the effects of their former actions the individual souls are implicated in the samsâra, the endless cycle of birth, action, and death, final escape from which is to be obtained only through the study of the *gñâna*-kânda of the Veda. Compliance with the injunctions of the karmakânda does not lead outside the samsâra; but he who, assisted by the grace of the Lord, cognizes—and meditates on—him in the way prescribed by the Upanishads reaches at his death final emancipation, i.e. he passes through the different stages of the path of the gods up to the world of Brahman and there enjoys an everlasting blissful existence from which there is no return into the sphere of transmigration. The characteristics of the released soul are similar to those of Brahman; it participates in all the latter's glorious qualities and powers, excepting only Brahman's power to emit, rule, and retract the entire world.

The chief points in which the two systems sketched above agree on the one hand and diverge on the other may be shortly stated as follows.—Both systems teach advaita, i.e. non-duality or monism. There exist not several fundamentally distinct principles, such as the prakriti and the purushas of the Sâṅkhyas, but there exists only one all-embracing being. While, however, the advaita taught by Saṅkara is a rigorous, absolute one, Râmânuga's doctrine has to be characterised as visishta advaita, i.e. qualified non-duality, non-duality with a difference. According to Saṅkara, whatever is, is Brahman, and Brahman itself is absolutely homogeneous, so that all difference and plurality must be illusory. According to Râmânuga also, whatever is, is Brahman; but Brahman is not of a homogeneous nature, but contains within itself elements of plurality owing to which it truly manifests itself in a diversified world. The world with its variety of material forms of existence and individual souls is not unreal Mâyâ, but a real part of Brahman's nature, the body investing the universal Self. The Brahman of Saṅkara is in itself impersonal, a homogeneous mass of objectless thought, transcending all attributes; a personal God it becomes only through its association with the unreal principle of Mâyâ, so that—strictly speaking—Saṅkara's personal God, his Îsvara, is himself something unreal. Râmânuga's Brahman, on the other hand, is essentially a personal God, the all-powerful and all-wise ruler of a real world permeated and animated by his spirit. There is thus no room for the distinction between a param nirgunam and an aparam sagunam brahma, between Brahman and Îsvara.—Saṅkara's individual soul is Brahman in so far as limited by the unreal upâdhis due to Mâyâ. The individual soul of Râmânuga, on the other hand, is really individual; it has indeed sprung from Brahman and is never outside Brahman, but nevertheless it enjoys a separate personal existence and will remain a personality for ever.—The release from sa*m*sâra means, according to *S*aṅkara, the absolute merging of the individual soul in Brahman, due to the dismissal of the erroneous notion that the soul is distinct from Brahman; according to Râmânu*g*a it only means the soul's passing from the troubles of earthly life into a kind of heaven or paradise where it will remain for ever in undisturbed personal bliss.—As Râmânu*g*a does not distinguish a higher and lower Brahman, the distinction of a higher and lower knowledge is likewise not valid for him; the teaching of the Upanishads is not twofold but essentially one, and leads the enlightened devotee to one result only [1].

I now proceed to give a conspectus of the contents of the Vedânta-sûtras according to *S*aṅkara in which at the same time all the more important points concerning which Râmânu*g*a disagrees will be noted. We shall here have to enter into details which to many may appear tedious. But it is only on a broad substratum of accurately stated details that we can hope to establish any definite conclusions regarding the comparative value of the different modes of interpretation which have been applied to the Sûtras. The line of investigation is an entirely new one, and for the present nothing can be taken for granted or known.—In stating the different heads of discussion (the so-called adhikara*n*as), each of which comprises one or more Sûtras, I shall follow the subdivision into adhikara*n*as adopted in the Vyâsâdhikara*n*amâlâ, the text of which is printed in the second volume of the Bibliotheca Indica edition of the Sûtras.

[1] The only 'sectarian' feature of the *S*rî-bhâshya is, that it identifies Brahman with Vish*n*u or Nârâya*n*a; but this in no way affects the interpretations put on the Sûtras and Upanishads. Nârâya*n*a is in fact nothing but another name of Brahman.

FIRST ADHYÂYA.

PÂDA I.

The first five adhikaranas lay down the fundamental positions with regard to Brahman. Adhik. I (1)[1] treats of what the study of the Vedânta presupposes. Adhik. II (2) defines Brahman as that whence the world originates, and so on. Adhik. III (3) declares that Brahman is the source of the Veda. Adhik. IV (4) proves Brahman to be the uniform topic of all Vedânta-texts. Adhik. V (5–11) is engaged in proving by various arguments that the Brahman, which the Vedânta-texts represent as the cause of the world, is an intelligent principle, and cannot be identified with the non-intelligent pradhâna from which the world springs according to the Sâṅkhyas.

With the next adhikarana there begins a series of discussions of essentially similar character, extending up to the end of the first adhyâya. The question is throughout whether certain terms met with in the Upanishads denote Brahman or some other being, in most cases the *g*îva, the individual soul. *S*aṅkara remarks at the outset that, as the preceding ten Sûtras had settled the all-important point that all the Vedânta-texts refer to Brahman, the question now arises why the enquiry should be continued any further, and thereupon proceeds to explain that the acknowledged distinction of a higher Brahman devoid of all qualities and a lower Brahman characterised by qualities necessitates an investigation whether certain Vedic texts of primâ facie doubtful import set forth the lower Brahman as the object of devout meditation, or the higher Brahman as the object of true knowledge. But that such an investigation is actually carried on in the remaining portion of the first adhyâya, appears neither from the wording of the Sûtras nor even from *S*aṅkara's own treatment of the Vedic

[1] The Roman numerals indicate the number of the adhikarana; the figures in parentheses state the Sûtras comprised in each adhikarana.

texts referred to in the Sûtras. In I, 1, 20, for instance, the question is raised whether the golden man within the sphere of the sun, with golden hair and beard and lotus-coloured eyes—of whom the *Kh*ândogya Upanishad speaks in I, 6, 6—is an individual soul abiding within the sun or the highest Lord. *S*aṅkara's answer is that the passage refers to the Lord, who, for the gratification of his worshippers, manifests himself in a bodily shape made of Mâyâ. So that according to *S*aṅkara himself the alternative lies between the sagu*n*a Brahman and some particular individual soul, not between the sagu*n*a Brahman and the nirgu*n*a Brahman.

Adhik. VI (12–19) raises the question whether the ânandamaya, mentioned in Taittirîya Upanishad II, 5, is merely a transmigrating individual soul or the highest Self. *S*aṅkara begins by explaining the Sûtras on the latter supposition—and the text of the Sûtras is certainly in favour of that interpretation—gives, however, finally the preference to a different and exceedingly forced explanation according to which the Sûtras teach that the ânandamaya is not Brahman, since the Upanishad expressly says that Brahman is the tail or support of the ânandamaya[1].—Râmânu*g*a's interpretation of Adhikara*n*a VI, although not agreeing in all particulars with the former explanation of *S*aṅkara, yet is at one with it in the chief point, viz. that the ânandamaya is Brahman. It further deserves notice that, while *S*aṅkara looks on Adhik. VI as the first of a series of interpretatory discussions, all of which treat the question whether certain Vedic passages refer to Brahman or not, Râmânu*g*a separates the adhikara*n*a from the subsequent part of the pâda and connects it with what had preceded. In Adhik. V it had been shown that Brahman cannot be

[1] Deussen's supposition (pp. 30, 150) that the passage conveying the second interpretation is an interpolation is liable to two objections. In the first place, the passage is accepted and explained by all commentators; in the second place, *S*aṅkara in the passage immediately preceding Sûtra 12 quotes the adhikara*n*a 'ânandamayo ' bhyâsât' as giving rise to a discussion whether the param or the aparam brahman is meant. Now this latter point is not touched upon at all in that part of the bhâshya which sets forth the former explanation, but only in the subsequent passage, which refutes the former and advocates the latter interpretation.

identified with the pradhâna; Adhik. VI shows that it is different from the individual soul, and the proof of the fundamental position of the system is thereby completed [1].—Adhik. VII (20, 21) demonstrates that the golden person seen within the sun and the person seen within the eye, mentioned in *Kh*. Up. I, 6, are not some individual soul of high eminence, but the supreme Brahman.—Adhik. VIII (22) teaches that by the ether from which, according to *Kh*. Up. I, 9, all beings originate, not the elemental ether has to be understood but the highest Brahman.—Adhik. IX (23). The prâ*n*a also mentioned in *Kh*. Up. I, 11, 5 denotes the highest Brahman [2].—Adhik. X (24–27) teaches that the light spoken of in *Kh*. Up. III, 13, 7 is not the ordinary physical light but the highest Brahman [3].—Adhik. XI (28–31) decides that the prâ*n*a mentioned in Kau. Up. III, 2 is Brahman.

Pâda II.

Adhik. I (1–8) shows that the being which consists of mind, whose body is breath, &c., mentioned in *Kh*. Up. III, 14, is not the individual soul, but Brahman. The Sûtras of this adhikara*n*a emphatically dwell on the difference of the individual soul and the highest Self, whence *S*aṅkara is obliged to add an explanation—in his comment on Sûtra 6—to the effect that that difference is to be understood as not real, but as due to the false limiting adjuncts of the highest Self.—The comment of Râmânuga throughout closely follows the words of the Sûtras; on Sûtra 6 it simply remarks that the difference of the highest Self

[1] Eva*m* *g*i*gñ*asitasya brahma*n*a*s* *k*etanabhogyabhûta*g*a*d*arûpasattvara*g*astamomayapradhânâd vyâv*ri*ttir uktâ, idânî*m* karmava*s*yât trigu*n*âtmakaprak*ri*tisa*m*sarganimittanânâvidhânantadukhasâgaranima*gg*anenâ*s*uddhâ*k* *k*a pratyagâtmano*s*nyan nikhilaheyapratyanîka*m* nirati*s*ayânandam brahmeti pratipâdyate, ânandamayo*s*bhyâsât.

[2] There is no reason to consider the passage 'atra ke*k*it' in *S*aṅkara's bhâshya on Sûtra 23 an interpolation as Deussen does (p. 30). It simply contains a criticism passed by *S*aṅkara on other commentators.

[3] To the passages on pp. 150 and 153 of the Sanskrit text, which Deussen thinks to be interpolations, there likewise applies the remark made in the preceding note.

from the individual soul rests thereon that the former as free from all evil is not subject to the effects of works in the same way as the soul is[1].—Adhik. II (9, 10) decides that he to whom the Brahmans and Kshattriyas are but food (Ka*th*a Up. I, 2, 25) is the highest Self.—Adhik. III (11, 12) shows that the two entered into the cave (Ka*th*a Up. I, 3, 1) are Brahman and the individual soul[2].—Adhik. IV (13–17) shows that the person within the eye mentioned in *Kh*. Up. IV, 15, 1 is Brahman.—Adhik. V (18–20) shows that the ruler within (antaryâmin) described in B*ri*. Up. III, 7, 3 is Brahman. Sûtra 20 clearly enounces the difference of the individual soul and the Lord; hence *S*aṅkara is obliged to remark that that difference is not real.—Adhik. VI (21–23) proves that that which cannot be seen, &c., mentioned in Mu*nd*aka Up. I, 1, 3 is Brahman.—Adhik. VII (24–32) shows that the âtman vai*s*vânara of *Kh*. Up. V, 11, 6 is Brahman.

Pâda III.

Adhik. I (1–7) proves that that within which the heaven, the earth, &c. are woven (Mu*nd*. Up. II, 2, 5) is Brahman.—Adhik. II (8, 9) shows that the bhûman referred to in *Kh*. Up. VII, 23 is Brahman.—Adhik. III (10–12) teaches that the Imperishable in which, according to B*ri*. Up. III, 8, 8, the ether is woven is Brahman.—Adhik. IV (13) decides that the highest person who is to be meditated upon with the syllable Om, according to Pra*s*na Up. V, 5, is not the

[1] *G*îvasya iva parasyâpi brahma*n*a*h* *s*arîrântarvartitvam abhyupagata*m* *k*et tadvad eva *s*arîrasambandhaprayuktasukhadukhopabhogaprâptir iti *k*en na, hetuvai*s*eshyât, na hi *s*arîrântarvartitvam eva sukhadukhopabhogahetu*h* api tu pu*n*yapâparûpakarmaparava*s*atva*m* ta*k* *k*âpahatapâpmana*h* paramâtmano na sambhavati.

[2] The second interpretation given on pp. 184–5 of the Sanskrit text (beginning with apara âha) Deussen considers to be an interpolation, caused by the reference to the Paiṅgi-upanishad in *S*aṅkara's comment on I, 3, 7 (p. 232). But there is no reason whatever for such an assumption. The passage on p. 232 shows that *S*aṅkara considered the explanation of the mantra given in the Paiṅgi-upanishad worth quoting, and is in fact fully intelligible only in case of its having been quoted before by *S*aṅkara himself.—That the 'apara' quotes the B*ri*hadâra*n*yaka not according to the Kâ*n*va text—to quote from which is *S*aṅkara's habit—but from the Mâdhyandina text, is due just to the circumstance of his being an 'apara,' i.e. not *S*aṅkara.

lower but the higher Brahman.—According to Râmânu*g*a the two alternatives are Brahman and Brahmâ (*g*îvasamash*t*irûpo*nd*âdhipati*s* *k*aturmukha*h*).—Adhik. V and VI (comprising, according to *S*añkara, Sûtras 14–21)[1] discuss the question whether the small ether within the lotus of the heart mentioned in *Kh*. Up. VIII, 1 is the elemental ether or the individual soul or Brahman; the last alternative being finally adopted. In favour of the second alternative the pûrvapakshin pleads the two passages *Kh*. Up. VIII, 3, 4 and VIII, 12, 3, about the serene being (samprasâda); for by the latter the individual soul only can be understood, and in the chapter, of which the latter passage forms part, there are ascribed to it the same qualities (viz. freeness from sin, old age, death, &c.) that were predicated in VIII, 1, of the small ether within the heart.—But the reply to this is, that the second passage refers not to the (ordinary) individual soul but to the soul in that state where its true nature has become manifest, i. e. in which it is Brahman; so that the subject of the passage is in reality not the so-called individual soul but Brahman. And in the former of the two passages the soul is mentioned not on its own account, but merely for the purpose of intimating that the highest Self is the cause through which the individual soul manifests itself in its true nature.—What Râmânu*g*a understands by the âvirbhâva of the soul will appear from the remarks on IV, 4.

The two next Sûtras (22, 23) constitute, according to *S*añkara, a new adhikara*n*a (VII), proving that he 'after whom everything shines, by whose light all this is lighted' (Ka*th*a Up. II, 5, 15) is not some material luminous body, but Brahman itself.—According to Râmânu*g*a the two Sûtras do not start a new topic, but merely furnish some further arguments strengthening the conclusion arrived at in the preceding Sûtras[2].

---

[1] Sûtras 14–21 are divided into two adhikara*n*as by the Adhikara*n*aratnamâlâ, but really constitute a simple adhikara*n*a only.

[2] Ita*s* *k*aitad evam. Anuk*ri*tes tasya *k*a. Tasya daharâkâ*s*asya parabrahma*n*o*s*nukârâd ayam apahatapâpmatvâdigu*n*ako vimuktabandha*h* pratyagâtmâ na daharâkâ*s*a*h* tadanukâras tatsâmya*m* tathâ hi pratyagâtmano*s*pi vimuktasya

Adhik. VIII (24, 25) decides that the person of the size of a thumb mentioned in Ka*th*a Up. II, 4, 12 is not the individual soul but Brahman.

The two next adhikara*n*as are of the nature of a digression. The passage about the aṅgush*th*amâtra was explained on the ground that the human heart is of the size of a span; the question may then be asked whether also such individuals as belong to other classes than mankind, more particularly the Gods, are capable of the knowledge of Brahman: a question finally answered in the affirmative.—This discussion leads in its turn to several other digressions, among which the most important one refers to the problem in what relation the different species of beings stand to the words denoting them (Sûtra 28). In connexion herewith *S*aṅkara treats of the nature of words (*s*abda), opposing the opinion of the Mîmâ*m*saka Upavarsha, according to whom the word is nothing but the aggregate of its constitutive letters, to the view of the grammarians who teach that over and above the aggregate of the letters there exists a supersensuous entity called 'spho*t*a,' which is the direct cause of the apprehension of the sense of a word (Adhik. IX; Sûtras 26–33).

Adhik. X (34–38) explains that *S*ûdras are altogether disqualified for Brahmavidyâ.

Sûtra 39 constitutes, according to *S*aṅkara, a new adhikara*n*a (XI), proving that the prâ*n*a in which everything trembles, according to Ka*th*a Up. II, 6, 2, is Brahman.—According to Râmânu*g*a the Sûtra does not introduce a new topic but merely furnishes an additional reason for the

---

parabrahmânukâra*h* *s*rûyate yadâ pa*s*ya*h* pa*s*yate rukmavar*n*a*m* kartâram î*s*a*m* purusha*m* brahmayoni*m* tadâ vidvân pu*n*yapâpe vidhûya nira*ñ*gana*h* parama*m* sâmyam upaitîty ato 'nukartâ pra*g*âpativâkyanirdish*t*a*h* anukârya*m* para*m* brahma na daharâkâ*s*a*h*. Api *k*a smaryate. Sa*m*sâri*n*o 'pi muktâvasthâyâ*m* paramasâmyâpattilaksha*n*a*h* parabrahmânukâra*h* smaryate ida*m* *gñ*ânam upâ*s*ritya, &c.—Ke*k*id anuk*ri*tes tasya *k*âpi smaryate iti *k*a sûtradvayam adhikara*n*ântara*m* tam eva bhântam anubhâti sarva*m* tasya bhâsâ sarvam ida*m* vibhâtîty asyâ*h* *s*rute*h* parabrahmaparatvanir*n*ayâya prav*ri*tta*m* vadanti. Tat tv ad*ris*yatvâdigu*n*ako dharmokte*h* dyubhvâdyâyatana*m* sva*s*abdâd ity adhikara*n*advayena tasya prakara*n*asya brahmavishayatvapratipâdanât *g*yotis*k*ara*n*âbhidhânât ity âdishu parasya brahma*n*o bhârûpatvâvagates *k*a pûrvapakshânutthânâd ayukta*m* sûtrâksharavairûpyâ*k* *k*a.

decision arrived at under Sûtras 24, 25, viz. that the angush*th*amâtra is Brahman. On this supposition, Sûtras 24-39 form one adhikara*n*a in which 26-38 constitute a mere digression led up to by the mention made of the heart in 25.—The angush*th*amâtra is referred to twice in the Ka*th*a Upanishad, once in the passage discussed (II, 4, 12), and once in II, 6, 17 ('the Person not larger than a thumb'). To determine what is meant by the angush*th*amâtra, Râmânu*g*a says, we are enabled by the passage II, 6, 2. 3, which is intermediate between the two passages concerning the angush*th*amâtra, and which clearly refers to the highest Brahman, of which alone everything can be said to stand in awe.

The next Sûtra (40) gives rise to a similar difference of opinion. According to *S*ankara it constitutes by itself a new adhikara*n*a (XII), proving that the 'light' (*g*yotis) mentioned in *Kh*. Up. VIII, 12, 3 is the highest Brahman. —According to Râmânu*g*a the Sûtra continues the preceding adhikara*n*a, and strengthens the conclusion arrived at by a further argument, referring to Ka*th*a Up. II. 5, 15 —a passage intermediate between the two passages about the angush*th*amâtra—which speaks of a primary light that cannot mean anything but Brahman. The Sûtra has in that case to be translated as follows: '(The angush*th*amâtra is Brahman) because (in a passage intervening between the two) a light is seen to be mentioned (which can be Brahman only).'

The three last Sûtras of the pâda are, according to *S*ankara, to be divided into two adhikara*n*as (XIII and XIV), Sûtra 41 deciding that the ether which reveals names and forms (*Kh*. Up. VIII, 14) is not the elemental ether but Brahman; and 42, 43 teaching that the vi*gñ*ânamaya, 'he who consists of knowledge,' of B*ri*. Up. IV, 3, 7 is not the individual soul but Brahman.—According to Râmânu*g*a the three Sûtras make up one single adhikara*n*a discussing whether the *Kh*andogya Upanishad passage about the ether refers to Brahman or to the individual soul in the state of release; the latter of these two alternatives being suggested by the circumstance that the released soul is the subject of the passage immediately preceding ('Shaking off all evil as a horse shakes off his hair,' &c.). Sûtra 41 decides that 'the ether (is Brahman) because the passage designates the nature of something else,' &c. (i.e. of something other than the individual soul; other because to the soul the revealing of names and forms cannot be ascribed, &c.)—But, an objection is raised, does not more than one scriptural passage show that the released soul and Brahman are identical, and is not therefore the ether which reveals names and forms the soul as well as Brahman?—(The two, Sûtra 42 replies, are different) 'because in the states of deep sleep and departing (the highest Self) is designated as different' (from the soul)—which point is proved by the same scriptural passages which *S*aṅkara adduces;—and 'because such terms as Lord and the like' cannot be applied to the individual soul (43). Reference is made to IV, 4, 14, where all *g*agadvyâpâra is said to belong to the Lord only, not to the soul even when in the state of release.

PÂDA IV.

The last pâda of the first adhyâya is specially directed against the Sâṅkhyas.

The first adhikara*n*a (1–7) discusses the passage Ka*th*a Up. I, 3, 10; 11, where mention is made of the Great and the Undeveloped—both of them terms used with a special technical sense in the Sâṅkhya-*s*âstra, avyakta being a synonym for pradhâna.—*S*aṅkara shows by an exhaustive review of the topics of the Ka*th*a Upanishad that the term avyakta has not the special meaning which the Sâṅkhyas attribute to it, but denotes the body, more strictly the subtle body (sûkshma *s*arîra), but at the same time the gross body also, in so far as it is viewed as an effect of the subtle one.

Adhik. II (8–10) demonstrates, according to *S*aṅkara, that the tricoloured a*g*â spoken of in *S*ve. Up. IV, 5 is not the pradhâna of the Sâṅkhyas, but either that power of the Lord from which the world springs, or else the primary causal matter first produced by that power.—What Râmânuga in contradistinction from *S*aṅkara understands by the primary causal matter, follows from the short sketch given above of the two systems.

Adhik. III (11–13) shows that the pa*ñk*a pa*ñk*aganâ*h* mentioned in B*ri*. Up. IV, 4, 17 are not the twenty-five principles of the Sâṅkhyas.—Adhik. IV (14, 15) proves that Scripture does not contradict itself on the all-important point of Brahman, i. e. a being whose essence is intelligence, being the cause of the world.

Adhik. V (16–18) is, according to *S*aṅkara, meant to prove that 'he who is the maker of those persons, of whom this is the work,' mentioned in Kau. Up. IV, 19, is not either the vital air or the individual soul, but Brahman.—The subject of the adhikara*n*a is essentially the same in Râmânu*g*a's view; greater stress is, however, laid on the adhikara*n*a being polemical against the Sâṅkhyas, who wish to turn the passage into an argument for the pradhâna doctrine.

The same partial difference of view is observable with regard to the next adhikara*n*a (VI; Sûtras 19–22) which decides that the 'Self to be seen, to be heard,' &c. (B*ri*. Up. II, 4, 5) is the highest Self, not the individual soul. This latter passage also is, according to Râmânu*g*a, made the subject of discussion in order to rebut the Sâṅkhya who is anxious to prove that what is there inculcated as the object of knowledge is not a universal Self but merely the Sâṅkhya purusha.

Adhik. VII (23–27) teaches that Brahman is not only the efficient or operative cause (nimitta) of the world, but its material cause as well. The world springs from Brahman by way of modification (pari*n*âma; Sûtra 26).—Râmânu*g*a views this adhikara*n*a as specially directed against the Se*s*vara-sâṅkhyas who indeed admit the existence of a highest Lord, but postulate in addition an independent pradhâna on which the Lord acts as an operative cause merely.

Adhik. VIII (28) remarks that the refutation of the Sâṅkhya views is applicable to other theories also, such as the doctrine of the world having originated from atoms.

After this rapid survey of the contents of the first adhyâya and the succinct indication of the most important points in which the views of *S*ankara and Râmânu*g*a diverge, we turn to a short consideration of two questions which here naturally present themselves, viz., firstly, which is the principle on which the Vedic passages referred to in the Sûtras have been selected and arranged; and, secondly, if, where *S*ankara and Râmânu*g*a disagree as to the subdivision of the Sûtras into Adhikara*n*as, and the determination of the Vedic passages discussed in the Sûtras, there are to be met with any indications enabling us to determine which of the two commentators is right. (The more general question as to how far the Sûtras favour either *S*ankara's or Râmânu*g*a's general views cannot be considered at present.)

The Hindu commentators here and there attempt to point out the reason why the discussion of a certain Vedic passage is immediately followed by the consideration of a certain other one. Their explanations—which have occasionally been referred to in the notes to the translation—rest on the assumption that the Sûtrakâra in arranging the texts to be commented upon was guided by technicalities of the Mîmâ*m*sâ-system, especially by a regard for the various so-called means of proof which the Mîmâ*m*saka employs for the purpose of determining the proper meaning and position of scriptural passages. But that this was the guiding principle, is rendered altogether improbable by a simple tabular statement of the Vedic passages referred to in the first adhyâya, such as given by Deussen on page 130; for from the latter it appears that the order in which the Sûtras exhibit the scriptural passages follows the order in which those passages themselves occur in the Upanishads, and it would certainly be a most strange coincidence if that order enabled us at the same time to exemplify the various pramâ*n*as of the Mîmâ*m*sâ in their due systematic succession.

As Deussen's statement shows, most of the passages discussed are taken from the *Kh*ândogya Upanishad, so many indeed that the whole first adhyâya may be said to consist of a discussion of all those *Kh*ândogya passages of which it is doubtful whether they are concerned with Brahman or not, passages from the other Upanishads being brought in wherever an opportunity offers. Considering the prominent position assigned to the Upanishad mentioned, I think it likely that the Sûtrakâra meant to begin the series of doubtful texts with the first doubtful passage from the *Kh*ândogya, and that hence the sixth adhikara*n*a which treats of the ânandamaya mentioned in the Taittirîya Upanishad has, in agreement with Râmânu*g*a's views, to be separated from the subsequent adhikara*n*as, and to be combined with the preceding ones whose task it is to lay down the fundamental propositions regarding Brahman's nature. —The remaining adhikara*n*as of the first pâda follow the order of passages in the *Kh*ândogya Upanishad, and therefore call for no remark; with the exception of the last adhikara*n*a, which refers to a Kaushîtaki passage, for whose being introduced in this place I am not able to account.—The first adhikara*n*a of the second pâda returns to the *Kh*ândogya Upanishad. The second one treats of a passage in the Ka*th*a Upanishad where a being is referred to which eats everything. The reason why that passage is introduced in this place seems to be correctly assigned in the *S*rî-bhâshya, which remarks that, as in the preceding Sûtra it had been argued that the highest Self is not an enjoyer, a doubt arises whether by that being which eats everything the highest Self can be meant [1].—The third adhikara*n*a again, whose topic is the 'two entered into the cave' (Ka*th*a Up. I, 3, 1), appears, as Râmânu*g*a remarks, to come in at this place owing to the preceding adhikara*n*a; for if it could not be proved that one of the two is the highest Self, a doubt would attach to the explanation given above of the 'eater,' since the 'two entered into the cave,' and the 'eater' stand under the same prakara*n*a, and must therefore be held to refer to the same matter.—The fourth adhikara*n*a is again occupied with a *Kh*ândogya passage.—The fifth adhikara*n*a, whose topic is the Ruler within (antaryâmin), manifestly owes its place, as remarked by Râmânu*g*a also,

[1] Yadi paramâtmâ na bhoktâ evam tarhi bhokt*ri*tayâ pratîyamâno *g*îva eva syâd ity âsankyâha attâ.

to the fact that the Vedic passage treated had been employed in the preceding adhikara*n*a (I, 2, 14) for the purpose of strengthening the argument [1].—The sixth adhikara*n*a, again, which discusses 'that which is not seen' (adre*s*ya; Mu*nd*. Up. I, 1, 6), is clearly introduced in this place because in the preceding adhikara*n*a it had been said that ad*ri*sh*t*a, &c. denote the highest Self.—The reasons to which the last adhikara*n*a of the second pâda and the first and third adhikara*n*as of the third pâda owe their places are not apparent (the second adhikara*n*a of the third pâda treats of a *Kh*ândogya passage). The introduction, on the other hand, of the passage from the Pra*s*na Upanishad treating of the akshara O*m*kâra is clearly due to the circumstance that an akshara, of a different nature, had been discussed in the preceding adhikara*n*a.—The fifth and sixth adhikara*n*as investigate *Kh*ândogya passages.—The two next Sûtras (22, 23) are, as remarked above, considered by *S*aṅkara to constitute a new adhikara*n*a treating of the 'being after which everything shines' (Mu*nd*. Up. II, 2, 10); while Râmânu*g*a looks on them as continuing the sixth adhikara*n*a. There is one circumstance which renders it at any rate probable that Râmânu*g*a. and not *S*aṅkara, here hits the intention of the author of the Sûtras. The general rule in the first three pâdas is that, wherever a new Vedic passage is meant to be introduced, the subject of the discussion, i. e. that being which in the end is declared to be Brahman is referred to by means of a special word, in most cases a nominative form [2]. From this rule there is in the preceding part of the adhyâya only one real exception, viz. in I, 2, 1, which possibly may be due to the fact that there a new pâda begins, and it therefore was considered super-

[1] Sthânâdivyapade*s*â*k k*a ity atra ya*h k*akshushi tish*th*ann ity âdinâ pratipâdyamâna*m k*akshushi sthitiniyamanâdika*m* paramâtmana eveti siddha*m* k*ri*tvâ akshipurushasya paramâtmatva*m* sâdhitam idâni*m* tad eva samarthayate antaryâ°.

[2] Ânandamaya*h* I, 1, 12; anta*h* I, 1, 20; âkâ*s*a*h* I. 1, 22; prâna*h* I, 1, 23; *g*yoti*h* I, 1, 24; prâna*h* I, 1, 28; attâ I, 2, 9; guhâ*m* pravish*t*au I, 2, 11; antara I, 2, 13; antaryâmî I, 2, 18; ad*ris*yatvâdigu*n*aka*h* I, 2, 21; vai*s*vânara*h* I. 2, 24; dyubhvâdyâyatanam I, 3, 1; bhûmâ I, 3, 8; aksharam I, 3. 10; sa*h* I, 3, 13; dahara*h* I, 3, 14; pramita*h* I, 3, 24; (*g*yoti*h* I, 3, 40;) âkâ*s*a*h* I, 3, 41.

fluous to indicate the introduction of a new topic by a special word. The exception supplied by I, 3, 19 is only an apparent one; for, as remarked above, Sûtra 19 does not in reality begin a new adhikara*n*a. A few exceptions occurring later on will be noticed in their places.—Now neither Sûtra 22 nor Sûtra 23 contains any word intimating that a new Vedic passage is being taken into consideration, and hence it appears preferable to look upon them, with Râmânu*g*a, as continuing the topic of the preceding adhikara*n*a.—This conclusion receives an additional confirmation from the position of the next adhikara*n*a, which treats of the being 'a span long' mentioned in Ka*th*a Up. II, 4, 12; for the reason of this latter passage being considered here is almost certainly the reference to the alpa*s*ruti in Sûtra 21, and, if so, the aṅgush*th*amâtra properly constitutes the subject of the adhikara*n*a immediately following on Adhik. V, VI; which, in its turn, implies that Sûtras 22, 23 do not form an independent adhikara*n*a.—The two next adhikara*n*as are digressions, and do not refer to special Vedic passages.—Sûtra 39 forms a new adhikara*n*a, according to *S*aṅkara, but not according to Râmânu*g*a, whose opinion seems again to be countenanced by the fact that the Sûtra does not exhibit any word indicative of a new topic. The same difference of opinion prevails with regard to Sûtra 40, and it appears from the translation of the Sûtra given above, according to Râmânu*g*a's view, that '*g*yoti*h*' need not be taken as a nominative.—The last two adhikara*n*as finally refer, according to Râmânu*g*a, to one *Kh*ândogya passage only, and here also we have to notice that Sûtra 42 does not comprise any word intimating that a new passage is about to be discussed.

From all this we seem entitled to draw the following conclusions. The Vedic passages discussed in the three first pâdas of the Vedânta-sûtras comprise all the doubtful—or at any rate all the more important doubtful—passages from the *Kh*ândogya Upanishad. These passages are arranged in the order in which the text of the Upanishad exhibits them. Passages from other Upanishads are discussed as opportunities offer, there being always a special reason why a certain *Kh*ândogya passage is followed by a certain passage from some other Upanishad. Those reasons can be assigned with sufficient certainty in a number of cases although not in all, and from among those passages whose introduction cannot be satisfactorily accounted for some are eliminated by our following the subdivision of the Sûtras into adhikara*n*as adopted by Râmânu*g*a, a subdivision countenanced by the external form of the Sûtras.

The fourth pâda of the first adhyâya has to be taken by itself. It is directed specially and avowedly against Sâṅkhya-interpretations of Scripture, not only in its earlier part which discusses isolated passages, but also—as is brought out much more clearly in the *S*rî-bhâshya than by *S*aṅkara—in its latter part which takes a general survey of the entire scriptural evidence for Brahman being the material as well as the operative cause of the world.

Deussen (p. 221) thinks that the selection made by the Sûtrakâra of Vedic passages setting forth the nature of Brahman is not in all cases an altogether happy one. But this reproach rests on the assumption that the passages referred to in the first adhyâya were chosen for the purpose of throwing light on what Brahman is, and this assumption can hardly be upheld. The Vedânta-sûtras as well as the Pûrvâ Mîmâ*m*sâ-sûtras are throughout Mîmâ*m*sâ, i.e. critical discussions of such scriptural passages as on a primâ facie view admit of different interpretations and therefore necessitate a careful enquiry into their meaning. Here and there we meet with Sûtras which do not directly involve a discussion of the sense of some particular Vedic passage, but rather make a mere statement on some important point. But those cases are rare, and it would be altogether contrary to the general spirit of the Sûtras to assume that a whole adhyâya should be devoted to the task of showing what Brahman is. The latter point is sufficiently determined in the first five (or six) adhikara*n*as; but after we once know what Brahman is we are at once confronted by a number of Upanishad passages concerning which it is doubtful whether they refer to Brahman or not. With their discussion all the remaining adhikara*n*as of the first adhyâya are occupied. That the Vedânta-sûtras view it as a particularly important task to controvert the doctrine of the Sâṅkhyas is patent (and has also been fully pointed out by Deussen, p. 23). The fifth adhikaraṇa already declares itself against the doctrine that the world has sprung from a non-intelligent principle, the pradhâna, and the fourth pâda of the first adhyâya returns to an express polemic against Sâṅkhya interpretations of certain Vedic statements. It is therefore perhaps not saying too much if we maintain that the entire first adhyâya is due to the wish, on the part of the Sûtrakâra, to guard his own doctrine against Sâṅkhya attacks. Whatever the attitude of the other so-called orthodox systems may be towards the Veda, the Sâṅkhya system is the only one whose adherents were anxious—and actually attempted—to prove that their views are warranted by scriptural passages. The Sâṅkhya tendency thus would be to show that all those Vedic texts which the Vedântin claims as teaching the existence of Brahman, the intelligent and sole cause of the world, refer either to the pradhâna or some product of the pradhâna, or else to the purusha in the Sâṅkhya sense, i. e. the individual soul. It consequently became the task of the Vedântin to guard the Upanishads against misinterpretations of the kind, and this he did in the first adhyâya of the Vedânta-sûtras, selecting those passages about whose interpretation doubts were, for some reason or other, likely to arise. Some of the passages singled out are certainly obscure, and hence liable to various interpretations; of others it is less apparent why it was thought requisite to discuss them at length. But this is hardly a matter in which we are entitled to find fault with the Sûtrakâra; for no modern scholar, either European or Hindu, is—or can possibly be—sufficiently at home, on the one hand, in the religious and philosophical views which prevailed at the time when the Sûtras may have been composed, and, on the other hand, in the intricacies of the Mîmâṃsâ, to judge with confidence which Vedic passages may give rise to discussions and which not.

SECOND ADHYÂYA.

The first adhyâya has proved that all the Vedânta-texts unanimously teach that there is only one cause of the world, viz. Brahman, whose nature is intelligence, and that there exists no scriptural passage which can be used to establish systems opposed to the Vedânta, more especially the Sâṅkhya system. The task of the two first pâdas of the second adhyâya is to rebut any objections which may be raised against the Vedânta doctrine on purely speculative grounds, apart from scriptural authority, and to show, again on purely speculative grounds, that none of the systems irreconcilable with the Vedânta can be satisfactorily established.

PÂDA I.

Adhikara*n*a I refutes the Sâṅkhya objection that the acceptation of the Vedânta system involves the rejection of the Sâṅkhya doctrine which after all constitutes a part of Sm*ri*ti, and as such has claims on consideration.—To accept the Sâṅkhya-sm*ri*ti, the Vedântin replies, would compel us to reject other Sm*ri*tis. such as the Manu-sm*ri*ti, which are opposed to the Sâṅkhya doctrine. The conflicting claims of Sm*ri*tis can be settled only on the ground of the Veda, and there can be no doubt that the Veda does not confirm the Sâṅkhya-sm*ri*ti, but rather those Sm*ri*tis which teach the origination of the world from an intelligent primary cause.

Adhik. II (3) extends the same line of argumentation to the Yoga-sm*ri*ti.

Adhik. III (4–11) shows that Brahman, although of the nature of intelligence, yet may be the cause of the non-intelligent material world. and that it is not contaminated by the qualities of the world when the latter is refunded into Brahman. For ordinary experience teaches us that like does not always spring from like, and that the qualities of effected things when the latter are refunded into their causes—as when golden ornaments, for instance, are melted and thereby become simple gold again—do not continue to exist in those causes.—Here also the argumentation is specially directed against the Sâṅkhyas, who, in order to account for the materiality and the various imperfections of the world, think it necessary to assume a causal substance participating in the same characteristics.

Adhik. IV (12) points out that the line of reasoning followed in the preceding adhikara*n*a is valid also against other theories, such as the atomistic doctrine.

The one Sûtra (13) constituting Adhik. V teaches, according to *S*aṅkara, that although the enjoying souls as well as the objects of fruition are in reality nothing but Brahman, and on that account identical, yet the two sets may practically be held apart, just as in ordinary life we hold apart, and distinguish as separate individual things, the waves, ripples, and foam of the sea, although at the bottom waves, ripples, and foam are all of them identical as being neither more nor less than sea-water.—The *S*rî-bhâshya gives a totally different interpretation of the Sûtra, according to which the latter has nothing whatever to do with the eventual non-distinction of enjoying souls and objects to be enjoyed. Translated according to Râmânu*g*a's view, the Sûtra runs as follows: 'If non-distinction (of the Lord and the individual souls) is said to result from the circumstance of (the Lord himself) becoming an enjoyer (a soul), we refute this objection by instances from every-day experience.' That is to say: If it be maintained that from our doctrine previously expounded, according to which this world springs from the Lord and constitutes his body, it follows that the Lord, as an embodied being, is not essentially different from other souls, and subject to fruition as they are; we reply that the Lord's having a body does not involve his being subject to fruition, not any more than in ordinary life a king, although himself an embodied being, is affected by the experiences of pleasure and pain which his servants have to undergo.—The construction which Râmânu*g*a puts on the Sûtra is not repugnant either to the words of the Sûtra or to the context in which the latter stands, and that it rests on earlier authority appears from a quotation made by Râmânu*g*a from the Drami*d*abhâshyakâra[1].

Adhik. VI (14–20) treats of the non-difference of the effect from the cause; a Vedânta doctrine which is defended by its adherents against the Vai*s*eshikas according to whom the effect is something different from the cause.—The divergent views of *S*aṅkara and Râmânu*g*a on this important point have been sufficiently illustrated in the general sketch of the two systems.

Adhik. VII (21–23) refutes the objection that, from the Vedic passages insisting on the identity of the Lord and the individual soul, it follows that the Lord must be like the individual soul the cause of evil, and that hence the entire doctrine of an all-powerful and all-wise Lord being the cause of the world has to be rejected. For, the Sûtrakâra remarks, the creative principle of the world is additional to, i.e. other than, the individual soul, the difference of the two being distinctly declared by Scripture.—The way in which the three Sûtras constituting this adhikara*n*a are treated by *S*aṅkara on the one hand and Râmânu*g*a on the other is characteristic. Râmânu*g*a throughout simply follows the words of the Sûtras, of which Sûtra 21 formulates the objection based on such texts as 'Thou art that,' while Sûtra 22 replies that Brahman is different from the soul, since that is expressly declared by Scripture. *S*aṅkara, on the other hand, sees himself obliged to add that the difference of the two, plainly maintained in Sûtra 22, is not real, but due to the soul's fictitious limiting adjuncts.

Adhik. VIII (24, 25) shows that Brahman, although destitute of material and instruments of action, may yet produce the world, just as gods by their mere power create

[1] Lokavat. Yathâ loke râ*g*a*s*âsanânuvartinâ*m* *k*a râ*g*ânugrahanigrahak*ri*tasukhadukhayoge'pi na sa*s*arîratvamâtre*n*a *s*âsake râ*g*any api *s*âsanânuv*ri*ttyativ*ri*ttinimittasukhadukhayor bhokt*ri*tvaprasaṅga*h*. Yathâha Drami*d*abhâshyakâra*h* yathâ loke râ*g*â pra*k*uradanda*s*ûke ghore'narthasa*m*ka*t*e'pi prade*s*e vartamâno'pi vya*g*anâdyavadhûtadeho doshair na sp*ris*yate abhipretâ*ms* *k*a lokân paripipâlayishati bhogâ*ms* *k*a gandhâdîn avi*s*va*g*anopabhogyân dhârayati tathâsau loke*s*varo bhramat*s*vasâmarthya*k*âmaro doshair na sp*ris*yate rakshati *k*a lokân brahmalokâdî*ms* *k*âvi*s*va*g*anopabhogyân dhârayatîti.

palaces, animals, and the like, and as milk by itself turns into curds.

Adhik. IX (26–29) explains that, according to the express doctrine of Scripture, Brahman does not in its entirety pass over into the world, and, although emitting the world from itself, yet remains one and undivided. This is possible, according to *S*ankara, because the world is unreal; according to Râmânu*g*a, because the creation is merely the visible and tangible manifestation of what previously existed in Brahman in a subtle imperceptible condition.

Adhik. X (30, 31) teaches that Brahman, although destitute of instruments of action, is enabled to create the world by means of the manifold powers which it possesses.

Adhik. XI (32, 33) assigns the motive of the creation, or, more properly expressed, teaches that Brahman, in creating the world, has no motive in the strict sense of the word, but follows a mere sportive impulse.

Adhik. XII (34–36) justifies Brahman from the charges of partiality and cruelty which might be brought against it owing to the inequality of position and fate of the various animate beings, and the universal suffering of the world. Brahman, as a creator and dispenser, acts with a view to the merit and demerit of the individual souls, and has so acted from all eternity.

Adhik. XIII (37) sums up the preceding argumentation by declaring that all the qualities of Brahman—omniscience and so on—are such as to capacitate it for the creation of the world.

Pâda II.

The task of the second pâda is to refute, by arguments independent of Vedic passages, the more important philosophical theories concerning the origin of the world which are opposed to the Vedânta view.—The first adhikara*n*a (1–10) is directed against the Sâṅkhyas, whose doctrine had already been touched upon incidentally in several previous places, and aims at proving that a non-intelligent first cause, such as the pradhâna of the Sâṅkhyas, is unable to create and dispose.—The second adhikara*n*a (11–17) refutes the

Vaiseshika tenet that the world originates from atoms set in motion by the adrishta.—The third and fourth adhikaranas are directed against various schools of Bauddha philosophers. Adhik. III (18–27) impugns the view of the so-called sarvâstitvavâdins, or bâhyârthavâdins, who maintain the reality of an external as well as an internal world; Adhik. IV (28–32) is directed against the vigñânavâdins, according to whom ideas are the only reality.—The last Sûtra of this adhikarana is treated by Râmânuga as a separate adhikarana refuting the view of the Mâdhyamikas, who teach that everything is void, i.e. that nothing whatever is real.—Adhik. V (33–36) is directed against the doctrine of the Gainas; Adhik. VI (37–41) against those philosophical schools which teach that a highest Lord is not the material but only the operative cause of the world.

The last adhikarana of the pâda (42–45) refers, according to the unanimous statement of the commentators, to the doctrine of the Bhâgavatas or Pâñkarâtras. But Sankara and Râmânuga totally disagree as to the drift of the Sûtrakâra's opinion regarding that system. According to the former it is condemned like the systems previously referred to; according to the latter it is approved of.—Sûtras 42 and 43, according to both commentators, raise objections against the system; Sûtra 42 being directed against the doctrine that from the highest being, called Vâsudeva, there is originated Sankarshana, i.e. the gîva, on the ground that thereby those scriptural passages would be contradicted which teach the soul's eternity; and Sûtra 43 impugning the doctrine that from Sankarshana there springs Pradyumna, i.e. the manas.—The Sûtra on which the difference of interpretation turns is 44. Literally translated it runs, 'Or, on account of there being' (or, 'their being') 'knowledge and so on, there is non-contradiction of that.'—This means, according to Sankara, 'Or, if in consequence of the existence of knowledge and so on (on the part of Sankarshana, &c. they be taken not as soul, mind, &c. but as Lords of pre-eminent knowledge, &c.), yet there is non-contradiction of that (viz. of the objection raised in Sûtra 42 against the Bhâgavata doctrine).'—

According to Râmânuga, on the other hand, the Sûtra has to be explained as follows: 'Or, rather there is non-contradiction of that (i. e. the Pâñkarâtra doctrine) on account of their being knowledge and so on (i. e. on account of their being Brahman).' Which means: Since Saṅkarshana and so on are merely forms of manifestation of Brahman, the Pâñkarâtra doctrine, according to which they spring from Brahman, is not contradicted.—The form of the Sûtra makes it difficult for us to decide which of the two interpretations is the right one; it, however, appears to me that the explanations of the 'vâ' and of the 'tat,' implied in Râmânuga's comment, are more natural than those resulting from Saṅkara's interpretation. Nor would it be an unnatural proceeding to close the polemical pâda with a defence of that doctrine which—in spite of objections—has to be viewed as the true one.

PÂDA III.

The third pâda discusses the question whether the different forms of existence which, in their totality, constitute the world have an origin or not, i.e. whether they are co-eternal with Brahman, or issue from it and are refunded into it at stated intervals.

The first seven adhikaranas treat of the five elementary substances.—Adhik. I (1–7) teaches that the ether is not co-eternal with Brahman, but springs from it as its first effect.—Adhik. II (8) shows that air springs from ether; Adhik. IV, V, VI (10; 11; 12) that fire springs from air, water from fire, earth from water.—Adhik. III (9) explains by way of digression that Brahman, which is not some special entity, but quite generally 'that which is,' cannot have originated from anything else.

Adhik. VII (13) demonstrates that the origination of one element from another is due, not to the latter in itself, but to Brahman acting in it.

Adhik. VIII (14) teaches that the reabsorption of the elements into Brahman takes place in the inverse order of their emission.

Adhik. IX (15) remarks that the indicated order in which

the emission and the reabsorption of the elementary substances take place is not interfered with by the creation and reabsorption of the organs of the soul, i.e. the sense organs and the internal organ (manas); for they also are of elemental nature, and as such created and retracted together with the elements of which they consist.

The remainder of the pâda is taken up by a discussion of the nature of the individual soul, the *g*îva.—Adhik. X (16) teaches that expressions such as 'Devadatta is born,' 'Devadatta has died,' strictly apply to the body only, and are transferred to the soul in so far only as it is connected with a body.

Adhik. XI (17) teaches that the individual soul is, according to Scripture, permanent, eternal, and therefore not, like the ether and the other elements, produced from Brahman at the time of creation.—This Sûtra is of course commented on in a very different manner by *S*aṅkara on the one hand and Râmânu*g*a on the other. According to the former, the *g*îva is in reality identical—and as such co-eternal—with Brahman; what originates is merely the soul's connexion with its limiting adjuncts, and that connexion is moreover illusory.—According to Râmânu*g*a, the *g*îva is indeed an effect of Brahman, but has existed in Brahman from all eternity as an individual being and as a mode (prakâra) of Brahman. So indeed have also the material elements; yet there is an important distinction owing to which the elements may be said to originate at the time of creation, while the same cannot be said of the soul. Previously to creation the material elements exist in a subtle condition in which they possess none of the qualities that later on render them the objects of ordinary experience; hence, when passing over into the gross state at the time of creation, they may be said to originate. The souls, on the other hand, possess at all times the same essential qualities, i.e. they are cognizing agents; only, whenever a new creation takes place, they associate themselves with bodies, and their intelligence therewith undergoes a certain expansion or development (vikâ*s*a), contrasting with the unevolved or contracted state (saṅko*k*a) which characterised it during the preceding pralaya. But this change is not a change of essential nature (svarûpânyathâbhâva), and hence we have to distinguish the souls as permanent entities from the material elements which at the time of each creation and reabsorption change their essential characteristics.

Adhik. XII (18) defines the nature of the individual soul. The Sûtra declares that the soul is '*gñ*a.' This means, according to *S*aṅkara, that intelligence or knowledge does not, as the Vai*s*eshikas teach, constitute a mere attribute of the soul which in itself is essentially non-intelligent, but is the very essence of the soul. The soul is not a knower, but knowledge; not intelligent, but intelligence.—Râmânu*g*a, on the other hand, explains '*gñ*a' by '*gñ*ât*ri*,' i. e. knower, knowing agent, and considers the Sûtra to be directed not only against the Vai*s*eshikas, but also against those philosophers who—like the Sâṅkhyas and the Vedântins of *S*aṅkara's school—maintain that the soul is not a knowing agent, but pure *k*aitanya.—The wording of the Sûtra certainly seems to favour Râmânu*g*a's interpretation; we can hardly imagine that an author definitely holding the views of *S*aṅkara should, when propounding the important dogma of the soul's nature, use the term *gñ*a of which the most obvious interpretation is *gñ*ât*ri*, not *gñ*ânam.

Adhik. XIII (19–32) treats the question whether the individual soul is a*n*u, i. e. of very minute size, or omnipresent, all-pervading (sarvagata, vyâpin). Here, again, we meet with diametrically opposite views.—In *S*aṅkara's opinion the Sûtras 19–28 represent the pûrvapaksha view, according to which the *g*îva is a*n*u, while Sûtra 29 formulates the siddhânta. viz. that the *g*îva, which in reality is all-pervading, is spoken of as a*n*u in some scriptural passages, because the qualities of the internal organ—which itself is a*n*u—constitute the essence of the individual soul as long as the latter is implicated in the sa*m*sâra.—According to Râmânu*g*a, on the other hand, the first Sûtra of the adhikara*n*a gives utterance to the siddhânta view, according to which the soul is of minute size; the Sûtras 20–25 confirm this view and refute objections raised against it; while the

Sûtras 26–29 resume the question already mooted under Sûtra 18, viz. in what relation the soul as knowing agent (*gñâtri*) stands to knowledge (*gñâna*).—In order to decide between the conflicting claims of these two interpretations we must enter into some details.—*S*aṅkara maintains that Sûtras 19–28 state and enforce a pûrvapaksha view, which is finally refuted in 29. What here strikes us at the outset, is the unusual length to which the defence of a mere prima facie view is carried; in no other place the Sûtras take so much trouble to render plausible what is meant to be rejected in the end, and an unbiassed reader will certainly feel inclined to think that in 19–28 we have to do, not with the preliminary statement of a view finally to be abandoned, but with an elaborate bonâ fide attempt to establish and vindicate an essential dogma of the system. Still it is not altogether impossible that the pûrvapaksha should here be treated at greater length than usual, and the decisive point is therefore whether we can, with *S*aṅkara, look upon Sûtra 29 as embodying a refutation of the pûrvapaksha and thus implicitly acknowledging the doctrine that the individual soul is all-pervading. Now I think there can be no doubt that *S*aṅkara's interpretation of the Sûtra is exceedingly forced. Literally translated (and leaving out the non-essential word 'prâg*ñ*avat') the Sûtra runs as follows: 'But on account of that quality (or "those qualities;" or else "on account of the quality—or qualities—of that") being the essence, (there is) that designation (or "the designation of that").' This *S*aṅkara maintains to mean, 'Because the qualities of the buddhi are the essence of the soul in the sa*m*sâra state, therefore the soul itself is sometimes spoken of as a*n*u.' Now, in the first place, nothing in the context warrants the explanation of the first 'tat' by buddhi. And—which is more important—in the second place, it is more than doubtful whether on *S*aṅkara's own system the qualities of the buddhi—such as pleasure, pain, desire, aversion, &c.—can with any propriety be said to constitute the essence of the soul even in the sa*m*sâra state. The essence of the soul in whatever state, according to *S*aṅkara's system, is knowledge or intelligence; whatever is due to its association with the buddhi is non-essential or, more strictly, unreal, false.

There are no similar difficulties in the way of Râmânu*g*a's interpretation of the adhikara*n*a. He agrees with *S*ankara in the explanation of Sûtras 19-25, with this difference that he views them as setting forth, not the pûrvapaksha, but the siddhânta. Sûtras 26-28 also are interpreted in a manner not very different from *S*ankara's, special stress being laid on the distinction made by Scripture between knowledge as a mere quality and the soul as a knowing agent, the substratum of knowledge. This discussion naturally gives rise to the question how it is that Scripture in some places makes use of the term vi*gñ*âna when meaning the individual soul. The answer is given in Sûtra 29, 'The soul is designated as knowledge because it has that quality for its essence,' i. e. because knowledge is the essential characteristic quality of the soul, therefore the term 'knowledge' is employed here and there to denote the soul itself. This latter interpretation gives rise to no doubt whatever. It closely follows the wording of the text and does not necessitate any forced supplementation. The 'tu' of the Sûtra which, according to *S*ankara, is meant to discard the pûrvapaksha, serves on Râmânu*g*a's view to set aside a previously-raised objection; an altogether legitimate assumption.

Of the three remaining Sûtras of the adhikara*n*a (30-32), 30 explains, according to *S*ankara, that the soul may be called a*n*u, since, as long as it exists in the sa*m*sâra condition, it is connected with the buddhi. According to Râmânu*g*a the Sûtra teaches that the soul may be called vi*gñ*âna because the latter constitutes its essential quality as long as it exists.—Sûtra 31 intimates, according to *S*ankara, that in the states of deep sleep, and so on, the soul is potentially connected with the buddhi, while in the waking state that connexion becomes actually manifest. The same Sûtra, according to Râmânu*g*a, teaches that *gñ*ât*ri*tva is properly said to constitute the soul's essential nature, although it is actually manifested in some states of the soul only.—In Sûtra 32, finally, *S*ankara sees a statement of the doctrine that, unless the soul had the buddhi for its limiting adjunct, it would either be permanently cognizing or permanently non-cognizing; while, according to Râmânuga, the Sûtra means that the soul would either be permanently cognizing or permanently non-cognizing, if it were pure knowledge and all-pervading (instead of being *gñâtri* and a*n*u, as it is in reality).—The three Sûtras can be made to fit in with either interpretation, although it must be noted that none of them explicitly refers to the soul's connexion with the buddhi.

Adhik. XIV and XV (33–39; 40) refer to the kart*ri*tva of the *g*îva, i.e. the question whether the soul is an agent. Sûtras 33–39 clearly say that it is such. But as, according to *S*aṅkara's system, this cannot be the final view,—the soul being essentially non-active, and all action belonging to the world of upâdhis,—he looks upon the next following Sûtra (40) as constituting an adhikara*n*a by itself, and teaching that the soul is an agent when connected with the instruments of action, buddhi, &c., while it ceases to be so when dissociated from them, 'just as the carpenter acts in both ways,' i.e. just as the carpenter works as long as he wields his instruments, and rests after having laid them aside.—Râmânuga, perhaps more naturally, does not separate Sûtra 40 from the preceding Sûtras, but interprets it as follows: Activity is indeed an essential attribute of the soul; but therefrom it does not follow that the soul is always actually active, just as the carpenter, even when furnished with the requisite instruments, may either work or not work, just as he pleases.

Adhik. XVI (41, 42) teaches that the soul in its activity is dependent on the Lord who impels it with a view to its former actions.

Adhik. XVII (43–53) treats of the relation of the individual soul to Brahman. Sûtra 43 declares that the individual soul is a part (a*ms*a) of Brahman, and the following Sûtras show how that relation does not involve either that Brahman is affected by the imperfections, sufferings, &c. of the souls, or that one soul has to participate in the experiences of other souls. The two commentators of course take entirely different views of the doctrine that the soul is a part of Brahman. According to Râmânu*g*a the souls are in reality parts of Brahman[1]; according to *S*aṅkara the 'a*m*sa' of the Sûtra must be understood to mean 'a*m*sa iva,' 'a part as it were;' the one universal indivisible Brahman having no real parts, but appearing to be divided owing to its limiting adjuncts.—One Sûtra (50) in this adhikara*n*a calls for special notice. According to *S*aṅkara the words 'âbhâsa eva *k*a' mean '(the soul is) a mere reflection,' which, as the commentators remark, is a statement of the so-called pratibimbavâda, i.e. the doctrine that the so-called individual soul is nothing but the reflection of the Self in the buddhi; while Sutra 43 had propounded the so-called ava*kkh*edavâda, i.e. the doctrine that the soul is the highest Self in so far as limited by its adjuncts.—According to Râmânu*g*a the âbhâsa of the Sûtra has to be taken in the

[1] *G*îvasya kart*ri*tva*m* paramapurushâyattam ity uktam. Idânî*m* kim aya*m* *g*îva*h* parasmâd atyantabhinna*h* uta param eva brahma bhrântam uta brahmaivopâdhyava*kkh*innam atha brahmâ*m*sa iti sa*m*sayyate *s*rutivipratipatte*h* sa*m*saya*h*. Nanu tadananyam ârambha*n*a*s*abdâdibhya*h* adhika*m* tu bhedanirde*s*âd ity atraivâyam artho nir*n*îta*h*. Satya*m* sa eva nânâtvaikatva*s*rutivipratipattyâ*s*kshipya *g*îvasya brahmâ*m*satvopapâdanena vi*s*eshato nir*n*îyate. Yâvad dhi *g*îvasya brahmâ*m*satva*m* na nir*n*îtam tâvag *g*îvasya brahmano*s*nanyatva*m* brahma*n*as tasmâd adhikatva*m* *k*a na pratitish*th*ati. Ki*m* tâvat prâptam. Atyanta*m* bhinna iti. Kuta*h*. *G*ñâ*g*ñau dvâv ityâdibhedanirde*s*ât. *G*ñâ*g*ñayor abheda*s*rutayas tv agninâ si*ñk*ed itivad viruddhârthapratipâdanâd aupa*k*ârikya*h*. Brahma*n*o*s* *m*so *g*îva ity api na sâdhîya*h*, ekavastvekade*s*avâ*k*î hy a*m*sa*s*abda*h*, *g*îvasya brahmaikade*s*atve tadgatâ doshâ brahma*n*i bhaveyu*h*. Na *k*a brahmakha*nd*o *g*îva ity a*m*satvopapatti*h* kha*nd*anânarhatvâd brahma*n*a*h* prâguktadoshaprasaṅgâ*k* *k*a, tasmâd atyantabhinnasya tada*m*satva*m* durupapâdam. Yadvâ bhrânta*m* brahmaiva *g*îva*h*. Kuta*h*. Tat tvam asi ayam âtmâ brahmetyâdibrahmâtmabhâvopade*s*ât, nânâtmatvavâdinyas tu pratyakshâdisiddhârthânuvâditvâd ananyathâsiddhâdvaitopade*s*aparâbhi*h* *s*rutibhi*h* pratyakshâdaya*s* *k*a avidyântargatâ*h* khyâpyante.—Athavâ brahmaivânâdyupâdhyava*kkh*inna*m* *g*îva*h*. Kuta*h*. Tata eva brahmâtmabhâvopade*s*ât. Na *k*âyam upâdhir bhrântiparikalpita ita vaktu*m* *s*akya*m* bandhamokshâdivyavasthânupapatter. Ity eva*m* prâpte*s*bhidhîyate. Brahmâ*m*sa iti. Kuta*h*. Nânâvyapade*s*âd anyathâ *k*aikatvena vyapade*s*âd ubhayathâ hi vyapade*s*o d*ri*syate. Nânâvyapade*s*as tâvat srash*t*ritvas*r*i*g*yatva — niyant*ri*tvaniyâmyatva — sarva*g*ñatvâ*g*ñatva—svâdhînatvaparâdhînatva — *s*uddhatvâ*s*uddhatva — kalyâ*n*agu*n*âkaratvaviparîtatva—patitva*s*eshatvâdibhir d*ri*syate. Anyathâ *k*âbhedena vyapade*s*o*s*pi tat tvam asi ayam âtmâ brahmetyâdibhir d*ri*syate. Api dâ*s*akitavâditvam apy adhîyate eke, brahma dâ*s*â brahma dâ*s*â brahmeme kitavâ ity âtharva*n*ikâ brahma*n*o dâ*s*akitavâditvam apy adhîyate, tata*s* *k*a sarva*g*îvavyâpitvena abhedo vyapadi*s*yata ity artha*h*. Evam ubhayavyapade*s*amukhyatvasiddhaye *g*îvo*s*ya*m* brahma*n*o*s* *m*sa ity abhyupagantavya*h*.

sense of hetvâbhâsa, a fallacious argument, and the Sûtra is explained as being directed against the reasoning of those Vedântins according to whom the soul is Brahman in so far as limited by non-real adjuncts [1].

Pâda IV.

Adhik. I, II, III (1–4; 5–6; 7) teach that the prâ*n*as (by which generic name are denoted the buddhîndriyas, karmendriyas, and the manas) spring from Brahman; are eleven in number; and are of minute size (a*n*u).

Adhik. IV, V, VI (8; 9–12; 13) inform us also that the mukhya prâ*n*a, i.e. the vital air, is produced from Brahman; that it is a principle distinct from air in general and from the prâ*n*as discussed above; and that it is minute (a*n*u).

Adhik. VII and VIII (14–16; 17–19) teach that the prâ*n*as are superintended and guided in their activity by special divinities, and that they are independent principles, not mere modifications of the mukhya prâ*n*a.

Adhik. IX (20–22) declares that the evolution of names and forms (the nâmarûpavyâkara*n*a) is the work, not of the individual soul, but of the Lord.

THIRD ADHYÂYA.

Pâda I.

Adhik. I (1–7) teaches that the soul, when passing out of the body at the time of death, remains invested with the subtle material elements (bhûtasûkshma) which serve as an abode to the prâ*n*as attached to the soul.

Adhik. II (8–11) shows that, when the souls of those who had enjoyed the reward of their good works in the moon descend to the earth in order to undergo a new embodiment, there cleaves to them a remainder (anu*s*aya) of their

[1] Nanu bhrântabrahma*g*îvavâde *s*py avidyâk*ri*topâdhibhedâd bhogavyavasthâdaya upapadyanta ata âha, âbhâsa eva *k*a. Akha*nd*aikarasaprakâ*s*amâtratvarûpasya svarûpatirodhânapûrvakopâdhibhedopapâdanahetur âbhâsa eva. Prakâ*s*aikasvarûpasya prakâ*s*atirodhâna*m* prakâ*s*anâ*s*a eveti prâg evopapâditam. Âbhâsâ eveti vâ pâ*th*a*h*, tathâ sati hetava âbhâsâ*h*.

former deeds which determines the nature of the new embodiment.

Adhik. III (12–21) discusses the fate after death of those whom their good works do not entitle to pass up to the moon.

Adhik. IV, V, VI (22; 23; 24–27) teach that the subtle bodies of the souls descending from the moon through the ether, air, &c., do not become identical with ether, air, &c., but only like them; that the entire descent occupies a short time only; and that, when the souls finally enter into plants and so on, they do not participate in the life of the latter, but are merely in external contact with them.

Pâda II.

Adhik. I (1–6) treats of the soul in the dreaming state. According to *S*ankara the three first Sûtras discuss the question whether the creative activity ascribed to the soul in some scriptural passages produces things as real as those by which the waking soul is surrounded, or not; Sûtra 3 settles the point by declaring that the creations of the dreaming soul are mere 'Mâyâ,' since they do not fully manifest the character of real objects. Sûtra 4 adds that dreams, although mere Mâyâ, yet have a prophetic quality. Sûtras 5 and 6 finally reply to the question why the soul, which after all is a part of the Lord and as such participates in his excellencies, should not be able to produce in its dreams a real creation, by the remark that the soul's knowledge and power are obscured by its connexion with the gross body.

The considerably diverging interpretation given of this adhikara*n*a by Râmânu*g*a has the advantage of more closely connecting the Sûtras with each other. According to him the question is not whether the creations of a dream are real or not, but whether they are the work of the individual soul or of the Lord acting within the soul. Sûtras 1 and 2 set forth the pûrvapaksha. The creations of dreams (are the work of the individual soul); for thus Scripture declares: 'And the followers of some *s*âkhâs declare (the soul to be) a creator,' &c. The third Sûtra states the siddhânta view: 'But the creations of dreams are Mâyâ, i.e. are of a wonderful nature (and as such cannot be effected by the individual soul), since (in this life) the nature (of the soul) is not fully manifested.' Concerning the word 'mâyâ,' Râmânu*g*a remarks, 'mâyâ*s*abdo hy â*sk*aryavâ*k*î *g*anaka*s*ya kule *g*âtâ devamâyeva nirmitâ ityâdishu tathâ dar*s*anât.' The three remaining Sûtras are exhibited in the *S*rî-bhâshya in a different order, the fourth Sûtra, according to *S*aṅkara, being the sixth according to Râmânu*g*a. Sûtras 4 and 5 (according to Râmânu*g*a's numeration) are explained by Râmânu*g*a very much in the same way as by *S*aṅkara; but owing to the former's statement of the subject-matter of the whole adhikara*n*a they connect themselves more intimately with the preceding Sûtras than is possible on *S*aṅkara's interpretation. In Sûtra 6 (sû*k*aka*s* *k*a hi) Râmânu*g*a sees a deduction from the siddhânta of the adhikara*n*a, 'Because the images of a dream are produced by the highest Lord himself, therefore they have prophetic significance.'

Adhik. II teaches that in the state of deep dreamless sleep the soul abides within Brahman in the heart.

Adhik. III (9) expounds the reasons entitling us to assume that the soul awakening from sleep is the same that went to sleep.—Adhik. IV (9) explains the nature of a swoon.

Adhik. V (11–21) is, according to *S*aṅkara, taken up with the question as to the nature of the highest Brahman in which the individual soul is merged in the state of deep sleep. Sûtra 11 declares that twofold characteristics (viz. absence and presence of distinctive attributes, nirvi*s*eshatva and savi*s*eshatva) cannot belong to the highest Brahman even through its stations, i.e. its limiting adjuncts; since all passages which aim at setting forth Brahman's nature declare it to be destitute of all distinctive attributes.—The fact, Sûtra 12 continues, that in many passages Brahman is spoken of as possessing distinctive attributes is of no relevancy, since wherever there are mentioned limiting adjuncts, on which all distinction depends, it is specially stated that Brahman in itself is free from all diversity; and—Sûtra 13 adds—in some places the assumption of diversity is specially objected to.—That Brahman is devoid of all form (Sûtra 14), is the pre-eminent meaning of all Vedânta-texts setting forth Brahman's nature.—That Brahman is represented as having different forms, as it were, is due to its connexion with its (unreal) limiting adjuncts; just as the light of the sun appears straight or crooked, as it were, according to the nature of the things he illuminates (15).—The B*ri*hadâra*n*yaka expressly declares that Brahman is one uniform mass of intelligence (16); and the same is taught in other scriptural passages and in Sm*ri*ti (17).—At the unreality of the apparent manifoldness of the Self, caused by the limiting adjuncts, aim those scriptural passages in which the Self is compared to the sun, which remains one although his reflections on the surface of the water are many (18).—Nor must the objection be raised that that comparison is unsuitable, because the Self is not material like the sun, and there are no real upâdhis separate from it as the water is from the sun; for the comparison merely means to indicate that, as the reflected image of the sun participates in the changes, increase, decrease, &c., which the water undergoes while the sun himself remains unaffected thereby, so the true Self is not affected by the attributes of the upâdhis, while, in so far as it is limited by the latter, it is affected by them as it were (19, 20).—That the Self is within the upâdhis, Scripture declares (21).

From the above explanation of this important adhikara*n*a the one given in the *S*rî-bhâshya differs totally. According to Râmânu*g*a the adhikara*n*a raises the question whether the imperfections clinging to the individual soul (the discussion of which has now come to an end) affect also the highest Lord who, according to Scripture, abides within the soul as antaryâmin. 'Notwithstanding the abode (of the highest Self within the soul) (it is) not (affected by the soul's imperfections) because everywhere (the highest Self is represented) as having twofold characteristics (viz. being, on one hand, free from all evil, apahatapâpman, vi*g*ara, vim*ri*tyu, &c., and, on the other hand, endowed with all auspicious qualities, satyakâma, satyasa*m*kalpa, &c.) (11).—Should it be objected that, just as the soul although essentially free from evil—according to the Pra*g*âpativâkya in the *Kh*ândogya—yet is liable to imperfections owing to its connexion with a variety of bodies, so the antaryâmin also is affected by abiding within bodies; we deny this because in every section of the chapter referring to the antaryâmin (in the B*ri*hadâra*n*yaka) he is expressly called the Immortal, the ruler within; which shows him to be free from the shortcomings of the *g*îva (12).—Some, moreover, expressly assert that, although the Lord and the soul are within one body, the soul only is imperfect, not the Lord (dvâ supar*n*â sayu*g*â sakhâyâ) (13).—Should it be said that, according to the *Kh*ândogya, Brahman entered together with the souls into the elements previously to the evolution of names and forms, and hence participates in the latter, thus becoming implicated in the sa*m*sâra; we reply that Brahman, although connected with such and such forms, is in itself devoid of form, since it is the principal element (agent; pradhâna) in the bringing about of names and forms (according to 'âkâ*s*o ha vai nâmarûpayor nirvahitâ') (14).—But does not the passage 'satya*m* *g*ñânam anantam brahma' teach that Brahman is nothing but light (intelligence) without any difference, and does not the passage 'neti neti' deny of it all qualities?—As in order, we reply, not to deprive passages as the one quoted from the Taittirîya of their purport, we admit that Brahman's nature is light, so we must also admit that Brahman is satyasa*m*kalpa, and so on; for if not, the passages in which those qualities are asserted would become purportless (15).—Moreover the Taittirîya passage only asserts so much, viz. the prakâ*s*arûpatâ of Brahman, and does not deny other qualities (16).—And the passage 'neti neti' will be discussed later on.—The ubhayaliṅgatva of Brahman in the sense assigned above is asserted in many places of *S*ruti and Sm*ri*ti (17).—Because Brahman although abiding in many places is not touched by their imperfections, the similes of the reflected sun, of the ether limited by jars, &c., are applicable to it (18).—Should it be said that the illustration is not an appropriate one, because the sun is apprehended in the water erroneously only while the antaryâmin really abides within all things, and therefore must be viewed as sharing their defects (19); we reply that what the simile means to negative is merely that Brahman should, owing to its inherence in many places, participate in the increase, decrease, and so on, of its abodes. On this view both similes are appropriate (20).—Analogous similes we observe to be employed in ordinary life, as when we compare a man to a lion (21).

Sûtras 22–30 constitute, according to *S*aṅkara, a new adhikara*n*a (VI), whose object it is to show that the clause 'not so, not so' (neti neti; B*ri*hadâr.) negatives, not Brahman itself, but only the two forms of Brahman described in the preceding part of the chapter. Sûtras 23–26 further dwell on Brahman being in reality devoid of all distinctive attributes which are altogether due to the upâdhis. The last four Sûtras return to the question how, Brahman being one only, the souls are in so many places spoken of as different from it, and, two explanatory hypotheses having been rejected, the conclusion is arrived at that all difference is unreal, due to fictitious limiting adjuncts.

According to Râmânu*g*a, Sûtras 22 ff. continue the discussion started in Sûtra 11. How, the question is asked, can the ubhayaliṅgatva of Brahman be maintained considering that the 'not so, not so' of the B*ri*hadâra*n*yaka denies of Brahman all the previously mentioned modes (prakâra), so that it can only be called that which is (sanmâtra)?—The reply given in Sûtra 22 is that 'not so, not so' does not deny of Brahman the distinctive qualities or modes declared previously (for it would be senseless at first to teach them, and finally to deny them again[1]), but merely denies the prâk*ri*taitâvattva, the previously stated limited nature of Brahman, i.e. it denies that Brahman possesses only the previously mentioned qualifications. With this agrees, that subsequently to 'neti neti' Scripture itself enunciates further qualifications of Brahman.—That Brahman as stated

[1] All the mentioned modes of Brahman are known from Scripture only, not from ordinary experience. If the latter were the case, then, and then only, Scripture might at first refer to them 'anuvâdena,' and finally negative them.

above is not the object of any other means of proof but Scripture is confirmed in Sûtra 23, 'Scripture declares Brahman to be the non-manifest.'—And the intuition (sâkshâtkâra) of Brahman ensues only upon its sa*m*râdhana, i.e. upon its being perfectly pleased by the worshipper's devotion, as Scripture and Sm*ri*ti declare (24).—That this interpretation of 'neti' is the right one, is likewise shown by the fact that in the same way as prakâ*s*a, luminousness, *gñ*âna, intelligence, &c., so also the quality of being differentiated by the world (prapa*ñk*avi*s*ish*t*atâ) is intuited as non-different, i.e. as likewise qualifying Brahman; and that prakâ*s*a, and so on, characterise Brahman, is known through repeated practice (on the part of *ri*shis like Vâmadeva) in the work of sa*m*râdhana mentioned before (25).—For all these reasons Brahman is connected with the infinite, i.e. the infinite number of auspicious qualities; for thus the twofold indications (liṅga) met with in Scripture are fully justified (26).—In what relation, then, does the a*k*id vastu, i.e. the non-sentient matter, which, according to the B*ri*hadâra*n*yaka, is one of the forms of Brahman, stand to the latter?—Non-sentient beings might, in the first place, be viewed as special arrangements (sa*m*sthânavi*s*eshâ*h*) of Brahman, as the coils are of the body of the snake; for Brahman is designated as both, i.e. sometimes as one with the world (Brahman is all this, &c.), sometimes as different from it (Let me enter into those elements, &c.) (27).—Or, in the second place, the relation of the two might be viewed as analogous to that of light and the luminous object which are two and yet one, both being fire (28).—Or, in the third place, the relation is like that stated before, i.e. the material world is, like the individual souls (whose case was discussed in II, 3, 43), a part—a*m*sa—of Brahman (29, 30).

Adhik. VII (31–37) explains how some metaphorical expressions, seemingly implying that there is something different from Brahman, have to be truly understood.

Adhik. VIII (38–41) teaches that the reward of works is not, as *G*aimini opines, the independent result of the works acting through the so-called apûrva, but is allotted by the Lord.

PÂDA III.

With the third pâda of the second adhyâya a new section of the work begins, whose task it is to describe how the individual soul is enabled by meditation on Brahman to obtain final release. The first point to be determined here is what constitutes a meditation on Brahman, and, more particularly, in what relation those parts of the Upanishads stand to each other which enjoin identical or partly identical meditations. The reader of the Upanishads cannot fail to observe that the texts of the different *s*âkhâs contain many chapters of similar, often nearly identical, contents, and that in some cases the text of even one and the same *s*âkhâ exhibits the same matter in more or less varied forms. The reason of this clearly is that the common stock of religious and philosophical ideas which were in circulation at the time of the composition of the Upanishads found separate expression in the different priestly communities; hence the same speculations, legends, &c. reappear in various places of the sacred Scriptures in more or less differing dress. Originally, when we may suppose the members of each Vedic school to have confined themselves to the study of their own sacred texts, the fact that the texts of other schools contained chapters of similar contents would hardly appear to call for special note or comment; not any more than the circumstance that the sacrificial performances enjoined on the followers of some particular *s*âkhâ were found described with greater or smaller modifications in the books of other *s*âkhâs also. But already at a very early period, at any rate long before the composition of the Vedânta-sûtras in their present form, the Vedic theologians must have apprehended the truth that, in whatever regards sacrificial acts, one *s*âkhâ may indeed safely follow its own texts, disregarding the texts of all other *s*âkhâs; that, however, all texts which aim at throwing light on the nature of Brahman and the relation to it of the human soul must somehow or other be combined into one consistent systematical whole equally valid for the followers of all Vedic schools. For, as we have had occasion to remark above, while acts may be performed by different individuals in different ways, cognition is defined by the nature of the object cognised, and hence can be one only, unless it ceases to be true cognition. Hence the attempts, on the one hand, of discarding by skilful interpretation all contradictions met with in the sacred text, and, on the other hand, of showing what sections of the different Upanishads have to be viewed as teaching the same matter, and therefore must be combined in one meditation. The latter is the special task of the present pâda.

Adhik. I and II (1–4; 5) are concerned with the question whether those vidyâs, which are met with in identical or similar form in more than one sacred text, are to be considered as constituting several vidyâs, or one vidyâ only. *S*a*n*kara remarks that the question affects only those vidyâs whose object is the qualified Brahman; for the knowledge of the non-qualified Brahman, which is of an absolutely uniform nature, can of course be one only wherever it is set forth. But things lie differently in those cases where the object of knowledge is the sagu*n*am brahma or some outward manifestation of Brahman; for the qualities as well as manifestations of Brahman are many. Anticipating the subject of a later adhikara*n*a, we may take for an example the so-called *Sâ*n*d*ilyavidyâ which is met with in *Kh*. Up. III, 14, again—in an abridged form—in B*ri*. Up. V, 6, and, moreover, in the tenth book of the *S*atapatha-brâhma*n*a (X, 6, 3). The three passages enjoin a meditation on Brahman as possessing certain attributes, some of which are specified in all the three texts (as, for instance, manomayatva, bhârûpatva), while others are peculiar to each separate passage (prâ*n*a*s*arîratva and satyasa*m*kalpatva, for instance, being mentioned in the *Kh*ândogya Upanishad and *S*atapatha-brâhma*n*a, but not in the B*ri*hadâra*n*yaka Upanishad, which, on its part, specifies sarvava*s*itva, not referred to in the two other texts). Here, then, there is room for a doubt whether the three passages refer to one object of knowledge or not. To the devout Vedântin the question is not a purely theoretical one, but of immediate practical interest. For if the three texts are to be held apart, there are three different meditations to be gone through; if, on the other hand, the vidyâ is one only, all the different qualities of Brahman mentioned in the three passages have to be combined into one meditation.—The decision is here, as in all similar cases, in favour of the latter alternative. A careful examination of the three passages shows that the object of meditation is one only; hence the meditation also is one only, comprehending all the attributes mentioned in the three texts.

Adhik. III (6–8) discusses the case of vidyâs being really separate, although apparently identical. The examples selected are the udgîthavidyâs of the *Kh*ândogya Upanishad (I, 1–3) and the B*ri*hadâra*n*yaka Upanishad (I, 3), which, although showing certain similarities—such as bearing the same name and the udgîtha being in both identified with prâ*n*a—yet are to be held apart, because the subject of the *Kh*ândogya vidyâ is not the whole udgîtha but only the sacred syllable Om, while the B*ri*hadâra*n*yaka Upanishad represents the whole udgîtha as the object of meditation.

Sûtra 9 constitutes in *S*aṅkara's view a new adhikara*n*a (IV), proving that in the passage, 'Let a man meditate' (*Kh*. Up. I, 1, 1), the O*m*kâra and the udgîtha stand in the relation of one specifying the other, the meaning being, 'Let a man meditate on that O*m*kâra which,' &c.—According to Râmânu*g*a's interpretation, which seems to fall in more satisfactorily with the form and the wording of the Sûtra, the latter merely furnishes an additional argument for the conclusion arrived at in the preceding adhikara*n*a.—Adhik. V (10) determines the unity of the so-called prâ*n*a-vidyâs and the consequent comprehension of the different qualities of the prâ*n*a, which are mentioned in the different texts, within one meditation.

Adhik. VI comprises, according to *S*aṅkara, the Sûtras 11–13. The point to be settled is whether in all the meditations on Brahman all its qualities are to be included or only those mentioned in the special vidyâ. The decision is that the essential and unalterable attributes of Brahman, such as bliss and knowledge, are to be taken into account everywhere, while those which admit of a more or less (as, for instance, the attribute of having joy for its head, mentioned in the Taitt. Up.) are confined to special meditations.—Adhik. VII (14, 15), according to *S*ankara, aims at proving that the object of Ka*th*a Up. III, 10, 11 is one only, viz. to show that the highest Self is higher than everything, so that the passage constitutes one vidyâ only. —Adhik. VIII (16, 17) determines, according to *S*ankara, that the Self spoken of in Ait. Âr. II, 4, 1, 1 is not a lower form of the Self (the so-called sûtrâtman), but the highest Self; the discussion of that point in this place being due to the wish to prove that the attributes of the highest Self have to be comprehended in the Aitareyaka meditation.

According to Râmânu*g*a the Sûtras 11–17 constitute a single adhikara*n*a whose subject is the same as that of *S*ankara's sixth adhikara*n*a. Sûtras 11–13 are, on the whole, explained as by *S*ankara; Sûtra 12, however, is said to mean, 'Such attributes as having joy for its head, &c. are not to be viewed as qualities of Brahman, and therefore not to be included in every meditation; for if they were admitted as qualities, difference would be introduced into Brahman's nature, and that would involve a more or less on Brahman's part.' Sûtras 14–17 continue the discussion of the passage about the priya*s*irastva.—If priya*s*irastva, &c. are not to be viewed as real qualities of Brahman, for what purpose does the text mention them?—'Because,' Sûtra 14 replies, 'there is no other purpose, Scripture mentions them for the purpose of pious meditation.'—But how is it known that the Self of delight is the highest Self? (owing to which you maintain that having limbs, head, &c. cannot belong to it as attributes.)—'Because,' Sûtra 15 replies, 'the term "Self" (âtmâ ânandamaya) is applied to it.'—But in the previous parts of the chapter the term Self (in âtmâ prâ*n*amaya, &c.) is applied to non-Selfs also; how then do you know that in âtmâ ânandamaya it denotes the real Self?—'The term Self,' Sûtra 16 replies, 'is employed here to denote the highest Self as in many other passages (âtmâ vâ idam eka, &c.), as we conclude from the subsequent passage, viz. he wished, May I be many.'—But, an objection is raised, does not the context show that the term 'Self,' which in all the preceding clauses about the prâ*n*amaya, &c. denoted something other than the Self, does the same in ânandamaya âtman, and is not the context of greater weight than a subsequent passage?—To this question asked in the former half of 17 (anvayâd iti *k*et) the latter half replies, 'Still it denotes the Self, owing to the affirmatory statement,' i.e. the fact of the highest Self having been affirmed in a previous passage also, viz. II, 1, 'From that Self sprang ether.'

Adhik. IX (18) discusses a minor point connected with the prâ*n*asa*m*vâda.—The subject of Adhik. X (19) has been indicated already above under Adhik. I.—Adhik. XI (20–22) treats of a case of a contrary nature; in B*ri*. Up. V, 5, Brahman is represented first as abiding in the sphere of the sun, and then as abiding within the eye; we therefore, in spite of certain counter-indications, have to do with two separate vidyâs.—Adhik. XII (23) refers to a similar case; certain attributes of Brahman mentioned in the Râ*n*âya-nîya-khila have not to be introduced into the corresponding *Kh*ândogya vidyâ, because the stated difference of Brahman's abode involves difference of vidyâ.—Adhik. XIII (24) treats of another instance of two vidyâs having to be held apart.

Adhik. XIV (25) decides that certain detached mantras and brâhma*n*a passages met with in the beginning of some Upanishads—as, for instance, a brâhma*n*a about the mahâvrata ceremony at the beginning of the Aitareya-âra*n*yaka—do, notwithstanding their position which seems to connect them with the brahmavidyâ, not belong to the latter, since they show unmistakable signs of being connected with sacrificial acts.

Adhik. XV (26) treats of the passages stating that the man dying in the possession of true knowledge shakes off all his good and evil deeds, and affirms that a statement, made in some of those passages only, to the effect that the good and evil deeds pass over to the friends and enemies of the deceased, is valid for all the passages.

Sûtras 27–30 constitute, according to *S*aṅkara, two adhikara*n*as of which the former (XVI; 27, 28) decides that the shaking off of the good and evil deeds takes place—not, as the Kaush. Up. states, on the road to Brahman's world—but at the moment of the soul's departure from the body; the Kaushîtaki statement is therefore not to be taken literally.—The latter adhikara*n*a (XVII; 29, 30) treats of the cognate question whether the soul that has freed itself from its deeds proceeds in all cases on the road of the gods (as said in the Kaush. Up.), or not. The decision is that he only whose knowledge does not pass beyond the sagu*n*am brahma proceeds on that road, while the soul of him who knows the nirgu*n*am brahma becomes one with it without moving to any other place.

The *S*rî-bhâshya treats the four Sûtras as one adhikara*n*a whose two first Sûtras are explained as by *S*añkara, while Sûtra 29 raises an objection to the conclusion arrived at, 'the going (of the soul on the path of the gods) has a sense only if the soul's freeing itself from its works takes place in both ways, i. e. partly at the moment of death, partly on the road to Brahman; for otherwise there would be a contradiction' (the contradiction being that, if the soul's works were all shaken off at the moment of death, the subtle body would likewise perish at that moment, and then the bodiless soul would be unable to proceed on the path of the gods).—To this Sûtra 30 replies, 'The complete shaking off of the works at the moment of death is possible, since matters of that kind are observed in Scripture,' i. e. since scriptural passages show that even he whose works are entirely annihilated, and who has manifested himself in his true shape, is yet connected with some kind of body; compare the passage, 'para*m* *g*yotir upasampadya svena rûpe*n*âbhinishpadyate sa tatra paryeti krî*d*an ramamâna*h* sa svarâ*d* bhavati tasya sarveshu lokeshu kâma*k*âro bhavati.' That subtle body is not due to karman, but to the soul's vidyâmâhâtmya.—That the explanation of the *S*rî-bhâshya agrees with the text as well as *S*añkara's, a comparison of the two will show; especially forced is *S*añkara's explanation of 'arthavattvam ubhayathâ,' which is said to mean that there is arthavattva in one case, and non-arthavattva in the other case.

The next Sûtra (31) constitutes an adhikara*n*a (XVIII)

deciding that the road of the gods is followed not only by those knowing the vidyâs which specially mention the going on that road, but by all who are acquainted with the saguna-vidyâs of Brahman.—The explanation given in the Srî-bhâshya (in which Sûtras 31 and 32 have exchanged places) is similar, with the difference however that all who meditate on Brahman—without any reference to the distinction of nirguna and saguna—proceed after death on the road of the gods. (The Srî-bhâshya reads 'sarveshâm,' i. e. all worshippers, not 'sarvâsâm,' all saguna-vidyâs.)

Adhik. XIX (32) decides that, although the general effect of true knowledge is release from all forms of body, yet even such beings as have reached perfect knowledge may retain a body for the purpose of discharging certain offices. —In the Srî-bhâshya, where the Sûtra follows immediately on Sûtra 30, the adhikarana determines, in close connexion with 30, that, although those who know Brahman as a rule divest themselves of the gross body—there remaining only a subtle body which enables them to move—and no longer experience pleasure and pain, yet certain beings, although having reached the cognition of Brahman, remain invested with a gross body, and hence liable to pleasure and pain until they have fully performed certain duties.

Adhik. XX (33) teaches that the negative attributes of Brahman mentioned in some vidyâs—such as its being not gross, not subtle, &c.—are to be included in all meditations on Brahman.—Adhik. XXI (34) determines that Kâtha Up. III, 1, and Mu. Up. III, 1, constitute one vidyâ only, because both passages refer to the highest Brahman. According to Râmânuga the Sûtra contains a reply to an objection raised against the conclusion arrived at in the preceding Sûtra.—Adhik. XXII (35, 36) maintains that the two passages, Bri. Up. III, 4 and III, 5, constitute one vidyâ only, the object of knowledge being in both cases Brahman viewed as the inner Self of all.—Adhik. XXIII (37) on the contrary decides that the passage Ait. Âr. II, 2, 4, 6 constitutes not one but two meditations.—Adhik. XXIV (38) again determines that the vidyâ of the True contained in Bri. Up. V, 4, 5, is one only.—According to Râmânuga,

Sûtras 35–38 constitute one adhikara*n*a only whose subject is the same as that of XXII according to *S*aṅkara.

Adhik. XXV (39) proves that the passages *Kh*. Up. VIII, 1 and B*ri*. Up. IV, 4, 22 cannot constitute one vidyâ, since the former refers to Brahman as possessing qualities, while the latter is concerned with Brahman as destitute of qualities.—Adhik. XXVI (40, 41) treats, according to *S*aṅkara, of a minor question connected with *Kh*. Up. V, 11 ff. —According to the *S*rî-bhâshya, Sûtras 39–41 form one adhikara*n*a whose first Sûtra reaches essentially the same conclusion as *S*aṅkara under 39. Sûtras 40, 41 thereupon discuss a general question concerning the meditations on Brahman. The qualities, an opponent is supposed to remark, which in the two passages discussed are predicated of Brahman—such as va*s*itva, satyakâmatva, &c.—cannot be considered real (pâramârthika), since other passages (sa esha neti neti, and the like) declare Brahman to be devoid of all qualities. Hence those qualities cannot be admitted into meditations whose purpose is final release.—To this objection Sûtra 40 replies, '(Those qualities) are not to be left out (from the meditations on Brahman), since (in the passages under discussion as well as in other passages) they are stated with emphasis [1].'—But, another objection is raised, Scripture says that he who meditates on Brahman as satyakâma, &c. obtains a mere perishable reward, viz. the world of the fathers, and similar results specified in *Kh*. Up. VIII, 2; hence, he who is desirous of final release, must not include those qualities of Brahman in his meditation.—To this objection Sûtra 41 replies, 'Because that (i. e. the free roaming in all the worlds, the world of the fathers, &c.) is stated as proceeding therefrom (i. e. the approach to Brahman which is final release) in the case of (the soul) which has approached Brahman;' (therefore a person desirous of release, may include satyakâmatva, &c. in his meditations.)

[1] Râmânuga has here some strong remarks on the improbability of qualities emphatically attributed to Brahman, in more than one passage, having to be set aside in any meditation: 'Na *k*a mâtâpit*ri*sahasrebhyo *s* pi vatsalatara*m* *s*âstra*m* pratârakavad apâramârthikau nirasanîyau gu*n*au pramâ*n*ântarâpratipannau âdare*n*opadi*s*ya sa*m*sâra*k*akraparivartanena pûrvam eva bambhramyamânân mumukshûn bhûyo *s* pi bhramayitum alam.'

Adhik. XXVII (42) decides that those meditations which are connected with certain matters forming constituent parts of sacrificial actions, are not to be considered as permanently requisite parts of the latter.—Adhik. XXVIII (43) teaches that, in a B*ri*. Up. passage and a similar *Kh*. Up. passage, Vâyu and Prâ*n*a are not to be identified, but to be held apart.—Adhik. XXIX (44–52) decides that the fire-altars made of mind, &c., which are mentioned in the Agnirahasya, do not constitute parts of the sacrificial action (so that the mental, &c. construction of the altar could optionally be substituted for the actual one), but merely subjects of meditations.

Adhik. XXX (53, 54) treats, according to *S*aṅkara, in the way of digression, of the question whether to the Self an existence independent of the body can be assigned, or not (as the Materialists maintain).—According to the *S*rî-bhâshya the adhikara*n*a does not refer to this wide question, but is concerned with a point more immediately connected with the meditations on Brahman, viz. the question as to the form under which, in those meditations, the Self of the meditating devotee has to be viewed. The two Sûtras then have to be translated as follows: 'Some (maintain that the soul of the devotee has, in meditations, to be viewed as possessing those attributes only which belong to it in its embodied state, such as *gñ*ât*ri*tva and the like), because the Self is (at the time of meditation) in the body.' —The next Sûtra rejects this view, 'This is not so, but the separatedness (i. e. the pure isolated state in which the Self is at the time of final release when it is freed from all evil, &c.) (is to be transferred to the meditating Self), because that will be[1] the state (of the Self in the condition of final release).'

Adhik. XXXI (55, 56) decides that meditations connected with constituent elements of the sacrifice, such as the udgîtha, are, in spite of difference of svara in the udgîtha, &c., valid, not only for that *s*âkhâ in which the meditation actually is met with, but for all *s*âkhâs.—Adhik.

[1] The *S*rî-bhâshya as well as several other commentaries reads tadbhâvabhâvitvât for *S*aṅkara's tadbhâvâbhâvitvât.

XXXII (57) decides that the Vaisvânara Agni of *Kh.* Up. V, 11 ff. is to be meditated upon as a whole, not in his single parts.—Adhik. XXXIII (58) teaches that those meditations which refer to one subject, but as distinguished by different qualities, have to be held apart as different meditations. Thus the daharavidyâ, *S*â*n*d*i*lyavidyâ, &c. remain separate.

Adhik. XXXIV (59) teaches that those meditations on Brahman for which the texts assign one and the same fruit are optional, there being no reason for their being cumulated.—Adhik. XXXV (60) decides that those meditations, on the other hand, which refer to special wishes may be cumulated or optionally employed according to choice.—Adhik. XXXVI (61–66) extends this conclusion to the meditations connected with constituent elements of action, such as the udgîtha.

Pâda IV.

Adhik. I (1–17) proves that the knowledge of Brahman is not kratvartha, i. e. subordinate to action, but independent.—Adhik. II (18–20) confirms this conclusion by showing that the state of the pravrâgins is enjoined by the sacred law, and that for them vidyâ only is prescribed, not action.—Adhik. III (21, 22) decides that certain clauses forming part of vidyâs are not mere stutis (arthavâdas), but themselves enjoin the meditation.—The legends recorded in the Vedânta-texts are not to be used as subordinate members of acts, but have the purpose of glorifying—as arthavâdas—the injunctions with which they are connected (Adhik. IV, 23, 24).—For all these reasons the ûrdhvaretasa*h* require no actions but only knowledge (Adhik. V, 25).—Nevertheless the actions enjoined by Scripture, such as sacrifices, conduct of certain kinds, &c., are required as conducive to the rise of vidyâ in the mind (Adhik. VI, 26, 27).—Certain relaxations, allowed by Scripture, of the laws regarding food, are meant only for cases of extreme need (Adhik. VII, 28–31).—The âsramakarmâ*n*i are obligatory on him also who does not strive after mukti (Adhik. VIII,

32–35).—Those also who, owing to poverty and so on, are anâsrama have claims to vidyâ (Adhik. IX, 36–39).—An ûrdhvaretas cannot revoke his vow (Adhik. X, 40).—Expiation of the fall of an ûrdhvaretas (Adhik. XI, 41, 42).—Exclusion of the fallen ûrdhvaretas in certain cases (Adhik. XII, 43).—Those meditations, which are connected with subordinate members of the sacrifice, are the business of the priest, not of the *yagamâna* (Adhik. XIII, 44–46).—B*ri*. Up. III, 5, 1 enjoins mauna as a third in addition to bâlya and pâ*nd*itya (Adhik. XIV, 47–49).—By bâlya is to be understood a childlike innocent state of mind (Adhik. XV, 50).

Sûtras 51 and 52 discuss, according to Râmânu*g*a, the question when the vidyâ, which is the result of the means described in III, 4, arises. Sûtra 51 treats of that vidyâ whose result is mere exaltation (abhyudaya), and states that 'it takes place in the present life, if there is not present an obstacle in the form of a prabalakarmântara (in which latter case the vidyâ arises later only), on account of Scripture declaring this (in various passages).'—Sûtra 52, 'Thus there is also absence of a definite rule as to (the time of origination of) that knowledge whose fruit is release, it being averred concerning that one also that it is in the same condition (i. e. of sometimes having an obstacle, sometimes not).—*S*aṅkara, who treats the two Sûtras as two adhikara*n*as, agrees as to the explanation of 51, while, putting a somewhat forced interpretation on 52, he makes it out to mean that a more or less is possible only in the case of the sagu*n*a-vidyâs.

FOURTH ADHYÂYA.

PÂDA I.

Adhikara*n*a I (1, 2).—The meditation on the Âtman enjoined by Scripture is not an act to be accomplished once only, but is to be repeated again and again.

Adhik. II (3).—The devotee engaged in meditation on Brahman is to view it as constituting his own Self.

Adhik. III (4).—To the rule laid down in the preceding adhikara*n*a the so-called pratîkopâsanas, i.e. those meditations in which Brahman is viewed under a symbol or outward manifestation (as, for instance, mano brahmety upâsîta) constitute an exception, i.e. the devotee is not to consider the pratîka as constituting his own Self.

Adhik. IV (5).—In the pratîkopâsanas the pratîka is to be meditatively viewed as being one with Brahman, not Brahman as being one with the pratîka.—Râmânu*g*a takes Sûtra 5 as simply giving a reason for the decision arrived at under Sûtra 4, and therefore as not constituting a new adhikara*n*a.

Adhik. V (6).—In meditations connected with constitutives of sacrificial works (as, for instance, ya evâsau tapati tam udgîtham upâsîta) the idea of the divinity, &c. is to be transferred to the sacrificial item, not vice versâ. In the example quoted, for instance, the udgîtha is to be viewed as Âditya, not Âditya as the udgîtha.

Adhik. VI (7–10).—The devotee is to carry on his meditations in a sitting posture.—*S*a*n*kara maintains that this rule does not apply to those meditations whose result is sa*m*yagdar*s*ana; but the Sûtra gives no hint to that effect.

Adhik. VII (11).—The meditations may be carried on at any time, and in any place, favourable to concentration of mind.

Adhik. VIII (12).—The meditations are to be continued until death.—*S*a*n*kara again maintains that those meditations which lead to sa*m*yagdar*s*ana are excepted.

Adhik. IX (13).—When through those meditations the knowledge of Brahman has been reached, the vidvân is no longer affected by the consequences of either past or future evil deeds.

Adhik. X (14).—Good deeds likewise lose their efficiency. —The literal translation of the Sûtra is, 'There is likewise non-attachment (to the vidvân) of the other (i.e. of the deeds other than the evil ones, i.e. of good deeds), but on the fall (of the body, i.e. when death takes place).' The last words of the Sûtra, 'but on the fall,' are separated by *S*a*n*kara from the preceding part of the Sûtra and interpreted to mean, 'when death takes place (there results mukti of the vidvân, who through his knowledge has freed himself from the bonds of works).'—According to Râmânuga the whole Sûtra simply means, 'There is likewise non-attachment of good deeds (not at once when knowledge is reached), but on the death of the vidvân[1].'

Adhik. XI (15).—The non-operation of works stated in the two preceding adhikaranas holds good only in the case of anârabdhakârya works, i.e. those works which have not yet begun to produce their effects, while it does not extend to the ârabdhakârya works on which the present existence of the devotee depends.

Adhik. XII (16, 17).—From the rule enunciated in Adhik. X are excepted such sacrificial performances as are enjoined permanently (nitya): so, for instance, the agnihotra, for they promote the origination of knowledge.

Adhik. XIII (18).—The origination of knowledge is promoted also by such sacrificial works as are not accompanied with the knowledge of the upâsanas referring to the different members of those works.

Adhik. XIV (19).—The ârabdhakârya works have to be worked out fully by the fruition of their effects; whereupon the vidvân becomes united with Brahman.—The 'bhoga' of the Sûtra is, according to Sankara, restricted to the present existence of the devotee, since the complete knowledge obtained by him destroys the nescience which otherwise would lead to future embodiments. According to Râmânuga a number of embodied existences may have to be gone through before the effects of the ârabdhakârya works are exhausted.

PÂDA II.

This and the two remaining pâdas of the fourth adhyâya describe the fate of the vidvân after death. According to Sankara we have to distinguish the vidvân who possesses the highest knowledge, viz. that he is one with the highest

[1] Nanu vidusho *pi setikartavyatákopâsananirvrittaye vrishtyannâdiphalânîshtâny eva katham teshâm virodhâd vinâsa ukyate. Tatrâha pâte tv iti. Sarîrapâte tu teshâm vinâsah sarîrapâtâd ûrdhvam tu vidyânugunadrishtaphalâni sukritâni nasyantîty arthah.

Brahman, and the vidvân who knows only the lower Brahman, and have to refer certain Sûtras to the former and others to the latter. According to Râmânu*g*a the vidvân is one only.

Adhik. I, II, III (1-6).—On the death of the vidvân (i.e. of him who possesses the lower knowledge, according to *S*añkara) his senses are merged in the manas, the manas in the chief vital air (prâ*n*a), the vital air in the individual soul (*g*îva), the soul in the subtle elements.—According to Râmânu*g*a the combination (sampatti) of the senses with the manas, &c. is a mere conjunction (sa*m*yoga), not a merging (laya).

Adhik. IV (7).—The vidvân (i.e. according to *S*añkara, he who possesses the lower knowledge) and the avidvân, i.e. he who does not possess any knowledge of Brahman, pass through the same stages (i.e. those described hitherto) up to the entrance of the soul, together with the subtle elements, and so on into the nâ*d*îs.—The vidvân also remains connected with the subtle elements because he has not yet completely destroyed avidyâ, so that the immortality which Scripture ascribes to him (am*ri*tatva*m* hi vidvân abhya*s*nute) is only a relative one.—Râmânu*g*a quotes the following text regarding the immortality of the vidvân:

'Yadâ sarve pramu*k*yante kâmâ ye-sya h*ri*di sthitâ*h*
atha martyo-m*ri*to bhavaty atra brahma sama*s*nute,'

and explains that the immortality which is here ascribed to the vidvân as soon as he abandons all desires can only mean the destruction—mentioned in the preceding pâda—of all the effects of good and evil works, while the 'reaching of Brahman' can only refer to the intuition of Brahman vouchsafed to the meditating devotee.

Adhik. V (8-11) raises, according to *S*añkara, the question whether the subtle elements of which Scripture says that they are combined with the highest deity (te*g*a*h* parasyâ*m* devatâyâm) are completely merged in the latter or not. The answer is that a complete absorption of the elements takes place only when final emancipation is reached; that, on the other hand, as long as the sa*m*sâra state lasts, the elements, although somehow combined with

Brahman, remain distinct so as to be able to form new bodies for the soul.

According to Râmânuga the Sûtras 8–11 do not constitute a new adhikarana, but continue the discussion of the point mooted in 7. The immortality there spoken of does not imply the separation of the soul from the body, 'because Scripture declares samsâra, i.e. embodiedness up to the reaching of Brahman' (tasya tâvad eva *k*iram yâvan na vimokshye atha sampatsye) (8).—That the soul after having departed from the gross body is not disconnected from the subtle elements, is also proved hereby, that the subtle body accompanies it, as is observed from authority[1] (9).—Hence the immortality referred to in the scriptural passage quoted is not effected by means of the total destruction of the body (10).

Adhik. VI (12–14) is of special importance.—According to *S*añkara the Sûtras now turn from the discussion of the departure of him who possesses the lower knowledge only to the consideration of what becomes of him who has reached the higher knowledge. So far it has been taught that in the case of relative immortality (ensuing on the apara vidyâ) the subtle elements, together with the senses and so on, depart from the body of the dying devotee; this implies at the same time that they do not depart from the body of the dying sage who knows himself to be one with Brahman. —Against this latter implied doctrine Sûtra 12 is supposed to formulate an objection. 'If it be said that the departure of the prânas from the body of the dying sage is denied (viz. in B*ri*. Up. IV, 4, 5, na tasya prânâ utkrâmanti, of him the prânas do not pass out); we reply that in that passage the genitive "tasya" has the sense of the ablative "tasmât," so that the sense of the passage is, "from him, i.e. from the *g*iva of the dying sage, the prânas do not depart, but remain with it."'—This objection *S*añkara supposes to be disposed of in Sûtra 13. 'By some there is given a clear denial of the departure of the prânas in the case of the

[1] Upalabhyate hi devayânena panthâ ga*kkh*ato vidushas tam pratibrûyât satyam brûyâd iti *k*andramasâ samvâdava*k*anena *s*arîrasadbhâva*h*, ata*h* sûkshma*s*arîram anuvartate.

dying sage,' viz. in the passage B*ri*. Up. III, 2, 11, where Yâ*gñ*avalkya instructs Ârtabhâga that, when this man dies, the prâ*n*as do not depart from it (asmât; the context showing that asmât means 'from it,' viz. from the body, and not 'from him,' viz. the *g*îva).—The same view is, moreover, confirmed by Sm*ri*ti passages.

According to Râmânu*g*a the three Sûtras forming *S*aṅkara's sixth adhikara*n*a do not constitute a new adhikara*n*a at all, and, moreover, have to be combined into two Sûtras. The topic continuing to be discussed is the utkrânti of the vidvân. If, Sûtra 12 says, the utkrânti of the prâ*n*as is not admitted, on the ground of the denial supposed to be contained in B*ri*. Up. IV, 4, 5; the reply is that the sense of the tasya there is '*s*ârîrât' (so that the passage means, 'from him, i.e. the *g*îva, the prâ*n*as do not depart'); for this is clearly shown by the reading of some, viz. the Mâdhyandinas, who, in their text of the passage, do not read 'tasya' but 'tasmât.'—With reference to the instruction given by Yâ*gñ*avalkya to Ârtabhâga, it is to be remarked that nothing there shows the 'ayam purusha' to be the sage who knows Brahman.—And, finally, there are Sm*ri*ti passages declaring that the sage also when dying departs from the body.

Adhik. VII and VIII (15, 16) teach, according to *S*aṅkara, that, on the death of him who possesses the higher knowledge, his prâ*n*as, elements, &c. are merged in Brahman, so as to be no longer distinct from it in any way.

According to Râmânu*g*a the two Sûtras continue the teaching about the prâ*n*as, bhûtas, &c. of the vidvân in general, and declare that they are finally merged in Brahman, not merely in the way of conjunction (sa*m*yoga), but completely[1].

Adhik. IX (17).—*S*aṅkara here returns to the owner of the aparâ vidyâ, while Râmânu*g*a continues the description of the utkrânti of his vidvân.—The *g*îva of the dying man

[1] When the *g*îva has passed out of the body and ascends to the world of Brahman, it remains enveloped by the subtle body until it reaches the river Vi*g*arâ. There it divests itself of the subtle body, and the latter is merged in Brahman.

passes into the heart, and thence departs out of the body by means of the nâ*d*îs; the vidvân by means of the nâ*d*î called sushum*n*â, the avidvân by means of some other nâ*d*î.

Adhik. X (18, 19).—The departing soul passes up to the sun by means of a ray of light which exists at night as well as during day.

Adhik. XI (20, 21).—Also that vidvân who dies during the dakshi*n*âyana reaches Brahman.

Pâda III.

Adhik. I, II, III (1–3) reconcile the different accounts given in the Upanishads as to the stations of the way which leads the vidvân up to Brahman.

Adhik. IV (4–6).—By the 'stations' we have, however, to understand not only the subdivisions of the way but also the divine beings which lead the soul on.

The remaining part of the pâda is by *S*aṅkara divided into two adhikara*n*as. Of these the former one (7–14) teaches that the Brahman to which the departed soul is led by the guardians of the path of the gods is not the highest Brahman, but the effected (kârya) or qualified (sagu*n*a) Brahman. This is the opinion propounded in Sûtras 7–11 by Bâdari, and, finally, accepted by *S*aṅkara in his commentary on Sûtra 14. In Sûtras 12–14 *G*aimini defends the opposite view, according to which the soul of the vidvân goes to the highest Brahman, not to the kâryam brahma. But *G*aimini's view, although set forth in the latter part of the adhikara*n*a, is, according to *S*aṅkara, a mere pûrvapaksha, while Bâdari's opinion represents the siddhânta.—The latter of the two adhikara*n*as (VI of the whole pâda; 15, 16) records the opinion of Bâdarâya*n*a on a collateral question, viz. whether, or not, all those who worship the effected Brahman are led to it. The decision is that those only are guided to Brahman who have not worshipped it under a pratika form.

According to Râmânu*g*a, Sûtras 7–16 form one adhikara*n*a only, in which the views of Bâdari and of *G*aimini represent two pûrvapakshas, while Bâdarâya*n*a's opinion is adopted as the siddhânta. The question is whether the guardians of the path lead to Brahman only those who worship the effected Brahman, i. e. Hira*n*yagarbha, or those who worship the highest Brahman, or those who worship the individual soul as free from Prak*ri*ti, and having Brahman for its Self (ye pratyagâtmâna*m* prak*ri*tiviyukta*m* brahmâtmakam upâsate).—The first view is maintained by Bâdari in Sûtra 7, 'The guardians lead to Brahman those who worship the effected Brahman, because going is possible towards the latter only;' for no movement can take place towards the highest and as such omnipresent Brahman.—The explanation of Sûtra 9 is similar to that of *S*añkara; but more clearly replies to the objection (that, if Hira*n*yagarbha were meant in the passage, 'purusho*mânava*h* sa etân brahma gamayati,' the text would read 'sa etân brahmâ*n*am gamayati') that Hira*n*yagarbha is called Brahman on account of his nearness to Brahman, i. e. on account of his prathama*g*atva.—The explanation of 10, 11 is essentially the same as in *S*añkara; so also of 12–14.—The siddhânta view is established in Sûtra 13, 'It is the opinion of Bâdarâya*n*a that it, i. e. the ga*n*a of the guardians, leads to Brahman those who do not take their stand on what is pratîka, i. e. those who worship the highest Brahman, and those who meditate on the individual Self as dissociated from prak*ri*ti, and having Brahman for its Self, but not those who worship Brahman under pratîkas. For both views—that of *G*aimini as well as that of Bâdari—are faulty.' The kârya view contradicts such passages as 'asmâ*k kh*arîrât samutthâya para*m g*yotir upasampadya,' &c.; the para view, such passages as that in the pa*ñk*âgni-vidyâ, which declares that ya ittha*m* vidu*h*, i. e. those who know the pa*ñk*âgni-vidyâ, are also led up to Brahman.

PÂDA IV.

Adhik. I (1–3) returns, according to *S*añkara, to the owner of the parâ vidyâ, and teaches that, when on his death his soul obtains final release, it does not acquire any new characteristics, but merely manifests itself in its true nature.—The explanation given by Râmânu*g*a is essentially the same, but of course refers to that vidvân whose going to Brahman had been described in the preceding pâda.

Adhik. II (4) determines that the relation in which the released soul stands to Brahman is that of avibhâga, non-separation. This, on *S*ankara's view, means absolute non-separation, identity.—According to Râmânu*g*a the question to be considered is whether the released soul views itself as separate (p*ri*thagbhûta) from Brahman, or as non-separate because being a mode of Brahman. The former view is favoured by those *S*ruti and Sm*ri*ti passages which speak of the soul as being with, or equal to, Brahman ; the latter by such passages as tat tvam asi and the like[1].

Adhik. III (5–7) discusses the characteristics of the released soul (i.e. of the truly released soul, according to *S*ankara). According to *G*aimini the released soul, when manifesting itself in its true nature, possesses all those qualities which in *Kh*. Up. VIII, 7, 1 and other places are ascribed to Brahman, such as apahatapâpmatva, satyasa*m*kalpatva, &c., ai*s*varya.—According to Au*d*ulomi the only characteristic of the released soul is *k*aitanya.—According to Bâdarâyana the two views can be combined (*S*ankara remarking that satyasa*m*kalpatva, &c. are ascribed to the released soul vyavahârâpekshayâ).

Adhik. IV (8–9) returns, according to *S*ankara, to the aparâ vidyâ, and discusses the question whether the soul of

[1] Kim aya*m* para*m* *g*yotir upasampanna*h* sarvabandhavinirmukta*h* pratyagâtmâ svâtmâna*m* paramâtmana*h* p*ri*thagbhûtam anubhavati uta tatprakâratayâ tadavibhaktam iti vi*s*aye so '*s*nute sarvân kâmân saha brahma*n*â vipa*sk*itâ pa*s*ya*h* pa*s*yate rukmavar*n*a*m* kartâram î*s*a*m* purusha*m* brahmayoni*m* tadâ vidvân pu*n*yapâpe vidhûya nira*ñg*ana*h* parama*m* sâmyam upaiti ida*m* *g*ñânam upâ*s*ritya mama sâdharmyam âgatâ*h* sarve 'pi nopa*g*âyante pralayena vyathanti *k*etyâdi*s*rutism*ri*tibhyo muktasya pare*n*a sâhityasâmyasâdharmyâvagamât p*ri*thagbhûtam anubhavatîti prâpte u*k*yate. Avibhâgeneti. Parasmâd brahma*n*ah svâtmânam avibhâgenânubhavati mukta*h*. Kuta*h*. D*ri*sh*t*atvât. Para*m* brahmopasampadya niv*ri*ttâvidyâtirodhânasya yâthâtathyena svâtmano d*ri*sh*t*atvât. Svâtmana*h* svarûpa*m* hi tat tvam asy ayam âtmâ brahma aitadâtmyam ida*m* sarva*m* sarva*m* khalv ida*m* brahmetyâdisâmânâdhikara*n*yanirde*s*ai*h* ya âtmani tish*th*an âtmano 'ntaro yam âtmâ na veda yasyâtmâ *s*arîra*m* ya âtmânam antaro yamayati âtmântaryâmy am*ri*ta*h* anta*h* pravish*t*a*h* *s*âstâ *g*anânâm ityâdibhi*s* *k*a paramâtmâtmaka*m* ta*kkh*arîratayâ tatprakârabhûtam iti pratipâditam avasthiter iti kâ*s*ak*ri*tsnety atrâto 'vibhâgenâha*m* brahmâsmîty evânubhavati.

the pious effects its desires by its mere determination, or uses some other means. The former alternative is accepted.—According to Râmânu*g*a the adhikara*n*a simply continues the consideration of the state of the released, begun in the preceding adhikara*n*a. Of the released soul it is said in *Kh*. Up. VIII, 12, 3 that after it has manifested itself in its true nature it moves about playing and rejoicing with women, carriages, and so on. The question then arises whether it effects all this by its mere sa*m*kalpa (it having been shown in the preceding adhikara*n*a that the released soul is, like the Lord, satyasa*m*kalpa), or not. The answer is in favour of the former alternative, on account of the explicit declaration made in *Kh*. Up. VIII, 2, 'By his mere will the fathers come to receive him.'

Adhik. V (10–14) decides that the released are embodied or disembodied according to their wish and will.

Adhik. VI (11, 12) explains how the soul of the released can animate several bodies at the same time.—Sûtra 12 gives, according to *S*aṅkara, the additional explanation that those passages which declare the absence of all specific cognition on the part of the released soul do not refer to the partly released soul of the devotee, but either to the soul in the state of deep sleep (svâpyaya = sushupti), or to the fully released soul of the sage (sampatti = kaivalya).—Râmânu*g*a explains that the passages speaking of absence of consciousness refer either to the state of deep sleep, or to the time of dying (sampatti = mara*n*am according to 'vâṅ manasi sampadyate,' &c.).

Adhik. VII (17–21).—The released *g*îvas participate in all the perfections and powers of the Lord, with the exception of the power of creating and sustaining the world. They do not return to new forms of embodied existence.

After having, in this way, rendered ourselves acquainted with the contents of the Brahma-sûtras according to the views of *S*aṅkara as well as Râmânu*g*a, we have now to consider the question which of the two modes of interpretation represents—or at any rate more closely approximates to—the true meaning of the Sûtras. That few of the Sûtras are intelligible if taken by themselves, we have already remarked above; but this does not exclude the possibility of our deciding with a fair degree of certainty which of the two interpretations proposed agrees better with the text, at least in a certain number of cases.

We have to note in the first place that, in spite of very numerous discrepancies,—of which only the more important ones have been singled out in the conspectus of contents,—the two commentators are at one as to the general drift of the Sûtras and the arrangement of topics. As a rule, the adhikara*n*as discuss one or several Vedic passages bearing upon a certain point of the system, and in the vast majority of cases the two commentators agree as to which are the special texts referred to. And, moreover, in a very large number of cases the agreement extends to the interpretation to be put on those passages and on the Sûtras. This far-reaching agreement certainly tends to inspire us with a certain confidence as to the existence of an old tradition concerning the meaning of the Sûtras on which the bulk of the interpretations of *S*añkara as well as of Râmânu*g*a are based.

But at the same time we have seen that, in a not inconsiderable number of cases, the interpretations of *S*añkara and Râmânu*g*a diverge more or less widely, and that the Sûtras affected thereby are, most of them, especially important because bearing on fundamental points of the Vedânta system. The question then remains which of the two interpretations is entitled to preference.

Regarding a small number of Sûtras I have already (in the conspectus of contents) given it as my opinion that Râmânu*g*a's explanation appears to be more worthy of consideration. We meet, in the first place, with a number of cases in which the two commentators agree as to the literal meaning of a Sûtra, but where *S*añkara sees himself reduced to the necessity of supplementing his interpretation by certain additions and reservations of his own for which the text gives no occasion, while Râmânu*g*a is able to take the Sûtra as it stands. To exemplify this remark, I again direct attention to all those Sûtras which in clear terms represent the individual soul as something different from the highest soul, and concerning which *S*aṅkara is each time obliged to have recourse to the plea of the Sûtra referring, not to what is true in the strict sense of the word, but only to what is conventionally looked upon as true. It is, I admit, not altogether impossible that *S*aṅkara's interpretation should represent the real meaning of the Sûtras; that the latter, indeed, to use the terms employed by Dr. Deussen, should for the nonce set forth an exoteric doctrine adapted to the common notions of mankind, which, however, can be rightly understood by him only to whose mind the esoteric doctrine is all the while present. This is not impossible, I say; but it is a point which requires convincing proofs before it can be allowed.—We have had, in the second place, to note a certain number of adhikara*n*as and Sûtras concerning whose interpretation *S*aṅkara and Râmânu*g*a disagree altogether; and we have seen that not unfrequently the explanations given by the latter commentator appear to be preferable because falling in more easily with the words of the text. The most striking instance of this is afforded by the 13th adhikara*n*a of II, 3, which treats of the size of the *g*îva, and where Râmânu*g*a's explanation seems to be decidedly superior to *S*aṅkara's, both if we look to the arrangement of the whole adhikara*n*a and to the wording of the single Sûtras. The adhikara*n*a is, moreover, a specially important one, because the nature of the view held as to the size of the individual soul goes far to settle the question what kind of Vedânta is embodied in Bâdarâya*n*a's work.

But it will be requisite not only to dwell on the interpretations of a few detached Sûtras, but to make the attempt at least of forming some opinion as to the relation of the Vedânta-sûtras as a whole to the chief distinguishing doctrines of *S*aṅkara as well as Râmânu*g*a. Such an attempt may possibly lead to very slender positive results; but in the present state of the enquiry even a merely negative result, viz. the conclusion that the Sûtras do not teach particular doctrines found in them by certain commentators, will not be without its value.

The first question we wish to consider in some detail is whether the Sûtras in any way favour *S*añkara's doctrine that we have to distinguish a twofold knowledge of Brahman, a higher knowledge which leads to the immediate absorption, on death, of the individual soul in Brahman, and a lower knowledge which raises its owner merely to an exalted form of individual existence. The adhyâya first to be considered in this connexion is the fourth one. According to *S*añkara the three latter pâdas of that adhyâya are chiefly engaged in describing the fate of him who dies in the possession of the lower knowledge, while two sections (IV, 2, 12–14; IV, 4, 1–7) tell us what happens to him who, before his death, had risen to the knowledge of the highest Brahman. According to Râmânu*g*a, on the other hand, the three pâdas, referring throughout to one subject only, give an uninterrupted account of the successive steps by which the soul of him who knows the Lord through the Upanishads passes, at the time of death, out of the gross body which it had tenanted, ascends to the world of Brahman, and lives there for ever without returning into the sa*m*sâra.

On an à priori view of the matter it certainly appears somewhat strange that the concluding section of the Sûtras should be almost entirely taken up with describing the fate of him who has after all acquired an altogether inferior knowledge only, and has remained shut out from the true sanctuary of Vedântic knowledge, while the fate of the fully initiated is disposed of in a few occasional Sûtras. It is, I think, not too much to say that no unbiassed student of the Sûtras would — before having allowed himself to be influenced by *S*añkara's interpretations — imagine for a moment that the solemn words, 'From thence is no return, from thence is no return,' with which the Sûtras conclude, are meant to describe, not the lasting condition of him who has reached final release, the highest aim of man, but merely a stage on the way of that soul which is engaged in the slow progress of gradual release, a stage which is indeed greatly superior to any earthly form of existence, but yet itself belongs to the essentially fictitious sa*m*sâra, and as such remains infinitely below the bliss of true mukti. And this à priori impression—which, although no doubt significant, could hardly be appealed to as decisive—is confirmed by a detailed consideration of the two sets of Sûtras which *S*aṅkara connects with the knowledge of the higher Brahman. How these Sûtras are interpreted by *S*aṅkara and Râmânu*g*a has been stated above in the conspectus of contents; the points which render the interpretation given by Râmânu*g*a more probable are as follows. With regard to IV, 2, 12–14, we have to note, in the first place, the circumstance—relevant although not decisive in itself—that Sûtra 12 does not contain any indication of a new topic being introduced. In the second place, it can hardly be doubted that the text of Sûtra 13, 'spash*t*o hy ekeshâm,' is more appropriately understood, with Râmânu*g*a, as furnishing a reason for the opinion advanced in the preceding Sûtra, than—with *S*aṅkara—as embodying the refutation of a previous statement (in which latter case we should expect not 'hi' but 'tu'). And, in the third place, the 'eke,' i.e. 'some,' referred to in Sûtra 13 would, on *S*aṅkara's interpretation, denote the very same persons to whom the preceding Sûtra had referred, viz. the followers of the Kâ*n*va-*s*âkhâ (the two Vedic passages referred to in 12 and 13 being B*ri*. Up. IV, 4, 5, and III, 2, 11, according to the Kâ*n*va recension); while it is the standing practice of the Sûtras to introduce, by means of the designation 'eke,' members of Vedic *s*âkhâs, teachers, &c. other than those alluded to in the preceding Sûtras. With this practice Râmânu*g*a's interpretation, on the other hand, fully agrees; for, according to him, the 'eke' are the Mâdhyandinas, whose reading in B*ri*. Up. IV, 4, 5, viz. 'tasmât,' clearly indicates that the 'tasya' in the corresponding passage of the Kâ*n*vas denotes the *s*ârîra, i.e. the *g*îva. I think it is not saying too much that *S*aṅkara's explanation, according to which the 'eke' would denote the very same Kâ*n*vas to whom the preceding Sûtra had referred—so that the Kâ*n*vas would be distinguished from themselves as it were—is altogether impossible.

The result of this closer consideration of the first set of

Sûtras, alleged by *S*aṅkara to concern the owner of the higher knowledge of Brahman, entitles us to view with some distrust *S*aṅkara's assertion that another set also—IV, 4, 1–7—has to be detached from the general topic of the fourth adhyâya, and to be understood as depicting the condition of those who have obtained final absolute release. And the Sûtras themselves do not tend to weaken this preliminary want of confidence. In the first place their wording also gives no indication whatever of their having to be separated from what precedes as well as what follows. And, in the second place, the last Sûtra of the set (7) obliges *S*aṅkara to ascribe to his truly released souls qualities which clearly cannot belong to them; so that he finally is obliged to make the extraordinary statement that those qualities belong to them 'vyavahârâpekshayâ,' while yet the purport of the whole adhikara*n*a is said to be the description of the truly released soul for which no vyavahâra exists! Very truly *S*aṅkara's commentator here remarks, 'atra ke*k*in muhyanti akha*nd*a-*k*inmâtra*g*ñânân muktasyâ*g*ñânâbhâvât kuta â*g*ñânika-dharmayoga*h*,' and the way in which thereupon he himself attempts to get over the difficulty certainly does not improve matters.

In connexion with the two passages discussed, we meet in the fourth adhyâya with another passage, which indeed has no direct bearing on the distinction of aparâ and parâ vidyâ, but may yet be shortly referred to in this place as another and altogether undoubted instance of *S*aṅkara's interpretations not always agreeing with the text of the Sûtras. The Sûtras 7–16 of the third pâda state the opinions of three different teachers on the question to which Brahman the soul of the vidvân repairs on death, or—according to Râmânu*g*a—the worshippers of which Brahman repair to (the highest) Brahman. Râmânu*g*a treats the views of Bâdari and *G*aimini as two pûrvapakshas, and the opinion of Bâdarâya*n*a—which is stated last—as the siddhânta. *S*aṅkara, on the other hand, detaching the Sûtras in which Bâdarâya*n*a's view is set forth from the preceding part of the adhikara*n*a (a proceeding which, although not plausible, yet cannot be said to be altogether illegitimate), maintains that Bâdari's view, which is expounded first, represents the siddhânta, while *G*aimini's view, set forth subsequently, is to be considered a mere pûrvapaksha. This, of course, is altogether inadmissible, it being the invariable practice of the Vedânta-sûtras as well as the Pûrva Mîmâ*m*sâ-sûtras to conclude the discussion of contested points with the statement of that view which is to be accepted as the authoritative one. This is so patent that *S*ankara feels himself called upon to defend his deviation from the general rule (Commentary on IV, 4, 13), without, however, bringing forward any arguments but such as are valid only if *S*ankara's system itself is already accepted.

The previous considerations leave us, I am inclined to think, no choice but to side with Râmânu*g*a as to the general subject-matter of the fourth adhyâya of the Sûtras. We need not accept him as our guide in all particular interpretations, but we must acknowledge with him that the Sûtras of the fourth adhyâya describe the ultimate fate of one and the same vidvân, and do not afford any basis for the distinction of a higher and lower knowledge of Brahman in *S*ankara's sense.

If we have not to discriminate between a lower and a higher knowledge of Brahman, it follows that the distinction of a lower and a higher Brahman is likewise not valid. But this is not a point to be decided at once on the negative evidence of the fourth adhyâya, but regarding which the entire body of the Vedânta-sûtras has to be consulted. And intimately connected with this investigation—in fact, one with it from a certain point of view—is the question whether the Sûtras afford any evidence of their author having held the doctrine of Mâyâ, the principle of illusion, by the association with which the highest Brahman, in itself transcending all qualities, appears as the lower Brahman or Î*s*vara. That Râmânu*g*a denies the distinction of the two Brahmans and the doctrine of Mâyâ we have seen above; we shall, however, in the subsequent investigation, pay less attention to his views and interpretations than to the indications furnished by the Sûtras themselves.

Placing myself at the point of view of a *S*ânkara, I am startled at the outset by the second Sûtra of the first adhyâya, which undertakes to give a definition of Brahman. 'Brahman is that whence the origination and so on (i. e. the sustentation and reabsorption) of this world proceed.' What, we must ask, is this Sûtra meant to define?—That Brahman, we are inclined to answer, whose cognition the first Sûtra declares to constitute the task of the entire Vedânta; that Brahman whose cognition is the only road to final release; that Brahman in fact which *S*ankara calls the highest.—But, here we must object to ourselves, the highest Brahman is not properly defined as that from which the world originates. In later Vedântic writings, whose authors were clearly conscious of the distinction of the higher absolute Brahman and the lower Brahman related to Mâyâ or the world, we meet with definitions of Brahman of an altogether different type. I need only remind the reader of the current definition of Brahman as sa*k*-*k*id-ânanda, or, to mention one individual instance, refer to the introductory *s*lokas of the Pa*ñk*adas*î dilating on the sa*m*vid svayamprabhâ, the self-luminous principle of thought which in all time, past or future, neither starts into being nor perishes (P. D. I, 7). 'That from which the world proceeds' can by a *S*ânkara be accepted only as a definition of Î*s*vara, of Brahman which by its association with Mâyâ is enabled to project the false appearance of this world, and it certainly is as improbable that the Sûtras should open with a definition of that inferior principle, from whose cognition there can accrue no permanent benefit, as, according to a remark made above, it is unlikely that they should conclude with a description of the state of those who know the lower Brahman only, and thus are debarred from obtaining true release. As soon, on the other hand, as we discard the idea of a twofold Brahman and conceive Brahman as one only, as the all-enfolding being which sometimes emits the world from its own substance and sometimes again retracts it into itself, ever remaining one in all its various manifestations—a conception which need not by any means be modelled in all its details on the views of the Râmânugas—the definition of Brahman given in the second Sûtra becomes altogether unobjectionable.

We next enquire whether the impression left on the mind by the manner in which Bâdarâyana defines Brahman, viz. that he does not distinguish between an absolute Brahman and a Brahman associated with Mâyâ, is confirmed or weakened by any other parts of his work. The Sûtras being throughout far from direct in their enunciations, we shall have to look less to particular terms and turns of expression than to general lines of reasoning. What in this connexion seems specially worthy of being taken into account, is the style of argumentation employed by the Sûtrakâra against the Sâṅkhya doctrine, which maintains that the world has originated, not from an intelligent being, but from the non-intelligent pradhâna. The most important Sûtras relative to this point are to be met with in the first pâda of the second adhyâya. Those Sûtras are indeed almost unintelligible if taken by themselves, but the unanimity of the commentators as to their meaning enables us to use them as steps in our investigation. The sixth Sûtra of the pâda mentioned replies to the Sâṅkhya objection that the non-intelligent world cannot spring from an intelligent principle, by the remark that 'it is thus seen,' i.e. it is a matter of common observation that non-intelligent things are produced from beings endowed with intelligence; hair and nails, for instance, springing from animals, and certain insects from dung.—Now, an argumentation of this kind is altogether out of place from the point of view of the true Sâṅkara. According to the latter the non-intelligent world does not spring from Brahman in so far as the latter is intelligence, but in so far as it is associated with Mâyâ. Mâyâ is the upâdâna of the material world, and Mâyâ itself is of a non-intelligent nature, owing to which it is by so many Vedântic writers identified with the prakriti of the Sâṅkhyas. Similarly the illustrative instances, adduced under Sûtra 9 for the purpose of showing that effects when being reabsorbed into their causal substances do not impart to the latter their own qualities, and that hence the material world also, when being refunded into Brahman, does not impart to it its own imperfections, are singularly inappropriate if viewed in connexion with the doctrine of Mâyâ, according to which the material world is no more in Brahman at the time of a pralaya than during the period of its subsistence. According to *S*ankara the world is not merged in Brahman, but the special forms into which the upâdâna of the world, i.e. Mâyâ, had modified itself are merged in non-distinct Mâyâ, whose relation to Brahman is not changed thereby.—The illustration, again, given in Sûtra 24 of the mode in which Brahman, by means of its inherent power, transforms itself into the world without employing any extraneous instruments of action, 'kshîravad dhi,' 'as milk (of its own accord turns into curds),' would be strangely chosen indeed if meant to bring nearer to our understanding the mode in which Brahman projects the illusive appearance of the world; and also the analogous instance given in the Sûtra next following, 'as Gods and the like (create palaces, chariots, &c. by the mere power of their will)'—which refers to the real creation of real things—would hardly be in its place if meant to illustrate a theory which considers unreality to be the true character of the world. The mere cumulation of the two essentially heterogeneous illustrative instances (kshîravad dhi; devâdivat), moreover, seems to show that the writer who had recourse to them held no very definite theory as to the particular mode in which the world springs from Brahman, but was merely concerned to render plausible in some way or other that an intelligent being can give rise to what is non-intelligent without having recourse to any extraneous means[1].

That the Mâyâ doctrine was not present to the mind of the Sûtrakâra, further appears from the latter part of the fourth pâda of the first adhyâya, where it is shown that Brahman is not only the operative but also the material cause of the world. If anywhere, there would have been

[1] *S*ankara's favourite illustrative instance of the magician producing illusive sights is—significantly enough—not known to the Sûtras.

the place to indicate, had such been the author's view, that Brahman is the material cause of the world through Mâyâ only, and that the world is unreal; but the Sûtras do not contain a single word to that effect. Sûtra 26, on the other hand, exhibits the significant term 'pari*n*âmât;' Brahman produces the world by means of a modification of itself. It is well known that later on, when the terminology of the Vedânta became definitely settled, the term 'pari*n*âmavâda' was used to denote that very theory to which the followers of *S*ankara are most violently opposed, viz. the doctrine according to which the world is not a mere vivarta, i.e. an illusory manifestation of Brahman, but the effect of Brahman undergoing a real change, may that change be conceived to take place in the way taught by Râmânu*g*a or in some other manner.—With regard to the last-quoted Sûtra, as well as to those touched upon above, the commentators indeed maintain that whatever terms and modes of expression are apparently opposed to the vivartavâda are in reality reconcilable with it; to Sûtra 26, for instance, Govindânanda remarks that the term 'pari*n*âma' only denotes an effect in general (kâryamâtra), without implying that the effect is real. But in cases of this nature we are fully entitled to use our own judgment, even if we were not compelled to do so by the fact that other commentators, such as Râmânu*g*a, are satisfied to take 'pari*n*âma' and similar terms in their generally received sense.

A further section treating of the nature of Brahman is met with in III, 2, 11 ff. It is, according to *S*ankara's view, of special importance, as it is alleged to set forth that Brahman is in itself destitute of all qualities, and is affected with qualities only through its limiting adjuncts (upâdhis), the offspring of Mâyâ. I have above (in the conspectus of contents) given a somewhat detailed abstract of the whole section as interpreted by *S*ankara on the one hand, and Râmânu*g*a on the other hand, from which it appears that the latter's opinion as to the purport of the group of Sûtras widely diverges from that of *S*ankara. The wording of the Sûtras is so eminently concise and vague that I find it impossible to decide which of the two commentators—if indeed either—is to be accepted as a trustworthy guide; regarding the sense of some Sûtras *S*ankara's explanation seems to deserve preference, in the case of others Râmânu*g*a seems to keep closer to the text. I decidedly prefer, for instance, Râmânu*g*a's interpretation of Sûtra 22, as far as the sense of the entire Sûtra is concerned, and more especially with regard to the term 'prak*ri*taitâvattvam,' whose proper force is brought out by Râmânu*g*a's explanation only. So much is certain that none of the Sûtras decidedly favours the interpretation proposed by *S*ankara. Whichever commentator we follow, we greatly miss coherence and strictness of reasoning, and it is thus by no means improbable that the section is one of those—perhaps not few in number—in which both interpreters had less regard to the literal sense of the words and to tradition than to their desire of forcing Bâdarâya*n*a's Sûtras to bear testimony to the truth of their own philosophic theories.

With special reference to the Mâyâ doctrine one important Sûtra has yet to be considered, the only one in which the term 'mâyâ' itself occurs, viz. III, 2, 3. According to *S*ankara the Sûtra signifies that the environments of the dreaming soul are not real but mere Mâyâ, i. e. unsubstantial illusion, because they do not fully manifest the character of real objects. Râmânu*g*a (as we have seen in the conspectus) gives a different explanation of the term 'mâyâ,' but in judging of *S*ankara's views we may for the time accept *S*ankara's own interpretation. Now, from the latter it clearly follows that if the objects seen in dreams are to be called Mâyâ, i.e. illusion, because not evincing the characteristics of reality, the objective world surrounding the waking soul must not be called Mâyâ. But that the world perceived by waking men is Mâyâ, even in a higher sense than the world presented to the dreaming consciousness, is an undoubted tenet of the *S*ânkara Vedânta; and the Sûtra therefore proves either that Bâdarâya*n*a did not hold the doctrine of the illusory character of the world, or else that, if after all he did hold that doctrine, he used the term 'mâyâ' in a sense altogether different from that in which *S*aṅkara employs it.—If, on the other hand, we, with Râmânu*g*a, understand the word 'mâyâ' to denote a wonderful thing, the Sûtra of course has no bearing whatever on the doctrine of Mâyâ in its later technical sense.

We now turn to the question as to the relation of the individual soul to Brahman. Do the Sûtras indicate anywhere that their author held *S*aṅkara's doctrine, according to which the *g*îva is in reality identical with Brahman, and separated from it, as it were, only by a false surmise due to avidyâ, or do they rather favour the view that the souls, although they have sprung from Brahman, and constitute elements of its nature, yet enjoy a kind of individual existence apart from it? This question is in fact only another aspect of the Mâyâ question, but yet requires a short separate treatment.

In the conspectus I have given it as my opinion that the Sûtras in which the size of the individual soul is discussed can hardly be understood in *S*aṅkara's sense, and rather seem to favour the opinion, held among others by Râmânu*g*a, that the soul is of minute size. We have further seen that Sûtra 18 of the third pâda of the second adhyâya, which describes the soul as '*gñ*a,' is more appropriately understood in the sense assigned to it by Râmânu*g*a; and, again, that the Sûtras which treat of the soul being an agent, can be reconciled with *S*aṅkara's views only if supplemented in a way which their text does not appear to authorise.—We next have the important Sûtra II, 3, 43 in which the soul is distinctly said to be a part (a*ms*a) of Brahman, and which, as we have already noticed, can be made to fall in with *S*aṅkara's views only if a*ms*a is explained, altogether arbitrarily, by 'a*ms*a iva,' while Râmânu*g*a is able to take the Sûtra as it stands.—We also have already referred to Sûtra 50, 'âbhâsa eva *k*a,' which *S*aṅkara interprets as setting forth the so-called pratibimbavâda according to which the individual Self is merely a reflection of the highest Self. But almost every Sûtra—and Sûtra 50 forms no exception—being so obscurely expressed, that viewed by itself it admits of various, often totally opposed, interpretations, the only safe method is to keep in view, in the case of each ambiguous aphorism, the general drift and spirit of the whole work, and that, as we have seen hitherto, is by no means favourable to the pratibimba doctrine. How indeed could Sûtra 50, if setting forth that latter doctrine, be reconciled with Sûtra 43, which says distinctly that the soul is a part of Brahman? For that 43 contains, as *S*aṅkara and his commentators aver, a statement of the ava*kkh*edavâda, can itself be accepted only if we interpret a*m*sa by a*m*sa iva, and to do so there is really no valid reason whatever. I confess that Râmânu*g*a's interpretation of the Sûtra (which however is accepted by several other commentators also) does not appear to me particularly convincing; and the Sûtras unfortunately offer us no other passages on the ground of which we might settle the meaning to be ascribed to the term âbhâsa, which may mean 'reflection,' but may mean hetvâbhâsa, i. e. fallacious argument, as well. But as things stand, this one Sûtra cannot, at any rate, be appealed to as proving that the pratibimbavâda which, in its turn, presupposes the mâyâvâda, is the teaching of the Sûtras.

To the conclusion that the Sûtrakâra did not hold the doctrine of the absolute identity of the highest and the individual soul in the sense of *S*aṅkara, we are further led by some other indications to be met with here and there in the Sûtras. In the conspectus of contents we have had occasion to direct attention to the important Sûtra II, 1, 22, which distinctly enunciates that the Lord is adhika, i. e. additional to, or different from, the individual soul, since Scripture declares the two to be different. Analogously I, 2, 20 lays stress on the fact that the *s*ârîra is not the antaryâmin, because the Mâdhyandinas, as well as the Kâ*n*vas, speak of him in their texts as different (bhedena enam adhîyate), and in 22 the *s*ârîra and the pradhâna are referred to as the two 'others' (itarau) of whom the text predicates distinctive attributes separating them from the highest Lord. The word 'itara' (the other one) appears in several other passages (I, 1, 16; I, 3, 16; II, 1, 21) as a kind of technical term denoting the individual soul in contradistinction from the Lord. The *S*âṅkaras indeed maintain that all those passages refer to an unreal distinction due to avidyâ. But this is just what we should like to see proved, and the proof offered in no case amounts to more than a reference to the system which demands that the Sûtras should be thus understood. If we accept the interpretations of the school of *S*ankara, it remains altogether unintelligible why the Sûtrakâra should never hint even at what *S*ankara is anxious again and again to point out at length, viz. that the greater part of the work contains a kind of exoteric doctrine only, ever tending to mislead the student who does not keep in view what its nature is. If other reasons should make it probable that the Sûtrakâra was anxious to hide the true doctrine of the Upanishads as a sort of esoteric teaching, we might be more ready to accept *S*ankara's mode of interpretation. But no such reasons are forthcoming; nowhere among the avowed followers of the *S*ânkara system is there any tendency to treat the kernel of their philosophy as something to be jealously guarded and hidden. On the contrary, they all, from Gau*d*apâda down to the most modern writer, consider it their most important, nay, only task to inculcate again and again in the clearest and most unambiguous language that all appearance of multiplicity is a vain illusion, that the Lord and the individual souls are in reality one, and that all knowledge but this one knowledge is without true value.

There remains one more important passage concerning the relation of the individual soul to the highest Self, a passage which attracted our attention above, when we were reviewing the evidence for early divergence of opinion among the teachers of the Vedânta. I mean I, 4, 20–22, which three Sûtras state the views of Â*s*marathya, Au*d*ulomi, and Kâ*s*ak*ri*tsna as to the reason why, in a certain passage of the B*ri*hadâra*n*yaka, characteristics of the individual soul are ascribed to the highest Self. The siddhânta view is enounced in Sûtra 22, 'avasthiter iti Kâ*s*ak*ri*tsna*h*,' i. e. Kâ*s*ak*ri*tsna (accounts for the circumstance mentioned) on the ground of the 'permanent abiding or abode.' By this 'permanent abiding' *S*ankara understands the Lord's abiding as, i. e. existing as—or in the condition of—the individual soul, and thus sees in the Sûtra an enunciation of his own view that the individual soul is nothing but the highest Self, 'avik*ri*ta*h* paramesvaro *g*îvo nânya*h*.' Râmâ-nu*g*a, on the other hand, likewise accepting Kâ*s*ak*ri*tsna's opinion as the siddhânta view, explains 'avasthiti' as the Lord's permanent abiding within the individual soul, as described in the antaryâmin-brâhma*n*a.—We can hardly maintain that the term 'avasthiti' cannot have the meaning ascribed to it by *S*ankara, viz. special state or condition, but so much must be urged in favour of Râmânu*g*a's interpretation that in the five other places where avasthiti (or anavasthiti) is met with in the Sûtras (I, 2, 17; II, 2, 4; II, 2, 13; II, 3, 24; III, 3, 32) it regularly means permanent abiding or permanent abode within something.

If, now, I am shortly to sum up the results of the preceding enquiry as to the teaching of the Sûtras, I must give it as my opinion that they do not set forth the distinction of a higher and lower knowledge of Brahman; that they do not acknowledge the distinction of Brahman and Î*s*vara in *S*ankara's sense; that they do not hold the doctrine of the unreality of the world; and that they do not, with *S*ankara, proclaim the absolute identity of the individual and the highest Self. I do not wish to advance for the present beyond these negative results. Upon Râmânu*g*a's mode of interpretation—although I accept it without reserve in some important details—I look on the whole as more useful in providing us with a powerful means of criticising *S*ankara's explanations than in guiding us throughout to the right understanding of the text. The author of the Sûtras may have held views about the nature of Brahman, the world, and the soul differing from those of *S*ankara, and yet not agreeing in all points with those of Râmânu*g*a. If, however, the negative conclusions stated above should be well founded, it would follow even from them that the system of Bâdarâya*n*a had greater affinities with that of the Bhâgavatas and Râmânu*g*a than with the one of which the *S*ankara-bhâshya is the classical exponent.

It appears from the above review of the teaching of the Sûtras that only a comparatively very small proportion of them contribute matter enabling us to form a judgment as to the nature of the philosophical doctrine advocated by Bâdarâyana. The reason of this is that the greater part of the work is taken up with matters which, according to Sankara's terminology, form part of the so-called lower knowledge, and throw no light upon philosophical questions in the stricter sense of the word. This circumstance is not without significance. In later works belonging to Sankara's school in which the distinction of a higher and lower vidyâ is clearly recognised, the topics constituting the latter are treated with great shortness; and rightly so, for they are unable to accomplish the highest aim of man, i. e. final release. When we therefore, on the other hand, find that the subjects of the so-called lower vidyâ are treated very fully in the Vedânta-sûtras, when we observe, for instance, the almost tedious length to which the investigation of the unity of vidyâs (most of which are so-called saguna, i. e. lower vidyâs) is carried in the third adhyâya, or the fact of almost the whole fourth adhyâya being devoted to the ultimate fate of the possessor of the lower vidyâ; we certainly feel ourselves confirmed in our conclusion that what Sankara looked upon as comparatively unimportant formed in Bâdarâyana's opinion part of that knowledge higher than which there is none, and which therefore is entitled to the fullest and most detailed exposition.

The question as to what kind of system is represented by the Vedânta-sûtras may be approached in another way also. While hitherto we have attempted to penetrate to the meaning of the Sûtras by means of the different commentaries, we might try the opposite road, and, in the first place, attempt to ascertain independently of the Sûtras what doctrine is set forth in the Upanishads, whose teaching the Sûtras doubtless aim at systematising. If, it might be urged, the Upanishads can be convincingly shown to embody a certain settled doctrine, we must consider it at the least highly probable that that very same doctrine—of whatever special nature it may be—is hidden in the enigmatical aphorisms of Bâdarâyana[1].

I do not, however, consider this line of argumentation

[1] Cp. Gough's Philosophy of the Upanishads, pp. 240 ff.

a safe one. Even if it could be shown that the teaching of all the chief Upanishads agrees in all essential points (a subject to which some attention will be paid later on), we should not on that account be entitled unhesitatingly to assume that the Sûtras set forth the same doctrine. Whatever the true philosophy of the Upanishads may be, there remains the undeniable fact that there exist and have existed since very ancient times not one but several essentially differing systems, all of which lay claim to the distinction of being the true representatives of the teaching of the Upanishads as well as of the Sûtras. Let us suppose, for argument's sake, that, for instance, the doctrine of Mâyâ is distinctly enunciated in the Upanishads; nevertheless Râmânu*g*a and, for all we know to the contrary, the whole series of more ancient commentators on whom he looked as authorities in the interpretation of the Sûtras, denied that the Upanishads teach Mâyâ, and it is hence by no means impossible that Bâdarâya*n*a should have done the same. The à priori style of reasoning as to the teaching of the Sûtras is therefore without much force.

But apart from any intention of arriving thereby at the meaning of the Sûtras there, of course, remains for us the all-important question as to the true teaching of the Upanishads, a question which a translator of the Sûtras and *S*aṅkara cannot afford to pass over in silence, especially after reason has been shown for the conclusion that the Sûtras and the *S*aṅkara-bhâshya do not agree concerning most important points of Vedântic doctrine. The Sûtras as well as the later commentaries claim, in the first place, to be nothing more than systematisations of the Upanishads, and for us a considerable part at least of their value and interest lies in this their nature. Hence the further question presents itself by whom the teaching of the Upanishads has been most adequately systematised, whether by Bâdarâya*n*a, or *S*aṅkara, or Râmânu*g*a, or some other commentator. This question requires to be kept altogether separate from the enquiry as to which commentator most faithfully renders the contents of the Sûtras, and it is by no means impossible that *S*aṅkara, for instance, should in the end have to be declared a more trustworthy guide with regard to the teaching of the Upanishads than concerning the meaning of the Sûtras.

We must remark here at once that, whatever commentator may be found to deserve preference on the whole, it appears fairly certain already at the outset that none of the systems which Indian ingenuity has succeeded in erecting on the basis of the Upanishads can be accepted in its entirety. The reason for this lies in the nature of the Upanishads themselves. To the Hindu commentator and philosopher the Upanishads came down as a body of revealed truth whose teaching had, somehow or other, to be shown to be thoroughly consistent and free from contradictions; a system had to be devised in which a suitable place could be allotted to every one of the multitudinous statements which they make on the various points of Vedântic doctrine. But to the European scholar, or in fact to any one whose mind is not bound by the doctrine of *S*ruti, it will certainly appear that all such attempts stand self-condemned. If anything is evident even on a cursory review of the Upanishads—and the impression so created is only strengthened by a more careful investigation—it is that they do not constitute a systematic whole. They themselves, especially the older ones, give the most unmistakable indications on that point. Not only are the doctrines expounded in the different Upanishads ascribed to different teachers, but even the separate sections of one and the same Upanishad are assigned to different authorities. It would be superfluous to quote examples of what a mere look at the *Kh*ândogya Upanishad, for instance, suffices to prove. It is of course not impossible that even a multitude of teachers should agree in imparting precisely the same doctrine; but in the case of the Upanishads that is certainly not antecedently probable. For, in the first place, the teachers who are credited with the doctrines of the Upanishads manifestly belonged to different sections of Brahminical society, to different Vedic *s*âkhâs; nay, some of them the tradition makes out to have been kshattriyas. And, in the second place, the period, whose mental activity is represented in the Upanishads, was a creative one, and as such cannot be judged according to the analogy of later periods of Indian philosophic development. The later philosophic schools as, for instance, the one of which *S*aṅkara is the great representative, were no longer free in their speculations, but strictly bound by a traditional body of texts considered sacred, which could not be changed or added to, but merely systematised and commented upon. Hence the rigorous uniformity of doctrine characteristic of those schools. But there had been a time when, what later writers received as a sacred legacy, determining and confining the whole course of their speculations, first sprang from the minds of creative thinkers not fettered by the tradition of any school, but freely following the promptings of their own heads and hearts. By the absence of school traditions, I do not indeed mean that the great teachers who appear in the Upanishads were free to make an entirely new start, and to assign to their speculations any direction they chose; for nothing can be more certain than that, at the period as the outcome of whose philosophical activity the Upanishads have to be considered, there were in circulation certain broad speculative ideas overshadowing the mind of every member of Brahminical society. But those ideas were neither very definite nor worked out in detail, and hence allowed themselves to be handled and fashioned in different ways by different individuals. With whom the few leading conceptions traceable in the teaching of all Upanishads first originated, is a point on which those writings themselves do not enlighten us, and which we have no other means for settling; most probably they are to be viewed not as the creation of any individual mind, but as the gradual outcome of speculations carried on by generations of Vedic theologians. In the Upanishads themselves, at any rate, they appear as floating mental possessions which may be seized and moulded into new forms by any one who feels within himself the required inspiration. A certain vague knowledge of Brahman, the great hidden being in which all this manifold world is one, seems to be spread everywhere, and often issues from the most unexpected sources. *S*vetaketu receives instruction from his father Uddâlaka; the proud Gârgya has to become the pupil of A*g*âta*s*atru, the king of Kâ*s*î; Bhu*g*yu Sâhyâyani receives answers to his questions from a Gandharva possessing a maiden; Satyakâma learns what Brahman is from the bull of the herd he is tending, from Agni and from a flamingo; and Upako*s*ala is taught by the sacred fires in his teacher's house. All this is of course legend, not history; but the fact that the philosophic and theological doctrines of the Upanishads are clothed in this legendary garb certainly does not strengthen the expectation of finding in them a rigidly systematic doctrine.

And a closer investigation of the contents of the Upanishads amply confirms this preliminary impression. If we avail ourselves, for instance, of M. Paul Régnaud's Matériaux pour servir à l'Histoire de la Philosophie de l'Inde, in which the philosophical lucubrations of the different Upanishads are arranged systematically according to topics, we can see with ease how, together with a certain uniformity of general leading conceptions, there runs throughout divergence in details, and very often not unimportant details. A look, for instance, at the collection of passages relative to the origination of the world from the primitive being, suffices to show that the task of demonstrating that whatever the Upanishads teach on that point can be made to fit into a homogeneous system is an altogether hopeless one. The accounts there given of the creation belong, beyond all doubt, to different stages of philosophic and theological development or else to different sections of priestly society. None but an Indian commentator would, I suppose, be inclined and sufficiently courageous to attempt the proof that, for instance, the legend of the âtman purushavidha, the Self in the shape of a person which is as large as man and woman together, and then splits itself into two halves from which cows, horses, asses, goats, &c. are produced in succession (B*ri*. Up. I, 1, 4), can be reconciled with the account given of the creation in the *Kh*ândogya Upanishad, where it is said that in the beginning there existed nothing but the sat, 'that which is,' and that feeling a desire of being many it emitted out of itself ether, and then all the other elements in due succession. The former is a primitive cosmogonic myth, which in its details shows striking analogies with the cosmogonic myths of other nations; the latter account is fairly developed Vedânta (although not Vedânta implying the Mâyâ doctrine). We may admit that both accounts show a certain fundamental similarity in so far as they derive the manifold world from one original being; but to go beyond this and to maintain, as *S*aṅkara does, that the âtman purushavidha of the B*ri*hadâra*n*yaka is the so-called Virâ*g* of the latter Vedânta—implying thereby that that section consciously aims at describing only the activity of one special form of Î*s*vara, and not simply the whole process of creation—is the ingenious shift of an orthodox commentator in difficulties, but nothing more.

How all those more or less conflicting texts came to be preserved and handed down to posterity, is not difficult to understand. As mentioned above, each of the great sections of Brahminical priesthood had its own sacred texts, and again in each of those sections there existed more ancient texts which it was impossible to discard when deeper and more advanced speculations began in their turn to be embodied in literary compositions, which in the course of time likewise came to be looked upon as sacred. When the creative period had reached its termination, and the task of collecting and arranging was taken in hand, older and newer pieces were combined into wholes, and thus there arose collections of such heterogeneous character as the *Kh*ândogya and B*ri*hadâra*n*yaka Upanishads. On later generations, to which the whole body of texts came down as revealed truth, there consequently devolved the inevitable task of establishing systems on which no exception could be taken to any of the texts; but that the task was, strictly speaking, an impossible one, i. e. one which it was impossible to accomplish fairly and honestly, there really is no reason to deny.

For a comprehensive criticism of the methods which the different commentators employ in systematising the contents of the Upanishads there is no room in this place. In order, however, to illustrate what is meant by the 'impossibility,' above alluded to, of combining the various doctrines of the Upanishads into a whole without doing violence to a certain number of texts, it will be as well to analyse in detail some few at least of *S*ankara's interpretations, and to render clear the considerations by which he is guided.

We begin with a case which has already engaged our attention when discussing the meaning of the Sûtras, viz. the question concerning the ultimate fate of those who have attained the knowledge of Brahman. As we have seen, *S*ankara teaches that the soul of him who has risen to an insight into the nature of the higher Brahman does not, at the moment of death, pass out of the body, but is directly merged in Brahman by a process from which all departing and moving, in fact all considerations of space, are altogether excluded. The soul of him, on the other hand, who has not risen above the knowledge of the lower qualified Brahman departs from the body by means of the artery called sushum*n*â, and following the so-called devayâna, the path of the gods, mounts up to the world of Brahman. A review of the chief Upanishad texts on which *S*ankara founds this distinction will show how far it is justified.

In a considerable number of passages the Upanishads contrast the fate of two classes of men, viz. of those who perform sacrifices and meritorious works only, and of those who in addition possess a certain kind of knowledge. Men of the former kind ascend after death to the moon, where they live for a certain time, and then return to the earth into new forms of embodiment; persons of the latter kind proceed on the path of the gods—on which the sun forms one stage—up to the world of Brahman, from which there is no return. The chief passages to that effect are *Kh*. Up. V, 10; Kaush. Up. I, 2 ff.; Mu*nd*. Up. I, 2, 9 ff.; B*ri*. Up. VI, 2, 15 ff.; Pra*s*na Up. I, 9 ff.—In other passages only the latter of the two paths is referred to, cp. *Kh*. Up. IV, 15; VIII, 6, 5; Taitt. Up. I, 6; B*ri*. Up. IV, 4, 8, 9; V, 10; Maitr. Up. VI, 30, to mention only the more important ones.

Now an impartial consideration of those passages shows

I think, beyond any doubt, that what is meant there by the knowledge which leads through the sun to the world of Brahman is the highest knowledge of which the devotee is capable, and that the world of Brahman to which his knowledge enables him to proceed denotes the highest state which he can ever reach, the state of final release, if we choose to call it by that name.—*Kh.* Up. V, 10 says, 'Those who know this (viz. the doctrine of the five fires), and those who in the forest follow faith and austerities go to light,' &c.—*Kh.* Up. IV, 15 is manifestly intended to convey the true knowledge of Brahman; Upakosala's teacher himself represents the instruction given by him as superior to the teaching of the sacred fires.—*Kh.* Up. VIII, 6, 5 quotes the old *s*loka which says that the man moving upwards by the artery penetrating the crown of the head reaches the Immortal.—Kaush. Up. I, 2—which gives the most detailed account of the ascent of the soul—contains no intimation whatever of the knowledge of Brahman, which leads up to the Brahman world, being of an inferior nature.—Mu*nd*. Up. I, 2, 9 agrees with the *Kh*ândogya in saying that 'Those who practise penance and faith in the forest, tranquil, wise, and living on alms, depart free from passion, through the sun, to where that immortal Person dwells whose nature is imperishable,' and nothing whatever in the context countenances the assumption that not the highest knowledge and the highest Person are there referred to.—B*ri*. Up. IV, 4, 8 quotes old *s*lokas clearly referring to the road of the gods ('the small old path'), on which 'sages who know Brahman move on to the svargaloka and thence higher on as entirely free.—That path was found by Brahman, and on it goes whoever knows Brahman.'—B*ri*. Up. VI, 2, 15 is another version of the Pa*ñk*âgnividyâ, with the variation, 'Those who know this, and those who in the forest worship faith and the True, go to light,' &c.—Pra*s*na Up. I, 10 says, 'Those who have sought the Self by penance, abstinence, faith, and knowledge gain by the northern path Âditya, the sun. There is the home of the spirits, the immortal free from danger, the highest. From thence they do not return, for it is the end.'—Maitr. Up. VI, 30 quotes *s*lokas, 'One of them (the arteries) leads upwards, piercing the solar orb: by it, having stepped beyond the world of Brahman, they go to the highest path.'

All these passages are as clear as can be desired. The soul of the sage who knows Brahman passes out by the sushum*n*â, and ascends by the path of the gods to the world of Brahman, there to remain for ever in some blissful state. But, according to *S*añkara, all these texts are meant to set forth the result of a certain inferior knowledge only, of the knowledge of the conditioned Brahman. Even in a passage apparently so entirely incapable of more than one interpretation as B*ri*. Up. VI, 2, 15, the 'True,' which the holy hermits in the forest are said to worship, is not to be the highest Brahman, but only Hira*n*yagarbha!—And why?—Only because the system so demands it, the system which teaches that those who know the highest Brahman become on their death one with it, without having to resort to any other place. The passage on which this latter tenet is chiefly based is B*ri*. Up. IV, 4, 6, 7, where, with the fate of him who at his death has desires, and whose soul therefore enters a new body after having departed from the old one, accompanied by all the prâ*n*as, there is contrasted the fate of the sage free from all desires. 'But as to the man who does not desire, who not desiring, freed from desires is satisfied in his desires, or desires the Self only, the vital spirits of him (tasya) do not depart—being Brahman he goes to Brahman.'

We have seen above (p. lxxx) that this passage is referred to in the important Sûtras on whose right interpretation it, in the first place, depends whether or not we must admit the Sûtrakâra to have acknowledged the distinction of a parâ and an aparâ vidyâ. Here the passage interests us as throwing light on the way in which *S*añkara systematises. He looks on the preceding part of the chapter as describing what happens to the souls of all those who do not know the highest Brahman, inclusive of those who know the lower Brahman only. They pass out of the old bodies followed by all prâ*n*as and enter new bodies. He, on the other hand, section 6 continues, who knows the true Brahman, does not pass out of the body, but becomes one with Brahman then and there. This interpretation of the purport of the entire chapter is not impossibly right, although I am rather inclined to think that the chapter aims at setting forth in its earlier part the future of him who does not know Brahman at all, while the latter part of section 6 passes on to him who does know Brahman (i.e. Brahman pure and simple, the text knowing of no distinction of the so-called lower and higher Brahman). In explaining section 6 *S*aṅkara lays stress upon the clause 'na tasya prâ*n*â utkrâmanti,' 'his vital spirits do not pass out,' taking this to signify that the soul with the vital spirits does not move at all, and thus does not ascend to the world of Brahman; while the purport of the clause may simply be that the soul and vital spirits do not go anywhere else, i.e. do not enter a new body, but are united, somehow or other, with Brahman. On *S*aṅkara's interpretation there immediately arises a new difficulty. In the *s*lokas, quoted under sections 8 and 9, the description of the small old path which leads to the svargaloka and higher on clearly refers—as noticed already above—to the path through the veins, primarily the sushum*n*â, on which, according to so many other passages, the soul of the wise mounts upwards. But that path is, according to *S*aṅkara, followed by him only who has not risen above the lower knowledge, and yet the *s*lokas have manifestly to be connected with what is said in the latter half of 6 about the owner of the parâ vidyâ. Hence *S*aṅkara sees himself driven to explain the *s*lokas in 8 and 9 (of which a faithful translation is given in Professor Max Müller's version) as follows:

8. 'The subtle old path (i.e. the path of knowledge on which final release is reached; which path is subtle, i.e. difficult to know, and old, i.e. to be known from the eternal Veda) has been obtained and fully reached by me. On it the sages who know Brahman reach final release (svargaloka*s*abda*h* samnihitaprakara*n*ât mokshâbhidhâyaka*h*).

9. 'On that path they say that there is white or blue or yellow or green or red (i.e. o t h e r s maintain that the path to final release is, in accordance with the colour of the arteries, either white or blue, &c.; but that is false, for the

paths through the arteries lead at the best to the world of Brahman, which itself forms part of the sa*m*sâra); that path (i.e. the only path to release, viz. the path of true knowledge) is found by Brahman, i.e. by such Brâhma*n*as as through true knowledge have become like Brahman,' &c.

A significant instance in truth of the straits to which thorough-going systematisers of the Upanishads see themselves reduced occasionally!

But we return to the point which just now chiefly interests us. Whether *S*añkara's interpretation of the chapter, and especially of section 6, be right or wrong, so much is certain that we are not entitled to view all those texts which speak of the soul going to the world of Brahman as belonging to the so-called lower knowledge, because a few other passages declare that the sage does not go to Brahman. The text which declares the sage free from desires to become one with Brahman could not, without due discrimination, be used to define and limit the meaning of other passages met with in the same Upanishad even—for as we have remarked above the B*ri*hadâra*n*yaka contains pieces manifestly belonging to different stages of development;—much less does it entitle us to put arbitrary constructions on passages forming part of other Upanishads. Historically the disagreement of the various accounts is easy to understand. The older notion was that the soul of the wise man proceeds along the path of the gods to Brahman's abode. A later—and, if we like, more philosophic—conception is that, as Brahman already is a man's Self, there is no need of any motion on man's part to reach Brahman. We may even apply to those two views the terms aparâ and parâ—lower and higher—knowledge. But we must not allow any commentator to induce us to believe that what he from his advanced standpoint looks upon as an inferior kind of cognition, was viewed in the same light by the authors of the Upanishads.

We turn to another Upanishad text likewise touching upon the point considered in what precedes, viz. the second Brâhma*n*a of the third adhyâya of the B*ri*hadâra*n*yaka. The discussion there first turns upon the grahas and atigrahas, i.e. the senses and organs and their objects, and Yâ*g*ñavalkya thereupon explains that death, by which everything is overcome, is itself overcome by water; for death is fire. The colloquy then turns to what we must consider an altogether new topic, Ârtabhâga asking, 'When this man (ayam purusha) dies, do the vital spirits depart from him or not?' and Yâ*g*ñavalkya answering, 'No, they are gathered up in him; he swells, he is inflated; inflated the dead (body) is lying.'—Now this is for *S*aṅkara an important passage, as we have already seen above (p. lxxxi); for he employs it, in his comment on Ved.-sûtra IV, 2, 13, for the purpose of proving that the passage B*ri*. Up. IV, 4, 6 really means that the vital spirits do not, at the moment of death, depart from the true sage. Hence the present passage also must refer to him who possesses the highest knowledge; hence the 'ayam purusha' must be 'that man,' i. e. the man who possesses the highest knowledge, and the highest knowledge then must be found in the preceding clause which says that death itself may be conquered by water. But, as Râmânu*g*a also remarks, neither does the context favour the assumption that the highest knowledge is referred to, nor do the words of section 11 contain any indication that what is meant is the merging of the Self of the true Sage in Brahman. With the interpretation given by Râmânu*g*a himself, viz. that the prâ*n*as do not depart from the *g*îva of the dying man, but accompany it into a new body, I can agree as little (although he no doubt rightly explains the 'ayam purusha' by 'man' in general), and am unable to see in the passage anything more than a crude attempt to account for the fact that a dead body appears swollen and inflated.—A little further on (section 13) Ârtabhâga asks what becomes of this man (ayam purusha) when his speech has entered into the fire, his breath into the air, his eye into the sun, &c. So much here is clear that we have no right to understand by the 'ayam purusha' of section 13 anybody different from the 'ayam purusha' of the two preceding sections; in spite of this *S*aṅkara—according to whose system the organs of the true sage do not enter into the elements, but are directly merged in Brahman—explains the 'ayam purusha' of section 13 to be the 'asa*m*yagdar*s*in,' i. e. the person who has not risen to the cognition of the highest Brahman. And still a further limiting interpretation is required by the system. The asa*m*yagdar*s*in also—who as such has to remain in the sa*m*sâra—cannot do without the organs, since his *g*îva when passing out of the old body into a new one is invested with the subtle body; hence section 13 cannot be taken as saying what it clearly does say, viz. that at death the different organs pass into the different elements, but as merely indicating that the organs are abandoned by the divinities which, during lifetime, presided over them!

The whole third adhyâya indeed of the B*ri*hadâra*n*yaka affords ample proof of the artificial character of *S*aṅkara's attempts to show that the teaching of the Upanishads follows a definite system. The eighth brâhma*n*a, for instance, is said to convey the doctrine of the highest non-related Brahman, while the preceding brâhma*n*as had treated only of Î*s*vara in his various aspects. But, as a matter of fact, brâhma*n*a 8, after having, in section 8, represented Brahman as destitute of all qualities, proceeds, in the next section, to describe that very same Brahman as the ruler of the world, 'By the command of that Imperishable sun and moon stand apart,' &c.; a clear indication that the author of the Upanishad does not distinguish a higher and lower Brahman in *S*aṅkara's sense.—The preceding brâhma*n*a (7) treats of the antaryâmin, i. e. Brahman viewed as the internal ruler of everything. This, according to *S*aṅkara, is the lower form of Brahman called Î*s*vara; but we observe that the antaryâmin as well as the so-called highest Brahman described in section 8 is, at the termination of the two sections, characterised by means of the very same terms (7, 23: Unseen but seeing, unheard but hearing, &c. There is no other seer but he, there is no other hearer but he, &c.; and 8, 11: That Brahman is unseen but seeing, unheard but hearing, &c. There is nothing that sees but it, nothing that hears but it, &c.).—Nothing can be clearer than that all these sections aim at describing one and the same being, and know nothing of the distinctions made by the developed

Vedânta, however valid the latter may be from a purely philosophic point of view.

We may refer to one more similar instance from the *Kh*ândogya Upanishad. We there meet in III, 14 with one of the most famous vidyâs describing the nature of Brahman, called after its reputed author the *S*â*nd*ilya-vidyâ. This small vidyâ is decidedly one of the finest and most characteristic texts; it would be difficult to point out another passage setting forth with greater force and eloquence and in an equally short compass the central doctrine of the Upanishads. Yet this text, which, beyond doubt, gives utterance to the highest conception of Brahman's nature that *S*â*nd*ilya's thought was able to reach, is by *S*aṅkara and his school again declared to form part of the lower vidyâ only, because it represents Brahman as possessing qualities. It is, according to their terminology, not *g*ñâna, i. e. knowledge, but the injunction of a mere upâsanâ, a devout meditation on Brahman in so far as possessing certain definite attributes such as having light for its form, having true thoughts, and so on. The Râmânu*g*as, on the other hand, quote this text with preference as clearly describing the nature of their highest, i. e. their one Brahman. We again allow that *S*aṅkara is free to deny that any text which ascribes qualities to Brahman embodies absolute truth; but we also again remark that there is no reason whatever for supposing that *S*â*nd*ilya, or whoever may have been the author of that vidyâ, looked upon it as anything else but a statement of the highest truth accessible to man.

We return to the question as to the true philosophy of the Upanishads, apart from the systems of the commentators.—From what precedes it will appear with sufficient distinctness that, if we understand by philosophy a philosophical system coherent in all its parts, free from all contradictions and allowing room for all the different statements made in all the chief Upanishads, a philosophy of the Upanishads cannot even be spoken of. The various lucubrations on Brahman, the world, and the human soul of which the Upanishads consist do not allow themselves to be systematised simply because they were never meant to form a system. *S*â*n*d*ilya's views as to the nature of Brahman did not in all details agree with those of Yâ*gñ*a-valkya, and Uddâlaka differed from both. In this there is nothing to wonder at, and the burden of proof rests altogether with those who maintain that a large number of detached philosophic and theological dissertations, ascribed to different authors, doubtless belonging to different periods, and not seldom manifestly contradicting each other, admit of being combined into a perfectly consistent whole.

The question, however, assumes a different aspect, if we take the terms 'philosophy' and 'philosophical system,' not in the strict sense in which *S*añkara and other commentators are not afraid of taking them, but as implying merely an agreement in certain fundamental features. In this latter sense we may indeed undertake to indicate the outlines of a philosophy of the Upanishads, only keeping in view that precision in details is not to be aimed at. And here we finally see ourselves driven back altogether on the texts themselves, and have to acknowledge that the help we receive from commentators, to whatever school they may belong, is very inconsiderable. Fortunately it cannot be asserted that the texts on the whole oppose very serious difficulties to a right understanding, however obscure the details often are. Concerning the latter we occasionally depend entirely on the explanations vouchsafed by the scholiasts, but as far as the general drift and spirit of the texts are concerned, we are quite able to judge by ourselves, and are even specially qualified to do so by having no particular system to advocate.

The point we will first touch upon is the same from which we started when examining the doctrine of the Sûtras, viz. the question whether the Upanishads acknowledge a higher and lower knowledge in *S*añkara's sense, i. e. a knowledge of a higher and a lower Brahman. Now this we find not to be the case. Knowledge is in the Upanishads frequently opposed to avidyâ, by which latter term we have to understand ignorance as to Brahman, absence of philosophic knowledge; and, again, in several places we find the knowledge of the sacrificial part of the Veda with its supplementary disciplines contrasted as inferior with the knowledge of the Self; to which latter distinction the Mu*nd*aka Up. (I. 4) applies the terms aparâ and parâ vidyâ. But a formal recognition of the essential difference of Brahman being viewed, on the one hand, as possessing distinctive attributes, and, on the other hand, as devoid of all such attributes is not to be met with anywhere. Brahman is indeed sometimes described as sagu*n*a and sometimes as nirgu*n*a (to use later terms); but it is nowhere said that thereon rests a distinction of two different kinds of knowledge leading to altogether different results. The knowledge of Brahman is one, under whatever aspects it is viewed; hence the circumstance (already exemplified above) that in the same vidyâs it is spoken of as sagu*n*a as well as nirgu*n*a. When the mind of the writer dwells on the fact that Brahman is that from which all this world originates, and in which it rests, he naturally applies to it distinctive attributes pointing at its relation to the world; Brahman, then, is called the Self and life of all, the inward ruler, the omniscient Lord, and so on. When, on the other hand, the author follows out the idea that Brahman may be viewed in itself as the mysterious reality of which the whole expanse of the world is only an outward manifestation, then it strikes him that no idea or term derived from sensible experience can rightly be applied to it, that nothing more may be predicated of it but that it is neither this nor that. But these are only two aspects of the cognition of one and the same entity.

Closely connected with the question as to the double nature of the Brahman of the Upanishads is the question as to their teaching Mâyâ.—From Colebrooke downwards the majority of European writers have inclined towards the opinion that the doctrine of Mâyâ, i.e. of the unreal illusory character of the sensible world, does not constitute a feature of the primitive philosophy of the Upanishads, but was introduced into the system at some later period, whether by Bâdarâya*n*a or *S*aṅkara or somebody else. The opposite view, viz. that the doctrine of Mâyâ forms an integral element of the teaching of the Upanishads, is implied in them everywhere, and enunciated more or less distinctly in more than one place, has in recent times been advocated with much force by Mr. Gough in the ninth chapter of his Philosophy of the Upanishads.

In his Matériaux, &c. M. Paul Régnaud remarks that 'the doctrine of Mâyâ, although implied in the teaching of the Upanishads, could hardly become clear and explicit before the system had reached a stage of development necessitating a choice between admitting two co-existent eternal principles (which became the basis of the Sâṅkhya philosophy), and accepting the predominance of the intellectual principle, which in the end necessarily led to the negation of the opposite principle.'—To the two alternatives here referred to as possible we, however, have to add a third one, viz. that form of the Vedânta of which the theory of the Bhâgavatas or Râmânu*g*as is the most eminent type, and according to which Brahman carries within its own nature an element from which the material universe originates; an element which indeed is not an independent entity like the pradhâna of the Sâṅkhyas, but which at the same time is not an unreal Mâyâ but quite as real as any other part of Brahman's nature. That a doctrine of this character actually developed itself on the basis of the Upanishads, is a circumstance which we clearly must not lose sight of, when attempting to determine what the Upanishads themselves are teaching concerning the character of the world.

In enquiring whether the Upanishads maintain the Mâyâ doctrine or not, we must proceed with the same caution as regards other parts of the system, i.e. we must refrain from using unhesitatingly, and without careful consideration of the merits of each individual case, the teaching—direct or inferred—of any one passage to the end of determining the drift of the teaching of other passages. We may admit that some passages, notably of the B*ri*hadâra*n*yaka, contain at any rate the germ of the later developed Mâyâ doctrine[1], and thus render it quite intelligible that a system like *S*aṅkara's

[1] It is well known that, with the exception of the *S*vetâ*s*vatara and Maitrâyanîya, none of the chief Upanishads exhibits the word 'mâyâ.' The term indeed occurs in one place in the B*ri*hadâra*n*yaka; but that passage is a quotation from the *Ri*k Sa*m*hitâ in which mâyâ means 'creative power.' Cp. P. Régnaud, La Mâyâ, in the Revue de l'Histoire des Religions, tome xii, No. 3 (1885).

should evolve itself, among others, out of the Upanishads; but that affords no valid reason for interpreting Mâyâ into other texts which give a very satisfactory sense without that doctrine, or are even clearly repugnant to it. This remark applies in the very first place to all the accounts of the creation of the physical universe. There, if anywhere, the illusional character of the world should have been hinted at, at least, had that theory been held by the authors of those accounts; but not a word to that effect is met with anywhere. The most important of those accounts—the one given in the sixth chapter of the *Kh*ândogya Upanishad—forms no exception. There is absolutely no reason to assume that the 'sending forth' of the elements from the primitive Sat, which is there described at length, was by the writer of that passage meant to represent a vivarta rather than a pari*n*âma, that the process of the origination of the physical universe has to be conceived as anything else but a real manifestation of real powers hidden in the primeval Self. The introductory words, addressed to *S*vetaketu by Uddâlaka, which are generally appealed to as intimating the unreal character of the evolution about to be described, do not, if viewed impartially, intimate any such thing[1]. For what is capable of being proved, and manifestly meant to be proved, by the illustrative instances of the lump of clay and the nugget of gold, through which there are known all things made of clay and gold? Merely that this whole world has Brahman for its causal substance, just as clay is the causal matter of every earthen pot, and gold of every golden ornament, but not that the process through which any causal substance becomes an effect is an unreal one. We—including Uddâlaka—may surely say that all earthen pots are in reality nothing but earth—the earthen pot being merely a special modification (vikâra) of clay which has a name of its own—without thereby committing ourselves to the doctrine that the change of form, which a lump of clay undergoes when being fashioned into a pot, is not real but a mere baseless illusion.

In the same light we have to view numerous other passages

[1] As is demonstrated very satisfactorily by Râmânuga.

which set forth the successive emanations proceeding from the first principle. When, for instance, we meet in the Ka*th*a Up. I, 3, 10, in the serial enumeration of the forms of existence intervening between the gross material world and the highest Self (the Person), with the 'avyâk*ri*ta,' the Undeveloped, immediately below the purusha; and when again the Mu*nd*aka Up. II, 1, 2, speaks of the 'high Imperishable' higher than which is the heavenly Person; there is no reason whatever to see in that 'Undeveloped' and that 'high Imperishable' anything but that real element in Brahman from which, as in the Râmânu*g*a system, the material universe springs by a process of real development. We must of course render it quite clear to ourselves in what sense the terms 'real' and 'unreal' have to be understood. The Upanishads no doubt teach emphatically that the material world does not owe its existence to any principle independent from the Lord like the pradhâna of the Sâṅkhyas; the world is nothing but a manifestation of the Lord's wonderful power, and hence is unsubstantial, if we take the term 'substance' in its strict sense. And, again, everything material is immeasurably inferior in nature to the highest spiritual principle from which it has emanated, and which it now hides from the individual soul. But neither unsubstantiality nor inferiority of the kind mentioned constitutes unreality in the sense in which the Mâyâ of *S*aṅkara is unreal. According to the latter the whole world is nothing but an erroneous appearance, as unreal as the snake, for which a piece of rope is mistaken by the belated traveller, and disappearing just as the imagined snake does as soon as the light of true knowledge has risen. But this is certainly not the impression left on the mind by a comprehensive review of the Upanishads which dwells on their general scope, and does not confine itself to the undue urging of what may be implied in some detached passages. The Upanishads do not call upon us to look upon the whole world as a baseless illusion to be destroyed by knowledge; the great error which they admonish us to relinquish is rather that things have a separate individual existence, and are not tied together by the bond of being all of them effects of Brahman, or Brahman itself. They do not say that true knowledge sublates this false world, as *S*aṅkara says, but that it enables the sage to extricate himself from the world —the inferior mûrta rûpa of Brahman, to use an expression of the B*ri*hadâra*n*yaka—and to become one with Brahman in its highest form. 'We are to see everything in Brahman, and Brahman in everything;' the natural meaning of this is, 'we are to look upon this whole world as a true manifestation of Brahman, as sprung from it and animated by it.' The mâyâvâdin has indeed appropriated the above saying also, and interpreted it so as to fall in with his theory; but he is able to do so only by perverting its manifest sense. For him it would be appropriate to say, not that everything we see is in Brahman, but rather that everything we see is out of Brahman, viz. as a false appearance spread over it and hiding it from us.

Stress has been laid[1] upon certain passages of the B*ri*hadâra*n*yaka which seem to hint at the unreality of this world by qualifying terms, indicative of duality or plurality of existence, by means of an added 'iva,' i.e. 'as it were' (yatrânyad iva syât; yatra dvaitam iva bhavati; âtmâ dhyâyatîva lelâyatîva). Those passages no doubt readily lend themselves to Mâyâ interpretations, and it is by no means impossible that in their author's mind there was something like an undeveloped Mâyâ doctrine. I must, however, remark that they, on the other hand, also admit of easy interpretations not in any way presupposing the theory of the unreality of the world. If Yâ*gñ*avalkya refers to the latter as that 'where there is something else as it were, where there is duality as it were,' he may simply mean to indicate that the ordinary opinion, according to which the individual forms of existence of the world are opposed to each other as altogether separate, is a mistaken one, all things being one in so far as they spring from—and are parts of—Brahman. This would in no way involve duality or plurality being unreal in *S*aṅkara's sense, not any more than, for instance, the modes of Spinoza are unreal because, according to that philosopher, there is only one universal

[1] Gough, Philosophy of the Upanishads, pp. 243 ff.

substance. And with regard to the clause 'the Self thinks as it were' it has to be noted that according to the commentators the 'as it were' is meant to indicate that truly not the Self is thinking, but the upâdhis, i. e. especially the manas with which the Self is connected. But whether these upâdhis are the mere offspring of Mâyâ, as *S*ankara thinks, or real forms of existence, as Râmânu*g*a teaches, is an altogether different question.

I do not wish, however, to urge these last observations, and am ready to admit that not impossibly those iva's indicate that the thought of the writer who employed them was darkly labouring with a conception akin to—although much less explicit than—the Mâyâ of *S*ankara. But what I object to is, that conclusions drawn from a few passages of, after all, doubtful import should be employed for introducing the Mâyâ doctrine into other passages which do not even hint at it, and are fully intelligible without it[1].

The last important point in the teaching of the Upanishads we have to touch upon is the relation of the *g*îvas, the individual souls to the highest Self. The special views regarding that point held by *S*ankara and Râmânu*g*a have been stated before. Confronting their theories with the texts of the Upanishads we must, I think, admit without hesitation, that *S*ankara's doctrine faithfully represents the prevailing teaching of the Upanishads in one important point at least, viz. therein that the soul or Self of the sage —whatever its original relation to Brahman may be—is in the end completely merged and indistinguishably lost in the universal Self. A distinction, repeatedly alluded to before, has indeed to be kept in view here also. Certain texts of the Upanishads describe the soul's going upwards, on the path of the gods, to the world of Brahman, where it dwells for unnumbered years, i. e. for ever. Those texts, as a type of which we may take the passage Kaushît. Up. I—the fundamental text of the Râmânu*g*as concerning the soul's

[1] I cannot discuss in this place the Mâyâ passages of the *S*vetâ*s*vatara and the Maitrâyanîya Upanishads. Reasons which want of space prevents me from setting forth in detail induce me to believe that neither of those two treatises deserves to be considered by us when wishing to ascertain the true unmixed doctrine of the Upanishads.

fate after death—belong to an earlier stage of philosophic development; they manifestly ascribe to the soul a continued individual existence. But mixed with texts of this class there are others in which the final absolute identification of the individual Self with the universal Self is indicated in terms of unmistakable plainness. 'He who knows Brahman and becomes Brahman;' 'he who knows Brahman becomes all this;' 'as the flowing rivers disappear in the sea losing their name and form, thus a wise man goes to the divine person.' And if we look to the whole, to the prevailing spirit of the Upanishads, we may call the doctrine embodied in passages of the latter nature the doctrine of the Upanishads. It is, moreover, supported by the frequently and clearly stated theory of the individual souls being merged in Brahman in the state of deep dreamless sleep.

It is much more difficult to indicate the precise teaching of the Upanishads concerning the original relation of the individual soul to the highest Self, although there can be no doubt that it has to be viewed as proceeding from the latter, and somehow forming a part of it. Negatively we are entitled to say that the doctrine, according to which the soul is merely brahma bhrântam or brahma mâyopâdhikam, is in no way countenanced by the majority of the passages bearing on the question. If the emission of the elements, described in the *Kh*ândogya and referred to above, is a real process—of which we saw no reason to doubt—the *g*îva âtman with which the highest Self enters into the emitted elements is equally real, a true part or emanation of Brahman itself.

After having in this way shortly reviewed the chief elements of Vedântic doctrine according to the Upanishads, we may briefly consider *S*aṅkara's system and mode of interpretation—with whose details we had frequent opportunities of finding fault—as a whole. It has been said before that the task of reducing the teaching of the whole of the Upanishads to a system consistent and free from contradictions is an intrinsically impossible one. But the task once being given, we are quite ready to admit that *S*aṅkara's system is most probably the best which can be devised.

While unable to allow that the Upanishads recognise a lower and higher knowledge of Brahman, in fact the distinction of a lower and higher Brahman, we yet acknowledge that the adoption of that distinction furnishes the interpreter with an instrument of extraordinary power for reducing to an orderly whole the heterogeneous material presented by the old theosophic treatises. This becomes very manifest as soon as we compare *S*ankara's system with that of Râmânu*g*a. The latter recognises only one Brahman which is, as we should say, a personal God, and he therefore lays stress on all those passages of the Upanishads which ascribe to Brahman the attributes of a personal God, such as omniscience and omnipotence. Those passages, on the other hand, whose decided tendency it is to represent Brahman as transcending all qualities, as one undifferenced mass of impersonal intelligence, Râmânu*g*a is unable to accept frankly and fairly, and has to misinterpret them more or less to make them fall in with his system. The same remark holds good with regard to those texts which represent the individual soul as finally identifying itself with Brahman; Râmânu*g*a cannot allow a complete identification but merely an assimilation carried as far as possible. *S*ankara, on the other hand, by skilfully ringing the changes on a higher and a lower doctrine, somehow manages to find room for whatever the Upanishads have to say. Where the text speaks of Brahman as transcending all attributes, the highest doctrine is set forth. Where Brahman is called the All-knowing ruler of the world, the author means to propound the lower knowledge of the Lord only. And where the legends about the primary being and its way of creating the world become somewhat crude and gross, Hira*n*yagarbha and Virâ*g* are summoned forth and charged with the responsibility. Of Virâ*g* Mr. Gough remarks (p. 55) that in him a place is provided by the poets of the Upanishads for the purusha of the ancient *ri*shis, the divine being out of whom the visible and tangible world proceeded. This is quite true if only we substitute for the 'poets of the Upanishads' the framers of the orthodox Vedânta system—for the Upanishads give no indication whatever that by their purusha they understand not the simple old purusha but the Virâg occupying a definite position in a highly elaborate system;—but the mere phrase,'providing a place' intimates with sufficient clearness the nature of the work in which systematisers of the Vedântic doctrine are engaged.

*S*ankara's method thus enables him in a certain way to do justice to different stages of historical development, to recognise clearly existing differences which other systematisers are intent on obliterating. And there has yet to be made a further and even more important admission in favour of his system. It is not only more pliable, more capable of amalgamating heterogeneous material than other systems, but its fundamental doctrines are manifestly in greater harmony with the essential teaching of the Upanishads than those of other Vedântic systems. Above we were unable to allow that the distinction made by *S*ankara between Brahman and Î*s*vara is known to the Upanishads; but we must now admit that if, for the purpose of determining the nature of the highest being, a choice has to be made between those texts which represent Brahman as nirgu*n*a, and those which ascribe to it personal attributes, *S*ankara is right in giving preference to texts of the former kind. The Brahman of the old Upanishads, from which the souls spring to enjoy individual consciousness in their waking state, and into which they sink back temporarily in the state of deep dreamless sleep and permanently in death, is certainly not represented adequately by the strictly personal Î*s*vara of Râmânuga, who rules the world in wisdom and mercy. The older Upanishads, at any rate, lay very little stress upon personal attributes of their highest being, and hence *S*ankara is right in so far as he assigns to his hypostatised personal Î*s*vara[1] a lower place than to his absolute Brahman. That he also faithfully represents the prevailing spirit of the Upanishads in his theory of the ultimate fate

[1] The Î*s*vara who allots to the individual souls their new forms of embodiment in strict accordance with their merit or demerit cannot be called anything else but a personal God. That this personal conscious being is at the same time identified with the totality of the individual souls in the unconscious state of deep dreamless sleep, is one of those extraordinary contradictions which thorough-going systematisers of Vedântic doctrine are apparently unable to avoid altogether.

of the soul, we have already remarked above. And although the Mâyâ doctrine cannot, in my opinion, be said to form part of the teaching of the Upanishads, it cannot yet be asserted to contradict it openly, because the very point which it is meant to elucidate, viz. the mode in which the physical universe and the multiplicity of individual souls originate, is left by the Upanishads very much in the dark. The later growth of the Mâyâ doctrine on the basis of the Upanishads is therefore quite intelligible, and I fully agree with Mr. Gough when he says regarding it that there has been no addition to the system from without but only a development from within, no graft but only growth. The lines of thought which finally led to the elaboration of the full-blown Mâyâ theory may be traced with considerable certainty. In the first place, deepening speculation on Brahman tended to the notion of advaita being taken in a more and more strict sense, as implying not only the exclusion of any second principle external to Brahman, but also the absence of any elements of duality or plurality in the nature of the one universal being itself; a tendency agreeing with the spirit of a certain set of texts from the Upanishads. And as the fact of the appearance of a manifold world cannot be denied, the only way open to thoroughly consistent speculation was to deny at any rate its reality, and to call it a mere illusion due to an unreal principle, with which Brahman is indeed associated, but which is unable to break the unity of Brahman's nature just on account of its own unreality. And, in the second place, a more thorough following out of the conception that the union with Brahman is to be reached through true knowledge only, not unnaturally led to the conclusion that what separates us in our unenlightened state from Brahman is such as to allow itself to be completely sublated by an act of knowledge; is. in other words, nothing else but an erroneous notion, an illusion.—A further circumstance which may not impossibly have co-operated to further the development of the theory of the world's unreality will be referred to later on[1].

[1] That section of the introduction in which the point referred to in the text

We have above been obliged to leave it an open question what kind of Vedânta is represented by the Vedânta-sûtras, although reason was shown for the supposition that in some important points their teaching is more closely related to the system of Râmânuga than to that of *S*ankara. If so, the philosophy of *S*ankara would on the whole stand nearer to the teaching of the Upanishads than the Sûtras of Bâdarâya*n*a. This would indeed be a somewhat unexpected conclusion—for, judging à priori, we should be more inclined to assume a direct propagation of the true doctrine of the Upanishads through Bâdarâya*n*a to *S*ankara—but à priori considerations have of course no weight against positive evidence to the contrary. There are, moreover, other facts in the history of Indian philosophy and theology which help us better to appreciate the possibility of Bâdarâya*n*a's Sûtras already setting forth a doctrine that lays greater stress on the personal character of the highest being than is in agreement with the prevailing tendency of the Upanishads. That the pure doctrine of those ancient Brahminical treatises underwent at a rather early period amalgamations with beliefs which most probably had sprung up in altogether different—priestly or non-priestly—communities is a well-known circumstance; it suffices for our purposes to refer to the most eminent of the early literary monuments in which an amalgamation of the kind mentioned is observable, viz. the Bhagavadgîtâ. The doctrine of the Bhagavadgîtâ represents a fusion of the Brahman theory of the Upanishads with the belief in a personal highest being—K*r*ishn*a* or Vish*n*u—which in many respects approximates very closely to the system of the Bhâgavatas; the attempts of a certain set of Indian commentators to explain it as setting forth pure Vedânta, i. e. the pure doctrine of the Upanishads, may simply be set aside. But this same Bhagavadgîtâ is quoted in Bâdarâya*n*a's Sûtras (at least according to the unanimous explanations of the most eminent scholiasts of different schools) as inferior to *S*ruti only in authority. The Sûtras,

is touched upon will I hope form part of the second volume of the translation. The same remark applies to a point concerning which further information had been promised above on page v.

moreover, refer in different places to certain Vedântic portions of the Mahâbhârata, especially the twelfth book, several of which represent forms of Vedânta distinctly differing from *S*aṅkara's teaching, and closely related to the system of the Bhâgavatas.

Facts of this nature—from entering into the details of which we are prevented by want of space—tend to mitigate the primâ facie strangeness of the assumption that the Vedânta-sûtras, which occupy an intermediate position between the Upanishads and *S*aṅkara, should yet diverge in their teaching from both. The Vedânta of Gau*d*apâda and *S*aṅkara would in that case mark a strictly orthodox reaction against all combinations of non-Vedic elements of belief and doctrine with the teaching of the Upanishads. But although this form of doctrine has ever since *S*aṅkara's time been the one most generally accepted by Brahminic students of philosophy, it has never had any wide-reaching influence on the masses of India. It is too little in sympathy with the wants of the human heart, which, after all, are not so very different in India from what they are elsewhere. Comparatively few, even in India, are those who rejoice in the idea of a universal non-personal essence in which their own individuality is to be merged and lost for ever, who think it sweet 'to be wrecked on the ocean of the Infinite[1].' The only forms of Vedântic philosophy which are—and can at any time have been—really popular, are those in which the Brahman of the Upanishads has somehow transformed itself into a being, between which and the devotee there can exist a personal relation, love and faith on the part of man, justice tempered by mercy on the part of the divinity. The only religious books of widespread influence are such as the Râmâyan of Tulsidâs, which lay no stress on the distinction between an absolute Brahman inaccessible to all human wants and sympathies, and a shadowy Lord whose very conception depends on the illusory principle of Mâyâ, but love to dwell on the delights of devotion

---

[1] Così tra questa
Immensità s' annega il pensier mio,
E il naufrago m' è dolce in questo mare.
LEOPARDI.

to one all-wise and merciful ruler, who is able and willing to lend a gracious ear to the supplication of the worshipper.

The present translation of the Vedânta-sûtras does not aim at rendering that sense which their author may have aimed at conveying, but strictly follows *S*ankara's interpretation. The question as to how far the latter agrees with the views held by Bâdarâya*n*a has been discussed above, with the result that for the present it must, on the whole, be left an open one. In any case it would not be feasible to combine a translation of *S*ankara's commentary with an independent version of the Sûtras which it explains. Similar considerations have determined the method followed in rendering the passages of the Upanishads referred to in the Sûtras and discussed at length by *S*ankara. There also the views of the commentator have to be followed closely; otherwise much of the comment would appear devoid of meaning. Hence, while of course following on the whole the critical translation published by Professor Max Müller in the earlier volumes of this Series, I had, in a not inconsiderable number of cases, to modify it so as to render intelligible *S*ankara's explanations and reasonings. I hope to find space in the introduction to the second volume of this translation for making some general remarks on the method to be followed in translating the Upanishads.

I regret that want of space has prevented me from extracting fuller notes from later scholiasts. The notes given are based, most of them, on the *t*ikâs composed by Ânandagiri and Govindânanda (the former of which is unpublished as yet, so far as I know), and on the Bhâmatî.

My best thanks are due to Pa*nd*its Râma Mi*s*ra *S*âstrin and Gangâdhara *S*âstrin of the Benares Sanskrit College, whom I have consulted on several difficult passages. Greater still are my obligations to Pa*nd*it Ke*s*ava *S*âstrin, of the same institution, who most kindly undertook to read a proof of the whole of the present volume, and whose advice has enabled me to render my version of more than one passage more definite or correct.

VEḌÂNTA-SÛTRAS

WITH

*S*AṄKARA BHÂSHYA.

SAṄKARA'S INTRODUCTION.

FIRST ADHYÂYA.

FIRST PÂDA.

REVERENCE TO THE AUGUST VÂSUDEVA!

IT is a matter not requiring any proof that the object and the subject [1] whose respective spheres are the notion of the 'Thou' (the Non-Ego [2]) and the 'Ego,' and which are opposed to each other as much as darkness and light are, cannot be identified. All the less can their respective attributes be identified. Hence it follows that it is wrong to superimpose [3] upon the subject—whose Self is intelligence, and which has for its sphere the notion of the Ego—the object whose sphere is the notion of the Non-Ego, and the attributes of the object, and vice versâ to superimpose the subject and the attributes of the subject on the object. In spite of this it is on the part of man a natural [4] procedure—

---

[1] The subject is the universal Self whose nature is intelligence (*k*it); the object comprises whatever is of a non-intelligent nature, viz. bodies with their sense-organs, internal organs, and the objects of the senses, i.e. the external material world.

[2] The object is said to have for its sphere the notion of the 'thou' (yushmat), not the notion of the 'this' or 'that' (idam), in order better to mark its absolute opposition to the subject or Ego. Language allows of the co-ordination of the pronouns of the first and the third person ('It is I,' 'I am he who,' &c.; ete vayam, ime vayam âsmahe), but not of the co-ordination of the pronouns of the first and second person.

[3] Adhyâsa, literally 'superimposition' in the sense of (mistaken) ascription or imputation, to something, of an essential nature or attributes not belonging to it. See later on.

[4] Natural, i.e. original, beginningless; for the modes of speech

which has its cause in wrong knowledge—not to distinguish the two entities (object and subject) and their respective attributes, although they are absolutely distinct, but to superimpose upon each the characteristic nature and the attributes of the other, and thus, coupling the Real and the Unreal[1], to make use of expressions such as 'That am I,' 'That is mine[2].'—But what have we to understand by the term 'superimposition?'—The apparent presentation, in the form of remembrance, to consciousness of something previously observed, in some other thing [3].

Some indeed define the term 'superimposition' as the superimposition of the attributes of one thing on another thing [4]. Others, again, define superimposition as the error

and action which characterise transmigratory existence have existed, with the latter, from all eternity.

[1] I. e. the intelligent Self which is the only reality and the non-real objects, viz. body and so on, which are the product of wrong knowledge.

[2] 'The body, &c. is my Self;' 'sickness, death, children, wealth, &c., belong to my Self.'

[3] Literally 'in some other place.' The clause 'in the form of remembrance' is added, the Bhâmatî remarks, in order to exclude those cases where something previously observed is recognised in some other thing or place; as when, for instance, the generic character of a cow which was previously observed in a black cow again presents itself to consciousness in a grey cow, or when Devadatta whom we first saw in Pâ*t*aliputra again appears before us in Mâhishmatî. These are cases of recognition where the object previously observed again presents itself to our senses; while in mere remembrance the object previously perceived is not in renewed contact with the senses. Mere remembrance operates in the case of adhyâsa, as when we mistake mother-of-pearl for silver which is at the time not present but remembered only.

[4] The so-called anyathâkhyâtivâdins maintain that in the act of adhyâsa the attributes of one thing, silver for instance, are superimposed on a different thing existing in a different place, mother-of-pearl for instance (if we take for our example of adhyâsa the case of some man mistaking a piece of mother-of-pearl before him for a piece of silver). The âtmakhyâtivâdins maintain that in adhyâsa the modification, in the form of silver, of the internal organ

founded on the non-apprehension of the difference of that which is superimposed from that on which it is superimposed[1]. Others[2], again, define it as the fictitious assumption of attributes contrary to the nature of that thing on which something else is superimposed. But all these definitions agree in so far as they represent superimposition as the apparent presentation of the attributes of one thing in another thing. And therewith agrees also the popular view which is exemplified by expressions such as the following: 'Mother-of-pearl appears like silver,' 'The moon although one only appears as if she were double.' But how is it possible that on the interior Self which itself is not an object there should be superimposed objects and their attributes? For every one superimposes an object only on such other objects as are placed before him (i. e. in contact with his sense organs), and you have said before that the interior Self which is entirely disconnected from the idea of the Thou (the Non-Ego) is never an object. It is not, we reply, non-object in the absolute sense. For it is the object of the notion of the Ego[3], and the interior Self is well-known to exist on account of its immediate (intuitive) presentation[4]. Nor is it an exceptionless rule that objects

is superimposed on the external thing mother-of-pearl and thus itself appears external. Both views fall under the above definition.

[1] This is the definition of the akhyâtivâdins.

[2] Some anyathâkhyâtivâdins and the Mâdhyamikas according to Ânanda Giri.

[3] The pratyagâtman is in reality non-object, for it is svayamprakâ*s*a, self-luminous, i. e. the subjective factor in all cognition. But it becomes the object of the idea of the Ego in so far as it is limited, conditioned by its adjuncts which are the product of Nescience, viz. the internal organ, the senses and the subtle and gross bodies, i. e. in so far as it is *g*îva, individual or personal soul. Cp. Bhâmatî, pp. 22, 23: '*k*idâtmaiva svayamprakâ*s*o-pi buddhyâdivishayavi*kkh*ura*n*ât katha*m**k*id asmatpratyayavishayo-ha*m*kârâspada*m* *g*îva iti *k*a *g*antur iti *k*a kshetra*g*ña iti *k*âkhyâyate.'

[4] Translated according to the Bhâmatî. We deny, the objector says, the possibility of adhyâsa in the case of the Self, not on the ground that it is not an object because self-luminous (for that it

can be superimposed only on such other objects as are before us, i. e. in contact with our sense-organs; for non-discerning men superimpose on the ether, which is not the object of sensuous perception, dark-blue colour.

Hence it follows that the assumption of the Non-Self being superimposed on the interior Self is not unreasonable.

This superimposition thus defined, learned men consider to be Nescience (avidyâ), and the ascertainment of the true nature of that which is (the Self) by means of the discrimination of that (which is superimposed on the Self), they call knowledge (vidyâ). There being such knowledge (neither the Self nor the Non-Self) are affected in the least by any blemish or (good) quality produced by their mutual superimposition [1]. The mutual superimposition of the Self and the Non-Self, which is termed Nescience, is the presupposition on which there base all the practical distinctions—those made in ordinary life as well as those laid down by the Veda—between means of knowledge, objects of knowledge (and knowing persons), and all scriptural texts, whether they are concerned with injunctions and prohibitions (of meritorious and non-meritorious actions), or with final release [2].—But how can the means of right

---

may be an object although it is self-luminous you have shown), but on the ground that it is not an object because it is not manifested either by itself or by anything else.—It is known or manifest, the Vedântin replies, on account of its immediate presentation (aparokshatvât), i. e. on account of the intuitional knowledge we have of it. Ânanda Giri construes the above clause in a different way: asmatpratyayâvishayatve *py aparokshatvâd ekântenâvishayatvâbbâvât tasminn ahaṅkârâdyadhyâsa ity arthaḥ. Aparokshatvam api kaiśḱid âtmano neshḱam ity âśaṅkyâha pratyagâtmeti.

[1] Tatraivam sati evambhûtavastutattvâvadhâraṇe sati. Bhâ. Tasminn adhyâse uktarîtyâ*vidyâtmake sati. Go. Yatrâtmani buddhyâdau vâ yasya buddhyâder âtmano vâdhyâsaḥ tena buddhyâdinâ*tmânâ va kṛitenâ*śanayâdidosheṇa ḱaitanyaguṇena ḱâtmânâtmâ vâ vastuto na svalpenâpi yugyate. Ânanda Giri.

[2] Whether they belong to the karmakâṇḍa, i. e. that part of the Veda which enjoins active religious duty or the gñânakâṇḍa, i. e. that part of the Veda which treats of Brahman.

knowledge such as perception, inference, &c., and scriptural texts have for their object that which is dependent on Nescience[1]?—Because, we reply, the means of right knowledge cannot operate unless there be a knowing personality, and because the existence of the latter depends on the erroneous notion that the body, the senses, and so on, are identical with, or belong to, the Self of the knowing person. For without the employment of the senses, perception and the other means of right knowledge cannot operate. And without a basis (i. e. the body[2]) the senses cannot act. Nor does anybody act by means of a body on which the nature of the Self is not superimposed[3]. Nor can, in the absence of all that[4], the Self which, in its own nature is free from all contact, become a knowing agent. And if there is no knowing agent, the means of right knowledge cannot operate (as said above). Hence perception and the other means of right knowledge, and the Vedic texts have for their object that which is dependent on Nescience. (That human cognitional activity has for its presupposition the superimposition described above), follows also from the non-difference in that respect of men from animals. Animals, when sounds or other sensible qualities affect their sense of hearing or other senses, recede or advance according as the idea derived from the sensation is a comforting or disquieting one. A cow, for instance, when she sees a man approaching with a raised stick in his hand, thinks that he wants to beat her, and therefore moves away; while she walks up to a man who advances with some fresh grass in his hand. Thus men also—who possess a higher intelligence—run away when

[1] It being of course the function of the means of right knowledge to determine Truth and Reality.

[2] The Bhâmatî takes adhish*th*ânam in the sense of superintendence, guidance. The senses cannot act unless guided by a superintending principle, i. e. the individual soul.

[3] If activity could proceed from the body itself, non-identified with the Self, it would take place in deep sleep also.

[4] I. e. in the absence of the mutual superimposition of the Self and the Non-Self and their attributes.

they see strong fierce-looking fellows drawing near with shouts and brandishing swords; while they confidently approach persons of contrary appearance and behaviour. We thus see that men and animals follow the same course of procedure with reference to the means and objects of knowledge. Now it is well-known that the procedure of animals bases on the non-distinction (of Self and Non-Self); we therefore conclude that, as they present the same appearances, men also—although distinguished by superior intelligence—proceed with regard to perception and so on, in the same way as animals do; as long, that is to say, as the mutual superimposition of Self and Non-Self lasts. With reference again to that kind of activity which is founded on the Veda (sacrifices and the like), it is true indeed that the reflecting man who is qualified to enter on it, does so not without knowing that the Self has a relation to another world; yet that qualification does not depend on the knowledge, derivable from the Vedânta-texts, of the true nature of the Self as free from all wants, raised above the distinctions of the Brâhma*n*a and Kshattriya-classes and so on, transcending transmigratory existence. For such knowledge is useless and even contradictory to the claim (on the part of sacrificers, &c. to perform certain actions and enjoy their fruits). And before such knowledge of the Self has arisen, the Vedic texts continue in their operation, to have for their object that which is dependent on Nescience. For such texts as the following, 'A Brâhma*n*a is to sacrifice,' are operative only on the supposition that on the Self are superimposed particular conditions such as caste, stage of life, age, outward circumstances, and so on. That by superimposition we have to understand the notion of something in some other thing we have already explained. (The superimposition of the Non-Self will be understood more definitely from the following examples.) Extra-personal attributes are superimposed on the Self, if a man considers himself sound and entire, or the contrary, as long as his wife, children, and so on are sound and entire or not. Attributes of the body are superimposed on the Self, if a man thinks of himself (his Self) as stout, lean, fair, as standing, walking, or jumping. Attributes of the sense-organs, if he thinks 'I am mute, or deaf, or one-eyed, or blind.' Attributes of the internal organ when he considers himself subject to desire, intention, doubt, determination, and so on. Thus the producer of the notion of the Ego (i. e. the internal organ) is superimposed on the interior Self, which, in reality, is the witness of all the modifications of the internal organ, and vice versâ the interior Self, which is the witness of everything, is superimposed on the internal organ, the senses, and so on. In this way there goes on this natural beginning—and endless superimposition, which appears in the form of wrong conception, is the cause of individual souls appearing as agents and enjoyers (of the results of their actions), and is observed by every one.

With a view to freeing one's self from that wrong notion which is the cause of all evil and attaining thereby the knowledge of the absolute unity of the Self the study of the Vedânta-texts is begun. That all the Vedânta-texts have the mentioned purport we shall show in this so-called *S*ârîraka-mîmâ*m*sâ[1].

Of this Vedânta-mîmâ*m*sâ about to be explained by us the first Sûtra is as follows.

1. Then therefore the enquiry into Brahman.

The word 'then' is here to be taken as denoting immediate consecution; not as indicating the introduction of a new subject to be entered upon; for the enquiry into Brahman (more literally, the desire of knowing Brahman) is not of that nature[2]. Nor has the word 'then' the sense

[1] The Mîmâ*m*sâ, i.e. the enquiry whose aim it is to show that the embodied Self, i.e. the individual or personal soul is one with Brahman. This Mîmâ*m*sâ being an enquiry into the meaning of the Vedânta-portions of the Veda, it is also called Vedânta-mîmâ*m*sâ.

[2] Nâdhikârârtha iti. Tatra hetur brahmeti. Asyârtha*h*, kim ayam atha*s*abdo brahmag*ñ*âne*kkh*âyâ*h* ki*m* vântar*n*îtavi*k*ârasya athave*kkh*âvisesha*n*ag*ñ*ânasyârambhârtha*h*. Nâdya*h* tasyâ mîmâ*m*sâpravartikâyâs tadapravartyatvâd anârabhyatvât tasyâ*s* *k*ottaratra

of auspiciousness (or blessing); for a word of that meaning could not be properly construed as a part of the sentence. The word 'then' rather acts as an auspicious term by being pronounced and heard merely, while it denotes at the same time something else, viz. immediate consecution as said above. That the latter is its meaning follows moreover from the circumstance that the relation in which the result stands to the previous topic (viewed as the cause of the result) is non-separate from the relation of immediate consecution [1].

If, then, the word 'then' intimates immediate consecution it must be explained on what antecedent the enquiry into Brahman specially depends; just as the enquiry into active religious duty (which forms the subject of the Pûrvâ Mîmâ*m*sâ) specially depends on the antecedent reading of the Veda. The reading of the Veda indeed is the common antecedent (for those who wish to enter on an enquiry into religious duty as well as for those desirous of knowing Brahman). The special question with regard to the enquiry into Brahman is whether it presupposes as its antecedent the understanding of the acts of religious duty (which is acquired by means of the Pûrvâ Mîmâ*m*sâ). To this question we reply in the negative, because for a man who has read the Vedânta-parts of the Veda it is possible to enter on the enquiry into Brahman even before engaging in the enquiry into religious duty. Nor is it the purport of the word 'then' to indicate order of succession; a purport which it serves in other passages, as, for instance, in the one enjoining the cutting off of pieces from the heart and other

---

pratyadhikara*n*am apratipâdanât. Na dvitîyo*thas*abdenânantaryoktidvârâ vi*s*ish*t*âdhikâryasamarpa*n*e sâdhana*k*atush*t*ayâsampannânâ*m* brahmadhîtadvi*k*ârayor anarthitvâd vi*k*ârânârambhân na *k*a vi*k*âravidhiva*s*âd adhikârî kalpya*h* prârambhasyâpi tulyatvâd adhikâri*n*as *k*a vidhyapekshitopâdhitvân na t*ri*tîya*h* brahma*g*ñânasyânandasâkshâtkâratvenâdhikâryatve*pyaprâdhânyâd atha*s*abdâsambandhât tasmân nârambhârthateti. Ânanda Giri.

[1] Any relation in which the result, i.e. here the enquiry into Brahman may stand to some antecedent of which it is the effect may be comprised under the relation of ânantarya.

parts of the sacrificial animal[1]. (For the intimation of order of succession could be intended only if the agent in both cases were the same; but this is not the case), because there is no proof for assuming the enquiry into religious duty and the enquiry into Brahman to stand in the relation of principal and subordinate matter or the relation of qualification (for a certain act) on the part of the person qualified[2]; and because the result as well as the object of the enquiry differs in the two cases. The knowledge of active religious duty has for its fruit transitory felicity, and that again depends on the performance of religious acts. The enquiry into Brahman, on the other hand, has for its fruit eternal bliss, and does not depend on the performance of any acts. Acts of religious duty do not yet exist at the time when they are enquired into, but are something to be accomplished (in the future); for they depend on the activity of man. In the Brahma-mîmâ*m*sâ, on the other hand, the object of enquiry, i.e. Brahman, is something already accomplished (existent),—for it is eternal,—and does not depend on human energy. The two enquiries differ moreover in so far as the operation of their respective fundamental texts is concerned. For the fundamental texts on which active religious duty depends convey information to man in so far only as they enjoin on him their own particular subjects (sacrifices, &c.); while the fundamental texts about Brahman merely instruct man, without laying on him the injunction of being instructed, instruction being their immediate result. The case is analogous to that of the information regarding objects of sense which ensues as soon as the objects are approximated to the senses. It therefore is requisite that something should be

[1] He cuts off from the heart, then from the tongue, then from the breast.

[2] Where one action is subordinate to another as, for instance, the offering of the prayâ*g*as is to the dar*s*apûr*n*amâsa-sacrifice, or where one action qualifies a person for another as, for instance, the offering of the dar*s*apûr*n*amâsa qualifies a man for the performance of the Soma-sacrifice, there is unity of the agent, and consequently an intimation of the order of succession of the actions is in its right place.

stated subsequent to which the enquiry into Brahman is proposed.—Well, then, we maintain that the antecedent conditions are the discrimination of what is eternal and what is non-eternal; the renunciation of all desire to enjoy the fruit (of one's actions) both here and hereafter; the acquirement of tranquillity, self-restraint, and the other means [1], and the desire of final release. If these conditions exist, a man may, either before entering on an enquiry into active religious duty or after that, engage in the enquiry into Brahman and come to know it; but not otherwise. The word 'then' therefore intimates that the enquiry into Brahman is subsequent to the acquisition of the above-mentioned (spiritual) means.

The word 'therefore' intimates a reason. Because the Veda, while declaring that the fruit of the agnihotra and similar performances which are means of happiness is non-eternal (as, for instance, *Kh.* Up. VIII, 1, 6, 'As here on earth whatever has been acquired by action perishes so perishes in the next world whatever is acquired by acts of religious duty'), teaches at the same time that the highest aim of man is realised by the knowledge of Brahman (as, for instance, Taitt. Up. II, 1, 'He who knows Brahman attains the highest'); therefore the enquiry into Brahman is to be undertaken subsequently to the acquirement of the mentioned means.

By Brahman is to be understood that the definition of which will be given in the next Sûtra (I, 1, 2); it is therefore not to be supposed that the word Brahman may here denote something else, as, for instance, the brahminical caste. In the Sûtra the genitive case ('of Brahman;' the literal translation of the Sûtra being 'then therefore the desire of knowledge of Brahman') denotes the object, not something generally supplementary (*s*esha [2]); for the desire of knowledge

[1] The 'means' in addition to *s*ama and dama are discontinuance of religious ceremonies (uparati), patience in suffering (titikshâ), attention and concentration of the mind (samâdhâna), and faith (*s*raddhâ).

[2] According to Pâ*n*ini II, 3, 50 the sixth (genitive) case expresses the relation of one thing being generally supplementary to, or connected with, some other thing.

demands an object of desire and no other such object is stated.—But why should not the genitive case be taken as expressing the general complementary relation (to express which is its proper office)? Even in that case it might constitute the object of the desire of knowledge, since the general relation may base itself on the more particular one.—This assumption, we reply, would mean that we refuse to take Brahman as the direct object, and then again indirectly introduce it as the object; an altogether needless procedure.—Not needless; for if we explain the words of the Sûtra to mean 'the desire of knowledge connected with Brahman' we thereby virtually promise that also all the heads of discussion which bear on Brahman will be treated.—This reason also, we reply, is not strong enough to uphold your interpretation. For the statement of some principal matter already implies all the secondary matters connected therewith. Hence if Brahman, the most eminent of all objects of knowledge, is mentioned, this implies already all those objects of enquiry which the enquiry into Brahman presupposes, and those objects need therefore not be mentioned, especially in the Sûtra. Analogously the sentence 'there the king is going' implicitly means that the king together with his retinue is going there. Our interpretation (according to which the Sûtra represents Brahman as the direct object of knowledge) moreover agrees with Scripture, which directly represents Brahman as the object of the desire of knowledge; compare, for instance, the passage, 'That from whence these beings are born, &c., desire to know that. That is Brahman' (Taitt. Up. III, 1). With passages of this kind the Sûtra only agrees if the genitive case is taken to denote the object. Hence we do take it in that sense. The object of the desire is the knowledge of Brahman up to its complete comprehension, desires having reference to results[1]. Knowledge thus constitutes the

[1] In the case of other transitive verbs, object and result may be separate; so, for instance, when it is said 'grâma*m* ga*kkh*ati,' the village is the object of the action of going, and the arrival at the village its result. But in the case of verbs of desiring object and result coincide.

means by which the complete comprehension of Brahman is desired to be obtained. For the complete comprehension of Brahman is the highest end of man, since it destroys the root of all evil such as Nescience, the seed of the entire Sa*m*sâra. Hence the desire of knowing Brahman is to be entertained.

But, it may be asked, is Brahman known or not known (previously to the enquiry into its nature)? If it is known we need not enter on an enquiry concerning it; if it is not known we can not enter on such an enquiry.

We reply that Brahman is known. Brahman, which is all-knowing and endowed with all powers, whose essential nature is eternal purity, intelligence, and freedom, exists. For if we consider the derivation of the word 'Brahman,' from the root b*ri*h, 'to be great,' we at once understand that eternal purity, and so on, belong to Brahman[1]. Moreover the existence of Brahman is known on the ground of its being the Self of every one. For every one is conscious of the existence of (his) Self, and never thinks 'I am not.' If the existence of the Self were not known, every one would think 'I am not.' And this Self (of whose existence all are conscious) is Brahman. But if Brahman is generally known as the Self, there is no room for an enquiry into it! Not so, we reply; for there is a conflict of opinions as to its special nature. Unlearned people and the Lokâyatikas are of opinion that the mere body endowed with the quality of intelligence is the Self; others that the organs endowed with intelligence are the Self; others maintain that the internal organ is the Self; others, again, that the Self is a mere momentary idea; others, again, that it is the Void. Others, again (to proceed to the opinion of such as acknowledge the authority of the Veda), maintain that there is a transmigrating being different from the body, and so on, which is both agent and enjoyer (of the fruits of action); others teach

[1] That Brahman exists we know, even before entering on the Brahma-mîmâ*m*sâ, from the occurrence of the word in the Veda, &c., and from the etymology of the word we at once infer Brahman's chief attributes.

that that being is enjoying only, not acting; others believe that in addition to the individual souls, there is an all-knowing, all-powerful Lord[1]. Others, finally, (i. e. the Vedântins) maintain that the Lord is the Self of the enjoyer (i. e. of the individual soul whose individual existence is apparent only, the product of Nescience).

Thus there are many various opinions, basing part of them on sound arguments and scriptural texts, part of them on fallacious arguments and scriptural texts misunderstood[2]. If therefore a man would embrace some one of these opinions without previous consideration, he would bar himself from the highest beatitude and incur grievous loss. For this reason the first Sûtra proposes, under the designation of an enquiry into Brahman, a disquisition of the Vedânta-texts, to be carried on with the help of conformable arguments, and having for its aim the highest beatitude.

So far it has been said that Brahman is to be enquired into. The question now arises what the characteristics of that Brahman are, and the reverend author of the Sûtras therefore propounds the following aphorism.

2. (Brahman is that) from which the origin, &c. (i. e. the origin, subsistence, and dissolution) of this (world proceed).

The term, &c. implies subsistence and re-absorption. That the origin is mentioned first (of the three) depends on the declaration of Scripture as well as on the natural development of a substance. Scripture declares the order

[1] The three last opinions are those of the followers of the Nyâya, the Sâṅkhya, and the Yoga-philosophy respectively. The three opinions mentioned first belong to various materialistic schools; the two subsequent ones to two sects of Bauddha philosophers.

[2] As, for instance, the passages 'this person consists of the essence of food;' 'the eye, &c. spoke;' 'non-existing this was in the beginning,' &c.

of succession of origin, subsistence, and dissolution in the passage, Taitt. Up. III, 1, 'From whence these beings are born,' &c. And with regard to the second reason stated, it is known that a substrate of qualities can subsist and be dissolved only after it has entered, through origination, on the state of existence. The words 'of this' denote that substrate of qualities which is presented to us by perception and the other means of right knowledge; the genitive case indicates it to be connected with origin, &c. The words 'from which' denote the cause. The full sense of the Sûtra therefore is: That omniscient omnipotent cause from which proceed the origin, subsistence, and dissolution of this world—which world is differentiated by names and forms, contains many agents and enjoyers, is the abode of the fruits of actions, these fruits having their definite places, times, and causes[1], and the nature of whose arrangement cannot even be conceived by the mind,—that cause, we say, is Brahman. Since the other forms of existence (such as increase, decline, &c.) are included in origination, subsistence, and dissolution, only the three latter are referred to in the Sûtra. As the six stages of existence enumerated by Yâska[2] are possible only during the period of the world's subsistence, it might—were they referred to in the Sûtra—be suspected that what is meant are not the origin, subsistence, and dissolution (of the world) as dependent on the first cause. To preclude this suspicion the Sûtra is to be taken as referring, in addition to the world's origination from Brahman, only to its subsistence in Brahman, and final dissolution into Brahman.

The origin, &c. of a world possessing the attributes stated above cannot possibly proceed from anything else but a Lord possessing the stated qualities; not either from a non-intelligent prâdhana[3], or from atoms, or from non-

[1] So the compound is to be divided according to Ân. Gi. and Go.; the Bhâ. proposes another less plausible division.

[2] According to Nirukta I, 2 the six bhâvavikârâ*h* are: origination, existence, modification, increase, decrease, destruction.

[3] The pradhâna, called also prak*ri*ti, is the primal causal matter of the world in the Sâṅkhya-system. It will be fully discussed in

being, or from a being subject to transmigration[1]; nor, again, can it proceed from its own nature (i.e. spontaneously, without a cause), since we observe that (for the production of effects) special places, times, and causes have invariably to be employed.

(Some of) those who maintain a Lord to be the cause of the world[2], think that the existence of a Lord different from mere transmigrating beings can be inferred by means of the argument stated just now (without recourse being had to Scripture at all).—But, it might be said, you yourself in the Sûtra under discussion have merely brought forward the same argument!—By no means, we reply. The Sûtras (i. e. literally 'the strings') have merely the purpose of stringing together the flowers of the Vedânta-passages. In reality the Vedânta-passages referred to by the Sûtras are discussed here. For the comprehension of Brahman is effected by the ascertainment, consequent on discussion, of the sense of the Vedânta-texts, not either by inference or by the other means of right knowledge. While, however, the Vedânta-passages primarily declare the cause of the origin, &c., of the world, inference also, being an instrument of right knowledge in so far as it does not contradict the Vedânta-texts, is not to be excluded as a means of confirming the meaning ascertained. Scripture itself, moreover, allows argumentation; for the passages, B*ri*. Up. II, 4, 5 ('the Self is to be heard, to be considered'), and *Kh*. Up. VI, 14, 2 ('as the man, &c., having been informed, and being able to judge for himself, would arrive at Gandhâra, in the same way a man who meets with a teacher obtains knowledge'), declare that human understanding assists Scripture[3].

Scriptural text, &c.[4], are not, in the enquiry into Brahman,

later parts of this work. To avoid ambiguities, the term pradhâna has been left untranslated. Cp. Sâṅkhya Kârikâ 3.

[1] Ke*k*it tu hira*n*yagarbha*m* sa*m*sâri*n*am evâgamâ*g* *g*agaddhetum â*k*akshate. Ânanda Giri.

[2] Viz. the Vai*s*eshikas.

[3] Âtmana*h* *s*ruter ity artha*h*. Ânanda Giri.

[4] Text (or direct statement), suggestive power (liṅga), syntactical

the only means of knowledge, as they are in the enquiry into active duty (i. e. in the Pûrva Mîmâ*m*sâ), but scriptural texts on the one hand, and intuition[1], &c., on the other hand, are to be had recourse to according to the occasion: firstly, because intuition is the final result of the enquiry into Brahman; secondly, because the object of the enquiry is an existing (accomplished) substance. If the object of the knowledge of Brahman were something to be accomplished, there would be no reference to intuition, and text, &c., would be the only means of knowledge. The origination of something to be accomplished depends, moreover, on man since any action either of ordinary life, or dependent on the Veda may either be done or not be done, or be done in a different way. A man, for instance, may move on either by means of a horse, or by means of his feet, or by some other means, or not at all. And again (to quote examples of actions dependent on the Veda), we meet in Scripture with sentences such as the following: 'At the atirâtra he takes the sho*d*a*s*in cup,' and 'at the atirâtra he does not take the sho*d*a*s*in cup;' or, 'he makes the oblation after the sun has risen,' and, 'he makes the oblation when the sun has not yet risen.' Just as in the quoted instances, injunctions and prohibitions, allowances of optional procedure, general rules and exceptions have their place, so they would have their place with regard to Brahman also (if the latter were a thing to be accomplished). But the fact is that no option is possible as to whether a substance is to be thus or thus, is to be or not to be. All option depends on the notions of man; but the knowledge of the real nature of a thing does not depend on the notions of man, but only on the thing itself. For to think with regard to a post, 'this is a post or a man, or something else,' is not knowledge of truth; the two ideas, 'it is a man or something else,' being false, and only the third idea, 'it

connection (vâkya), &c., being the means of proof made use of in the Pûrva Mîmâ*m*sâ.

[1] The so-called sâkshâtkâra of Brahman. The &c. comprises inference and so on.

is a post,' which depends on the thing itself, falling under the head of true knowledge. Thus true knowledge of all existing things depends on the things themselves, and hence the knowledge of Brahman also depends altogether on the thing, i. e. Brahman itself.—But, it might be said, as Brahman is an existing substance, it will be the object of the other means of right knowledge also, and from this it follows that a discussion of the Vedânta-texts is purposeless.—This we deny; for as Brahman is not an object of the senses, it has no connection with those other means of knowledge. For the senses have, according to their nature, only external things for their objects, not Brahman. If Brahman were an object of the senses, we might perceive that the world is connected with Brahman as its effect; but as the effect only (i. e. the world) is perceived, it is impossible to decide (through perception) whether it is connected with Brahman or something else. Therefore the Sûtra under discussion is not meant to propound inference (as the means of knowing Brahman), but rather to set forth a Vedânta-text.—Which, then, is the Vedânta-text which the Sûtra points at as having to be considered with reference to the characteristics of Brahman?—It is the passage Taitt. Up. III, 1, 'Bh*ri*gu Vâru*n*i went to his father Varu*n*a, saying, Sir, teach me Brahman,' &c., up to 'That from whence these beings are born, that by which, when born, they live, that into which they enter at their death, try to know that. That is Brahman.' The sentence finally determining the sense of this passage is found III, 6: 'From bliss these beings are born; by bliss, when born, they live; into bliss they enter at their death.' Other passages also are to be adduced which declare the cause to be the almighty Being, whose essential nature is eternal purity, intelligence, and freedom.

That Brahman is omniscient we have been made to infer from it being shown that it is the cause of the world. To confirm this conclusion, the Sûtrakâra continues as follows:

3. (The omniscience of Brahman follows) from its being the source of Scripture.

Brahman is the source, i. e. the cause of the great body of Scripture, consisting of the *Ri*g-veda and other branches, which is supported by various disciplines (such as grammar, nyâya, purâ*n*a, &c.); which lamp-like illuminates all things; which is itself all-knowing as it were. For the origin of a body of Scripture possessing the quality of omniscience cannot be sought elsewhere but in omniscience itself. It is generally understood that the man from whom some special body of doctrine referring to one province of knowledge only originates, as, for instance, grammar from Pâ*n*ini possesses a more extensive knowledge than his work, comprehensive though it be; what idea, then, shall we have to form of the supreme omniscience and omnipotence of that great Being, which in sport as it were, easily as a man sends forth his breath, has produced the vast mass of holy texts known as the *Ri*g-veda, &c., the mine of all knowledge, consisting of manifold branches, the cause of the distinction of all the different classes and conditions of gods, animals, and men! See what Scripture says about him, 'The *Ri*g-veda, &c., have been breathed forth from that great Being' (B*ri*. Up. II, 4, 10).

Or else we may interpret the Sûtra to mean that Scripture consisting of the *Ri*g-veda, &c., as described above, is the source or cause, i. e. the means of right knowledge through which we understand the nature of Brahman. So that the sense would be: through Scripture only as a means of knowledge Brahman is known to be the cause of the origin, &c., of the world. The special scriptural passage meant has been quoted under the preceding Sûtra 'from which these beings are born,' &c.—But as the preceding Sûtra already has pointed out a text showing that Scripture is the source of Brahman, of what use then is the present Sûtra?—The words of the preceding Sûtra, we reply, did not clearly indicate the scriptural passage, and room was thus left for the suspicion that the origin, &c., of the world were adduced merely as determining an inference (independent of Scripture). To obviate this suspicion the Sûtra under discussion has been propounded.

But, again, how can it be said that Scripture is the means of knowing Brahman? Since it has been declared that Scripture aims at action (according to the Pûrva Mîmâ*m*sâ

Sûtra I, 2, 1, 'As the purport of Scripture is action, those scriptural passages whose purport is not action are purportless'), the Vedânta-passages whose purport is not action are purportless. Or else if they are to have some sense, they must either, by manifesting the agent, the divinity or the fruit of the action, form supplements to the passages enjoining actions, or serve the purpose of themselves enjoining a new class of actions, such as devout meditation and the like. For the Veda cannot possibly aim at conveying information regarding the nature of accomplished substances, since the latter are the objects of perception and the other means of proof (which give sufficient information about them; while it is the recognised object of the Veda to give information about what is not known from other sources). And if it did give such information, it would not be connected with things to be desired or shunned, and thus be of no use to man. For this very reason Vedic passages, such as 'he howled, &c.,' which at first sight appear purposeless, are shown to have a purpose in so far as they glorify certain actions (cp. Pû. Mî. Sû. I, 2, 7, 'Because they stand in syntactical connection with the injunctions, therefore their purport is to glorify the injunctions'). In the same way mantras are shown to stand in a certain relation to actions, in so far as they notify the actions themselves and the means by which they are accomplished. So, for instance, the mantra, 'For strength thee (I cut;' which accompanies the cutting of a branch employed in the dar*s*apûr*n*amâsa-sacrifice). In short, no Vedic passage is seen or can be proved to have a meaning but in so far as it is related to an action. And injunctions which are defined as having actions for their objects cannot refer to accomplished existent things. Hence we maintain that the Vedânta-texts are mere supplements to those passages which enjoin actions; notifying the agents, divinities, and results connected with those actions. Or else, if this be not admitted, on the ground of its involving the introduction of a subject-matter foreign to the Vedânta-texts (viz. the subject-matter of the Karmakâ*nd*a of the Veda), we must admit (the second of the two alternatives proposed above, viz.) that the

Vedânta-texts refer to devout meditation (upâsanâ) and similar actions which are mentioned in those very (Vedânta) texts. The result of all of which is that Scripture is not the source of Brahman.

To this argumentation the Sûtrakâra replies as follows:

4. But that (Brahman is to be known from Scripture), because it is connected (with the Vedânta-texts) as their purport.

The word 'but' is meant to rebut the pûrva-paksha (the primâ facie view as urged above). That all-knowing, all-powerful Brahman, which is the cause of the origin, subsistence, and dissolution of the world, is known from the Vedânta-part of Scripture. How? Because in all the Vedânta-texts the sentences construe in so far as they have for their purport, as they intimate that matter (viz. Brahman). Compare, for instance, 'Being only this was in the beginning, one, without a second' (*Kh.* Up. VI, 2, 1); 'In the beginning all this was Self, one only' (Ait. Âr. II, 4, 1, 1); 'This is the Brahman without cause and without effect, without anything inside or outside; this Self is Brahman perceiving everything' (B*ri*. Up. II, 5, 19); 'That immortal Brahman is before' (Mu. Up. II, 2, 11); and similar passages. If the words contained in these passages have once been determined to refer to Brahman, and their purport is understood thereby, it would be improper to assume them to have a different sense; for that would involve the fault of abandoning the direct statements of the text in favour of mere assumptions. Nor can we conclude the purport of these passages to be the intimation of the nature of agents, divinities, &c. (connected with acts of religious duty); for there are certain scriptural passages which preclude all actions, actors, and fruits, as, for instance, B*ri*. Up. II, 4, 13, 'Then by what should he see whom?' (which passage intimates that there is neither an agent, nor an object of action, nor an instrument.) Nor again can Brahman, though it is of the nature of an accomplished thing, be the object of perception and the other means of knowledge; for the fact of everything having its Self in Brahman cannot be grasped without the aid of the scriptural passage 'That art thou' (*Kh.* Up. VI, 8, 7). Nor can it rightly be objected that instruction is purportless if not connected with something either to be striven after or shunned; for from the mere comprehension of Brahman's Self, which is not something either to be avoided or endeavoured after, there results cessation of all pain, and thereby the attainment of man's highest aim. That passages notifying certain divinities, and so on, stand in subordinate relation to acts of devout meditation mentioned in the same chapters may readily be admitted. But it is impossible that Brahman should stand in an analogous relation to injunctions of devout meditation, for if the knowledge of absolute unity has once arisen there exists no longer anything to be desired or avoided, and thereby the conception of duality, according to which we distinguish actions, agents, and the like, is destroyed. If the conception of duality is once uprooted by the conception of absolute unity, it cannot arise again, and so no longer be the cause of Brahman being looked upon as the complementary object of injunctions of devotion. Other parts of the Veda may have no authority except in so far as they are connected with injunctions; still it is impossible to impugn on that ground the authoritativeness of passages conveying the knowledge of the Self; for such passages have their own result. Nor, finally, can the authoritativeness of the Veda be proved by inferential reasoning so that it would be dependent on instances observed elsewhere. From all which it follows that the Veda possesses authority as a means of right knowledge of Brahman.

Here others raise the following objection:—Although the Veda is the means of gaining a right knowledge of Brahman, yet it intimates Brahman only as the object of certain injunctions, just as the information which the Veda gives about the sacrificial post, the âhavanîya-fire and other objects not known from the practice of common life is merely supplementary to certain injunctions[1]. Why so?

[1] So, for instance, the passage 'he carves the sacrificial post and

Because the Veda has the purport of either instigating to action or restraining from it. For men fully acquainted with the object of the Veda have made the following declaration, 'The purpose of the Veda is seen to be the injunction of actions' (Bhâshya on *G*aimini Sûtra I, 1, 1); 'Injunction means passages impelling to action' (Bh. on *G*aim. Sû. I, 1, 2); 'Of this (viz. active religious duty) the knowledge comes from injunction' (part of *G*aim. Sû. I, 1, 5); 'The (words) denoting those (things) are to be connected with (the injunctive verb of the vidhi-passage) whose purport is action' (*G*aim. Sû. I, 1, 25); 'As action is the purport of the Veda, whatever does not refer to action is purportless' (*G*aim. Sû. I, 2, 1). Therefore the Veda has a purport in so far only as it rouses the activity of man with regard to some actions and restrains it with regard to others; other passages (i.e. all those passages which are not directly injunctive) have a purport only in so far as they supplement injunctions and prohibitions. Hence the Vedânta-texts also as likewise belonging to the Veda can have a meaning in the same way only. And if their aim is injunction, then just as the agnihotra-oblation and other rites are enjoined as means for him who is desirous of the heavenly world, so the knowledge of Brahman is enjoined as a means for him who is desirous of immortality.—But—somebody might object—it has been declared that there is a difference in the character of the objects enquired into, the object of enquiry in the karma-kâ*nd*a (that part of the Veda which treats of active religious duty) being something to be accomplished, viz. duty, while here the object is the already existent absolutely accomplished Brahman. From this it follows that the fruit of the knowledge of Brahman must be of a different nature from the fruit of the knowledge of duty which depends on the performance of actions[1].—We reply that it must not be such because the

makes it eight-cornered,' has a purpose only as being supplementary to the injunction 'he ties the victim to the sacrificial post.'

[1] If the fruits of the two *s*âstras were not of a different nature, there would be no reason for the distinction of two *s*âstras; if they

Vedânta-texts give information about Brahman only in so far as it is connected with injunctions of actions. We meet with injunctions of the following kind, 'Verily the Self is to be seen' (B*ri*. Up. II, 4, 5); 'The Self which is free from sin that it is which we must search out, that it is which we must try to understand' (*Kh*. Up. VIII, 7, 1); 'Let a man worship him as Self' (B*ri*. Up. I, 4, 7); 'Let a man worship the Self only as his true state' (B*ri*. Up. I, 4, 15); 'He who knows Brahman becomes Brahman' (Mu. Up. III, 2, 9). These injunctions rouse in us the desire to know what that Brahman is. It, therefore, is the task of the Vedânta-texts to set forth Brahman's nature, and they perform that task by teaching us that Brahman is eternal, all-knowing, absolutely self-sufficient, ever pure, intelligent and free, pure knowledge, absolute bliss. From the devout meditation on this Brahman there results as its fruit, final release, which, although not to be discerned in the ordinary way, is discerned by means of the *s*âstra. If, on the other hand, the Vedânta-texts were considered to have no reference to injunctions of actions, but to contain statements about mere (accomplished) things, just as if one were saying 'the earth comprises seven dvîpas,' 'that king is marching on,' they would be purportless, because then they could not possibly be connected with something to be shunned or endeavoured after.—Perhaps it will here be objected that sometimes a mere statement about existent things has a purpose, as, for instance, the affirmation, 'This is a rope, not a snake,' serves the purpose of removing the fear engendered by an erroneous opinion, and that so likewise the Vedânta-passages making statements about the non-transmigrating Self, have a purport of their own (without reference to any action), viz. in so far as they remove the erroneous opinion of the Self being liable to transmigration.—We reply that this might

are of a different nature, it cannot be said that the knowledge of Brahman is enjoined for the purpose of final release, in the same way as sacrifices are enjoined for the purpose of obtaining the heavenly world and the like.

be so if just as the mere hearing of the true nature of the rope dispels the fear caused by the imagined snake, so the mere hearing of the true nature of Brahman would dispel the erroneous notion of one's being subject to transmigration. But this is not the case; for we observe that even men to whom the true nature of Brahman has been stated continue to be affected by pleasure, pain, and the other qualities attaching to the transmigratory condition. Moreover, we see from the passage, B*ri*. Up. II, 4, 5, 'The Self is to be heard, to be considered, to be reflected upon,' that consideration and reflection have to follow the mere hearing. From all this it results that the *s*âstra can be admitted as a means of knowing Brahman in so far only as the latter is connected with injunctions.

To all this, we, the Vedântins, make the following reply:—The preceding reasoning is not valid, on account of the different nature of the fruits of actions on the one side, and of the knowledge of Brahman on the other side. The enquiry into those actions, whether of body, speech, or mind, which are known from *S*ruti and Sm*ri*ti, and are comprised under the name 'religious duty' (dharma), is carried on in the *G*aimini Sûtra, which begins with the words 'then therefore the enquiry into duty;' the opposite of duty also (adharma), such as doing harm, &c., which is defined in the prohibitory injunctions, forms an object of enquiry to the end that it may be avoided. The fruits of duty, which is good, and its opposite, which is evil, both of which are defined by original Vedic statements, are generally known to be sensible pleasure and pain, which make themselves felt to body, speech, and mind only, are produced by the contact of the organs of sense with the objects, and affect all animate beings from Brahman down to a tuft of grass. Scripture, agreeing with observation, states that there are differences in the degree of pleasure of all embodied creatures from men upward to Brahman. From those differences it is inferred that there are differences in the degrees of the merit acquired by actions in accordance with religious duty; therefrom again are inferred differences in degree between those qualified to perform acts of religious duty. Those latter differences are moreover known to be affected by the desire of certain results (which entitles the man so desirous to perform certain religious acts), worldly possessions, and the like. It is further known from Scripture that those only who perform sacrifices proceed, in consequence of the pre-eminence of their knowledge and meditation, on the northern path (of the sun; *Kh.* Up. V, 10, 1), while mere minor offerings, works of public utility and alms, only lead through smoke and the other stages to the southern path. And that there also (viz. in the moon which is finally reached by those who have passed along the southern path) there are degrees of pleasure and the means of pleasure is understood from the passage 'Having dwelt there till their works are consumed.' Analogously it is understood that the different degrees of pleasure which are enjoyed by the embodied creatures, from man downward to the inmates of hell and to immovable things, are the mere effects of religious merit as defined in Vedic injunctions. On the other hand, from the different degrees of pain endured by higher and lower embodied creatures, there is inferred difference of degree in its cause, viz. religious demerit as defined in the prohibitory injunctions, and in its agents. This difference in the degree of pain and pleasure, which has for its antecedent embodied existence, and for its cause the difference of degree of merit and demerit of animated beings, liable to faults such as ignorance and the like, is well known—from *S*ruti, Sm*ri*ti, and reasoning—to be non-eternal, of a fleeting, changing nature (sa*m*sâra). The following text, for instance, 'As long as he is in the body he cannot get free from pleasure and pain' (*Kh.* Up. VIII, 12, 1), refers to the sa*m*sâra-state as described above. From the following passage, on the other hand, 'When he is free from the body then neither pleasure nor pain touches him,' which denies the touch of pain or pleasure, we learn that the unembodied state called 'final release' (moksha) is declared not to be the effect of religious merit as defined by Vedic injunctions. For if it were the effect of merit it would not be denied that it is subject to pain and pleasure. Should it be said that the very circumstance of its being an unembodied state is the effect of merit, we reply that that cannot be, since Scripture declares that state to be naturally and originally an unembodied one. 'The wise who knows the Self as bodiless within the bodies, as unchanging among changing things, as great and omnipresent does never grieve' (Ka. Up. II, 22); 'He is without breath, without mind, pure' (Mu. Up. II, 1, 2); 'That person is not attached to anything' (B*ri*. Up. IV, 3, 15)[1]. All which passages establish the fact that so-called release differs from all the fruits of action, and is an eternally and essentially disembodied state. Among eternal things, some indeed may be 'eternal, although changing' (pari*n*âminitya), viz. those, the idea of whose identity is not destroyed, although they may undergo changes; such, for instance, are earth and the other elements in the opinion of those who maintain the eternity of the world, or the three gu*n*as in the opinion of the Sâṅkhyas. But this (moksha) is eternal in the true sense, i. e. eternal without undergoing any changes (kû*t*asthanitya), omnipresent as ether, free from all modifications, absolutely self-sufficient, not composed of parts, of self-luminous nature. That bodiless entity in fact, to which merit and demerit with their consequences and threefold time do not apply, is called release; a definition agreeing with scriptural passages, such as the following: 'Different from merit and demerit, different from effect and cause, different from past and future' (Ka. Up. I, 2, 14). It[2] (i. e. moksha) is, therefore, the same as Brahman in the enquiry into which we are at present engaged. If Brahman were represented as supplementary to certain actions, and re-

[1] The first passage shows that the Self is not joined to the gross body; the second that it is not joined to the subtle body; the third that is independent of either.

[2] Ânanda Giri omits 'ata*h*.' His comment is: p*ri*thaggig*ñ*âsâvishayatvâ*k k*a dharmâdyasp*ri*sh*t*atva*m* brahma*n*o yuktam ityâha । tad iti । ata*h s*abdapâ*th*e dharmâdyaspar*s*e karmaphalavailaksha*n*ya*m* hetûk*ri*tam.—The above translation follows Govindânanda's first explanation. Tat kaivalyam brahmaiva karmaphalavilaksha*n*atvâd ity artha*h*.

lease were assumed to be the effect of those actions, it would be non-eternal, and would have to be considered merely as something holding a pre-eminent position among the described non-eternal fruits of actions with their various degrees. But that release is something eternal is acknowledged by whoever admits it at all, and the teaching concerning Brahman can therefore not be merely supplementary to actions.

There are, moreover, a number of scriptural passages which declare release to follow immediately on the cognition of Brahman, and which thus preclude the possibility of an effect intervening between the two; for instance, 'He who knows Brahman becomes Brahman' (Mu. Up. III, 2, 9); 'All his works perish when He has been beheld, who is the higher and the lower' (Mu. Up. II, 2, 8); 'He who knows the bliss of Brahman fears nothing' (Taitt. Up. II, 9); 'O *G*anaka, you have indeed reached fearlessness' (B*ri*. Up. IV, 2, 4); 'That Brahman knew its Self only, saying, I am Brahman. From it all this sprang' (B*ri*. Up. I, 4, 10); 'What sorrow, what trouble can there be to him who beholds that unity?' (Î*s*. Up. 7.) We must likewise quote the passage, B*ri*. Up. I, 4, 10, ('Seeing this the *Ri*shi Vâmadeva understood: I was Manu, I was the sun,') in order to exclude the idea of any action taking place between one's seeing Brahman and becoming one with the universal Self; for that passage is analogous to the following one, 'standing he sings,' from which we understand that no action due to the same agent intervenes between the standing and the singing. Other scriptural passages show that the removal of the obstacles which lie in the way of release is the only fruit of the knowledge of Brahman; so, for instance, 'You indeed are our father, you who carry us from our ignorance to the other shore' (Pr. Up. VI, 8); 'I have heard from men like you that he who knows the Self overcomes grief. I am in grief. Do, Sir, help me over this grief of mine' (*Kh*. Up. VII, 1, 3); 'To him after his faults had been rubbed out, the venerable Sanatkumâra showed the other side of darkness' (*Kh*. Up. VII, 26, 2). The same is the purport of the Sûtra, supported by arguments, of (Gautama) Â*k*ârya, 'Final release results from the successive removal of wrong knowledge, faults, activity, birth, pain, the removal of each later member of the series depending on the removal of the preceding member' (Nyây. Sû. I, 1, 2); and wrong knowledge itself is removed by the knowledge of one's Self being one with the Self of Brahman.

Nor is this knowledge of the Self being one with Brahman a mere (fanciful) combination[1], as is made use of, for instance, in the following passage, 'For the mind is endless, and the Visvedevas are endless, and he thereby gains the endless world' (Bri. Up. III, 1, 9)[2]; nor is it an (in reality unfounded) ascription (superimposition)[3], as in the passages, 'Let him meditate on mind as Brahman,' and 'Âditya is Brahman, this is the doctrine' (*Kh.* Up. III, 18, 1; 19, 1), where the contemplation as Brahman is superimposed on the mind, Âditya and so on; nor, again, is it (a figurative conception of identity) founded on the connection (of the things viewed as identical) with some special activity, as in the passage, 'Air is indeed the absorber; breath is indeed the absorber[4]' (*Kh.* Up. IV, 3, 1; 3); nor is it a mere (ceremonial) purification of (the Self constituting a subordinate member) of an action (viz. the action of seeing, &c., Brahman), in the same way as, for instance, the act of looking at the sacri-

---

[1] Sampat. Sampan nâmâlpe vastuny âlambane sâmânyena kenakin mahato vastunah sampâdanam. Ânanda Giri.

[2] In which passage the mind, which may be called endless on account of the infinite number of modifications it undergoes, is identified with the Visvedevas, which thereby constitute the chief object of the meditation; the fruit of the meditation being immortality. The identity of the Self with Brahman, on the other hand, is real, not only meditatively imagined, on account of the attribute of intelligence being common to both.

[3] Adhyâsah sâstrato-tasmims taddhîh. Sampadi sampâdyamânasya prâdhânyenânudhyânam, adhyâse tu âlambanasyeti viseshah. Ânanda Giri.

[4] Air and breath each absorb certain things, and are, therefore, designated by the same term 'absorber.' Seyam samvargadrishtir vâyau prâne ka dasâsâgatam gagad darsayati yathâ gîvâtmani brimhanakriyayâ brahmadrishtir amritatvâya phalâya kalpata iti. Bhâmatî.

ficial butter[1]. For if the knowledge of the identity of the Self and Brahman were understood in the way of combination and the like, violence would be done thereby to the connection of the words whose object, in certain passages, it clearly is to intimate the fact of Brahman and the Self being really identical; so, for instance, in the following passages, 'That art thou' (*Kh.* Up. VI, 8, 7); 'I am Brahman' (B*ri*. Up. I, 4, 10); 'This Self is Brahman' (B*ri*. Up. II, 5, 19). And other texts which declare that the fruit of the cognition of Brahman is the cessation of Ignorance would be contradicted thereby; so, for instance, 'The fetter of the heart is broken, all doubts are solved' (Mu. Up. II, 2, 8). Nor, finally, would it be possible, in that case, satisfactorily to explain the passages which speak of the individual Self becoming Brahman: such as 'He who knows Brahman becomes Brahman' (Mu. Up. III, 2, 9). Hence the knowledge of the unity of Brahman and the Self cannot be of the nature of figurative combination and the like. The knowledge of Brahman does, therefore, not depend on the active energy of man, but is analogous to the knowledge of those things which are the objects of perception, inference, and so on, and thus depends on the object of knowledge only. Of such a Brahman or its knowledge it is impossible to establish, by reasoning, any connection with actions.

Nor, again, can we connect Brahman with acts by representing it as the object of the action of knowing. For that it is not such is expressly declared in two passages, viz. 'It is different from the known and again above (i.e. different from) the unknown' (Ken. Up. I, 3); and 'How should he know him by whom he knows all this?' (B*ri*. Up. II, 4, 13.) In the same way Brahman is expressly declared not to be the object of the act of devout meditation, viz. in the second half of the verse, Ken. Up. I, 5, whose first half

[1] The butter used in the upâ*ms*uyâ*g*a is ceremonially purified by the wife of the sacrificer looking at it; so, it might be said, the Self of him who meditates on Brahman (and who as kart*ri*—agent—stands in a subordinate aṅga-relation to the karman of meditation) is merely purified by the cognition of its being one with Brahman.

declares it not to be an object (of speech, mind, and so on), 'That which is not proclaimed by speech, by which speech is proclaimed, that only know to be Brahman, not that on which people devoutly meditate as this.' If it should be objected that if Brahman is not an object (of speech, mind, &c.) the *s*âstra can impossibly be its source, we refute this objection by the remark that the aim of the *s*âstra is to discard all distinctions fictitiously created by Nescience. The *s*âstra's purport is not to represent Brahman definitely as this or that object, its purpose is rather to show that Brahman as the eternal subject (pratyagâtman, the inward Self) is never an object, and thereby to remove the distinction of objects known, knowers, acts of knowledge, &c., which is fictitiously created by Nescience. Accordingly the *s*âstra says, 'By whom it is not thought by him it is thought, by whom it is thought he does not know it; unknown by those who know it, it is known by those who do not know it' (Ken. Up. II, 3); and 'Thou couldst not see the seer of sight, thou couldst not hear the hearer of hearing, nor perceive the perceiver of perception, nor know the knower of knowledge' (B*ri*. Up. III, 4, 2). As thereby (i. e. by the knowledge derived from the *s*âstra) the imagination of the transitoriness of Release which is due to Nescience is discarded, and Release is shown to be of the nature of the eternally free Self, it cannot be charged with the imperfection of non-eternality. Those, on the other hand, who consider Release to be something to be effected properly maintain that it depends on the action of mind, speech, or body. So, likewise, those who consider it to be a mere modification. Non-eternality of Release is the certain consequence of these two opinions; for we observe in common life that things which are modifications, such as sour milk and the like, and things which are effects, such as jars, &c., are non-eternal. Nor, again, can it be said that there is a dependance on action in consequence of (Brahman or Release) being something which is to be obtained[1]; for as Brahman constitutes a person's Self it is

[1] An hypothesis which might be proposed for the purpose of

not something to be attained by that person. And even if Brahman were altogether different from a person's Self still it would not be something to be obtained; for as it is omnipresent it is part of its nature that it is ever present to every one, just as the (all-pervading) ether is. Nor, again, can it be maintained that Release is something to be ceremonially purified, and as such depends on an activity. For ceremonial purification (sa*m*skâra) results either from the accretion of some excellence or from the removal of some blemish. The former alternative does not apply to Release as it is of the nature of Brahman, to which no excellence can be added; nor, again, does the latter alternative apply, since Release is of the nature of Brahman, which is eternally pure.—But, it might be said, Release might be a quality of the Self which is merely hidden and becomes manifest on the Self being purified by some action; just as the quality of clearness becomes manifest in a mirror when the mirror is cleaned by means of the action of rubbing.—This objection is invalid, we reply, because the Self cannot be the abode of any action. For an action cannot exist without modifying that in which it abides. But if the Self were modified by an action its non-eternality would result therefrom, and texts such as the following, 'unchangeable he is called,' would thus be stultified; an altogether unacceptable result. Hence it is impossible to assume that any action should abide in the Self. On the other hand, the Self cannot be purified by actions abiding in something else as it stands in no relation to that extraneous something. Nor will it avail to point out (as a quasi-analogous case) that the embodied Self (dehin, the individual soul) is purified by certain ritual actions which abide in the body, such as bathing, rinsing one's mouth, wearing the sacrificial thread, and the like. For what is purified by those actions is that Self merely which is joined to the body, i.e. the Self in so far as it is under the power of Nescience. For it is a matter of per-

obviating the imputation to moksha of non-eternality which results from the two preceding hypotheses.

ception that bathing and similar actions stand in the relation of inherence to the body, and it is therefore only proper to conclude that by such actions only that something is purified which is joined to the body. If a person thinks 'I am free from disease,' he predicates health of that entity only which is connected with and mistakenly identifies itself with the harmonious condition of matter (i.e. the body) resulting from appropriate medical treatment applied to the body (i.e. the 'I' constituting the subject of predication is only the individual embodied Self). Analogously that I which predicates of itself, that it is purified by bathing and the like, is only the individual soul joined to the body. For it is only this latter principle of egoity (aha*m*kart*ri*), the object of the notion of the ego and the agent in all cognition, which accomplishes all actions and enjoys their results. Thus the mantras also declare, 'One of them eats the sweet fruit, the other looks on without eating' (Mu. Up. III, 1, 1); and 'When he is in union with the body, the senses, and the mind, then wise people call him the Enjoyer' (Ka. Up. III, 1, 4). Of Brahman, on the other hand, the two following passages declare that it is incapable of receiving any accretion and eternally pure, 'He is the one God, hidden in all beings, all-pervading, the Self within all beings, watching over all works, dwelling in all beings, the witness, the perceiver, the only one; free from qualities' (*S*v. Up. VI, 11); and 'He pervaded all, bright, incorporeal, scatheless, without muscles, pure, untouched by evil' (Î*s*. Up. 8). But Release is nothing but being Brahman. Therefore Release is not something to be purified. And as nobody is able to show any other way in which Release could be connected with action, it is impossible that it should stand in any, even the slightest, relation to any action, excepting knowledge.

But, it will be said here, knowledge itself is an activity of the mind. By no means, we reply; since the two are of different nature. An action is that which is enjoined as being independent of the nature of existing things and dependent on the energy of some person's mind; compare, for instance, the following passages, 'To whichever divinity the offering is made on that one let him meditate when about to say vasha*t*' (Ait. Brâhm. III, 8, 1); and 'Let him meditate in his mind on the sandhyâ.' Meditation and reflection are indeed mental, but as they depend on the (meditating, &c.) person they may either be performed or not be performed or modified. Knowledge, on the other hand, is the result of the different means of (right) knowledge, and those have for their objects existing things; knowledge can therefore not be either made or not made or modified, but depends entirely on existing things, and not either on Vedic statements or on the mind of man. Although mental it thus widely differs from meditation and the like.

The meditation, for instance, on man and woman as fire, which is founded on *Kh*. Up. V, 7, 1; 8, 1, 'The fire is man, O Gautama; the fire is woman, O Gautama,' is on account of its being the result of a Vedic statement, merely an action and dependent on man; that conception of fire, on the other hand, which refers to the well-known (real) fire, is neither dependent on Vedic statements nor on man, but only on a real thing which is an object of perception; it is therefore knowledge and not an action. The same remark applies to all things which are the objects of the different means of right knowledge. This being thus that knowledge also which has the existent Brahman for its object is not dependent on Vedic injunction. Hence, although imperative and similar forms referring to the knowledge of Brahman are found in the Vedic texts, yet they are ineffective because they refer to something which cannot be enjoined, just as the edge of a razor becomes blunt when it is applied to a stone. For they have for their object something which can neither be endeavoured after nor avoided.—But what then, it will be asked, is the purport of those sentences which, at any rate, have the appearance of injunctions; such as, 'The Self is to be seen, to be heard about?'—They have the purport, we reply, of diverting (men) from the objects of natural activity. For when a man acts intent on external things, and only anxious to attain the objects of his desire and to eschew the objects of his aversion, and does not thereby reach the highest aim of man although desirous of attaining it; such texts as the one quoted divert him from the objects of natural activity and turn the stream of his thoughts on the inward (the highest) Self. That for him who is engaged in the enquiry into the Self, the true nature of the Self is nothing either to be endeavoured after or to be avoided, we learn from texts such as the following: 'This everything, all is that Self' (B*ri*. Up. II, 4, 6); 'But when the Self only is all this, how should he see another, how should he know another, how should he know the knower?' (B*ri*. Up. IV, 5, 15); 'This Self is Brahman' (B*ri*. Up. II, 5, 19). That the knowledge of Brahman refers to something which is not a thing to be done, and therefore is not concerned either with the pursuit or the avoidance of any object, is the very thing we admit; for just that constitutes our glory, that as soon as we comprehend Brahman, all our duties come to an end and all our work is over. Thus *S*ruti says, 'If a man understands the Self, saying, "I am he," what could he wish or desire that he should pine after the body?' (B*ri*. Up. IV, 4, 12.) And similarly Sm*ri*ti declares, 'Having understood this the understanding man has done with all work, O Bhârata' (Bha. Gîtâ XV, 20). Therefore Brahman is not represented as the object of injunctions.

We now proceed to consider the doctrine of those who maintain that there is no part of the Veda which has the purport of making statements about mere existent things, and is not either an injunction or a prohibition, or supplementary to either. This opinion is erroneous, because the soul (purusha), which is the subject of the Upanishads, does not constitute a complement to anything else. Of that soul which is to be comprehended from the Upanishads only, which is non-transmigratory, Brahman, different in nature from the four classes of substances[1], which forms a topic of its own and is not a complement to anything else; of that

[1] Viz. things to be originated (for instance, gha*t*a*m* karoti), things to be obtained (grâma*m* ga*kkh*ati), things to be modified (suvar*n*a*m* ku*nd*ala*m* karoti), and things to be ceremonially purified (vrîhîn prokshati).

soul it is impossible to say that it is not or is not apprehended; for the passage, 'That Self is to be described by No, no!' (B*ri*. Up. III, 9, 26) designates it as the Self, and that the Self is cannot be denied. The possible objection that there is no reason to maintain that the soul is known from the Upanishads only, since it is the object of self-consciousness, is refuted by the fact that the soul of which the Upanishads treat is merely the witness of that (i. e. of the object of self-consciousness, viz. the *g*îvâtman). For neither from that part of the Veda which enjoins works nor from reasoning, anybody apprehends that soul which, different from the agent that is the object of self-consciousness, merely witnesses it; which is permanent in all (transitory) beings; uniform; one; eternally unchanging; the Self of everything. Hence it can neither be denied nor be represented as the mere complement of injunctions; for of that very person who might deny it it is the Self. And as it is the Self of all, it can neither be striven after nor avoided. All perishable things indeed perish, because they are mere modifications, up to (i. e. exclusive of) the soul. But the soul is imperishable[1], as there is no cause why it should perish; and eternally unchanging, as there is no cause for its undergoing any modification; hence it is in its essence eternally pure and free. And from passages, such as 'Beyond the soul there is nothing; this is the goal, the highest road' (Ka. Up. I, 3, 11), and 'That soul, taught in the Upanishads, I ask thee' (B*ri*. Up. III, 9, 26), it appears that the attribute of resting on the Upanishads is properly given to the soul, as it constitutes their chief topic. To say, therefore, that there is no portion of the Veda referring to existing things, is a mere bold assertion.

With regard to the quotations made of the views of men acquainted with the purport of the *S*âstra (who alone were stated to have declared that the Veda treats of actions) it is to be understood that they, having to do with the enquiry into duty, refer to that part of the *S*âstra which consists of

[1] Whence it follows that it is not something to be avoided like transitory things.

injunctions and prohibitions. With regard to the other passage quoted ('as action is the purport of the Veda, whatever does not refer to action is purportless') we remark that if that passage were taken in an absolutely strict sense (when it would mean that only those words which denote action have a meaning), it would follow that all information about existent things is meaningless[1]. If, on the other hand, the Veda—in addition to the injunctions of activity and cessation of activity—does give information about existent things as being subservient to some action to be accomplished, why then should it not give information also about the existent eternally unchangeable Self? For an existent thing, about which information is given, does not become an act (through being stated to be subservient to an act).—But, it will be said, although existent things are not acts, yet, as they are instrumental to action, the information given about such things is merely subservient to action.—This, we reply, does not matter; for although the information may be subservient to action, the things themselves about which information is given are already intimated thereby as things which have the power of bringing about certain actions. Their final end (prayogana) indeed may be subserviency to some action, but thereby they do not cease to be, in the information given about them, intimated in themselves.—Well, and if they are thus intimated, what is gained thereby for your purpose[2]? We reply that the information about the Self, which is an existing thing not comprehended from other sources, is of the same nature (as the information about other existent things); for by the comprehension of the Self a stop is put to all false knowledge, which is the cause of transmigration, and thus a

[1] That, for instance, in the passage 'he is to sacrifice with Soma,' the word 'soma,' which does not denote an action, is devoid of sense.

[2] I.e. for the purpose of showing that the passages conveying information about Brahman as such are justified. You have (the objector maintains) proved hitherto only that passages containing information about existent things are admissible, if those things have a purpose; but how does all this apply to the information about Brahman of which no purpose has been established?

purpose is established which renders the passages relative to Brahman equal to those passages which give information about things instrumental to actions. Moreover, there are found (even in that part of the Veda which treats of actions) such passages as 'a Brâhma*n*a is not to be killed,' which teach abstinence from certain actions. Now abstinence from action is neither action nor instrumental to action. If, therefore, the tenet that all those passages which do not express action are devoid of purport were insisted on, it would follow that all such passages as the one quoted, which teach abstinence from action, are devoid of purport—a consequence which is of course unacceptable. Nor, again, can the connexion in which the word 'not' stands with the action expressed by the verb 'is to be killed'—which action is naturally established [1]—be used as a reason for assuming that 'not' denotes an action non-established elsewhere [2], different from the state of mere passivity implied in the abstinence from the act of killing. For the peculiar function of the particle 'not' is to intimate the idea of the non-existence of that with which it is connected, and the conception of the non-existence (of something to be done) is the cause of the state of passivity. (Nor can it be objected that, as soon as that momentary idea has passed away, the state of passivity will again make room for activity; for) that idea itself passes away (only after having completely destroyed the natural impulse prompting to the murder of a Brâhma*n*a, &c.), just as a fire is extinguished only after having completely consumed its fuel. Hence we are of opinion that the aim of prohibitory passages, such as 'a Brâhma*n*a is not to be killed,' is a merely passive state, consisting in the abstinence from some possible action; excepting some special cases, such as the so-called Pra*g*âpati-vow, &c.[3] Hence the charge of want of purpose is to be

---

[1] It is 'naturally established' because it has natural motives—not dependent on the injunctions of the Veda, viz. passion and the like.

[2] Elsewhere, i.e. outside the Veda.

[3] The above discussion of the prohibitory passages of the Veda

considered as referring (not to the Vedânta-passages, but only) to such statements about existent things as are of the nature of legends and the like, and do not serve any purpose of man.

The allegation that a mere statement about an actually existent thing not connected with an injunction of something to be done, is purposeless (as, for instance, the statement that the earth contains seven dvîpas) has already been refuted on the ground that a purpose is seen to exist in some such statements, as, for instance, 'this is not a snake, but a rope.'—But how about the objection raised above that the information about Brahman cannot be held to have a purpose in the same way as the statement about a rope has one, because a man even after having heard about Brahman continues to belong to this transmigratory

is of a very scholastic nature, and various clauses in it are differently interpreted by the different commentators. *S*aṅkara endeavours to fortify his doctrine, that not all parts of the Veda refer to action by an appeal to prohibitory passages which do not enjoin action but abstinence from action. The legitimacy of this appeal might be contested on the ground that a prohibitory passage also, (as, for instance, 'a Brâhma*n*a is not to be killed,') can be explained as enjoining a positive action, viz. some action opposed in nature to the one forbidden, so that the quoted passage might be interpreted to mean 'a determination, &c. of not killing a Brâhma*n*a is to be formed;' just as we understand something positive by the expression 'a non-Brâhma*n*a,' viz. some man who is a kshattriya or something else. To this the answer is that, wherever we can, we must attribute to the word 'not' its primary sense which is the absolute negation of the word to which it is joined; so that passages where it is joined to words denoting action must be considered to have for their purport the entire absence of action. Special cases only are excepted, as the one alluded to in the text where certain prohibited actions are enumerated under the heading of vows; for as a vow is considered as something positive, the non-doing of some particular action must there be understood as intimating the performance of some action of an opposite nature. The question as to the various meanings of the particle 'not' is discussed in all treatises on the Pûrvâ Mîmâ*m*sâ; see, for instance, Arthasamgraha, translation, p. 39 ff.

world?—We reply as follows: It is impossible to show that a man who has once understood Brahman to be the Self, belongs to the transmigratory world in the same sense as he did before, because that would be contrary to the fact of his being Brahman. For we indeed observe that a person who imagines the body, and so on, to constitute the Self, is subject to fear and pain, but we have no right to assume that the same person after having, by means of the Veda, comprehended Brahman to be the Self, and thus having got over his former imaginings, will still in the same manner be subject to pain and fear whose cause is wrong knowledge. In the same way we see that a rich householder, puffed up by the conceit of his wealth, is grieved when his possessions are taken from him; but we do not see that the loss of his wealth equally grieves him after he has once retired from the world and put off the conceit of his riches. And, again, we see that a person possessing a pair of beautiful earrings derives pleasure from the proud conceit of ownership; but after he has lost the earrings and the conceit established thereon, the pleasure derived from them vanishes. Thus *S*ruti also declares, 'When he is free from the body, then neither pleasure nor pain touches him' (*Kh*. Up. VIII, 12, 1). If it should be objected that the condition of being free from the body follows on death only, we demur, since the cause of man being joined to the body is wrong knowledge. For it is not possible to establish the state of embodiedness upon anything else but wrong knowledge. And that the state of disembodiedness is eternal on account of its not having actions for its cause, we have already explained. The objection again, that embodiedness is caused by the merit and demerit effected by the Self (and therefore real), we refute by remarking that as the (reality of the) conjunction of the Self with the body is itself not established, the circumstance of merit and demerit being due to the action of the Self is likewise not established; for (if we should try to get over this difficulty by representing the Self's embodiedness as caused by merit and demerit) we should commit the logical fault of making embodiedness dependent on merit and demerit, and again merit and demerit on embodiedness. And the assumption of an endless retrogressive chain (of embodied states and merit and demerit) would be no better than a chain of blind men (who are unable to lead one another). Moreover, the Self can impossibly become an agent, as it cannot enter into intimate relation to actions. If it should be said that the Self may be considered as an agent in the same way as kings and other great people are (who without acting themselves make others act) by their mere presence, we deny the appositeness of this instance; for kings may become agents through their relation to servants whom they procure by giving them wages, &c., while it is impossible to imagine anything, analogous to money, which could be the cause of a connexion between the Self as lord and the body, and so on (as servants). Wrong imagination, on the other hand, (of the individual Self, considering itself to be joined to the body,) is a manifest reason of the connexion of the two (which is not based on any assumption). This explains also in how far the Self can be considered as the agent in sacrifices and similar acts[1]. Here it is objected that the Self's imagination as to the body, and so on, belonging to itself is not false, but is to be understood in a derived (figurative) sense. This objection we invalidate by the remark that the distinction of derived and primary senses of words is known to be applicable only where an actual difference of things is known to exist. We are, for instance, acquainted with a certain species of animals having a mane, and so on, which is the exclusive primary object of the idea and word 'lion,' and we are likewise acquainted with persons possessing in an eminent degree certain leonine qualities, such as fierceness, courage, &c.; here, a well settled difference of objects existing, the idea and the name 'lion' are applied to those persons in a derived or figurative sense. In those cases, however, where the difference of the objects is not well established, the transfer of the conception and

[1] The Self is the agent in a sacrifice, &c. only in so far as it imagines itself to be joined to a body; which imagination is finally removed by the cognition of Brahman.

name of the one to the other is not figurative, but simply founded on error. Such is, for instance, the case of a man who at the time of twilight does not discern that the object before him is a post, and applies to it the conception and designation of a man; such is likewise the case of the conception and designation of silver being applied to a shell of mother-of-pearl somehow mistaken for silver. How then can it be maintained that the application of the word and the conception of the Ego to the body, &c., which application is due to the non-discrimination of the Self and the Not-Self, is figurative (rather than simply false)? considering that even learned men who know the difference of the Self and the Not-Self confound the words and ideas just as common shepherds and goatherds do.

As therefore the application of the conception of the Ego to the body on the part of those who affirm the existence of a Self different from the body is simply false, not figurative, it follows that the embodiedness of the Self is (not real but) caused by wrong conception, and hence that the person who has reached true knowledge is free from his body even while still alive. The same is declared in the *S*ruti passages concerning him who knows Brahman: 'And as the slough of a snake lies on an ant-hill, dead and cast away, thus lies this body; but that disembodied immortal spirit is Brahman only, is only light' (B*ri*. Up. IV, 4, 7); and 'With eyes he is without eyes as it were, with ears without ears as it were, with speech without speech as it were, with a mind without mind as it were, with vital airs without vital airs as it were.' Sm*ri*ti also, in the passage where the characteristic marks are enumerated of one whose mind is steady (Bha. Gîtâ II, 54), declares that he who knows is no longer connected with action of any kind. Therefore the man who has once comprehended Brahman to be the Self, does not belong to this transmigratory world as he did before. He, on the other hand, who still belongs to this transmigratory world as before, has not comprehended Brahman to be the Self. Thus there remain no unsolved contradictions.

With reference again to the assertion that Brahman is not

fully determined in its own nature, but stands in a complementary relation to injunctions, because the hearing about Brahman is to be followed by consideration and reflection, we remark that consideration and reflection are themselves merely subservient to the comprehension of Brahman. If Brahman, after having been comprehended, stood in a subordinate relation to some injunctions, it might be said to be merely supplementary. But this is not the case, since consideration and reflection no less than hearing are subservient to comprehension. It follows that the *S*âstra cannot be the means of knowing Brahman only in so far as it is connected with injunctions, and the doctrine that on account of the uniform meaning of the Vedânta-texts, an independent Brahman is to be admitted, is thereby fully established. Hence there is room for beginning the new *S*âstra indicated in the first Sûtra, 'Then therefore the enquiry into Brahman.' If, on the other hand, the Vedânta-texts were connected with injunctions, a new *S*âstra would either not be begun at all, since the *S*âstra concerned with injunctions has already been introduced by means of the first Sûtra of the Pûrva Mîmâ*m*sâ, 'Then therefore the enquiry into duty;' or if it were begun it would be introduced as follows: 'Then therefore the enquiry into the remaining duties;' just as a new portion of the Pûrva Mîmâ*m*sâ Sûtras is introduced with the words, 'Then therefore the enquiry into what subserves the purpose of the sacrifice, and what subserves the purpose of man' (Pû. Mî. Sû. IV, 1, 1). But as the comprehension of the unity of Brahman and the Self has not been propounded (in the previous *S*âstra), it is quite appropriate that a new *S*âstra, whose subject is Brahman, should be entered upon. Hence all injunctions and all other means of knowledge end with the cognition expressed in the words, 'I am Brahman;' for as soon as there supervenes the comprehension of the non-dual Self, which is not either something to be eschewed or something to be appropriated, all objects and knowing agents vanish, and hence there can no longer be means of proof. In accordance with this, they (i. e. men knowing Brahman) have made the following declaration:—

'When there has arisen (in a man's mind) the knowledge, "I am that which is, Brahman is my Self," and when, owing to the sublation of the conceptions of body, relatives, and the like, the (imagination of) the figurative and the false Self has come to an end[1]; how should then the effect[2] (of that wrong imagination) exist any longer? As long as the knowledge of the Self, which Scripture tells us to search after, has not arisen, so long the Self is knowing subject; but that same subject is that which is searched after, viz. (the highest Self) free from all evil and blemish. Just as the idea of the Self being the body is assumed as valid (in ordinary life), so all the ordinary sources of knowledge (perception and the like) are valid only until the one Self is ascertained.'

(Herewith the section comprising the four Sûtras is finished[3].)

So far it has been declared that the Vedânta-passages, whose purport is the comprehension of Brahman being the Self, and which have their object therein, refer exclusively to Brahman without any reference to actions. And it has further been shown that Brahman is the omniscient omnipotent cause of the origin, subsistence, and dissolution of the world. But now the Sâṅkhyas and others being of opinion that an existent substance is to be known through other means of proof (not through the Veda) infer different causes, such as the pradhâna and the like, and thereupon interpret the Vedânta-passages as referring to the latter. All the Vedânta-passages, they maintain, which treat of the creation of the world distinctly point out that the cause (of the world) has to be concluded from the effect by inference; and the cause which is to be inferred is the connexion of the pradhâna with the souls (purusha). The followers of Ka*n*âda again infer from the very same

[1] The figurative Self, i. e. the imagination that wife, children, possessions, and the like are a man's Self; the false Self, i. e. the imagination that the Self acts, suffers, enjoys, &c.

[2] I. e. the apparent world with all its distinctions.

[3] The words in parentheses are not found in the best manuscripts.

passages that the Lord is the efficient cause of the world while the atoms are its material cause. And thus other argumentators also taking their stand on passages apparently favouring their views and on fallacious arguments raise various objections. For this reason the teacher (Vyâsa)—thoroughly acquainted as he is with words, passages, and means of proof—proceeds to state as primâ facie views, and afterwards to refute, all those opinions founded on deceptive passages and fallacious arguments. Thereby he at the same time proves indirectly that what the Vedânta-texts aim at is the comprehension of Brahman.

The Sâṅkhyas who opine that the non-intelligent pradhâna consisting of three constituent elements (guṇa) is the cause of the world argue as follows. The Vedânta-passages which you have declared to intimate that the all-knowing all-powerful Brahman is the cause of the world can be consistently interpreted also on the doctrine of the pradhâna being the general cause. Omnipotence (more literally: the possession of all powers) can be ascribed to the pradhâna in so far as it has all its effects for its objects. All-knowingness also can be ascribed to it, viz. in the following manner. What you think to be knowledge is in reality an attribute of the guṇa of Goodness[1], according to the Smṛiti passage 'from Goodness springs knowledge' (Bha. Gîtâ XIV, 17). By means of this attribute of Goodness, viz. knowledge, certain men endowed with organs which are effects (of the pradhâna) are known as all-knowing Yogins; for omniscience is acknowledged to be connected with the very highest degree of 'Goodness.' Now to the soul (purusha) which is isolated, destitute of effected organs, consisting of pure (undifferenced) intelligence it is quite impossible to ascribe either all-knowingness or limited knowledge; the pradhâna, on the other hand, because consisting of the three guṇas, comprises also in its pradhâna state the element of Goodness which is the cause of all-knowingness. The Vedânta-passages therefore in

[1] The most exalted of the three constituent elements whose state of equipoise constitutes the pradhâna.

a derived (figurative) sense ascribe all-knowingness to the pradhâna, although it is in itself non-intelligent. Moreover you (the Vedântin) also who assume an all-knowing Brahman can ascribe to it all-knowingness in so far only as that term means capacity for all knowledge. For Brahman cannot always be actually engaged in the cognition of everything; for from this there would follow the absolute permanency of his cognition, and this would involve a want of independence on Brahman's part with regard to the activity of knowing. And if you should propose to consider Brahman's cognition as non-permanent it would follow that with the cessation of the cognition Brahman itself would cease. Therefore all-knowingness is possible only in the sense of capacity for all knowledge. Moreover you assume that previously to the origination of the world Brahman is without any instruments of action. But without the body, the senses, &c. which are the instruments of knowledge, cognition cannot take place in any being. And further it must be noted that the pradhâna, as consisting of various elements, is capable of undergoing modifications, and may therefore act as a (material) cause like clay and other substances; while the uncompounded homogeneous Brahman is unable to do so.

To these conclusions he (Vyâsa) replies in the following Sûtra.

5. On account of seeing (i. e. thinking being attributed in the Upanishads to the cause of the world; the pradhâna) is not (to be identified with the cause indicated by the Upanishads; for) it is not founded on Scripture.

It is impossible to find room in the Vedânta-texts for the non-intelligent pradhâna, the fiction of the Sâṅkhyas; because it is not founded on Scripture. How so? Because the quality of seeing, i. e. thinking, is in Scripture ascribed to the cause. For the passage, *Kh.* Up. VI, 2, (which begins: 'Being only, my dear, this was in the beginning, one only, without a second,' and goes on, 'It thought (saw), may I be many, may I grow forth. It sent forth fire,') declares that this world differentiated by name and form, which is there denoted by the word 'this,' was before its origination identical with the Self of that which is and that the principle denoted by the term 'the being' (or 'that which is') sent forth fire and the other elements after having thought. The following passage also ('Verily in the beginning all this was Self, one only; there was nothing else blinking whatsoever. He thought, shall I send forth worlds? He sent forth these worlds,' Ait. Âr. II, 4, 1, 2) declares the creation to have had thought for its antecedent. In another passage also (Pr. Up. VI, 3) it is said of the person of sixteen parts, 'He thought, &c. He sent forth Prâ*n*a.' By 'seeing' (i. e. the verb 'seeing' exhibited in the Sûtra) is not meant that particular verb only, but any verbs which have a cognate sense; just as the verb 'to sacrifice' is used to denote any kind of offering. Therefore other passages also whose purport it is to intimate that an all-knowing Lord is the cause of the world are to be quoted here, as, for instance, Mu. Up. I, 1, 9, 'From him who perceives all and who knows all, whose brooding consists of knowledge, from him is born that Brahman, name and form and food.'

The argumentation of the Sâṅkhyas that the pradhâna may be called all-knowing on account of knowledge constituting an attribute of the gu*n*a Goodness is inadmissible. For as in the pradhâna-condition the three gu*n*as are in a state of equipoise, knowledge which is a quality of Goodness only is not possible[1]. Nor can we admit the explanation that the pradhâna is all-knowing because endowed with the capacity for all knowledge. For if, in the condition of equipoise of the gu*n*as, we term the pradhâna all-knowing with reference to the power of knowledge residing in Goodness, we must likewise term it little-knowing, with reference to the power impeding knowledge which resides in Passion and Dark-

[1] Knowledge can arise only where Goodness is predominant, not where the three qualities mutually counterbalance one another.

ness. Moreover a modification of Goodness which is not connected with a witnessing (observing) principle (sâkshin) is not called knowledge, and the non-intelligent pradhâna is destitute of such a principle. It is therefore impossible to ascribe to the pradhâna all-knowingness. The case of the Yogins finally does not apply to the point under consideration; for as they possess intelligence, they may, owing to an excess of Goodness in their nature, rise to omniscience[1].—Well then (say those Sâṅkhyas who believe in the existence of a Lord) let us assume that the pradhâna possesses the quality of knowledge owing to the witnessing principle (the Lord), just as the quality of burning is imparted to an iron ball by fire.—No, we reply; for if this were so, it would be more reasonable to assume that that which is the cause of the pradhâna having the quality of thought i.e. the all-knowing primary Brahman itself is the cause of the world.

The objection that to Brahman also all-knowingness in its primary sense cannot be ascribed because, if the activity of cognition were permanent, Brahman could not be considered as independent with regard to it, we refute as follows. In what way, we ask the Sâṅkhya, is Brahman's all-knowingness interfered with by a permanent cognitional activity? To maintain that he, who possesses eternal knowledge capable to throw light on all objects, is not all-knowing, is contradictory. If his knowledge were considered non-permanent, he would know sometimes, and sometimes he would not know; from which it would follow indeed that he is not all-knowing. This fault is however avoided if we admit Brahman's knowledge to be permanent.—But, it may be objected, on this latter alternative the knower cannot be designated as independent with reference to the act of knowing.—Why not? we reply; the sun also, although his heat and light are permanent, is nevertheless designated as independent

[1] The excess of Sattva in the Yogin would not enable him to rise to omniscience if he did not possess an intelligent principle independent of Sattva.

when we say, 'he burns, he gives light[1].'—But, it will again be objected, we say that the sun burns or gives light when he stands in relation to some object to be heated or illuminated; Brahman, on the other hand, stands, before the creation of the world, in no relation to any object of knowledge. The cases are therefore not parallel.—This objection too, we reply, is not valid; for as a matter of fact we speak of the Sun as an agent, saying 'the sun shines,' even without reference to any object illuminated by him, and hence Brahman also may be spoken of as an agent, in such passages as 'it thought,' &c., even without reference to any object of knowledge. If, however, an object is supposed to be required ('knowing' being a transitive verb while 'shining' is intransitive), the texts ascribing thought to Brahman will fit all the better.—What then is that object to which the knowledge of the Lord can refer previously to the origin of the world?—Name and form, we reply, which can be defined neither as being identical with Brahman nor as different from it, unevolved but about to be evolved. For if, as the adherents of the Yoga-*s*âstra assume, the Yogins have a perceptive knowledge of the past and the future through the favour of the Lord; in what terms shall we have to speak of the eternal cognition of the ever pure Lord himself, whose objects are the creation, subsistence, and dissolution of the world! The objection that Brahman, previously to the origin of the world, is not able to think because it is not connected with a body, &c. does not apply; for Brahman, whose nature is eternal cognition—as the sun's nature is eternal luminous-

[1] Ânanda Giri comments as follows: paroktânupapattim nirasitum p*rikkh*ati idam iti. Prak*ri*tyarthâbhâvât pratyayârthâbhâvâd vâ brahma*n*o sarva*gñ*ateti pra*s*nam eva praka*t*ayati katham iti. Pratharna*m* pratyâha yasyeti. Ukta*m* vyatirekadvârâ viv*ri*noti anityatve hîti. Dvitîya*m* *s*a*n*kate *gñ*âneti. Svato nityasyâpi *gñ*ânasya tattadarthâva*kkh*innasya kâryatvât tatra svâtantryam pratyayârtho brahma*n*a*h* sidhyatîty âha.—The knowledge of Brahman is eternal, and in so far Brahman is not independent with regard to it, but it is independent with regard to each particular act of knowledge; the verbal affix in '*g*ânâti' indicating the particularity of the act.

ness—can impossibly stand in need of any instruments of knowledge. The transmigrating soul (sa*m*sârin) indeed, which is under the sway of Nescience, &c., may require a body in order that knowledge may arise in it; but not so the Lord, who is free from all impediments of knowledge. The two following Mantras also declare that the Lord does not require a body, and that his knowledge is without any obstructions. 'There is no effect and no instrument known of him, no one is seen like unto him or better; his high power is revealed as manifold, as inherent, acting as knowledge and force.' 'Grasping without hands, hasting without feet, he sees without eyes, he hears without ears. He knows what can be known, but no one knows him; they call him the first, the great person' (*S*v. Up. VI, 8; III, 19).

But, to raise a new objection, there exists no transmigrating soul different from the Lord and obstructed by impediments of knowledge; for *S*ruti expressly declares that 'there is no other seer but he; there is no other knower but he' (B*ri*. Up. III, 7, 23). How then can it be said that the origination of knowledge in the transmigrating soul depends on a body, while it does not do so in the case of the Lord?—True, we reply. There is in reality no transmigrating soul different from the Lord. Still the connexion (of the Lord) with limiting adjuncts, consisting of bodies and so on, is assumed, just as we assume the ether to enter into connexion with divers limiting adjuncts such as jars, pots, caves, and the like. And just as in consequence of connexion of the latter kind such conceptions and terms as 'the hollow (space) of a jar,' &c. are generally current, although the space inside a jar is not really different from universal space, and just as in consequence thereof there generally prevails the false notion that there are different spaces such as the space of a jar and so on; so there prevails likewise the false notion that the Lord and the transmigrating soul are different; a notion due to the non-discrimination of the (unreal) connexion of the soul with the limiting conditions, consisting of the body and so on. That the Self, although in reality the only existence, imparts the quality of Selfhood to bodies and the like which are Not-Self is a matter of observation, and is due to mere wrong conception, which depends in its turn on antecedent wrong conception. And the consequence of the soul thus involving itself in the transmigratory state is that its thought depends on a body and the like.

The averment that the pradhâna, because consisting of several elements, can, like clay and similar substances, occupy the place of a cause while the uncompounded Brahman cannot do so, is refuted by the fact of the pradhâna not basing on Scripture. That, moreover, it is possible to establish by argumentation the causality of Brahman, but not of the pradhâna and similar principles, the Sûtrakâra will set forth in the second Adhyâya (II, 1, 4, &c.).

Here the Sâṅkhya comes forward with a new objection. The difficulty started by you, he says, viz. that the non-intelligent pradhâna cannot be the cause of the world, because thought is ascribed to the latter in the sacred texts, can be got over in another way also, viz. on the ground that non-intelligent things are sometimes figuratively spoken of as intelligent beings. We observe, for instance, that people say of a river-bank about to fall, 'the bank is inclined to fall (pipatishati),' and thus speak of a non-intelligent bank as if it possessed intelligence. So the pradhâna also, although non-intelligent, may, when about to create, be figuratively spoken of as thinking. Just as in ordinary life some intelligent person after having bathed, and dined, and formed the purpose of driving in the afternoon to his village, necessarily acts according to his purpose, so the pradhâna also acts by the necessity of its own nature, when transforming itself into the so-called great principle and the subsequent forms of evolution; it may therefore figuratively be spoken of as intelligent.—But what reason have you for setting aside the primary meaning of the word 'thought' and for taking it in a figurative sense?—The observation, the Sâṅkhya replies, that fire and water also are figuratively spoken of as intelligent beings in the two following scriptural passages, 'That fire thought; that water thought' (*Kh.* Up. VI, 2, 3; 4). We therefrom conclude that thought is to be taken in a figurative sense there also where Being (Sat) is the agent, because it is mentioned in a chapter where (thought) is generally taken in a figurative sense[1].

To this argumentation of the Sâṅkhya the next Sûtra replies:

6. If it is said that (the word 'seeing') has a figurative meaning, we deny that, on account of the word Self (being applied to the cause of the world).

Your assertion that the term 'Being' denotes the non-intelligent pradhâna, and that thought is ascribed to it in a figurative sense only, as it is to fire and water, is untenable. Why so? On account of the term 'Self.' For the passage *Kh*. Up. VI, 2, which begins 'Being only, my dear, this was in the beginning,' after having related the creation of fire, water, and earth ('it thought,' &c.; 'it sent forth fire,' &c.), goes on—denoting the thinking principle of which the whole chapter treats, and likewise fire, water, and earth, by the term 'divinities'—as follows, 'That divinity thought: Let me now enter those three divinities with this living Self (*g*îva âtman) and evolve names and forms.' If we assumed that in this passage the non-intelligent pradhâna is figuratively spoken of as thinking, we should also have to assume that the same pradhâna—as once constituting the subject-matter of the chapter—is referred to by the term 'that divinity.' But in that case the divinity would not speak of the *g*îva as 'Self.' For by the term '*G*îva' we must understand, according to the received meaning and the etymology of the word, the intelligent (principle) which rules over the body and sustains the vital airs. How could such a principle be the Self of the non-intelligent pradhâna? By 'Self' we understand (a being's) own nature, and it is clear that the intelligent *G*îva cannot constitute the nature of the non-intelligent pradhâna. If, on the other hand, we refer the whole chapter to the intelligent Brahman, to

[1] In the second Kha*nd*a of the sixth Prapâ*th*aka of the *Kh*. Up. 'aikshata' is twice used in a figurative sense (with regard to fire and water); it is therefore to be understood figuratively in the third passage also where it occurs.

which thought in its primary sense belongs, the use of the word 'Self' with reference to the *G*îva is quite adequate. Then again there is the other passage, 'That which is that subtle essence, in it all that exists has its self. It is the true. It is the Self. That art thou, O *S*vetaketu' (*Kh*. Up. VI, 8, 7, &c.). Here the clause 'It is the Self' designates the Being of which the entire chapter treats, viz. the subtle Self, by the word 'Self,' and the concluding clause, 'that art thou, O *S*vetaketu,' declares the intelligent *S*vetaketu to be of the nature of the Self. Fire and water, on the other hand, are non-intelligent, since they are objects (of the mind), and since they are declared to be implicated in the evolution of names and forms. And as at the same time there is no reason for ascribing to them thought in its primary sense—while the employment of the word 'Self' furnishes such a reason with reference to the Sat—the thought attributed to them must be explained in a figurative sense, like the inclination of the river-bank. Moreover, the thinking on the part of fire and water is to be understood as dependent on their being ruled over by the Sat. On the other hand, the thought of the Sat is, on account of the word 'Self,' not to be understood in a figurative sense[1].

Here the Sâṅkhya comes forward with a new objection. The word 'Self,' he says, may be applied to the pradhâna, although unintelligent, because it is sometimes figuratively used in the sense of 'that which effects all purposes of another;' as, for instance, a king applies the word 'Self' to some servant who carries out all the king's intentions, 'Bhadrasena is my (other) Self.' For the pradhâna, which effects the enjoyment and the emancipation of the soul, serves the latter in the same way as a minister serves his king in the affairs of peace and war. Or else, it may be said, the one word 'Self' may refer to non-intelligent things as well as to intelligent beings, as we see that such expressions as 'the Self of the elements,' 'the Self of the senses,' are made use of, and as the one word 'light' (*g*yotis) denotes a certain

[1] So that, on this latter explanation, it is unnecessary to assume a figurative sense of the word 'thinking' in any of the three passages.

sacrifice (the *g*yotish*t*oma) as well as a flame. How then does it follow from the word 'Self' that the thinking (ascribed to the cause of the world) is not to be taken in a figurative sense?

To this last argumentation the Sûtrakâra replies:

7. (The pradhâna cannot be designated by the term 'Self') because release is taught of him who takes his stand on that (the Sat).

The non-intelligent pradhâna cannot be the object of the term 'Self' because in the passage *Kh*. Up. VI, 2 ff., where the subtle Sat which is under discussion is at first referred to in the sentence, 'That is the Self,' and where the subsequent clause, 'That art thou, O *S*vetaketu,' declares the intelligent *S*vetaketu to have his abode in the Self, a passage subsequent to the two quoted (viz. 'a man who has a teacher obtains true knowledge; for him there is only delay as long as he is not delivered, then he will be perfect') declares final release. For if the non-intelligent pradhâna were denoted by the term 'Sat,' and did comprehend—by means of the phrase 'That art thou'—persons desirous of final release who as such are intelligent, the meaning could only be 'Thou art non-intelligent;' so that Scripture would virtually make contradictory statements to the disadvantage of man, and would thus cease to be a means of right knowledge. But to assume that the faultless *s*âstra is not a means of right knowledge, would be contrary to reason. And if the *s*âstra, considered as a means of right knowledge, should point out to a man desirous of release, but ignorant of the way to it, a non-intelligent Self as the real Self, he would—comparable to the blind man who had caught hold of the ox's tail[1]—cling to the view of that being the Self,

[1] A wicked man meets in a forest a blind person who has lost his way, and implores him to lead him to his village; instead of doing so the wicked man persuades the blind one to catch hold of the tail of an ox, which he promises would lead him to his place. The consequence is that the blind man is, owing to his trustfulness, led even farther astray, and injured by the bushes, &c., through which the ox drags him.

and thus never be able to reach the real Self different from the false Self pointed out to him; hence he would be debarred from what constitutes man's good, and would incur evil. We must therefore conclude that, just as the *s*âstra teaches the agnihotra and similar performances in their true nature as means for those who are desirous of the heavenly world, so the passage 'that is the Self, that art thou, O *S*vetaketu,' teaches the Self in its true nature also. Only on that condition release for him whose thoughts are true can be taught by means of the simile in which the person to be released is compared to the man grasping the heated axe (*Kh*. Up. VI, 16). For in the other case, if the doctrine of the Sat constituting the Self had a secondary meaning only, the cognition founded on the passage 'that art thou' would be of the nature of a fanciful combination only[1], like the knowledge derived from the passage, 'I am the hymn' (Ait. Âr. II, 1, 2, 6), and would lead to a mere transitory reward; so that the simile quoted could not convey the doctrine of release. Therefore the word 'Self' is applied to the subtle Sat not in a merely figurative sense. In the case of the faithful servant, on the other hand, the word 'Self' can—in such phrases as 'Bhadrasena is my Self'—be taken in a figurative sense, because the difference between master and servant is well established by perception. Moreover, to assume that, because words are sometimes seen to be used in figurative senses, a figurative sense may be resorted to in the case of those things also for which words (i.e. Vedic words) are the only means of knowledge, is altogether indefensible; for an assumption of that nature would lead to a general want of confidence. The assertion that the word 'Self' may (primarily) signify what is non-intelligent as well as what is intelligent, just as the word '*g*yotis' signifies a certain sacrifice as well as light, is inadmissible, because we have no right to attribute to words a plurality of meanings. Hence (we rather assume that) the word 'Self' in its primary meaning refers to what is intelligent only and is then, by a figurative

[1] Cp. above, p. 30.

attribution of intelligence, applied to the elements and the like also; whence such phrases as 'the Self of the elements,' 'the Self of the senses.' And even if we assume that the word 'Self' primarily signifies both classes of beings, we are unable to settle in any special case which of the two meanings the word has, unless we are aided either by the general heading under which it stands, or some determinative attributive word. But in the passage under discussion there is nothing to determine that the word refers to something non-intelligent, while, on the other hand, the Sat distinguished by thought forms the general heading, and *S*vetaketu, i.e. a being endowed with intelligence, is mentioned in close proximity. That a non-intelligent Self does not agree with *S*vetaketu, who possesses intelligence, we have already shown. All these circumstances determine the object of the word 'Self' here to be something intelligent. The word '*g*yotis' does moreover not furnish an appropriate example; for according to common use it has the settled meaning of 'light' only, and is used in the sense of sacrifice only on account of the arthavâda assuming a similarity (of the sacrifice) to light.

A different explanation of the Sûtra is also possible. The preceding Sûtra may be taken completely to refute all doubts as to the word 'Self' having a figurative or double sense, and then the present Sûtra is to be explained as containing an independent reason, proving that the doctrine of the pradhâna being the general cause is untenable.

Hence the non-intelligent pradhâna is not denoted by the word 'Self.' This the teacher now proceeds to prove by an additional reason.

8. And (the pradhâna cannot be denoted by the word 'Self') because there is no statement of its having to be set aside.

If the pradhâna which is the Not-Self were denoted by the term 'Being' (Sat), and if the passage 'That is the Self, that art thou, O *S*vetaketu,' referred to the pradhâna; the teacher whose wish it is to impart instruction about the true Brahman would subsequently declare that the pradhâna is to be set aside (and the true Brahman to be considered); for otherwise his pupil, having received the instruction about the pradhâna, might take his stand on the latter, looking upon it as the Non-Self. In ordinary life a man who wishes to point out to a friend the (small) star Arundhatî at first directs his attention to a big neighbouring star, saying 'that is Arundhatî,' although it is really not so; and thereupon he withdraws his first statement and points out the real Arundhatî. Analogously the teacher (if he intended to make his pupil understand the Self through the Non-Self) would in the end definitely state that the Self is not of the nature of the pradhâna. But no such statement is made; for the sixth Prapâ*th*aka arrives at a conclusion based on the view that the Self is nothing but that which is (the Sat).

The word 'and' (in the Sûtra) is meant to notify that the contradiction of a previous statement (which would be implied in the rejected interpretation) is an additional reason for the rejection. Such a contradiction would result even if it were stated that the pradhâna is to be set aside. For in the beginning of the Prapâ*th*aka it is intimated that through the knowledge of the cause everything becomes known. Compare the following consecutive sentences, 'Have you ever asked for that instruction by which we hear what cannot be heard, by which we perceive what cannot be perceived, by which we know what cannot be known? What is that instruction? As, my dear, by one clod of clay all that is made of clay is known, the modification (i.e. the effect) being a name merely which has its origin in speech, while the truth is that it is clay merely,' &c. Now if the term 'Sat' denoted the pradhâna, which is merely the cause of the aggregate of the objects of enjoyment, its knowledge, whether to be set aside or not to be set aside, could never lead to the knowledge of the aggregate of enjoyers (souls), because the latter is not an effect of the pradhâna. Therefore the pradhâna is not denoted by the term 'Sat.'—For this the Sûtrakâra gives a further reason.

9. On account of (the individual Soul) going to the Self (the Self cannot be the pradhâna).

With reference to the cause denoted by the word 'Sat,' Scripture says, 'When a man sleeps here, then, my dear, he becomes united with the Sat, he is gone to his own (Self). Therefore they say of him, "he sleeps" (svapiti), because he is gone to his own (svam apîta).' (*Kh*. Up. VI, 8, 1.) This passage explains the well-known verb 'to sleep,' with reference to the soul. The word, 'his own,' denotes the Self which had before been denoted by the word Sat; to the Self he (the individual soul) goes, i.e. into it it is resolved, according to the acknowledged sense of api-i, which means 'to be resolved into.' The individual soul (*g*îva) is called awake as long as being connected with the various external objects by means of the modifications of the mind—which thus constitute limiting adjuncts of the soul—it apprehends those external objects, and identifies itself with the gross body, which is one of those external objects[1]. When, modified by the impressions which the external objects have left, it sees dreams, it is denoted by the term 'mind[2].' When, on the cessation of the two limiting adjuncts (i.e. the subtle and the gross bodies), and the consequent absence of the modifications due to the adjuncts, it is, in the state of deep sleep, merged in the Self as it were, then it is said to be asleep (resolved into the Self). A similar etymology of the word 'h*ri*daya' is given by *s*ruti, 'That Self abides in the heart. And this is the etymological explanation: he is in the heart (h*ri*di ayam).' (*Kh*. Up. VIII, 3, 3.) The words a*s*anâya and udanyâ are similarly etymologised: 'water is carrying away what has been eaten by him;' 'fire carries away what has been drunk by him' (*Kh*. Up. VI, 8, 3; 5). Thus the passage quoted above explains the resolution (of the soul) into the Self, denoted by the term 'Sat,' by means of the etymology of the word 'sleep.' But the intelligent

[1] So according to the commentators, not to accept whose guidance in the translation of scholastic definitions is rather hazardous. A simpler translation of the clause might however be given.

[2] With reference to *Kh*. Up. VI, 8, 2.

Self can clearly not resolve itself into the non-intelligent pradhâna. If, again, it were said that the pradhâna is denoted by the word 'own,' because belonging to the Self (as being the Self's own), there would remain the same absurd statement as to an intelligent entity being resolved into a non-intelligent one. Moreover another scriptural passage (viz. 'embraced by the intelligent—prâ*gñ*a—Self he knows nothing that is without, nothing that is within,' B*ri*. Up. IV, 3, 21) declares that the soul in the condition of dreamless sleep is resolved into an intelligent entity. Hence that into which all intelligent souls are resolved is an intelligent cause of the world, denoted by the word 'Sat,' and not the pradhâna.—A further reason for the pradhâna not being the cause is subjoined.

10. On account of the uniformity of view (of the Vedânta-texts, Brahman is to be considered the cause).

If, as in the argumentations of the logicians, so in the Vedânta-texts also, there were set forth different views concerning the nature of the cause, some of them favouring the theory of an intelligent Brahman being the cause of the world, others inclining towards the pradhâna doctrine, and others again tending in a different direction; then it might perhaps be possible to interpret such passages as those, which speak of the cause of the world as thinking, in such a manner as to make them fall in with the pradhâna theory. But the stated condition is absent since all the Vedânta-texts uniformly teach that the cause of the world is the intelligent Brahman. Compare, for instance, 'As from a burning fire sparks proceed in all directions, thus from that Self the prâ*n*as proceed each towards its place; from the prâ*n*as the gods, from the gods the worlds' (Kau. Up. III, 3). And 'from that Self sprang ether'.(Taitt. Up. II, 1). And 'all this springs from the Self' (*Kh*. Up. VII, 26, 1). And 'this prâ*n*a is born from the Self' (Pr. Up. III, 3); all which passages declare the Self to be the cause. That the word 'Self' denotes an intelligent being, we have already shown.

And that all the Vedânta-texts advocate the same view as to an intelligent cause of the world, greatly strengthens their claim to be considered a means of right knowledge, just as the corresponding claims of the senses are strengthened by their giving us information of a uniform character regarding colour and the like. The all-knowing Brahman is therefore to be considered the cause of the world, 'on account of the uniformity of view (of the Vedânta-texts).'—A further reason for this conclusion is advanced.

11. And because it is directly stated in Scripture (therefore the all-knowing Brahman is the cause of the world).

That the all-knowing Lord is the cause of the world, is also declared in a text directly referring to him (viz. the all-knowing one), viz. in the following passage of the mantropanishad of the *S*vetâ*s*vataras (VI, 9) where the word 'he' refers to the previously mentioned all-knowing Lord, 'He is the cause, the lord of the lords of the organs, and there is of him neither parent nor lord.' It is therefore finally settled that the all-knowing Brahman is the general cause, not the non-intelligent pradhâna or anything else.

In what precedes we have shown, availing ourselves of appropriate arguments, that the Vedânta-texts exhibited under Sûtras I, 1–11, are capable of proving that the all-knowing, all-powerful Lord is the cause of the origin, subsistence, and dissolution of the world. And we have explained, by pointing to the prevailing uniformity of view (I, 10), that all Vedânta-texts whatever maintain an intelligent cause. The question might therefore be asked, 'What reason is there for the subsequent part of the Vedânta-sûtras?' (as the chief point is settled already.)

To this question we reply as follows: Brahman is apprehended under two forms; in the first place as qualified by limiting conditions owing to the multiformity of the evolutions of name and form (i. e. the multiformity of the created world); in the second place as being the opposite of this, i. e. free from all limiting conditions whatever. Compare the following passages: B*ri*. Up. IV, 5, 15, 'For where there is duality as it were, then one sees the other; but when the Self only is all this, how should he see another?' *Kh*. Up. VII, 24, 1, 'Where one sees nothing else, hears nothing else, understands nothing else, that is the greatest. Where one sees something else, hears something else, understands something else, that is the little. The greatest is immortal; the little is mortal;' Taitt. Âr. III, 12, 7, 'The wise one, who having produced all forms and made all names, sits calling (the things by their names [1]);' *S*v. Up. VI, 19, 'Who is without parts, without actions, tranquil, without faults, without taint, the highest bridge of immortality, like a fire that has consumed its fuel;' B*ri*. Up. II, 3, 6, 'Not so, not so;' B*ri*. Up. III, 8, 8, 'It is neither coarse nor fine, neither short nor long;' and 'defective is one place, perfect the other.' All these passages, with many others, declare Brahman to possess a double nature, according as it is the object either of Knowledge or of Nescience. As long as it is the object of Nescience, there are applied to it the categories of devotee, object of devotion, and the like [2]. The different modes of devotion lead to different results, some to exaltation, some to gradual emancipation, some to success in works; those modes are distinct on account of the distinction of the different qualities and limiting conditions [3]. And although the one highest Self only, i. e. the Lord distinguished by those different qualities constitutes the object of devotion, still the fruits (of devotion) are distinct, according as the devotion refers to different qualities. Thus Scripture says, 'According as man worships him, that he becomes;' and, 'According to what his thought is in this world, so will he be when he has departed

[1] The wise one, i. e. the highest Self; which as *g*îvâtman is conversant with the names and forms of individual things.

[2] I. e. it is looked upon as the object of the devotion of the individual souls; while in reality all those souls and Brahman are one.

[3] Qualities, i. e. the attributes under which the Self is meditated on; limiting conditions, i. e. the localities—such as the heart and the like—which in pious meditation are ascribed to the Self.

this life' (*Kh*. Up. III, 14, 1). Sm*ri*ti also makes an analogous statement, 'Remembering whatever form of being he leaves this body in the end, into that form he enters, being impressed with it through his constant meditation' (Bha. Gîtâ VIII, 6).

Although one and the same Self is hidden in all beings movable as well as immovable, yet owing to the gradual rise of excellence of the minds which form the limiting conditions (of the Self), Scripture declares that the Self, although eternally unchanging and uniform, reveals itself[1] in a graduated series of beings, and so appears in forms of various dignity and power; compare, for instance (Ait. Âr. II, 3, 2, 1), 'He who knows the higher manifestation of the Self in him[2],' &c. Similarly Sm*ri*ti remarks, 'Whatever being there is of power, splendour or might, know it to have sprung from portions of my glory' (Bha. Gîtâ X, 41); a passage declaring that wherever there is an excess of power and so on, there the Lord is to be worshipped. Accordingly here (i. e. in the Sûtras) also the teacher will show that the golden person in the disc of the Sun is the highest Self, on account of an indicating sign, viz. the circumstance of his being unconnected with any evil (Ved. Sû. I, 1, 20); the same is to be observed with regard to I, 1, 22 and other Sûtras. And, again, an enquiry will have to be undertaken into the meaning of the texts, in order that a settled conclusion may be reached concerning that knowledge of the Self which leads to instantaneous release; for although that knowledge is conveyed by means of various limiting conditions, yet no special connexion with limiting conditions is intended to be intimated, in consequence of which there arises a doubt whether it (the

---

[1] Ânanda Giri reads âvish*t*asya for âvishk*ri*tasya.

[2] Cp. the entire passage. All things are manifestations of the highest Self under certain limiting conditions, but occupying different places in an ascending scale. In unsentient things, stones, &c. only the sattâ, the quality of being manifests itself; in plants, animals, and men the Self manifests itself through the vital sap; in animals and men there is understanding; higher thought in man alone.

knowledge) has the higher or the lower Brahman for its object; so, for instance, in the case of Sûtra I, 1, 12[1]. From all this it appears that the following part of the *S*âstra has a special object of its own, viz. to show that the Vedânta-texts teach, on the one hand, Brahman as connected with limiting conditions and forming an object of devotion, and on the other hand, as being free from the connexion with such conditions and constituting an object of knowledge. The refutation, moreover, of non-intelligent causes different from Brahman, which in I, 1, 10 was based on the uniformity of the meaning of the Vedânta-texts, will be further detailed by the Sûtrakâra, who, while explaining additional passages relating to Brahman, will preclude all causes of a nature opposite to that of Brahman.

12. (The Self) consisting of bliss (is the highest Self) on account of the repetition (of the word 'bliss,' as denoting the highest Self).

The Taittirîya-upanishad (II, 1–5), after having enumerated the Self consisting of food, the Self consisting of the vital airs, the Self consisting of mind, and the Self consisting of understanding, says, 'Different from this which consists of understanding is the other inner Self which consists of bliss.' Here the doubt arises whether the phrase, 'that which consists of bliss,' denotes the highest Brahman of which it had been said previously, that 'It is true Being, Knowledge, without end,' or something different from Brahman, just as the

[1] Ânanda Giri on the preceding passage beginning from 'thus here also:' na kevala*m* dvaividhyam brahma*n*a*h* *s*rutism*ri*tyor eva siddha*m* ki*m* tu sûtrak*ri*to*-pi matam ity âha, evam iti, *s*rutism*ri*tyor iva prak*ri*te*-pi *s*âstre dvairûpyam brahma*n*o bhavati; tatra sopâdhikabrahmavishayam antastaddharmâdhikara*n*am udâharati âdityeti; uktanyâya*m* tulyade*s*eshu prasârayati evam iti; sopâdhikopade*s*avan nirupâdhikopade*s*a*m* dar*s*ayati evam ityâdinâ, âtma*gñ*âna*m* nir*n*etavyam iti sambandha*h*; nir*n*ayaprasa*n*gam âha pareti; annamayâdyupâdhidvâroktasya katham paravidyâvishayatva*m* tatrâha upâdhîti; nir*n*ayakramam âha vâkyeti, uktârtham adhikara*n*a*m* kvâstîty â*s*a*n*kyokta*m* yatheti.

Self consisting of food, &c., is different from it.—The pûrvapakshin maintains that the Self consisting of bliss is a secondary (not the principal) Self, and something different from Brahman; as it forms a link in a series of Selfs, beginning with the Self consisting of food, which all are not the principal Self. To the objection that even thus the Self consisting of bliss may be considered as the primary Self, since it is stated to be the innermost of all, he replies that this cannot be admitted, because the Self of bliss is declared to have joy and so on for its limbs, and because it is said to be embodied. If it were identical with the primary Self, joy and the like would not touch it; but the text expressly says 'Joy is its head;' and about its being embodied we read, 'Of that former one this one is the embodied Self' (Taitt. Up. II, 6), i.e. of that former Self of Understanding this Self of bliss is the embodied Self. And of what is embodied, the contact with joy and pain cannot be prevented. Therefore the Self which consists of bliss is nothing but the transmigrating Soul.

To this reasoning we make the following reply:—By the Self consisting of bliss we have to understand the highest Self, 'on account of repetition.' For the word 'bliss' is repeatedly applied to the highest Self. So Taitt. Up. II, 7, where, after the clause 'That is flavour'—which refers back to the Self consisting of bliss, and declares it to be of the nature of flavour—we read, 'For only after having perceived flavour can any one perceive delight. Who could breathe, who could breathe forth if that Bliss existed not in the ether (of the heart)? For he alone causes blessedness;' and again, II, 8, 'Now this is an examination of Bliss;' 'He reaches that Self consisting of Bliss;' and again, II, 9, 'He who knows the Bliss of Brahman fears nothing;' and in addition, 'He understood that Bliss is Brahman' (III, 6). And in another scriptural passage also (B*ri*. Up. III, 9, 28), 'Knowledge and bliss is Brahman,' we see the word 'bliss' applied just to Brahman. As, therefore, the word 'bliss' is repeatedly used with reference to Brahman, we conclude that the Self consisting of bliss is Brahman also. The objection that the Self consisting of bliss can only denote the secondary Self (the Sa*m*sârin), because it forms a link in a series of secondary Selfs, beginning with the one consisting of food, is of no force, for the reason that the Self consisting of bliss is the innermost of all. The *S*âstra, wishing to convey information about the primary Self, adapts itself to common notions, in so far as it at first refers to the body consisting of food, which, although not the Self, is by very obtuse people identified with it; it then proceeds from the body to another Self, which has the same shape with the preceding one, just as the statue possesses the form of the mould into which the molten brass had been poured; then, again, to another one, always at first representing the Non-Self as the Self, for the purpose of easier comprehension; and it finally teaches that the innermost Self[1], which consists of bliss, is the real Self. Just as when a man, desirous of pointing out the star Arundhatî to another man, at first points to several stars which are not Arundhatî as being Arundhatî, while only the star pointed out in the end is the real Arundhatî; so here also the Self consisting of bliss is the real Self on account of its being the innermost (i.e. the last). Nor can any weight be allowed to the objection that the attribution of joy and so on, as head, &c., cannot possibly refer to the real Self; for this attribution is due to the immediately preceding limiting condition (viz. the Self consisting of understanding, the so-called vig*ñ*ânako*s*a), and does not really belong to the real Self. The possession of a bodily nature also is ascribed to the Self of bliss, only because it is represented as a link in the chain of bodies which begins with the Self consisting of food, and is not ascribed to it in the same direct sense in which it is predicated of the transmigrating Self. Hence the Self consisting of bliss is the highest Brahman.

13. If (it be objected that the term ânandamaya, consisting of bliss, can) not (denote the highest Self) on account of its being a word denoting a modifica-

[1] After which no other Self is mentioned.

tion (or product); (we declare the objection to be) not (valid) on account of abundance, (the idea of which may be expressed by the affix maya.)

Here the pûrvapakshin raises the objection that the word ânandamaya (consisting of bliss) cannot denote the highest Self.—Why?—Because the word ânandamaya is understood to denote something different from the original word (i. e. the word ânanda without the derivative affix maya), viz. a modification; according to the received sense of the affix maya. 'Ânandamaya' therefore denotes a modification, just as annamaya (consisting of food) and similar words do.

This objection is, however, not valid, because 'maya' is also used in the sense of abundance, i. e. denotes that where there is abundance of what the original word expresses. So, for instance, the phrase 'the sacrifice is annamaya' means 'the sacrifice is abounding in food' (not 'is some modification or product of food'). Thus here Brahman also, as abounding in bliss, is called ânandamaya. That Brahman does abound in bliss follows from the passage (Taitt. Up. II, 8), where, after the bliss of each of the different classes of beings, beginning with man, has been declared to be a hundred times greater than the bliss of the immediately preceding class, the bliss of Brahman is finally proclaimed to be absolutely supreme. Maya therefore denotes abundance.

14. And because he is declared to be the cause of it, (i. e. of bliss; therefore maya is to be taken as denoting abundance.)

Maya must be understood to denote abundance, for that reason also that Scripture declares Brahman to be the cause of bliss, 'For he alone causes bliss' (Taitt. Up. II, 7). For he who causes bliss must himself abound in bliss; just as we infer in ordinary life, that a man who enriches others must himself possess abundant wealth. As, therefore, maya may be taken to mean 'abundant,' the Self consisting of bliss is the highest Self.

15. Moreover (the ânandamaya is Brahman be-

cause) the same (Brahman) which had been referred to in the mantra is sung, (i. e. proclaimed in the Brâhma*n*a passage as the ânandamaya.)

The Self, consisting of joy, is the highest Brahman for the following reason also[1]. On the introductory words 'he who knows Brahman attains the highest' (Taitt. Up. II, 1), there follows a mantra proclaiming that Brahman, which forms the general topic of the chapter, possesses the qualities of true existence, intelligence, infinity; after that it is said that from Brahman there sprang at first the ether and then all other moving and non-moving things, and that, entering into the beings which it had emitted, Brahman stays in the recess, inmost of all; thereupon, for its better comprehension, the series of the different Selfs ('different from this is the inner Self,' &c.) are enumerated, and then finally the same Brahman which the mantra had proclaimed, is again proclaimed in the passage under discussion, 'different from this is the other inner Self, which consists of bliss.' To assume that a mantra and the Brâhma*n*a passage belonging to it have the same sense is only proper, on account of the absence of contradiction (which results therefrom); for otherwise we should be driven to the unwelcome inference that the text drops the topic once started, and turns to an altogether new subject.

Nor is there mentioned a further inner Self different from the Self consisting of bliss, as in the case of the Self consisting of food, &c.[2] On the same (i. e. the Self consisting of bliss) is founded, 'This same knowledge of Bh*ri*gu and Varu*n*a; he understood that bliss is Brahman' (Taitt. Up. III, 6). Therefore the Self consisting of bliss is the highest Self.

---

[1] The previous proofs were founded on liṅga; the argument which is now propounded is founded on prakara*n*a.

[2] While, in the case of the Selfs consisting of food and so on, a further inner Self is duly mentioned each time. It cannot, therefore, be concluded that the Selfs consisting of food, &c., are likewise identical with the highest Self referred to in the mantra.

16. (The Self consisting of bliss is the highest Self,) not the other (i. e. the individual Soul), on account of the impossibility (of the latter assumption).

And for the following reason also the Self consisting of bliss is the highest Self only, not the other, i. e. the one which is other than the Lord, i.e. the transmigrating individual soul. The personal soul cannot be denoted by the term 'the one consisting of bliss.' Why? On account of the impossibility. For Scripture says, with reference to the Self consisting of bliss, 'He wished, may I be many, may I grow forth. He brooded over himself. After he had thus brooded, he sent forth whatever there is.' Here, the desire arising before the origination of a body, &c., the non-separation of the effects created from the creator, and the creation of all effects whatever, cannot possibly belong to any Self different from the highest Self.

17. And on account of the declaration of the difference (of the two, the ânandamaya cannot be the transmigrating soul).

The Self consisting of bliss cannot be identical with the transmigrating soul, for that reason also that in the section treating of the Self of bliss, the individual soul and the Self of bliss are distinctly represented as different; Taitt. Up. II, 7, 'It (i. e. the Self consisting of bliss) is a flavour; for only after perceiving a flavour can this (soul) perceive bliss.' For he who perceives cannot be that which is perceived.—But, it may be asked, if he who perceives or attains cannot be that which is perceived or attained, how about the following *S*ruti- and Sm*ri*ti-passages, 'The Self is to be sought;' 'Nothing higher is known than the attainment of the Self[1]?'—This objection, we reply, is legitimate (from the point of view of absolute truth). Yet we see that in ordinary life, the Self, which in reality is never anything

[1] Yadi labdhâ na labdhavya*h* katha*m* tarhi paramâtmano vastuto bhinnena *g*îvâtmanâ paramâtmâ labhyata ity artha*h*. Bhâmatî.

but the Self, is, owing to non-comprehension of the truth, identified with the Non-Self, i. e. the body and so on; whereby it becomes possible to speak of the Self in so far as it is identified with the body, and so on, as something not searched for but to be searched for, not heard but to be heard, not seized but to be seized, not perceived but to be perceived, not known but to be known, and the like. Scripture, on the other hand, denies, in such passages as 'there is no other seer but he' (*Bri*. Up. III, 7, 23), that there is in reality any seer or hearer different from the all-knowing highest Lord. (Nor can it be said that the Lord is unreal because he is identical with the unreal individual soul; for)[1] the Lord differs from the soul (vig*ñ*â-nâtman) which is embodied, acts and enjoys, and is the product of Nescience, in the same way as the real juggler who stands on the ground differs from the illusive juggler, who, holding in his hand a shield and a sword, climbs up to the sky by means of a rope; or as the free unlimited ether differs from the ether of a jar, which is determined by its limiting adjunct, (viz. the jar.) With reference to this fictitious difference of the highest Self and the individual Self, the two last Sûtras have been propounded.

18. And on account of desire (being mentioned as belonging to the ânandamaya) no regard is to be had to what is inferred, (i. e. to the pradhâna inferred by the Sâṅkhyas.)

Since in the passage 'he desired, may I be many, may I grow forth,' which occurs in the chapter treating of the ânandamaya (Taitt. Up. II, 6), the quality of feeling desire is mentioned, that which is inferred, i. e. the non-intelligent pradhâna assumed by the Sâṅkhyas, cannot be regarded as being the Self consisting of bliss and the cause of the world. Although the opinion that the pradhâna is the

[1] Yathâ paramesvarâd bhinno *g*îvâtmâ drash*t*â na bhavaty evam *g*îvâtmano-pi drash*t*ur na bhinna*h* paramesvara iti *g*îvasyânirvâ*k*-yatve paramesvaro-py anirvâ*k*ya*h* syâd ity ata âha paramesvaras tv avidyâkalpitâd iti. Ânanda Giri.

cause of the world, has already been refuted in the Sûtra I, 1, 5, it is here, where a favourable opportunity presents itself, refuted for a second time on the basis of the scriptural passage about the cause of the world feeling desire, for the purpose of showing the uniformity of view (of all scriptural passages).

19. And, moreover, it (i. e. Scripture) teaches the joining of this (i. e. the individual soul) with that, (i. e. the Self consisting of bliss), on that (being fully known).

And for the following reason also the term, 'the Self consisting of bliss,' cannot denote either the pradhâna or the individual soul. Scripture teaches that the individual soul when it has reached knowledge is joined, i. e. identified, with the Self of bliss under discussion, i. e. obtains final release. Compare the following passage (Taitt. Up. II, 7), 'When he finds freedom from fear, and rest in that which is invisible, incorporeal, undefined, unsupported, then he has obtained the fearless. For if he makes but the smallest distinction in it there is fear for him.' That means, if he sees in that Self consisting of bliss even a small difference in the form of non-identity, then he finds no release from the fear of transmigratory existence. But when he, by means of the cognition of absolute identity, finds absolute rest in the Self consisting of bliss, then he is freed from the fear of transmigratory existence. But this (finding absolute rest) is possible only when we understand by the Self consisting of bliss, the highest Self, and not either the pradhâna or the individual soul. Hence it is proved that the Self consisting of bliss is the highest Self.

But, in reality, the following remarks have to be made concerning the true meaning of the word 'ânandamaya [1].' On what grounds, we ask, can it be maintained that the

[1] The explanation of the ânandamaya given hitherto is here recalled, and a different one given. The previous explanation is attributed by Go. Ân. to the vr*i*ttikâra.

affix 'maya' after having, in the series of compounds beginning with annamaya and ending with vig*ñ*ânamaya, denoted mere modifications, should all at once, in the word ânandamaya, which belongs to the same series, denote abundance, so that ânandamaya would refer to Brahman? If it should be said that the assumption is made on account of the governing influence of the Brahman proclaimed in the mantra (which forms the beginning of the chapter, Taitt. Up. II), we reply that therefrom it would follow that also the Selfs consisting of food, breath, &c., denote Brahman (because the governing influence of the mantra extends to them also).—The advocate of the former interpretation will here, perhaps, restate an argument already made use of above, viz. as follows: To assume that the Selfs consisting of food, and so on, are not Brahman is quite proper, because after each of them an inner Self is mentioned. After the Self of bliss, on the other hand, no further inner Self is mentioned, and hence it must be considered to be Brahman itself; otherwise we should commit the mistake of dropping the subject-matter in hand (as which Brahman is pointed out by the mantra), and taking up a new topic.—But to this we reply that, although unlike the case of the Selfs consisting of food, &c., no inner Self is mentioned after the Self consisting of bliss, still the latter cannot be considered as Brahman, because with reference to the Self consisting of bliss Scripture declares, 'Joy is its head. Satisfaction is its right arm. Great satisfaction is its left arm. Bliss is its trunk. Brahman is its tail, its support.' Now, here the very same Brahman which, in the mantra, had been introduced as the subject of the discussion, is called the tail, the support; while the five involucra, extending from the involucrum of food up to the involucrum of bliss, are merely introduced for the purpose of setting forth the knowledge of Brahman. How, then, can it be maintained that our interpretation implies the needless dropping of the general subject-matter and the introduction of a new topic?—But, it may again be objected, Brahman is called the tail, i.e. a member of the Self consisting of bliss; analogously to those passages in which a tail and other members are ascribed to the Selfs consisting of food and so on. On what grounds, then, can we claim to know that Brahman (which is spoken of as a mere member, i. e. a subordinate matter) is in reality the chief matter referred to?—From the fact, we reply, of Brahman being the general subject-matter of the chapter.—But, it will again be said, that interpretation also according to which Brahman is cognised as a mere member of the ânandamaya does not involve a dropping of the subject-matter, since the ânandamaya himself is Brahman.—But, we reply, in that case one and the same Brahman would at first appear as the whole, viz. as the Self consisting of bliss, and thereupon as a mere part, viz. as the tail; which is absurd. And as one of the two alternatives must be preferred, it is certainly appropriate to refer to Brahman the clause 'Brahman is the tail' which contains the word 'Brahman,' and not the sentence about the Self of Bliss in which Brahman is not mentioned. Moreover, Scripture, in continuation of the phrase, 'Brahman is the tail, the support,' goes on, 'On this there is also the following *s*loka: He who knows the Brahman as non-existing becomes himself non-existing. He who knows Brahman as existing him we know himself as existing.' As this *s*loka, without any reference to the Self of bliss, states the advantage and disadvantage connected with the knowledge of the being and non-being of Brahman only, we conclude that the clause, 'Brahman is the tail, the support,' represents Brahman as the chief matter (not as a merely subordinate matter). About the being or non-being of the Self of bliss, on the other hand, a doubt is not well possible, since the Self of bliss distinguished by joy, satisfaction, &c., is well known to every one.—But if Brahman is the principal matter, how can it be designated as the mere tail of the Self of bliss ('Brahman is the tail, the support')?—Its being called so, we reply, forms no objection; for the word tail here denotes that which is of the nature of a tail, so that we have to understand that the bliss of Brahman is not a member (in its literal sense), but the support or abode, the one nest (resting-place) of all worldly bliss. Analogously another scriptural passage declares, 'All other creatures live on a small portion of that bliss' (*Bri*. Up. IV, 3, 32). Further, if by the Self consisting of bliss we were to understand Brahman, we should have to assume that the Brahman meant is the Brahman distinguished by qualities (savi*s*esha), because it is said to have joy and the like for its members. But this assumption is contradicted by a complementary passage (II, 9) which declares that Brahman is the object neither of mind nor speech, and so shows that the Brahman meant is the (absolute) Brahman (devoid of qualities), 'From whence all speech, with the mind, turns away unable to reach it, he who knows the bliss of that Brahman fears nothing.' Moreover, if we speak of something as 'abounding in bliss[1],' we thereby imply the co-existence of pain; for the word 'abundance' in its ordinary sense implies the existence of a small measure of what is opposed to the thing whereof there is abundance. But the passage so understood would be in conflict with another passage (*Kh*. Up. VII, 24), 'Where one sees nothing else, hears nothing else, understands nothing else, that is the Infinite;' which declares that in the Infinite, i. e. Brahman, there is nothing whatever different from it. Moreover, as joy, &c. differ in each individual body, the Self consisting of bliss also is a different one in each body. Brahman, on the other hand, does not differ according to bodies; for the mantra at the beginning of the chapter declares it to be true Being, knowledge, infinite, and another passage says, 'He is the one God, hidden in all beings, all-pervading, the Self within all beings' (*S*v. Up. VI, 11). Nor, again, does Scripture exhibit a frequent repetition of the word 'ânandamaya;' for merely the radical part of the compound (i.e. the word ânanda without the affix maya) is repeated in all the following passages: 'It is a flavour, for only after seizing flavour can any one seize bliss. Who could breathe, who could breathe forth, if that bliss existed not in the ether? For he alone causes blessedness;' 'Now this is an examination of bliss;' 'He who

[1] In which sense, as shown above, the word ânandamaya must be taken if understood to denote Brahman.

knows the bliss of that Brahman fears nothing;' 'He understood that bliss is Brahman.' If it were a settled matter that Brahman is denoted by the term, 'the Self consisting of bliss,' then we could assume that in the subsequent passages, where merely the word 'bliss' is employed, the term 'consisting of bliss' is meant to be repeated; but that the Self consisting of bliss is not Brahman, we have already proved by means of the reason of joy being its head, and so on. Hence, as in another scriptural passage, viz. 'Brahman is knowledge and bliss' (*Bri.* Up. III, 9, 28), the mere word 'bliss' denotes Brahman, we must conclude that also in such passages as, 'If that bliss existed not in the ether,' the word bliss is used with reference to Brahman, and is not meant to repeat the term 'consisting of bliss.' The repetition of the full compound, 'consisting of bliss,' which occurs in the passage, 'He reaches that Self consisting of bliss' (Taitt. Up. II, 8), does not refer to Brahman, as it is contained in the enumeration of Non-Selfs, comprising the Self of food, &c., all of which are mere effects, and all of which are represented as things to be reached.—But, it may be said, if the Self consisting of bliss, which is said to have to be reached, were not Brahman—just as the Selfs consisting of food, &c. are not Brahman—then it would not be declared (in the passage immediately following) that he who knows obtains for his reward Brahman.—This objection we invalidate by the remark that the text makes its declaration as to Brahman—which is the tail, the support—being reached by him who knows, by the very means of the declaration as to the attainment of the Self of bliss; as appears from the passage, 'On this there is also this *s*loka, from which all speech returns,' &c. With reference, again, to the passage, 'He desired: may I be many, may I grow forth,' which is found in proximity to the mention of the Self consisting of bliss, we remark that it is in reality connected (not with the Self of bliss but with) Brahman, which is mentioned in the still nearer passage, 'Brahman is the tail, the support,' and does therefore not intimate that the Self of bliss is Brahman. And, on account of its referring to the passage last quoted ('it desired,' &c.), the later passage also, 'That is flavour,' &c., has not the Self of bliss for its subject.—But, it may be objected, the (neuter word) Brahman cannot possibly be designated by a masculine word as you maintain is done in the passage, 'He desired.' &c.—In reply to this objection we point to the passage (Taitt. Up. II, 1), 'From that Self sprang ether,' where, likewise, the masculine word 'Self' can refer to Brahman only, since the latter is the general topic of the chapter. In the knowledge of Bh*ri*gu and Varu*n*a finally ('he knew that bliss is Brahman'), the word 'bliss' is rightly understood to denote Brahman, since we there meet neither with the affix 'maya,' nor with any statement as to joy being its head, and the like. To ascribe to Brahman in itself joy, and so on, as its members, is impossible, unless we have recourse to certain, however minute, distinctions qualifying Brahman; and that the whole chapter is not meant to convey a knowledge of the qualified (savi*s*esha) Brahman is proved by the passage (quoted above), which declares that Brahman transcends speech and mind. We therefore must conclude that the affix maya, in the word ânandamaya, does not denote abundance, but expresses a mere effect, just as it does in the words annamaya and the subsequent similar compounds.

The Sûtras are therefore to be explained as follows. There arises the question whether the passage, 'Brahman is the tail, the support,' is to be understood as intimating that Brahman is a mere member of the Self consisting of bliss, or that it is the principal matter. If it is said that it must be considered as a mere member, the reply is, 'The Self consisting of bliss on account of the repetition.' That means: Brahman, which in the passage 'the Self consisting of bliss,' &c., is spoken of as the tail, the support, is designated as the principal matter (not as something subordinate). On account of the repetition; for in the memorial *s*loka, 'he becomes himself non-existing,' Brahman alone is reiterated. 'If not, on account of the word denoting a modification; not so, on account of abundance.' In this Sûtra the word 'modification' is meant to convey the sense of member. The objection that on account of the word 'tail,' which denotes a mere member, Brahman cannot be taken as the principal matter must be refuted. This we do by remarking that there is no difficulty, since a word denoting a member may be introduced into the passage on account of prâkurya[1]. Prâkurya here means a phraseology abounding in terms denoting members. After the different members, beginning with the head and ending with the tail, of the Selfs, consisting of food, &c. have been enumerated, there are also mentioned the head and the other limbs of the Self of bliss, and then it is added, 'Brahman is the tail, the support;' the intention being merely to introduce some more terms denoting members, not to convey the meaning of 'member,' (an explanation which is impossible) because the preceding Sûtra already has proved Brahman (not to be a member, but) to be the principal matter. 'And because he is declared to be the cause of it.' That means: Brahman is declared to be the cause of the entire aggregate of effects, inclusive of the Self, consisting of bliss, in the following passage, 'He created all whatever there is' (Taitt. Up. II, 6). And as Brahman is the cause, it cannot at the same time be called the member, in the literal sense of the word, of the Self of bliss, which is nothing but one of Brahman's effects. The other Sûtras also (which refer to the Self of bliss[2]) are to be considered, as well as they may, as conveying a knowledge of Brahman, which (Brahman) is referred to in the passage about the tail.

20. The one within (the sun and the eye) (is the highest Lord), on account of his qualities being declared[3].

The following passage is found in Scripture (*Kh.* Up. I, 6, 6 ff.), 'Now that person bright as gold who is seen within

---

[1] I.e. the word translated hitherto by abundance.

[2] See I, 1, 15–19.

[3] The preceding adhikara*n*a had shown that the five Selfs (consisting of food, mind, and so on), which the Taitt. Up. enumerates, are introduced merely for the purpose of facilitating the cognition of Brahman considered as devoid of all qualities; while that Brahman

the sun, with beard bright as gold and hair bright as gold, bright as gold altogether to the very tips of his nails, whose eyes are like blue lotus; his name is Ut, for he has risen (udita) above all evil. He also who knows this rises above all evil. So much with reference to the devas.' And further on, with reference to the body, 'Now the person who is seen in the eye,' &c. Here the following doubt presents itself. Do these passages point out, as the object of devotion directed on the sphere of the sun and the eye, merely some special individual soul, which, by means of a large measure of knowledge and pious works, has raised itself to a position of eminence; or do they refer to the eternally perfect highest Lord?

The pûrvapakshin takes the former view. An individual soul, he says, is referred to, since Scripture speaks of a definite shape. To the person in the sun special features are ascribed, such as the possession of a beard as bright as gold and so on, and the same features manifestly belong to the person in the eye also, since they are expressly transferred to it in the passage, 'The shape of this person is the same as the shape of that person.' That, on the other hand, no shape can be ascribed to the highest Lord, follows from the passage (Kau. Up. I, 3. 15), 'That which is without sound, without touch, without form, without decay.' That an individual soul is meant follows moreover from the fact that a definite abode is mentioned, 'He who is in the sun; he who is in the eye.' About the highest Lord, who has no special abode, but abides in his own glory, no similar statement can be made; compare, for instance, the two following passages, 'Where does he rest? In his own glory?' (*Kh.* Up. VII, 24. 1); and 'like the ether he is omnipresent, eternal.' A further argument for our view is supplied by the fact that the might (of the being in question) is said to be limited; for the passage, 'He is lord of the worlds beyond that, and of the wishes of the devas,' indicates the

itself is the real object of knowledge. The present adhikara*n*a undertakes to show that the passage about the golden person represents he savi*s*esha Brahman as the object of devout meditation.

limitation of the might of the person in the sun; and the passage, 'He is lord of the worlds beneath that and of the wishes of men,' indicates the limitation of the might of the person in the eye. No limit, on the other hand, can be admitted of the might of the highest Lord, as appears from the passage (B*ri*. Up. IV, 4, 22), 'He is the Lord of all, the king of all things, the protector of all things. He is a bank and a boundary so that these worlds may not be confounded;' which passage intimates that the Lord is free from all limiting distinctions. For all these reasons the person in the eye and the sun cannot be the highest Lord.

To this reasoning the Sûtra replies, 'The one within, on account of his qualities being declared.' The person referred to in the passages concerning the person within the sun and the person within the eye is not a transmigrating being, but the highest Lord. Why? Because his qualities are declared. For the qualities of the highest Lord are indicated in the text as follows. At first the name of the person within the sun is mentioned—'his name is Ut'—and then this name is explained on the ground of that person being free from all evil, 'He has risen above all evil.' The same name thus explained is then transferred to the person in the eye, in the clause, 'the name of the one is the name of the other.' Now, entire freedom from sin is attributed in Scripture to the highest Self only; so, for instance (*Kh*. Up. VIII, 7, 1), 'The Self which is free from sin,' &c. Then, again, there is the passage, 'He is *Ri*k, he is Sâman, Uktha, Ya*g*us, Brahman,' which declares the person in the eye to be the Self of the *Ri*k, Sâman, and so on; which is possible only if that person is the Lord who, as being the cause of all, is to be considered as the Self of all. Moreover, the text, after having stated in succession *Ri*k and Sâman to have earth and fire for their Self with reference to the Devas, and, again, speech and breath with reference to the body, continues, '*Ri*k and Sâman are his joints,' with reference to the Devas, and 'the joints of the one are the joints of the other,' with reference to the body. Now this statement also can be made only with regard to that which is the Self of all. Further, the passage, 'Therefore all who sing to the Vînâ sing him, and from him also they obtain wealth,' shows that the being spoken of is the sole topic of all worldly songs; which again holds true of the highest Lord only. That absolute command over the objects of worldly desires (as displayed, for instance, in the bestowal of wealth) entitles us to infer that the Lord is meant, appears also from the following passage of the Bhagavad-gîtâ (X, 41), 'Whatever being there is possessing power, glory, or strength, know it to be produced from a portion of my energy[1].' To the objection that the statements about bodily shape contained in the clauses, 'With a beard bright as gold,' &c., cannot refer to the highest Lord, we reply that the highest Lord also may, when he pleases, assume a bodily shape formed of Mâyâ, in order to gratify thereby his devout worshippers. Thus Sm*ri*ti also says, 'That thou seest me, O Nârada, is the Mâyâ emitted by me; do not then look on me as endowed with the qualities of all beings.' We have further to note that expressions such as, 'That which is without sound, without touch, without form, without decay,' are made use of where instruction is given about the nature of the highest Lord in so far as he is devoid of all qualities; while passages such as the following one, 'He to whom belong all works, all desires, all sweet odours and tastes' (*Kh*. Up. III, 14, 2), which represent the highest Lord as the object of devotion, speak of him, who is the cause of everything, as possessing some of the qualities of his effects. Analogously he may be spoken of, in the passage under discussion, as having a beard bright as gold and so on. With reference to the objection that the highest Lord cannot be meant because an abode is spoken of, we remark that, for the purposes of devout meditation, a special abode may be assigned to Brahman, although it abides in its own glory only; for as Brahman is, like ether, all-pervading, it may be viewed as

[1] So that the real giver of the gifts bestowed by princes on poets and singers is Brahman.

being within the Self of all beings. The statement, finally, about the limitation of Brahman's might, which depends on the distinction of what belongs to the gods and what to the body, has likewise reference to devout meditation only. From all this it follows that the being which Scripture states to be within the eye and the sun is the highest Lord.

21. And there is another one (i. e. the Lord who is different from the individual souls animating the sun, &c.), on account of the declaration of distinction.

There is, moreover, one distinct from the individual souls which animate the sun and other bodies, viz. the Lord who rules within; whose distinction (from all individual souls) is proclaimed in the following scriptural passage, 'He who dwells in the sun and within the sun, whom the sun does not know, whose body the sun is, and who rules the sun within; he is thy Self, the ruler within, the immortal' (B*ri*. Up. III, 7, 9). Here the expression, 'He within the sun whom the sun does not know,' clearly indicates that the Ruler within is distinct from that cognising individual soul whose body is the sun. With that Ruler within we have to identify the person within the sun, according to the tenet of the sameness of purport of all Vedânta-texts. It thus remains a settled conclusion that the passage under discussion conveys instruction about the highest Lord.

22. The âkâ*s*a, i. e. ether (is Brahman) on account of characteristic marks (of the latter being mentioned).

In the *Kh*ândogya (I, 9) the following passage is met with, 'What is the origin of this world?' 'Ether,' he replied. 'For all these beings take their rise from the ether only, and return into the ether. Ether is greater than these, ether is their rest.'—Here the following doubt arises. Does the word 'ether' denote the highest Brahman or the elemental ether?—Whence the doubt?—Because the word is seen to be used in both senses. Its use in the sense of 'elemental ether' is well established in ordinary as well as in Vedic speech;

and, on the other hand, we see that it is sometimes used to denote Brahman, viz. in cases where we ascertain, either from some complementary sentence or from the fact of special qualities being mentioned, that Brahman is meant. So, for instance, Taitt. Up. II, 7, 'If that bliss existed not in the ether;' and *Kh*. Up. VIII, 14, 'That which is called ether is the revealer of all forms and names; that within which forms and names are[1] that is Brahman.' Hence the doubt.—Which sense is then to be adopted in our case?—The sense of elemental ether, the pûrvapakshin replies; because this sense belongs to the word more commonly, and therefore presents itself to the mind more readily. The word 'ether' cannot be taken in both senses equally, because that would involve a (faulty) attribution of several meanings to one and the same word. Hence the term 'ether' applies to Brahman in a secondary (metaphorical) sense only; on account of Brahman being in many of its attributes, such as all pervadingness and the like, similar to ether. The rule is, that when the primary sense of a word is possible, the word must not be taken in a secondary sense. And in the passage under discussion only the primary sense of the word 'ether' is admissible. Should it be objected that, if we refer the passage under discussion to the elemental ether, a complementary passage ('for all these beings take their rise from the ether only, &c.') cannot be satisfactorily accounted for; we reply that the elemental ether also may be represented as a cause, viz. of air, fire, &c. in due succession. For we read in Scripture (Taitt. Up. II, 1), 'From that Self sprang ether, from ether air, from air fire, and so on.' The qualities also of being greater and of being a place of rest may be ascribed to the elemental ether, if we consider its relations to all other beings. Therefore we conclude that the word 'ether' here denotes the elemental ether.

To this we reply as follows:—The word ether must here be taken to denote Brahman, on account of characteristic marks of the latter being mentioned. For the sentence,

[1] Or else 'that which is within forms and names.'

'All these beings take their rise from the ether only,' clearly indicates the highest Brahman, since all Vedânta-texts agree in definitely declaring that all beings spring from the highest Brahman.—But, the opponent may say, we have shown that the elemental ether also may be represented as the cause, viz. of air, fire, and the other elements in due succession.—We admit this. But still there remains the difficulty, that, unless we understand the word to apply to the fundamental cause of all, viz. Brahman, the affirmation contained in the word 'only' and the qualification expressed by the word 'all' (in 'all beings') would be out of place. Moreover, the clause, 'They return into the ether,' again points to Brahman, and so likewise the phrase, 'Ether is greater than these, ether is their rest;' for absolute superiority in point of greatness Scripture attributes to the highest Self only; cp. *Kh.* Up. III, 14, 3, 'Greater than the earth, greater than the sky, greater than heaven, greater than all these worlds.' The quality of being a place of rest likewise agrees best with the highest Brahman, on account of its being the highest cause. This is confirmed by the following scriptural passage: 'Knowledge and bliss is Brahman, it is the rest of him who gives gifts' (B*ri*. Up. III, 9, 28). Moreover, *G*aivali finding fault with the doctrine of *S*âlâvatya, on account of (his sâman) having an end (*Kh.* Up. I, 8, 8), and wishing to proclaim something that has no end chooses the ether, and then, having identified the ether with the Udgîtha, concludes, 'He is the Udgîtha greater than great; he is without end.' Now this endlessness is a characteristic mark of Brahman. To the remark that the sense of 'elemental ether' presents itself to the mind more readily, because it is the better established sense of the word âkâ*s*a, we reply, that, although it may present itself to the mind first, yet it is not to be accepted, because we see that qualities of Brahman are mentioned in the complementary sentences. That the word âkâ*s*a is also used to denote Brahman has been shown already; cp. such passages as, 'Ether is the revealer of all names and forms.' We see, moreover, that various synonyma of âkâ*s*a are employed to denote Brahman. So, for instance, *Ri*k Sa*m*h.

I, 164, 39, 'In which the Vedas are[1], in the Imperishable one (i. e. Brahman), the highest, the ether (vyoman), on which all gods have their seat.' And Taitt. Up. III, 6, 'This is the knowledge of Bh*ri*gu and Varu*n*a, founded on the highest ether (vyoman).' And again, 'Om, ka is Brahman, ether (kha) is Brahman' (*Kh.* Up. IV, 10, 5), and 'the old ether' (B*ri.* Up. V, 1)[2]. And other similar passages. On account of the force of the complementary passage we are justified in deciding that the word 'ether,' although occurring in the beginning of the passage, refers to Brahman. The case is analogous to that of the sentence, 'Agni (lit. the fire) studies a chapter,' where the word agni, although occurring in the beginning, is at once seen to denote a boy[3]. It is therefore settled that the word 'ether' denotes Brahman.

23. For the same reason breath (is Brahman).

Concerning the udgîtha it is said (*Kh.* Up I, 10, 9), 'Prastot*ri*, that deity which belongs to the prastâva, &c.,' and, further on (I, 11, 4; 5), 'Which then is that deity? He said: Breath. For all these beings merge into breath alone, and from breath they arise. This is the deity belonging to the prastâva.' With reference to this passage doubt and decision are to be considered as analogous to those stated under the preceding Sûtra. For while in some passages—as, for instance, 'For indeed, my son, mind is fastened to prâ*n*a,' *Kh.* Up. VI, 8, 2; and, 'the prâ*n*a of prâ*n*a,' B*ri.* Up. IV, 4, 18—the word 'breath' is seen to denote Brahman, its use

[1] Viz. as intimating it. Thus Ân. Gi. and Go. Ân. against the accent of *rikâh.* Sâya*n*a explains *rikâh* as genitive.

[2] O*m*kârasya pratîkatvena vâ*k*akatvena lakshakatvena vâ brahmatvam uktam, om iti, ka*m* sukha*m* tasyârthendriyayogagatva*m* vârayitu*m* kham iti, tasya bhûtâkâ*s*atva*m* vyâseddhum purâ*n*am ity uktam. Ân. Gi.

[3] The doubt about the meaning of a word is preferably to be decided by means of a reference to preceding passages; where that is not possible (the doubtful word occurring at the beginning of some new chapter) complementary, i. e. subsequent passages have to be taken into consideration.

in the sense of a certain modification of air is better established in common as well as in Vedic language. Hence there arises a doubt whether in the passage under discussion the word prâ*n*a denotes Brahman or (ordinary) breath. In favour of which meaning have we then to decide?

Here the pûrvapakshin maintains that the word must be held to denote the fivefold vital breath, which is a peculiar modification of wind (or air); because, as has been remarked already, that sense of the word prâ*n*a is the better established one.—But no, an objector will say, just as in the case of the preceding Sûtra, so here also Brahman is meant, on account of characteristic marks being mentioned; for here also a complementary passage gives us to understand that all beings spring from and merge into prâ*n*a; a process which can take place in connexion with the highest Lord only.—This objection, the pûrvapakshin replies, is futile, since we see that the beings enter into and proceed from the principal vital air also. For Scripture makes the following statement (*S*at. Br. X, 3, 3, 6), 'When man sleeps, then into breath indeed speech merges, into breath the eye, into breath the ear, into breath the mind; when he awakes then they spring again from breath alone.' What the Veda here states is, moreover, a matter of observation, for during sleep, while the process of breathing goes on uninterruptedly, the activity of the sense organs is interrupted and again becomes manifest at the time of awaking only. And as the sense organs are the essence of all material beings, the complementary passage which speaks of the merging and emerging of the beings can be reconciled with the principal vital air also. Moreover, subsequently to prâ*n*a being mentioned as the divinity of the prastâva the sun and food are designated as the divinities of the udgîtha and the pratihâra. Now as they are not Brahman, the prâ*n*a also, by parity of reasoning, cannot be Brahman.

To this argumentation the author of the Sûtras replies: For the same reason prâ*n*a—that means: on account of the presence of characteristic marks—which constituted the reason stated in the preceding Sûtra—the word prâ*n*a also must be held to denote Brahman. For Scripture says of prâ*n*a also, that it is connected with marks characteristic of Brahman. The sentence, 'All these beings merge into breath alone, and from breath they arise,' which declares that the origination and retractation of all beings depend on prâ*n*a, clearly shows prâ*n*a to be Brahman. In reply to the assertion that the origination and retractation of all beings can be reconciled equally well with the assumption of prâ*n*a denoting the chief vital air, because origination and retractation take place in the state of waking and of sleep also, we remark that in those two states only the senses are merged into, and emerge from, the chief vital air, while, according to the scriptural passage, 'For all these beings, &c.,' all beings whatever into which a living Self has entered, together with their senses and bodies, merge and emerge by turns. And even if the word 'beings' were taken (not in the sense of animated beings, but) in the sense of material elements in general, there would be nothing in the way of interpreting the passage as referring to Brahman.—But, it may be said, that the senses together with their objects do, during sleep, enter into prâ*n*a, and again issue from it at the time of waking, we distinctly learn from another scriptural passage, viz. Kau. Up. III, 3, 'When a man being thus asleep sees no dream whatever, he becomes one with that prâ*n*a alone. Then speech goes to him with all names,' &c.—True, we reply, but there also the word prâ*n*a denotes (not the vital air) but Brahman, as we conclude from characteristic marks of Brahman being mentioned. The objection, again, that the word prâ*n*a cannot denote Brahman because it occurs in proximity to the words 'food' and 'sun' (which do not refer to Brahman), is altogether baseless; for proximity is of no avail against the force of the complementary passage which intimates that prâ*n*a is Brahman. That argument, finally, which rests on the fact that the word prâ*n*a commonly denotes the vital air with its five modifications, is to be refuted in the same way as the parallel argument which the pûrvapakshin brought forward with reference to the word 'ether.' From all this it follows that the prâ*n*a, which is the deity of the prastâva, is Brahman.

Some (commentators)[1] quote under the present Sûtra the following passages, 'the prâ*n*a of prâ*n*a' (B*ri*. Up. IV, 4, 18), and 'for to prâ*n*a mind is fastened' (*Kh*. Up. VI, 8, 2). But that is wrong since these two passages offer no opportunity for any discussion, the former on account of the separation of the words, the latter on account of the general topic. When we meet with a phrase such as 'the father of the father' we understand at once that the genitive denotes a father different from the father denoted by the nominative. Analogously we infer from the separation of words contained in the phrase, 'the breath of breath,' that the 'breath of breath' is different from the ordinary breath (denoted by the genitive 'of breath'). For one and the same thing cannot, by means of a genitive, be predicated of—and thus distinguished from—itself. Concerning the second passage we remark that, if the matter constituting the general topic of some chapter is referred to in that chapter under a different name, we yet conclude, from the general topic, that that special matter is meant. For instance, when we meet in the section which treats of the *g*yotish*t*oma sacrifice with the passage, 'in every spring he is to offer the *g*yotis sacrifice,' we at once understand that the word *g*yotis denotes the *g*yotish*t*oma. If we therefore meet with the clause 'to prâ*n*a mind is fastened' in a section of which the highest Brahman is the topic, we do not for a moment suppose that the word prâ*n*a should there denote the ordinary breath which is a mere modification of air. The two passages thus do not offer any matter for discussion, and hence do not furnish appropriate instances for the Sûtra. We have shown, on the other hand, that the passage about the prâ*n*a, which is the deity of the prastâva, allows room for doubt, pûrvapaksha and final decision.

24. The 'light' (is Brahman), on account of the mention of feet (in a passage which is connected with the passage about the light).

Scripture says (*Kh*. Up. III, 13, 7), 'Now that light which shines above this heaven, higher than all, higher than every-

[1] The v*ri*ttikâra, the commentators say.

thing, in the highest worlds beyond which there are no other worlds, that is the same light which is within man.' Here the doubt presents itself whether the word 'light' denotes the light of the sun and the like, or the highest Self. Under the preceding Sûtras we had shown that some words which ordinarily have different meanings yet in certain passages denote Brahman, since characteristic marks of the latter are mentioned. Here the question has to be discussed whether, in connexion with the passage quoted, characteristic marks of Brahman are mentioned or not.

The pûrvapakshin maintains that the word 'light' denotes nothing else but the light of the sun and the like, since that is the ordinary well-established meaning of the term. The common use of language, he says, teaches us that the two words 'light' and 'darkness' denote mutually opposite things, darkness being the term for whatever interferes with the function of the sense of sight, as, for instance, the gloom of the night, while sunshine and whatever else favours the action of the eye is called light. The word 'shines' also, which the text exhibits, is known ordinarily to refer to the sun and similar sources of light; while of Brahman, which is devoid of colour, it cannot be said, in the primary sense of the word, that it 'shines.' Further, the word *g*yotis must here denote light because it is said to be bounded by the sky ('that light which shines above this heaven'). For while it is impossible to consider the sky as being the boundary of Brahman, which is the Self of all and the source of all things movable or immovable, the sky may be looked upon as forming the boundary of light, which is a mere product and as such limited; accordingly the text says, 'the light beyond heaven.'—But light, although a mere product, is perceived everywhere; it would therefore be wrong to declare that it is bounded by the sky!—Well, then, the pûrvapakshin replies, let us assume that the light meant is the first-born (original) light which has not yet become tripartite[1]. This explanation again cannot be

[1] I.e. which has not been mixed with water and earth, according to *Kh*. Up. VI, 3, 3. Before that mixture took place light was

admitted, because the non-tripartite light does not serve any purpose.—But, the pûrvapakshin resumes, Why should its purpose not be found therein that it is the object of devout meditation?—That cannot be, we reply; for we see that only such things are represented as objects of devotion as have some other independent use of their own; so, for instance, the sun (which dispels darkness and so on). Moreover the scriptural passage, 'Let me make each of these three (fire, water, and earth) tripartite,' does not indicate any difference[1]. And even of the non-tripartite light it is not known that the sky constitutes its boundary.—Well, then (the pûrvapakshin resumes, dropping the idea of the non-tripartite light), let us assume that the light of which the text speaks is the tripartite (ordinary) light. The objection that light is seen to exist also beneath the sky, viz. in the form of fire and the like, we invalidate by the remark that there is nothing contrary to reason in assigning a special locality to fire, although the latter is observed everywhere; while to assume a special place for Brahman, to which the idea of place does not apply at all, would be most unsuitable. Moreover, the clause 'higher than everything, in the highest worlds beyond which there are no other worlds,' which indicates a multiplicity of abodes, agrees much better with light, which is a mere product (than with Brahman). There is moreover that other clause also, 'That is the same light which is within man,' in which the highest light is identified with the gastric fire (the fire within man). Now such identifications can be made only where there is a certain similarity of nature; as is seen, for instance, in the passage, 'Of that person Bhû*h* is the head, for the head is one and that syllable is one' (*Bri*. Up. V, 5, 3). But that the fire within the human body is not Brahman clearly appears from the passage, 'Of this we have visible and audible proof' (*Kh*. Up. III, 13, 7; 8), which declares that

entirely separated from the other elements, and therefore bounded by the latter.

[1] So as to justify the assumption that such a thing as non-tripartite light exists at all.

the fire is characterised by the noise it makes, and by heat; and likewise from the following passage, 'Let a man meditate on this as that which is seen and heard.' The same conclusion may be drawn from the passage, 'He who knows this becomes conspicuous and celebrated,' which proclaims an inconsiderable reward only, while to the devout meditation on Brahman a high reward would have to be allotted. Nor is there mentioned in the entire passage about the light any other characteristic mark of Brahman, while such marks are set forth in the passages (discussed above) which refer to prâ*n*a and the ether. Nor, again, is Brahman indicated in the preceding section, 'the Gâyatrî is everything whatsoever exists,' &c. (III, 12); for that passage makes a statement about the Gâyatrî metre only. And even if that section did refer to Brahman, still Brahman would not be recognised in the passage at present under discussion; for there (in the section referred to) it is declared—in the clause, 'Three feet of it are the Immortal in heaven'—that heaven constitutes the abode; while in our passage the words 'the light above heaven' declare heaven to be a boundary. For all these reasons the word *g*yotis is here to be taken in its ordinary meaning, viz. light.

To this we make the following reply. The word *g*yotis must be held to denote Brahman. Why? On account of the feet (quarters) being mentioned. In a preceding passage Brahman had been spoken of as having four feet (quarters). 'Such is the greatness of it; greater than it is the Person (purusha). One foot of it are all the beings, three feet of it are the Immortal in heaven.' That which in this passage is said to constitute the three-quarter part, immortal and connected with heaven, of Brahman, which altogether comprises four quarters; this very same entity we recognise as again referred to in the passage under discussion, because there also it is said to be connected with heaven. If therefore we should set it aside in our interpretation of the passage and assume the latter to refer to the ordinary light, we should commit the mistake of dropping, without need, the topic started and introducing a new subject. Brahman, in fact, continues to form the subject-matter, not only of the passage about the light, but likewise of the subsequent section, the so-called *Sândilya*-vidyâ (*Kh*. Up. III, 14). Hence we conclude that in our passage the word 'light' must be held to denote Brahman. The objection (raised above) that from common use the words 'light' and 'to shine' are known to denote effected (physical) light is without force; for as it is known from the general topic of the chapter that Brahman is meant, those two words do not necessarily denote physical light only to the exclusion of Brahman[1], but may also denote Brahman itself, in so far as it is characterised by the physical shining light which is its effect. Analogously another mantra declares, 'that by which the sun shines kindled with heat' (Taitt. Br. III, 12, 9, 7). Or else we may suppose that the word *g*yotis here does not denote at all that light on which the function of the eye depends. For we see that in other passages it has altogether different meanings; so, for instance, B*ri*. Up. IV, 3, 5, 'With speech only as light man sits,' and Taitt. Sa. I, 6, 3, 3, 'May the mind, the light, accept,' &c. It thus appears that whatever illuminates (in the different senses of the word) something else may be spoken of as 'light.' Hence to Brahman also, whose nature is intelligence, the term 'light' may be applied; for it gives light to the entire world. Similarly, other scriptural passages say, 'Him the shining one, everything shines after; by his light all this is lighted' (Kau. Up. II, 5, 15); and 'Him the gods worship as the light of lights, as the immortal' (B*ri*. Up. IV, 4, 16). Against the further objection that the omnipresent Brahman cannot be viewed as bounded by heaven we remark that the assignment, to Brahman, of a special locality is not contrary to reason because it subserves the purpose of devout meditation. Nor does it avail anything to say that it is impossible to assign any place to Brahman because Brahman is out of connexion with all place. For it is possible to make such

[1] Brahma*n*o vyava*kkh*idya te*gah*samarpakatva*m* vi*s*eshakatvam, tadabhâvo*s*vi*s*eshakatvam. Ân. Gi.

an assumption, because Brahman is connected with certain limiting adjuncts. Accordingly Scripture speaks of different kinds of devout meditation on Brahman as specially connected with certain localities, such as the sun, the eye, the heart. For the same reason it is also possible to attribute to Brahman a multiplicity of abodes, as is done in the clause (quoted above) 'higher than all.' The further objection that the light beyond heaven is the mere physical light because it is identified with the gastric fire, which itself is a mere effect and is inferred from perceptible marks such as the heat of the body and a certain sound, is equally devoid of force; for the gastric fire may be viewed as the outward appearance (or symbol) of Brahman, just as Brahman's name is a mere outward symbol. Similarly in the passage, 'Let a man meditate on it (the gastric light) as seen and heard,' the visibility and audibility (here implicitly ascribed to Brahman) must be considered as rendered possible through the gastric fire being the outward appearance of Brahman. Nor is there any force in the objection that Brahman cannot be meant because the text mentions an inconsiderable reward only; for there is no reason compelling us to have recourse to Brahman for the purpose of such and such a reward only, and not for the purpose of such and such another reward. Wherever the text represents the highest Brahman—which is free from all connexion with distinguishing attributes—as the universal Self, it is understood that the result of that instruction is one only, viz. final release. Wherever, on the other hand, Brahman is taught to be connected with distinguishing attributes or outward symbols, there, we see, all the various rewards which this world can offer are spoken of; cp. for instance, B*ri*. Up. IV, 4, 24, 'This is he who eats all food, the giver of wealth. He who knows this obtains wealth.' Although in the passage itself which treats of the light no characteristic mark of Brahman is mentioned, yet, as the Sûtra intimates, the mark stated in a preceding passage (viz. the mantra, 'Such is the greatness of it,' &c.) has to be taken in connexion with the passage about the light as well. The question how the mere circumstance of Brahman being mentioned in a not distant passage can have the power of divorcing from its natural object and transferring to another object the direct statement about light implied in the word 'light,' may be answered without difficulty. The passage under discussion runs[1], 'which above this heaven, the light.' The relative pronoun with which this clause begins intimates, according to its grammatical force[2], the same Brahman which was mentioned in the previous passage, and which is here recognised (as being the same which was mentioned before) through its connexion with heaven; hence the word *g*yotis also—which stands in grammatical co-ordination to 'which'—must have Brahman for its object. From all this it follows that the word 'light' here denotes Brahman.

25. If it be objected that (Brahman is) not (denoted) on account of the metre being denoted; (we reply) not so, because thus (i.e. by means of the metre) the direction of the mind (on Brahman) is declared; for thus it is seen (in other passages also).

We now address ourselves to the refutation of the assertion (made in the pûrvapaksha of the preceding Sûtra) that in the previous passage also Brahman is not referred to, because in the sentence, 'Gâyatrî is everything whatsoever here exists,' the metre called Gâyatrî is spoken of.—How (we ask the pûrvapakshin) can it be maintained that, on account of the metre being spoken of, Brahman is not denoted, while yet the mantra 'such is the greatness of it,' &c., clearly sets forth Brahman with its four quarters? —You are mistaken (the pûrvapakshin replies). The sentence, 'Gâyatrî is everything,' starts the discussion of Gâyatrî. The same Gâyatrî is thereupon described under the various forms of all beings, earth, body, heart, speech, breath; to which there refers also the verse, 'that Gâyatrî

---

1 If we strictly follow the order of words in the original.

2 Svasâmarthyena sarvanâmna*h* sannihitaparâmar*s*itvava*s*ena.

has four feet and is sixfold.' After that we meet with the mantra, 'Such is the greatness of it,' &c. How then, we ask, should this mantra, which evidently is quoted with reference to the Gâyatrî (metre) as described in the preceding clauses, all at once denote Brahman with its four quarters? Since therefore the metre Gâyatrî is the subject-matter of the entire chapter, the term 'Brahman' which occurs in a subsequent passage ('the Brahman which has thus been described') must also denote the metre. This is analogous to a previous passage (*Kh*. Up. III, 11, 3, 'He who thus knows this Brahma-upanishad'), where the word Brahma-upanishad is explained to mean Veda-upanishad. As therefore the preceding passage refers (not to Brahman, but) to the Gâyatrî metre, Brahman does not constitute the topic of the entire section.

This argumentation, we reply, proves nothing against our position. 'Because thus direction of the mind is declared,' i. e. because the Brâhma*n*a passage, 'Gâyatrî indeed is all this,' intimates that by means of the metre Gâyatrî the mind is to be directed on Brahman which is connected with that metre. Of the metre Gâyatrî, which is nothing but a certain special combination of syllables, it could not possibly be said that it is the Self of everything. We therefore have to understand the passage as declaring that Brahman, which, as the cause of the world, is connected with that product also whose name is Gâyatrî, is 'all this;' in accordance with that other passage which directly says, 'All this indeed is Brahman' (*Kh*. Up. III, 14, 1). That the effect is in reality not different from the cause, we shall prove later on, under Sûtra II, 1, 14. Devout meditation on Brahman under the form of certain effects (of Brahman) is seen to be mentioned in other passages also, so, for instance, Ait. Âr. III, 2, 3, 12, 'For the Bahv*rik*as consider him in the great hymn, the Adhvaryus in the sacrificial fire, the *Kh*andogas in the Mahâvrata ceremony.' Although, therefore, the previous passage speaks of the metre, Brahman is what is meant, and the same Brahman is again referred to in the passage about the light, whose purport it is to enjoin another form of devout meditation.

Another commentator[1] is of opinion that the term Gâyatrî (does not denote Brahman in so far as viewed under the form of Gâyatrî, but) directly denotes Brahman, on account of the equality of number; for just as the Gâyatrî metre has four feet consisting of six syllables each, so Brahman also has four feet, (i. e. quarters.) Similarly we see that in other psssages also the names of metres are used to denote other things which resemble those metres in certain numerical relations; cp. for instance, *Kh.* Up. IV, 3, 8, where it is said at first, 'Now these five and the other five make ten and that is the K*ri*ta,' and after that 'these are again the Virâ*g* which eats the food.' If we adopt this interpretation, Brahman only is spoken of, and the metre is not referred to at all. In any case Brahman is the subject with which the previous passage is concerned.

26. And thus also (we must conclude, viz. that Brahman is the subject of the previous passage), because (thus only) the declaration as to the beings, &c. being the feet is possible.

That the previous passage has Brahman for its topic, we must assume for that reason also that the text designates the beings and so on as the feet of Gâyatrî. For the text at first speaks of the beings, the earth, the body, and the heart[2], and then goes on 'that Gâyatrî has four feet and is sixfold.' For of the mere metre, without any reference to Brahman, it would be impossible to say that the beings and so on are its feet. Moreover, if Brahman were not meant, there would be no room for the verse, 'Such is the greatness,' &c. For that verse clearly describes Brahman in its own nature; otherwise it would be impossible to represent the Gâyatrî as the Self of everything as is done in the words, 'One foot of it are all the beings; three feet of it are what is immortal in heaven.' The purusha-sûkta also (*Rik*

[1] The v*ri*ttikâra according to Go. Ân. in his *t*ikâ on the bhâshya to the next Sûtra.

[2] Concerning the difficulty involved in this interpretation, cp. Deussen, p. 183, note.

Sa*m*h. X, 90) exhibits the verse with sole reference to Brahman. Sm*ri*ti likewise ascribes to Brahman a like nature, 'I stand supporting all this world by a single portion of myself' (Bha. Gîtâ X, 42). Our interpretation moreover enables us to take the passage, 'that Brahman indeed which,' &c. (III, 12, 7), in its primary sense, (i. e. to understand the word Brahman to denote nothing but Brahman.) And, moreover, the passage, 'these are the five men of Brahman' (III, 13, 6), is appropriate only if the former passage about the Gâyatrî is taken as referring to Brahman (for otherwise the 'Brahman' in 'men of Brahman' would not be connected with the previous topic). Hence Brahman is to be considered as the subject-matter of the previous passage also. And the decision that the same Brahman is referred to in the passage about the light where it is recognised (to be the same) from its connexion with heaven, remains unshaken.

27. The objection that (the Brahman of the former passage cannot be recognised in the latter) on account of the difference of designation, is not valid because in either (designation) there is nothing contrary (to the recognition).

The objection that in the former passage ('three feet of it are what is immortal in heaven'), heaven is designated as the abode, while in the latter passage ('that light which shines above this heaven'), heaven is designated as the boundary, and that, on account of this difference of designation, the subject-matter of the former passage cannot be recognised in the latter, must likewise be refuted. This we do by remarking that in either designation nothing is contrary to the recognition. Just as in ordinary language a falcon, although in contact with the top of a tree, is not only said to be on the tree but also above the tree, so Brahman also, although being in heaven, is here referred to as being beyond heaven as well.

Another (commentator) explains: just as in ordinary language a falcon, although not in contact with the top of a tree, is not only said to be above the top of the tree but also on the top of the tree, so Brahman also, which is in reality beyond heaven, is (in the former of the two passages) said to be in heaven. Therefore the Brahman spoken of in the former passage can be recognised in the latter also, and it remains therefore a settled conclusion that the word 'light' denotes Brahman.

28. Prâ*n*a (breath) is Brahman, that being understood from a connected consideration (of the passages referring to prâ*n*a).

In the Kaushîtaki-brâhma*n*a-upanishad there is recorded a legend of Indra and Pratardana which begins with the words, 'Pratardana, forsooth, the son of Divodâsa came by means of fighting and strength to the beloved abode of Indra' (Kau. Up. III, 1). In this legend we read: 'He said: I am prâ*n*a, the intelligent Self (pra*gñ*âtman), meditate on me as Life, as Immortality' (III, 2). And later on (III, 3), 'Prâ*n*a alone, the intelligent Self, having laid hold of this body, makes it rise up.' Then, again (III, 8), 'Let no man try to find out what speech is, let him know the speaker.' And in the end (III, 8), 'That breath indeed is the intelligent Self, bliss, imperishable, immortal.'—Here the doubt presents itself whether the word prâ*n*a denotes merely breath, the modification of air, or the Self of some divinity, or the individual soul, or the highest Brahman.—But, it will be said at the outset, the Sûtra I, 1, 21 already has shown that the word prâ*n*a refers to Brahman, and as here also we meet with characteristic marks of Brahman, viz. the words 'bliss, imperishable, immortal,' what reason is there for again raising the same doubt?—We reply: Because there are observed here characteristic marks of different kinds. For in the legend we meet not only with marks indicating Brahman, but also with marks pointing to other beings. Thus Indra's words, 'Know me only' (III, 1), point to the Self of a divinity; the words, 'Having laid hold of this body it makes it rise up,' point to the breath; the words, 'Let no man try to find out what speech is, let him know the speaker,' point to the individual soul. There is thus room for doubt.

If, now, the pûrvapakshin maintains that the term prâ*n*a here denotes the well-known modification of air, i. e. breath, we, on our side, assert that the word prâ*n*a must be understood to denote Brahman.—For what reason?—On account of such being the consecutive meaning of the passages. For if we examine the connexion of the entire section which treats of the prâ*n*a, we observe that all the single passages can be construed into a whole only if they are viewed as referring to Brahman. At the beginning of the legend Pratardana, having been allowed by Indra to choose a boon, mentions the highest good of man, which he selects for his boon, in the following words, 'Do you yourself choose that boon for me which you deem most beneficial for a man.' Now, as later on prâ*n*a is declared to be what is most beneficial for man, what should prâ*n*a denote but the highest Self? For apart from the cognition of that Self a man cannot possibly attain what is most beneficial for him, as many scriptural passages declare. Compare, for instance, *S*ve. Up. III, 8, 'A man who knows him passes over death; there is no other path to go.' Again, the further passage, 'He who knows me thus by no deed of his is his life harmed, not by theft, not by bhrû*n*ahatyâ' (III, 1), has a meaning only if Brahman is supposed to be the object of knowledge. For, that subsequently to the cognition of Brahman all works and their effects entirely cease, is well known from scriptural passages, such as the following, 'All works perish when he has been beheld who is the higher and the lower' (Mu. Up. II, 2, 8). Moreover, prâ*n*a can be identified with the intelligent Self only if it is Brahman. For the air which is non-intelligent can clearly not be the intelligent Self. Those characteristic marks, again, which are mentioned in the concluding passage (viz. those intimated by the words 'bliss,' 'imperishable,' 'immortal') can, if taken in their full sense, not be reconciled with any being except Brahman. There are, moreover, the following passages, 'He does not increase by a good action, nor decrease by a bad action. For he makes him whom he wishes to lead up from these worlds do a good deed; and the same makes him whom he wishes to lead down from these worlds do a bad deed;' and, 'He is the guardian of the world, he is the king of the world, he is the Lord of the world' (Kau. Up. III, 8). All this can be properly understood only if the highest Brahman is acknowledged to be the subject-matter of the whole chapter, not if the vital air is substituted in its place. Hence the word prâ*n*a denotes Brahman.

29. If it be said that (Brahman is) not (denoted) on account of the speaker denoting himself; (we reply that this objection is not valid) because there is in that (chapter) a multitude of references to the interior Self.

An objection is raised against the assertion that prâ*n*a denotes Brahman. The word prâ*n*a, it is said, does not denote the highest Brahman, because the speaker designates himself. The speaker, who is a certain powerful god called Indra, at first says, in order to reveal himself to Pratardana, 'Know me only,' and later on, 'I am prâ*n*a, the intelligent Self.' How, it is asked, can the prâ*n*a, which this latter passage, expressive of personality as it is, represents as the Self of the speaker, be Brahman to which, as we know from Scripture, the attribute of being a speaker cannot be ascribed; compare, for instance, B*ri*. Up. III, 8, 8, 'It is without speech, without mind.' Further on, also, the speaker, i. e. Indra, glorifies himself by enumerating a number of attributes, all of which depend on personal existence and can in no way belong to Brahman, 'I slew the three-headed son of Tvash*tri*; I delivered the Arunmukhas, the devotees, to the wolves,' and so on. Indra may be called prâ*n*a on account of his strength. Scripture says, 'Strength indeed is prâ*n*a,' and Indra is known as the god of strength; and of any deed of strength people say, 'It is Indra's work.' The personal Self of a deity may, moreover, be called an intelligent Self; for the gods, people say, possess unobstructed knowledge. It thus being a settled matter that some passages convey information about the personal Self of some deity, the other passages also—as, for instance, the one about what is most beneficial for man—must be interpreted as well as they may with reference to the same deity. Hence prâ*n*a does not denote Brahman.

This objection we refute by the remark that in that chapter there are found a multitude of references to the interior Self. For the passage, 'As long as prâ*n*a dwells in this body so long surely there is life,' declares that that prâ*n*a only which is the intelligent interior Self—and not some particular outward deity—has power to bestow and to take back life. And where the text speaks of the eminence of the prâ*n*as as founded on the existence of the prâ*n*a, it shows that that prâ*n*a is meant which has reference to the Self and is the abode of the sense-organs[1].

Of the same tendency is the passage, 'Prâ*n*a, the intelligent Self, alone having laid hold of this body makes it rise up;' and the passage (which occurs in the passus, 'Let no man try to find out what speech is,' &c.), 'For as in a car the circumference of the wheel is set on the spokes and the spokes on the nave, thus are these objects set on the subjects (the senses) and the subjects on the prâ*n*a. And that prâ*n*a indeed is the Self of prag*ñ*â, blessed, imperishable, immortal.' So also the following passage which, referring to this interior Self, forming as it were the centre of the peripherical interaction of the objects and senses, sums up as follows, 'He is my Self, thus let it be known;' a summing up which is appropriate only if prâ*n*a is meant to denote not some outward existence, but the interior Self. And another scriptural passage declares 'this Self is Brahman, omniscient[2]' (B*ri*. Up. II, 5, 19). We therefore arrive at

[1] The text runs, 'astitve *k*a prâ*n*ânâ*m* ni*h*s*reyasam,' and Go. Ân. explains 'astitve prâ*n*asthitau prâ*n*ânâ*m* indriyâ*n*âm sthitir ity arthata*h* s*rutim âha.' He as well as Ân. Gi. quotes as the text of the scriptural passage referred to 'athâto ni*h*s*reyasâdânam ity âdi.' But if instead of 'astitve *k*a' we read 'asti tv eva,' we get the concluding clause of Kau. Up. III, 2, as given in Cowell's edition.

[2] Whence we know that the interior Self referred to in the Kau. Up. is Brahman.

the conclusion that, on account of the multitude of references to the interior Self, the chapter contains information regarding Brahman, not regarding the Self of some deity.—How then can the circumstance of the speaker (Indra) referring to himself be explained?

30. The declaration (made by Indra about himself, viz. that he is one with Brahman) (is possible) through intuition vouched for by Scripture, as in the case of Vâmadeva.

The individual divine Self called Indra perceiving by means of *ri*shi-like intuition[1]—the existence of which is vouched for by Scripture—its own Self to be identical with the supreme Self, instructs Pratardana (about the highest Self) by means of the words 'Know me only.'

By intuition of the same kind the *ri*shi Vâmadeva reached the knowledge expressed in the words, 'I was Manu and Sûrya;' in accordance with the passage, 'Whatever deva was awakened (so as to know Brahman) he indeed became that' (B*ri*. Up. I, 4, 10). The assertion made above (in the pûrvapaksha of the preceding Sûtra) that Indra after saying, 'Know me only,' glorifies himself by enumerating the slaying of Tvash*tri*'s son and other deeds of strength, we refute as follows. The death of Tvash*tri*'s son and similar deeds are referred to, not to the end of glorifying Indra as the object of knowledge—in which case the sense of the passage would be, 'Because I accomplished such and such deeds, therefore know me'—but to the end of glorifying the cognition of the highest Self. For this reason the text, after having referred to the slaying of Tvash*tri*'s son and the like, goes on in the clause next following to exalt knowledge, 'And not one hair of me is harmed there. He who knows me thus by no deed of his is his life harmed.'—(But how does this passage convey praise of knowledge?)—Because, we reply, its meaning is as follows: 'Although I do such cruel deeds,

[1] I. e. spontaneous intuition of supersensible truth, rendered possible through the knowledge acquired in former existences.

yet not even a hair of mine is harmed because I am one with Brahman; therefore the life of any other person also who knows me thus is not harmed by any deed of his.' And the object of the knowledge (praised by Indra) is nothing else but Brahman which is set forth in a subsequent passage, 'I am prâ*n*a, the intelligent Self.' Therefore the entire chapter refers to Brahman.

31. If it be said (that Brahman is) not (meant), on account of characteristic marks of the individual soul and the chief vital air (being mentioned); we say no, on account of the threefoldness of devout meditation (which would result from your interpretation); on account of (the meaning advocated by us) being accepted (elsewhere); and on account of (characteristic marks of Brahman) being connected (with the passage under discussion).

Although we admit, the pûrvapakshin resumes, that the chapter about the prâ*n*a does not furnish any instruction regarding some outward deity, since it contains a multitude of references to the interior Self; still we deny that it is concerned with Brahman.—For what reason?—Because it mentions characteristic marks of the individual soul on the one hand, and of the chief vital air on the other hand. The passage, 'Let no man try to find out what speech is, let him know the speaker,' mentions a characteristic mark of the individual soul, and must therefore be held to point out as the object of knowledge the individual soul which rules and employs the different organs of action such as speech and so on. On the other hand, we have the passage, 'But prâ*n*a alone, the intelligent Self, having laid hold of this body makes it rise up,' which points to the chief vital air; for the chief attribute of the vital air is that it sustains the body. Similarly, we read in the colloquy of the vital airs (Pra. Up. II, 3), concerning speech and the other vital airs, 'Then prâ*n*a (the chief vital air) as the best said to them: Be not deceived; I alone dividing myself fivefold support this body and keep it.' Those, again, who in the passage quoted above read 'this one (masc.), the body[1]' must give the following explanation, Prâ*n*a having laid hold of this one, viz. either the individual soul or the aggregate of the sense organs, makes the body rise up. The individual soul as well as the chief vital air may justly be designated as the intelligent Self; for the former is of the nature of intelligence, and the latter (although non-intelligent in itself) is the abode of other prâ*n*as, viz. the sense organs, which are the instruments of intelligence. Moreover, if the word prâ*n*a be taken to denote the individual soul as well as the chief vital air, the prâ*n*a and the intelligent Self may be spoken of in two ways, either as being non-different on account of their mutual concomitance, or as being different on account of their (essentially different) individual character; and in these two different ways they are actually spoken of in the two following passages, 'What is prâ*n*a that is pra*gñ*â, what is pra*gñ*â that is prâ*n*a;' and, 'For together do these two live in the body and together do they depart.' If, on the other hand, prâ*n*a denoted Brahman, what then could be different from what? For these reasons prâ*n*a does not denote Brahman, but either the individual soul or the chief vital air or both.

All this argumentation, we reply, is wrong, 'on account of the threefoldness of devout meditation.' Your interpretation would involve the assumption of devout meditation of three different kinds, viz. on the individual soul, on the chief vital air, and on Brahman. But it is inappropriate to assume that a single sentence should enjoin three kinds of devout meditation; and that all the passages about the prâ*n*a really constitute one single sentence (one syntactical whole) appears from the beginning and the concluding part. In the beginning we have the clause 'Know me only,' followed by 'I am prâ*n*a, the intelligent Self, meditate on me as Life, as Immortality;' and in the end we read, 'And that prâ*n*a indeed is the intelligent Self, blessed, imperishable, immortal.' The beginning and the concluding part are thus seen to be similar, and we

[1] Ima*m s*arîram instead of ida*m s*arîram.

therefore must conclude that they refer to one and the same matter. Nor can the characteristic mark of Brahman be so turned as to be applied to something else; for the ten objects and the ten subjects (subjective powers)[1] cannot rest on anything but Brahman. Moreover, prâ*n*a must denote Brahman 'on account of (that meaning) being accepted,' i. e. because in the case of other passages where characteristic marks of Brahman are mentioned the word prâ*n*a is taken in the sense of 'Brahman.' And another reason for assuming the passage to refer to Brahman is that here also, i. e. in the passage itself there is 'connexion' with characteristic marks of Brahman, as, for instance, the reference to what is most beneficial for man. The assertion that the passage, 'Having laid hold of this body it makes it rise up,' contains a characteristic mark of the chief vital air, is untrue; for as the function of the vital air also ultimately rests on Brahman it can figuratively be ascribed to the latter. So Scripture also declares, 'No mortal lives by the breath that goes up and by the breath that goes down. We live by another in whom these two repose' (Ka. Up. II, 5, 5). Nor does the indication of the individual soul which you allege to occur in the passage, 'Let no man try to find out what speech is, let him know the speaker,' preclude the view of prâ*n*a denoting Brahman. For, as the passages, 'I am Brahman,' 'That art thou,' and others, prove, there is in reality no such thing as an individual soul absolutely different from Brahman, but Brahman, in so far as it differentiates itself through the mind (buddhi) and other limiting conditions, is called individual soul, agent, enjoyer. Such passages therefore as the one alluded to, (viz. 'let no man try to find out what speech is, let him know the speaker,') which, by setting aside all the differences due to limiting conditions, aim at directing the mind on the internal Self and thus showing that the

[1] Pa*ñk*a *s*abdâdaya*h* pa*ñk*a p*ri*thivyâdaya*s* *k*a da*s*a bhûtamâtrâ*h* pa*ñk*a buddhîndriyâ*n*i pa*ñk*a buddhaya iti da*s*a pra*gñ*âmâtrâ*h*. Yadvâ *gñ*ânendriyârthâ*h* pa*ñk*a karmendriyârthâ*s* *k*a pa*ñk*eti da*s*a bhûtamâtrâ*h* dvividhânîndriyâ*n*i pra*gñ*âmâtrâ da*s*eti bhâva*h*. Ân. Gi.

individual soul is one with Brahman, are by no means out of place. That the Self which is active in speaking and the like is Brahman appears from another scriptural passage also, viz. Ke. Up. I, 5, 'That which is not expressed by speech and by which speech is expressed that alone know as Brahman, not that which people here adore.' The remark that the statement about the difference of prâ*n*a and pra*g*ñâ (contained in the passage, 'Together they dwell in this body, together they depart') does not agree with that interpretation according to which prâ*n*a is Brahman, is without force; for the mind and the vital air which are the respective abodes of the two powers of cognition and action, and constitute the limiting conditions of the internal Self may be spoken of as different. The internal Self, on the other hand, which is limited by those two adjuncts, is in itself non-differentiated, so that the two may be identified, as is done in the passage 'prâ*n*a is pra*g*ñâ.'

The second part of the Sûtra is explained in a different manner also[1], as follows: Characteristic marks of the individual soul as well as of the chief vital air are not out of place even in a chapter whose topic is Brahman. How so? 'On account of the threefoldness of devout meditation.' The chapter aims at enjoining three kinds of devout meditation on Brahman, according as Brahman is viewed under the aspect of prâ*n*a, under the aspect of pra*g*ñâ, and in itself. The passages, 'Meditate (on me) as life, as immortality. Life is prâ*n*a,' and 'Having laid hold of this body it makes it rise up. Therefore let man worship it alone as uktha,' refer to the prâ*n*a aspect. The introductory passage, 'Now we shall explain how all things become one in that pra*g*ñâ,' and the subsequent passages, 'Speech verily milked one portion thereof; the word is its object placed outside;' and, 'Having by pra*g*ñâ taken possession of speech he obtains by speech all words &c.,' refer to the pra*g*ñâ aspect. The Brahman aspect finally is referred to in the following passage, 'These ten

[1] Viz. by the v*ri*ttikâra.

objects have reference to pragñâ, the ten subjects have reference to objects. If there were no objects there would be no subjects; and if there were no subjects there would be no objects. For on either side alone nothing could be achieved. But that is not many. For as in a car the circumference of the wheel is set on the spokes and the spokes on the nave, thus are these objects set on the subjects and the subjects on the prâna.' Thus we see that the one meditation on Brahman is here represented as threefold, according as Brahman is viewed either with reference to two limiting conditions or in itself. In other passages also we find that devout meditation on Brahman is made dependent on Brahman being qualified by limiting adjuncts; so, for instance (*Kh.* Up. III, 14, 2), 'He who consists of mind, whose body is prâna.' The hypothesis of Brahman being meditated upon under three aspects perfectly agrees with the prâna chapter[1]; as, on the one hand, from a comparison of the introductory and the concluding clauses we infer that the subject-matter of the whole chapter is one only, and as, on the other hand, we meet with characteristic marks of prâna, pragñâ, and Brahman in turns. It therefore remains a settled conclusion that Brahman is the topic of the whole chapter.

[1] Ihâpi tad yugyate explaining the 'iha tadyogât' of the Sûtra.

SECOND PÂDA.

REVERENCE TO THE HIGHEST SELF!

IN the first pâda Brahman has been shown to be the cause of the origin, subsistence, and reabsorption of the entire world, comprising the ether and the other elements. Moreover, of this Brahman, which is the cause of the entire world, certain qualities have (implicitly) been declared, such as all-pervadingness, eternity, omniscience, its being the Self of all, and so on. Further, by producing reasons showing that some words which are generally used in a different sense denote Brahman also, we have been able to determine that some passages about whose sense doubts are entertained refer to Brahman. Now certain other passages present themselves which because containing only obscure indications of Brahman give rise to the doubt whether they refer to the highest Self or to something else. We therefore begin the second and third pâdas in order to settle those doubtful points.

1. (That which consists of mind is Brahman) because there is taught what is known from everywhere.

Scripture says, 'All this indeed is Brahman, beginning, ending, and breathing in it; thus knowing let a man meditate with calm mind. Now man is made of determination (kratu); according to what his determination is in this world so will he be when he has departed this life. Let him therefore form this determination: he who consists of mind, whose body is breath (the subtle body),' &c. (*Kh.* Up. III, 14). Concerning this passage the doubt presents itself whether what is pointed out as the object of meditation, by means of attributes such as consisting of mind, &c., is the embodied (individual) soul or the highest Brahman.

The embodied Self, the pûrvapakshin says.—Why?—Because the embodied Self as the ruler of the organs of action is well known to be connected with the mind and so on, while the highest Brahman is not, as is declared in several scriptural passages, so, for instance (Mu. Up. II, 1, 2),

'He is without breath, without mind, pure.'—But, it may be objected, the passage, 'All this indeed is Brahman,' mentions Brahman directly; how then can you suppose that the embodied Self forms the object of meditation?—This objection does not apply, the pûrvapakshin rejoins, because the passage does not aim at enjoining meditation on Brahman, but rather at enjoining calmness of mind, the sense being: because Brahman is all this, ta*gg*alân, let a man meditate with a calm mind. That is to say: because all this aggregate of effects is Brahman only, springing from it, ending in it, and breathing in it; and because, as everything constitutes one Self only, there is no room for passion; therefore a man is to meditate with a calm mind. And since the sentence aims at enjoining calmness of mind, it cannot at the same time enjoin meditation on Brahman[1]; but meditation is separately enjoined in the clause, 'Let him form the determination, i.e. reflection.' And thereupon the subsequent passage, 'He who consists of mind, whose body is breath,' &c. states the object of the meditation in words indicatory of the individual soul. For this reason we maintain that the meditation spoken of has the individual soul for its object. The other attributes also subsequently stated in the text, 'He to whom all works, all desires belong,' &c. may rightly be held to refer to the individual soul. The attributes, finally, of being what abides in the heart and of being extremely minute which are mentioned in the passage, 'He is my Self within the heart, smaller than a corn of rice, smaller than a corn of barley,' may be ascribed to the individual soul which has the size of the point of a goad, but not to the unlimited Brahman. If it be objected that the immediately following passage, 'greater than the earth,' &c., cannot refer to something limited, we reply that smallness and greatness which are mutually opposite cannot indeed be ascribed to one and the same thing; and that, if one attribute

[1] The clause 'he is to meditate with a calm mind' if taken as a gu*n*avidhi, i.e. as enjoining some secondary matter, viz. calmness of mind of the meditating person, cannot at the same time enjoin meditation; for that would involve a so-called split of the sentence (vâkyabheda).

only is to be ascribed to the subject of the passage, smallness is preferable because it is mentioned first; while the greatness mentioned later on may be attributed to the soul in so far as it is one with Brahman. If it is once settled that the whole passage refers to the individual soul, it follows that the declaration of Brahman also, contained in the passage, 'That is Brahman' (III, 14, 4), refers to the individual soul[1], as it is clearly connected with the general topic. Therefore the individual soul is the object of meditation indicated by the qualities of consisting of mind and so on.

To all this we reply: The highest Brahman only is what is to be meditated upon as distinguished by the attributes of consisting of mind and so on.—Why?—'On account of there being taught here what is known from everywhere.' What is known from all Vedânta-passages to be the sense of the word Brahman, viz. the cause of the world, and what is mentioned here in the beginning words of the passage, ('all this indeed is Brahman,') the same we must assume to be taught here as distinguished by certain qualities, viz. consisting of mind and so on. Thus we avoid the fault of dropping the subject-matter under discussion and needlessly introducing a new topic.—But, it may be said, it has been shown that Brahman is, in the beginning of the passage, introduced merely for the purpose of intimating the injunction of calmness of mind, not for the purpose of intimating Brahman itself.—True, we reply; but the fact nevertheless remains that, where the qualities of consisting of mind, &c. are spoken of, Brahman only is proximate (i. e. mentioned not far off so that it may be concluded to be the thing referred to), while the individual soul is neither proximate nor intimated by any word directly pointing to it. The cases of Brahman and the individual soul are therefore not equal.

2. And because the qualities desired to be expressed are possible (in Brahman; therefore the passage refers to Brahman).

[1] *G*îve*x*pi dehâdib*rim*hanâ*g* *g*yâstvanyâyâd vâ brahmatety artha*h*. Ân. Gi.

Although in the Veda which is not the work of man no wish in the strict sense can be expressed [1], there being no speaker, still such phrases as 'desired to be expressed,' may be figuratively used on account of the result, viz. (mental) comprehension. For just as in ordinary language we speak of something which is intimated by a word and is to be received (by the hearer as the meaning of the word), as 'desired to be expressed;' so in the Veda also whatever is denoted as that which is to be received is 'desired to be expressed,' everything else 'not desired to be expressed.' What is to be received as the meaning of a Vedic sentence, and what not, is inferred from the general purport of the passage. Those qualities which are here desired to be expressed, i. e. intimated as qualities to be dwelt on in meditation, viz. the qualities of having true purposes, &c. are possible in the highest Brahman; for the quality of having true purposes may be ascribed to the highest Self which possesses unimpeded power over the creation, subsistence, and reabsorption of this world. Similarly the qualities of having true desires and true purposes are attributed to the highest Self in another passage, viz. the one beginning, 'The Self which is free from sin' (*Kh.* Up. VIII, 7, 1). The clause, 'He whose Self is the ether,' means 'he whose Self is like the ether;' for Brahman may be said to be like the ether on account of its omnipresence and other qualities. This is also expressed by the clause, 'Greater than the earth.' And the other explanation also, according to which the passage means 'he whose Self is the ether' is possible, since Brahman which as the cause of the whole world is the Self of everything is also the Self of the ether. For the same reasons he is called 'he to whom all works belong, and so on.' Thus the qualities here intimated as topics of meditation agree with the nature of Brahman. We further maintain that the terms 'consisting of mind,' and 'having breath for its body,' which the pûrvapakshin asserts

[1] The discussion is brought on by the term 'vivakshita' in the Sûtra whose meaning is 'expressed, aimed at,' but more literally 'desired to be expressed.'

cannot refer to Brahman, may refer to it. For as Brahman is the Self of everything, qualities such as consisting of mind and the like, which belong to the individual soul, belong to Brahman also. Accordingly *S*ruti and Sm*ri*ti say of Brahman, 'Thou art woman, thou art man; thou art youth, thou art maiden; thou as an old man totterest along on thy staff; thou art born with thy face turned everywhere' (*S*ve. Up. IV, 3), and 'its hands and feet are everywhere, its eyes and head are everywhere, its ears are everywhere, it stands encompassing all in the world' (Bha. Gîtâ III, 13).

The passage (quoted above against our view), 'Without breath, without mind, pure,' refers to the pure (unrelated) Brahman. The terms 'consisting of mind; having breath for its body,' on the other hand, refer to Brahman as distinguished by qualities. Hence, as the qualities mentioned are possible in Brahman, we conclude that the highest Brahman only is represented as the object of meditation.

3. On the other hand, as (those qualities) are not possible (in it), the embodied (soul is) not (denoted by manomaya, &c.).

The preceding Sûtra has declared that the qualities mentioned are possible in Brahman; the present Sûtra states that they are not possible in the embodied Self. Brahman only possesses, in the manner explained, the qualities of consisting of mind, and so on; not the embodied individual soul. For qualities such as expressed in the words, 'He whose purposes are true, whose Self is the ether, who has no speech, who is not disturbed, who is greater than the earth,' cannot easily be attributed to the embodied Self. By the term 'embodied' (*s*ârîra) we have to understand 'residing' in a body. If it be objected that the Lord also resides in the body[1], we reply, True, he does reside in the body, but not in the body only; for *s*ruti declares him to be all-pervading; compare, 'He is greater than the earth; greater than the atmosphere, omnipresent like the ether, eternal.' The individual soul, on the other

[1] Because he is vyâpin.

hand, is in the body only, apart from which as the abode of fruition it does not exist.

4. And because there is a (separate) denotation of the object of activity and of the agent.

The attributes of consisting of mind, and so on, cannot belong to the embodied Self for that reason also, that there is a (separate) denotation of the object of activity and of the agent. In the passage, 'When I shall have departed from hence I shall obtain him' (*Kh*. Up. III, 14, 4), the word 'him' refers to that which is the topic of discussion, viz. the Self which is to be meditated upon as possessing the attributes of consisting of mind, &c., as the object of an activity, viz. as something to be obtained; while the words, 'I shall obtain,' represent the meditating individual Self as the agent, i. e. the obtainer. Now, wherever it can be helped, we must not assume that one and the same being is spoken of as the agent and the object of the activity at the same time. The relation existing between a person meditating and the thing meditated upon requires, moreover, different abodes.—And thus for the above reason, also, that which is characterised by the attributes of consisting of mind, and so on, cannot be the individual soul.

5. On account of the difference of words.

That which possesses the attributes of consisting of mind, and so on, cannot be the individual soul, for that reason also that there is a difference of words.

That is to say, we meet with another scriptural passage of kindred subject-matter (*S*at. Brâ. X, 6, 3, 2), 'Like a rice grain, or a barley grain, or a canary seed or the kernel of a canary seed, thus that golden person is in the Self.' There one word, i. e. the locative 'in the Self,' denotes the embodied Self, and a different word, viz. the nominative 'person,' denotes the Self distinguished by the qualities of consisting of mind, &c. We therefrom conclude that the two are different.

6. And on account of Sm*ri*ti.

Sm*ri*ti also declares the difference of the embodied Self

and the highest Self, viz. Bha. Gîtâ XVIII, 61, 'The Lord, O Arguna, is seated in the heart of all beings, driving round by his magical power all beings (as if they were) mounted on a machine.'

But what, it may be asked, is that so-called embodied Self different from the highest Self which is to be set aside according to the preceding Sûtras? *S*ruti passages, as well as Sm*ri*ti, expressly deny that there is any Self apart from the highest Self; compare, for instance, B*ri*. Up. III, 7, 23, 'There is no other seer but he; there is no other hearer but he;' and Bha. Gîtâ XIII, 2, 'And know me also, O Bhârata, to be the kshetrag*ñ*a in all kshetras.'

True, we reply, (there is in reality one universal Self only.) But the highest Self in so far as it is limited by its adjuncts, viz. the body, the senses, and the mind (mano-buddhi), is, by the ignorant, spoken of as if it were embodied. Similarly the ether, although in reality unlimited, appears limited owing to certain adjuncts, such as jars and other vessels. With regard to this (unreal limitation of the one Self) the distinction of objects of activity and of agents may be practically assumed, as long as we have not learned—from the passage, 'That art thou'—that the Self is one only. As soon, however, as we grasp the truth that there is only one universal Self, there is an end to the whole practical view of the world with its distinction of bondage, final release, and the like.

7. If it be said that (the passage does) not (refer to Brahman) on account of the smallness of the abode (mentioned), and on account of the denotations of that (i. e. of minuteness); we say, no; because (Brahman) has thus to be contemplated, and because the case is analogous to that of ether.

On account of the limitation of its abode, which is mentioned in the clause, 'He is my Self within the heart,' and on account of the declaration as to its minuteness contained in the direct statement, 'He is smaller than a grain of rice,' &c.; the embodied soul only, which is of the size of an awl's point, is spoken of in the passage under discussion, and not the highest Self. This assertion made above (in the pûrvapaksha of Sûtra I, and restated in the pûrvapaksha of the present Sûtra) has to be refuted. We therefore maintain that the objection raised does not invalidate our view of the passage. It is true that a thing occupying a limited space only cannot in any way be spoken of as omnipresent; but, on the other hand, that which is omnipresent, and therefore in all places may, from a certain point of view, be said to occupy a limited space. Similarly, a prince may be called the ruler of Ayodhyâ although he is at the same time the ruler of the whole earth.—But from what point of view can the omnipresent Lord be said to occupy a limited space and to be minute?—He may, we reply, be spoken of thus, 'because he is to be contemplated thus.' The passage under discussion teaches us to contemplate the Lord as abiding within the lotus of the heart, characterised by minuteness and similar qualities—which apprehension of the Lord is rendered possible through a modification of the mind—just as Hari is contemplated in the sacred stone called *S*âlagrâm. Although present everywhere, the Lord is pleased when meditated upon as dwelling in the heart. The case is, moreover, to be viewed as analogous to that of the ether. The ether, although all-pervading, is spoken of as limited and minute, if considered in its connexion with the eye of a needle; so Brahman also. But it is an understood matter that the attributes of limitation of abode and of minuteness depend, in Brahman's case, entirely on special forms of contemplation, and are not real. The latter consideration disposes also of the objection, that if Brahman has its abode in the heart, which heart-abode is a different one in each body, it would follow that it is affected by all the imperfections which attach to beings having different abodes, such as parrots shut up in different cages, viz. want of unity, being made up of parts, non-permanency, and so on.

8. If it is said that (from the circumstance of Brahman and the individual soul being one) there follows fruition (on the part of Brahman); we say, no; on account of the difference of nature (of the two).

But, it may be said, as Brahman is omnipresent like ether, and therefore connected with the hearts of all living beings, and as it is of the nature of intelligence and therefore not different from the individual soul, it follows that Brahman also has the same fruition of pleasure, pain, and so on (as the individual soul). The same result follows from its unity. For in reality there exists no transmigratory Self different from the highest Self; as appears from the text, 'There is no other knower but he' (B*ri*. Up. III, 7, 23), and similar passages. Hence the highest Self is subject to the fruition connected with transmigratory existence.

This is not so, we reply; because there is a difference of nature. From the circumstance that Brahman is connected with the hearts of all living beings it does not follow that it is, like the embodied Self, subject to fruition. For, between the embodied Self and the highest Self, there is the difference that the former acts and enjoys, acquires merit and demerit, and is affected by pleasure, pain, and so on; while the latter is of the opposite nature, i.e. characterised by being free from all evil and the like. On account of this difference of the two, the fruition of the one does not extend to the other. To assume merely on the ground of the mutual proximity of the two, without considering their essentially different powers, that a connexion with effects exists (in Brahman's case also), would be no better than to suppose that space is on fire (when something in space is on fire). The same objection and refutation apply to the case of those also who teach the existence of more than one omnipresent Self. In reply to the assertion, that because Brahman is one and there are no other Selfs outside it, Brahman must be subject to fruition since the individual soul is so, we ask the question: How have you, our wise opponent, ascertained that there is no other Self? You will reply, we suppose, from scriptural texts such as, 'That art thou,' 'I am Brahman,' 'There is no other knower but he,' and so on. Very well, then, it appears that the truth about scriptural matters is to be ascertained from Scripture, and that Scripture is not sometimes to be appealed to, and on other occasions to be disregarded.

Scriptural texts, such as 'that art thou,' teach that Brahman which is free from all evil is the Self of the embodied soul, and thus dispel even the opinion that the embodied soul is subject to fruition; how then should fruition on the part of the embodied soul involve fruition on the part of Brahman?—Let, then, the unity of the individual soul and Brahman not be apprehended on the ground of Scripture.—In that case, we reply, the fruition on the part of the individual soul has wrong knowledge for its cause, and Brahman as it truly exists is not touched thereby, not any more than the ether becomes really dark-blue in consequence of ignorant people presuming it to be so. For this reason the Sûtrakâra says[1] 'no, on account of the difference.' In spite of their unity, fruition on the part of the soul does not involve fruition on the part of Brahman; because there is a difference. For there is a difference between false knowledge and perfect knowledge, fruition being the figment of false knowledge while the unity (of the Self) is revealed by perfect knowledge. Now, as the substance revealed by perfect knowledge cannot be affected by fruition which is nothing but the figment of false knowledge, it is impossible to assume even a shadow of fruition on Brahman's part.

9. The eater (is the highest Self) since what is movable and what is immovable is mentioned (as his food).

We read in the Ka*th*avallî (I, 2, 25), 'Who then knows where He is, He to whom the Brahmans and Kshattriyas are but food, and death itself a condiment?' This passage intimates, by means of the words 'food' and 'condiment,' that there is some eater. A doubt then arises whether the eater be Agni or the individual soul or the highest Self; for no distinguishing characteristic is stated, and Agni as well as the individual soul and the highest Self is observed to form, in that Upanished, the subjects of questions[2].

---

[1] Another interpretatio 1 of the later part of Sûtra.

[2] Cp. Ka*th*a Up. I, 1, 13; 20; I, 2, 14.

The pûrvapakshin maintains that the eater is Agni, fire being known from Scripture as well (cp. Br*i*. Up. I, 4, 6) as from ordinary life to be the eater of food. Or else the individual soul may be the eater, according to the passage, 'One of them eats the sweet fruit' (Mu. Up. III, 1, 1). On the other hand, the eater cannot be Brahman on account of the passage (which forms the continuation of the one quoted from the Mu. Up.), 'The other looks on without eating.'

The eater, we reply, must be the highest Self 'because there is mentioned what is movable and what is immovable.' For all things movable and immovable are here to be taken as constituting the food, while death is the condiment. But nothing beside the highest Self can be the consumer of all these things in their totality; the highest Self, however, when reabsorbing the entire aggregate of effects may be said to eat everything. If it is objected that here no express mention is made of things movable and things immovable, and that hence we have no right to use the (alleged) mention made of them as a reason, we reply that this objection is unfounded; firstly, because the aggregate of all living beings is seen to be meant from the circumstance of death being the condiment; and, secondly, because the Brahmans and Kshattriyas may here, on account of their pre-eminent position, be viewed as instances only (of all beings). Concerning the objection that the highest Self cannot be an eater on account of the passage quoted ('the other looks on without eating'), we remark that that passage aims at denying the fruition (on the part of the highest Self) of the results of works, such fruition being mentioned in immediate proximity, but is not meant to negative the reabsorption of the world of effects (into Brahman); for it is well established by all the Vedânta-texts that Brahman is the cause of the creation, subsistence, and reabsorption of the world. Therefore the eater can here be Brahman only.

10. And on account of the topic under discussion.

That the highest Self only can be the eater referred to

is moreover evident from the passage (Ka. Up. I, 2, 18), ('The knowing Self is not born, it dies not'), which shows that the highest Self is the general topic. And to adhere to the general topic is the proper proceeding. Further, the clause, 'Who then knows where he is,' shows that the cognition is connected with difficulties; which circumstance again points to the highest Self.

11. The 'two entered into the cave' (are the individual soul and the highest Self), for the two are (intelligent) Selfs (and therefore of the same nature), as it is seen (that numerals denote beings of the same nature).

In the same Ka*th*avallî we read (I, 3, 1), 'There are the two drinking the reward of their works in the world, (i.e. the body,) entered into the cave, dwelling on the highest summit. Those who know Brahman call them shade and light; likewise those householders who perform the Tri*n*â-*k*iketa sacrifice.'

Here the doubt arises whether the mind (buddhi) and the individual soul are referred to, or the individual soul and the highest Self. If the mind and the individual soul, then the individual soul is here spoken of as different from the aggregate of the organs of action, (i. e. the body,) among which the mind occupies the first place. And a statement on this point is to be expected, as a question concerning it is asked in a preceding passage, viz. I, 1, 20, 'There is that doubt when a man is dead—some saying he is; others, he is not. This I should like to know taught by thee; this is the third of my boons.' If, on the other hand, the passage refers to the individual soul and the highest Self, then it intimates that the highest Self is different from the individual soul; and this also requires to be declared here, on account of the question contained in the passage (I, 2, 14), 'That which thou seest as different from religious duty and its contrary, from effect and cause, from the past and the future, tell me that.'

The doubt to which the passage gives rise having thus

been stated, a caviller starts the following objection: neither of the stated views can be maintained.—Why?—On account of the characteristic mark implied in the circumstance that the two are said to drink, i. e. to enjoy, the fruit of their works in the world. For this can apply to the intelligent individual soul only, not to the non-intelligent buddhi. And as the dual form 'drinking' (pibantau) shows that both are drinking, the view of the two being the buddhi and the individual soul is not tenable. For the same reason the other opinion also, viz. of the two being the individual soul and the highest Self, cannot be maintained; for drinking (i. e. the fruition of reward) cannot be predicated of the highest Self, on account of the mantra (Mu. Up. III, 1, 1), 'The other looks on without eating.'

These objections, we reply, are without any force. Just as we see that in phrases such as 'the men with the umbrella (lit. the umbrella-men) are walking,' the attribute of being furnished with an umbrella which properly speaking belongs to one man only is secondarily ascribed to many, so here two agents are spoken of as drinking because one of them is really drinking. Or else we may explain the passage by saying that, while the individual soul only drinks, the Lord also is said to drink because he makes the soul drink. On the other hand, we may also assume that the two are the buddhi and the individual soul, the instrument being figuratively spoken of as the agent—a figure of speech exemplified by phrases such as 'the fuel cooks (the food).' And in a chapter whose topic is the soul no two other beings can well be represented as enjoying rewards. Hence there is room for the doubt whether the two are the buddhi and the individual soul, or the individual soul and the highest Self.

Here the pûrvapakshin maintains that the former of the two stated views is the right one, because the two beings are qualified as 'entered into the cave.' Whether we understand by the cave the body or the heart, in either case the buddhi and the individual soul may be spoken of as 'entered into the cave.' Nor would it be appropriate, as long as another interpretation is possible, to assume that a special place is here ascribed to the omnipresent Brahman. Moreover, the words 'in the world of their good deeds' show that the two do not pass beyond the sphere of the results of their good works. But the highest Self is not in the sphere of the results of either good or bad works; according to the scriptural passage, 'It does not grow larger by works nor does it grow smaller.' Further, the words 'shade and light' properly designate what is intelligent and what is non-intelligent, because the two are opposed to each other like light and shade. Hence we conclude that the buddhi and the individual soul are spoken of.

To this we make the following reply:—In the passage under discussion the individual soul (vi*g*ñânâtman) and the highest Self are spoken of, because these two, being both intelligent Selfs, are of the same nature. For we see that in ordinary life also, whenever a number is mentioned, beings of the same class are understood to be meant; when, for instance, the order is given, 'Look out for a second (i. e. a fellow) for this bull,' people look out for a second bull, not for a horse or a man. So here also, where the mention of the fruition of rewards enables us to determine that the individual soul is meant, we understand at once, when a second is required, that the highest Self has to be understood; for the highest Self is intelligent, and therefore of the same nature as the soul.—But has it not been said above that the highest Self cannot be meant here, on account of the text stating that it is placed in the cave?—Well, we reply, *s*ruti as well as smri*ti* speaks of the highest Self as placed in the cave. Compare, for instance (Ka. Up. I, 2, 12), 'The Ancient who is hidden in the cave, who dwells in the abyss;' Taitt. Up. II, 1, 'He who knows him hidden in the cave, in the highest ether;' and, 'Search for the Self entered into the cave.' That it is not contrary to reason to assign to the omnipresent Brahman a special locality, for the purpose of clearer perception, we have already demonstrated. The attribute of existing in the world of its good works, which properly belongs to one of the two only, viz. to the individual soul, may be assigned to both, analogously to the case of the men, one of whom carries an umbrella. Their being compared to light and shade also is unobjectionable, because the qualities of belonging and not belonging to this transmigratory world are opposed to each other, like light and shade; the quality of belonging to it being due to Nescience, and the quality of not belonging to it being real. We therefore understand by the two 'entered into the cave,' the individual soul and the highest Self.—Another reason for this interpretation follows.

12. And on account of the distinctive qualities (mentioned).

Moreover, the distinctive qualities mentioned in the text agree only with the individual Self and the highest Self. For in a subsequent passage (I, 3, 3), 'Know the Self to be the charioteer, the body to be the chariot,' which contains the simile of the chariot, the individual soul is represented as a charioteer driving on through transmigratory existence and final release, while the passage (9), 'He reaches the end of his journey, and that is the highest place of Vish*n*u,' represents the highest Self as the goal of the driver's course. And in a preceding passage also, (I, 2, 12, 'The wise, who by means of meditation on his Self, recognises the Ancient who is difficult to be seen, who has entered into the dark, who is hidden in the cave, who dwells in the abyss, as God, he indeed leaves joy and sorrow far behind,') the same two beings are distinguished as thinker and as object of thought. The highest Self is, moreover, the general topic. And further, the clause, 'Those who know Brahman call them,' &c., which brings forward a special class of speakers, is in its place only if the highest Self is accepted (as one of the two beings spoken of). It is therefore evident that the passage under discussion refers to the individual soul and the highest Self.

The same reasoning applies to the passage (Mu. Up. III, 1, 1), 'Two birds, inseparable friends,' &c. There also the Self is the general topic, and hence no two ordinary birds can be meant; we therefore conclude from the characteristic mark of eating, mentioned in the passage, 'One of them eats the sweet fruit,' that the individual soul is meant, and from the characteristic marks of abstinence from eating and of intelligence, implied in the words, 'The other looks on without eating,' that the highest Self is meant. In a subsequent mantra again the two are distinguished as the seer and the object of sight. 'Merged into the same tree (as it were into water) man grieves at his own impotence (anîsâ), bewildered; but when he sees the other Lord (îsa) contented and knows his glory, then his grief passes away.'

Another (commentator) gives a different interpretation of the mantra, 'Two birds inseparable,' &c. To that mantra, he says, the final decision of the present head of discussion does not apply, because it is differently interpreted in the Paiṅgi-rahasya Brâhmana. According to the latter the being which eats the sweet fruit is the sattva; the other being which looks on without eating, the individual soul (gña); so that the two are the sattva and the individual soul (kshetragña). The objection that the word sattva might denote the individual soul, and the word kshetragña, the highest Self, is to be met by the remark that, in the first place, the words sattva and kshetragña have the settled meaning of internal organ and individual soul, and are, in the second place, expressly so interpreted there, (viz. in the Paiṅgi-rahasya,) 'The sattva is that by means of which man sees dreams; the embodied one, the seer, is the kshetragña; the two are therefore the internal organ and the individual soul.' Nor does the mantra under discussion fall under the pûrvapaksha propounded above. For it does not aim at setting forth the embodied individual soul, in so far as it is characterised by the attributes connected with the transmigratory state, such as acting and enjoying; but in so far rather as it transcends all attributes connected with the samsâra and is of the nature of Brahman, i. e. is pure intelligence; as is evident from the clause, 'The other looks on without eating.' That agrees, moreover, with sruti and smriti passages, such as, 'That art thou,' and 'Know me also to be the individual soul' (Bha. Gîtâ XIII, 2). Only on such an explanation of the passage as the preceding one there is room for the declaration made in the concluding passage of the section, 'These two are the sattva and the kshetragña; to him indeed who knows this no impurity attaches[1].'—But how can, on the above interpretation, the non-intelligent sattva (i. e. the internal organ) be spoken of as an enjoyer, as is actually done in the clause, 'One of them eats the sweet fruit?'—The whole passage, we reply, does not aim at setting forth the fact that the sattva is an enjoyer, but rather the fact that the intelligent individual soul is not an enjoyer, but is of the nature of Brahman. To that end[2] the passage under discussion metaphorically ascribes the attribute of being an enjoyer to the internal organ, in so far as it is modified by pleasure, pain, and the like. For all acting and enjoying is at the bottom based on the non-discrimination (by the soul) of the respective nature of internal organ and soul; while in reality neither the internal organ nor the soul either act or enjoy; not the former, because it is non-intelligent; not the latter, because it is not capable of any modification. And the internal organ can be considered as acting and enjoying, all the less as it is a mere presentment of Nescience. In agreement with what we have here maintained, Scripture ('For where there is as it were duality there one sees the other,' &c.; B*ri*. Up. IV, 5, 15) declares that the practical assumption of agents, and so on—comparable to the assumption of the existence of elephants, and the like, seen in a dream—holds good in the sphere of Nescience only; while the passage, 'But when the Self only is all this, how should he see another?' declares that all that practically postulated existence vanishes for him who has arrived at discriminative knowledge.

13. The person within (the eye) (is Brahman) on account of the agreement (of the attributes of that person with the nature of Brahman).

[1] Freedom from impurity can result only from the knowledge that the individual soul is in reality Brahman. The commentators explain ragas by avidyâ.

[2] Tadartham iti, *g*îvasya brahmasiddhyartham iti yâvat, *k*aitanya*kh*âyâpannâ dhî*h* sukhâdinâ pari*n*amata iti, tatra purusho-pi bhaktri*t*vam ivânubhavati na tattvata iti vaktum adhyâropayati. Ânanda Giri.

Scripture says, 'He spoke: The person that is seen in the eye that is the Self. This is the immortal, the fearless, this is Brahman. Even though they drop melted butter or water on it (the eye) it runs away on both sides,' &c. (*Kh.* Up. IV, 15, 1).

The doubt here arises whether this passage refers to the reflected Self which resides in the eye, or to the individual Self, or to the Self of some deity which presides over the sense of sight, or to the Lord.

With reference to this doubt the pûrvapakshin argues as follows: What is meant (by the person in the eye) is the reflected Self, i. e. the image of a person (reflected in the eye of another); for of that it is well known that it is seen, and the clause, 'The person that is seen in the eye,' refers to it as something well known. Or else we may appropriately take the passage as referring to the individual Self. For the individual Self (cognitional Self, vi*gñ*ânâtman) which perceives the colours by means of the eye is, on that account, in proximity to the eye; and, moreover, the word 'Self' (which occurs in the passage) favours this interpretation. Or else the passage is to be understood as referring to the soul animating the sun which assists the sense of sight; compare the passage (B*ri*. Up. V, 5, 2), 'He (the person in the sun) rests with his rays in him (the person in the right eye).' Moreover, qualities such as immortality and the like (which are ascribed to the subject of the scriptural passage) may somehow belong to individual deities. The Lord, on the other hand[1], cannot be meant, because a particular locality is spoken of.

Against this we remark that the highest Lord only can be meant here by the person within the eye.—Why?—'On account of the agreement.' For the qualities mentioned in the passage accord with the nature of the highest Lord. The quality of being the Self, in the first place, belongs to the highest Lord in its primary (non-figurative or non-derived) sense, as we know from such texts as 'That

[1] Who, somebody might say, is to be understood here, because immortality and similar qualities belong to him not somehow only, but in their true sense.

is the Self,' 'That art thou.' Immortality and fearlessness again are often ascribed to him in Scripture. The location in the eye also is in consonance with the nature of the highest Lord. For just as the highest Lord whom Scripture declares to be free from all evil is not stained by any imperfections, so the station of the eye also is declared to be free from all stain, as we see from the passage, 'Even though they drop melted butter or water on it it runs away on both sides.' The statement, moreover, that he possesses the qualities of sa*m*yadvâma, &c. can be reconciled with the highest Lord only (*Kh*. Up. IV. 15, 2, 'They call him Sa*m*yadvâma, for all blessings (vâma) go towards him (sa*m*yanti). He is also vâmanî, for he leads (nayati) all blessings (vâma). He is also Bhâmanî, for he shines (bhâti) in all worlds'). Therefore, on account of agreement, the person within the eye is the highest Lord.

14. And on account of the statement of place, and so on.

But how does the confined locality of the eye agree with Brahman which is omnipresent like the ether?—To this question we reply that there would indeed be a want of agreement if that one locality only were assigned to the Lord. For other localities also, viz. the earth and so on, are attributed to him in the passage, 'He who dwells in the earth,' &c. (B*ri*. Up. III, 7, 3). And among those the eye also is mentioned, viz. in the clause, 'He who dwells in the eye,' &c. The phrase 'and so on,' which forms part of the Sûtra, intimates that not only locality is assigned to Brahman, although not (really) appropriate to it, but that also such things as name and form, although not appropriate to Brahman which is devoid of name and form, are yet seen to be attributed to it. That, in such passages as 'His name is ut, he with the golden beard' (*Kh*. Up. I, 6, 7, 6), Brahman although devoid of qualities is spoken of, for the purposes of devotion, as possessing qualities depending on name and form, we have already shown. And we have, moreover, shown that to attribute to Brahman a definite locality, in spite of his omnipresence, subserves the purposes of contemplation, and is therefore not contrary to reason [1]; no more than to contemplate Vish*n*u in the sacred *s*âlagrâm.

15. And on account of the passage referring to that which is distinguished by pleasure (i. e. Brahman).

There is, moreover, really no room for dispute whether Brahman be meant in the passage under discussion or not, because the fact of Brahman being meant is established 'by the reference to that which is distinguished by pleasure.' For the same Brahman which is spoken of as characterised by pleasure in the beginning of the chapter [2], viz. in the clauses, 'Breath is Brahman, Ka is Brahman, Kha is Brahman,' that same Brahman we must suppose to be referred to in the present passage also, it being proper to adhere to the subject-matter under discussion; the clause, 'The teacher will tell you the way [3],' merely announcing that the way will be proclaimed [by the teacher; not that a new subject will be started].—How then, it may be asked, is it known that Brahman, as distinguished by pleasure, is spoken of in the beginning of the passage?—We reply: On hearing the speech of the fires, viz. 'Breath is Brahman, Ka is Brahman. Kha is Brahman,' Upako*s*ala says, 'I understand that breath is Brahman, but I do not understand that Ka or Kha is Brahman.' Thereupon the fires reply, 'What is Ka is Kha, what is Kha is Ka.' Now the word Kha denotes in ordinary language the elemental ether. If therefore the word Ka which means pleasure were not applied to qualify the sense of 'Kha,' we should conclude

[1] The *T*îkâs say that the contents of this last sentence are hinted at by the word 'and' in the Sûtra.

[2] I. e. at the beginning of the instruction which the sacred fires give to Upako*s*ala, *Kh*. Up. IV, 10 ff.

[3] Which words conclude the instruction given by the fires, and introduce the instruction given by the teacher, of which the passage 'the person that is seen in the eye,' &c. forms a part.

that the name Brahman is here symbolically[1] given to the mere elemental ether as it is (in other places) given to mere names and the like. Thus also with regard to the word Ka, which, in ordinary language, denotes the imperfect pleasure springing from the contact of the sense-organs with their objects. If the word Kha were not applied to qualify the sense of Ka we should conclude that ordinary pleasure is here called Brahman. But as the two words Ka and Kha (occur together and therefore) qualify each other, they intimate Brahman whose Self is pleasure. If[2] in the passage referred to (viz. 'Breath is Brahman, Ka is Brahman, Kha is Brahman') the second Brahman (i.e. the word Brahman in the clause 'Ka is Brahman') were not added, and if the sentence would run 'Ka, Kha is Brahman,' the word Ka would be employed as a mere qualifying word, and thus pleasure as being a mere quality would not be represented as a subject of meditation. To prevent this, both words—Ka as well as Kha—are joined with the word Brahman ('Ka (is) Brahman, Kha (is) Brahman'). For the passage wishes to intimate that pleasure also, although a quality, should be meditated upon as something in which qualities inhere. It thus appears that at the beginning of the chapter Brahman, as characterised by pleasure, is spoken of. After that the Gârhapatya and the other sacred fires proclaim in turns their own glory, and finally conclude with the words, 'This is our knowledge, O friend, and the knowledge of the Self;' wherein they point back to the Brahman spoken of before. The words, 'The teacher will tell you the way' (which form the last clause of the concluding passage), merely promise an explanation of the way, and thus preclude the idea of another topic being started. The teacher thereupon saying, 'As water does not cling to a lotus leaf, so no evil deed clings to one who knows it' (which words intervene between the concluding

[1] Â*s*rayântarapratyayasyâ*s*rayântare kshepa*h* pratîka*h*, yathâ brahma*s*abda*h* paramâtmavishayo nâmâdishu kshipyate. Bhâ.

[2] The following sentences give the reason why, although there is only one Brahman, the word Brahman is repeated.

speech of the fires and the information given by the teacher about the person within the eye) declares that no evil attacks him who knows the person within the eye, and thereby shows the latter to be Brahman. It thus appears that the teacher's intention is to speak about that Brahman which had formed the topic of the instruction of the fires; to represent it at first as located in the eye and possessing the qualities of Sa*m*yadvâma and the like, and to point out afterwards that he who thus knows passes on to light and so on. He therefore begins by saying, 'That person that is seen in the eye that is the Self.'

16. And on account of the statement of the way of him who has heard the Upanishads.

The person placed in the eye is the highest lord for the following reason also. From *s*ruti as well as sm*ri*ti we are acquainted with the way of him who has heard the Upanishads or the secret knowledge, i. e. who knows Brahman. That way, called the path of the gods, is described (Pra. Up. I, 10), 'Those who have sought the Self by penance, abstinence, faith, and knowledge gain by the northern path the sun. This is the home of the spirits, the immortal, free from fear, the highest. From thence they do not return;' and also (Bha. Gîtâ VIII, 24), 'Fire, light, the bright fortnight, the six months of the northern progress of the sun, on that way those who know Brahman go, when they have died, to Brahman.' Now that very same way is seen to be stated, in our text, for him who knows the person within the eye. For we read (*Kh*. Up. IV, 15, 5), 'Now whether people perform obsequies for him or no he goes to light;' and later on, 'From the sun (he goes) to the moon, from the moon to lightning. There is a person not human, he leads them to Brahman. This is the path of the gods, the path that leads to Brahman. Those who proceed on that path do not return to the life of man.' From this description of the way which is known to be the way of him who knows Brahman we ascertain that the person within the eye is Brahman.

17. (The person within the eye is the highest), not any other Self; on account of the non-permanency (of the other Selfs) and on account of the impossibility (of the qualities of the person in the eye being ascribed to the other Selfs).

To the assertion made in the pûrvapaksha that the person in the eye is either the reflected Self or the cognitional Self (the individual soul) or the Self of some deity the following answer is given.—No other Self such as, for instance, the reflected Self can be assumed here, on account of non-permanency.—The reflected Self, in the first place, does not permanently abide in the eye. For when some person approaches the eye the reflection of that person is seen in the eye, but when the person moves away the reflection is seen no longer. The passage 'That person within the eye' must, moreover, be held, on the ground of proximity, to intimate that the person seen in a man's own eye is the object of (that man's) devout meditation (and not the reflected image of his own person which he may see in the eye of another man). [Let, then, another man approach the devout man, and let the latter meditate on the image reflected in his own eye, but seen by the other man only. No, we reply, for] we have no right to make the (complicated) assumption that the devout man is, at the time of devotion, to bring close to his eye another man in order to produce a reflected image in his own eye. Scripture, moreover, (viz. *Kh.* Up. VIII, 9, 1, 'It (the reflected Self) perishes as soon as the body perishes,') declares the non-permanency of the reflected Self.—And, further, 'on account of impossibility' (the person in the eye cannot be the reflected Self). For immortality and the other qualities ascribed to the person in the eye are not to be perceived in the reflected Self.—Of the cognitional Self, in the second place, which is in general connexion with the whole body and all the senses, it can likewise not be said that it has its permanent station in the eye only. That, on the other hand, Brahman although all-pervading may, for the purpose of contemplation, be spoken of as connected with particular places such as the heart and the like, we have seen already. The cognitional Self shares (with the reflected Self) the impossibility of having the qualities of immortality and so on attributed to it. Although the cognitional Self is in reality not different from the highest Self, still there are fictitiously ascribed to it (adhyâropita) the effects of nescience, desire and works, viz. mortality and fear; so that neither immortality nor fearlessness belongs to it. The qualities of being the sa*m*yadvâma, &c. also cannot properly be ascribed to the cognitional Self, which is not distinguished by lordly power (ai*s*varya).—In the third place, although the Self of a deity (viz. the sun) has its station in the eye—according to the scriptural passage, 'He rests with his rays in him'—still Selfhood cannot be ascribed to the sun, on account of his externality (parâgrûpatva). Immortality, &c. also cannot be predicated of him, as Scripture speaks of his origin and his dissolution. For the (so-called) deathlessness of the gods only means their (comparatively) long existence. And their lordly power also is based on the highest Lord and does not naturally belong to them; as the mantra declares, 'From terror of it (Brahman) the wind blows, from terror the sun rises; from terror of it Agni and Indra, yea, Death runs as the fifth.'—Hence the person in the eye must be viewed as the highest Lord only. In the case of this explanation being adopted the mention (of the person in the eye) as something well known and established, which is contained in the words 'is seen' (in the phrase 'the person that is seen in the eye'), has to be taken as referring to (the mental perception founded on) the *s*âstra which belongs to those who know; and the glorification (of devout meditation) has to be understood as its purpose.

18. The internal ruler over the devas and so on (is Brahman), because the attributes of that (Brahman) are designated.

In B*ri*. Up. III, 7, 1 ff. we read, 'He who within rules this world and the other world and all beings,' and later on, 'He who dwells in the earth and within the earth, whom the earth does not know, whose body the earth is, who rules the earth within, he is thy Self, the ruler within, the immortal,' &c. The entire chapter (to sum up its contents) speaks of a being, called the antaryâmin (the internal ruler), who, dwelling within, rules with reference to the gods, the world, the Veda, the sacrifice, the beings, the Self.—Here now, owing to the unusualness of the term (antaryâmin), there arises a doubt whether it denotes the Self of some deity which presides over the gods and so on, or some Yogin who has acquired extraordinary powers, such as, for instance, the capability of making his body subtle, or the highest Self, or some other being. What alternative then does recommend itself?

As the term is an unknown one, the pûrvapakshin says, we must assume that the being denoted by it is also an unknown one, different from all those mentioned above.—Or else it may be said that, on the one hand, we have no right to assume something of an altogether indefinite character, and that, on the other hand, the term antaryâmin—which is derived from antaryamana (ruling within)—cannot be called altogether unknown, that therefore antaryâmin may be assumed to denote some god presiding over the earth, and so on. Similarly, we read (B*ri*. Up. III, 9, 16), 'He whose dwelling is the earth, whose sight is fire, whose mind is light,' &c. A god of that kind is capable of ruling the earth, and so on, dwelling within them, because he is endowed with the organs of action; rulership is therefore rightly ascribed to him.—Or else the rulership spoken of may belong to some Yogin whom his extraordinary powers enable to enter within all things.—The highest Self, on the other hand, cannot be meant, as it does not possess the organs of action (which are required for ruling).

To this we make the following reply.—The internal ruler, of whom Scripture speaks with reference to the gods, must be the highest Self, cannot be anything else.—Why so?—Because its qualities are designated in the passage under discussion. The universal rulership implied in the statement that, dwelling within, it rules the entire aggregate of created beings, inclusive of the gods, and so on, is an appropriate attribute of the highest Self, since omnipotence depends on (the omnipotent ruler) being the cause of all created things.—The qualities of Selfhood and immortality also, which are mentioned in the passage, 'He is thy Self, the ruler within, the immortal,' belong in their primary sense to the highest Self.—Further, the passage, 'He whom the earth does not know,' which declares that the internal ruler is not known by the earth-deity, shows him to be different from that deity; for the deity of the earth knows itself to be the earth.—The attributes 'unseen,' 'unheard,' also point to the highest Self, which is devoid of shape and other sensible qualities.—The objection that the highest Self is destitute of the organs of action, and hence cannot be a ruler, is without force, because organs of action may be ascribed to him owing to the organs of action of those whom he rules.—If it should be objected that [if we once admit an internal ruler in addition to the individual soul] we are driven to assume again another and another ruler ad infinitum; we reply that this is not the case, as actually there is no other ruler (but the highest Self[1]). The objection would be valid only in the case of a difference of rulers actually existing.—For all these reasons, the internal ruler is no other but the highest Self.

19. And (the internal ruler is) not that which the Sm*ri*ti assumes, (viz. the pradhâna,) on account of the statement of qualities not belonging to it.

Good so far, a Sâṅkhya opponent resumes. The attributes, however, of not being seen, &c., belong also to the pradhâna assumed by the Sâṅkhya-sm*ri*ti, which is acknowledged to be devoid of form and other sensible qualities. For their

[1] According to Scripture, Niraṅku*s*a*m* sarvaniyantritva*m* *s*rauta*m* na *k*a tâdri*s*e sarvaniyantari bhedo na *k*ânumâna*m* *s*rutibhâditam uttish*th*ati. Ânanda Giri. Or else, as Go. Ân. remarks, we may explain: as the highest Self is not really different from the individual soul. So also Bhâmatî: Na *k*ânavasthâ, na hi niyantrantara*m* tena niyamyate ki*m* tu yo *g*îvo niyantâ lokasiddha*h* sa paramâtmevopâdhyava*kkh*edakalpitabheda*h*.

Smr*i*ti says, 'Undiscoverable, unknowable, as if wholly in sleep.' (Manu I, 5). To this pradhâna also the attribute of rulership belongs, as it is the cause of all effects. Therefore the internal ruler may be understood to denote the pradhâna. The pradhâna has, indeed, been set aside already by the Sûtra I, 1, 5, but we bring it forward again, because we find that attributes belonging to it, such as not being seen and the like, are mentioned in Scripture.

To this argumentation the Sûtrakâra replies that the word 'internal ruler' cannot denote the pradhâna, because qualities not belonging to the latter are stated. For, although the pradhâna may be spoken of as not being seen, &c., it cannot be spoken of as seeing, since the Sâṅkhyas admit it to be non-intelligent. But the scriptural passage which forms the complement to the passage about the internal ruler (B*ri*. Up. III, 7, 23) says expressly, 'Unseen but seeing, unheard but hearing, unperceived but perceiving, unknown but knowing.'—And Selfhood also cannot belong to the pradhâna.

Well, then, if the term 'internal ruler' cannot be admitted to denote the pradhâna, because the latter is neither a Self nor seeing; let us suppose it to denote the embodied (individual) soul, which is intelligent, and therefore hears, sees, perceives, knows; which is internal (pratya*ñk*), and therefore of the nature of Self; and which is immortal, because it is able to enjoy the fruits of its good and evil actions. It is, moreover, a settled matter that the attributes of not being seen, &c., belong to the embodied soul, because the agent of an action, such as seeing, cannot at the same time be the object of the action. This is declared in scriptural passages also, as, for instance (B*ri*. Up. III, 4, 2), 'Thou couldst not see the seer of sight.' The individual soul is, moreover, capable of inwardly ruling the complex of the organs of action, as it is the enjoyer. Therefore the internal ruler is the embodied soul.—To this reasoning the following Sûtra replies.

20. And the embodied soul (also cannot be understood by the internal ruler), for both also (i. e. both

recensions of the B*ri*had Âra*n*yaka) speak of it as different (from the internal ruler).

The word 'not' (in the Sûtra) has to be supplied from the preceding Sûtra. Although the attributes of seeing, &c., belong to the individual soul, still as the soul is limited by its adjuncts, as the ether is by a jar, it is not capable of dwelling completely within the earth and the other beings mentioned, and to rule them. Moreover, the followers of both *s*âkhâs, i. e. the Kâ*n*vas as well as the Mâdhyandinas, speak in their texts of the individual soul as different from the internal ruler, viz. as constituting, like the earth, and so on, his abode and the object of his rule. The Kâ*n*vas read (B*ri*. Up. III, 7, 22), 'He who dwells in knowledge;' the Mâdhyandinas, 'He who dwells in the Self.' If the latter reading is adopted, the word 'Self' denotes the individual soul; if the former, the individual soul is denoted by the word 'knowledge;' for the individual soul consists of knowledge. It is therefore a settled matter that some being different from the individual soul, viz. the lord, is denoted by the term 'internal ruler.'—But how, it may be asked, is it possible that there should be within one body two seers, viz. the lord who rules internally and the individual soul different from him?—Why—we ask in return—should that be impossible?—Because, the opponent replies, it is contrary to scriptural passages, such as, 'There is no other seer but he,' &c., which deny that there is any seeing, hearing, perceiving, knowing Self, but the internal ruler under discussion.—May, we rejoin, that passage not have the purpose of denying the existence of another ruler?—No, the opponent replies, for there is no occasion for another ruler (and therefore no occasion for denying his existence), and the text does not contain any specification, (but merely denies the existence of any other seer in general.)

We therefore advance the following final refutation of the opponent's objection.—The declaration of the difference of the embodied Self and the internal ruler has its reason in the limiting adjunct, consisting of the organs of action, presented by Nescience, and is not absolutely true. For the

Self within is one only; two internal Selfs are not possible. But owing to its limiting adjunct the one Self is practically treated as if it were two; just as we make a distinction between the ether of the jar and the universal ether. Hence there is room for those scriptural passages which set forth the distinction of knower and object of knowledge, for perception and the other means of proof, for the intuitive knowledge of the apparent world, and for that part of Scripture which contains injunctions and prohibitions. In accordance with this, the scriptural passage, 'Where there is duality, as it were, there one sees another,' declares that the whole practical world exists only in the sphere of Nescience; while the subsequent passage, 'But when the Self only is all this, how should he see another?' declares that the practical world vanishes in the sphere of true knowledge.

21. That which possesses the attributes of invisibility and so on (is Brahman), on account of the declaration of attributes.

Scripture says, 'The higher knowledge is this by which the Indestructible is apprehended. That which cannot be seen nor seized, which is without origin and qualities, without eyes and ears, without hands and feet, the eternal, all-pervading, omnipresent, infinitesimal, that which is imperishable, that it is which the wise regard as the source of all beings' (Mu. Up. I, 1, 5; 6).—Here the doubt arises whether the source of all beings which is spoken of as characterised by invisibility, &c. be the pradhâna, or the embodied soul, or the highest Lord.

We must, the pûrvapakshin says, understand by the source of all beings the non-intelligent pradhâna because (in the passage immediately subsequent to the one quoted) only non-intelligent beings are mentioned as parallel instances. 'As the spider sends forth and draws in its thread, as plants grow on the earth, as from the living man hairs spring forth on the head and the body, thus everything arises here from the Indestructible.'—But, it may be objected, men and spiders which are here quoted as parallel instances are of intelligent nature.—No, the pûrvapakshin replies; for the intelligent being as such is not the source of the threads and the hair, but everybody knows that the non-intelligent body of the spider ruled by intelligence is the source of the threads; and so in the case of man also.—While, moreover, in the case of the preceding Sûtra, the pradhâna hypothesis could not be accepted, because, although some qualities mentioned, such as invisibility and so on, agreed with it, others such as being the seer and the like did not; we have here to do only with attributes such as invisibility which agree with the pradhâna, no attribute of a contrary nature being mentioned.—But the qualities mentioned in the complementary passage (Mu. Up. I, 1, 9), 'He who knows all and perceives all,' do not agree with the non-intelligent pradhâna; how, then, can the source of all beings be interpreted to mean the pradhâna?—To this the pûrvapakshin replies: The passage, 'The higher knowledge is that by which the Indestructible is apprehended, that which cannot be seen,' &c., points, by means of the term 'the Indestructible,' to the source of all beings characterised by invisibility and similar attributes. This same 'Indestructible' is again mentioned later on in the passage, 'It is higher than the high Imperishable.' Now that which in this latter passage is spoken of as higher than the Imperishable may possess the qualities of knowing and perceiving everything, while the pradhâna denoted by the term 'the Imperishable' is the source of all beings.—If, however, the word 'source' (yoni) be taken in the sense of operative cause, we may by 'the source of the beings' understand the embodied Self also, which, by means of merit and demerit, is the cause of the origin of the complex of things.

To this we make the following reply.—That which here is spoken of as the source of all beings, distinguished by such qualities as invisibility and so on, can be the highest Lord only, nothing else.—Whereupon is this conclusion founded?—On the statement of attributes. For the clause, 'He who is all-knowing, all-perceiving,' clearly states an attribute belonging to the highest Lord only, since the attributes of knowing all and perceiving all cannot be predicated either of the non-intelligent pradhâna or the embodied soul whose power of sight is narrowed by its limiting conditions. To the objection that the qualities of knowing and perceiving all are, in the passage under discussion, attributed to that which is higher than the source of all beings—which latter is denoted by the term 'the Imperishable'—not to the source itself, we reply that this explanation is inadmissible because the source of all beings, which—in the clause, 'From the Indestructible everything here arises'—is designated as the material cause of all created beings, is later on spoken of as all-knowing, and again as the cause of all created beings, viz. in the passage (I, 1, 9), 'From him who knows all and perceives all, whose brooding consists of knowledge, from him is born that Brahman, name, form, and food.' As therefore the Indestructible which forms the general topic of discussion is, owing to the identity of designation, recognised (as being referred to in the later passage also), we understand that it is the same Indestructible to which the attributes of knowing and perceiving all are ascribed.—We further maintain that also the passage, 'Higher than the high Imperishable,' does not refer to any being different from the imperishable source of all beings which is the general topic of discussion. We conclude this from the circumstance that the passage, 'He truly told that knowledge of Brahman through which he knows the imperishable true person,' (I, 2, 13; which passage leads on to the passage about that which is higher than the Imperishable,) merely declares that the imperishable source of all beings, distinguished by invisibility and the like—which formed the subject of the preceding chapter—will be discussed. The reason why that imperishable source is called higher than the high Imperishable, we shall explain under the next Sûtra.—Moreover, two kinds of knowledge are enjoined there (in the Upanishad), a lower and a higher one. Of the lower one it is said that it comprises the *Ri*g-veda and so on, and then the text continues, 'The higher knowledge is that by which the Indestructible is apprehended.' Here the Indestructible is declared to be the subject of the higher knowledge. If we now were to assume that the Indestructible distinguished by invisibility and like qualities is something different from the highest Lord, the knowledge referring to it would not be the higher one. For the distinction of lower and higher knowledge is made on account of the diversity of their results, the former leading to mere worldly exaltation, the latter to absolute bliss; and nobody would assume absolute bliss to result from the knowledge of the pradhâna.—Moreover, as on the view we are controverting the highest Self would be assumed to be something higher than the imperishable source of all beings, three kinds of knowledge would have to be acknowledged, while the text expressly speaks of two kinds only.—Further, the reference to the knowledge of everything being implied in the knowledge of one thing—which is contained in the passage (I, 1, 3), 'Sir, what is that through which if it is known everything else becomes known?'—is possible only if the allusion is to Brahman the Self of all, and not either to the pradhâna which comprises only what is non-intelligent or to the enjoyer viewed apart from the objects of enjoyment.—The text, moreover, by introducing the knowledge of Brahman as the chief subject—which it does in the passage (I, 1, 1), 'He told the knowledge of Brahman, the foundation of all knowledge, to his eldest son Atharvan'—and by afterwards declaring that out of the two kinds of knowledge, viz. the lower one and the higher one, the higher one leads to the comprehension of the Imperishable, shows that the knowledge of the Imperishable is the knowledge of Brahman. On the other hand, the term 'knowledge of Brahman' would become meaningless if that Imperishable which is to be comprehended by means of it were not Brahman. The lower knowledge of works which comprises the *Ri*g-veda, and so on, is mentioned preliminarily to the knowledge of Brahman for the mere purpose of glorifying the latter; as appears from the passages in which it (the lower knowledge) is spoken of slightingly, such as (I, 2, 7), 'But frail indeed are those boats, the sacrifices, the eighteen in which this lower ceremonial has been told. Fools who praise this as the highest good are subject again and again to old age and death.' After these slighting remarks the text declares that he who turns away from the lower knowledge is prepared for the highest one (I, 2, 12), 'Let a Brâhma*n*a after he has examined all these worlds which are gained by works acquire freedom from all desires. Nothing that is eternal (not made) can be gained by what is not eternal (made). Let him in order to understand this take fuel in his hand and approach a guru who is learned and dwells entirely in Brahman.'—The remark that, because the earth and other non-intelligent things are adduced as parallel instances, that also which is compared to them, viz. the source of all beings must be non-intelligent, is without foundation, since it is not necessary that two things of which one is compared to the other should be of absolutely the same nature. The things, moreover, to which the source of all beings is compared, viz. the earth and the like, are material, while nobody would assume the source of all beings to be material.—For all these reasons the source of all beings, which possesses the attributes of invisibility and so on, is the highest Lord.

22. The two others (i. e. the individual soul and the pradhâna) are not (the source of all beings) because there are stated distinctive attributes and difference.

The source of all beings is the highest Lord, not either of the two others, viz. the pradhâna and the individual soul, on account of the following reason also. In the first place, the text distinguishes the source of all beings from the embodied soul, as something of a different nature; compare the passage (II, 1, 2), 'That heavenly person is without body, he is both without and within, not produced, without breath and without mind, pure.' The distinctive attributes mentioned here, such as being of a heavenly nature, and so on, can in no way belong to the individual soul, which erroneously considers itself to be limited by name and form as presented by Nescience, and erroneously imputes their attributes to itself. Therefore the passage manifestly refers to the Person which is the subject of all the Upanishads.—In the second place, the source of all beings which forms the general topic is represented in the text as something different from the pradhâna, viz. in the passage, 'Higher than the high Imperishable.' Here the term 'Imperishable' means that undeveloped entity which represents the seminal potentiality of names and forms, contains the fine parts of the material elements, abides in the Lord, forms his limiting adjunct, and being itself no effect is high in comparison to all effects; the whole phrase, 'Higher than the high Imperishable,' which expresses a difference then clearly shows that the highest Self is meant here.—We do not on that account assume an independent entity called pradhâna and say that the source of all beings is stated separately therefrom; but if a pradhâna is to be assumed at all (in agreement with the common opinion) and if being assumed it is assumed of such a nature as not to be opposed to the statements of Scripture, viz. as the subtle cause of all beings denoted by the terms 'the Undeveloped' and so on, we have no objection to such an assumption, and declare that, on account of the separate statement therefrom, i. e. from that pradhâna, 'the source of all beings' must mean the highest Lord.—A further argument in favour of the same conclusion is supplied by the next Sûtra.

23. And on account of its form being mentioned.

Subsequently to the passage, 'Higher than the high Imperishable,' we meet (in the passage, 'From him is born breath,' &c.) with a description of the creation of all things, from breath down to earth, and then with a statement of the form of this same source of beings as consisting of all created beings, 'Fire is his head, his eyes the sun and the moon, the quarters his ears, his speech the Vedas disclosed, the wind his breath, his heart the universe; from his feet came the earth; he is indeed the inner Self of all things.' This statement of form can refer only to the highest Lord, and not either to the embodied soul, which, on account of its small power, cannot be the cause of all effects, or to the pradhâna, which cannot be the inner Self of all beings. We therefore conclude that the source of all beings is the highest Lord, not either of the other two.—But wherefrom do you conclude that the quoted declaration of form refers to the source of all beings?—From the general topic, we reply. The word 'he' (in the clause, 'He is indeed the inner Self of all things') connects the passage with the general topic. As the source of all beings constitutes the general topic, the whole passage, from 'From him is born breath,' up to, 'He is the inner Self of all beings,' refers to that same source. Similarly, when in ordinary conversation a certain teacher forms the general topic of the talk, the phrase, 'Study under him; he knows the Veda and the Vedâṅgas thoroughly,' as a matter of course, refers to that same teacher.—But how can a bodily form be ascribed to the source of all beings which is characterised by invisibility and similar attributes?—The statement as to its nature, we reply, is made for the purpose of showing that the source of all beings is the Self of all beings, not of showing that it is of a bodily nature. The case is analogous to such passages as, 'I am food, I am food, I am the eater of food' (Taitt. Up. III, 10, 6).—Others, however, are of opinion[1] that the statement quoted does not refer to the source of all beings, because that to which it refers is spoken of as something produced. For, on the one hand, the immediately preceding passage ('From him is born health, mind, and all organs of sense, ether, air, light, water, and the earth, the support of all') speaks of the aggregate of beings from air down to earth as something produced, and, on the other

[1] V*ri*ttik*ri*dvyâkhyâm dûshayati, Go. Ân.; ekade*s*ina*m* dûshayati, Ânanda Giri; tad etat paramatenâkshepasamâdhânâbhyâ*m* vyâkhyâya svamatena vyâ*k*ash*t*e, puna*h* *s*abdo*pi pûrvasmâd vi*s*esha*m* dyotayann asyesh*t*atâ*m* sû*k*ayati, Bhâmatî.—The statement of the two former commentators must be understood to mean—in agreement with the Bhâmatî—that *S*aṅkara is now going to refute the preceding explanation by the statement of his own view. Thus Go. Ân. later on explains 'asmin pakshe' by 'svapakshe.'

hand, a passage met with later on ('From him comes Agni, the sun being his fuel,' up to 'All herbs and juices') expresses itself to the same purpose. How then should all at once, in the midst of these two passages (which refer to the creation). a statement be made about the nature of the source of all beings?—The attribute of being the Self of all beings (which above was said to be mentioned in the passage about the creation, 'Fire is his head,' &c., is not mentioned there but) is stated only later on in a passage subsequent to that which refers to the creation, viz. 'The Person is all this, sacrifice,' &c. (II, 1, 10).—Now, we see that *s*ruti as well as sm*ri*ti speaks of the birth of Pra*g*âpati, whose body is this threefold world; compare *Ri*g-veda Sa*m*h. X, 121, 1, 'Hira*n*yagarbha arose in the beginning; he was the one born Lord of things existing. He established the earth and this sky; to what God shall we offer our oblation?' where the expression 'arose' means 'he was born.' And in sm*ri*ti we read, 'He is the first embodied one, he is called the Person; as the primal creator of the beings Brahman was evolved in the beginning.' This Person which is (not the original Brahman but) an effect (like other created beings) may be called the internal Self of all beings (as it is called in II, 1, 4), because in the form of the Self of breath it abides in the Selfs of all beings.—On this latter explanation (according to which the passage, 'Fire is his head,' &c., does not describe the nature of the highest Lord, and can therefore not be referred to in the Sûtra) the declaration as to the Lord being the 'nature' of all which is contained in the passage, 'The Person is all this, sacrifice,' &c., must be taken as the reason for establishing the highest Lord, (i. e. as the passage which, according to the Sûtra, proves that the source of all beings is the highest Lord [1].)

[1] The question is to what passage the 'rûpopanyâsât' of the Sûtra refers.—According to the opinion set forth first it refers to Mu. Up. II, 1, 4 ff.—But, according to the second view, II, 1, 4 to II, 1, 9, cannot refer to the source of all beings, i. e. the highest Self, because that entire passage describes the creation, the inner Self of which is not the highest Self but Pra*g*âpati, i. e. the Hira*n*yagarbha or Sûtrâtman of the later Vedânta, who is himself an

24. Vaiѕvânara (is the highest Lord) on account of the distinction qualifying the common terms (Vaiѕvânara and Self).

(In *Kh.* Up. V, 11 ff.) a discussion begins with the words, 'What is our Self, what is Brahman?' and is carried on in the passage, 'You know at present that Vaiѕvânara Self, tell us that;' after that it is declared with reference to Heaven, sun, air, ether, water, and earth, that they are connected with the qualities of having good light, &c., and, in order to disparage devout meditation on them singly, that they stand to the Vaiѕvânara in the relation of being his head, &c., merely; and then finally (V, 18) it is said, 'But he who meditates on the Vaiѕvânara Self as measured by a span, as abhivimâna [1], he eats food in all worlds, in all beings, in all Selfs. Of that Vaiѕvânara Self the head is Sute*g*as (having good light), the eye Viѕvarûpa (multiform), the breath P*ri*thagvartman (moving in various courses), the trunk Bahula (full), the bladder Rayi (wealth), the feet the earth, the chest the altar, the hairs the grass on the altar, the heart the Gârhapatya fire, the mind the Anvâhârya fire, the mouth the Âhavanîya fire.'—Here the doubt arises whether by the term 'Vaiѕvânara' we have to understand the gastric fire, or the elemental fire, or the divinity presiding over the latter, or the embodied soul, or the highest Lord.—But what, it may be asked, gives rise to this doubt?—The circumstance, we reply, of 'Vaiѕvânara' being employed as a common term for the gastric fire, the elemental fire, and the divinity of the latter, while 'Self' is a term applying to the embodied soul as well as to the highest Lord. Hence the doubt arises which meaning of the term is to be accepted and which to be set aside.

Which, then, is the alternative to be embraced?—Vaiѕvânara, the pûrvapakshin maintains, is the gastric fire, because we meet, in some passages, with the term used in

'effect,' and who is called the inner Self, because he is the breath of life (prâ*n*a) in everything.—Hence the Sûtra must be connected with another passage, and that passage is found in II, 1, 10, where it is said that the Person (i. e. the highest Self) is all this, &c.

[1] About which term see later on.

that special sense; so, for instance (Bri. Up. V, 9), 'Agni Vaisvânara is the fire within man by which the food that is eaten is cooked.'—Or else the term may denote fire in general, as we see it used in that sense also; so, for instance (Rig-veda Samh. X, 88, 12), 'For the whole world the gods have made the Agni Vaisvânara a sign of the days.' Or, in the third place, the word may denote that divinity whose body is fire. For passages in which the term has that sense are likewise met with; compare, for instance, Rig-veda Samh. I, 98, 1, 'May we be in the favour of Vaisvânara; for he is the king of the beings, giving pleasure, of ready grace;' this and similar passages properly applying to a divinity endowed with power and similar qualities. Perhaps it will be urged against the preceding explanations, that, as the word Vaisvânara is used in co-ordination with the term 'Self,' and as the term 'Self' alone is used in the introductory passage ('What is our Self, what is Brahman?'), Vaisvânara has to be understood in a modified sense, so as to be in harmony with the term Self. Well, then, the pûrvapakshin rejoins, let us suppose that Vaisvânara is the embodied Self which, as being an enjoyer, is in close vicinity to the Vaisvânara fire,[1] (i. e. the fire within the body,) and with which the qualification expressed by the term, 'Measured by a span,' well agrees, since it is restricted by its limiting condition (viz. the body and so on).—In any case it is evident that the term Vaisvânara does not denote the highest Lord.

To this we make the following reply.—The word Vaisvânara denotes the highest Self, on account of the distinction qualifying the two general terms.—Although the term 'Self,' as well as the term 'Vaisvânara,' has various meanings—the latter term denoting three beings while the former denotes two—yet we observe a distinction from which we conclude that both terms can here denote the highest Lord only; viz. in the passage, 'Of that Vaisvânara Self the head is Sutegas,' &c. For it is clear that that passage refers to the highest Lord in so far as he is distinguished by having heaven, and so on, for his head and limbs, and in so far as

[1] Sârîre lakshanayâ vaisvânarasabdopapattim âha tasyeti. Ân. Gi.

he has entered into a different state (viz. into the state of being the Self of the threefold world); represents him, in fact, for the purpose of meditation, as the internal Self of everything. As such the absolute Self may be represented, because it is the cause of everything; for as the cause virtually contains all the states belonging to its effects, the heavenly world, and so on, may be spoken of as the members of the highest Self.—Moreover, the result which Scripture declares to abide in all worlds—viz. in the passage, 'He eats food in all worlds, in all beings, in all Selfs'—is possible only if we take the term Vai*s*vânara to denote the highest Self.—The same remark applies to the declaration that all the sins are burned of him who has that knowledge, 'Thus all his sins are burned,' &c. (*Kh*. Up. V, 24, 3).—Moreover, we meet at the beginning of the chapter with the words 'Self' and 'Brahman;' viz. in the passage, 'What is our Self, what is Brahman?' Now these are marks of Brahman, and indicate the highest Lord only. Hence he only can be meant by the term Vai*s*vânara.

25. (And) because that which is stated by Sm*ri*ti (i. e. the shape of the highest Lord as described by Sm*ri*ti) is an inference (i. e. an indicatory mark from which we infer the meaning of *S*ruti).

The highest Lord only is Vai*s*vânara, for that reason also that Sm*ri*ti ascribes to the highest Lord only a shape consisting of the threefold world, the fire constituting his mouth, the heavenly world his head, &c. So, for instance, in the following passage, 'He whose mouth is fire, whose head the heavenly world, whose navel the ether, whose feet the earth, whose eye the sun, whose ears the regions, reverence to him the Self of the world.' The shape described here in Sm*ri*ti allows us to infer a *S*ruti passage on which the Sm*ri*ti rests, and thus constitutes an inference, i. e. a sign indicatory of the word 'Vai*s*vânara' denoting the highest Lord. For, although the quoted Sm*ri*ti passage contains a glorification[1],

[1] And as such might be said not to require a basis for its statements.

still even a glorification in the form in which it there appears is not possible, unless it has a Vedic passage to rest on.—Other Smriti passages also may be quoted in connexion with this Sûtra, so, for instance, the following one, 'He whose head the wise declare to be the heavenly world, whose navel the ether, whose eyes sun and moon, whose ears the regions, and whose feet the earth, he is the inscrutable leader of all beings.'

26. If it be maintained that (Vaisvânara is) not (the highest Lord) on account of the term (viz. Vaisvânara, having a settled different meaning), &c., and on account of his abiding within (which is a characteristic of the gastric fire); (we say) no, on account of the perception (of the highest Lord), being taught thus (viz. in the gastric fire), and on account of the impossibility (of the heavenly world, &c. being the head, &c. of the gastric fire), and because they (the Vâgasaneyins) read of him (viz. the Vaisvânara) as man (which term cannot apply to the gastric fire).

Here the following objection is raised.—Vaisvânara cannot be the highest Lord, on account of the term, &c., and on account of the abiding within. The term, viz. the term Vaisvânara, cannot be applied to the highest Lord, because the settled use of language assigns to it a different sense. Thus, also, with regard to the term Agni (fire) in the passage (*S*at. Brâ. X, 6, 1, 11), 'He is the Agni Vaisvânara.' The word '&c.' (in the Sûtra) hints at the fiction concerning the three sacred fires, the gârhapatya being represented as the heart, and so on, of the Vaisvânara Self (*Kh*. Up. V, 18, 2 [1]).—Moreover, the passage, 'Therefore the first food which a man may take is in the place of homa' (*Kh*. Up. V, 19, 1), contains a glorification of (Vaisvânara) being the abode of the oblation to Prâna [2]. For these reasons we have to under-

[1] Na *k*a gârhapatyâdihridayâditâ brahmana*h* sambhavinî. Bhâmatî.

[2] Na *k*a prânâhutyadhikaranatâ *nyatra ga*th*arâgner yugyate. Bhâmatî.

stand by Vaisvânara the gastric fire.—Moreover, Scripture speaks of the Vaisvânara as abiding within, 'He knows him abiding within man;' which again applies to the gastric fire only.—With reference to the averment that on account of the specifications contained in the passage, 'His head is Sutegas,' &c., Vaisvânara is to be explained as the highest Self, we (the pûrvapakshin) ask: How do you reach the decision that those specifications, although agreeing with both interpretations, must be assumed to refer to the highest Lord only, and not to the gastric fire?—Or else we may assume that the passage speaks of the elemental fire which abides within and without; for that that fire is also connected with the heavenly world, and so on, we understand from the mantra, 'He who with his light has extended himself over earth and heaven, the two halves of the world, and the atmosphere' (*Rig*-veda Sa*m*h. X, 88, 3).—Or else the attribute of having the heavenly world, and so on, for its members may, on account of its power, be attributed to that divinity which has the elemental fire for its body.—Therefore Vaisvânara is not the highest Lord.

To all this we reply as follows.—Your assertions are unfounded, 'because there is taught the perception in this manner.' The reasons (adduced in the former part of the Sûtra), viz. the term, and so on, are not sufficient to make us abandon the interpretation according to which Vaisvânara is the highest Lord.—Why?—On account of perception being taught in this manner, i. e. without the gastric fire being set aside. For the passages quoted teach the perception of the highest Lord in the gastric fire, analogously to such passages as 'Let a man meditate on the mind as Brahman' (*Kh*. Up. III, 18, 1).—Or else they teach that the object of perception is the highest Lord, in so far as he has the gastric fire called Vaisvânara for his limiting condition; analogously to such passages as 'He who consists of mind, whose body is breath, whose form is light' (*Kh*. Up. III, 14, 2[1]). If it were the aim of the passages about the Vais-

[1] According to the former explanation the gastric fire is to be looked on as the outward manifestation (pratika) of the highest Lord; according to the latter as his limiting condition.

vânara to make statements not concerning the highest Lord, but merely concerning the gastric fire, there would be no possibility of specifications such as contained in the passage 'His head is Sute*g*as,' &c. That also on the assumption of Vai*s*vânara being either the divinity of fire or the elemental fire no room is to be found for the said specifications, we shall show under the following Sûtra.—Moreover, if the mere gastric fire were meant, there would be room only for a declaration that it abides within man, not that it is man. But, as a matter of fact, the Vâ*g*asaneyins speak of him—in their sacred text—as man, 'This Agni Vai*s*vânara is man; he who knows this Agni Vai*s*vânara as man-like, as abiding within man,' &c. (*S*at. Brâ. X, 6, 1, 11). The highest Lord, on the other hand, who is the Self of everything, may be spoken of as well as man, as abiding within man.—Those who, in the latter part of the Sûtra, read 'man-like' (purushavidham) instead of 'man' (purusham), wish to express the following meaning: If Vai*s*vânara were assumed to be the gastric fire only, he might be spoken of as abiding within man indeed, but not as man-like. But the Vâ*g*asaneyins do speak of him as man-like, 'He who knows him as man-like, as abiding within man.'—The meaning of the term man-like is to be concluded from the context, whence it will be seen that, with reference to nature, it means that the highest Lord has the heaven for his head, &c., and is based on the earth; and with reference to man, that he forms the head, &c., and is based on the chin (of the devout worshipper[1]).

27. For the same reasons (the Vai*s*vânara) cannot be the divinity (of fire), or the element (of fire).

The averment that the fanciful attribution of members contained in the passage 'His head is Sute*g*as,' &c. may apply to the elemental fire also which from the mantras is seen to be connected with the heavenly world, &c., or else to the divinity whose body is fire, on account of its power, is refuted by the following remark: For the reasons

[1] I. e. that he may be fancifully identified with the head and so on of the devout worshipper.

already stated Vaisvânara is neither the divinity nor the element. For to the elemental fire which is mere heat and light the heavenly world and so on cannot properly be ascribed as head and so on, because an effect cannot be the Self of another effect.—Again, the heavenly world cannot be ascribed as head, &c. to the divinity of fire, in spite of the power of the latter; for, on the one hand, it is not a cause (but a mere effect), and on the other hand its power depends on the highest Lord. Against all these interpretations there lies moreover the objection founded on the inapplicability of the term 'Self.'

28. *G*aimini (declares that there is) no contradiction even on the assumption of a direct (worship of the highest Lord as Vaisvânara).

Above (Sûtra 26) it has been said that Vaisvânara is the highest Lord, to be meditated upon as having the gastric fire either for his outward manifestation or for his limiting condition; which interpretation was accepted in deference to the circumstance that he is spoken of as abiding within—and so on.—The teacher *G*aimini however is of opinion that it is not necessary to have recourse to the assumption of an outward manifestation or limiting condition, and that there is no objection to refer the passage about Vaisvânara to the direct worship of the highest Lord.—But, if you reject the interpretation based on the gastric fire, you place yourself in opposition to the statement that Vaisvânara abides within, and to the reasons founded on the term, &c. (Sû. 26).—To this we reply that we in no way place ourselves in opposition to the statement that Vaisvânara abides within. For the passage, 'He knows him as man-like, as abiding within man,' does not by any means refer to the gastric fire, the latter being neither the general topic of discussion nor having been mentioned by name before.—What then does it refer to?—It refers to that which forms the subject of discussion, viz. that similarity to man (of the highest Self) which is fancifully found in the members of man from the upper part of the head down to the chin; the text therefore says, 'He knows him as man-like, as abiding within man,' just as we say of a branch that it abides within the tree[1].—Or else we may adopt another interpretation and say that after the highest Self has been represented as having the likeness to man as a limiting condition, with regard to nature as well as to man, the passage last quoted ('He knows him as abiding within man') speaks of the same highest Self as the mere witness (sâkshin; i. e. as the pure Self, non-related to the limiting conditions).—The consideration of the context having thus shown that the highest Self has to be resorted to for the interpretation of the passage, the term 'Vai*s*vânara' must denote the highest Self in some way or other. The word 'Vi*s*vânara' is to be explained either as 'he who is all and man (i. e. the individual soul),' or 'he to whom souls belong' (in so far as he is their maker or ruler), and thus denotes the highest Self which is the Self of all. And the form 'Vai*s*vânara' has the same meaning as 'Vi*s*vânara,' the taddhita-suffix, by which the former word is derived from the latter, not changing the meaning; just as in the case of râkshasa (derived from rakshas), and vâyasa (derived from vayas).—The word 'Agni' also may denote the highest Self if we adopt the etymology agni=agra*n*î, i. e. he who leads in front.—As the Gârhapatya-fire finally, and as the abode of the oblation to breath the highest Self may be represented because it is the Self of all.

But, if it is assumed that Vai*s*vânara denotes the highest Self, how can Scripture declare that he is measured by a span?—On the explanation of this difficulty we now enter.

29. On account of the manifestation, so Â*s*marathya opines.

The circumstance of the highest Lord who transcends all measure being spoken of as measured by a span has for its reason 'manifestation.' The highest Lord manifests

[1] Whereby we mean not that it is inside the tree, but that it forms a part of the tree.—The Vai*s*vânara Self is identified with the different members of the body, and these members abide within, i. e. form parts of the body.

himself as measured by a span, i.e. he specially manifests himself for the benefit of his worshippers in some special places, such as the heart and the like, where he may be perceived. Hence, according to the opinion of the teacher Âsmarathya, the scriptural passage which speaks of him who is measured by a span may refer to the highest Lord.

30. On account of remembrance; so Bâdari opines.

Or else the highest Lord may be called 'measured by a span' because he is remembered by means of the mind which is seated in the heart which is measured by a span. Similarly, barley-corns which are measured by means of prasthas are themselves called prasthas. It must be admitted that barley-grains themselves have a certain size which is merely rendered manifest through their being connected with a prastha measure; while the highest Lord himself does not possess a size to be rendered manifest by his connexion with the heart. Still the remembrance (of the Lord by means of the mind) may be accepted as offering a certain foundation for the Sruti passage concerning him who is measured by a span.—Or else[1] the Sûtra may be interpreted to mean that the Lord, although not really measured by a span, is to be remembered (meditated upon) as being of the measure of a span; whereby the passage is furnished with an appropriate sense.—Thus the passage about him who is measured by a span may, according to the opinion of the teacher Bâdari, be referred to the highest Lord, on account of remembrance.

31. On the ground of imaginative identification (the highest Lord may be called prâdesamâtra), Gaimini thinks; for thus (Scripture) declares.

Or else the passage about him who is measured by a span may be considered to rest on imaginative combination.—Why?—Because the passage of the Vâgasaneyi-

[1] Parimânasya hridayadvârâropitasya smaryamâne katham âropo vishayavishayitvena bhedâd ity âsankya vyâkhyântaram âha prâdeseti. Ânanda Giri.

brâhma*n*a which treats of the same topic identifies heaven, earth, and so on—which are the members of Vai*s*vânara viewed as the Self of the threefold world—with certain parts of the human frame, viz. the parts comprised between the upper part of the head and the chin, and thus declares the imaginative identity of Vai*s*vânara with something whose measure is a span. There we read, 'The Gods indeed reached him, knowing him as measured by a span as it were. Now I will declare them (his members) to you so as to identify him (the Vai*s*vânara) with that whose measure is a span; thus he said. Pointing to the upper part of the head he said: This is what stands above (i. e. the heavenly world) as Vai*s*vânara (i. e. the head of Vai*s*vânara [1]). Pointing to the eyes he said: This is he with good light (i. e. the sun) as Vai*s*vânara (i. e. the eye of V.). Pointing to the nose he said: This is he who moves on manifold paths (i. e. the air) as Vai*s*vânara (i. e. the breath of V.). Pointing to the space (ether) within his mouth he said: This is the full one (i. e. the ether) as Vai*s*vânara. Pointing to the saliva within his mouth he said: This is wealth as Vai*s*vânara (i. e. the water in the bladder of V.). Pointing to the chin he said: This is the base as Vai*s*vânara (i. e. the feet of V.).'—Although in the Vâ*g*asaneyi-brâhma*n*a the heaven is denoted as that which has the attribute of standing above and the sun as that which has the attribute of good light, while in the *Kh*ândogya the heaven is spoken of as having good light and the sun as being multiform; still this difference does not interfere (with the unity of the vidyâ) [2], because both texts equally use the term 'measured by a span,' and because all *s*âkhâs intimate the same.—The above explanation of the term 'measured by a span,' which rests on imaginative identification, the teacher *G*aimini considers the most appropriate one.

32. Moreover they (the *G*âbâlas) speak of him

[1] Atra sarvatra vai*s*vânara*s*abdas tadangapara*h*. Go. Ân.

[2] Which unity entitles us to use the passage from the *S*at. Brâ. for the explanation of the passage from the *Kh*. Up.

(the highest Lord) in that (i.e. the interstice between the top of the head and the chin which is measured by a span).

Moreover the *G*âbâlas speak in their text of the highest Lord as being in the interstice between the top of the head and the chin. 'The unevolved infinite Self abides in the avimukta (i.e. the non-released soul). Where does that avimukta abide? It abides in the Vara*n*â and the Nâsî, in the middle. What is that Vara*n*â, what is that Nâsî?' The text thereupon etymologises the term Vara*n*â as that which wards off (vârayati) all evil done by the senses, and the term Nâsî as that which destroys (nâ*s*ayati) all evil done by the senses; and then continues, 'And what is its place?—The place where the eyebrows and the nose join. That is the joining place of the heavenly world (represented by the upper part of the head) and of the other (i.e. the earthly world represented by the chin).' (*G*âbâla Up. I.)—Thus it appears that the scriptural statement which ascribes to the highest Lord the measure of a span is appropriate. That the highest Lord is called abhivimâna refers to his being the inward Self of all. As such he is directly measured, i.e. known by all animate beings. Or else the word may be explained as 'he who is near everywhere—as the inward Self—and who at the same time is measureless' (as being infinite). Or else it may denote the highest Lord as him who, as the cause of the world, measures it out, i.e. creates it. By all this it is proved that Vai*s*vânara is the highest Lord.

THIRD PÂDA.

Reverence to the highest Self!

1. The abode of heaven, earth, and so on (is Brahman), on account of the term 'own,' i.e. Self.

We read (Mu. Up. II, 2, 5), 'He in whom the heaven, the earth, and the sky are woven, the mind also with all the vital airs, know him alone as the Self, and leave off other words! He is the bridge of the Immortal.'—Here the doubt arises whether the abode which is intimated by the statement of the heaven and so on being woven in it is the highest Brahman or something else.

The pûrvapakshin maintains that the abode is something else, on account of the expression, 'It is the bridge of the Immortal.' For, he says, it is known from every-day experience that a bridge presupposes some further bank to which it leads, while it is impossible to assume something further beyond the highest Brahman, which in Scripture is called 'endless, without a further shore' (B*ri*. Up. II, 4, 12). Now if the abode is supposed to be something different from Brahman, it must be supposed to be either the pradhâna known from Sm*ri*ti, which, as being the (general) cause, may be called the (general) abode; or the air known from *S*ruti, of which it is said (B*ri*. Up. III, 7, 2, 'Air is that thread, O Gautama. By air as by a thread, O Gautama, this world and the other world and all beings are strung together'), that it supports all things; or else the embodied soul which, as being the enjoyer, may be considered as an abode with reference to the objects of its fruition.

Against this view we argue with the sûtrakâra as follows:—'Of the world consisting of heaven, earth, and so on, which in the quoted passage is spoken of as woven (upon something), the highest Brahman must be the abode.'—Why?—On account of the word 'own,' i. e. on account of the word 'Self.' For we meet with the word 'Self' in the passage, 'Know him alone as the Self.' This term 'Self' is thoroughly appropriate only if we understand the highest Self and not anything else.—(To propound another interpretation of the phrase 'svasabdât' employed in the Sûtra.) Sometimes also Brahman is spoken of in *S*ruti as the general abode by its own terms (i.e. by terms properly designating Brahman), as, for instance (*Kh*. Up. VI, 8, 4), 'All these creatures, my dear, have their root in the being, their abode in the being, their rest in the being[1].'—(Or else we have to explain 'svasabdena' as follows), In the passages preceding and following the passage under discussion Brahman is glorified with its own names[2]; cp. Mu. Up. II, 1, 10, 'The Person is all this, sacrifice, penance, Brahman, the highest Immortal,' and II, 2, 11, 'That immortal Brahman is before, is behind, Brahman is to the right and left.' Here, on account of mention being made of an abode and that which abides, and on account of the co-ordination expressed in the passage, 'Brahman is all' (Mu. Up. II, 2, 11), a suspicion might arise that Brahman is of a manifold variegated nature, just as in the case of a tree consisting of different parts we distinguish branches, stem, and root. In order to remove this suspicion the text declares (in the passage under discussion), 'Know him alone as the Self.' The sense of which is: The Self is not to be known as manifold, qualified by the universe of effects; you are rather to dissolve by true knowledge the universe of effects, which is the mere product of Nescience, and to know that one Self, which is the general abode, as uniform. Just as when somebody says, 'Bring that on which Devadatta sits,' the person addressed brings the chair only (the abode of Devadatta), not Devadatta himself; so the passage, 'Know him alone as the Self,' teaches that the object to be known is the one uniform Self which constitutes the general abode. Similarly another scriptural passage reproves him who believes in the unreal world of effects,

[1] From passages of which nature we may infer that in the passage under discussion also the 'abode' is Brahman.

[2] From which circumstance we may conclude that the passage under discussion also refers to Brahman.

'From death to death goes he who sees any difference here' (Ka. Up. II, 4, 11). The statement of co-ordination made in the clause 'All is Brahman' aims at dissolving (the wrong conception of the reality of) the world, and not in any way at intimating that Brahman is multiform in nature[1]; for the uniformity (of Brahman's nature) is expressly stated in other passages such as the following one, 'As a mass of salt has neither inside nor outside, but is altogether a mass of taste, thus indeed has that Self neither inside nor outside, but is altogether a mass of knowledge' (B*ri*. Up. IV, 5, 13).—For all these reasons the abode of heaven, earth, &c. is the highest Brahman.—Against the objection that on account of the text speaking of a 'bridge,' and a bridge requiring a further bank, we have to understand by the abode of heaven and earth something different from Brahman, we remark that the word 'bridge' is meant to intimate only that that which is called a bridge supports, not that it has a further bank. We need not assume by any means that the bridge meant is like an ordinary bridge made of clay and wood. For as the word setu (bridge) is derived from the root si, which means 'to bind,' the idea of holding together, supporting is rather implied in it than the idea of being connected with something beyond (a further bank).

According to the opinion of another (commentator) the word 'bridge' does not glorify the abode of heaven, earth, &c., but rather the knowledge of the Self which is glorified in the preceding clause, 'Know him alone as the Self,' and the abandonment of speech advised in the clause, 'leave off other words;' to them, as being the means of obtaining immortality, the expression 'the bridge of the immortal' applies[2]. On that account we have to set aside the assertion that, on account of the word 'bridge,' something different from Brahman is to be understood by the abode of heaven, earth, and so on.

---

[1] Yat sarvam avidyâropita*m* tat sarva*m* paramârthato brahma na tu yad brahma tat sarvam ity artha*h*. Bhâmatî.

[2] So that the passage would have to be translated, 'That, viz. knowledge, &c. is the bridge of the Immortal.'

2. And on account of its being designated as that to which the Released have to resort.

By the abode of heaven, earth, and so on, we have to understand the highest Brahman for that reason also that we find it denoted as that to which the Released have to resort.—The conception that the body and other things contained in the sphere of the Not-self are our Self, constitutes Nescience; from it there spring desires with regard to whatever promotes the well-being of the body and so on, and aversions with regard to whatever tends to injure it; there further arise fear and confusion when we observe anything threatening to destroy it. All this constitutes an endless series of the most manifold evils with which we all are acquainted. Regarding those on the other hand who have freed themselves from the stains of Nescience desire aversion and so on, it is said that they have to resort to that, viz. the abode of heaven, earth, &c. which forms the topic of discussion. For the text, after having said, 'The fetter of the heart is broken, all doubts are solved, all his works perish when He has been beheld who is the higher and the lower' (Mu. Up. II, 2, 8), later on remarks, 'The wise man freed from name and form goes to the divine Person who is greater than the great' (Mu. Up. III, 2, 8). That Brahman is that which is to be resorted to by the released, is known from other scriptural passages, such as 'When all desires which once entered his heart are undone then does the mortal become immortal, then he obtains Brahman' (B*ri*. Up. IV, 4, 7). Of the pradhâna and similar entities, on the other hand, it is not known from any source that they are to be resorted to by the released. Moreover, the text (in the passage, 'Know him alone as the Self and leave off other words') declares that the knowledge of the abode of heaven and earth, &c. is connected with the leaving off of all speech; a condition which, according to another scriptural passage, attaches to (the knowledge of) Brahman; cp. B*ri*. Up. IV, 4, 21, 'Let a wise Brâhma*n*a, after he has discovered him, practise wisdom. Let him not seek after many words, for that is mere weariness of the tongue.'—For that reason also the abode of heaven, earth, and so on, is the highest Brahman.

3. Not (i. e. the abode of heaven, earth, &c. cannot be) that which is inferred, (i. e. the pradhâna), on account of the terms not denoting it.

While there has been shown a special reason in favour of Brahman (being the abode), there is no such special reason in favour of anything else. Hence he (the sûtrakâra) says that that which is inferred, i. e. the pradhâna assumed by the Sâṅkhya-sm*ri*ti, is not to be accepted as the abode of heaven, earth, &c.—Why?—On account of the terms not denoting it. For the sacred text does not contain any term intimating the non-intelligent pradhâna, on the ground of which we might understand the latter to be the general cause or abode; while such terms as 'he who perceives all and knows all' (Mu. Up. I, 1, 9) intimate an intelligent being opposed to the pradhâna in nature.—For the same reason the air also cannot be accepted as the abode of heaven, earth, and so on.

4. (Nor) also the individual soul (prâ*n*abh*ri*t).

Although to the cognitional (individual) Self the qualities of Selfhood and intelligence do belong, still omniscience and similar qualities do not belong to it as its knowledge is limited by its adjuncts; thus the individual soul also cannot be accepted as the abode of heaven, earth, &c., for the same reason, i. e. on account of the terms not denoting it.—Moreover, the attribute of forming the abode of heaven, earth, and so on, cannot properly be given to the individual soul because the latter is limited by certain adjuncts and therefore non-pervading (not omnipresent)[1].—The special enunciation (of the individual soul) is caused by what follows[2].—The individual soul is not to be

[1] Bhogyasya bhokt*ris*eshatvât tasyâyatanatvam uktam â*s*aṅkyâha na *k*eti, *g*îvasyâd*r*ish*t*advârâ dyubhvâdinimittatve-pi na sâkshât tadâyatanatvam aupâdhikatvenâvibhutvâd ity artha*h*. Ânanda Giri.

[2] It would not have been requisite to introduce a special Sûtra

accepted as the abode of heaven, earth, &c. for the following reason also.

5. On account of the declaration of difference.

The passage 'Know him alone as the Self' moreover implies a declaration of difference, viz. of the difference of the object of knowledge and the knower. Here the individual soul as being that which is desirous of release is the knower, and consequently Brahman, which is denoted by the word 'self' and represented as the object of knowledge, is understood to be the abode of heaven, earth, and so on. —For the following reason also the individual soul cannot be accepted as the abode of heaven, earth, &c.

6. On account of the subject-matter.

The highest Self constitutes the subject-matter (of the entire chapter), as we see from the passage 'Sir, what is that through which, when it is known, everything else becomes known?' (Mu. Up. I, 1, 3), in which the knowledge of everything is declared to be dependent on the knowledge of one thing. For all this (i.e. the entire world) becomes known if Brahman the Self of all is known, not if only the individual soul is known.—Another reason against the individual soul follows.

7. And on account of the two conditions of standing and eating (of which the former is characteristic of the highest Lord, the latter of the individual soul).

With reference to that which is the abode of heaven, earth, and so on, the text says, 'Two birds, inseparable friends,' &c. (Mu. Up. III, 1, 1). This passage describes the two states of mere standing, i.e. mere presence, and of eating, the clause, 'One of them eats the sweet fruit,' referring to the eating, i.e. the fruition of the results of works,

for the individual soul—which, like the air, is already excluded by the preceding Sûtra—if it were not for the new argument brought forward in the following Sûtra which applies to the individual soul only.

and the clause, 'The other one looks on without eating,' describing the condition of mere inactive presence. The two states described, viz. of mere presence on the one hand and of enjoyment on the other hand, show that the Lord and the individual soul are referred to. Now there is room for this statement which represents the Lord as separate from the individual soul, only if the passage about the abode of heaven and earth likewise refers to the Lord; for in that case only there exists a continuity of topic. On any other supposition the second passage would contain a statement about something not connected with the general topic, and would therefore be entirely uncalled for.—But, it may be objected, on your interpretation also the second passage makes an uncalled-for statement, viz. in so far as it represents the individual soul as separate from the Lord.—Not so, we reply. It is nowhere the purpose of Scripture to make statements regarding the individual soul. From ordinary experience the individual soul, which in the different individual bodies is joined to the internal organs and other limiting adjuncts, is known to every one as agent and enjoyer, and we therefore must not assume that it is that which Scripture aims at setting forth. The Lord, on the other hand, about whom ordinary experience tells us nothing, is to be considered as the special topic of all scriptural passages, and we therefore cannot assume that any passage should refer to him merely casually[1].—

[1] If the individual soul were meant by the abode of heaven, earth, &c., the statement regarding Î*s*vara made in the passage about the two birds would be altogether abrupt, and on that ground objectionable. The same difficulty does not present itself with regard to the abrupt mention of the individual soul which is well known to everybody, and to which therefore casual allusions may be made.—I subjoin Ânanda Giri's commentary on the entire passage: *G*îvasyopâdhyaikyenâvivakshitatvât tad*g*ñâne-pi sarva*g*ñânasiddhes tasyâyatanatvâdyabhâve hetvantara*m* vâ*k*yam ity â*s*ankya sûtre*n*a pariharati kuta*s*ketyâdinâ. Tad vyâ*k*ash*t*e dyubhvâdîti. Nirde*s*am eva dar*s*ayati tayor iti. Vibhaktyartham âha tâbhyâ*m* *k*eti. Sthitye*s*varasyâdanâ*g* *g*îvasa*m*grahe-pi katham î*s*varasyaiva vi*s*vâyatanatva*m* tadâha yadîti. Î*s*varasyâyanatvenâprak*ri*tatve *g*îvap*ri*-

That the mantra 'two birds,' &c. speaks of the Lord and the individual soul we have already shown under I, 2, 11.—And if, according to the interpretation given in the Paiṅgi-upanishad (and quoted under I, 2, 11), the verse is understood to refer to the internal organ (sattva) and the individual soul (not to the individual soul and the Lord), even then there is no contradiction (between that interpretation and our present averment that the individual soul is not the abode of heaven and earth).—How so?—Here (i.e. in the present Sûtra and the Sûtras immediately preceding) it is denied that the individual soul which, owing to its imagined connexion with the internal organ and other limiting adjuncts, has a separate existence in separate bodies—its division being analogous to the division of universal space into limited spaces such as the spaces within jars and the like—is that which is called the abode of heaven and earth. That same soul, on the other hand, which exists in all bodies, if considered apart from the limiting adjuncts, is nothing else but the highest Self. Just as the spaces within jars, if considered apart from their limiting conditions, are merged in universal space, so the individual soul also is incontestably that which is denoted as the abode of heaven and earth, since it (the soul) cannot really be separate from the highest Self. That it is not the abode of heaven and earth, is therefore said of the individual soul in so far only as it imagines itself to be connected with the internal organ and so on. Hence it follows that the highest Self is the abode of heaven, earth, and so on.—The same conclusion has already been arrived at under I, 2, 21; for in the passage concerning the source of all beings (which passage is discussed under the Sûtra quoted) we meet with the clause, 'In which heaven and

thakkathanânupapattir ity uktam eva vyatirekadvârâha anyatheti. *G*îvasyâyatanatvenâprak*ri*tatve tulyânupapattir iti *s*aṅkate nanviti. Tasyaikyârtha*m* lokasiddhasyânuvâdatvân naivam ity âha neti. *G*îvasyâpûrvatvâbhâvenâpratipâdyatvam eva praka*t*ayati kshetra*gñ*o hîti. Î*s*varasyâpi lokavâdisiddhatvâd apratipâdyatety â*s*aṅkyâha î*s*varas tv iti.

earth and the sky are woven.' In the present adhikara*n*a the subject is resumed for the sake of further elucidation.

8. The bhûman (is Brahman), as the instruction about it is additional to that about the state of deep sleep (i. e. the vital air which remains awake even in the state of deep sleep).

We read (*Kh*. Up. VII, 23; 24), 'That which is much (bhûman) we must desire to understand.—Sir, I desire to understand it.—Where one sees nothing else, hears nothing else, understands nothing else, that is what is much (bhûman). Where one sees something else, hears something else, understands something else, that is the Little.'—Here the doubt arises whether that which is much is the vital air (prâ*n*a) or the highest Self.—Whence the doubt?—The word 'bhûman,' taken by itself, means the state of being much, according to its derivation as taught by Pâ*n*ini, VI, 4, 158. Hence there is felt the want of a specification showing what constitutes the Self of that muchness. Here there presents itself at first the approximate passage, 'The vital air is more than hope' (*Kh*. Up. VII, 15, 1), from which we may conclude that the vital air is bhûman.—On the other hand, we meet at the beginning of the chapter, where the general topic is stated, with the following passage, 'I have heard from men like you that he who knows the Self overcomes grief. I am in grief. Do, Sir, help me over this grief of mine;' from which passage it would appear that the bhûman is the highest Self.—Hence there arises a doubt as to which of the two alternatives is to be embraced, and which is to be set aside.

The pûrvapakshin maintains that the bhûman is the vital air, since there is found no further series of questions and answers as to what is more. For while we meet with a series of questions and answers (such as, 'Sir, is there something which is more than a name?'—'Speech is more than name.'—'Is there something which is more than speech?'—'Mind is more than speech'), which extends from name up to vital air, we do not meet with a similar question and answer as to what might be more than vital air (such as, 'Is there something which is more than vital air?'—'Such and such a thing is more than vital air'). The text rather at first declares at length (in the passage, 'The vital air is more than hope,' &c.) that the vital air is more than all the members of the series from name up to hope; it then acknowledges him who knows the vital air to be an ativâdin, i. e. one who makes a statement surpassing the preceding statements (in the passage, 'Thou art an ativâdin. He may say I am an ativâdin; he need not deny it'); and it thereupon (in the passage, 'But he in reality is an ativâdin who declares something beyond by means of the True'[1]),—not leaving off, but rather continuing to refer to the quality of an ativâdin which is founded on the vital air,—proceeds, by means of the series beginning with the True, to lead over to the bhûman; so that we conclude the meaning to be that the vital air is the bhûman.—But, if the bhûman is interpreted to mean the vital air, how have we to explain the passage in which the bhûman is characterised, 'Where one sees nothing else?' &c.—As, the pûrvapakshin replies, in the state of deep sleep we observe a cessation of all activity, such as seeing, &c., on the part of the organs merged in the vital air, the vital air itself may be characterised by a passage such as, 'Where one sees nothing else.' Similarly, another scriptural passage (Pra. Up. IV, 2; 3) describes at first (in the words, 'He does not hear, he does not see,' &c.) the state of deep sleep as characterised by the cessation of the activity of all bodily organs, and then by declaring that in that state the vital air, with its five modifications, remains awake ('The fires of the prâ*n*as are awake in that town'), shows the vital air to occupy the principal position in the state of deep sleep.—That passage also, which speaks of the bliss of the bhûman ('The bhûman is bliss,' *Kh*. Up. VII, 23), can be reconciled with our explanation, because Pra. Up. IV, 6 declares bliss to attach to the state of deep sleep ('Then that god sees no dreams and at that time that happiness arises in his body').—Again, the statement, 'The bhûman is immortality' (*Kh*. Up. VII, 24, 1), may

[1] As might be the primâ facie conclusion from the particle 'but' introducing the sentence 'but he in reality,' &c.

likewise refer to the vital air; for another scriptural passage says, 'Prâ*n*a is immortality' (Kau. Up. III, 2).—But how can the view according to which the bhûman is the vital air be reconciled with the fact that in the beginning of the chapter the knowledge of the Self is represented as the general topic ('He who knows the Self overcomes grief,' &c.)? —By the Self there referred to, the pûrvapakshin replies, nothing else is meant but the vital air. For the passage, 'The vital air is father, the vital air is mother, the vital air is brother, the vital air is sister, the vital air is teacher, the vital air is Brâhma*n*a' (*Kh.* Up. VII, 15, 1), represents the vital air as the Self of everything. As, moreover, the passage, 'As the spokes of a wheel rest in the nave, so all this rests in prâ*n*a,' declares the prâ*n*a to be the Self of all—by means of a comparison with the spokes and the nave of a wheel—the prâ*n*a may be conceived under the form of bhûman, i. e. plenitude.—Bhûman, therefore, means the vital air.

To this we make the following reply.—Bhûman can mean the highest Self only, not the vital air.—Why?—'On account of information being given about it, subsequent to bliss.' The word 'bliss' (samprasâda) means the state of deep sleep, as may be concluded, firstly, from the etymology of the word ('In it he, i.e. man, is altogether pleased—samprasîdati')—and, secondly, from the fact of samprasâda being mentioned in the B*ri*hadâra*n*yaka together with the state of dream and the waking state. And as in the state of deep sleep the vital air remains awake, the word 'samprasâda' is employed in the Sûtra to denote the vital air; so that the Sûtra means, 'on account of information being given about the bhûman, subsequently to (the information given about) the vital air.' If the bhûman were the vital air itself, it would be a strange proceeding to make statements about the bhûman in addition to the statements about the vital air. For in the preceding passages also we do not meet, for instance, with a statement about name subsequent to the previous statement about name (i. e. the text does not say 'name is more than name'), but after something has been said about name, a new statement is made about speech, which is something different from name (i. e. the text says, 'Speech is more than name'), and so on up to the statement about vital air, each subsequent statement referring to something other than the topic of the preceding one. We therefore conclude that the bhûman also, the statement about which follows on the statement about the vital air, is something other than the vital air.—But—it may be objected—we meet here neither with a question, such as, 'Is there something more than vital air?' nor with an answer, such as, 'That and that is more than vital air.' How, then, can it be said that the information about the bhûman is given subsequently to the information about the vital air?—Moreover, we see that the circumstance of being an ativâdin, which is exclusively connected with the vital air, is referred to in the subsequent passage (viz. 'But in reality he is an ativâdin who makes a statement surpassing (the preceding statements) by means of the True'). There is thus no information additional to the information about the vital air.—To this objection we reply that it is impossible to maintain that the passage last quoted merely continues the discussion of the quality of being an ativâdin, as connected with the knowledge of the vital air; since the clause, 'He who makes a statement surpassing, &c. by means of the True,' states a specification.—But, the objector resumes, this very statement of a specification may be explained as referring to the vital air. If you ask how, we refer you to an analogous case. If somebody says, 'This Agnihotrin speaks the truth,' the meaning is not that the quality of being an Agnihotrin depends on speaking the truth; that quality rather depends on the (regular performance of the) agnihotra only, and speaking the truth is mentioned merely as a special attribute of that special Agnihotrin. So our passage also ('But in reality he is an ativâdin who makes a statement, &c. by means of the True') does not intimate that the quality of being an ativâdin depends on speaking the truth, but merely expresses that speaking the truth is a special attribute of him who knows the vital air; while the quality of being an ativâdin must be considered to depend on the knowledge of the vital air.—This objection we rebut by the remark that it involves an abandonment of the direct meaning of the sacred text. For from the text, as it stands, we understand that the quality of being an ativâdin depends on speaking the truth; the sense being: An ativâdin is he who is an ativâdin by means of the True. The passage does not in any way contain a eulogisation of the knowledge of the vital air. It could be connected with the latter only on the ground of general subject-matter (prakara*n*a)[1]; which would involve an abandonment of the direct meaning of the text in favour of prakara*n*a[2].—Moreover, the particle but ('But in reality he is,' &c.), whose purport is to separate (what follows) from the subject-matter of what precedes, would not agree (with the prâ*n*a explanation). The following passage also, 'But we must desire to know the True' (VII, 16), which presupposes a new effort, shows that a new topic is going to be entered upon.—For these reasons we have to consider the statement about the ativâdin in the same light as we should consider the remark—made in a conversation which previously had turned on the praise of those who study one Veda—that he who studies the four Vedas is a great Brâhma*n*a; a remark which we should understand to be laudatory of persons different from those who study one Veda, i.e. of those who study all the four Vedas. Nor is there any reason to assume that a new topic can be introduced in the form of question and answer only; for that the matter propounded forms a new topic is sufficiently clear from the circumstance that no connexion can be established between it and the preceding topic. The succession of topics in the chapter under discussion is as follows: Nârada at first listens to the instruction which Sanatkumâra gives him about various matters, the last of which is Prâ*n*a, and then becomes silent. Thereupon Sanatkumâra explains to him spontaneously (without being

[1] It being maintained that the passage referred to is to be viewed in connexion with the general subject-matter of the preceding part of the chapter.

[2] And would thus involve a violation of a fundamental principle of the Mîmâ*m*sâ.

asked) that the quality of being an ativâdin, if merely based on the knowledge of the vital air—which knowledge has for its object an unreal product,—is devoid of substance, and that he only is an ativâdin who is such by means of the True. By the term 'the True' there is meant the highest Brahman; for Brahman is the Real, and it is called the 'True' in another scriptural passage also, viz. Taitt. Up. II, 1, 'The True, knowledge, infinite is Brahman.' Nârada, thus enlightened, starts a new line of enquiry ('Might I, Sir, become an ativâdin by the True?') and Sanatkumâra then leads him, by a series of instrumental steps, beginning with understanding, up to the knowledge of bhûman. We therefrom conclude that the bhûman is that very True whose explanation had been promised in addition to the (knowledge of the) vital air. We thus see that the instruction about the bhûman is additional to the instruction about the vital air, and bhûman must therefore mean the highest Self, which is different from the vital air. With this interpretation the initial statement, according to which the enquiry into the Self forms the general subject-matter, agrees perfectly well. The assumption, on the other hand (made by the pûrvapakshin), that by the Self we have here to understand the vital air is indefensible. For, in the first place, Self-hood does not belong to the vital air in any non-figurative sense. In the second place, cessation of grief cannot take place apart from the knowledge of the highest Self; for, as another scriptural passage declares, 'There is no other path to go' (*S*vet. Up. VI, 15). Moreover, after we have read at the outset, 'Do, Sir, lead me over to the other side of grief' (*Kh*. Up. VII, 1, 3), we meet with the following concluding words (VII, 26, 2), 'To him, after his faults had been rubbed out, the venerable Sanatkumâra showed the other side of darkness.' The term 'darkness' here denotes Nescience, the cause of grief, and so on.—Moreover, if the instruction terminated with the vital air, it would not be said of the latter that it rests on something else. But the brâhma*n*a (*Kh*. Up. VII, 26, 1) does say, 'The vital air springs from the Self.' Nor can it be objected against this last argument that the concluding part of the chapter may refer to the highest Self, while, all the same, the bhûman (mentioned in an earlier part of the chapter) may be the vital air. For, from the passage (VII, 24, 1), ('Sir, in what does the bhûman rest? In its own greatness,' &c.), it appears that the bhûman forms the continuous topic up to the end of the chapter.—The quality of being the bhûman—which quality is plenitude—agrees, moreover, best with the highest Self, which is the cause of everything.

9. And on account of the agreement of the attributes (mentioned in the text).

The attributes, moreover, which the sacred text ascribes to the bhûman agree well with the highest Self. The passage, 'Where one sees nothing else, hears nothing else, understands nothing else, that is the bhûman,' gives us to understand that in the bhûman the ordinary activities of seeing and so on are absent; and that this is characteristic of the highest Self, we know from another scriptural passage, viz. 'But when the Self only is all this, how should he see another?' &c. (B*ri*. Up. IV, 5, 15). What is said about the absence of the activities of seeing and so on in the state of deep sleep (Pra. Up. IV, 2) is said with the intention of declaring the non-attachedness of the Self, not of describing the nature of the prâ*n*a; for the highest Self (not the vital air) is the topic of that passage. The bliss also of which Scripture speaks as connected with that state is mentioned only in order to show that bliss constitutes the nature of the Self. For Scripture says (B*ri*. Up. IV, 3, 32), 'This is his highest bliss. All other creatures live on a small portion of that bliss.'—The passage under discussion also ('The bhûman is bliss. There is no bliss in that which is little (limited). The bhûman only is bliss') by denying the reality of bliss on the part of whatever is perishable shows that Brahman only is bliss as bhûman, i. e. in its plenitude.—Again, the passage, 'The bhûman is immortality,' shows that the highest cause is meant; for the immortality of all effected things is a merely relative one, and another scriptural passage says that 'whatever is different from that (Brahman) is perishable' (B*ri*. Up. III, 4, 2).—Similarly, the qualities of being the True, and of resting in its own greatness, and of being omnipresent, and of being the Self of everything which the text mentions (as belonging to the bhûman) can belong to the highest Self only, not to anything else.—By all this it is proved that the bhûman is the highest Self.

10. The Imperishable (is Brahman) on account of (its) supporting (all things) up to ether.

We read (B*ri*. Up. III, 8, 7; 8), 'In what then is the ether woven, like warp and woof?—He said: O Gârgî, the Brâhma*n*as call this the akshara (the Imperishable). It is neither coarse nor fine,' and so on.—Here the doubt arises whether the word 'akshara' means 'syllable' or 'the highest Lord.'

The pûrvapakshin maintains that the word 'akshara' means 'syllable' merely, because it has, in such terms as akshara-samâmnâya, the meaning of 'syllable;' because we have no right to disregard the settled meaning of a word; and because another scriptural passage also ('The syllable Om is all this,' *Kh*. Up. II, 23, 4) declares a syllable, represented as the object of devotion, to be the Self of all.

To this we reply that the highest Self only is denoted by the word 'akshara.'—Why?—Because it (the akshara) is said to support the entire aggregate of effects, from earth up to ether. For the sacred text declares at first that the entire aggregate of effects beginning with earth and differentiated by threefold time is based on ether, in which it is 'woven like warp and woof;' leads then (by means of the question, 'In what then is the ether woven, like warp and woof?') over to the akshara, and, finally, concludes with the words, 'In that akshara then, O Gârgî, the ether is woven, like warp and woof.'—Now the attribute of supporting everything up to ether cannot be ascribed to any being but Brahman. The text (quoted from the *Kh*. Up.) says indeed that the syllable Om is all this, but that statement is to be understood as a mere glorification of the syllable Om considered as a means to obtain Brahman.—Therefore we take akshara to mean either 'the Imperishable' or 'that which pervades;' on the ground of either of which explanations it must be identified with the highest Brahman.

But—our opponent resumes—while we must admit that the above reasoning holds good so far that the circumstance of the akshara supporting all things up to ether is to be accepted as a proof of all effects depending on a cause, we point out that it may be employed by those also who declare the pradhâna to be the general cause. How then does the previous argumentation specially establish Brahman (to the exclusion of the pradhâna)?—The reply to this is given in the next Sûtra.

11. This (supporting can), on account of the command (attributed to the Imperishable, be the work of the highest Lord only).

The supporting of all things up to ether is the work of the highest Lord only.—Why?—On account of the command.—For the sacred text speaks of a command ('By the command of that akshara, O Gârgî, sun and moon stand apart!' III, 8, 9), and command can be the work of the highest Lord only, not of the non-intelligent pradhâna. For non-intelligent causes such as clay and the like are not capable of command, with reference to their effects, such as jars and the like.

12. And on account of (Scripture) separating (the akshara) from that whose nature is different (from Brahman).

Also on account of the reason stated in this Sûtra Brahman only is to be considered as the Imperishable, and the supporting of all things up to ether is to be looked upon as the work of Brahman only, not of anything else. The meaning of the Sûtra is as follows. Whatever things other than Brahman might possibly be thought to be denoted by the term 'akshara,' from the nature of all those things Scripture separates the akshara spoken of as the support of all things up to ether. The scriptural passage alluded to is III, 8, 11, 'That akshara, O Gârgî, is unseen but seeing, unheard but hearing, unperceived but perceiving, unknown but knowing.' Here the designation of being unseen, &c. agrees indeed with the pradhâna also, but not so the designation of seeing, &c., as the pradhâna is non-intelligent.—Nor can the word akshara denote the embodied soul with its limiting conditions, for the passage following on the one quoted declares that there is nothing different from the Self ('there is nothing that sees but it, nothing that hears but it, nothing that perceives but it, nothing that knows but it'); and, moreover, limiting conditions are expressly denied (of the akshara) in the passage, 'It is without eyes, without ears, without speech, without mind,' &c. (III, 8, 8). An embodied soul without limiting conditions does not exist[1].—It is therefore certain beyond doubt that the Imperishable is nothing else but the highest Brahman.

13. On account of his being designated as the object of sight (the highest Self is meant, and) the same (is meant in the passage speaking of the meditation on the highest person by means of the syllable Om).

(In Pra. Up. V, 2) the general topic of discussion is set forth in the words, 'O Satyakâmâ, the syllable Om is the highest and also the other Brahman; therefore he who knows it arrives by the same means at one of the two.' The text then goes on, 'Again, he who meditates with this syllable Om of three mâtrâs on the highest Person,' &c.—Here the doubt presents itself, whether the object of meditation referred to in the latter passage is the highest Brahman or the other Brahman; a doubt based on the former passage, according to which both are under discussion.

The pûrvapakshin maintains that the other, i.e. the lower

[1] A remark directed against the possible attempt to explain the passage last quoted as referring to the embodied soul.

Brahman, is referred to, because the text promises only a reward limited by a certain locality for him who knows it. For, as the highest Brahman is omnipresent, it would be inappropriate to assume that he who knows it obtains a fruit limited by a certain locality. The objection that, if the lower Brahman were understood, there would be no room for the qualification, 'the highest person,' is not valid, because the vital principle (prâ*n*a) may be called 'higher' with reference to the body[1].

To this we make the following reply: What is here taught as the object of meditation is the highest Brahman only. —Why?—On account of its being spoken of as the object of sight. For the person to be meditated upon is, in a complementary passage, spoken of as the object of the act of seeing, 'He sees the person dwelling in the castle (of the body; purusham puri*s*ayam), higher than that one who is of the shape of the individual soul, and who is himself higher (than the senses and their objects).' Now, of an act of meditation an unreal thing also can be the object, as, for instance, the merely imaginary object of a wish. But of the act of seeing, real things only are the objects, as we know from experience; we therefore conclude, that in the passage last quoted, the highest (only real) Self which corresponds to the mental act of complete intuition[2] is spoken of as the object of sight. This same highest Self we recognise in the passage under discussion as the object of meditation, in consequence of the term, 'the highest person.'—But—an objection will be raised—as the object of meditation we have the highest person, and as the object of sight the person higher than that one who is himself higher, &c.; how, then, are we to know that those two are identical?—The two passages, we

---

[1] Pi*nd*a*h* sthûlo deha*h*, prâ*n*a*h* sûtrâtmâ. Ânanda Giri.—The lower Brahman (hira*n*yagarbha on sûtrâtman) is the vital principle (prâ*n*a) in all creatures.

[2] Sa*m*yagdar*s*ana, i.e. complete seeing or intuition; the same term which in other places—where it is not requisite to insist on the idea of 'seeing' in contradistinction from 'reflecting' or 'meditating'—is rendered by perfect knowledge.

reply, have in common the terms 'highest' (or 'higher,' para) and 'person.' And it must not by any means be supposed that the term *g*îvaghana[1] refers to that highest person which, considered as the object of meditation, had previously been introduced as the general topic. For the consequence of that supposition would be that that highest person which is the object of sight would be different from that highest person which is represented as the object of meditation. We rather have to explain the word *g*îvaghana as 'He whose shape[2] is characterised by the *g*îvas;' so that what is really meant by that term is that limited condition of the highest Self which is owing to its adjuncts, and manifests itself in the form of *g*îvas, i. e. individual souls; a condition analogous to the limitation of salt (in general) by means of the mass of a particular lump of salt. That limited condition of the Self may itself be called 'higher,' if viewed with regard to the senses and their objects.

Another (commentator) says that we have to understand by the word '*g*îvaghana' the world of Brahman spoken of in the preceding sentence ('by the Sâman verses he is led up to the world of Brahman'), and again in the following sentence (v. 7), which may be called 'higher,' because it is higher than the other worlds. That world of Brahman may be called *g*îvaghana because all individual souls (*g*îva) with their organs of action may be viewed as comprised (saṅghâta = ghana) within Hira*n*yagarbha, who is the Self of all organs, and dwells in the Brahma-world. We thus understand that he who is higher than that *g*îvaghana, i. e. the highest Self, which constitutes the object of sight, also constitutes the object of meditation. The qualification, moreover, expressed in the term 'the highest person' is in its place only if we understand the highest Self to be meant. For the name, 'the highest person,' can be given only to the highest Self, higher than which there is nothing. So another scriptural passage also says, 'Higher than the person there is nothing—this is the goal, the highest road.' Hence the

[1] Translated above by 'of the shape of the individual soul.'

[2] Pâ*n*ini III, 3, 77, 'mûrtta*m* ghana*h*.'

sacred text, which at first distinguishes between the higher and the lower Brahman ('the syllable Om is the higher and the lower Brahman'), and afterwards speaks of the highest Person to be meditated upon by means of the syllable Om, gives us to understand that the highest Person is nothing else but the highest Brahman. That the highest Self constitutes the object of meditation, is moreover intimated by the passage declaring that release from evil is the fruit (of meditation), 'As a snake is freed from its skin, so is he freed from evil.'—With reference to the objection that a fruit confined to a certain place is not an appropriate reward for him who meditates on the highest Self, we finally remark that the objection is removed, if we understand the passage to refer to emancipation by degrees. He who meditates on the highest Self by means of the syllable Om, as consisting of three mâtrâs, obtains for his (first) reward the world of Brahman, and after that, gradually, complete intuition.

14. The small (ether) (is Brahman) on account of the subsequent (arguments).

We read (*Kh.* Up. VIII, 1, 1), 'There is this city of Brahman, and in it the palace, the small lotus, and in it that small ether. Now what exists within that small ether that is to be sought for, that is to be understood,' &c.—Here the doubt arises whether the small ether within the small lotus of the heart of which Scripture speaks, is the elemental ether, or the individual soul (vi*gñ*ânâtman), or the highest Self. This doubt is caused by the words 'ether' and 'city of Brahman.' For the word 'ether,' in the first place, is known to be used in the sense of elemental ether as well as of highest Brahman. Hence the doubt whether the small ether of the text be the elemental ether or the highest ether, i.e. Brahman. In explanation of the expression 'city of Brahman,' in the second place, it might be said either that the individual soul is here called Brahman and the body Brahman's city, or else that the city of Brahman means the city of the highest Brahman. Here (i.e. in consequence of this latter doubt) a further doubt arises as to the nature of the small ether, according as the individual soul or the highest Self is understood by the Lord of the city.

The pûrvapakshin maintains that by the small ether we have to understand the elemental ether, since the latter meaning is the conventional one of the word âkâsa. The elemental ether is here called small with reference to its small abode (the heart).—In the passage, 'As large as this ether is, so large is that ether within the heart,' it is represented as constituting at the same time the two terms of a comparison, because it is possible to make a distinction between the outer and the inner ether[1]; and it is said that 'heaven and earth are contained within it,' because the whole ether, in so far as it is space, is one[2].—Or else, the pûrvapakshin continues, the 'small one' may be taken to mean the individual soul, on account of the term, 'the city of Brahman.' The body is here called the city of Brahman because it is the abode of the individual soul; for it is acquired by means of the actions of the soul. On this interpretation we must assume that the individual soul is here called Brahman metaphorically. The highest Brahman cannot be meant, because it is not connected with the body as its lord. The lord of the city, i. e. the soul, is represented as dwelling in one spot of the city (viz. the heart), just as a real king resides in one spot of his residence. Moreover, the mind (manas) constitutes the limiting adjunct of the individual soul, and the mind chiefly abides in the heart; hence the individual soul only can be spoken of as dwelling in the heart. Further, the individual soul only can be spoken of as small, since it is (elsewhere; Svet. Up. V, 8) compared in size to the point of a goad. That it is compared (in the passage under discussion) to the ether must be understood to intimate its non-difference from Brahman.—

[1] So that the interpretation of the pûrvapakshin cannot be objected to on the ground of its involving the comparison of a thing to itself.

[2] So that no objection can be raised on the ground that heaven and earth cannot be contained in the small ether of the heart.

Nor does the scriptural passage say that the 'small' one is to be sought for and to be understood, since in the clause, 'That which is within that,' &c., it is represented as a mere distinguishing attribute of something else [1].

To all this we make the following reply:—The small ether can mean the highest Lord only, not either the elemental ether or the individual soul.—Why?—On account of the subsequent reasons, i.e. on account of the reasons implied in the complementary passage. For there, the text declares at first, with reference to the small ether, which is enjoined as the object of sight, 'If they should say to him,' &c.; thereupon follows an objection, 'What is there that deserves to be sought for or that is to be understood?' and thereon a final decisive statement, 'Then he should say: As large as this ether is, so large is that ether within the heart. Both heaven and earth are contained within it.' Here the teacher, availing himself of the comparison of the ether within the heart with the known (universal) ether, precludes the conception that the ether within the heart is small—which conception is based on the statement as to the smallness of the lotus, i.e. the heart—and thereby precludes the possibility of our understanding by the term 'the small ether,' the elemental ether. For, although the ordinary use of language gives to the word 'ether' the sense of elemental ether, here the elemental ether cannot be thought of, because it cannot possibly be compared with itself.—But, has it not been stated above, that the ether, although one only, may be compared with itself, in consequence of an assumed difference between the outer and the inner ether?—That explanation, we reply, is impossible; for we cannot admit that a comparison of a thing with itself may be based upon a merely imaginary difference. And even if we admitted

[1] Viz. of that which is within it. Ânanda Giri proposes two explanations: na *k*eti, paravi*s*esha*n*atvenety atra paro daharâkâ*s*a upâdânât tasminn iti saptamyanta-ta*kkh*abdasyeti *s*esha*h*. Yadvâ para*s*abdo *'*nta*h*sthavastuvishayas tadvi*s*esha*n*atvena tasminn iti daharâkâ*s*asyokter ity artha*h*. Ta*kkh*abdasya samnik*ri*sh*t*ânvaya-yoge viprak*ri*sh*t*ânvayasya *g*aghanyatvâd âkâ*s*ântargata*m* dhyeyam iti bhâva*h*.

the possibility of such a comparison, the extent of the outer ether could never be ascribed to the limited inner ether. Should it be said that to the highest Lord also the extent of the (outer) ether cannot be ascribed, since another scriptural passage declares that he is greater than ether (*S*a. Brâ. X, 6, 3, 2), we invalidate this objection by the remark, that the passage (comparing the inner ether with the outer ether) has the purport of discarding the idea of smallness (of the inner ether), which is prima facie established by the smallness of the lotus of the heart in which it is contained, and has not the purport of establishing a certain extent (of the inner ether). If the passage aimed at both, a split of the sentence[1] would result.—Nor, if we allowed the assumptive difference of the inner and the outer ether, would it be possible to represent that limited portion of the ether which is enclosed in the lotus of the heart, as containing within itself heaven, earth, and so on. Nor can we reconcile with the nature of the elemental ether the qualities of Self-hood, freeness from sin, and so on, (which are ascribed to the 'small' ether) in the following passage, 'It is the Self free from sin, free from old age, from death and grief, from hunger and thirst, of true desires, of true purposes.'—Although the term 'Self' (occurring in the passage quoted) may apply to the individual soul, yet other reasons exclude all idea of the individual soul being meant (by the small ether). For it would be impossible to dissociate from the individual soul, which is restricted by limiting conditions and elsewhere compared to the point of a goad, the attribute of smallness attaching to it, on account of its being enclosed in the lotus of the heart.—Let it then be assumed—our opponent remarks—that the qualities of all-pervadingness, &c. are ascribed to the individual soul with the intention of intimating its non-difference from Brahman.—Well, we reply, if you suppose that the small ether is called all-pervading because it is one with Brahman, our own suppo-

[1] A vâkyabheda—split of the sentence—takes place according to the Mîmâ*m*sâ when one and the same sentence contains two new statements which are different.

sition, viz. that the all-pervadingness spoken of is directly predicated of Brahman itself, is the much more simple one.—Concerning the assertion that the term 'city of Brahman' can only be understood, on the assumption that the individual soul dwells, like a king, in one particular spot of the city of which it is the Lord, we remark that the term is more properly interpreted to mean 'the body in so far as it is the city of the highest Brahman;' which interpretation enables us to take the term 'Brahman' in its primary sense[1]. The highest Brahman also is connected with the body, for the latter constitutes an abode for the perception of Brahman[2]. Other scriptural passages also express the same meaning, so, for instance, Pra. Up. V, 5, 'He sees the highest person dwelling in the city' (purusha = puri*s*aya), &c., and B*ri*. Up. II, 5, 18, 'This person (purusha) is in all cities (bodies) the dweller within the city (puri*s*aya).'—Or else (taking brahmapura to mean *g*îvapura) we may understand the passage to teach that Brahman is, in the city of the individual soul, near (to the devout worshipper), just as Vish*n*u is near to us in the *S*âlagrâma-stone.—Moreover, the text (VIII, 1, 6) at first declares the result of works to be perishable ('as here on earth whatever has been acquired by works perishes, so perishes whatever is acquired for the next world by good actions,' &c.), and afterwards declares the imperishableness of the results flowing from a knowledge of the small ether, which forms the general subject of discussion ('those who depart from hence after having discovered the Self and those true desires, for them there is freedom in all worlds'). From this again it is manifest that the small ether is the highest Self.—We now turn to the statement made by the pûrvapakshin, 'that the sacred text does not represent the small ether as that

---

[1] While the explanation of Brahman by *g*îva would compel us to assume that the word Brahman secondarily denotes the individual soul.

[2] Upalabdher adhish*th*ânam brahma*n*a deha ishyate I
Tenâsâdhâra*n*atvena deho brahmapuram bhavet II
Bhâmatî.

which is to be sought for and to be understood, because it is mentioned as a distinguishing attribute of something else,' and reply as follows: If the (small) ether were not that which is to be sought for and to be understood, the description of the nature of that ether, which is given in the passage ('as large as this ether is, so large is that ether within the heart'), would be devoid of purport.—But—the opponent might say—that descriptive statement also has the purport of setting forth the nature of the thing abiding within (the ether); for the text after having raised an objection (in the passage, 'And if they should say to him: Now with regard to that city of Brahman and the palace in it, i. e. the small lotus of the heart, and the small ether within the heart, what is there within it that deserves to be sought for or that is to be understood?') declares, when replying to that objection, that heaven, earth, and so on, are contained within it (the ether), a declaration to which the comparison with the ether forms a mere introduction.—Your reasoning, we reply, is faulty. If it were admitted, it would follow that heaven, earth, &c., which are contained within the small ether, constitute the objects of search and enquiry. But in that case the complementary passage would be out of place. For the text carrying on, as the subject of discussion, the ether that is the abode of heaven, earth, &c.—by means of the clauses, 'In it all desires are contained,' 'It is the Self free from sin,' &c., and the passage, 'But those who depart from hence having discovered the Self, and the true desires' (in which passage the conjunction 'and' has the purpose of joining the desires to the Self)—declares that the Self as well, which is the abode of the desires, as the desires which abide in the Self, are the objects of knowledge. From this we conclude that in the beginning of the passage also, the small ether abiding within the lotus of the heart, together with whatever is contained within it as earth, true desires, and so on, is represented as the object of knowledge. And, for the reasons explained, that ether is the highest Lord.

15. (The small ether is Brahman) on account of

the action of going (into Brahman) and of the word (brahmaloka); for thus it is seen (i. e. that the individual souls go into Brahman is seen elsewhere in Scripture); and (this going of the souls into Brahman constitutes) an inferential sign (by means of which we may properly interpret the word 'brahmaloka').

It has been declared (in the preceding Sûtra) that the small (ether) is the highest Lord, on account of the reasons contained in the subsequent passages. These subsequent reasons are now set forth.—For this reason also the small (ether) can be the highest Lord only, because the passage complementary to the passage concerning the small (ether) contains a mention of going and a word, both of which intimate the highest Lord. In the first place, we read (*Kh.* Up. VIII, 3, 2), 'All these creatures, day after day going into that Brahma-world, do not discover it.' This passage which refers back, by means of the word 'Brahma-world,' to the small ether which forms the general subject-matter, speaks of the going to it of the creatures, i. e. the individual souls, wherefrom we conclude that the small (ether) is Brahman. For this going of the individual souls into Brahman, which takes place day after day in the state of deep sleep, is seen, i. e. is met with in another scriptural passage, viz. *Kh.* Up. VI, 8, 1, 'He becomes united with the True,' &c. In ordinary life also we say of a man who lies in deep sleep, 'he has become Brahman,' 'he is gone into the state of Brahman.'—In the second place, the word 'Brahma-world,' which is here applied to the small (ether) under discussion, excludes all thought of the individual soul or the elemental ether, and thus gives us to understand that the small (ether) is Brahman.—But could not the word 'Brahma-world' convey as well the idea of the world of him whose throne is the lotus[1]?—It might do so indeed, if we explained the compound 'Brahma-world' as 'the world of Brahman.' But if we explain it on the ground of the co-ordination of both members of the compound—so that

[1] I. e. Brahmâ, the lower Brahman.

'Brahma-world' denotes that world which is Brahman—then it conveys the idea of the highest Brahman only.—And that daily going (of the souls) into Brahman (mentioned above) is, moreover, an inferential sign for explaining the compound 'Brahma-world,' on the ground of the co-ordination of its two constituent members. For it would be impossible to assume that all those creatures daily go into the world of the effected (lower) Brahman; which world is commonly called the Satyaloka, i. e. the world of the True.

16. And on account of the supporting also (attributed to it), (the small ether must be the Lord) because that greatness is observed in him (according to other scriptural passages).

And also on account of the 'supporting' the small ether can be the highest Lord only.—How?—The text at first introduces the general subject of discussion in the passage, 'In it is that small ether;' declares thereupon that the small one is to be compared with the universal ether, and that everything is contained in it; subsequently applies to it the term 'Self,' and states it to possess the qualities of being free from sin, &c.; and, finally, declares with reference to the same general subject of discussion, 'That Self is a bank, a limitary support (vidh*ri*ti), that these worlds may not be confounded.' As 'support' is here predicated of the Self, we have to understand by it a supporting agent. Just as a dam stems the spreading water so that the boundaries of the fields are not confounded, so that Self acts like a limitary dam in order that these outer and inner worlds, and all the different castes and â*s*ramas may not be confounded. In accordance with this our text declares that greatness, which is shown in the act of holding asunder, to belong to the small (ether) which forms the subject of discussion; and that such greatness is found in the highest Lord only, is seen from other scriptural passages, such as 'By the command of that Imperishable, O Gârgî, sun and moon are held apart' (B*ri*. Up. III, 8, 9). Similarly, we read in another passage also, about whose referring to the highest

Lord there is no doubt, 'He is the Lord of all, the king of all things, the protector of all things. He is a bank and a limitary support, so that these worlds may not be confounded' (B*ri*. Up. IV, 4, 22).—Hence, on account of the 'supporting,' also the small (ether) is nothing else but the highest Lord.

17. And on account of the settled meaning.

The small ether within cannot denote anything but the highest Lord for this reason also, that the word 'ether' has (among other meanings) the settled meaning of 'highest Lord.' Compare, for instance, the sense in which the word 'ether' is used in *Kh*. Up. VIII, 14, 'He who is called ether is the revealer of all forms and names;' and *Kh*. Up. I, 9, 1, 'All these beings take their rise from the ether,' &c. On the other hand, we do not meet with any passage in which the word 'ether' is used in the sense of 'individual soul.' —We have already shown that the word cannot, in our passage, denote the elemental ether; for, although the word certainly has that settled meaning, it cannot have it here, because the elemental ether cannot possibly be compared to itself, &c. &c.

18. If it be said that the other one (i. e. the individual soul) (is meant) on account of a reference to it (made in a complementary passage), (we say) no, on account of the impossibility.

If the small (ether) is to be explained as the highest Lord on account of a complementary passage, then, the pûrvapakshin resumes, we point out that another complementary passage contains a reference to the other one, i. e. to the individual soul: 'Now that serene being (literally: serenity, complete satisfaction), which after having risen out from this earthly body and having reached the highest light, appears in its true form, that is, the Self; thus he spoke' (*Kh*. Up. VIII, 3, 4). For there the word 'serenity,' which is known to denote, in another scriptural passage, the state of deep sleep, can convey the idea of the individual soul only when it is in that state, not of anything else. The 'rising from the body' also can be predicated of the individual soul only whose abode the body is; just as air, &c., whose abode is the ether, are said to arise from the ether. And just as the word 'ether,' although in ordinary language not denoting the highest Lord, yet is admitted to denote him in such passages as, 'The ether is the revealer of forms and names,' because it there occurs in conjunction with qualities of the highest Lord, so it may likewise denote the individual soul. Hence the term 'the small ether' denotes in the passage under discussion the individual soul, 'on account of the reference to the other.'

Not so, we reply, 'on account of the impossibility.' In the first place, the individual soul, which imagines itself to be limited by the internal organ and its other adjuncts, cannot be compared with the ether. And, in the second place, attributes such as freedom from evil, and the like, cannot be ascribed to a being which erroneously transfers to itself the attributes of its limiting adjuncts. This has already been set forth in the first Sûtra of the present adhikara*n*a, and is again mentioned here in order to remove all doubt as to the soul being different from the highest Self. That the reference pointed out by the pûrvapakshin is not to the individual soul will, moreover, be shown in one of the next Sûtras (I, 3, 21).

19. If it be said that from the subsequent (chapter it appears that the individual soul is meant), (we point out that what is there referred to is) rather (the individual soul in so far) as its true nature has become manifest (i. e. as it is non-different from Brahman).

The doubt whether, 'on account of the reference to the other,' the individual soul might not possibly be meant, has been discarded on the ground of 'impossibility.' But, like a dead man on whom am*ri*ta has been sprinkled, that doubt rises again, drawing new strength from the subsequent chapter which treats of Pra*g*âpati. For there he (Pra*g*âpati) at the outset declares that the Self, which is free from sin and the like, is that which is to be searched out, that which we must try to understand (*Kh.* Up. VIII, 7, 1); after that he points out that the seer within the eye, i. e. the individual soul, is the Self ('that person that is seen in the eye is the Self,' VIII, 7, 3); refers again and again to the same entity (in the clauses 'I shall explain him further to you,' VIII, 9, 3; VIII, 10, 4); and (in the explanations fulfilling the given promises) again explains the (nature of the) same individual soul in its different states ('He who moves about happy in dreams is the Self,' VIII, 10, 1; 'When a man being asleep, reposing, and at perfect rest sees no dreams, that is the Self,' VIII, 11, 1). The clause attached to both these explanations (viz. 'That is the immortal, the fearless; that is Brahman') shows, at the same time, the individual soul to be free from sin, and the like. After that Pra*g*âpati, having discovered a shortcoming in the condition of deep sleep (in consequence of the expostulation of Indra, 'In that way he does not know himself that he is I, nor does he know these beings,' VIII, 11, 2), enters on a further explanation ('I shall explain him further to you, and nothing more than this'), begins by blaming the (soul's) connexion with the body, and finally declares the individual soul, when it has risen from the body, to be the highest person. ('Thus does that serene being, arising from this body, appear in its own form as soon as it has approached the highest light. That is the highest person.')—From this it appears that there is a possibility of the qualities of the highest Lord belonging to the individual soul also, and on that account we maintain that the term, 'the small ether within it,' refers to the individual soul.

This position we counter-argue as follows. 'But in so far as its nature has become manifest.' The particle 'but' (in the Sûtra) is meant to set aside the view of the pûrvapakshin, so that the sense of the Sûtra is, 'Not even on account of the subsequent chapter a doubt as to the small ether being the individual soul is possible, because there also that which is meant to be intimated is the individual soul, in so far only as its (true) nature has become manifest.' The Sûtra uses the expression 'he whose nature has become manifest,' which qualifies *g*îva, the individual soul, with reference to its previous condition[1]. — The meaning is as follows. Pra*g*âpati speaks at first of the seer characterised by the eye ('That person which is within the eye,' &c.); shows thereupon, in the passage treating of (the reflection in) the waterpan, that he (viz. the seer) has not his true Self in the body; refers to him repeatedly as the subject to be explained (in the clauses 'I shall explain him further to you'); and having then spoken of him as subject to the states of dreaming and deep sleep, finally explains the individual soul in its real nature, i.e. in so far as it is the highest Brahman, not in so far as it is individual soul ('As soon as it has approached the highest light it appears in its own form'). The highest light mentioned, in the passage last quoted, as what is to be approached, is nothing else but the highest Brahman, which is distinguished by such attributes as freeness from sin, and the like. That same highest Brahman constitutes —as we know from passages such as 'that art thou'—the real nature of the individual soul, while its second nature, i.e. that aspect of it which depends on fictitious limiting conditions, is not its real nature. For as long as the individual soul does not free itself from Nescience in the form of duality—which Nescience may be compared to the mistake of him who in the twilight mistakes a post for a man—and does not rise to the knowledge of the Self, whose nature is unchangeable, eternal Cognition—which expresses itself in the form 'I am Brahman'—so long it remains the individual soul. But when, discarding the aggregate of body, sense-organs and mind, it arrives, by means of Scripture, at the knowledge that it is not itself that aggregate, that it does not form part of transmigratory existence, but is the True, the Real, the Self, whose nature is pure intelligence; then

[1] The masculine 'âvirbhûtasvarûpa*h*' qualifies the substantive *g*îva*h* which has to be supplied. Properly speaking the *g*îva whose true nature has become manifest, i.e. which has become Brahman, is no longer *g*îva; hence the explanatory statement that the term *g*îva is used with reference to what the *g*îva was before it became Brahman.

knowing itself to be of the nature of unchangeable, eternal Cognition, it lifts itself above the vain conceit of being one with this body, and itself becomes the Self, whose nature is unchanging, eternal Cognition. As is declared in such scriptural passages as 'He who knows the highest Brahman becomes even Brahman' (Mu. Up. III, 2, 9). And this is the real nature of the individual soul by means of which it arises from the body and appears in its own form.

Here an objection may be raised. How, it is asked, can we speak of the true nature (svarûpa) of that which is unchanging and eternal, and then say that 'it appears in its own form (true nature)?' Of gold and similar substances, whose true nature becomes hidden, and whose specific qualities are rendered non-apparent by their contact with some other substance, it may be said that their true nature is rendered manifest when they are cleaned by the application of some acid substance; so it may be said, likewise, that the stars, whose light is during daytime overpowered (by the superior brilliancy of the sun), become manifest in their true nature at night when the overpowering (sun) has departed. But it is impossible to speak of an analogous overpowering of the eternal light of intelligence by whatever agency, since, like ether, it is free from all contact, and since, moreover, such an assumption would be contradicted by what we actually observe. For the (energies of) seeing, hearing, noticing, cognising constitute the character of the individual soul, and that character is observed to exist in full perfection, even in the case of that individual soul which has not yet risen beyond the body. Every individual soul carries on the course of its practical existence by means of the activities of seeing, hearing, cognising; otherwise no practical existence at all would be possible. If, on the other hand, that character would realise itself in the case of that soul only which has risen above the body, the entire aggregate of practical existence, as it actually presents itself prior to the soul's rising, would thereby be contradicted. We therefore ask: Wherein consists that (alleged) rising from the body? Wherein consists that appearing (of the soul) in its own form?

To this we make the following reply.—Before the rise of

discriminative knowledge the nature of the individual soul, which is (in reality) pure light, is non-discriminated as it were from its limiting adjuncts consisting of body, senses, mind, sense-objects and feelings, and appears as consisting of the energies of seeing and so on. Similarly—to quote an analogous case from ordinary experience—the true nature of a pure crystal, i. e. its transparency and whiteness, is, before the rise of discriminative knowledge (on the part of the observer), non-discriminated as it were from any limiting adjuncts of red or blue colour; while, as soon as through some means of true cognition discriminative knowledge has arisen, it is said to have now accomplished its true nature, i. e. transparency and whiteness, although in reality it had already done so before. Thus the discriminative knowledge, effected by *S*ruti, on the part of the individual soul which previously is non-discriminated as it were from its limiting adjuncts, is (according to the scriptural passage under discussion) the soul's rising from the body, and the fruit of that discriminative knowledge is its accomplishment in its true nature, i. e. the comprehension that its nature is the pure Self. Thus the embodiedness and the non-embodiedness of the Self are due merely to discrimination and non-discrimination, in agreement with the mantra, 'Bodiless within the bodies,' &c. (Ka. Up. I, 2, 22), and the statement of Sm*ri*ti as to the non-difference between embodiedness and non-embodiedness 'Though dwelling in the body, O Kaunteya, it does not act and is not tainted' (Bha. Gî. XIII, 31). The individual soul is therefore called 'That whose true nature is non-manifest' merely on account of the absence of discriminative knowledge, and it is called 'That whose nature has become manifest' on account of the presence of such knowledge. Manifestation and non-manifestation of its nature of a different kind are not possible, since its nature is nothing but its nature (i. e. in reality is always the same). Thus the difference between the individual soul and the highest Lord is owing to wrong knowledge only, not to any reality, since, like ether, the highest Self is not in real contact with anything.

And wherefrom is all this to be known?—From the instruction given by Pra*g*âpati who, after having referred to the *g*iva ('the person that is seen in the eye,' &c.), continues 'This is the immortal, the fearless, this is Brahman.' If the well-known seer within the eye were different from Brahman which is characterised as the immortal and fearless, it would not be co-ordinated (as it actually is) with the immortal, the fearless, and Brahman. The reflected Self, on the other hand, is not spoken of as he who is characterised by the eye (the seer within the eye), for that would render Pra*g*âpati obnoxious to the reproach of saying deceitful things.—So also, in the second section, the passage, 'He who moves about happy in dreams,' &c. does not refer to a being different from the seeing person within the eye spoken of in the first chapter, (but treats of the same topic) as appears from the introductory clause, 'I shall explain him further to you.' Moreover[1], a person who is conscious of having seen an elephant in a dream and of no longer seeing it when awake discards in the waking state the object which he had seen (in his sleep), but recognises himself when awake to be the same person who saw something in the dream.—Thus in the third section also Pra*g*âpati does indeed declare the absence of all particular cognition in the state of deep sleep, but does not contest the identity of the cognising Self ('In that way he does not know himself that he is I, nor all these beings'). The following clause also, 'He is gone to utter annihilation,' is meant to intimate only the annihilation of all specific cognition, not the annihilation of the cogniser. For there is no destruction of the knowing of the knower as—according to another scriptural passage (B*ri*. Up. IV, 3, 30)—that is imperishable.—Thus, again, in the fourth section the introductory phrase of Pra*g*âpati is, 'I shall explain him further to you and nothing different from this;' he thereupon refutes the connexion (of the Self) with the body and other limiting conditions ('Maghavat, this body is mortal,' &c.), shows the individual soul—which is there called 'the serene being'—

[1] To state another reason showing that the first and second chapters of Pra*g*âpati's instruction refer to the same subject.

in the state when it has reached the nature of Brahman ('It appears in its own form'), and thus proves the soul to be non-different from the highest Brahman whose characteristics are immortality and fearlessness.

Some (teachers) however are of opinion that if the highest Self is meant (in the fourth section) it would be inappropriate to understand the words 'This (him) I will explain further,' &c., as referring to the individual soul, and therefore suppose that the reference is (not to the individual soul forming the topic of the three preceding sections, but) to the Self possessing the qualities of freeness from sin, &c., which Self is pointed out at the beginning of the entire chapter (VII, 1).—Against this interpretation we remark that, in the first place, it disregards the direct enunciation of the pronoun (i.e. the 'this' in 'this I will explain') which rests on something approximate (i.e. refers to something mentioned not far off), and, in the second place, is opposed to the word 'further' (or 'again') met with in the text, since from that interpretation it would follow that what had been discussed in the preceding sections is not again discussed in the subsequent section. Moreover, if Pra*g*âpati, after having made a promise in the clause, 'This I shall explain' (where that clause occurs for the first time), did previously to the fourth section explain a different topic in each section, we should have to conclude that he acted deceitfully.—Hence (our opinion about the purport of the whole chapter remains valid, viz. that it sets forth how) the unreal aspect of the individual soul as such—which is a mere presentation of Nescience, is stained by all the desires and aversions attached to agents and enjoyers, and is connected with evils of various kinds—is dissolved by true knowledge, and how the soul is thus led over into the opposite state, i.e. into its true state in which it is one with the highest Lord and distinguished by freedom from sin and similar attributes. The whole process is similar to that by which an imagined snake passes over into a rope as soon as the mind of the beholder has freed itself from its erroneous imagination.

Others again, and among them some of ours (asmadîyâ*s* *k*a ke*k*it), are of opinion that the individual soul as such is real. To the end of refuting all these speculators who obstruct the way to the complete intuition of the unity of the Self this *s*ârîraka-*s*âstra has been set forth, whose aim it is to show that there is only one highest Lord ever unchanging, whose substance is cognition [1], and who, by means of Nescience, manifests himself in various ways, just as a thaumaturg appears in different shapes by means of his magical power. Besides that Lord there is no other substance of cognition.—If, now, the Sûtrakâra raises and refutes the doubt whether a certain passage which (in reality) refers to the Lord does refer to the individual soul, as he does in this and the preceding Sûtras [2], he does so for the following purpose. To the highest Self which is eternally pure, intelligent and free, which is never changing, one only, not in contact with anything, devoid of form, the opposite characteristics of the individual soul are erroneously ascribed; just as ignorant men ascribe blue colour to the colourless ether. In order to remove this erroneous opinion by means of Vedic passages tending either to prove the unity of the Self or to disprove the doctrine of duality —which passages he strengthens by arguments—he insists on the difference of the highest Self from the individual soul, does however not mean to prove thereby that the soul is different from the highest Self, but, whenever speaking of the soul, refers to its distinction (from the Self) as forming an item of ordinary thought, due to the power of Nescience. For thus, he thinks, the Vedic injunctions of works which are given with a view to the states of acting and enjoying, natural (to the non-enlightened soul), are not stultified.—That, however, the absolute unity of the Self is the real purport of the *s*âstra's teaching, the Sûtrakâra declares, for instance, in I, 1, 30 [3]. The refutation of the reproach of

[1] I. e. of whom cognition is not a mere attribute.

[2] Although in reality there is no such thing as an individual soul.

[3] Nanu *g*îvabrahma*n*or aikyam na kvâpi sûtrakâro mukhato vadati kim tu sarvatra bhedam eva, ato naikyam ish*t*am tatrâha pratipâdyam tv iti.

futility raised against the injunctions of works has already been set forth by us, on the ground of the distinction between such persons as possess full knowledge, and such as do not.

20. And the reference (to the individual soul) has a different meaning.

The alleged reference to the individual soul which has been pointed out (by the pûrvapakshin) in the passage complementary to the passage about the small ether ('Now that serene being,' &c., VIII, 3, 4) teaches, if the small ether is interpreted to mean the highest Lord, neither the worship of the individual soul nor any qualification of the subject under discussion (viz. the small ether), and is therefore devoid of meaning.—On that account the Sûtra declares that the reference has another meaning, i. e. that the reference to the individual soul is not meant to determine the nature of the individual soul, but rather the nature of the highest Lord. In the following manner. The individual soul which, in the passage referred to, is called the serene being, acts in the waking state as the ruler of the aggregate comprising the body and the sense-organs; permeates in sleep the na*d*is of the body, and enjoys the dream visions resulting from the impressions of the waking state; and, finally, desirous of reaching an inner refuge, rises in the state of deep sleep beyond its imagined connexion with the gross and the subtle body, reaches the highest light, i. e. the highest Brahman previously called ether, and thus divesting itself of the state of specific cognition appears in its own (true) nature. The highest light which the soul is to reach and through which it is manifested in its true nature is the Self, free from sin and so on, which is there represented as the object of worship.—In this sense the reference to the individual soul can be admitted by those also who maintain that in reality the highest Lord is meant.

21. If it be said that on account of the scriptural

declaration of the smallness (of the ether) (the Lord cannot be meant; we reply that) that has been explained (before).

The pûrvapakshin has remarked that the smallness of the ether stated by Scripture ('In it is that small ether') does not agree with the highest Lord, that it may however be predicated of the individual soul which (in another passage) is compared to the point of a goad. As that remark calls for a refutation we point out that it has been refuted already, it having been shown—under I, 2, 7—that a relative smallness may be attributed to the Lord. The same refutation is—as the Sûtra points out—to be applied here also.—That smallness is, moreover, contradicted by that scriptural passage which compares (the ether within the heart) with the known (universal) ether. ('As large as is this ether, so large is the ether within the heart.')

22. On account of the acting after (i.e. the shining after), (that after which sun, moon, &c. are said to shine is the highest Self), and (because by the light) of him (all this is said to be lighted).

We read (Mu. Up. II, 2, 10, and Ka. Up. V, 15), 'The sun does not shine there, nor the moon and the stars, nor these lightnings, much less this fire. After him when he shines everything shines; by the light of him all this is lighted.' The question here arises whether he 'after whom when he shines everything shines, and by whose light all this is lighted,' is some luminous substance, or the highest Self (prâ*gñ*a âtman).

A luminous substance, the pûrvapakshin maintains.—Why?—Because the passage denies the shining only of such luminous bodies as the sun and the like. It is known (from every-day experience) that luminous bodies such as the moon and the stars do not shine at daytime when the sun, which is itself a luminous body, is shining. Hence we infer that that thing on account of which all this, including the moon, the stars, and the sun himself, does not shine is likewise a thing of light. The 'shining after' also is possible only if there is a luminous body already; for we know from experience that 'acting after' (imitation) of any kind takes place only when there are more than one agent of similar nature; one man, for instance, walks after another man who walks himself. Therefore we consider it settled that the passage refers to some luminous body.

To this we reply that the highest Self only can be meant.—Why?—On account of the acting after. The shining after mentioned in the passage, 'After him when he shines everything shines,' is possible only if the prâ*gñ*a Self, i. e. the highest Self, is understood. Of that prâ*gñ*a Self another scriptural passage says, 'His form is light, his thoughts are true' (*Kh*. Up. III, 14, 2). On the other hand, it is not by any means known that the sun, &c. shines after some other luminous body. Moreover, on account of the equality of nature of all luminous bodies such as the sun and the like, there is no need for them of any other luminous body after which they should shine; for we see that a lamp, for instance, does not 'shine after' another lamp. Nor is there any such absolute rule (as the pûrvapakshin asserted) that acting after is observed only among things of similar nature. It is rather observed among things of dissimilar nature also; for a red-hot iron ball acts after, i. e. burns after the burning fire, and the dust of the ground blows (is blown) after the blowing wind.—The clause 'on account of the acting after' (which forms part of the Sûtra) points to the shining after (mentioned in the scriptural *s*loka under discussion); the clause 'and of him' points to the fourth pâda of the same *s*loka. The meaning of this latter clause is that the cause assigned for the light of the sun, &c. (in the passage 'by the light of him everything is lighted') intimates the prâ*gñ*a Self. For of that Self Scripture says, 'Him the gods worship as the light of lights, as immortal time' (B*ri*. Up. IV, 4, 16). That, on the other hand, the light of the sun, the moon, &c. should shine by some other (physical) light is, in the first place, not known; and, in the second place, absurd as one (physical) light is counteracted by another.—Or else the cause assigned for the shining does not apply only to the sun and the other bodies mentioned in the *s*loka; but the meaning (of the last pâda) rather is—as we may conclude from the comprehensive statement 'all this'—that the manifestation of this entire world consisting of names and forms, acts, agents and fruits (of action) has for its cause the existence of the light of Brahman; just as the existence of the light of the sun is the cause of the manifestation of all form and colour.—Moreover, the text shows by means of the word 'there' ('the sun does not shine there,' &c.) that the passage is to be connected with the general topic, and that topic is Brahman as appears from Mu. Up. II, 2, 5, 'In whom the heaven, the earth, and the sky are woven,' &c. The same appears from a passage subsequent (on the one just quoted and immediately preceding the passage under discussion). 'In the highest golden sheath there is the Brahman without passion and without parts; that is pure, that is the light of lights, that is it which they know who know the Self.' This passage giving rise to the question, 'How is it the light of lights?' there is occasion for the reply given in 'The sun does not shine there,' &c.—In refutation of the assertion that the shining of luminous bodies such as the sun and the moon can be denied only in case of there being another luminous body—as, for instance, the light of the moon and the stars is denied only when the sun is shining—we point out that it has been shown that he (the Self) only can be the luminous being referred to, nothing else. And it is quite possible to deny the shining of sun, moon, and so on with regard to Brahman; for whatever is perceived is perceived by the light of Brahman only so that sun, moon, &c. can be said to shine in it; while Brahman as self-luminous is not perceived by means of any other light. Brahman manifests everything else, but is not manifested by anything else; according to such scriptural passages as, 'By the Self alone as his light man sits,' &c. (B*ri*. Up. IV, 3, 6), and 'He is incomprehensible, for he cannot be comprehended' (B*ri*. Up. IV, 2, 4).

23. Moreover Smriti also speaks of him (i. e. of the prâgña Self as being the universal light).

Moreover that aspect of the prâgña Self is spoken of in Smriti also, viz. in the Bhagavad Gîtâ (XV, 6, 12), 'Neither the sun, nor the moon, nor the fire illumines that; having gone into which men do not return, that is my highest seat.' And 'The light which abiding in the sun illumines the whole world, and that which is in the moon and that which is in the fire, all that light know to be mine.'

24. On account of the term, (viz. the term 'lord' applied to it) the (person) measured (by a thumb) (is the highest Lord).

We read (Ka. Up. II, 4, 12), 'The person of the size of a thumb stands in the middle of the Self,' &c., and (II, 4, 13), 'That person, of the size of a thumb, is like a light without smoke, lord of the past and of the future, he is the same to-day and to-morrow. This is that.'—The question here arises whether the person of the size of a thumb mentioned in the text is the cognitional (individual) Self or the highest Self.

The pûrvapakshin maintains that on account of the declaration of the person's size the cognitional Self is meant. For to the highest Self which is of infinite length and breadth Scripture would not ascribe the measure of a span; of the cognitional Self, on the other hand, which is connected with limiting adjuncts, extension of the size of a span may, by means of some fictitious assumption, be predicated. Smriti also confirms this, 'Then Yama drew forth, by force, from the body of Satyavat the person of the size of a thumb tied to Yama's noose and helpless' (Mahâbh. III, 16763). For as Yama could not pull out by force the highest Self, the passage is clearly seen to refer to the transmigrating (individual soul) of the size of a thumb, and we thence infer that the same Self is meant in the Vedic passage under discussion.

To this we reply that the person a thumb long can only

be the highest Lord.—Why?—On account of the term 'lord of the past and of the future.' For none but the highest Lord is the absolute ruler of the past and the future.—Moreover, the clause 'this is that' connects the passage with that which had been enquired about, and therefore forms the topic of discussion. And what had been enquired about is Brahman, 'That which thou seest as neither this nor that, as neither effect nor cause, as neither past nor future, tell me that' (I, 2, 14).—'On account of the term,' i. e. on account of the direct statement, in the text, of a designation, viz. the term 'Lord,' we understand that the highest Lord is meant[1].—But still the question remains how a certain extension can be attributed to the omnipresent highest Self.—The reply to this is given in the next Sûtra.

25. But with reference to the heart (the highest Self is said to be of the size of a span), as men are entitled (to the study of the Veda).

The measure of a span is ascribed to the highest Lord, although omnipresent with reference to his abiding within the heart; just as to ether (space) the measure of a cubit is ascribed with reference to the joint of a bamboo. For, on the one hand, the measure of a span cannot be ascribed directly to the highest Self which exceeds all measure, and, on the other hand, it has been shown that none but the highest Lord can be meant here, on account of the term 'Lord,' and so on.—But—an objection may be raised—as the size of the heart varies in the different classes of living beings it cannot be maintained that the declaration

---

[1] This last sentence is directed against the possible objection that '*s*abda,' which the Sûtra brings forward as an argument in favour of the highest Lord being meant, has the sense of 'sentence' (vâkya), and is therefore of less force than liṅga, i. e. indicatory or inferential mark which is represented in our passage by the aṅgush*th*amâtratâ of the purusha, and favours the *g*îva-interpretation. *S*abda, the text remarks, here means *s*ruti, i. e. direct enunciation, and *s*ruti ranks, as a means of proof, higher than liṅga.

of the highest Self being of the size of a thumb can be explained with reference to the heart.—To this objection the second half of the Sûtra replies: On account of men (only) being entitled. For the *s*âstra, although propounded without distinction (i. e. although not itself specifying what class of beings is to proceed according to its precepts), does in reality entitle men[1] only (to act according to its precepts); for men only (of the three higher castes) are, firstly, capable (of complying with the precepts of the *s*âstra); are, secondly, desirous (of the results of actions enjoined by the *s*âstra); are, thirdly, not excluded by prohibitions; and are, fourthly, subject to the precepts about the upanayana ceremony and so on[2]. This point has been explained in the section treating of the definition of adhikâra (Pûrva Mîm. S. VI, 1).—Now the human body has ordinarily a fixed size, and hence the heart also has a fixed size, viz. the size of a thumb. Hence, as men (only) are entitled to study and practise the *s*âstra, the highest Self may, with reference to its dwelling in the human heart, be spoken of as being of the size of a thumb.—In reply to the pûrvapakshin's reasoning that on account of the statement of size and on account of Smriti we can understand by him who is of the size of a thumb the transmigrating soul only, we remark that—analogously to such passages as 'That is the Self,' 'That art thou'—our passage

[1] I. e. men belonging to the three upper castes.

[2] The first reason excludes animals, gods, and *ri*shis. Gods cannot themselves perform sacrifices, the essential feature of which is the parting, on the part of the sacrificer, with an offering meant for the gods. *Ri*shis cannot perform sacrifices in the course of whose performance the ancestral *ri*shis of the sacrificer are invoked. —The second reason excludes those men whose only desire is emancipation and who therefore do not care for the perishable fruits of sacrifices.—The third and fourth reasons exclude the *S*ûdras who are indirectly disqualified for *s*âstric works because the Veda in different places gives rules for the three higher castes only, and for whom the ceremony of the upanayana—indispensable for all who wish to study the Veda—is not prescribed.—Cp. Pûrva Mîmâmsâ Sûtras VI, 1.

teaches that the transmigrating soul which is of the size of a thumb is (in reality) Brahman. For the Vedânta-passages have a twofold purport; some of them aim at setting forth the nature of the highest Self, some at teaching the unity of the individual soul with the highest Self. Our passage teaches the unity of the individual soul with the highest Self, not the size of anything. This point is made clear further on in the Upanishad, 'The person of the size of a thumb, the inner Self, is always settled in the heart of men. Let a man draw that Self forth from his body with steadiness, as one draws the pith from a reed. Let him know that Self as the Bright, as the Immortal' (II, 6, 17).

26. Also (beings) above them, (viz. men) (are qualified for the study and practice of the Veda), on account of the possibility (of it), according to Bâdarâya*n*a.

It has been said above that the passage about him who is of the size of a thumb has reference to the human heart, because men are entitled to study and act according to the *s*âstra. This gives us an occasion for the following discussion. —It is true that the *s*âstra entitles men, but, at the same time, there is no exclusive rule entitling men only to the knowledge of Brahman; the teacher, Bâdarâya*n*a, rather thinks that the *s*âstra entitles those (classes of beings) also which are above men, viz. gods, and so on.—On what account?—On the account of possibility.—For in their cases also the different causes on which the qualification depends, such as having certain desires, and so on, may exist. In the first place, the gods also may have the desire of final release, caused by the reflection that all effects, objects, and powers are non-permanent. In the second place, they may be capable of it as their corporeality appears from mantras, arthavâdas, itihâsas, purâ*n*as, and ordinary experience. In the third place, there is no prohibition (excluding them like *S*ûdras). Nor does, in the fourth place, the scriptural rule about the upanayana-ceremony annul their title; for that ceremony merely subserves the study of the Veda, and to the gods the Veda is manifest of itself (without study). That the gods, moreover, for the purpose of acquiring knowledge, undergo discipleship, and the like, appears from such scriptural passages as 'One hundred and one years Indra lived as a disciple with Pra*g*âpati' (*Kh.* Up. VIII, 11, 3), and 'Bh*ri*gu Vâru*n*i went to his father Varu*n*a, saying, "Sir, teach me Brahman"' (Taitt. Up. III, 1).—And the reasons which have been given above against gods and *ri*shis being entitled to perform religious works (such as sacrifices), viz. the circumstance of there being no other gods (to whom the gods could offer sacrifices), and of there being no other *ri*shis (who could be invoked during the sacrifice), do not apply to the case of branches of knowledge. For Indra and the other gods, when applying themselves to knowledge, have no acts to perform with a view to Indra, and so on; nor have Bh*ri*gu and other *ri*shis, in the same case, to do anything with the circumstance of their belonging to the same gotra as Bh*ri*gu, &c. What, then, should stand in the way of the gods' and *ri*shis' right to acquire knowledge? —Moreover, the passage about that which is of the size of a thumb remains equally valid, if the right of the gods, &c. is admitted; it has then only to be explained in each particular case by a reference to the particular size of the thumb (of the class of beings spoken of).

27. If it be said that (the corporeal individuality of the gods involves) a contradiction to (sacrificial) works; we deny that, on account of the observation of the assumption (on the part of the gods) of several (forms).

If the right of the gods, and other beings superior to men, to the acquisition of knowledge is founded on the assumption of their corporeality, &c., we shall have to admit, in consequence of that corporeality, that Indra and the other gods stand in the relation of subordinate members (aṅga) to sacrificial acts, by means of their being present in person just as the priests are. But this admission will lead to 'a contradiction in the sacrificial acts,' because the circumstance of the gods forming the members of sacrificial acts by means of their personal presence, is neither actually observed nor possible. For it is not possible that one and the same Indra should, at the same time, be present in person at many sacrifices.

To this we reply, that there is no such contradiction.—Why?—On account of the assumption of several (forms). For it is possible for one and the same divine Self to assume several forms at the same time.—How is that known?—From observation.—For a scriptural passage at first replies to the question how many gods there are, by the declaration that there are 'Three and three hundred, three and three thousand,' and subsequently, on the question who they are, declares 'They (the 303 and 3003) are only the various powers of them, in reality there are only thirty-three gods' (B*ri*. Up. III, 9, 1, 2); showing thereby that one and the same divine Self may at the same time appear in many forms. After that it proceeds to show that these thirty-three gods themselves are in reality contained in six, five, &c., and finally, by replying to the question, 'Who is the one god?' that Breath is the one god, shows that the gods are all forms of Breath, and that Breath, therefore, can at the same time appear in many forms.—Sm*ri*ti also has a similar statement, 'A Yogin, O hero of the Bharatas, may, by his power, multiply his Self in many thousand shapes, and in them walk about on the earth. In some he may enjoy the objects, in others he may undergo dire penance, and, finally, he may again retract them all, just as the sun retracts the multitude of his rays.' If such Sm*ri*ti passages as the above declare that even Yogins, who have merely acquired various extraordinary powers, such as subtlety of body, and the like, may animate several bodies at the same time, how much more capable of such feats must the gods be, who naturally possess all supernatural powers? The gods thus being able to assume several shapes, a god may divide himself into many forms and enter into relation with many sacrifices at the same time, remaining all the while unseen by others, in consequence of his power to render himself invisible.

The latter part of the Sûtra may be explained in a different manner also, viz. as meaning that even beings enjoying corporeal individuality are seen to enter into mere subordinate relation to more than one action. Sometimes, indeed, one individual does not at the same time enter into subordinate relation to different actions; one Brâhma*n*a, for instance, is not at the same time entertained by many entertainers. But in other cases one individual stands in subordinate relation to many actions at the same time; one Brâhma*n*a, for instance, may constitute the object of the reverence done to him by many persons at the same time. Similarly, it is possible that, as the sacrifice consists in the parting (on the part of the sacrificer with some offering) with a view (to some divinity), many persons may at the same time part with their respective offerings, all of them having in view one and the same individual divinity. The individuality of the gods does not, therefore, involve any contradiction in sacrificial works.

28. If it be said (that a contradiction will result) in respect of the word; we refute this objection on the ground that (the world) originates from the word, as is shown by perception and inference.

Let it then be granted that, from the admission of the corporeal individuality of the gods, no contradiction will result in the case of sacrificial works. Still a contradiction will result in respect of the 'word' (*s*abda).—How?—The authoritativeness of the Veda has been proved 'from its independence,' basing on the original (eternal) connexion of the word with its sense ('the thing signified')[1]. But now, although a divinity possessing corporeal individuality, such as admitted above, may, by means of its supernatural powers, be able to enjoy at the same time the oblations

[1] The reference is to Pûrva Mîmâ*m*sâ Sûtras I, 1, 5 (not to I, 2, 21, as stated in Muir's Sanskrit Texts, III, p. 69).

which form part of several sacrifices, yet it will, on account of its very individuality, be subject to birth and death just as we men are, and hence, the eternal connexion of the eternal word with a non-eternal thing being destroyed, a contradiction will arise with regard to the authoritativeness proved to belong to the word of the Veda.

To this we reply that no such contradiction exists.—Why? —'On account of their origin from it.' For from that very same word of the Veda the world, with the gods and other beings, originates.—But—an objection will be raised—in Sûtra I, 1, 2 ('That whence there is the origin, &c. of this world') it has been proved that the world originates from Brahman; how then can it be said here that it originates from the word? And, moreover, even if the origin of the world from the word of the Veda be admitted, how is the contradiction in regard to the word removed thereby, inasmuch as the Vasus, the Rudras, the Âdityas, the Visvedevas, and the Maruts[1] are non-eternal beings, because produced; and if they are non-eternal, what is there to preclude the non-eternality of the Vedic words Vasu, &c. designating them? For it is known from every-day life that only when the son of Devadatta is born, the name Yagñadatta is given to him (lit. made for him)[2]. Hence we adhere to our opinion that a contradiction does arise with regard to the 'word.'

This objection we negative, on the ground that we observe the eternity of the connexion between such words as cow, and so on, and the things denoted by them. For, although the individuals of the (species denoted by the word) cow have an origin, their species[3] does not have an origin, since of (the three categories) substances, qualities, and actions the individuals only originate, not the species. Now it is with the species that the words are connected, not with the individuals, which, as being infinite in number, are not capable of entering into that connexion. Hence, although

[1] In which classes of beings all the gods are comprised.

[2] Which shows that together with the non-eternality of the thing denoted there goes the non-eternality of the denoting word.

[3] Âkriti, best translated by εἶδος.

the individuals do not originate, no contradiction arises in the case of words such as cow, and the like, since the species are eternal. Similarly, although individual gods are admitted to originate, there arises no contradiction in the case of such words as Vasu, and the like, since the species denoted by them are eternal. And that the gods, and so on, belong to different species, is to be concluded from the descriptions of their various personal appearance, such as given in the mantras, arthavâdas, &c. Terms such as 'Indra' rest on the connexion (of some particular being) with some particular place, analogously to terms such as 'army-leader;' hence, whoever occupies that particular place is called by that particular name.—The origination of the world from the 'word' is not to be understood in that sense, that the word constitutes the material cause of the world, as Brahman does; but while there exist the ever-lasting words, whose essence is the power of denotation in connexion with their eternal sense (i.e. the âk*ri*tis denoted), the accomplishment of such individual things as are capable of having those words applied to them is called an origination from those words.

How then is it known that the world originates from the word?—'From perception and inference.' Perception here denotes Scripture which, in order to be authoritative, is independent (of anything else). 'Inference' denotes Sm*ri*ti which, in order to be authoritative, depends on something else (viz. Scripture). These two declare that creation is preceded by the word. Thus a scriptural passage says, 'At the word t h e s e Pra*g*âpati created the gods; at the words w e r e p o u r e d o u t he created men; at the word d r o p s he created the fathers; at the words t h r o u g h t h e f i l t e r he created the Soma cups; at the words t h e s w i f t o n e s he created the stotra; at the words t o a l l he created the *s*astra; at the word b l e s s i n g s he created the other beings.' And another passage says, 'He with his mind united himself with speech (i.e. the word of the Veda.—B*ri*. Up. I, 2, 4). Thus Scripture declares in different places that the word precedes the creation.—Sm*ri*ti also delivers itself as follows, 'In the beginning a divine voice, eternal, without beginning or end, formed of the Vedas was uttered by Svayambhû, from which all activities proceeded.' By the 'uttering' of the voice we have here to understand the starting of the oral tradition (of the Veda), because of a voice without beginning or end 'uttering' in any other sense cannot be predicated.—Again, we read, 'In the beginning Mahesvara shaped from the words of the Veda the names and forms of all beings and the procedure of all actions.' And again, 'The several names, actions, and conditions of all things he shaped in the beginning from the words of the Veda' (Manu I, 21). Moreover, we all know from observation that any one when setting about some thing which he wishes to accomplish first remembers the word denoting the thing, and after that sets to work. We therefore conclude that before the creation the Vedic words became manifest in the mind of Pragâpati the creator, and that after that he created the things corresponding to those words. Scripture also, where it says (Taitt. Brâ. II, 2, 4, 2) 'uttering bhûr he created the earth,' &c., shows that the worlds such as the earth, &c. became manifest, i.e. were created from the words bhûr, &c. which had become manifest in the mind (of Pragâpati).

Of what nature then is the 'word' with a view to which it is said that the world originates from the 'word?'—It is the sphota, the pûrvapakshin says[1]. For on the as-

[1] The pûrvapakshin, i.e. here the grammarian maintains, for the reasons specified further on, that there exists in the case of words a supersensuous entity called sphota which is manifested by the letters of the word, and, if apprehended by the mind, itself manifests the sense of the word. The term sphota may, according as it is viewed in either of these lights, be explained as the manifestor or that which is manifested.—The sphota is a grammatical fiction, the word in so far as it is apprehended by us as a whole. That we cannot identify it with the 'notion' (as Deussen seems inclined to do, p. 80) follows from its being distinctly called vâkaka or abhidhâyaka, and its being represented as that which causes the conception of the sense of a word (arthadhîhetu).

sumption that the letters are the word, the doctrine that the individual gods, and so on, originates from the eternal words of the Veda could not in any way be proved, since the letters perish as soon as they are produced (i.e. pronounced). These perishable letters are moreover apprehended as differing according to the pronunciation of the individual speaker. For this reason we are able to determine, merely from the sound of the voice of some unseen person whom we hear reading, who is reading, whether Devadatta or Ya*gñ*adatta or some other man. And it cannot be maintained that this apprehension of difference regarding the letters is an erroneous one; for we do not apprehend anything else whereby it is refuted. Nor is it reasonable to maintain that the apprehension of the sense of a word results from the letters. For it can neither be maintained that each letter by itself intimates the sense, since that would be too wide an assumption [1]; nor that there takes place a simultaneous apprehension of the whole aggregate of letters; since the letters succeed one another in time. Nor can we admit the explanation that the last letter of the word together with the impressions produced by the perception of the preceding letters is that which makes us apprehend the sense. For the word makes us apprehend the sense only if it is itself apprehended in so far as having reference to the mental grasp of the constant connexion (of the word and the sense), just as smoke makes us infer the existence of fire only when it is itself apprehended; but an apprehension of the last letter combined with the impressions produced by the preceding letters does not actually take place, because those impressions are not objects of perception [2]. Nor, again, can it be maintained that (although those im-

---

[1] For that each letter by itself expresses the sense is not observed; and if it did so, the other letters of the word would have to be declared useless.

[2] In order to enable us to apprehend the sense from the word, there is required the actual consciousness of the last letter plus the impressions of the preceding letters; just as smoke enables us to

pressions are not objects of perception, yet they may be inferred from their effects, and that thus) the actual perception of the last letter combined with the impressions left by the preceding letters—which impressions are apprehended from their effects—is that which intimates the sense of the word; for that effect of the impressions, viz. the remembrance of the entire word, is itself something consisting of parts which succeed each other in time.—From all this it follows that the spho*t*a is the word. After the apprehending agent, i.e. the buddhi, has, through the apprehension of the several letters of the word, received rudimentary impressions, and after those impressions have been matured through the apprehension of the last letter, the spho*t*a presents itself in the buddhi all at once as the object of one mental act of apprehension.—And it must not be maintained that that one act of apprehension is merely an act of remembrance having for its object the letters of the word; for the letters which are more than one cannot form the object of one act of apprehension.—As that spho*t*a is recognised as the same as often as the word is pronounced, it is eternal; while the apprehension of difference referred to above has for its object the letters merely. From this eternal word, which is of the nature of the spho*t*a and possesses denotative power, there is produced the object denoted, i.e. this world which consists of actions, agents, and results of action.

Against this doctrine the reverend Upavarsha maintains that the letters only are the word.—But—an objection is raised—it has been said above that the letters no sooner produced pass away!—That assertion is not true, we reply; for they are recognised as the same letters (each time they are produced anew).—Nor can it be maintained that the recognition is due to similarity only, as in the case of hairs, for instance; for the fact of the recognition being a recognition in the strict sense of the word is not contradicted by any other means of proof.—Nor, again, can it be said

infer the existence of fire only if we are actually conscious of the smoke. But that actual consciousness does not take place because the impressions are not objects of perceptive consciousness.

that the recognition has its cause in the species (so that not the same individual letter would be recognised, but only a letter belonging to the same species as other letters heard before); for, as a matter of fact, the same individual letters are recognised. That the recognition of the letters rests on the species could be maintained only if whenever the letters are pronounced different individual letters were apprehended, just as several cows are apprehended as different individuals belonging to the same species. But this is actually not the case; for the (same) individual letters are recognised as often as they are pronounced. If, for instance, the word cow is pronounced twice, we think not that two different words have been pronounced, but that the same individual word has been repeated.—But, our opponent reminds us, it has been shown above, that the letters are apprehended as different owing to differences of pronunciation, as appears from the fact that we apprehend a difference when merely hearing the sound of Devadatta or Ya*gñ*adatta reading.—Although, we reply, it is a settled matter that the letters are recognised as the same, yet we admit that there are differences in the apprehension of the letters; but as the letters are articulated by means of the conjunction and disjunction (of the breath with the palate, the teeth, &c.), those differences are rightly ascribed to the various character of the articulating agents and not to the intrinsic nature of the letters themselves. Those, moreover, who maintain that the individual letters are different have, in order to account for the fact of recognition, to assume species of letters, and further to admit that the apprehension of difference is conditioned by external factors. Is it then not much simpler to assume, as we do, that the apprehension of difference is conditioned by external factors while the recognition is due to the intrinsic nature of the letters? And this very fact of recognition is that mental process which prevents us from looking on the apprehension of difference as having the letters for its object (so that the opponent was wrong in denying the existence of such a process). For how should, for instance, the one syllable ga, when it is pronounced in the same moment by several persons, be at the same time of different nature, viz. accented with the udâtta, the anudâtta, and the Svarita and nasal as well as non-nasal[1]? Or else[2]—and this is the preferable explanation—we assume that the difference of apprehension is caused not by the letters but by the tone (dhvani). By this tone we have to understand that which enters the ear of a person who is listening from a distance and not able to distinguish the separate letters, and which, for a person standing near, affects the letters with its own distinctions, such as high or low pitch and so on. It is on this tone that all the distinctions of udâtta, anudâtta, and so on depend, and not on the intrinsic nature of the letters; for they are recognised as the same whenever they are pronounced. On this theory only we gain a basis for the distinctive apprehension of the udâtta, the anudâtta, and the like. For on the theory first propounded (but now rejected), we should have to assume that the distinctions of udâtta and so on are due to the processes of conjunction and disjunction described above, since the letters themselves, which are ever recognised as the same, are not different. But as those processes of conjunction and disjunction are not matter of perception, we cannot definitely ascertain in the letters any differences based on those processes, and hence the apprehension of the udâtta and so on remains without a basis.—Nor should it be urged that from the difference of the udâtta and so on there results also a difference of the letters recognised. For a difference in one matter does not involve a difference in some other matter which in itself is free from difference. Nobody, for instance, thinks that because the individuals

[1] 'How should it be so?' i.e. it cannot be so; and on that account the differences apprehended do not belong to the letters themselves, but to the external conditions mentioned above.

[2] With 'or else' begins the exposition of the finally accepted theory as to the cause why the same letters are apprehended as different. Hitherto the cause had been found in the variety of the upâdhis of the letters. Now a new distinction is made between articulated letters and non-articulated tone.

are different from each other the species also contains a difference in itself.

The assumption of the sphoṭa is further gratuitous, because the sense of the word may be apprehended from the letters.—But—our opponent here objects—I do not assume the existence of the sphoṭa. I, on the contrary, actually perceive it; for after the buddhi has been impressed by the successive apprehension of the letters of the word, the sphoṭa all at once presents itself as the object of cognition. —You are mistaken, we reply. The object of the cognitional act of which you speak is simply the letters of the word. That one comprehensive cognition which follows upon the apprehension of the successive letters of the word has for its object the entire aggregate of the letters constituting the word, and not anything else. We conclude this from the circumstance that in that final comprehensive cognition there are included those letters only of which a definite given word consists, and not any other letters. If that cognitional act had for its object the sphoṭa—i. e. something different from the letters of the given word—then those letters would be excluded from it just as much as the letters of any other word. But as this is not the case, it follows that that final comprehensive act of cognition is nothing but an act of remembrance which has the letters of the word for its object.—Our opponent has asserted above that the letters of a word being several cannot form the object of one mental act. But there he is wrong again. The ideas which we have of a row, for instance, or a wood or an army, or of the numbers ten, hundred, thousand, and so on, show that also such things as comprise several unities can become the objects of one and the same cognitional act. The idea which has for its object the word as one whole is a derived one, in so far as it depends on the determination of one sense in many letters[1]; in the same way as the idea of a

[1] I. e. it is not directly one idea, for it has for its object more than one letter; but it may be called one in a secondary sense because it is based on the determinative knowledge that the letters, although more than one, express one sense only.

wood, an army, and so on.—But—our opponent may here object—if the word were nothing else but the letters which in their aggregate become the object of one mental act, such couples of words as *g*ârâ and râ*g*â or pika and kapi would not be cognised as different words ; for here the same letters are presented to consciousness in each of the words constituting one couple.—There is indeed, we reply, in both cases a comprehensive consciousness of the same totality of letters ; but just as ants constitute the idea of a row only if they march one after the other, so the letters also constitute the idea of a certain word only if they follow each other in a certain order. Hence it is not contrary to reason that the same letters are cognised as different words, in consequence of the different order in which they are arranged.

The hypothesis of him who maintains that the letters are the word may therefore be finally formulated as follows. The letters of which a word consists—assisted by a certain order and number—have, through traditional use, entered into a connexion with a definite sense. At the time when they are employed they present themselves as such (i. e. in their definite order and number) to the buddhi, which, after having apprehended the several letters in succession, finally comprehends the entire aggregate, and they thus unerringly intimate to the buddhi their definite sense. This hypothesis is certainly simpler than the complicated hypothesis of the grammarians who teach that the spho*t*a is the word. For they have to disregard what is given by perception, and to assume something which is never perceived ; the letters apprehended in a definite order are said to manifest the spho*t*a, and the spho*t*a in its turn is said to manifest the sense.

Or let it even be admitted that the letters are different ones each time they are pronounced ; yet, as in that case we necessarily must assume species of letters as the basis of the recognition of the individual letters, the function of conveying the sense which we have demonstrated in the case of the (individual) letters has then to be attributed to the species.

From all this it follows that the theory according to which the individual gods and so on originate from the eternal words is unobjectionable.

29. And from this very reason there follows the eternity of the Veda.

As the eternity of the Veda is founded on the absence of the remembrance of an agent only, a doubt with regard to it had been raised owing to the doctrine that the gods and other individuals have sprung from it. That doubt has been refuted in the preceding Sûtra.—The present Sûtra now confirms the, already established, eternity of the Veda. The eternity of the word of the Veda has to be assumed for this very reason, that the world with its definite (eternal) species, such as gods and so on, originates from it.—A mantra also ('By means of the sacrifice they followed the trace of speech; they found it dwelling in the *ri*shis,' *Ri*g-veda Sa*m*h. X, 71, 3) shows that the speech found (by the *ri*shis) was permanent.—On this point Vedavyâsa also speaks as follows: 'Formerly the great *ri*shis, being allowed to do so by Svayambhû, obtained, through their penance, the Vedas together with the itihâsas, which had been hidden at the end of the yuga.'

30. And on account of the equality of names and forms there is no contradiction (to the eternity of the word of the Veda) in the renovation (of the world); as is seen from *S*ruti and Sm*ri*ti.

If—the pûrvapakshin resumes—the individual gods and so on did, like the individual animals, originate and pass away in an unbroken succession so that there would be no break of the course of practical existence including denominations, things denominated and agents denominating; the connexion (between word and thing) would be eternal, and the objection as to a contradiction with reference to the word (raised in Sûtra 27) would thereby be refuted. But if, as *S*ruti and Sm*ri*ti declare, the whole threefold world periodically divests itself of name and form, and is entirely dissolved (at the end of a kalpa), and is after that produced anew; how can the contradiction be considered to have been removed?

To this we reply: 'On account of the sameness of name and form.'—Even then the beginninglessness of the world will have to be admitted (a point which the teacher will prove later on: II, 1, 36). And in the beginningless sa*m*sâra we have to look on the (relative) beginning, and the dissolution connected with a new kalpa in the same light in which we look on the sleeping and waking states, which, although in them according to Scripture (a kind of) dissolution and origination take place, do not give rise to any contradiction, since in the later waking state (subsequent to the state of sleep) the practical existence is carried on just as in the former one. That in the sleeping and the waking states dissolution and origination take place is stated Kaush. Up. III, 3, 'When a man being asleep sees no dream whatever he becomes one with that prâ*n*a alone. Then speech goes to him with all names, the eye with all forms, the ear with all sounds, the mind with all thoughts. And when he awakes then, as from a burning fire, sparks proceed in all directions, thus from that Self the prâ*n*as proceed, each towards its place; from the prâ*n*as the gods, from the gods the worlds.'

Well, the pûrvapakshin resumes, it may be that no contradiction arises in the case of sleep, as during the sleep of one person the practical existence of other persons suffers no interruption, and as the sleeping person himself when waking from sleep may resume the very same form of practical existence which was his previously to his sleep. The case of a mahâpralaya (i. e. a general annihilation of the world) is however a different one, as then the entire current of practical existence is interrupted, and the form of existence of a previous kalpa can be resumed in a subsequent kalpa no more than an individual can resume that form of existence which it enjoyed in a former birth.

This objection, we reply, is not valid. For although a mahâpralaya does cut short the entire current of practical existence, yet, by the favour of the highest Lord, the Lords (îsvara), such as Hira*n*yagarbha and so on, may continue the same form of existence which belonged to them in the preceding kalpa. Although ordinary animated beings do not, as we see, resume that form of existence which belonged to them in a former birth; still we cannot judge of the Lords as we do of ordinary beings. For as in the series of beings which descends from man to blades of grass a successive diminution of knowledge, power, and so on, is observed—although they all have the common attribute of being animated—so in the ascending series extending from man up to Hira*n*yagarbha, a gradually increasing manifestation of knowledge, power, &c. takes place; a circumstance which *S*ruti and Sm*ri*ti mention in many places, and which it is impossible to deny. On that account it may very well be the case that the Lords, such as Hira*n*yagarbha and so on, who in a past kalpa were distinguished by superior knowledge and power of action, and who again appear in the present kalpa, do, if favoured by the highest Lord, continue (in the present kalpa) the same kind of existence which they enjoyed in the preceding kalpa; just as a man who rises from sleep continues the same form of existence which he enjoyed previously to his sleep. Thus Scripture also declares, 'He who first creates Brahman (Hira*n*yagarbha) and delivers the Vedas to him, to that God who is the light of his own thoughts, I, seeking for release, go for refuge' (*S*vet. Up. VI, 18). *S*aunaka and others moreover declare (in the Anukrama*n*îs of the Veda) that the ten books (of the *Ri*g-veda) were seen by Madhu*kkh*andas and other *ri*shis[1]. And, similarly, Sm*ri*ti tells us, for every Veda, of men of exalted mental vision (*ri*shis) who 'saw' the subdivisions of their respective Vedas, such as kâ*nd*as and so on. Scripture also declares that the performance of the sacrificial action by means of the mantra is to be preceded by the knowledge of the *ri*shi and so on, 'He who makes another person sacrifice or read by means of a mantra of which he

[1] Which circumstance proves that exalted knowledge appertains not only to Hira*n*yagarbha, but to many beings.

does not know the *ri*shi, the metre, the divinity, and the Brâhma*n*a, runs against a post, falls into a pit[1], &c. &c., therefore one must know all those matters for each mantra' (Ârsheya Brâhma*n*a, first section).—Moreover, religious duty is enjoined and its opposite is forbidden, in order that the animate beings may obtain pleasure and escape pain. Desire and aversion have for their objects pleasure and pain, known either from experience or from Scripture, and do not aim at anything of a different nature. As therefore each new creation is (nothing but) the result of the religious merit and demerit (of the animated beings of the preceding creation), it is produced with a nature resembling that of the preceding creation. Thus Sm*ri*ti also declares, 'To whatever actions certain of these (animated beings) had turned in a former creation, to the same they turn when created again and again. Whether those actions were harmful or harmless, gentle or cruel, right or wrong, true or untrue, influenced by them they proceed; hence a certain person delights in actions of a certain kind.'—Moreover, this world when being dissolved (in a mahâpralaya) is dissolved to that extent only that the potentiality (*s*akti) of the world remains, and (when it is produced again) it is produced from the root of that potentiality; otherwise we should have to admit an effect without a cause. Nor have we the right to assume potentialities of different kind (for the different periods of the world). Hence, although the series of worlds from the earth upwards, and the series of different classes of animate beings such as gods, animals, and men, and the different conditions based on caste, â*s*rama, religious duty and fruit (of works), although all these we say are again and again interrupted and thereupon produced anew; we yet have to understand that they are, in the beginningless sa*m*sâra, subject to a certain determinateness analogous to the determinateness governing the connexion between the senses and their objects. For it is impossible to imagine that the relation of senses and sense-objects should be a different one in different creations, so

[1] Viz. naraka, the commentaries say.

that, for instance, in some new creation a sixth sense and a corresponding sixth sense-object should manifest themselves. As, therefore, the phenomenal world is the same in all kalpas and as the Lords are able to continue their previous forms of existence, there manifest themselves, in each new creation, individuals bearing the same names and forms as the individuals of the preceding creations, and, owing to this equality of names and forms, the admitted periodical renovations of the world in the form of general pralayas and general creations do not conflict with the authoritativeness of the word of the Veda. The permanent identity of names and forms is declared in *S*ruti as well as Sm*ri*ti; compare, for instance, *Ri*k. Sa*m*h. X, 190, 3, 'As formerly the creator ordered sun and moon, and the sky, and the air, and the heavenly world;' which passage means that the highest Lord arranged at the beginning of the present kalpa the entire world with sun and moon, and so on, just as it had been arranged in the preceding kalpa. Compare also Taitt. Brâhm. III, 1, 4, 1, 'Agni desired: May I become the consumer of the food of the gods; for that end he offered a cake on eight potsherds to Agni and the K*ri*ttikâs.' This passage, which forms part of the injunction of the ish*t*i to the Nakshatras, declares equality of name and form connecting the Agni who offered and the Agni to whom he offered [1].

Sm*ri*ti also contains similar statements to be quoted here; so, for instance, 'Whatever were the names of the *ri*shis and their powers to see the Vedas, the same the Unborn one again gives to them when they are produced afresh at the end of the night (the mahâpralaya). As the various signs of the seasons return in succession in their due time, thus the same beings again appear in the different yugas. And of whatever individuality the gods of the

---

[1] Asmin kalpe sarveshâm prâ*n*inâm dâhapâkaprakâ*s*akârî *y*o *s*yam agnir d*ris*yate so*s*yam agni*h* pûrvasmin kalpe manushya*h* san devatvapadaprâpaka*m* karmânush*th*âyâsmin kalpa eta*g* *g*anma labdhavân ata*h* pûrvasmin kalpe sa manushyo bhâvinî*m* sa*mgñ*âm â*sri*tyâgnir iti vyapadi*s*yate.—Sâya*n*a on the quoted passage.

past ages were, equal to them are the present gods in name and form.'

31. On account of the impossibility of (the gods being qualified) for the madhu-vidyâ, &c. *G*aimini (maintains) the non-qualification (of the gods for the Brahma-vidyâ).

A new objection is raised against the averment that the gods, &c. also are entitled to the knowledge of Brahman. The teacher, *G*aimini, considers the gods and similar beings not to have any claim.—Why?—On account of the impossibility, in the case of the so-called Madhu-vidyâ, &c. If their claim to the knowledge of Brahman were admitted, we should have to admit their claim to the madhu-vidyâ ('the knowledge of the honey') also, because that also is a kind of knowledge not different (from the knowledge of Brahman). But to admit this latter claim is not possible; for, according to the passage, 'The Sun is indeed the honey of the devas' (*Kh.* Up. III, 1, 1), men are to meditate on the sun (the god Âditya) under the form of honey, and how, if the gods themselves are admitted as meditating worshippers, can Âditya meditate upon another Âditya?—Again, the text, after having enumerated five kinds of nectar, the red one, &c. residing in the sun, and after having stated that the five classes of gods, viz. the Vasus, Rudras, Âdityas, Maruts, and Sâdhyas, live on one of these nectars each, declares that 'he who thus knows this nectar becomes one of the Vasus, with Agni at their head, he sees the nectar and rejoices,' &c., and indicates thereby that those who know the nectars enjoyed by the Vasus, &c., attain the greatness of the Vasus, &c. But how should the Vasus themselves know other Vasus enjoying the nectar, and what other Vasu-greatness should they desire to attain?—We have also to compare the passages 'Agni is one foot, Âditya is one foot, the quarters are one foot' (*Kh.* Up. III, 18, 2); 'Air is indeed the absorber' (*Kh.* Up. IV, 3, 1); 'Âditya is Brahman, this is the doctrine.' All these passages treat of the meditation on the Self of certain divinities, for which meditation these divinities themselves are not qualified.—So it is likewise impossible that the *ri*shis themselves should be qualified for meditations connected with *ri*shis, such as expressed in passages like *Bri*. Up. II, 2, 4, 'These two are the *ri*shis Gautama and Bharadvâ*g*a; the right Gautama, the left Bharadvâ*g*a.'—Another reason for the non-qualification of the gods is stated in the following Sûtra.

32. And (the devas, &c. are not qualified) on account of (the words denoting the devas, &c.) being (used) in the sense of (sphere of) light.

To that sphere of light, the pûrvapakshin resumes, which is stationed in the sky, and during its diurnal revolutions illumines the world, terms such as Âditya, i.e. the names of devas, are applied, as we know from the use of ordinary language, and from Vedic complementary passages[1]. But of a mere sphere of light we cannot understand how it should be endowed with either a bodily form, consisting of the heart and the like, or intelligence, or the capability of forming wishes[2]. For mere light we know to be, like earth, entirely devoid of intelligence. The same observation applies to Agni (fire), and so on. It will perhaps be said that our objection is not valid, because the personality of the devas is known from the mantras, arthavâdas, itihâsas, purâ*n*as, and from the conceptions of ordinary life[3]; but we contest the relevancy of this remark. For the conceptions of ordinary life do not constitute an independent means of knowledge; we rather say that a thing is known from ordinary life if it is known by the (acknowledged) means of knowledge, perception, &c. But none of the recognised means of knowledge, such as perception and the like, apply to the

[1] As, for instance, 'So long as Âditya rises in the east and sets in the west' (*Kh*. Up. III, 6, 4).

[2] Whence it follows that the devas are not personal beings, and therefore not qualified for the knowledge of Brahman.

[3] Yama, for instance, being ordinarily represented as a person with a staff in his hand, Varu*n*a with a noose, Indra with a thunderbolt, &c. &c.

matter under discussion. Itihâsas and purâ*n*as again being of human origin, stand themselves in need of other means of knowledge on which to base. The arthavâda passages also, which, as forming syntactical wholes with the injunctory passages, have merely the purpose of glorifying (what is enjoined in the latter), cannot be considered to constitute by themselves reasons for the existence of the personality, &c. of the devas. The mantras again, which, on the ground of direct enunciation, &c., are to be employed (at the different stages of the sacrificial action), have merely the purpose of denoting things connected with the sacrificial performance, and do not constitute an independent means of authoritative knowledge for anything[1].—For these reasons the devas, and similar beings, are not qualified for the knowledge of Brahman.

33. Bâdarâya*n*a, on the other hand, (maintains) the existence (of qualification for Brahma-vidyâ on the part of the gods); for there are (passages indicatory of that).

The expression 'on the other hand' is meant to rebut the pûrvapaksha. The teacher, Bâdarâya*n*a, maintains the existence of the qualification on the part of the gods, &c. For, although the qualification of the gods cannot be admitted with reference to the madhu-vidyâ, and similar topics of knowledge, in which the gods themselves are implicated, still they may be qualified for the pure knowledge of Brahman, qualification in general depending on the presence of desire, capability, &c.[2] Nor does the impossibility of qualification in certain cases interfere with the presence of qualification in those other cases where it is not impossible. To the case of the gods the same reasoning applies as to the case of men; for among men also, all are not qualified for everything, Brâhma*n*as, for instance, not for the râ*g*asûya-sacrifice[3].

[1] On the proper function of arthavâda and mantra according to the Mîmâ*m*sâ, cp. Arthasa*m*graha, Introduction.

[2] See above, p. 197.

[3] Which can be offered by kshattriyas only.

And, with reference to the knowledge of Brahman, Scripture, moreover, contains express hints notifying that the devas are qualified; compare, for instance, B*ri*. Up. I, 4, 10, 'Whatever Deva was awakened (so as to know Brahman) he indeed became that; and the same with *ri*shis;' *Kh*. Up. VIII, 7, 2, 'They said: Well, let us search for that Self by which, if one has searched it out, all worlds and all desires are obtained. Thus saying, Indra went forth from the Devas, Viro*k*ana from the Asuras.' Similar statements are met with in Sm*ri*ti, so, for instance, in the colloquy of the Gandharva and Yâ*g*ñavalkya[1].—Against the objection raised in the preceding Sûtra (32) we argue as follows. Words like âditya, and so on, which denote devas, although having reference to light and the like, yet convey the idea of certain divine Selfs (persons) endowed with intelligence and pre-eminent power; for they are used in that sense in mantras and arthavâda passages. For the devas possess, in consequence of their pre-eminent power, the capability of residing within the light, and so on, and to assume any form they like. Thus we read in Scripture, in the arthavâda passage explaining the words 'ram of Medhâtithi,' which form part of the Subrahma*n*ya-formula, that 'Indra, having assumed the shape of a ram, carried off Medhâtithi, the descendant of Ka*n*va' (Sha*d*v. Br. I, 1). And thus Sm*ri*ti says that 'Âditya, having assumed the shape of a man, came to Kuntî.' Moreover, even in such substances as earth, intelligent ruling beings must be admitted to reside, for that appears from such scriptural passages as 'the earth spoke,' 'the waters spoke,' &c. The non-intelligence of light and the like, in so far as they are mere material elements, is admitted in the case of the sun (âditya), &c. also; but—as already remarked—from the use of the words in mantras and

---

[1] *S*rautalingenânumânabâdha*m* dar*s*ayitvâ smârtenâpi tadbâdha*m* dar*s*ayati smârtam iti. Ki*m* atra brahma am*ri*ta*m* ki*m* svid vedyam anuttamam, *k*intayet tatra vai gatvâ gandharvo mâm ap*rikkh*ata, Vi*s*vâvasus tato râ*g*an vedânta*g*ñânakovida iti moksha-dharme *g*anakayâ*g*ñavalkyasa*m*vâdât prahlâdâ*g*agarasa*m*vâdâ*k* *k*oktânumânâsiddhir ity artha*h*.

ar'havâdas it appears that there are intelligent beings of divine nature (which animate those material elements).

We now turn to the objection (raised above by the pûrvapakshin) that mantras and arthavâdas, as merely subserving other purposes, have no power of setting forth the personality of the devas, and remark that not the circumstance of subordination or non-subordination to some other purpose, but rather the presence or absence of a certain idea furnishes a reason for (our assuming) the existence of something. This is exemplified by the case of a person who, having set out for some other purpose, (nevertheless) forms the conviction of the existence of leaves, grass, and the like, which he sees lying on the road.—But, the pûrvapakshin may here object, the instance quoted by you is not strictly analogous. In the case of the wanderer, perception, whose objects the grass and leaves are, is active, and through it he forms the conception of their existence. In the case of an arthavâda, on the other hand, which, as forming a syntactical unity with the corresponding injunctory passage, merely subserves the purpose of glorifying (the latter), it is impossible to determine any energy having a special object of its own. For in general any minor syntactical unity, which is included in a more comprehensive syntactical unity conveying a certain meaning, does not possess the power of expressing a separate meaning of its own. Thus, for instance, we derive, from the combination of the three words constituting the negative sentence, '(Do) not drink wine,' one meaning only, i.e. a prohibition of drinking wine, and do not derive an additional meaning, viz. an order to drink wine, from the combination of the last two words, 'drink wine.'—To this objection we reply, that the instance last quoted is not analogous (to the matter under discussion). The words of the sentence prohibiting the drinking of wine form only one whole, and on that account the separate sense which any minor syntactical unity included in the bigger sentence may possess cannot be accepted. In the case of injunction and arthavâda, on the other hand, the words constituting the arthavâda form a separate group of their own which refers to some accomplished thing[1], and only subsequently to that, when it comes to be considered what purpose they subserve, they enter on the function of glorifying the injunction. Let us examine, as an illustrative example, the injunctive passage, 'He who is desirous of prosperity is to offer to Vâyu a white animal.' All the words contained in this passage are directly connected with the injunction. This is, however, not the case with the words constituting the corresponding arthavâda passage, 'For Vâyu is the swiftest deity; Vâyu he approaches with his own share; he leads him to prosperity.' The single words of this arthavâda are not grammatically connected with the single words of the injunction, but form a subordinate unity of their own, which contains the praise of Vâyu, and glorify the injunction, only in so far as they give us to understand that the action enjoined is connected with a distinguished divinity. If the matter conveyed by the subordinate (arthavâda) passage can be known by some other means of knowledge, the arthavâda acts as a mere anuvâda, i. e. a statement referring to something (already known)[2]. When its contents are contradicted by other means of knowledge it acts as a so-called gu*n*avâda, i. e. a statement of a quality[3]. Where, again, neither of the two mentioned conditions is found, a doubt may arise whether the arthavâda is to be taken as a gu*n*avâda on account of the absence of other means of knowledge, or as an arthavâda referring to something known (i. e. an anuvâda) on account of the absence of contradiction by other means of proof. The latter alternative is, however, to be embraced by reflecting people. —The same reasoning applies to mantras also.

There is a further reason for assuming the personality of the gods. The Vedic injunctions, as enjoining sacrificial offerings to Indra and the other gods, presuppose certain characteristic shapes of the individual divinities, because

[1] As opposed to an action to be accomplished.

[2] Of this nature is, for instance, the arthavâda, 'Fire is a remedy for cold.'

[3] Of this nature is, for instance, the passage 'the sacrificial post is the sun' (i. e. possesses the qualities of the sun, luminousness, &c.; a statement contradicted by perception).

without such the sacrificer could not represent Indra and the other gods to his mind. And if the divinity were not represented to the mind it would not be possible to make an offering to it. So Scripture also says, 'Of that divinity for which the offering is taken he is to think when about to say vausha*t*' (Ai. Br. III, 8, 1). Nor is it possible to consider the essential form (or character) of a thing to consist in the word only[1]; for word (denoting) and thing (denoted) are different. He therefore who admits the authoritativeness of the scriptural word has no right to deny that the shape of Indra, and the other gods, is such as we understand it to be from the mantras and arthavâdas.—Moreover, itihâsas and purâ*n*as also—because based on mantra and arthavâda which possess authoritative power in the manner described—are capable of setting forth the personality, &c. of the devas. Itihâsa and purâ*n*a can, besides, be considered as based on perception also. For what is not accessible to our perception may have been within the sphere of perception of people in ancient times. Sm*ri*ti also declares that Vyâsa and others conversed with the gods face to face. A person maintaining that the people of ancient times were no more able to converse with the gods than people are at present, would thereby deny the (incontestable) variety of the world. He might as well maintain that because there is at present no prince ruling over the whole earth, there were no such princes in former times; a position by which the scriptural injunction of the râ*g*asûya-sacrifice[2] would be stultified. Or he might maintain that in former times the spheres of duty of the different castes and â*s*ramas were as generally unsettled as they are now, and, on that account, declare those parts of Scripture which define those different duties to be purposeless. It is therefore altogether unobjectionable to assume that the men of ancient times, in consequence of their eminent religious

[1] And therefore to suppose that a divinity is nothing but a certain word forming part of a mantra.

[2] The râ*g*asûya-sacrifice is to be offered by a prince who wishes to become the ruler of the whole earth.

merit, conversed with the gods face to face. Sm*ri*ti also declares that 'from the reading of the Veda there results intercourse with the favourite divinity' (Yoga Sûtra II, 44). And that Yoga does, as Sm*ri*ti declares, lead to the acquirement of extraordinary powers, such as subtlety of body, and so on, is a fact which cannot be set aside by a mere arbitrary denial. Scripture also proclaims the greatness of Yoga, 'When, as earth, water, light, heat, and ether arise, the fivefold quality of Yoga takes place, then there is no longer illness, old age, or pain for him who has obtained a body produced by the fire of Yoga' (*S*vet. Up. II, 12). Nor have we the right to measure by our capabilities the capability of the *ri*shis who see the mantras and brâhma*n*a passages (i. e. the Veda).—From all this it appears that the itihâsas and purâ*n*as have an adequate basis.—And the conceptions of ordinary life also must not be declared to be unfounded, if it is at all possible to accept them.

The general result is that we have the right to conceive the gods as possessing personal existence, on the ground of mantras, arthavâdas, itihâsas, purâ*n*as, and ordinarily prevailing ideas. And as the gods may thus be in the condition of having desires and so on, they must be considered as qualified for the knowledge of Brahman. Moreover, the declarations which Scripture makes concerning gradual emancipation [1] agree with this latter supposition only.

34. Grief of him (i. e. of *G*ânas*r*uti) (arose) on account of his hearing a disrespectful speech about himself; on account of the rushing on of that (grief) (Raikva called him *S*ûdra); for it (the grief) is pointed at (by Raikva).

(In the preceding adhikara*n*a) the exclusiveness of the claim of men to knowledge has been refuted, and it has been declared that the gods, &c. also possess such a claim. The present adhikara*n*a is entered on for the purpose of removing the doubt whether, as the exclusiveness of the

[1] In one of whose stages the being desirous of final emancipation becomes a deva.

claim of twice-born men is capable of refutation, the *S*ûdras also possess such a claim.

The pûrvapakshin maintains that the *S*ûdras also have such a claim, because they may be in the position of desiring that knowledge, and because they are capable of it; and because there is no scriptural prohibition (excluding them from knowledge) analogous to the text, 'Therefore[1] the *S*ûdra is unfit for sacrificing' (Taitt. Sa*m*h. VII, 1, 1, 6). The reason, moreover, which disqualifies the *S*ûdras for sacrificial works, viz. their being without the sacred fires, does not invalidate their qualification for knowledge, as knowledge can be apprehended by those also who are without the fires. There is besides an inferential mark supporting the claim of the *S*ûdras; for in the so-called sa*m*varga-knowledge he (Raikva) refers to *G*ânа*s*ruti Pautrâyа*n*a, who wishes to learn from him, by the name of *S*ûdra 'Fie, necklace and carriage be thine, O *S*ûdra, together with the cows' (*Kh*. Up. IV, 2, 3). Sm*ri*ti moreover speaks of Vidûra and others who were born from *S*ûdra mothers as possessing eminent knowledge.—Hence the *S*ûdra has a claim to the knowledge of Brahman.

To this we reply that the *S*ûdras have no such claim, on account of their not studying the Veda. A person who has studied the Veda and understood its sense is indeed qualified for Vedic matters; but a *S*ûdra does not study the Veda, for such study demands as its antecedent the upanayana-ceremony, and that ceremony belongs to the three (higher) castes only. The mere circumstance of being in a condition of desire does not furnish a reason for qualification, if capability is absent. Mere temporal capability again does not constitute a reason for qualification, spiritual capability being required in spiritual matters. And spiritual capability is (in the case of the *S*ûdras) excluded by their being excluded from the study of the Veda.—The Vedic statement, moreover, that the *S*ûdra is unfit for sacrifices intimates, because

[1] The commentaries explain 'therefore' by 'on account of his being devoid of the three sacred fires.' This explanation does not, however, agree with the context of the Taitt. Sa*m*h.

founded on reasoning, that he is unfit for knowledge also; for the argumentation is the same in both cases[1].—With reference to the pûrvapakshin's opinion that the fact of the word 'Sûdra' being enounced in the samvarga-knowledge constitutes an inferential mark (of the Sûdra's qualification for knowledge), we remark that that inferential mark has no force, on account of the absence of arguments. For the statement of an inferential mark possesses the power of intimation only in consequence of arguments being adduced; but no such arguments are brought forward in the passage quoted[2]. Besides, the word 'Sûdra' which occurs in the samvarga-vidyâ would establish a claim on the part of the Sûdras to that one vidyâ only, not to all vidyâs. In reality, however, it is powerless, because occurring in an arthavâda, to establish the Sûdras' claim to anything.—The word 'Sûdra' can moreover be made to agree with the context in which it occurs in the following manner. When Gânasruti Pautrâyana heard himself spoken of with disrespect by the flamingo ('How can you speak of him, being what he is, as if he were like Raikva with the car?' IV, 1, 3), grief (suk) arose in his mind, and to that grief the rishi Raikva alludes with the word Sûdra, in order to show thereby his knowledge of what is remote. This explanation must be accepted because a (real) born Sûdra is not qualified (for the samvarga-vidyâ). If it be asked how the grief (suk) which had arisen in Gânasruti's mind can be referred to by means of the word Sûdra, we reply: On account of the rushing on (âdravana) of the grief. For we may etymologise the word Sûdra by dividing it into its parts, either as 'he rushed into grief' (Sukam abhidudrâva) or as 'grief rushed on

[1] The Sûdra not having acquired a knowledge of Vedic matters in the legitimate way, i.e. through the study of the Veda under the guidance of a guru, is unfit for sacrifices as well as for vidyâ.

[2] The linga contained in the word 'Sûdra' has no proving power as it occurs in an arthavâda-passage which has no authority if not connected with a corresponding injunctive passage. In our case the linga in the arthavâda-passage is even directly contradicted by those injunctions which militate against the Sûdras' qualification for Vedic matters.

him,' or as 'he in his grief rushed to Raikva;' while on the other hand it is impossible to accept the word in its ordinary conventional sense. The circumstance (of the king actually being grieved) is moreover expressly touched upon in the legend[1].

35. And because the kshattriyahood (of *G*ânasruti) is understood from the inferential mark (supplied by his being mentioned) later on with *K*aitraratha (who was a kshattriya himself).

*G*ânasruti cannot have been a *S*ûdra by birth for that reason also that his being a kshattriya is understood from an inferential sign, viz. his being mentioned together (in one chapter) with the kshattriya *K*aitraratha Abhipratârin. For, later on, i.e. in the passage complementary to the sa*m*varga-vidyâ, a kshattriya *K*aitrarathi Abhipratârin is glorified, 'Once while *S*aunaka Kâpeya and Abhipratârin Kâkshaseni were being waited on at their meal a religious student begged of them' (*Kh*. Up. IV, 3, 5). That this Abhipratârin was a *K*aitrarathi (i.e. a descendant of *K*itraratha) we have to infer from his connexion with a Kâpeya. For we know (from *S*ruti) about the connexion of *K*itraratha himself with the Kâpeyas ('the Kâpeyas made *K*itraratha perform that sacrifice;' Tâ*nd*ya Br. XX, 12, 5), and as a rule sacrificers of one and the same family employ officiating priests of one and the same family. Moreover, as we understand from Scripture ('from him a *K*aitrarathi descended who was a prince[2]') that he (*K*aitraratha) was a prince, we must

---

[1] Ha*m*savâkyâd âtmano*s*nâdara*m* srutvâ gânasrute*h* *s*ug ut-pannety etad eva katha*m* gamyate yenâsau *s*ûdra*s*abdena sû*k*yate tatrâha spr*is*yate *k*eti. Ânanda Giri.

[2] I translate this passage as I find it in all MSS. of *S*ankara consulted by me (noting, however, that some MSS. read *k*aitrarathi-nâmaika*h*). Ânanda Giri expressly explains tasmâd by *k*itrarathâd ity artha*h*.—The text of the Tâ*nd*ya Br. runs: tasmâ*k* *k*aitrarathînâm eka*h* kshatrapatir gâyate, and the commentary explains: tasmât kâra*n*âd adyâpi *k*itravam*s*otpannâmâ*m* madhye eka eva râ*g*â kshatra-

understand him to have been a kshattriya. The fact now of *G*ânas*r*uti being praised in the same vidyâ with the kshattriya Abhipratârin intimates that the former also was a kshattriya. For as a rule equals are mentioned together with equals. That *G*ânas*r*uti was a kshattriya we moreover conclude from his sending his door-keeper and from other similar signs of power (mentioned in the text).—Hence the *S*ûdras are not qualified (for the knowledge of Brahman).

36. On account of the reference to ceremonial purifications (in the case of the higher castes) and on account of their absence being declared (in the case of the *S*ûdras).

That the *S*ûdras are not qualified, follows from that circumstance also that in different places of the vidyâs such ceremonies as the upanayana and the like are referred to. Compare, for instance, *S*at. Br. XI, 5, 3, 13, 'He initiated him as a pupil;' *Kh*. Up. VII, 1, 1, 'Teach me, Sir! thus he approached him;' Pra. Up. I, 1, 'Devoted to Brahman, firm in Brahman, seeking for the highest Brahman they, carrying fuel in their hands, approached the venerable Pippalâda, thinking that he would teach them all that.'—Thus the following passage also, 'He without having made them undergo the upanayana (said) to them' (*Kh*. Up. V, 11, 7), shows that the upanayana is a well-established ceremony[1].—With reference to the *S*ûdras, on the other hand, the absence of ceremonies is frequently mentioned; so, for instance, Manu X, 4, where they are spoken of as 'once-born' only ('the *S*ûdra is the fourth caste, once-born'), and Manu X, 126, 'In the *S*ûdra there is not any sin, and he is not fit for any ceremony.'

patir balâdhipatir bhavati.—Grammar does not authorise the form *k*aitraratha used in the Sûtra.

[1] The king As*v*apati receives some Brâhma*n*as as his pupils without insisting on the upanayana. This express statement of the upanayana having been omitted in a certain case shows it to be the general rule.

37. And on account of (Gautama) proceeding (to initiate *G*âbâla) on the ascertainment of (his) not being that (i.e. a *S*ûdra).

The *S*ûdras are not qualified for that reason also that Gautama, having ascertained *G*âbâla not to be a *S*ûdra from his speaking the truth, proceeded to initiate and instruct him. 'None who is not a Brâhma*n*a would thus speak out. Go and fetch fuel, friend, I shall initiate you. You have not swerved from the truth' (*Kh*. Up. IV, 4, 5); which scriptural passage furnishes an inferential sign (of the *S*ûdras not being capable of initiation).

38. And on account of the prohibition, in Sm*ri*ti, of (the *S*ûdras') hearing and studying (the Veda) and (knowing and performing) (Vedic) matters.

The *S*ûdras are not qualified for that reason also that Sm*ri*ti prohibits their hearing the Veda, their studying the Veda, and their understanding and performing Vedic matters. The prohibition of hearing the Veda is conveyed by the following passages: 'The ears of him who hears the Veda are to be filled with (molten) lead and lac,' and 'For a *S*ûdra is (like) a cemetery, therefore (the Veda) is not to be read in the vicinity of a *S*ûdra.' From this latter passage the prohibition of studying the Veda results at once; for how should he study Scripture in whose vicinity it is not even to be read? There is, moreover, an express prohibition (of the *S*ûdras studying the Veda). 'His tongue is to be slit if he pronounces it; his body is to be cut through if he preserves it.' The prohibitions of hearing and studying the Veda already imply the prohibition of the knowledge and performance of Vedic matters; there are, however, express prohibitions also, such as 'he is not to impart knowledge to the *S*ûdra,' and 'to the twice-born belong study, sacrifice, and the bestowal of gifts.'—From those *S*ûdras, however, who, like Vidura and 'the religious hunter,' acquire knowledge in consequence of the after effects of former deeds, the fruit of their knowledge cannot be withheld, since knowledge in all cases brings about its fruit. Smriti, moreover, declares that all the four castes are qualified for acquiring the knowledge of the itihâsas and purânas; compare the passage, 'He is to teach the four castes' (Mahâbh.).—It remains, however, a settled point that they do not possess any such qualification with regard to the Veda.

39. (The prâna is Brahman), on account of the trembling (predicated of the whole world).

The discussion of qualification for Brahma-knowledge—on which we entered as an opportunity offered—being finished we return to our chief topic, i. e. the enquiry into the purport of the Vedânta-texts.—We read (Ka. Up. II, 6, 2), 'Whatever there is, the whole world when gone forth trembles in the prâna. It (the prâna) is a great terror, a raised thunderbolt. Those who know it become immortal[1].'—This passage declares that this whole world trembles, abiding in prâna, and that there is raised something very terrible, called a thunderbolt, and that through its knowledge immortality is obtained. But as it is not immediately clear what the prâna is, and what that terrible thunderbolt, a discussion arises.

The pûrvapakshin maintains that, in accordance with the ordinary meaning of the term, prâna denotes the air with its five modifications, that the word 'thunderbolt' also is to be taken in its ordinary sense, and that thus the whole passage contains a glorification of air. For, he says, this whole world trembles, abiding within air with its five forms—which is here called prâna—and the terrible thunderbolts also spring from air (or wind) as their cause. For in the air, people say, when it manifests itself in the form of Parganya, lightning, thunder, rain, and thunderbolts manifest themselves.—Through the knowledge of that air immortality

[1] As the words stand in the original they might be translated as follows (and are so translated by the pûrvapakshin), 'Whatever there is, the whole world trembles in the prâna, there goes forth (from it) a great terror, viz. the raised thunderbolt.'

also can be obtained; for another scriptural passage says, 'Air is everything by itself, and air is all things together. He who knows this conquers death.'—We therefore conclude that the same air is to be understood in the passage under discussion.

To this we make the following reply.—Brahman only can be meant, on account of what precedes as well as what follows. In the preceding as well as the subsequent part of the chapter Brahman only is spoken of; how then can it be supposed that in the intermediate part all at once the air should be referred to? The immediately preceding passage runs as follows, 'That only is called the Bright, that is called Brahman, that alone is called the Immortal. All worlds are contained in it, and no one goes beyond it.' That the Brahman there spoken of forms the topic of our passage also, we conclude, firstly, from proximity; and, secondly, from the circumstance that in the clause, 'The whole world trembles in prâ*n*a,' we recognise a quality of Brahman, viz. its constituting the abode of the whole world. That the word prâ*n*a can denote the highest Self also, appears from such passages as 'the prâ*n*a of prâ*n*a' (B*ri*. Up. IV, 4, 18). Being the cause of trembling, moreover, is a quality which properly appertains to the highest Self only, not to mere air. Thus Scripture says, 'No mortal lives by the prâ*n*a and the breath that goes down. We live by another in whom these two repose' (Ka. Up. II, 5, 5). And also in the passage subsequent to the one under discussion, ('From terror of it fire burns, from terror the sun burns, from terror Indra and Vâyu, and Death as the fifth run away,') Brahman, and not the air, must be supposed to be spoken of, since the subject of that passage is represented as the cause of fear on the part of the whole world inclusive of the air itself. Thence we again conclude that the passage under discussion also refers to Brahman, firstly, on the ground of proximity; and, secondly, because we recognise a quality of Brahman, viz. its being the cause of fear, in the words, 'A great terror, a raised thunderbolt.' The word 'thunderbolt' is here used to denote a cause of fear in general. Thus in ordinary life also a man strictly carries out a king's command because he fearfully considers in his mind, 'A thunderbolt (i. e. the king's wrath, or threatened punishment) is hanging over my head; it might fall if I did not carry out his command.' In the same manner this whole world inclusive of fire, air, sun, and so on, regularly carries on its manifold functions from fear of Brahman; hence Brahman as inspiring fear is compared to a thunderbolt. Similarly, another scriptural passage, whose topic is Brahman, declares, 'From terror of it the wind blows, from terror the sun rises; from terror of it Agni and Indra, yea, Death runs as the fifth.'—That Brahman is what is referred to in our passage, further follows from the declaration that the fruit of its cognition is immortality. For that immortality is the fruit of the knowledge of Brahman is known, for instance, from the mantra, 'A man who knows him only passes over death, there is no other path to go' (*S*vet. Up. VI, 15).—That immortality which the pûrvapakshin asserts to be sometimes represented as the fruit of the knowledge of the air is a merely relative one; for there (i.e. in the chapter from which the passage is quoted) at first the highest Self is spoken of, by means of a new topic being started (B*ri*. Up. III, 4), and thereupon the inferior nature of the air and so on is referred to. ('Everything else is evil.')—That in the passage under discussion the highest Self is meant appears finally from the general subject-matter; for the question (asked by Na*k*iketas in I, 2, 14, 'That which thou seest as neither this nor that, as neither effect nor cause, as neither past nor future tell me that') refers to the highest Self.

40. The light (is Brahman), on account of that (Brahman) being seen (in the scriptural passage).

We read in Scripture, 'Thus does that serene being, arising from this body, appear in its own form as soon as it has approached the highest light' (*Kh*. Up. VIII, 12, 3). Here the doubt arises whether the word 'light' denotes the (physical) light, which is the object of sight and dispels darkness, or the highest Brahman.

The pûrvapakshin maintains that the word 'light' denotes the well-known (physical) light, because that is the conventional sense of the world. For while it is to be admitted that in another passage, discussed under I, 1, 24, the word 'light' does, owing to the general topic of the chapter, divest itself of its ordinary meaning and denote Brahman, there is in our passage no similar reason for setting the ordinary meaning aside. Moreover, it is stated in the chapter treating of the nâ*d*is of the body, that a man going to final release reaches the sun ('When he departs from this body then he departs upwards by those very rays;' *Kh.* Up. VIII, 6, 5). Hence we conclude that the word 'light' denotes, in our passage, the ordinary light.

To this we make the following reply.—The word 'light' can denote the highest Brahman only, on account of that being seen. We see that in the whole chapter Brahman is carried on as the topic of discussion. For the Self, which is free from sin, &c. is introduced as the general subject-matter in VIII, 7, 1 ('the Self which is free from sin'); it is thereupon set forth as that which is to be searched out and to be understood (VIII, 7, 1); it is carried on by means of the clauses, 'I shall explain that further to you' (VIII, 9, 3 ff.); after that freedom from body is said to belong to it, because it is one with light ('when he is free from the body then neither pleasure nor pain touches him,' VIII, 12, 1)—and freedom from body is not possible outside Brahman—and it is finally qualified as 'the highest light, the highest person' (VIII, 12, 3).—Against the statement, made by the pûrvapakshin, that Scripture speaks of a man going to release as reaching the sun, we remark that the release there referred to is not the ultimate one, since it is said to be connected with going and departing upwards. That the ultimate release has nothing to do with going and departing upwards we shall show later on.

41. The ether is (Brahman), as it is designated as something different, &c. (from name and form).

Scripture says, 'He who is called ether (âkâ*s*a) is the revealer of all forms and names. That within which these forms and names are contained is the Brahman, the Immortal, the Self' (*Kh.* Up. VIII, 14, 1).

There arising a doubt whether that which here is called ether is the highest Brahman or the ordinary elemental ether, the pûrvapakshin declares that the latter alternative is to be embraced, firstly, because it is founded on the conventional meaning of the word 'ether;' and, secondly, because the circumstance of revealing names and forms can very well be reconciled with the elemental ether, as that which affords room (for all things). Moreover, the passage contains no clear indicatory mark of Brahman, such as creative power, and the like.

To this we reply, that the word 'ether' can here denote the highest Brahman only, because it is designated as a different thing, &c. For the clause, 'That within which these two are contained is Brahman,' designates the ether as something different from names and forms. But, excepting Brahman, there is nothing whatever different from name and form, since the entire world of effects is evolved exclusively by names and forms. Moreover, the complete revealing of names and forms cannot be accomplished by anything else but Brahman, according to the text which declares Brahman's creative agency, 'Let me enter (into those beings) with this living Self (*g*îva âtman), and evolve names and forms' (*Kh.* Up. VI, 3, 2). But—it may be said—from this very passage it is apparent that the living Self also (i. e. the individual soul) possesses revealing power with regard to names and forms.—True, we reply, but what the passage really wishes to intimate, is the non-difference (of the individual soul from the highest Self). And the very statement concerning the revealing of names and forms implies the statement of signs indicatory of Brahman, viz. creative power and the like.—Moreover, the terms 'the Brahman, the Immortal, the Self' (VIII, 14) indicate that Brahman is spoken of.

42. And (on account of the designation) (of the highest Self) as different (from the individual soul) in the states of deep sleep and departing.

In the sixth prapâ*th*aka of the B*ri*hadâra*n*yaka there is given, in reply to the question, 'Who is that Self?' a lengthy exposition of the nature of the Self, 'He who is within the heart, among the prâ*n*as, the person of light, consisting of knowledge' (B*ri*. Up. IV, 3, 7). Here the doubt arises, whether the passage merely aims at making an additional statement about the nature of the transmigrating soul (known already from other sources), or at establishing the nature of the non-transmigrating Self.

The pûrvapakshin maintains that the passage is concerned with the nature of the transmigrating soul, on account of the introductory and concluding statements. For the introductory statement, 'He among the prâ*n*as who consists of knowledge,' contains marks indicatory of the embodied soul, and so likewise the concluding passage, 'And that great unborn Self is he who consists of cognition,' &c. (IV, 4, 22). We must therefore adhere to the same subject-matter in the intermediate passages also, and look on them as setting forth the same embodied Self, represented in its different states, viz. the waking state, and so on.

In reply to this, we maintain that the passage aims only at giving information about the highest Lord, not at making additional statements about the embodied soul.—Why?—On account of the highest Lord being designated as different from the embodied soul, in the states of deep sleep and of departing from the body. His difference from the embodied soul in the state of deep sleep is declared in the following passage, 'This person embraced by the intelligent (prâ*g*ña) Self knows nothing that is without, nothing that is within.' Here the term, 'the person,' must mean the embodied soul; for of him it is possible to deny that he knows, because he, as being the knower, may know what is within and without. The 'intelligent Self,' on the other hand, is the highest Lord, because he is never dissociated from intelligence, i. e.—in his case—all-embracing knowledge.—Similarly, the passage treating of departure, i. e. death ('this bodily Self mounted by the intelligent Self moves along groaning'), refers to the highest Lord as different from the individual Self. There also we have to understand by the 'embodied one' the individual soul which is the Lord of the body, while the 'intelligent one' is again the Lord. We thus understand that 'on account of his being designated as something different, in the states of deep sleep and departure,' the highest Lord forms the subject of the passage.—With reference to the pûrvapakshin's assertion that the entire chapter refers to the embodied Self, because indicatory marks of the latter are found in its beginning, middle, and end, we remark that in the first place the introductory passage ('He among the prâ*n*as who consists of cognition') does not aim at setting forth the character of the transmigrating Self, but rather, while merely referring to the nature of the transmigrating Self as something already known, aims at declaring its identity with the highest Brahman; for it is manifest that the immediately subsequent passage, 'as if thinking, as if moving[1],' aims at discarding the attributes of the transmigrating Self. The concluding passage again is analogous to the initial one; for the words, 'And that great unborn Self is he who,' &c., mean: We have shown that that same cognitional Self, which is observed among the prâ*n*as, is the great unborn Self, i. e. the highest Lord.—He, again, who imagines that the passages intervening (between the two quoted) aim at setting forth the nature of the transmigrating Self by representing it in the waking state, and so on, is like a man who, setting out towards the east, wants to set out at the same time towards the west. For in representing the states of waking, and so on, the passage does not aim at describing the soul as subject to different states or transmigration, but rather as free from all particular conditions and transmigration. This is evident from the circumstance that on *G*anaka's question, which is repeated in every section, 'Speak on for the sake of emancipation,' Yâ*gñ*avalkya replies each time, 'By all that he is not affected, for that person is not attached to anything' (B*ri*. Up. IV, 3, 14–16). And later on he says (IV, 3, 22), 'He is not followed by

[1] The stress lies here on the 'as if,' which intimate that the Self does not really think or move.

good, not followed by evil, for he has then overcome all the sorrows of the heart.' We have, therefore, to conclude that the chapter exclusively aims at setting forth the nature of the non-transmigrating Self.

43. And on account of such words as Lord, &c.

That the chapter aims at setting forth the nature of the non-transmigrating Self, we have to conclude from that circumstance also that there occur in it terms such as Lord and so on, intimating the nature of the non-transmigrating Self, and others excluding the nature of the transmigrating Self. To the first class belongs, for instance, 'He is the lord of all, the king of all things, the protector of all things.' To the latter class belongs the passage, 'He does not become greater by good works, nor smaller by evil works.'—From all which we conclude that the chapter refers to the non-transmigrating highest Lord.

FOURTH PÂDA.

REVERENCE TO THE HIGHEST SELF!

1. If it be said that some (mention) that which is based on inference (i.e. the pradhâna); we deny this, because (the term alluded to) refers to what is contained in the simile of the body (i.e. the body itself); and (that the text) shows.

In the preceding part of this work—as whose topic there has been set forth an enquiry into Brahman—we have at first defined Brahman (I, 1, 2); we have thereupon refuted the objection that that definition applies to the pradhâna also, by showing that there is no scriptural authority for the latter (I, 1, 5), and we have shown in detail that the common purport of all Vedânta-texts is to set forth the doctrine that Brahman, and not the pradhâ*n*a, is the cause of the world. Here, however, the Sâṅkhya again raises an objection which he considers not to have been finally disposed of.

It has not, he says, been satisfactorily proved that there is no scriptural authority for the pradhâna; for some *s*âkhâs contain expressions which seem to convey the idea of the pradhâna. From this it follows that Kapila and other supreme *ri*shis maintain the doctrine of the pradhâna being the general cause only because it is based on the Veda.—As long therefore as it has not been proved that those passages to which the Sâṅkhyas refer have a different meaning (i. e. do not allude to the pradhâna), all our previous argumentation as to the omniscient Brahman being the cause of the world must be considered as unsettled. We therefore now begin a new chapter which aims at proving that those passages actually have a different meaning.

The Sâṅkhyas maintain that that also which is based on inference, i. e. the pradhâna, is perceived in the text of some *s*âkhâs. We read, for instance, they say, in the Kâ*th*aka (I, 3, 11), 'Beyond the Great there is the Undeveloped, beyond the Undeveloped there is the Person.' There we recognise, named by the same names and enumerated in the same order, the three entities with which we are acquainted from the Sâṅkhya-smriti, viz. the great principle, the Undeveloped (the pradhâna), and the soul [1]. That by the Undeveloped is meant the pradhâna is to be concluded from the common use of Smriti and from the etymological interpretation of which the word admits, the pradhâna being called undeveloped because it is devoid of sound and other qualities. It cannot therefore be asserted that there is no scriptural authority for the pradhâna. And this pradhâna vouched for by Scripture we declare to be the cause of the world, on the ground of Scripture, Smriti, and ratiocination.

Your reasoning, we reply, is not valid. The passage from the Kâthaka quoted by you intimates by no means the existence of that great principle and that Undeveloped which are known from the Sâṅkhya-smriti. We do not recognise there the pradhâna of the Sâṅkhyas, i.e. an independent general cause consisting of three constituting elements; we merely recognise the word 'Undeveloped,' which does not denote any particular determined thing, but may—owing to its etymological meaning, 'that which is not developed, not manifest'—denote anything subtle and difficult to distinguish. The Sâṅkhyas indeed give to the word a settled meaning, as they apply it to the pradhâna; but then that meaning is valid for their system only, and has no force in the determination of the sense of the Veda. Nor does mere equality of position prove equality of being, unless the latter be recognised independently. None but a fool would think a cow to be a horse because he sees it tied in the usual place of a horse. We, moreover, conclude, on the strength of the general subject-matter, that the passage does not refer to the pradhâna the fiction of the Sâṅkhyas, 'on account of there being referred

[1] The Great one is the technical Sâṅkhya-term for buddhi, avyakta is a common designation of pradhâna or prakriti, and purusha is the technical name of the soul. Compare, for instance, Sâṅkhya Kâr. 2, 3.

to that which is contained in the simile of the body.' This means that the body which is mentioned in the simile of the chariot is here referred to as the Undeveloped. We infer this from the general subject-matter of the passage and from the circumstance of nothing else remaining.—The immediately preceding part of the chapter exhibits the simile in which the Self, the body, and so on, are compared to the lord of a chariot, a chariot, &c., 'Know the Self to be the lord of the chariot, the body to be the chariot, the intellect the charioteer, and the mind the reins. The senses they call the horses, the objects of the senses their roads. When he (the Self) is in union with the body, the senses and the mind, then wise people call him the enjoyer.' The text then goes on to say that he whose senses, &c. are not well controlled enters into sa*m*sâra, while he who has them under control reaches the end of the journey, the highest place of Vish*n*u. The question then arises: What is the end of the journey, the highest place of Vish*n*u? Whereupon the text explains that the highest Self which is higher than the senses, &c., spoken of is the end of the journey, the highest place of Vish*n*u. 'Beyond the senses there are the objects, beyond the objects there is the mind, beyond the mind there is the intellect, the great Self is beyond the intellect. Beyond the great there is the Undeveloped, beyond the Undeveloped there is the Person. Beyond the Person there is nothing—this is the goal, the highest Road.' In this passage we recognise the senses, &c. which in the preceding simile had been compared to horses and so on, and we thus avoid the mistake of abandoning the matter in hand and taking up a new subject. The senses, the intellect, and the mind are referred to in both passages under the same names. The objects (in the second passage) are the objects which are (in the former passage) designated as the roads of the senses; that the objects are beyond (higher than) the senses is known from the scriptural passage representing the senses as grahas, i.e. graspers, and the objects as atigrahas, i.e. superior to the grahas (B*ri*. Up. III, 2). The mind (manas) again is superior to the objects, because the relation of the senses and their objects is based on the mind. The intellect (buddhi) is higher than the mind, since the objects of enjoyment are conveyed to the soul by means of the intellect. Higher than the intellect is the great Self which was represented as the lord of the chariot in the passage, 'Know the Self to be the lord of the chariot.' That the same Self is referred to in both passages is manifest from the repeated use of the word 'Self;' that the Self is superior to intelligence is owing to the circumstance that the enjoyer is naturally superior to the instrument of enjoyment. The Self is appropriately called great as it is the master.—Or else the phrase 'the great Self' may here denote the intellect of the first-born Hira*n*yagarbha which is the basis of all intellects; in accordance with the following Sm*ri*ti-passage 'it is called mind, the great one; reflection, Brahman; the stronghold, intellect; enunciation, the Lord; highest knowledge, consciousness; thought, remembrance[1],' and likewise with the following scriptural passage, 'He (Hira*n*yagarbha) who first creates Brahman and delivers the Vedas to him' (*S*vet. Up. VI, 18). The intellect, which in the former passage had been referred to under its common name buddhi, is here mentioned separately, since it may be represented as superior to our human intellects. On this latter explanation of the term 'the great Self,' we must assume that the personal Self which in the simile had been compared to the charioteer is, in the latter passage, included in the highest person (mentioned last); to which there is no objection, since in reality the personal Self and the highest Self are identical.—Thus there remains now the body only which had before been compared to a chariot. We therefore con-

[1] Sa*m*kalpavikalparûpamananas*a*ktyâ haira*n*yagarbhî buddhir manas tasyâ*h* vyash*t*imana*h*su samash*t*itayâ vyâptim âha mahân iti. Sa*m*kalpâdi*s*aktitayâ tarhi sa*m*dehâtmatva*m* tatrâha matir iti. Mahatvam upapâdayati brahmeti. Bhogyag*â*tâdhâratvam âha pûr iti. Nis*k*ayâtmakatvam âha buddhir iti. Kîrti*s*aktimattvam âha khyâtir iti. Niyamana*s*aktimatvam âha î*s*vara iti. Loke yat prak*ri*sh*t*a*m* g*ñ*ânam tato*-*natirekam âha prag*ñ*eti. Tatphalam api tato nârthântaravishayam ity âha sa*m*vid iti. *K*itpradhânatvam âha *k*itir iti. G*ñ*âtasarvârthânusa*m*dhâna*s*aktim âha sm*ri*ti*s* *k*eti. Ânanda Giri.

clude that the text after having enumerated the senses and all the other things mentioned before, in order to point out the highest place, points out by means of the one remaining word, viz. avyakta, the only thing remaining out of those which had been mentioned before, viz. the body. The entire passage aims at conveying the knowledge of the unity of the inward Self and Brahman, by describing the soul's passing through sa*m*sâra and release under the form of a simile in which the body, &c. of the soul—which is affected by Nescience and therefore joined to a body, senses, mind, intellect, objects, sensations, &c.—are compared to a chariot, and so on.—In accordance with this the subsequent verse states the difficulty of knowing the highest place of Vish*n*u ('the Self is hidden in all beings and does not shine forth, but it is seen by subtle seers through their sharp and subtle intellect'), and after that the next verse declares Yoga to be the means of attaining that cognition. 'A wise man should keep down speech in the mind, he should keep down the mind in intelligence, intelligence he should keep down within the great Self, and he should keep that within the quiet Self.'—That means: The wise man should restrain the activity of the outer organs such as speech, &c., and abide within the mind only; he should further restrain the mind which is intent on doubtful external objects within intelligence, whose characteristic mark is decision, recognising that indecision is evil; he should further restrain intelligence within the great Self, i. e. the individual soul or else the fundamental intellect; he should finally fix the great Self on the calm Self, i. e. the highest Self, the highest goal, of which the whole chapter treats.—If we in this manner review the general context, we perceive that there is no room for the pradhâna imagined by the Sâṅkhyas.

2. But the subtle (body is meant by the term avyakta) on account of its capability (of being so designated).

It has been asserted, under the preceding Sûtra, that the term 'the Undeveloped' signifies, on account of the general subject-matter and because the body only remains, the body and not the pradhâna of the Sâṅkhyas.—But here the following doubt arises: How can the word 'undeveloped' appropriately denote the body which, as a gross and clearly appearing thing, should rather be called vyakta, i. e. that which is developed or manifested?

To this doubt the Sûtra replies that what the term avyakta denotes is the subtle causal body. Anything subtle may be spoken of as Undeveloped. The gross body indeed cannot directly be termed 'undeveloped,' but the subtle parts of the elements from which the gross body originates may be called so, and that the term denoting the causal substance is applied to the effect also is a matter of common occurrence; compare, for instance, the phrase 'mix the Soma with cows, i.e. milk' (*Ri*g-veda S. IX, 46, 4). Another scriptural passage also—'now all this was then undeveloped' (B*ri*. Up. I, 4, 7)—shows that this, i. e. this developed world with its distinction of names and forms, is capable of being termed undeveloped in so far as in a former condition it was in a merely seminal or potential state, devoid of the later evolved distinctions of name and form.

3. (Such a previous seminal condition of the world may be admitted) on account of its dependency on him (the Lord); (for such an admission is) according to reason.

Here a new objection is raised.—If, the opponent says, in order to prove the possibility of the body being called undeveloped you admit that this world in its antecedent seminal condition before either names or forms are evolved can be called undeveloped, you virtually concede the doctrine that the pradhâna is the cause of the world. For we Sâṅkhyas understand by the term pradhâna nothing but that antecedent condition of the world.

Things lie differently, we rejoin. If we admitted some antecedent state of the world as the independent cause of the actual world, we should indeed implicitly admit the pradhâna doctrine. What we admit is, however, only a previous state dependent on the highest Lord, not an independent state. A previous stage of the world such as the one assumed by us must necessarily be admitted, since it is according to sense and reason. For without it the highest Lord could not be conceived as creator, as he could not become active if he were destitute of the potentiality of action. The existence of such a causal potentiality renders it moreover possible that the released souls should not enter on new courses of existence, as it is destroyed by perfect knowledge. For that causal potentiality is of the nature of Nescience; it is rightly denoted by the term 'undeveloped;' it has the highest Lord for its substratum; it is of the nature of an illusion; it is a universal sleep in which are lying the transmigrating souls destitute for the time of the consciousness of their individual character[1]. This undeveloped principle is sometimes denoted by the term âkâ*s*a, ether; so, for instance, in the passage, 'In that Imperishable then, O Gârgî, the ether is woven like warp and woof' (B*ri*. Up. III, 8, 11). Sometimes, again, it is denoted by the term akshara, the Imperishable; so, for instance (Mu. Up. II, 1, 2), 'Higher, than the high Imperishable.' Sometimes it is spoken of as Mâyâ, illusion; so, for instance (*S*ve. Up. IV, 10), 'Know then Prak*ri*ti is Mâyâ, and the great Lord he who is affected with Mâyâ.' For Mâyâ is properly called undeveloped or non-manifested since it cannot be defined either as that which is or that which is not.—The statement of the Kâ*th*aka that 'the Undeveloped is beyond the Great

[1] Nanu na bî*g*a*s*aktir vidyayâ dahyate vastutvâd âtmavan nety âha avidyeti. Ke*k*it tu prati*g*îvam avidya*s*aktibhedam i*kkh*anti tan na avyaktâvyâk*ri*tâdi*s*abdâyâs tasyâ bhedakâbhâvâd ekatve*s*pi sva*s*aktyâ vi*k*itrakâryakaratvâd ity âha avyakteti. Na *k*a tasyâ *g*îvâ*s*rayatva*m* *g*îva*s*abdavâ*k*yasya kalpitatvâd avidyârûpatvât ta*kkh*abdalakshyasya brahmâvyatirekâd ity âha parame*s*vareti. Mâyâvidyayor bhedâd î*s*varasya mâyâ*s*rayatva*m* *g*îvânâm avidyâ*s*rayateti vadanta*m* pratyâha mâyâmayîti. Yathâ mâyâvino mâyâ paratantrâ tathaishâpîty artha*h*. Pratîtau tasyâ*s* *k*etanâpekshâm âha mahâsuptir iti. Ânanda Giri.

one' is based on the fact of the Great one originating from the Undeveloped, if the Great one be the intellect of Hira*n*yagarbha. If, on the other hand, we understand by the Great one the individual soul, the statement is founded on the fact of the existence of the individual soul depending on the Undeveloped, i. e. Nescience. For the continued existence of the individual soul as such is altogether owing to the relation in which it stands to Nescience. The quality of being beyond the Great one which in the first place belongs to the Undeveloped, i. e. Nescience, is attributed to the body which is the product of Nescience, the cause and the effect being considered as identical. Although the senses, &c. are no less products of Nescience, the term 'the Undeveloped' here refers to the body only, the senses, &c. having already been specially mentioned by their individual names, and the body alone being left.—Other interpreters of the two last Sûtras give a somewhat different explanation[1].—There are, they say, two kinds of body, the gross one and the subtle one. The gross body is the one which is perceived; the nature of the subtle one will be explained later on. (Ved. Sû. III, 1, 1.) Both these bodies together were in the simile compared to the chariot; but here (in the passage under discussion) only the subtle body is referred to as the Undeveloped, since the subtle body only is capable of being denoted by that term. And as the soul's passing through bondage and release depends on the subtle body, the latter is said to be beyond the soul, like the things (arthavat), i. e. just as the objects are said to be beyond the senses because the activity of the latter depends on the objects.—But how—we ask those interpreters—is it possible that the word 'Undeveloped' should refer to the subtle body only, while, according to your opinion, both bodies had in the simile been represented as a chariot, and so equally constitute part of the topic of the chapter, and equally remain (to be mentioned in the

[1] Sûtradvayasya v*ri*ttik*ri*dvyâkhyânam utthâpayati. Go. Ân. Â*k*âryade*s*iyamatam utthâpayati. Ân. Gi.

passage under discussion)?—If you should rejoin that you are authorised to settle the meaning of what the text actually mentions, but not to find fault with what is not mentioned, and that the word avyakta which occurs in the text can denote only the subtle body, but not the gross body which is vyakta, i. e. developed or manifest; we invalidate this rejoinder by remarking that the determination of the sense depends on the circumstance of the passages interpreted constituting a syntactical whole. For if the earlier and the later passage do not form a whole they convey no sense, since that involves the abandonment of the subject started and the taking up of a new subject. But syntactical unity cannot be established unless it be on the ground of there being a want of a complementary part of speech or sentence. If you therefore construe the connexion of the passages without having regard to the fact that the latter passage demands as its complement that both bodies (which had been spoken of in the former passage) should be understood as referred to, you destroy all syntactical unity and so incapacitate yourselves from arriving at the true meaning of the text. Nor must you think that the second passage occupies itself with the subtle body only, for that reason that the latter is not easily distinguished from the Self, while the gross body is easily so distinguished on account of its readily perceived loathsomeness. For the passage does not by any means refer to such a distinction—as we conclude from the circumstance of there being no verb enjoining it—but has for its only subject the highest place of Vish*n*u, which had been mentioned immediately before. For after having enumerated a series of things in which the subsequent one is always superior to the one preceding it, it concludes by saying that nothing is beyond the Person.—We might, however, accept the interpretation just discussed without damaging our general argumentation; for whichever explanation we receive, so much remains clear that the Kâ*th*aka passage does not refer to the pradhâna.

4. And (the pradhâna cannot be meant) because

there is no statement as to (the avyakta) being something to be cognised.

The Sâṅkhyas, moreover, represent the pradhâna as something to be cognised in so far as they say that from the knowledge of the difference of the constitutive elements of the pradhâna and of the soul there results the desired isolation of the soul. For without a knowledge of the nature of those constitutive elements it is impossible to cognise the difference of the soul from them. And somewhere they teach that the pradhâna is to be cognised by him who wishes to attain special powers.—Now in the passage under discussion the avyakta is not mentioned as an object of knowledge; we there meet with the mere word avyakta, and there is no sentence intimating that the avyakta is to be known or meditated upon. And it is impossible to maintain that a knowledge of things which (knowledge) is not taught in the text is of any advantage to man.—For this reason also we maintain that the word avyakta cannot denote the pradhâna.—Our interpretation, on the other hand, is unobjectionable, since according to it the passage mentions the body (not as an object of knowledge, but merely) for the purpose of throwing light on the highest place of Vish*n*u, in continuation of the simile in which the body had been compared to a chariot.

5. And if you maintain that the text does speak (of the pradhâna as an object of knowledge) we deny that; for the intelligent (highest) Self is meant, on account of the general subject-matter.

Here the Sâṅkhya raises a new objection, and maintains that the averment made in the last Sûtra is not proved, since the text later on speaks of the pradhâna—which had been referred to as the Undeveloped—as an object of knowledge. 'He who has perceived that which is without sound, without touch, without form, without decay, without taste, eternal, without smell, without beginning, without end, beyond the great and unchangeable, is freed from the jaws of death' (Ka. Up. II, 3, 15). For here the text speaks of the pradhâna, which is beyond the great, describing it as possessing the same qualities which the Sâṅkhya-smṛiti ascribes to it, and designating it as the object of perception. Hence we conclude that the pradhâna is denoted by the term avyakta.

To this we reply that the passage last quoted does represent as the object of perception not the pradhâna but the intelligent, i. e. the highest Self. We conclude this from the general subject-matter. For that the highest Self continues to form the subject-matter is clear from the following reasons. In the first place, it is referred to in the passage, 'Beyond the person there is nothing, this is the goal, the highest Road;' it has further to be supplied as the object of knowledge in the passage, 'The Self is hidden in all beings and does not shine forth,' because it is there spoken of as difficult to know; after that the restraint of passion, &c. is enjoined as conducive to its cognition, in the passage, 'A wise man should keep down speech within the mind;' and, finally, release from the jaws of death is declared to be the fruit of its knowledge. The Sâṅkhyas, on the other hand, do not suppose that a man is freed from the jaws of death merely by perceiving the pradhâna, but connect that result rather with the cognition of the intelligent Self.—The highest Self is, moreover, spoken of in all Vedânta-texts as possessing just those qualities which are mentioned in the passage quoted above, viz. absence of sound, and the like. Hence it follows, that the pradhâna is in the text neither spoken of as the object of knowledge nor denoted by the term avyakta.

6. And there is question and explanation relative to three things only (not to the pradhâna).

To the same conclusion we are led by the consideration of the circumstance that the Kaṭhavallî-upanishad brings forward, as subjects of discussion, only three things, viz. the fire sacrifice, the individual soul, and the highest Self. These three things only Yama explains, bestowing thereby the boons he had granted, and to them only the questions of Naḱiketas refer. Nothing else is mentioned or enquired about. The question relative to the fire sacrifice is contained in the passage (Ka. Up. I, 1, 13), 'Thou knowest, O Death, the fire sacrifice which leads us to Heaven; tell it to me, who am full of faith.' The question as to the individual soul is contained in I, 1, 20, 'There is that doubt when a man is dead, some saying, he is; others, he is not. This I should like to know, taught by thee; this is the third of my boons.' And the question about the highest Self is asked in the passage (I, 2, 14), 'That which thou seest as neither this nor that, as neither effect nor cause, as neither past nor future, tell me that.'—The corresponding answers are given in I, 1, 15, 'Yama then told him that fire sacrifice, the beginning of all the worlds, and what bricks are required for the altar, and how many;' in the passage met with considerably later on (II, 5, 6; 7), 'Well then, O Gautama, I shall tell thee this mystery, the old Brahman and what happens to the Self after reaching death. Some enter the womb in order to have a body as organic beings, others go into inorganic matter according to their work and according to their knowledge;' and in the passage (I, 2, 18), 'The knowing Self is not born nor does it die,' &c.; which latter passage dilates at length on the highest Self. But there is no question relative to the pradhâna, and hence no opportunity for any remarks on it.

Here the Sâṅkhya advances a new objection. Is, he asks, the question relative to the Self which is asked in the passage, 'There is that doubt when a man is dead,' &c., again resumed in the passage, 'That which thou seest as neither this nor that,' &c., or does the latter passage raise a distinct new question? If the former, the two questions about the Self coalesce into one, and there are therefore altogether two questions only, one relative to the fire sacrifice, the other relative to the Self. In that case the Sûtra has no right to speak of questions and explanations relating to three subjects.—If the latter, you do not consider it a mistake to assume a question in excess of the number of boons granted, and can therefore not object to us if we assume an explanation about the pradhâna in excess of the number of questions asked.

To this we make the following reply.—We by no means assume a question in excess of the number of boons granted, being prevented from doing so by the influence of the opening part of that syntactical whole which constitutes the Ka*th*avallî-upanishad. The Upanishad starts with the topic of the boons granted by Yama, and all the following part of the Upanishad—which is thrown into the form of a colloquy of Yama and Na*k*iketas—carries on that topic up to the very end. Yama grants to Na*k*iketas, who had been sent by his father, three boons. For his first boon Na*k*iketas chooses kindness on the part of his father towards him, for his second boon the knowledge of the fire sacrifice, for his third boon the knowledge of the Self. That the knowledge of the Self is the third boon appears from the indication contained in the passage (I, 1, 20), 'There is that doubt —; this is the third of my boons.'—If we therefore supposed that the passage, 'That which thou seest as neither this nor that,' &c., raises a new question, we should thereby assume a question in excess of the number of boons granted, and thus destroy the connexion of the entire Upanishad.—But—the Sâṅkhya will perhaps interpose—it must needs be admitted that the passage last quoted does raise a new question, because the subject enquired about is a new one. For the former question refers to the individual soul, as we conclude from the doubt expressed in the words, 'There is that doubt when a man is dead—some saying, he is; others, he is not.' Now this individual soul, as having definite attributes, &c., cannot constitute the object of a question expressed in such terms as, 'This which thou seest as neither this nor that,' &c.; the highest Self, on the other hand, may be enquired about in such terms, since it is above all attributes. The appearance of the two questions is, moreover, seen to differ; for the former question refers to existence and non-existence, while the latter is concerned with an entity raised above all definite attributes, &c. Hence we conclude that the latter question, in which the former one cannot be recognised, is a separate question, and does not merely resume the subject of the former one.—All this argumentation is not valid, we reply, since we maintain the unity of the highest Self and the individual Self. If the individual Self were different from the highest Self, we should have to declare that the two questions are separate independent questions, but the two are not really different, as we know from other scriptural passages, such as 'Thou art that.' And in the Upanishad under discussion also the answer to the question, 'That which thou seest as neither this nor that,' viz. the passage, 'The knowing Self is not born, it dies not'—which answer is given in the form of a denial of the birth and death of the Self—clearly shows that the embodied Self and the highest Self are non-different. For there is room for a denial of something only when that something is possible, and the possibility of birth and death exists in the embodied Self only, since it is connected with the body, but not in the highest Self.—There is, moreover, another passage conveying the same meaning, viz. II, 4, 4, 'The wise when he knows that that by which he perceives all objects in sleep or in waking, is the great omnipresent Self, grieves no more.' This passage makes the cessation of all grief dependent on the knowledge of the individual Self, in so far as it possesses the qualities of greatness and omnipresence, and thereby declares that the individual Self is not different from the highest Self. For that the cessation of all sorrow is consequent on the knowledge of the highest Self, is a recognised Vedânta tenet.—There is another passage also warning men not to look on the individual Self and the highest Self as different entities, viz. II, 4, 10, 'What is here the same is there; and what is there the same is here. He who sees any difference here goes from death to death.'—The following circumstance, too, is worthy of consideration. When Na*k*iketas has asked the question relating to the existence or non-existence of the soul after death, Yama tries to induce him to choose another boon, tempting him with the offer of various objects of desire. But Na*k*iketas remains firm. Thereupon Death, dwelling on the distinction of the Good and the Pleasant, and the distinction of wisdom and ignorance, praises Na*k*iketas, 'I believe Na*k*iketas to be one who desires knowledge, for even many pleasures did not tear thee away' (I, 2, 4); and later on praises the question asked by Na*k*iketas, 'The wise who, by means of meditation on his Self, recognises the Ancient who is difficult to be seen, who has entered into the dark, who is hidden in the cave, who dwells in the abyss, as God, he indeed leaves joy and sorrow far behind' (I, 2, 12). Now all this means to intimate that the individual Self and the highest Self are non-different. For if Na*k*iketas set aside the question, by asking which he had earned for himself the praise of Yama, and after having received that praise asked a new question, all that praise would have been bestowed on him unduly. Hence it follows that the question implied in I, 2, 14, 'That which thou seest as neither this nor that,' merely resumes the topic to which the question in I, 1, 20 had referred.—Nor is there any basis to the objection that the two questions differ in form. The second question, in reality, is concerned with the same distinction as the first. The first enquires about the existence of the soul apart from the body, &c.; the second refers to the circumstance of that soul not being subject to sa*m*sâra. For as long as Nescience remains, so long the soul is affected with definite attributes, &c.; but as soon as Nescience comes to an end, the soul is one with the highest Self, as is taught by such scriptural texts as 'Thou art that.' But whether Nescience be active or inactive, no difference is made thereby in the thing itself (viz. the soul). A man may, in the dark, mistake a piece of rope lying on the ground for a snake, and run away from it, frightened and trembling; thereon another man may tell him, 'Do not be afraid, it is only a rope, not a snake;' and he may then dismiss the fear caused by the imagined snake, and stop running. But all the while the presence and subsequent absence of his erroneous notion, as to the rope being a snake, make no difference whatever in the rope itself. Exactly analogous is the case of the individual soul which is in reality one with the highest soul, although Nescience makes it appear different. Hence the reply contained in the passage, 'It is not born, it dies not,' is also to be considered as furnishing an answer to the question asked in I, 1, 20.—The Sûtra is to be understood with reference to the distinction of the individual Self and the highest Self which results from Nescience. Although the question relating to the Self is in reality one only, yet its former part (I, 1, 20) is seen specially to refer to the individual Self, since there a doubt is set forth as to the existence of the soul when, at the time of death, it frees itself from the body, and since the specific marks of the *samsâra*-state, such as activity, &c. are not denied; while the latter part of the question (I, 2, 14), where the state of being beyond all attributes is spoken of, clearly refers to the highest Self.—For these reasons the Sûtra is right in assuming three topics of question and explanation, viz. the fire sacrifice, the individual soul, and the highest Self. Those, on the other hand, who assume that the pradhâna constitutes a fourth subject discussed in the Upanishad, can point neither to a boon connected with it, nor to a question, nor to an answer. Hence the pradhâna hypothesis is clearly inferior to our own.

7. And (the case of the term avyakta) is like that of the term mahat.

While the Sâṅkhyas employ the term 'the Great one,' to denote the first-born entity, which is mere existence[1] (? viz. the intellect), the term has a different meaning in Vedic use. This we see from its being connected with the Self, &c. in such passages as the following, 'The great Self is beyond the Intellect' (Ka. Up. I, 3, 10); 'The great omnipresent Self' (Ka. Up. I, 2, 22); 'I know that great person' (*S*ve. Up. III, 8). We thence conclude that the word avyakta also, where it occurs in the Veda, cannot denote the pradhâna.—The pradhâna is therefore a mere thing of inference, and not vouched for by Scripture.

8. (It cannot be maintained that *ag*â means the

[1] The commentators give different explanations of the Sattâmâtra of the text.—Sattâmâtre sattvapradhânaprak*ri*ter âdyapari*n*âme. Go. Ân.—Bhogâpavargapurushârthasya maha*kkh*abditabuddhikâryatvât purushâpekshitaphalakâra*n*am sad u*k*yate tatra bhâvapratyayo*-*pi svarûpârtho na sâmânyavâ*k*î kâryânumeya*m* mahan na pratyaksham iti mâtra*s*abda*h*. Ânanda Giri.

pradhâna) because no special characteristic is stated; as in the case of the cup.

Here the advocate of the pradhâna comes again forward and maintains that the absence of scriptural authority for the pradhâna is not yet proved. For, he says, we have the following mantra (*S*ve. Up. IV, 5), 'There is one a*g*â[1], red, white, and black, producing manifold offspring of the same nature. There is one a*g*a who loves her and lies by her; there is another who leaves her after having enjoyed her.'—In this mantra the words 'red,' 'white,' and 'black' denote the three constituent elements of the pradhâna. Passion is called red on account of its colouring, i. e. influencing property; Goodness is called white, because it is of the nature of Light; Darkness is called black on account of its covering and obscuring property. The state of equipoise of the three constituent elements, i. e. the pradhâna, is denoted by the attributes of its parts, and is therefore called red—white—black. It is further called a*g*â, i. e. unborn, because it is acknowledged to be the fundamental matter out of which everything springs, not a mere effect.—But has not the word a*g*â the settled meaning of she-goat?—True; but the ordinary meaning of the word cannot be accepted in this place, because true knowledge forms the general subject-matter.—That pradhâna produces many creatures participating in its three constituent elements. One unborn being loves her and lies by her, i. e. some souls, deluded by ignorance, approach her, and falsely imagining that they experience pleasure or pain, or are in a state of dulness, pass through the course of transmigratory existence. Other souls, again, which have attained to discriminative knowledge, lose their attachment to prak*ri*ti, and leave her after having enjoyed her, i. e. after she has afforded to them enjoyment and release.—On the ground of this passage, as interpreted above, the

[1] As the meaning of the word a*g*â is going to be discussed, and as the author of the Sûtras and *S*aṅkara seem to disagree as to its meaning (see later on), I prefer to leave the word untranslated in this place.—*S*aṅkara reads—and explains,—in the mantra, sarûpâ*h* (not sarûpâm) and bhuktabhogâm, not bhuktabhogyâm.

followers of Kapila claim the authority of Scripture for their pradhâna hypothesis.

To this argumentation we reply, that the quoted mantra by no means proves the Sâṅkhya doctrine to be based on Scripture. That mantra, taken by itself, is not able to give additional strength to any doctrine. For, by means of some supposition or other, the terms *ag*â, &c. can be reconciled with any doctrine, and there is no reason for the special assertion that the Sâṅkhya doctrine only is meant. The case is analogous to that of the cup mentioned in the mantra, 'There is a cup having its mouth below and its bottom above' (B*ri*. Up. II, 2, 3). Just as it is impossible to decide on the ground of this mantra taken by itself what special cup is meant—it being possible to ascribe, somehow or other, the quality of the mouth being turned downward to any cup—; so here also there is no special quality stated, so that it is not possible to decide from the mantra itself whether the pradhâna is meant by the term *ag*â, or something else.—But in connexion with the mantra about the cup we have a supplementary passage from which we learn what kind of cup is meant, 'What is called the cup having its mouth below and its bottom above is this head.'—Whence, however, can we learn what special being is meant by the *ag*â of the *S*vetâ*s*vatara-upanishad?—To this question the next Sûtra replies.

9. But the (elements) beginning with light (are meant by the term *ag*â); for some read so in their text.

By the term *ag*â we have to understand the causal matter of the four classes of beings, which matter has sprung from the highest Lord and begins with light, i. e. comprises fire, water, and earth.—The word 'but' (in the Sûtra) gives emphasis to the assertion.—This *ag*â is to be considered as comprising three elementary substances, not as consisting of three gu*n*as in the Sâṅkhya sense. We draw this conclusion from the fact that one *s*âkhâ, after having related how fire, water, and earth sprang from the highest Lord, assigns to them red colour, and so on. 'The red colour of burning fire (agni) is the colour of the elementary fire (tegas), its white colour is the colour of water, its black colour the colour of earth,' &c. Now those three elements—fire, water, and earth—we recognise in the *S*vetâ*s*vatara passage, as the words red, white, and black are common to both passages, and as these words primarily denote special colours and can be applied to the Sâṅkhya gu*n*as in a secondary sense only. That passages whose sense is beyond doubt are to be used for the interpretation of doubtful passages, is a generally acknowledged rule. As we therefore find that in the *S*vetâ*s*vatara—after the general topic has been started in I, 1, 'The Brahman-students say, Is Brahman the cause?'—the text, previous to the passage under discussion, speaks of a power of the highest Lord which arranges the whole world ('the Sages devoted to meditation and concentration have seen the power belonging to God himself, hidden in its own qualities'); and as further that same power is referred to in two subsequent complementary passages ('Know then, Prak*ri*ti is Mâyâ, and the great Lord he who is affected with Mâyâ;' 'who being one only rules over every germ;' IV, 10, 11); it cannot possibly be asserted that the mantra treating of the agâ refers to some independent causal matter called pradhâna. We rather assert, on the ground of the general subject-matter, that the mantra describes the same divine power referred to in the other passages, in which names and forms lie unevolved, and which we assume as the antecedent condition of that state of the world in which names and forms are evolved. And that divine power is represented as three-coloured, because its products, viz. fire, water, and earth, have three distinct colours.—But how can we maintain, on the ground of fire, water, and earth having three colours, that the causal matter is appropriately called a three-coloured agâ? if we consider, on the one hand, that the exterior form of the genus agâ (i. e. goat) does not inhere in fire, water, and earth; and, on the other hand, that Scripture teaches fire, water, and earth to have been produced, so that the word agâ cannot be taken in the sense 'non-produced[1].'—To this question the next Sûtra replies.

[1] Here there seems to be a certain discrepancy between the

10. And on account of the statement of the assumption (of a metaphor) there is nothing contrary to reason (in *ag*â denoting the causal matter); just as in the case of honey (denoting the sun) and similar cases.

The word *ag*â neither expresses that fire, water, and earth belong to the goat species, nor is it to be explained as meaning 'unborn;' it rather expresses an assumption, i. e. it intimates the assumption of the source of all beings (which source comprises fire, water, and earth), being compared to a she-goat. For as accidentally some she-goat might be partly red, partly white, partly black, and might have many young goats resembling her in colour, and as some he-goat might love her and lie by her, while some other he-goat might leave her after having enjoyed her; so the universal causal matter which is tri-coloured, because comprising fire, water, and earth, produces many inanimate and animate beings similar to itself, and is enjoyed by the souls fettered by Nescience, while it is abandoned by those souls which have attained true knowlege.—Nor must we imagine that the distinction of individual souls, which is implied in the preceding explanation, involves that reality of the multiplicity of souls which forms one of the tenets of other philosophical schools. For the purport of the passage is to intimate, not the multiplicity of souls, but the distinction of

---

views of the Sûtra writer and *S*aṅkara. Govindânanda notes that according to the Bhâshyak*ri*t *ag*â means simply mâyâ—which interpretation is based on prakara*n*a—while, according to the Sûtrak*ri*t, who explains *ag*â on the ground of the *Kh*ândogya-passage treating of the three primary elements, *ag*â denotes the aggregate of those three elements constituting an avântaraprak*ri*ti.—On *S*aṅkara's explanation the term *ag*â presents no difficulties, for mâyâ is *ag*â, i.e. unborn, not produced. On the explanation of the Sûtra writer, however, *ag*â cannot mean unborn, since the three primary elements are products. Hence we are thrown back on the rû*d*hi signification of *ag*â, according to which it means she-goat. But how can the avântara-prak*ri*ti be called a she-goat? To this question the next Sûtra replies.

the states of bondage and release. This latter distinction is explained with reference to the multiplicity of souls as ordinarily conceived; that multiplicity, however, depends altogether on limiting adjuncts, and is the unreal product of wrong knowledge merely; as we know from scriptural passages such as, 'He is the one God hidden in all beings, all-pervading, the Self in all beings,' &c.—The words 'like the honey' (in the Sûtra) mean that just as the sun, although not being honey, is represented as honey (*Kh.* Up. III, 1), and speech as a cow (B*ri.* Up. V, 8), and the heavenly world, &c. as the fires (B*ri.* Up. VI, 2, 9), so here the causal matter, although not being a she-goat, is metaphorically represented as one. There is therefore nothing contrary to reason in the circumstance of the term a*g*â being used to denote the aggregate of fire, water, and earth.

11. (The assertion that there is scriptural authority for the pradhâna, &c. can) also not (be based) on the mention of the number (of the Sâṅkhya categories), on account of the diversity (of the categories) and on account of the excess (over the number of those categories).

The attempt to base the Sâṅkhya doctrine on the mantra speaking of the a*g*â having failed, the Sâṅkhya again comes forward and points to another mantra: 'He in whom the five "five-people" and the ether rest, him alone I believe to be the Self; I who know believe him to be Brahman' (B*ri.* Up. IV, 4, 17). In this mantra we have one word which expresses the number five, viz. the five-people, and then another word, viz. five, which qualifies the former; these two words together therefore convey the idea of five pentads, i.e. twenty-five. Now as many beings as the number twenty-five presupposes, just so many categories the Sâṅkhya system counts. Cp. Sâṅkhya Kârikâ, 3: 'The fundamental causal substance (i.e. the pradhâna) is not an effect. Seven (substances), viz. the Great one (Intellect), and so on, are causal substances as well as effects. Sixteen are effects. The soul is neither a causal substance nor an effect.'

As therefore the number twenty-five, which occurs in the scriptural passage quoted, clearly refers to the twenty-five categories taught in the Sâṅkhya-smṛiti, it follows that the doctrine of the pradhâna, &c. rests on a scriptural basis.

To this reasoning we make the following reply.—It is impossible to base the assertion that the pradhâna, &c. have Scripture in their favour on the reference to their number which you pretend to find in the text, 'on account of the diversity of the Sâṅkhya categories.' The Sâṅkhya categories have each their individual difference, and there are no attributes belonging in common to each pentad on account of which the number twenty-five could be divided into five times five. For a number of individually separate things can, in general, not be combined into smaller groups of two or three, &c. unless there be a special reason for such combination.—Here the Sâṅkhya will perhaps rejoin that the expression five (times) five is used only to denote the number twenty-five which has five pentads for its constituent parts; just as the poem says, 'five years and seven Indra did not rain,' meaning only that there was no rain for twelve years.—But this explanation also is not tenable. In the first place, it is liable to the objection that it has recourse to indirect indication[1].—In the second place, the second 'five' constitutes a compound with the word 'people,' the Brâhmaṇa-accent showing that the two form one word only[2]. To the same conclusion we are led by another passage also (Taitt. Saṃh. I, 6, 2, 2, pañkânâṃ tvâ pañkaganânâm, &c.) where the two terms constitute one word, have one accent and one case-

[1] Indication (lakshaṇâ, which consists in this case in five times five being used instead of twenty-five) is considered as an objectionable mode of expression, and therefore to be assumed in interpretation only where a term can in no way be shown to have a direct meaning.

[2] That pañkaganâḥ is only one word appears from its having only one accent, viz. the udâtta on the last syllable, which udâtta becomes anudâtta according to the rules laid down in the Bhâshika Sûtra for the accentuation of the Satapatha-brâhmaṇa.

termination. The word thus being a compound there is neither a repetition of the word 'five,' involving two pentads, nor does the one five qualify the other, as the mere secondary member of a compound cannot be qualified by another word.—But as the people are already denoted to be five by the compound 'five-people,' the effect of the other 'five' qualifying the compound will be that we understand twenty-five people to be meant; just as the expression 'five five-bundles' (pa*ñk*a pa*ñk*apûlya*h*) conveys the idea of twenty-five bundles.—The instance is not an analogous one, we reply. The word 'pa*ñk*apûli' denotes a unity (i.e. one bundle made up of five bundles), and hence when the question arises, 'How many such bundles are there?' it can be qualified by the word 'five,' indicating that there are five such bundles. The word pa*ñk*a*g*anâ*h*, on the other hand, conveys at once the idea of distinction (i.e. of five distinct things), so that there is no room at all for a further desire to know how many people there are, and hence no room for a further qualification. And if the word 'five' be taken as a qualifying word it can only qualify the numeral five (in five-people); the objection against which assumption has already been stated.—For all these reasons the expression the five five-people cannot denote the twenty-five categories of the Sâṅkhyas.—This is further not possible 'on account of the excess.' For on the Sâṅkhya interpretation there would be an excess over the number twenty-five, owing to the circumstance of the ether and the Self being mentioned separately. The Self is spoken of as the abode in which the five five-people rest, the clause 'Him I believe to be the Self' being connected with the 'in whom' of the antecedent clause. Now the Self is the intelligent soul of the Sâṅkhyas which is already included in the twenty-five categories, and which therefore, on their interpretation of the passage, would here be mentioned once as constituting the abode and once as what rests in the abode! If, on the other hand, the soul were supposed not to be comprised in the twenty-five categories, the Sâṅkhya would thereby abandon his own doctrine of the categories being twenty-five. The same remarks apply to the separate mention made of the ether. —How, finally, can the mere circumstance of a certain number being referred to in the sacred text justify the assumption that what is meant are the twenty-five Sâṅkhya categories of which Scripture speaks in no other place? especially if we consider that the word *g*ana has not the settled meaning of category, and that the number may be satisfactorily accounted for on another interpretation of the passage.

How, then, the Sâṅkhya will ask, do you interpret the phrase 'the five five-people?'—On the ground, we reply, of the rule Pâ*n*ini II, 1, 50, according to which certain compounds formed with numerals are mere names. The word pa*ñk*a*g*anâ*h* thus is not meant to convey the idea of the number five, but merely to denote certain classes of beings. Hence the question may present itself, How many such classes are there? and to this question an answer is given by the added numeral 'five.' There are certain classes of beings called five-people, and these classes are five. Analogously we may speak of the seven seven-*ri*shis, where again the compound denotes a class of beings merely, not their number.—Who then are those five-people?—To this question the next Sûtra replies.

12. (The pa*ñk*a*g*anâ*h* are) the breath and so on, (as is seen) from the complementary passage.

The mantra in which the pa*ñk*a*g*anâ*h* are mentioned is followed by another one in which breath and four other things are mentioned for the purpose of describing the nature of Brahman. 'They who know the breath of breath, the eye of the eye, the ear of the ear, the food of food, the mind of mind [1].' Hence we conclude, on the ground of proximity, that the five-people are the beings mentioned in this latter mantra.—But how, the Sâṅkhya asks, can the word 'people' be applied to the breath, the eye, the ear, and so on?—How, we ask in return, can it be

[1] So in the Mâdhyandina recension of the Upanishad; the Kâ*n*va recension has not the clause 'the food of food.'

applied to your categories? In both cases the common meaning of the word 'people' has to be disregarded; but in favour of our explanation is the fact that the breath, the eye, and so on, are mentioned in a complementary passage. The breath, the eye, &c. may be denoted by the word 'people' because they are connected with people. Moreover, we find the word 'person,' which means as much as 'people,' applied to the prâ*n*as in the passage, 'These are the five persons of Brahman' (*Kh*. Up. III, 13, 6); and another passage runs, 'Breath is father, breath is mother,' &c. (*Kh*. Up. VII, 15, 1). And, owing to the force of composition, there is no objection to the compound being taken in its settled conventional meaning [1].—But how can the conventional meaning be had recourse to, if there is no previous use of the word in that meaning?—That may be done, we reply, just as in the case of udbhid and similar words [2]. We often infer that a word of unknown meaning refers to some known thing because it is used in connexion with the latter. So, for instance, in the case of the following words: 'He is to sacrifice with the udbhid; he cuts the yûpa; he makes the vedi.' Analogously we conclude that the term pa*ñk*a*g*anâ*h*, which, from the grammatical rule quoted, is known to be a name, and which therefore demands a thing of which it is the name, denotes the breath, the eye, and so on, which are connected with it through their being mentioned in a complementary passage.—Some commentators explain the word pa*ñk*a-

[1] This in answer to the Sâṅkhya who objects to *g*ana when applied to the prâna, &c. being interpreted with the help of laksha*n*â; while if referred to the pradhâna, &c. it may be explained to have a direct meaning, on the ground of yaugika interpretation (the pradhâna being *g*ana because it produces, the mahat &c. being *g*ana because they are produced). The Vedântin points out that the compound pa*ñk*a*g*anâ*h* has its own rû*dh*i-meaning, just as a*s*vakar*n*a, literally horse-ear, which conventionally denotes a certain plant.

[2] We infer that udbhid is the name of a sacrifice because it is mentioned in connexion with the act of sacrificing; we infer that the yûpa is a wooden post because it is said to be cut, and so on.

ganâh to mean the Gods, the Fathers, the Gandharvas, the Asuras, and the Rakshas. Others, again, think that the four castes together with the Nishâdas are meant. Again, some scriptural passage (*Ri*g-veda Sa*m*h. VIII, 53, 7) speaks of the tribe of 'the five-people,' meaning thereby the created beings in general; and this latter explanation also might be applied to the passage under discussion. The teacher (the Sûtrakâra), on the other hand, aiming at showing that the passage does not refer to the twenty-five categories of the Sâṅkhyas, declares that on the ground of the complementary passage breath, &c. have to be understood.

Well, let it then be granted that the five-people mentioned in the Mâdhyandina-text are breath, &c. since that text mentions food also (and so makes up the number five). But how shall we interpret the Kâ*n*va-text which does not mention food (and thus altogether speaks of four things only)?—To this question the next Sûtra replies.

13. In the case of (the text of) some (the Kâ*n*vas) where food is not mentioned, (the number five is made full) by the light (mentioned in the preceding mantra).

The Kâ*n*va-text, although not mentioning food, makes up the full number five, by the light mentioned in the mantra preceding that in which the five-people are spoken of. That mantra describes the nature of Brahman by saying, 'Him the gods worship as the light of lights.'—If it be asked how it is accounted for that the light mentioned in both texts equally is in one text to be employed for the explanation of the five-people, and not in the other text; we reply that the reason lies in the difference of the requirements. As the Mâdhyandinas meet in one and the same mantra with breath and four other entities enabling them to interpret the term, 'the five-people,' they are in no need of the light mentioned in another mantra. The Kâ*n*vas, on the other hand, cannot do without the light. The case is analogous to that of the Sho*d*a*s*in-cup, which, according to different passages, is either to be offered or not to be offered at the atirâtra-sacrifice.

We have proved herewith that Scripture offers no basis for the doctrine of the pradhâna. That this doctrine cannot be proved either by Smriti or by ratiocination will be shown later on.

14. (Although there is a conflict of the Vedânta-passages with regard to the things created, such as) ether and so on; (there is no such conflict with regard to the Lord) on account of his being represented (in one passage) as described (in other passages), viz. as the cause (of the world).

In the preceding part of the work the right definition of Brahman has been established; it has been shown that all the Vedânta-texts have Brahman for their common topic; and it has been proved that there is no scriptural authority for the doctrine of the pradhâna.—But now a new objection presents itself.

It is not possible—our opponent says—to prove either that Brahman is the cause of the origin, &c. of the world, or that all Vedânta-texts refer to Brahman; because we observe that the Vedânta-texts contradict one another. All the Vedânta-passages which treat of the creation enumerate its successive steps in different order, and so in reality speak of different creations. In one place it is said that from the Self there sprang the ether (Taitt. Up. II, 1); in another place that the creation began with fire (*Kh*. Up. VI, 2, 3); in another place, again, that the Person created breath and from breath faith (Pr. Up. VI, 4); in another place, again, that the Self created these worlds, the water (above the heaven), light, the mortal (earth), and the water (below the earth) (Ait. Âr. II, 4, 1, 2; 3). There no order is stated at all. Somewhere else it is said that the creation originated from the Non-existent. 'In the beginning this was non-existent; from it was born what exists' (Taitt. Up. II, 7); and, 'In the beginning this was non-existent; it became existent; it grew' (*Kh*. Up. III, 19, 1). In another place, again, the doctrine of the Non-existent being the antecedent of the creation is impugned, and the Existent mentioned in its stead. 'Others say, in the beginning there was that only which is not; but how could it be thus, my dear? How could that which is be born of that which is not?' (*Kh*. Up. VI, 2, 1; 2.) And in another place, again, the development of the world is spoken of as having taken place spontaneously, 'Now all this was then undeveloped. It became developed by form and name' (B*ri*. Up. I, 4, 7).—As therefore manifold discrepancies are observed, and as no option is possible in the case of an accomplished matter [1], the Vedânta-passages cannot be accepted as authorities for determining the cause of the world, but we must rather accept some other cause of the world resting on the authority of Sm*ri*ti and Reasoning.

To this we make the following reply.—Although the Vedânta-passages may be conflicting with regard to the order of the things created, such as ether and so on, they do not conflict with regard to the creator, 'on account of his being represented as described.' That means: such as the creator is described in any one Vedânta-passage, viz. as all-knowing, the Lord of all, the Self of all, without a second, so he is represented in all other Vedânta-passages also. Let us consider, for instance, the description of Brahman (given in Taitt. Up. II, 1 ff.). There it is said at first, 'Truth, knowledge, infinite is Brahman.' Here the word 'knowledge,' and so likewise the statement, made later on, that Brahman desired (II, 6), intimate that Brahman is of the nature of intelligence. Further, the text declares [2] that the cause of the world is the general Lord, by representing it as not dependent on anything else. It further applies to the cause of the world the term 'Self' (II, 1), and it represents it as abiding within the series of sheaths begin-

[1] Option being possible only in the case of things to be accomplished, i.e. actions.

[2] According to Go. Ân. in the passage, 'That made itself its Self' (II, 7); according to Ân. Giri in the passage, 'He created all' (II, 6).

ning with the gross body; whereby it affirms it to be the internal Self within all beings. Again—in the passage, 'May I be many, may I grow forth'—it tells how the Self became many, and thereby declares that the creator is non-different from the created effects. And—in the passage, 'He created all this whatever there is'—it represents the creator as the Cause of the entire world, and thereby declares him to have been without a second previously to the creation. The same characteristics which in the above passages are predicated of Brahman, viewed as the Cause of the world, we find to be predicated of it in other passages also, so, for instance, 'Being only, my dear, was this in the beginning, one only, without a second. It thought, may I be many, may I grow forth. It sent forth fire' (*Kh.* Up. VI, 2, 1; 3), and 'In the beginning all this was Self, one only; there was nothing else blinking whatsoever. He thought, shall I send forth worlds?' (Ait. Âr. II, 4, 1, 1; 2.) The Vedânta-passages which are concerned with setting forth the cause of the world are thus in harmony throughout.—On the other hand, there are found conflicting statements concerning the world, the creation being in some places said to begin with ether, in other places with fire, and so on. But, in the first place, it cannot be said that the conflict of statements concerning the world affects the statements concerning the cause, i. e. Brahman, in which all the Vedânta-texts are seen to agree—for that would be an altogether unfounded generalization;—and, in the second place, the teacher will reconcile later on (II, 3) those conflicting passages also which refer to the world. And, to consider the matter more thoroughly, a conflict of statements regarding the world would not even matter greatly, since the creation of the world and similar topics are not at all what Scripture wishes to teach. For we neither observe nor are told by Scripture that the welfare of man depends on those matters in any way; nor have we the right to assume such a thing; because we conclude from the introductory and concluding clauses that the passages about the creation and the like form only subordinate members of passages treating of Brahman. That all the passages setting forth the creation and so on subserve the purpose of teaching Brahman, Scripture itself declares; compare *Kh.* Up. VI, 8, 4, 'As food too is an offshoot, seek after its root, viz. water. And as water too is an offshoot, seek after its root, viz. fire. And as fire too is an offshoot, seek after its root, viz. the True.' We, moreover, understand that by means of comparisons such as that of the clay (*Kh.* Up. VI, 1, 4) the creation is described merely for the purpose of teaching us that the effect is not really different from the cause. Analogously it is said by those who know the sacred tradition, 'If creation is represented by means of (the similes of) clay, iron, sparks, and other things; that is only a means for making it understood that (in reality) there is no difference whatever' (Gau*d*ap. Kâ. III, 15).—On the other hand, Scripture expressly states the fruits connected with the knowledge of Brahman, 'He who knows Brahman obtains the highest' (Taitt. Up. II, 1); 'He who knows the Self overcomes grief' (*Kh.* Up. VII, 1, 3); 'A man who knows him passes over death' (*S*ve. Up. III, 8). That fruit is, moreover, apprehended by intuition (pratyaksha), for as soon as, by means of the doctrine, 'That art thou,' a man has arrived at the knowledge that the Self is non-transmigrating, its transmigrating nature vanishes for him.

It remains to dispose of the assertion that passages such as 'Non-being this was in the beginning' contain conflicting statements about the nature of the cause. This is done in the next Sûtra.

15. On account of the connexion (with passages treating of Brahman, the passages speaking of the Non-being do not intimate absolute Non-existence).

The passage 'Non-being indeed was this in the beginning' (Taitt. Up. II, 7) does not declare that the cause of the world is the absolutely Non-existent which is devoid of all Selfhood. For in the preceding sections of the Upanishad Brahman is distinctly denied to be the Non-existing, and is defined to be that which is ('He who knows the Brahman as non-existing becomes himself non-existing.

He who knows the Brahman as existing him we know himself as existing'); it is further, by means of the series of sheaths, viz. the sheath of food, &c., represented as the inner Self of everything. This same Brahman is again referred to in the clause, 'He wished, may I be many;' is declared to have originated the entire creation; and is finally referred to in the clause, 'Therefore the wise call it the true.' Thereupon the text goes on to say, with reference to what has all along been the topic of discussion, 'On this there is also this *s*loka, Non-being indeed was this in the beginning,' &c. If here the term 'Non-being' denoted the absolutely Non-existent, the whole context would be broken; for while ostensibly referring to one matter the passage would in reality treat of a second altogether different matter. We have therefore to conclude that, while the term 'Being' ordinarily denotes that which is differentiated by names and forms, the term 'Non-being' denotes the same substance previous to its differentiation, i.e. that Brahman is, in a secondary sense of the word, called Non-being, previously to the origination of the world. The same interpretation has to be applied to the passage 'Non-being this was in the beginning' (*Kh*. Up. III, 19, 1); for that passage also is connected with another passage which runs, 'It became being;' whence it is evident that the 'Non-being' of the former passage cannot mean absolute Non-existence. And in the passage, 'Others say, Non-being this was in the beginning' (*Kh*. Up. VI, 2, 1), the reference to the opinion of 'others' does not mean that the doctrine referred to (according to which the world was originally absolutely non-existent) is propounded somewhere in the Veda; for option is possible in the case of actions but not in the case of substances. The passage has therefore to be looked upon as a refutation of the tenet of primitive absolute non-existence as fancifully propounded by some teachers of inferior intelligence; a refutation undertaken for the purpose of strengthening the doctrine that this world has sprung from that which is.—The following passage again, 'Now this was then undeveloped,' &c. (B*ri*. Up. I, 4, 7), does not by any means assert that the evolution of the world took place without a ruler; as we conclude from the circumstance of its being connected with another passage in which the ruler is represented as entering into the evolved world of effects, 'He entered thither to the very tips of the finger-nails,' &c. If it were supposed that the evolution of the world takes place without a ruler, to whom could the subsequent pronoun 'he' refer (in the passage last quoted) which manifestly is to be connected with something previously intimated? And as Scripture declares that the Self, after having entered into the body, is of the nature of intelligence ('when seeing, eye by name; when hearing, ear by name; when thinking, mind by name'), it follows that it is intelligent at the time of its entering also.—We, moreover, must assume that the world was evolved at the beginning of the creation in the same way as it is at present seen to develop itself by names and forms, viz. under the rulership of an intelligent creator; for we have no right to make assumptions contrary to what is at present actually observed. Another scriptural passage also declares that the evolution of the world took place under the superintendence of a ruler, 'Let me now enter these beings with this living Self, and let me then evolve names and forms' (*Kh*. Up. VI, 3, 2). The intransitive expression 'It developed itself' (vyâkriyata; it became developed) is to be viewed as having reference to the ease with which the real agent, viz. the Lord, brought about that evolution. Analogously it is said, for instance, that 'the cornfield reaps itself' (i. e. is reaped with the greatest ease), although there is the reaper sufficient (to account for the work being done).—Or else we may look on the form vyâkriyata as having reference to a necessarily implied agent; as is the case in such phrases as 'the village is being approached' (where we necessarily have to supply 'by Devadatta or somebody else').

16. (He whose work is this is Brahman), because (the 'work') denotes the world.

In the Kaushîtaki-brâhma*n*a, in the dialogue of Bâlâki and A*g*âta*s*atru, we read, 'O Bâlâki, he who is the maker of those persons, he of whom this is the work, he alone is to be known' (Kau. Up. IV, 19). The question here arises whether what is here inculcated as the object of knowledge is the individual soul or the chief vital air or the highest Self.

The pûrvapakshin maintains that the vital air is meant. For, in the first place, he says, the clause 'of whom this is the work' points to the activity of motion, and that activity rests on the vital air. In the second place, we meet with the word 'prâ*n*a' in a complementary passage ('Then he becomes one with that prâ*n*a alone'), and that word is well known to denote the vital air. In the third place, prâ*n*a is the maker of all the persons, the person in the sun, the person in the moon, &c., who in the preceding part of the dialogue had been enumerated by Bâlâki; for that the sun and the other divinities are mere differentiations of prâ*n*a we know from another scriptural passage, viz. 'Who is that one god (in whom all the other gods are contained)? Prâ*n*a and he is Brahman, and they call him That' (B*ri*. Up. III, 9, 9).—Or else, the pûrvapakshin continues, the passage under discussion represents the individual soul as the object of knowledge. For of the soul also it can be said that 'this is the work,' if we understand by 'this' all meritorious and non-meritorious actions; and the soul also, in so far as it is the enjoyer, can be viewed as the maker of the persons enumerated in so far as they are instrumental to the soul's fruition. The complementary passage, moreover, contains an inferential mark of the individual soul. For A*g*âta*s*atru, in order to instruct Bâlâki about the 'maker of the persons' who had been proposed as the object of knowledge, calls a sleeping man by various names and convinces Bâlâki, by the circumstance that the sleeper does not hear his shouts, that the prâ*n*a and so on are not the enjoyers; he thereupon wakes the sleeping man by pushing him with his stick, and so makes Bâlâki comprehend that the being capable of fruition is the individual soul which is distinct from the prâ*n*a. A subsequent passage also contains an inferential mark of the individual soul, viz. 'And as the master feeds with his people, nay, as his people feed on the master, thus does this conscious Self feed with the other Selfs, thus those Selfs feed on the conscious Self' (Kau. Up. IV, 20). And as the individual soul is the support of the prâ*n*a, it may itself be called prâ*n*a.—We thus conclude that the passage under discussion refers either to the individual soul or to the chief vital air; but not to the Lord, of whom it contains no inferential marks whatever.

To this we make the following reply.—The Lord only can be the maker of the persons enumerated, on account of the force of the introductory part of the section. Bâlâki begins his colloquy with A*g*âta*s*atru with the offer, 'Shall I tell you Brahman?' Thereupon he enumerates some individual souls residing in the sun, the moon, and so on, which participate in the sight of the secondary Brahman, and in the end becomes silent. A*g*âta*s*atru then sets aside Bâlâki's doctrine as not referring to the chief Brahman—with the words, 'Vainly did you challenge me, saying, Shall I tell you Brahman,' &c.—and proposes the maker of all those individual souls as a new object of knowledge. If now that maker also were merely a soul participating in the sight of the secondary Brahman, the introductory statement which speaks of Brahman would be futile. Hence it follows that the highest Lord himself is meant.—None, moreover, but the highest Lord is capable of being the maker of all those persons as he only is absolutely independent.—Further, the clause 'of whom this is the work' does not refer either to the activity of motion nor to meritorious and non-meritorious actions; for neither of those two is the topic of discussion or has been mentioned previously. Nor can the term 'work' denote the enumerated persons, since the latter are mentioned separately—in the clause, 'He who is the maker of those persons'—and as inferential marks (viz. the neuter gender and the singular number of the word karman, work) contradict that assumption. Nor, again, can the term 'work' denote either the activity whose object the persons are, or the result of that activity, since those two are already implied in the mention of the agent (in the clause, 'He who is the maker'). Thus there remains no other alternative than to take the pronoun 'this' (in 'He of whom this is the work') as denoting the perceptible world and to understand the same world—as that which is made—by the term 'work.' —We may indeed admit that the world also is not the previous topic of discussion and has not been mentioned before; still, as no specification is mentioned, we conclude that the term 'work' has to be understood in a general sense, and thus denotes what first presents itself to the mind, viz. everything which exists in general. It is, moreover, not true that the world is not the previous topic of discussion; we are rather entitled to conclude from the circumstance that the various persons (in the sun, the moon, &c.) which constitute a part of the world had been specially mentioned before, that the passage in question is concerned with the whole world in general. The conjunction 'or' (in 'or he of whom,' &c.) is meant to exclude the idea of limited makership; so that the whole passage has to be interpreted as follows, 'He who is the maker of those persons forming a part of the world, or rather—to do away with this limitation—he of whom this entire world without any exception is the work.' The special mention made of the persons having been created has for its purpose to show that those persons whom Bâlâki had proclaimed to be Brahman are not Brahman. The passage therefore sets forth the maker of the world in a double aspect, at first as the creator of a special part of the world and thereupon as the creator of the whole remaining part of the world; a way of speaking analogous to such every-day forms of expression as, 'The wandering mendicants are to be fed, and then the Brâhma*n*as[1].' And that the maker of the world is the highest Lord is affirmed in all Vedânta-texts.

17. If it be said that this is not so, on account of the inferential marks of the individual soul and the chief vital air; we reply that that has already been explained.

---

[1] By the Brâhma*n*as being meant all those Brâhma*n*as who are not at the same time wandering mendicants.

It remains for us to refute the objection that on account of the inferential marks of the individual soul and the chief vital air, which are met with in the complementary passage, either the one or the other must be meant in the passage under discussion, and not the highest Lord.—We therefore remark that that objection has already been disposed of under I, 1, 31. There it was shown that from an interpretation similar to the one here proposed by the pûrvapakshin there would result a threefold meditation, one having Brahman for its object, a second one directed on the individual soul, and a third one connected with the chief vital air. Now the same result would present itself in our case, and that would be unacceptable as we must infer from the introductory as well as the concluding clauses, that the passage under discussion refers to Brahman. With reference to the introductory clause this has been already proved; that the concluding passage also refers to Brahman, we infer from the fact of there being stated in it a pre-eminently high reward, 'Warding off all evil he who knows this obtains pre-eminence among all beings, sovereignty, supremacy.'—But if this is so, the sense of the passage under discussion is already settled by the discussion of the passage about Pratarda*n*a (I, 1, 31); why, then, the present Sûtra?—No, we reply; the sense of our passage is not yet settled, since under I, 1, 31 it has not been proved that the clause, 'Or he whose work is this,' refers to Brahman. Hence there arises again, in connexion with the present passage, a doubt whether the individual soul and the chief vital air may not be meant, and that doubt has again to be refuted.—The word prâ*n*a occurs, moreover, in the sense of Brahman, so in the passage, 'The mind settles down on prâ*n*a' (*Kh*. Up. VI, 8, 2).—The inferential marks of the individual soul also have, on account of the introductory and concluding clauses referring to Brahman, to be explained so as not to give rise to any discrepancy.

18. But *G*aimini thinks that (the reference to the individual soul) has another purport, on account of

the question and answer; and thus some also (read in their text).

Whether the passage under discussion is concerned with the individual soul or with Brahman, is, in the opinion of the teacher *G*aimini, no matter for dispute, since the reference to the individual soul has a different purport, i. e. aims at intimating Brahman. He founds this his opinion on a question and a reply met with in the text. After A*g*âta*s*atru has taught Bâlâki, by waking the sleeping man, that the soul is different from the vital air, he asks the following question, 'Bâlâki, where did this person here sleep? Where was he? Whence came he thus back?' This question clearly refers to something different from the individual soul. And so likewise does the reply, 'When sleeping he sees no dream, then he becomes one with that prâ*n*a alone;' and, 'From that Self all prâ*n*as proceed, each towards its place, from the prâ*n*as the gods, from the gods the worlds.'—Now it is the general Vedânta doctrine that at the time of deep sleep the soul becomes one with the highest Brahman, and that from the highest Brahman the whole world proceeds, inclusive of prâ*n*a, and so on. When Scripture therefore represents as the object of knowledge that in which there takes place the deep sleep of the soul, characterised by absence of consciousness and utter tranquillity, i. e. a state devoid of all those specific cognitions which are produced by the limiting adjuncts of the soul, and from which the soul returns when the sleep is broken; we understand that the highest Self is meant.—Moreover, the Vâ*g*asaneyi*s*âkhâ, which likewise contains the colloquy of Bâlâki and A*g*âta*s*atru, clearly refers to the individual soul by means of the term, 'the person consisting of cognition' (vi*gñ*ânamaya), and distinguishes from it the highest Self ('Where was then the person consisting of cognition? and from whence did he thus come back?' B*ri*. Up. II, 1, 16); and later on, in the reply to the above question, declares that 'the person consisting of cognition lies in the ether within the heart.' Now we know that the word 'ether' may be used to denote the highest Self, as, for instance, in the passage about the small ether within the lotus of the heart (*Kh*. Up. VIII, 1, 1). Further on the B*ri*. Up. says, 'All the Selfs came forth from that Self;' by which statement of the coming forth of all the conditioned Selfs it intimates that the highest Self is the one general cause. —The doctrine conveyed by the rousing of the sleeping person, viz. that the individual soul is different from the vital air, furnishes at the same time a further argument against the opinion that the passage under discussion refers to the vital air.

19. (The Self to be seen, to be heard, &c. is the highest Self) on account of the connected meaning of the sentences.

We read in the B*ri*hadâra*n*yaka, in the Maitreyî-brâhma*n*a the following passage, 'Verily, a husband is not dear that you may love the husband, &c. &c.; verily, everything is not dear that you may love everything; but that you may love the Self therefore everything is dear. Verily, the Self is to be seen, to be heard, to be perceived, to be marked, O Maitreyî! When the Self has been seen, heard, perceived, and known, then all this is known' (B*ri*. Up. IV, 5, 6).—Here the doubt arises whether that which is represented as the object to be seen, to be heard, and so on, is the cognitional Self (the individual soul) or the highest Self.—But whence the doubt?—Because, we reply, the Self is, on the one hand, by the mention of dear things such as husband and so on, indicated as the enjoyer whence it appears that the passage refers to the individual soul; and because, on the other hand, the declaration that through the knowledge of the Self everything becomes known points to the highest Self.

The pûrvapakshin maintains that the passage refers to the individual soul, on account of the strength of the initial statement. The text declares at the outset that all the objects of enjoyment found in this world, such as husband, wife, riches, and so on, are dear on account of the Self, and thereby gives us to understand that the enjoying (i. e. the individual) Self is meant; if thereupon it refers to the Self as the object of sight and so on, what other Self should it mean than the same individual Self?—A subsequent passage also (viz. 'Thus does this great Being, endless, unlimited, consisting of nothing but knowledge, rise from out of these elements, and vanish again after them. When he has departed there is no more knowledge'), which describes how the great Being under discussion rises, as the Self of knowledge, from the elements, shows that the object of sight is no other than the cognitional Self, i.e. the individual soul. The concluding clause finally, 'How, O beloved, should he know the knower?' shows, by means of the term 'knower,' which denotes an agent, that the individual soul is meant. The declaration that through the cognition of the Self everything becomes known must therefore not be interpreted in the literal sense, but must be taken to mean that the world of objects of enjoyment is known through its relation to the enjoying soul.

To this we make the following reply.—The passage makes a statement about the highest Self, on account of the connected meaning of the entire section. If we consider the different passages in their mutual connexion, we find that they all refer to the highest Self. After Maitreyî has heard from Yâ*gñ*avalkya that there is no hope of immortality by wealth, she expresses her desire of immortality in the words, 'What should I do with that by which I do not become immortal? What my Lord knoweth tell that to me;' and thereupon Yâ*gñ*avalkya expounds to her the knowledge of the Self. Now Scripture as well as Sm*ri*ti declares that immortality is not to be reached but through the knowledge of the highest Self.—The statement further that through the knowledge of the Self everything becomes known can be taken in its direct literal sense only if by the Self we understand the highest cause. And to take it in a non-literal sense (as the pûrvapakshin proposes) is inadmissible, on account of the explanation given of that statement in a subsequent passage, viz. 'Whosoever looks for the Brahman class elsewhere than in the Self, is abandoned by the Brahman class.' Here it is said that whoever erroneously views this world with its Brahmans and so on, as having an independent existence apart from the Self, is abandoned by that very world of which he has taken an erroneous view; whereby the view that there exists any difference is refuted. And the immediately subsequent clause, 'This everything is the Self,' gives us to understand that the entire aggregate of existing things is non-different from the Self; a doctrine further confirmed by the similes of the drum and so on.—By explaining further that the Self about which he had been speaking is the cause of the universe of names, forms, and works ('There has been breathed forth from this great Being what we have as *Ri*g-veda,' &c.) Yâ*g*ñavalkya again shows that it is the highest Self.—To the same conclusion he leads us by declaring, in the paragraph which treats of the natural centres of things, that the Self is the centre of the whole world with the objects, the senses and the mind, that it has neither inside nor outside, that it is altogether a mass of knowledge.—From all this it follows that what the text represents as the object of sight and so on is the highest Self.

We now turn to the remark made by the pûrvapakshin that the passage teaches the individual soul to be the object of sight, because it is, in the early part of the chapter, denoted as something dear.

20. (The circumstance of the soul being represented as the object of sight) indicates the fulfilment of the promissory statement; so Â*s*marathya thinks.

The fact that the text proclaims as the object of sight that Self which is denoted as something dear indicates the fulfilment of the promise made in the passages, 'When the Self is known all this is known,' 'All this is that Self.' For if the individual soul were different from the highest Self, the knowledge of the latter would not imply the knowledge of the former, and thus the promise that through the knowledge of one thing everything is to be known would not be fulfilled. Hence the initial statement aims at representing the individual Self and the highest Self as non-different for the purpose of fulfilling the promise made.—This is the opinion of the teacher Â*s*marathya [1].

21. (The initial statement identifies the individual soul and the highest Self) because the soul when it will depart (from the body) is such (i. e. one with the highest Self); thus Au*d*ulomi thinks.

The individual soul which is inquinated by the contact with its different limiting adjuncts, viz. body, senses, and mind (mano-buddhi), attains through the instrumentality of knowledge, meditation, and so on, a state of complete serenity, and thus enables itself, when passing at some future time out of the body, to become one with the highest Self; hence the initial statement in which it is represented as non-different from the highest Self. This is the opinion of the teacher Au*d*ulomi.—Thus Scripture says, 'That serene being arising from this body appears in its own form as soon as it has approached the highest light' (*Kh.* Up. VIII, 12, 3).—In another place Scripture intimates, by means of the simile of the rivers, that name and form abide in the individual soul, 'As

[1] The comment of the Bhâmatî on the Sûtra runs as follows: As the sparks issuing from a fire are not absolutely different from the fire, because they participate in the nature of the fire; and, on the other hand, are not absolutely non-different from the fire, because in that case they could be distinguished neither from the fire nor from each other; so the individual souls also—which are effects of Brahman—are neither absolutely different from Brahman, for that would mean that they are not of the nature of intelligence; nor absolutely non-different from Brahman, because in that case they could not be distinguished from each other, and because, if they were identical with Brahman and therefore omniscient, it would be useless to give them any instruction. Hence the individual souls are somehow different from Brahman and somehow non-different.—The technical name of the doctrine here represented by Â*s*marathya is bhedâbhedavâda.

the flowing rivers disappear in the sea, having lost their name and their form, thus a wise man freed from name and form goes to the divine Person who is greater than the great' (Mu. Up. III, 2, 8). I. e. as the rivers losing the names and forms abiding in them disappear in the sea, so the individual soul also losing the name and form abiding in it becomes united with the highest person. That the latter half of the passage has the meaning here assigned to it, follows from the parallelism which we must assume to exist between the two members of the comparison[1].

22. (The initial statement is made) because (the highest Self) exists in the condition (of the individual soul); so Kâ*s*ak*ri*tsna thinks.

Because the highest Self exists also in the condition of the individual soul, therefore, the teacher Kâ*s*ak*ri*tsna thinks, the initial statement which aims at intimating the non-difference of the two is possible. That the highest Self only is that which appears as the individual soul, is evident from the Brâhma*n*a-passage, 'Let me enter into them with this living Self and evolve names and forms,' and similar passages. We have also mantras to the same effect, for instance, 'The wise one who, having produced all forms and made all names, sits calling the things by their names' (Taitt. Âr. III, 12, 7)[2].

[1] Bhâmatî: The individual soul is absolutely different from the highest Self; it is inquinated by the contact with its different limiting adjuncts. But it is spoken of, in the Upanishad, as non-different from the highest Self because after having purified itself by means of knowledge and meditation it may pass out of the body and become one with the highest Self. The text of the Upanishad thus transfers a future state of non-difference to that time when difference actually exists. Compare the saying of the Pâ*ñk*arâtrikas: 'Up to the moment of emancipation being reached the soul and the highest Self are different. But the emancipated soul is no longer different from the highest Self, since there is no further cause of difference.'—The technical name of the doctrine advocated by Au*d*ulomi is satyabhedavâda.

[2] Compare the note to the same mantra as quoted above under I, 1, 11.

And where Scripture relates the creation of fire and the other elements, it does not at the same time relate a separate creation of the individual soul; we have therefore no right to look on the soul as a product of the highest Self, different from the latter.—In the opinion of the teacher Kâ*s*ak*ri*tsna the non-modified highest Lord himself is the individual soul, not anything else. Â*s*marathya, although meaning to say that the soul is not (absolutely) different from the highest Self, yet intimates by the expression, 'On account of the fulfilment of the promise'—which declares a certain mutual dependence—that there does exist a certain relation of cause and effect between the highest Self and the individual soul[1]. The opinion of Au*d*ulomi again clearly implies that the difference and non-difference of the two depend on difference of condition[2]. Of these three opinions we conclude that the one held by Kâ*s*ak*ri*tsna accords with Scripture, because it agrees with what all the Vedânta-texts (so, for instance, the passage, 'That art thou') aim at inculcating. Only on the opinion of Kâ*s*ak*ri*tsna immortality can be viewed as the result of the knowledge of the soul; while it would be impossible to hold the same view if the soul were a modification (product) of the Self and as such liable to lose its existence by being merged in its causal substance. For the same reason, name and form cannot abide in the soul (as was above attempted to prove by means of the simile of the rivers), but abide in the limiting adjunct and are ascribed to the soul itself in a figurative sense only. For the same reason the origin of the souls from the highest Self, of which Scripture speaks in some places as analogous to the issuing of sparks from the fire, must be viewed as based only on the limiting adjuncts of the soul.

The last three Sûtras have further to be interpreted so as to furnish replies to the second of the pûrvapakshin's arguments, viz. that the B*ri*hadâra*n*yaka passage represents as

---

[1] And not the relation of absolute identity.

[2] I.e. upon the state of emancipation and its absence.

the object of sight the individual soul, because it declares that the great Being which is to be seen arises from out of these elements. 'There is an indication of the fulfilment of the promise; so Âsmarathya thinks.' The promise is made in the two passages, 'When the Self is known, all this is known,' and 'All this is that Self.' That the Self is everything, is proved by the declaration that the whole world of names, forms, and works springs from one being, and is merged in one being [1]; and by its being demonstrated, with the help of the similes of the drum, and so on, that effect and cause are non-different. The fulfilment of the promise is, then, finally indicated by the text declaring that that great Being rises, in the form of the individual soul, from out of these elements; thus the teacher Âsmarathya thinks. For if the soul and the highest Self are non-different, the promise that through the knowledge of one everything becomes known is capable of fulfilment.—'Because the soul when it will depart is such; thus Audulomi thinks.' The statement as to the non-difference of the soul and the Self (implied in the declaration that the great Being rises, &c.) is possible, because the soul when—after having purified itself by knowledge, and so on—it will depart from the body, is capable of becoming one with the highest Self. This is Audulomi's opinion.—'Because it exists in the condition of the soul; thus Kâsakritsna opines.' Because the highest Self itself is that which appears as the individual soul, the statement as to the non-difference of the two is well-founded. This is the view of the teacher Kâsakritsna.

But, an objection may be raised, the passage, 'Rising from out of these elements he vanishes again after them. When he has departed there is no more knowledge,' intimates the final destruction of the soul, not its identity with the highest Self!—By no means, we reply. The passage means to say

[1] Upapâditam keti, sarvasyâtmamâtratvam iti seshah. Upapâdanaprakâram sûkayati eketi. Sa yathârdrendhanâgner ityâdinaikaprasavatvam, yathâ sarvâsâm apâm ityâdinâ kaikapralayatvam sarvasyoktam. Ân. Gi.

only that on the soul departing from the body all specific cognition vanishes, not that the Self is destroyed. For an objection being raised—in the passage, 'Here thou hast bewildered me, Sir, when thou sayest that having departed there is no more knowledge'—Scripture itself explains that what is meant is not the annihilation of the Self, 'I say nothing that is bewildering. Verily, beloved, that Self is imperishable, and of an indestructible nature. But there takes place non-connexion with the mâtrâs.' That means: The eternally unchanging Self, which is one mass of knowledge, cannot possibly perish; but by means of true knowledge there is effected its dissociation from the mâtrâs, i. e. the elements and the sense organs, which are the product of Nescience. When the connexion has been solved, specific cognition, which depended on it, no longer takes place, and thus it can be said, that 'When he has departed there is no more knowledge.'

The third argument also of the pûrvapakshin, viz. that the word 'knower'—which occurs in the concluding passage, 'How should he know the knower?'—denotes an agent, and therefore refers to the individual soul as the object of sight, is to be refuted according to the view of Kâ*s*ak*ri*tsna.—Moreover, the text after having enumerated—in the passage, 'For where there is duality as it were, there one sees the other,' &c.—all the kinds of specific cognition which belong to the sphere of Nescience declares—in the subsequent passage, 'But when the Self only is all this, how should he see another?'—that in the sphere of true knowledge all specific cognition such as seeing, and so on, is absent. And, again, in order to obviate the doubt whether in the absence of objects the knower might not know himself, Yâ*gñ*avalkya goes on, 'How, O beloved, should he know himself, the knower?' As thus the latter passage evidently aims at proving the absence of specific cognition, we have to conclude that the word 'knower' is here used to denote that being which is knowledge, i. e. the Self.—That the view of Kâ*s*ak*ri*tsna is scriptural, we have already shown above. And as it is so, all the adherents of the Vedânta must admit that the difference of the soul and the highest Self is not real, but due to the limiting adjuncts, viz. the body, and so on, which are the product of name and form as presented by Nescience. That view receives ample confirmation from Scripture; compare, for instance, 'Being only, my dear, this was in the beginning, one, without a second' (*Kh.* Up. VI, 2, 1); 'The Self is all this' (*Kh.* Up. VII, 25, 2); 'Brahman alone is all this' (Mu. Up. II, 2, 11); 'This everything is that Self' (B*ri.* Up. II, 4, 6); 'There is no other seer but he' (B*ri.* Up. III, 7, 23); 'There is nothing that sees but it' (B*ri.* Up. III, 8, 11).—It is likewise confirmed by Sm*ri*ti; compare, for instance, 'Vâsudeva is all this' (Bha. Gî. VII, 19): 'Know me, O Bhârata, to be the soul in all bodies' (Bha. Gî. XIII, 2); 'He who sees the highest Lord abiding alike within all creatures' (Bha. Gî. XIII, 27).—The same conclusion is supported by those passages which deny all difference; compare, for instance, 'If he thinks, that is one and I another; he does not know' (B*ri.* Up. I, 4, 10); 'From death to death he goes who sees here any diversity' (B*ri.* Up. IV, 4, 19). And, again, by those passages which negative all change on the part of the Self; compare, for instance, 'This great unborn Self, undecaying, undying, immortal, fearless is indeed Brahman' (B*ri.* Up. IV, 24).—Moreover, if the doctrine of general identity were not true, those who are desirous of release could not be in the possession of irrefutable knowledge, and there would be no possibility of any matter being well settled; while yet the knowledge of which the Self is the object is declared to be irrefutable and to satisfy all desire, and Scripture speaks of those, 'Who have well ascertained the object of the knowledge of the Vedânta' (Mu. Up. III, 2, 6). Compare also the passage, 'What trouble, what sorrow can there be to him who has once beheld that unity?' (I*s*. Up. 7.)—And Sm*ri*ti also represents the mind of him who contemplates the Self as steady (Bha. Gî. II, 54).

As therefore the individual soul and the highest Self differ in name only, it being a settled matter that perfect knowledge has for its object the absolute oneness of the two; it is senseless to insist (as some do) on a plurality of Selfs, and to maintain that the individual soul is different from the highest Self, and the highest Self from the individual soul. For the Self is indeed called by many different names, but it is one only. Nor does the passage, 'He who knows Brahman which is real, knowledge, infinite, as hidden in the cave' (Taitt. Up. II, 1), refer to some one cave (different from the abode of the individual soul)[1]. And that nobody else but Brahman is hidden in the cave we know from a subsequent passage, viz. 'Having sent forth he entered into it' (Taitt. Up. II, 6), according to which the creator only entered into the created beings.—Those who insist on the distinction of the individual and the highest Self oppose themselves to the true sense of the Vedânta-texts, stand thereby in the way of perfect knowledge, which is the door to perfect beatitude, and groundlessly assume release to be something effected, and therefore non-eternal[2]. (And if they attempt to show that moksha, although effected, is eternal) they involve themselves in a conflict with sound logic.

23. (Brahman is) the material cause also, on account of (this view) not being in conflict with the promissory statements and the illustrative instances.

It has been said that, as practical religious duty has to be enquired into because it is the cause of an increase of happiness, so Brahman has to be enquired into because it is the cause of absolute beatitude. And Brahman has been defined as that from which there proceed the origination, sustentation, and retractation of this world. Now as this definition comprises alike the relation of substantial causality in which clay and gold, for instance, stand to golden ornaments and earthen pots, and the relation of operative

---

[1] So according to Go. Ân. and Ân. Gi., although their interpretations seem not to account sufficiently for the ekâm of the text. —Kâ*mk*id evaikâm iti *g*îvasthânâd anyâm ity artha*h*. Go. Ân.—*G*îvabhâvena pratibimbâdhârâtiriktâm ity artha*h*. Ân. Gi.

[2] While release, as often remarked, is eternal, it being in fact not different from the eternally unchanging Brahman.

causality in which the potter and the goldsmith stand to the things mentioned; a doubt arises to which of these two kinds the causality of Brahman belongs.

The pûrvapakshin maintains that Brahman evidently is the operative cause of the world only, because Scripture declares his creative energy to be preceded by reflection. Compare, for instance, Pra. Up. VI, 3; 4: 'He reflected, he created prâ*n*a.' For observation shows that the action of operative causes only, such as potters and the like, is preceded by reflection, and moreover that the result of some activity is brought about by the concurrence of several factors[1]. It is therefore appropriate that we should view the prime creator in the same light. The circumstance of his being known as 'the Lord' furnishes another argument. For lords such as kings and the son of Vivasvat are known only as operative causes, and the highest Lord also must on that account be viewed as an operative cause only.—Further, the effect of the creator's activity, viz. this world, is seen to consist of parts, to be non-intelligent and impure; we therefore must assume that its cause also is of the same nature; for it is a matter of general observation that cause and effect are alike in kind. But that Brahman does not resemble the world in nature, we know from many scriptural passages, such as 'It is without parts, without actions, tranquil, without fault, without taint' (*S*ve. Up. VI, 19). Hence there remains no other alternative but to admit that in addition to Brahman there exists a material cause of the world of impure nature, such as is known from Sm*r*iti[2], and to limit the causality of Brahman, as declared by Scripture, to operative causality.

To this we make the following reply.—Brahman is to be acknowledged as the material cause as well as the operative cause; because this latter view does not conflict with the promissory statements and the illustrative instances. The promissory statement chiefly meant is the following one,

---

[1] I.e. that the operative cause and the substantial cause are separate things.

[2] Viz. the Sâṅkhya-sm*r*iti.

'Have you ever asked for that instruction by which that which is not heard becomes heard; that which is not perceived, perceived; that which is not known, known?' (*Kh*. Up. VI, 1, 3.) This passage intimates that through the cognition of one thing everything else, even if (previously) unknown, becomes known. Now the knowledge of everything is possible through the cognition of the material cause, since the effect is non-different from the material cause. On the other hand, effects are not non-different from their operative causes; for we know from ordinary experience that the carpenter, for instance, is different from the house he has built.—The illustrative example referred to is the one mentioned (*Kh*. Up. VI, 1, 4), 'My dear, as by one clod of clay all that is made of clay is known, the modification (i. e. the effect) being a name merely which has its origin in speech, while the truth is that it is clay merely;' which passage again has reference to the material cause. The text adds a few more illustrative instances of similar nature, 'As by one nugget of gold all that is made of gold is known; as by one pair of nail-scissors all that is made of iron is known.'—Similar promissory statements are made in other places also, for instance, 'What is that through which if it is known everything else becomes known?' (Mu. Up. I, 1, 3.) An illustrative instance also is given in the same place, 'As plants grow on the earth' (I, 1, 7).—Compare also the promissory statement in B*ri*. Up. IV, 5, 6, 'When the Self has been seen, heard, perceived, and known, then all this is known;' and the illustrative instance quoted (IV, 5, 8), 'Now as the sounds of a drum if beaten cannot be seized externally, but the sound is seized when the drum is seized or the beater of the drum.'—Similar promissory statements and illustrative instances which are to be found in all Vedânta-texts are to be viewed as proving, more or less, that Brahman is also the material cause of the world. The ablative case also in the passage, 'That from whence (yata*h*) these beings are born,' has to be considered as indicating the material cause of the beings, according to the grammatical rule, Pâ*n*. I, 4, 30.—That Brahman is at the same time the operative cause of the world, we have to conclude from the circumstance that there is no other guiding being. Ordinary material causes, indeed, such as lumps of clay and pieces of gold, are dependent, in order to shape themselves into vessels and ornaments, on extraneous operative causes such as potters and goldsmiths; but outside Brahman as material cause there is no other operative cause to which the material cause could look; for Scripture says that previously to creation Brahman was one without a second.—The absence of a guiding principle other than the material cause can moreover be established by means of the argument made use of in the Sûtra, viz. accordance with the promissory statements and the illustrative examples. If there were admitted a guiding principle different from the material cause, it would follow that everything cannot be known through one thing, and thereby the promissory statements as well as the illustrative instances would be stultified.—The Self is thus the operative cause, because there is no other ruling principle, and the material cause because there is no other substance from which the world could originate.

24. And on account of the statement of reflection (on the part of the Self).

The fact of the sacred texts declaring that the Self reflected likewise shows that it is the operative as well as the material cause. Passages like 'He wished, may I be many, may I grow forth,' and 'He thought, may I be many, may I grow forth,' show, in the first place, that the Self is the agent in the independent activity which is preceded by the Self's reflection; and, in the second place, that it is the material cause also, since the words 'May I be many' intimate that the reflective desire of multiplying itself has the inward Self for its object.

25. And on account of both (i.e. the origin and the dissolution of the world) being directly declared (to have Brahman for their material cause).

This Sûtra supplies a further argument for Brahman's

being the general material cause.—Brahman is the material cause of the world for that reason also that the origination as well as the dissolution of the world is directly spoken of in the sacred texts as having Brahman for their material cause, 'All these beings take their rise from the ether and return into the ether' (*Kh.* Up. I, 9, 1). That that from which some other thing springs and into which it returns is the material cause of that other thing is well known. Thus the earth, for instance, is the material cause of rice, barley, and the like.—The word 'directly' (in the Sûtra) notifies that there is no other material cause, but that all this sprang from the ether only.—Observation further teaches that effects are not re-absorbed into anything else but their material causes.

26. (Brahman is the material cause) on account of (the Self) making itself; (which is possible) owing to modification.

Brahman is the material cause for that reason also that Scripture—in the passage, 'That made itself its Self' (Taitt. Up. II, 7)—represents the Self as the object of action as well as the agent.—But how can the Self which as agent was in full existence previously to the action be made out to be at the same time that which is effected by the action?—Owing to modification, we reply. The Self, although in full existence previously to the action, modifies itself into something special, viz. the Self of the effect. Thus we see that causal substances, such as clay and the like, are, by undergoing the process of modification, changed into their products.—The word 'itself' in the passage quoted intimates the absence of any other operative cause but the Self.

The word 'pari*n*âmât' (in the Sûtra) may also be taken as constituting a separate Sûtra by itself, the sense of which would be: Brahman is the material cause of the world for that reason also, that the sacred text speaks of Brahman and its modification into the Self of its effect as co-ordinated, viz. in the passage, 'It became sat and tyat, defined and undefined' (Taitt. Up. II, 6).

27. And because Brahman is called the source.

Brahman is the material cause for that reason also that it is spoken of in the sacred texts as the source (yoni); compare, for instance, 'The maker, the Lord, the person who has his source in Brahman' (Mu. Up. III, 1, 3); and 'That which the wise regard as the source of all beings' (Mu. Up. I, 1, 6). For that the word 'source' denotes the material cause is well known from the use of ordinary language; the earth, for instance, is called the yoni of trees and herbs. In some places indeed the word yoni means not source, but merely place; so, for instance, in the mantra, 'A yoni, O Indra, was made for you to sit down upon' (*Ri*k. Sa*m*h. I, 104, 1). But that in the passage quoted it means 'source' follows from a complementary passage, 'As the spider sends forth and draws in its threads,' &c.—It is thus proved that Brahman is the material cause of the world.—Of the objection, finally, that in ordinary life the activity of operative causal agents only, such as potters and the like, is preceded by reflection, we dispose by the remark that, as the matter in hand is not one which can be known through inferential reasoning, ordinary experience cannot be used to settle it. For the knowledge of that matter we rather depend on Scripture altogether, and hence Scripture only has to be appealed to. And that Scripture teaches that the Lord who reflects before creation is at the same time the material cause, we have already explained. The subject will, moreover, be discussed more fully later on.

28. Hereby all (the doctrines concerning the origin of the world which are opposed to the Vedânta) are explained, are explained.

The doctrine according to which the pradhâna is the cause of the world has, in the Sûtras beginning with I, 1, 5, been again and again brought forward and refuted. The chief reason for the special attention given to that doctrine is that the Vedânta-texts contain some passages which, to people deficient in mental penetration, may appear to contain inferential marks pointing to it. The doctrine, moreover, stands somewhat near to the Vedânta doctrine since, like the latter, it admits the non-difference of cause and effect, and it, moreover, has been accepted by some of the authors of the Dharma-sûtras, such as Devala, and so on. For all these reasons we have taken special trouble to refute the pradhâna doctrine, without paying much attention to the atomic and other theories. These latter theories, however, must likewise be refuted, as they also are opposed to the doctrine of Brahman being the general cause, and as slow-minded people might think that they also are referred to in some Vedic passages. Hence the Sûtrakâra formally extends, in the above Sûtra, the refutation already accomplished of the pradhâna doctrine to all similar doctrines which need not be demolished in detail after their great protagonist, the pradhâna doctrine, has been so completely disposed of. They also are, firstly, not founded on any scriptural authority; and are, secondly, directly contradicted by various Vedic passages.—The repetition of the phrase 'are explained' is meant to intimate that the end of the adhyâya has been reached.

SECOND ADHYÂYA.

FIRST PÂDA.

REVERENCE TO THE HIGHEST SELF!

1. If it be objected that (from the doctrine expounded hitherto) there would result the fault of there being no room for (certain) Smritis; we do not admit that objection, because (from the rejection of our doctrine) there would result the fault of want of room for other Smritis.

It has been shown in the first adhyâya that the omniscient Lord of all is the cause of the origin of this world in the same way as clay is the material cause of jars and gold of golden ornaments; that by his rulership he is the cause of the subsistence of this world once originated, just as the magician is the cause of the subsistence of the magical illusion; and that he, lastly, is the cause of this emitted world being finally reabsorbed into his essence, just as the four classes of creatures are reabsorbed into the earth. It has further been proved, by a demonstration of the connected meaning of all the Vedânta-texts, that the Lord is the Self of all of us. Moreover, the doctrines of the pradhâna, and so on, being the cause of this world have been refuted as not being scriptural.—The purport of the second adhyâya, which we now begin, is to refute the objections (to the doctrine established hitherto) which might be founded on Smriti and Reasoning, and to show that the doctrines of the pradhâna, &c. have only fallacious arguments to lean upon, and that the different Vedânta-texts do not contradict one another with regard to the mode of creation and similar topics.—The first point is to refute the objections based on Smriti.

Your doctrine (the pûrvapakshin says) that the omniscient

Brahman only is the cause of this world cannot be maintained, 'because there results from it the fault of there being no room for (certain) Smritis.' Such Smritis are the one called Tantra which was composed by a rishi and is accepted by authoritative persons, and other Smritis based on it[1]; for all of which there would be no room if your interpretation of the Veda were the true one. For they all teach that the non-intelligent pradhâna is the independent cause of the world. There is indeed room (a raison d'être) for Smritis like the Manu-smriti, which give information about matters connected with the whole body of religious duty, characterised by injunction[2] and comprising the agnihotra and similar performances. They tell us at what time and with what rites the members of the different castes are to be initiated; how the Veda has to be studied; in what way the cessation of study has to take place; how marriage has to be performed, and so on. They further lay down the manifold religious duties, beneficial to man, of the four castes and âsramas[3]. The Kâpila Smriti, on the other hand, and similar books are not concerned with things to be done, but were composed with exclusive reference to perfect knowledge as the means of final release. If then no room were left for them in that connexion also, they would be altogether purposeless; and hence we must explain the Vedânta-texts in such a manner as not to bring them into conflict with the Smritis mentioned[4].—But how, somebody may ask the pûrvapakshin, can the eventual fault of there being left no room for certain Smritis be used as an objection against that sense of Sruti which—from various

[1] The Smriti called Tantra is the Sâṅkhyasâstra as taught by Kapila; the Smriti-writers depending on him are Âsuri, Pañkasikha, and others.

[2] Mîmâmsâ Sû. I, 1, 2: kodanâlakshano*rtho dharmah. Commentary: kodanâ iti kriyâyâh pravartakam vakanam âhuh.

[3] Purushârtha; in opposition to the rules referred to in the preceding sentence which are kratvartha, i.e. the acting according to which secures the proper performance of certain rites.

[4] It having been decided by the Pûrvâ Mimâmsâ already that Smritis contradicted by Sruti are to be disregarded.

reasons as detailed under I, 1 and ff.—has been ascertained by us to be the true one, viz. that the omniscient Brahman alone is the cause of the world?—Our objection, the pûrvapakshin replies, will perhaps not appear valid to persons of independent thought; but as most men depend in their reasonings on others, and are unable to ascertain by themselves the sense of *S*ruti, they naturally rely on Sm*ri*tis, composed by celebrated authorities, and try to arrive at the sense of *S*ruti with their assistance; while, owing to their esteem for the authors of the Sm*ri*tis, they have no trust in our explanations. The knowledge of men like Kapila Sm*ri*ti declares to have been *ri*shi-like and unobstructed, and moreover there is the following *S*ruti-passage, 'It is he who, in the beginning, bears in his thoughts the son, the *ri*shi, kapila [1], whom he wishes to look on while he is born' (*S*ve. Up. V, 2). Hence their opinion cannot be assumed to be erroneous, and as they moreover strengthen their position by argumentation, the objection remains valid, and we must therefore attempt to explain the Vedânta-texts in conformity with the Sm*ri*tis.

This objection we dispose of by the remark, 'It is not so because therefrom would result the fault of want of room for other Sm*ri*tis.'—If you object to the doctrine of the Lord being the cause of the world on the ground that it would render certain Sm*ri*tis purposeless, you thereby render purposeless other Sm*ri*tis which declare themselves in favour of the said doctrine. These latter Sm*ri*ti-texts we will quote in what follows. In one passage the highest Brahman is introduced as the subject of discussion, 'That which is subtle and not to be known;' the text then goes on, 'That is the internal Self of the creatures, their soul,' and after that remarks 'From that sprang the Unevolved, consisting of the three gu*n*as, O best of Brâhma*n*as.' And in another place it is said that 'the Unevolved is

[1] On the meaning of 'kapila' in the above passage, compare the Introduction to the Upanishads, translated by Max Müller, vol. ii, p. xxxviii ff.—As will be seen later on, *S*añkara, in this bhâshya, takes the Kapila referred to to be some *ri*shi.

dissolved in the Person devoid of qualities, O Brâhma*n*a.'—Thus we read also in the Purâ*n*a, 'Hear thence this short statement: The ancient Nârâya*n*a is all this; he produces the creation at the due time, and at the time of reabsorption he consumes it again.' And so in the Bhagavadgîtâ also (VII, 6), 'I am the origin and the place of reabsorption of the whole world.' And Âpastamba too says with reference to the highest Self, 'From him spring all bodies; he is the primary cause, he is eternal, he is unchangeable' (Dharma Sûtra I, 8, 23, 2). In this way Sm*ri*ti, in many places, declares the Lord to be the efficient as well as the material cause of the world. As the pûrvapakshin opposes us on the ground of Sm*ri*ti, we reply to him on the ground of Sm*ri*ti only; hence the line of defence taken up in the Sûtra. Now it has been shown already that the *S*ruti-texts aim at conveying the doctrine that the Lord is the universal cause, and as wherever different Sm*ri*tis conflict those maintaining one view must be accepted, while those which maintain the opposite view must be set aside, those Sm*ri*tis which follow *S*ruti are to be considered as authoritative, while all others are to be disregarded; according to the Sûtra met with in the chapter treating of the means of proof (Mîm. Sûtra I, 3, 3), 'Where there is contradiction (between *S*ruti and Sm*ri*ti) (Sm*ri*ti) is to be disregarded; in case of there being no (contradiction) (Sm*ri*ti is to be recognised) as there is inference (of Sm*ri*ti being founded on *S*ruti).'—Nor can we assume that some persons are able to perceive supersensuous matters without *S*ruti, as there exists no efficient cause for such perception. Nor, again, can it be said that such perception may be assumed in the case of Kapila and others who possessed supernatural powers, and consequently unobstructed power of cognition. For the possession of supernatural powers itself depends on the performance of religious duty, and religious duty is that which is characterised by injunction[1]; hence the sense of injunctions (i. e. of the Veda)

[1] I.e. religious duty is known only from the injunctive passages of the Veda.

which is established first must not be fancifully interpreted in reference to the dicta of men 'established' (i. e. made perfect, and therefore possessing supernatural powers) afterwards only. Moreover, even if those 'perfect' men were accepted as authorities to be appealed to, still, as there are many such perfect men, we should have, in all those cases where the Sm*ri*tis contradict each other in the manner described, no other means of final decision than an appeal to *S*ruti.—As to men destitute of the power of independent judgment, we are not justified in assuming that they will without any reason attach themselves to some particular Sm*ri*ti; for if men's inclinations were so altogether unregulated, truth itself would, owing to the multiformity of human opinion, become unstable. We must therefore try to lead their judgment in the right way by pointing out to them the conflict of the Sm*ri*tis, and the distinction founded on some of them following *S*ruti and others not.—The scriptural passage which the pûrvapakshin has quoted as proving the eminence of Kapila's knowledge would not justify us in believing in such doctrines of Kapila (i. e. of some Kapila) as are contrary to Scripture; for that passage mentions the bare name of Kapila (without specifying which Kapila is meant), and we meet in tradition with another Kapila, viz. the one who burned the sons of Sagara and had the surname Vâsudeva. That passage, moreover, serves another purpose, (viz. the establishment of the doctrine of the highest Self,) and has on that account no force to prove what is not proved by any other means, (viz. the supereminence of Kapila's knowledge.) On the other hand, we have a *S*ruti-passage which proclaims the excellence of Manu[1], viz. 'Whatever Manu said is medicine' (Taitt. Sa*m*h. II, 2, 10, 2). Manu himself, where he glorifies the seeing of the one Self in everything ('he who equally sees the Self in all beings and all beings in the Self, he as a sacrificer to the Self attains self-

[1] After it has been shown that Kapila the dvaitavâdin is not mentioned in *S*ruti, it is now shown that Manu the sarvâtmavâdin is mentioned there.

luminousness,' i.e. becomes Brahman, Manu Smriti XII, 91), implicitly blames the doctrine of Kapila. For Kapila, by acknowledging a plurality of Selfs, does not admit the doctrine of there being one universal Self. In the Mahâbhârata also the question is raised whether there are many persons (souls) or one; thereupon the opinion of others is mentioned, 'There are many persons, O King, according to the Sânkhya and Yoga philosophers;' that opinion is controverted 'just as there is one place of origin, (viz. the earth,) for many persons, so I will proclaim to you that universal person raised by his qualities;' and, finally, it is declared that there is one universal Self, 'He is the internal Self of me, of thee, and of all other embodied beings, the internal witness of all, not to be apprehended by any one. He the all-headed, all-armed, all-footed, all-eyed, all-nosed one moves through all beings according to his will and liking.' And Scripture also declares that there is one universal Self, 'When to a man who understands the Self has become all things, what sorrow, what trouble can there be to him who once beheld that unity?' (Îs. Up. 7); and other similar passages. All which proves that the system of Kapila contradicts the Veda, and the doctrine of Manu who follows the Veda, by its hypothesis of a plurality of Selfs also, not only by the assumption of an independent pradhâna. The authoritativeness of the Veda with regard to the matters stated by it is independent and direct, just as the light of the sun is the direct means of our knowledge of form and colour; the authoritativeness of human dicta, on the other hand, is of an altogether different kind, as it depends on an extraneous basis (viz. the Veda), and is (not immediate but) mediated by a chain of teachers and tradition.

Hence the circumstance that the result (of our doctrine) is want of room for certain Smritis, with regard to matters contradicted by the Veda, furnishes no valid objection.—An additional reason for this our opinion is supplied by the following Sûtra.

2. And on account of the non-perception of the

others (i.e. the effects of the pradhâna, according to the Sâṅkhya system).

The principles different from the pradhâna, but to be viewed as its modifications which the (Sâṅkhya) Smriti assumes, as, for instance, the great principle, are perceived neither in the Veda nor in ordinary experience. Now things of the nature of the elements and the sense organs, which are well known from the Veda, as well as from experience, may be referred to in Smriti; but with regard to things which, like Kapila's great principle, are known neither from the Veda nor from experience—no more than, for instance, the objects of a sixth sense—Smriti is altogether impossible. That some scriptural passages which apparently refer to such things as the great principle have in reality quite a different meaning has already been shown under I, 4, 1. But if that part of Smriti which is concerned with the effects (i.e. the great principle, and so on) is without authority, the part which refers to the cause (the pradhâna) will be so likewise. This is what the Sûtra means to say.—We have thus established a second reason, proving that the circumstance of there being no room left for certain Smritis does not constitute a valid objection to our doctrine.—The weakness of the trust in reasoning (apparently favouring the Sâṅkhya doctrine) will be shown later on under II, 1, 4 ff.

3. Thereby the Yoga (Smriti) is refuted.

This Sûtra extends the application of the preceding argumentation, and remarks that by the refutation of the Sâṅkhya-smriti the Yoga-smriti also is to be considered as refuted; for the latter also assumes, in opposition to Scripture, a pradhâna as the independent cause of the world, and the 'great principle,' &c. as its effects, although neither the Veda nor common experience favour these views.—But, if the same reasoning applies to the Yoga also, the latter system is already disposed of by the previous arguments; of what use then is it formally to extend them to the Yoga? (as the Sûtra does.)—We reply that here an additional cause of doubt presents itself, the practice of Yoga being enjoined in the Veda as a means of obtaining perfect knowledge; so, for instance, B*ri*. Up. II, 4, 5, '(The Self) is to be heard, to be thought, to be meditated upon[1].' In the *S*vetâ*s*vatara Upanishad, moreover, we find various injunctions of Yoga-practice connected with the assumption of different positions of the body, &c.; so, for instance, 'Holding his body with its three erect parts even,' &c. (II, 8).

Further, we find very many passages in the Veda which (without expressly enjoining it) point to the Yoga, as, for instance, Ka. Up. II, 6, 11, 'This, the firm holding back of the senses, is what is called Yoga;' 'Having received this knowledge and the whole rule of Yoga' (Ka. Up. II, 6, 18); and so on. And in the Yoga-*s*âstra itself the passage, 'Now then Yoga, the means of the knowledge of truth,' &c. defines the Yoga as a means of reaching perfect knowledge. As thus one topic of the *s*âstra at least (viz. the practice of Yoga) is shown to be authoritative, the entire Yoga-sm*ri*ti will have to be accepted as unobjectionable, just as the Sm*ri*ti referring to the ash*t*akâs[2].—To this we reply that the formal extension (to the Yoga, of the arguments primarily directed against the Sâṅkhya) has the purpose of removing the additional doubt stated in the above lines; for in spite of a part of the Yoga-sm*ri*ti being authoritative, the disagreement (between Sm*ri*ti and *S*ruti) on other topics remains as shown above.—Although[3] there are many Sm*ri*tis treating of the soul, we have singled out for refutation the Sâṅkhya and Yoga because they are widely known as offering the means for accomplishing the highest

---

[1] In which passage the phrase 'to be meditated upon' (nididhyâsâ) indicates the act of mental concentration characteristic of the Yoga.

[2] The ash*t*akâs (certain oblations to be made on the eighth days after the full moons of the seasons hemanta and *s*i*s*ira) furnish the stock illustration for the doctrine of the Pûrvâ Mîm. that Sm*ri*ti is authoritative in so far as it is based on *S*ruti.

[3] But why—it will be asked—do you apply yourself to the refutation of the Sâṅkhya and Yoga only, and not also to that of other Sm*ri*tis conflicting with the Vedânta views?

end of man and have found favour with many competent persons. Moreover, their position is strengthened by a Vedic passage referring to them, 'He who has known that cause which is to be apprehended by Sâṅkhya and Yoga he is freed from all fetters' (*S*ve. Up. VI, 13). (The claims which on the ground of this last passage might be set up for the Sâṅkhya and Yoga-sm*ri*tis in their entirety) we refute by the remark that the highest beatitude (the highest aim of man) is not to be attained by the knowledge of the Sâṅkhya-sm*ri*ti irrespective of the Veda, nor by the road of Yoga-practice. For Scripture itself declares that there is no other means of obtaining the highest beatitude but the knowledge of the unity of the Self which is conveyed by the Veda, 'Over death passes only the man who knows him; there is no other path to go' (*S*ve. Up. III, 8). And the Sâṅkhya and Yoga-systems maintain duality, do not discern the unity of the Self. In the passage quoted ('That cause which is to be apprehended by Sâṅkhya and Yoga') the terms 'Sâṅkhya' and 'Yoga' denote Vedic knowledge and meditation, as we infer from proximity[1]. We willingly allow room for those portions of the two systems which do not contradict the Veda. In their description of the soul, for instance, as free from all qualities the Sâṅkhyas are in harmony with the Veda which teaches that the person (purusha) is essentially pure; cp. B*ri*. Up. IV, 3, 16, 'For that person is not attached to anything.' The Yoga again in giving rules for the condition of the wandering religious mendicant admits that state of retirement from the concerns of life which is known from scriptural passages such as the following one, 'Then the parivrâ*g*aka with discoloured (yellow) dress, shaven, without any possessions,' &c. (*G*âbâla Upan. IV).

The above remarks will serve as a reply to the claims of all argumentative Sm*ri*tis. If it be said that those Sm*ri*tis also assist, by argumentation and proof, the cognition of truth, we do not object to so much, but we maintain

[1] I.e. from the fact of these terms being employed in a passage standing close to other passages which refer to Vedic knowledge.

all the same that the truth can be known from the Vedânta-texts only; as is stated by scriptural passages such as 'None who does not know the Veda perceives that great one' (Taitt. Br. III, 12, 9, 7); 'I now ask thee that person taught in the Upanishads' (B*ri*. Up. III, 9, 26); and others.

4. (Brahman can)not (be the cause of the world) on account of the difference of character of that, (viz. the world); and its being such, (i.e. different from Brahman) (we learn) from Scripture.

The objections, founded on Sm*ri*ti, against the doctrine of Brahman being the efficient and the material cause of this world have been refuted; we now proceed to refute those founded on Reasoning.—But (to raise an objection at the outset) how is there room for objections founded on Reasoning after the sense of the sacred texts has once been settled? The sacred texts are certainly to be considered absolutely authoritative with regard to Brahman as well as with regard to religious duty (dharma).—(To this the pûrvapakshin replies), The analogy between Brahman and dharma would hold good if the matter in hand were to be known through the holy texts only, and could not be approached by the other means of right knowledge also. In the case of religious duties, i. e. things to be done, we indeed entirely depend on Scripture. But now we are concerned with Brahman which is an accomplished existing thing, and in the case of accomplished things there is room for other means of right knowledge also, as, for instance, the case of earth and the other elements shows. And just as in the case of several conflicting scriptural passages we explain all of them in such a manner as to make them accord with one, so *S*ruti, if in conflict with other means of right knowledge, has to be bent so as to accord with the latter. Moreover, Reasoning, which enables us to infer something not actually perceived in consequence of its having a certain equality of attributes with what is actually perceived, stands nearer to perception than *S*ruti which conveys its sense by tradition merely. And the knowledge of Brahman which discards Nescience and effects final release terminates in a perception (viz. the intuition—sâkshâtkâra—of Brahman), and as such must be assumed to have a seen result (not an unseen one like dharma)[1]. Moreover, the scriptural passage, 'He is to be heard, to be thought,' enjoins thought in addition to hearing, and thereby shows that Reasoning also is to be resorted to with regard to Brahman. Hence an objection founded on Reasoning is set forth, 'Not so, on account of the difference of nature of this (effect).'—The Vedântic opinion that the intelligent Brahman is the material cause of this world is untenable because the effect would in that case be of an altogether different character from the cause. For this world, which the Vedântin considers as the effect of Brahman, is perceived to be non-intelligent and impure, consequently different in character from Brahman; and Brahman again is declared by the sacred texts to be of a character different from the world, viz. intelligent and pure. But things of an altogether different character cannot stand to each other in the relation of material cause and effect. Such effects, for instance, as golden ornaments do not have earth for their material cause, nor is

[1] The cognition of Brahman terminates in an act of anubhava; hence as it has been shown that reasoning is more closely connected with anubhava than *S*ruti is, we have the right to apply reasoning to *S*ruti.—Ânanda Giri comments on the passage from anubhavâvasânam as follows: brahmasâkshâtkârasya mokshopâyatayâ prâdhânyât tatra *s*abdâd api parokshago*k*arâd aparokshârthasâdharmyago*k*aras tarko*s*ntarangam iti tasyaiva balavatvam ity artha*h*. Aitihyamâtre*n*a pravâdapâramparyamâtre*n*a parokshatayeti yâvat. Anubhavasya prâdhânye tarkasyoktanyâyena tasminn antarangatvâd âgamasya *k*a bahirangatvâd antarangabahirangayor antaranga*m* balavad ity nyâyâd ukta*m* tarkasya balavattvam. Anubhavaprâdhânya*m* tu nâdyâpi siddham ity â*s*ankyâhânubhaveti. Nanu Brahmag*ñ*âna*m* vaidikatvâd dharmavad ad*r*ish*t*aphalam esh*t*avya*m* tat kuto*s* syânubhavâvasânâvidyânivartakatva*m* tatrâha moksheti. Adhish*th*ânasâkshâtkârasya *s*uktyâdig*ñ*âne tadavidyâtatkâryanivartakatvad*r*ish*t*e*h*, brahmag*ñ*ânasyâpi tarkava*s*âd asambhâvanâdinirâsadvârâ sâkshâtkârâvasâyinas tadavidyâdinivartakatvenaiva muktihetuteti nâd*r*ish*t*aphalatety artha*h*.

gold the material cause of earthen vessels; but effects of an earthy nature originate from earth and effects of the nature of gold from gold. In the same manner this world, which is non-intelligent and comprises pleasure, pain, and dulness, can only be the effect of a cause itself non-intelligent and made up of pleasure, pain, and dulness; but not of Brahman which is of an altogether different character. The difference in character of this world from Brahman must be understood to be due to its impurity and its want of intelligence. It is impure because being itself made up of pleasure, pain, and dulness, it is the cause of delight, grief, despondency, &c., and because it comprises in itself abodes of various character such as heaven, hell, and so on. It is devoid of intelligence because it is observed to stand to the intelligent principle in the relation of subserviency, being the instrument of its activity. For the relation of subserviency of one thing to another is not possible on the basis of equality; two lamps, for instance, cannot be said to be subservient to each other (both being equally luminous).—But, it will be said, an intelligent instrument also might be subservient to the enjoying soul; just as an intelligent servant is subservient to his master.—This analogy, we reply, does not hold good, because in the case of servant and master also only the non-intelligent element in the former is subservient to the intelligent master. For a being endowed with intelligence subserves another intelligent being only with the non-intelligent part belonging to it, viz. its internal organ, sense organs, &c.; while in so far as it is intelligent itself it acts neither for nor against any other being. For the Sâṅkhyas are of opinion that the intelligent beings (i. e. the souls) are incapable of either taking in or giving out anything[1], and are non-active. Hence that only which is devoid of intelligence can be an instrument. Nor[2] is there anything

[1] Niratis*a*yâ*h*, upa*g*anâpâyadharmas*û*nyatva*m* niratis*a*yatvam. Ân. Gi.

[2] A sentence replying to the possible objection that the world, as being the effect of the intelligent Brahman, might itself be intelligent.

to show that things like pieces of wood and clods of earth are of an intelligent nature; on the contrary, the dichotomy of all things which exist into such as are intelligent and such as are non-intelligent is well established. This world therefore cannot have its material cause in Brahman from which it is altogether different in character.—Here somebody might argue as follows. Scripture tells us that this world has originated from an intelligent cause; therefore, starting from the observation that the attributes of the cause survive in the effect, I assume this whole world to be intelligent. The absence of manifestation of intelligence (in this world) is to be ascribed to the particular nature of the modification[1]. Just as undoubtedly intelligent beings do not manifest their intelligence in certain states such as sleep, swoon, &c., so the intelligence of wood and earth also is not manifest (although it exists). In consequence of this difference produced by the manifestation and non-manifestation of intelligence (in the case of men, animals, &c., on the one side, and wood, stones, &c. on the other side), and in consequence of form, colour, and the like being present in the one case and absent in the other, nothing prevents the instruments of action (earth, wood, &c.) from standing to the souls in the relation of a subordinate to a superior thing, although in reality both are equally of an intelligent nature. And just as such substances as flesh, broth, pap, and the like may, owing to their individual differences, stand in the relation of mutual subserviency, although fundamentally they are all of the same nature, viz. mere modifications of earth, so it will be in the case under discussion also, without there being done any violence to the well-known distinction (of beings intelligent and non-intelligent).—This reasoning—the pûrvapakshin replies—if valid might remove to a certain extent that difference of character between

[1] In the case of things commonly considered non-intelligent, intelligence is not influenced by an internal organ, and on that account remains unperceived; samaste *g*agati sato*pi *k*aitanyasya tatra tatrânta*h*kara*n*apari*n*âmânuparâgâd anupalabdhir aviruddhâ. Ân. Gi.

Brahman and the world which is due to the circumstance of the one being intelligent and the other non-intelligent; there would, however, still remain that other difference which results from the fact that the one is pure and the other impure. But in reality the argumentation of the objector does not even remove the first-named difference; as is declared in the latter part of the Sûtra, 'And its being such we learn from Scripture.' For the assumption of the intellectuality of the entire world—which is supported neither by perception nor by inference, &c.—must be considered as resting on Scripture only in so far as the latter speaks of the world as having originated from an intelligent cause; but that scriptural statement itself is contradicted by other texts which declare the world to be 'of such a nature,' i. e. of a nature different from that of its material cause. For the scriptural passage, 'It became that which is knowledge and that which is devoid of knowledge' (Taitt. Up. II, 6), which teaches that a certain class of beings is of a non-intelligent nature intimates thereby that the non-intelligent world is different from the intelligent Brahman.—But—somebody might again object—the sacred texts themselves sometimes speak of the elements and the bodily organs, which are generally considered to be devoid of intelligence, as intelligent beings. The following passages, for instance, attribute intelligence to the elements. 'The earth spoke;' 'The waters spoke' (*S*at. Br. VI, 1, 3, 2; 4); and, again, 'Fire thought;' 'Water thought' (*Kh*. Up. VI, 2, 3; 4). Other texts attribute intelligence to the bodily organs, 'These prâ*n*as when quarrelling together as to who was the best went to Brahman' (B*ri*. Up. VI, 1, 7); and, again, 'They said to Speech: Do thou sing out for us' (B*ri*. Up. I, 3, 2).—To this objection the pûrvapakshin replies in the following Sûtra.

5. But (there takes place) denotation of the superintending (deities), on account of the difference and the connexion.

The word 'but' discards the doubt raised. We are

not entitled to base the assumption of the elements and the sense organs being of an intellectual nature on such passages as 'the earth spoke,' &c. because 'there takes place denotation of that which presides.' In the case of actions like speaking, disputing, and so on, which require intelligence, the scriptural passages denote not the mere material elements and organs, but rather the intelligent divinities which preside over earth, &c., on the one hand, and Speech, &c., on the other hand. And why so? 'On account of the difference and the connexion.' The difference is the one previously referred to between the enjoying souls, on the one hand, and the material elements and organs, on the other hand, which is founded on the distinction between intelligent and non-intelligent beings; that difference would not be possible if all beings were intelligent. Moreover, the Kaushîtakins in their account of the dispute of the prâ*n*as make express use of the word 'divinities' in order to preclude the idea of the mere material organs being meant, and in order to include the superintending intelligent beings. They say, 'The deities contending with each for who was the best;' and, again, 'All these deities having recognised the pre-eminence in prâ*n*a' (Kau. Up. II, 14).—And, secondly, Mantras, Arthavâdas, Itihâsas, Purâ*n*as, &c. all declare that intelligent presiding divinities are connected with everything. Moreover, such scriptural passages as 'Agni having become Speech entered into the mouth' (Ait. Âr. II, 4, 2, 4) show that each bodily organ is connected with its own favouring divinity. And in the passages supplementary to the quarrel of the prâ*n*as we read in one place how, for the purpose of settling their relative excellence, they went to Pra*g*âpati, and how they settled their quarrel on the ground of presence and absence, each of them, as Pra*g*âpati had advised, departing from the body for some time ('They went to their father Pra*g*âpati and said,' &c.; *Kh*. Up. V, 1, 7); and in another place it is said that they made an offering to prâ*n*a (B*ri*. Up. VI, 1, 13), &c.; all of them proceedings which are analogous to those of men, &c., and therefore strengthen the hypothesis that the text refers to the superintending deities. In the case of such passages as, 'Fire thought,' we must assume that the thought spoken of is that of the highest deity which is connected with its effects as a superintending principle.—From all this it follows that this world is different in nature from Brahman, and hence cannot have it for its material cause.

To this objection raised by the pûrvapakshin the next Sûtra replies.

6. But it is seen.

The word 'but' discards the pûrvapaksha.

Your assertion that this world cannot have originated from Brahman on account of the difference of its character is not founded on an absolutely true tenet. For we see that from man, who is acknowledged to be intelligent, non-intelligent things such as hair and nails originate, and that, on the other hand, from avowedly non-intelligent matter, such as cow-dung, scorpions and similar animals are produced.—But—to state an objection—the real cause of the non-intelligent hair and nails is the human body which is itself non-intelligent, and the non-intelligent bodies only of scorpions are the effects of non-intelligent dung.—Even thus, we reply, there remains a difference in character (between the cause, for instance, the dung, and the effect, for instance, the body of the scorpion), in so far as some non-intelligent matter (the body) is the abode of an intelligent principle (the scorpion's soul), while other non-intelligent matter (the dung) is not. Moreover, the difference of nature — due to the cause passing over into the effect—between the bodies of men on the one side and hair and nails on the other side, is, on account of the divergence of colour, form, &c., very considerable after all. The same remark holds good with regard to cow-dung and the bodies of scorpions, &c. If absolute equality were insisted on (in the case of one thing being the effect of another), the relation of material cause and effect (which after all requires a distinction of the two) would be annihilated. If, again, it be remarked that in the case of men and hair as well as in that of scorpions and cow-dung there is one characteristic feature, at least, which is found in the effect as well as in the cause, viz. the quality of being of an earthy nature; we reply that in the case of Brahman and the world also one characteristic feature, viz. that of existence (sattâ), is found in ether, &c. (which are the effects) as well as in Brahman (which is the cause).—He, moreover, who on the ground of the difference of the attributes tries to invalidate the doctrine of Brahman being the cause of the world, must assert that he understands by difference of attributes either the non-occurrence (in the world) of the entire complex of the characteristics of Brahman, or the non-occurrence of any (some or other) characteristic, or the non-occurrence of the characteristic of intelligence. The first assertion would lead to the negation of the relation of cause and effect in general, which relation is based on the fact of there being in the effect something over and above the cause (for if the two were absolutely identical they could not be distinguished). The second assertion is open to the charge of running counter to what is well known; for, as we have already remarked, the characteristic quality of existence which belongs to Brahman is found likewise in ether and so on. For the third assertion the requisite proving instances are wanting; for what instances could be brought forward against the upholder of Brahman, in order to prove the general assertion that whatever is devoid of intelligence is seen not to be an effect of Brahman? (The upholder of Brahman would simply not admit any such instances) because he maintains that this entire complex of things has Brahman for its material cause. And that all such assertions are contrary to Scripture, is clear, as we have already shown it to be the purport of Scripture that Brahman is the cause and substance of the world. It has indeed been maintained by the pûrvapakshin that the other means of proof also (and not merely sacred tradition) apply to Brahman, on account of its being an accomplished entity (not something to be accomplished as religious duties are); but such an assertion is entirely gratuitous. For Brahman, as being devoid of form and so on, cannot become an object of perception; and as there are in its case no characteristic marks (on which conclusions, &c. might be based), inference also and the other means of proof do not apply to it; but, like religious duty, it is to be known solely on the ground of holy tradition. Thus Scripture also declares, 'That doctrine is not to be obtained by argument, but when it is declared by another then, O dearest! it is easy to understand' (Ka. Up. I, 2, 9). And again, 'Who in truth knows it? Who could here proclaim it, whence this creation sprang?' (*Ri*g-v. Sa*m*h. X, 129, 6.) These two mantras show that the cause of this world is not to be known even by divine beings (îsvara)[1] of extraordinary power and wisdom.

There are also the following Sm*ri*ti passages to the same effect: 'Do not apply reasoning to those things which are uncognisable[2];' 'Unevolved he is called, uncognisable, unchangeable;' 'Not the legions of the gods know my origin, not the great *ri*shis. For I myself am in every way the origin of the gods and great *ri*shis' (Bha. Gî. X, 2).—And if it has been maintained above that the scriptural passage enjoining thought (on Brahman) in addition to mere hearing (of the sacred texts treating of Brahman) shows that reasoning also is to be allowed its place, we reply that the passage must not deceitfully be taken as enjoining bare independent ratiocination, but must be understood to represent reasoning as a subordinate auxiliary of intuitional knowledge. By reasoning of the latter type we may, for instance, arrive at the following conclusions; that because the state of dream and the waking state exclude each other the Self is not connected with those states; that, as the soul in the state of deep sleep leaves the phenomenal world behind and becomes one with that whose Self is pure Being, it has for its Self pure Being apart from the phenomenal world; that as the world springs from Brahman it cannot be separate from Brahman,

[1] On îsvara in the above meaning, compare Deussen, p. 69, note 41.

[2] The line 'prak*ri*tibhya*h* param,' &c. is wanting in all MSS. I have consulted.

according to the principle of the non-difference of cause and effect, &c.[1] The fallaciousness of mere reasoning will moreover be demonstrated later on (II, 1, 11).—He[2], moreover, who merely on the ground of the sacred tradition about an intelligent cause of the world would assume this entire world to be of an intellectual nature would find room for the other scriptural passage quoted above ('He became knowledge and what is devoid of knowledge') which teaches a distinction of intellect and non-intellect; for he could avail himself of the doctrine of intellect being sometimes manifested and sometimes non-manifested. His antagonist, on the other hand (i.e. the Sâṅkhya), would not be able to make anything of the passage, for it distinctly teaches that the highest cause constitutes the Self of the entire world.

If, then, on account of difference of character that which is intelligent cannot pass over into what is non-intelligent, that also which is non-intelligent (i.e. in our case, the non-intelligent pradhâna of the Sâṅkhyas) cannot pass over into what is intelligent.—(So much for argument's sake,) but apart from that, as the argument resting on difference of character has already been refuted, we must assume an intelligent cause of the world in agreement with Scripture.

---

[1] Ânanda Giri on the above passage: *s*rutyâkâṅkshita*m* tarkam eva mananavidhivishayam udâharati svapnânteti. Svapna*g*âgaritayor mithovyabhi*k*ârâd âtmana*h* svabhâvatas tadvattvâbhâvâd avasthâdvayena tasya svato*s*sa*m*p*ri*ktatvam ato *g*îvasyâvasthâvatvena nâbrahmatvam ity artha*h*. Tathâpi dehâditâdâtmyenâtmano bhâvân na ni*h*prapa*ñk*abrahmatety â*s*aṅkyâha sa*m*prasâde *k*eti. Satâ somya tadâ sa*m*panno bhavatîti *s*rute*h* sushupte ni*h*prapa*ñk*asadâtmatvâvagamâd âtmanas tathâvidhabrahmatvasiddhir ity artha*h*. Dvaitagrâhipratyakshâdivirodhât katham âtmano*s*dvitîyabrahmatvam ity â*s*aṅkya ta*gg*atvâdihetunâ brahmâtiriktavastvabhâvasiddher adhyakshâdînâm atatvâvedakaprâmâ*n*yâd avirodhâd yuktam âtmano*s*dvitîyabrahmatvam ity âha prapa*ñk*asyeti.

[2] Let us finally assume, merely for argument's sake, that a vailaksha*n*ya of cause and effect is not admissible, and enquire whether that assumption can be reconciled more easily with an intelligent or a non-intelligent cause of the world.

7. If (it is said that the effect is) non-existent (before its origination); we do not allow that because it is a mere negation (without an object).

If Brahman, which is intelligent, pure, and devoid of qualities such as sound, and so on, is supposed to be the cause of an effect which is of an opposite nature, i.e. non-intelligent, impure, possessing the qualities of sound, &c., it follows that the effect has to be considered as non-existing before its actual origination. But this consequence cannot be acceptable to you—the Vedântin—who maintain the doctrine of the effect existing in the cause already.

This objection of yours, we reply, is without any force, on account of its being a mere negation. If you negative the existence of the effect previous to its actual origination, your negation is a mere negation without an object to be negatived. The negation (implied in 'non-existent') can certainly not have for its object the existence of the effect previous to its origination, since the effect must be viewed as 'existent,' through and in the Self of the cause, before its origination as well as after it; for at the present moment also this effect does not exist independently, apart from the cause; according to such scriptural passages as 'Whosoever looks for anything elsewhere than in the Self is abandoned by everything' (B*ri*. Up. II, 4, 6). In so far, on the other hand, as the effect exists through the Self of the cause, its existence is the same before the actual beginning of the effect (as after it).—But Brahman, which is devoid of qualities such as sound, &c., is the cause of this world (possessing all those qualities)!—True, but the effect with all its qualities does not exist without the Self of the cause either now or before the actual beginning (of the effect); hence it cannot be said that (according to our doctrine) the effect is non-existing before its actual beginning.—This point will be elucidated in detail in the section treating of the non-difference of cause and effect.

8. On account of such consequences at the time

of reabsorption (the doctrine maintained hitherto) is objectionable.

The pûrvapakshin raises further objections.—If an effect which is distinguished by the qualities of grossness, consisting of parts, absence of intelligence, limitation, impurity, &c., is admitted to have Brahman for its cause, it follows that at the time of reabsorption (of the world into Brahman), the effect, by entering into the state of non-division from its cause, inquinates the latter with its properties. As therefore—on your doctrine—the cause (i. e. Brahman) as well as the effect is, at the time of reabsorption, characterised by impurity and similar qualities, the doctrine of the Upanishads, according to which an omniscient Brahman is the cause of the world, cannot be upheld.—Another objection to that doctrine is that in consequence of all distinctions passing at the time of reabsorption into the state of non-distinction there would be no special causes left at the time of a new beginning of the world, and consequently the new world could not arise with all the distinctions of enjoying souls, objects to be enjoyed and so on (which are actually observed to exist).—A third objection is that, if we assume the origin of a new world even after the annihilation of all works, &c. (which are the causes of a new world arising) of the enjoying souls which enter into the state of non-difference from the highest Brahman, we are led to the conclusion that also those (souls) which have obtained final release again appear in the new world.—If you finally say, 'Well, let this world remain distinct from the highest Brahman even at the time of reabsorption,' we reply that in that case a reabsorption will not take place at all, and that, moreover, the effect's existing separate from the cause is not possible.—For all these reasons the Vedânta doctrine is objectionable.

To this the next Sûtra replies.

9. Not so; as there are parallel instances.

There is nothing objectionable in our system.—The objection that the effect when being reabsorbed into its cause would inquinate the latter with its qualities does not damage our position 'because there are parallel instances,' i. e. because there are instances of effects not inquinating with their qualities the causes into which they are reabsorbed. Things, for instance, made of clay, such as pots, &c., which in their state of separate existence are of various descriptions, do not, when they are reabsorbed into their original matter (i. e. clay), impart to the latter their individual qualities; nor do golden ornaments impart their individual qualities to their elementary material, i. e. gold, into which they may finally be reabsorbed. Nor does the fourfold complex of organic beings which springs from earth impart its qualities to the latter at the time of reabsorption. You (i. e. the pûrvapakshin), on the other hand, have not any instances to quote in your favour. For reabsorption could not take place at all if the effect when passing back into its causal substance continued to subsist there with all its individual properties. And [1] that in spite of the non-difference of cause and effect the effect has its Self in the cause, but not the cause in the effect, is a point which we shall render clear later on, under II, 1, 14.

Moreover, the objection that the effect would impart its qualities to the cause at the time of reabsorption is formulated too narrowly because, the identity of cause and effect being admitted, the same would take place during the time of the subsistence (of the effect, previous to its reabsorption). That the identity of cause and effect (of Brahman and the world) holds good indiscriminately with regard to all time (not only the time of reabsorption), is declared in many scriptural passages, as, for instance, 'This everything is that Self' (B*ri*. Up. II, 4, 6); 'The Self is all this' (*Kh*. Up. VII, 25, 2); 'The immortal Brahman is this before' (Mu. Up. II, 2, 11); 'All this is Brahman' (*Kh*. Up. III, 14, 1).

With regard to the case referred to in the *S*ruti-passages we refute the assertion of the cause being affected by the

---

[1] Nanu pralayakâle kâryadharmâ*s k*en nâvatish*th*eran na tarhi kâra*n*adharmâ api tish*th*eyus tayor abhedât tatrâhânanyatve›pîti. Ân. Gi.

effect and its qualities by showing that the latter are the mere fallacious superimpositions of nescience, and the very same argument holds good with reference to reabsorption also.—We can quote other examples in favour of our doctrine. As the magician is not at any time affected by the magical illusion produced by himself, because it is unreal, so the highest Self is not affected by the world-illusion. And as one dreaming person is not affected by the illusory visions of his dream because they do not accompany the waking state and the state of dreamless sleep; so the one permanent witness of the three states (viz. the highest Self which is the one unchanging witness of the creation, subsistence, and reabsorption of the world) is not touched by the mutually exclusive three states. For that the highest Self appears in those three states, is a mere illusion, not more substantial than the snake for which the rope is mistaken in the twilight. With reference to this point teachers knowing the true tradition of the Vedânta have made the following declaration, 'When the individual soul which is held in the bonds of slumber by the beginningless Mâyâ awakes, then it knows the eternal, sleepless, dreamless non-duality' (Gau*d*ap. Kâr. I, 16).

So far we have shown that—on our doctrine—there is no danger of the cause being affected at the time of reabsorption by the qualities of the effect, such as grossness and the like.—With regard to the second objection, viz. that if we assume all distinctions to pass (at the time of reabsorption) into the state of non-distinction there would be no special reason for the origin of a new world affected with distinctions, we likewise refer to the 'existence of parallel instances.' For the case is parallel to that of deep sleep and trance. In those states also the soul enters into an essential condition of non-distinction; nevertheless, wrong knowledge being not yet finally overcome, the old state of distinction re-establishes itself as soon as the soul awakes from its sleep or trance. Compare the scriptural passage, 'All these creatures when they have become merged in the True, know not that they are merged in the True. Whatever these creatures are here, whether a lion, or a wolf, or a boar, or a worm, or a midge, or a gnat, or a musquito, that they become again' (*Kh.* Up. VI, 9, 2; 3). For just as during the subsistence of the world the phenomenon of multifarious distinct existence, based on wrong knowledge, proceeds unimpeded like the vision of a dream, although there is only one highest Self devoid of all distinction; so, we conclude, there remains, even after reabsorption, the power of distinction (potential distinction) founded on wrong knowledge.—Herewith the objection that—according to our doctrine—even the finally released souls would be born again is already disposed of. They will not be born again because in their case wrong knowledge has been entirely discarded by perfect knowledge. —The last alternative finally (which the pûrvapakshin had represented as open to the Vedântin), viz. that even at the time of reabsorption the world should remain distinct from Brahman, precludes itself because it is not admitted by the Vedântins themselves.—Hence the system founded on the Upanishads is in every way unobjectionable.

10. And because the objections (raised by the Sâṅkhya against the Vedânta doctrine) apply to his view also.

The doctrine of our opponent is liable to the very same objections which he urges against us, viz. in the following manner. — The objection that this world cannot have sprung from Brahman on account of its difference of character applies no less to the doctrine of the pradhâna being the cause of the world; for that doctrine also assumes that from a pradhâna devoid of sound and other qualities a world is produced which possesses those very qualities. The beginning of an effect different in character being thus admitted, the Sâṅkhya is equally driven to the doctrine that before the actual beginning the effect was non-existent. And, moreover, it being admitted (by the Sâṅkhya also) that at the time of reabsorption the effect passes back into the state of non-distinction from the cause, the case of the Sâṅkhya here also is the same as ours.—And, further, if (as the Sâṅkhya also must admit) at the time of reabsorption the differences of all the special effects are obliterated and pass into a state of general non-distinction, the special fixed conditions, which previous to reabsorption were the causes of the different worldly existence of each soul, can, at the time of a new creation, no longer be determined, there being no cause for them; and if you assume them to be determined without a cause, you are driven to the admission that even the released souls have to re-enter a state of bondage, there being equal absence of a cause (in the case of the released and the non-released souls). And if you try to avoid this conclusion by assuming that at the time of reabsorption some individual differences pass into the state of non-distinction, others not, we reply that in that case the latter could not be considered as effects of the pradhâna[1].—It thus appears that all those difficulties (raised by the Sâṅkhya) apply to both views, and cannot therefore be urged against either only. But as either of the two doctrines must necessarily be accepted, we are strengthened —by the outcome of the above discussion—in the opinion that the alleged difficulties are no real difficulties[2].

11. If it be said that, in consequence of the ill-foundedness of reasoning, we must frame our conclusions otherwise; (we reply that) thus also there would result non-release.

In matters to be known from Scripture mere reasoning is not to be relied on for the following reason also. As the thoughts of man are altogether unfettered, reasoning which disregards the holy texts and rests on individual opinion only has no proper foundation. We see how arguments, which some clever men had excogitated with great pains, are shown, by people still more ingenious, to be fallacious, and how the arguments of the latter again are refuted in their turn

[1] For if they are effects of the pradhâna they must as such be reabsorbed into it at the time of general reabsorption.

[2] And that the Vedânta view is preferable because the nullity of the objections has already been demonstrated in its case.

by other men; so that, on account of the diversity of men's opinions, it is impossible to accept mere reasoning as having a sure foundation. Nor can we get over this difficulty by accepting as well-founded the reasoning of some person of recognised mental eminence, may he now be Kapila or anybody else; since we observe that even men of the most undoubted mental eminence, such as Kapila, Ka*n*âda, and other founders of philosophical schools, have contradicted one another.

But (our adversary may here be supposed to say), we will fashion our reasoning otherwise, i.e. in such a manner as not to lay it open to the charge of having no proper foundation. You cannot, after all, maintain that no reasoning whatever is well-founded; for you yourself can found your assertion that reasoning has no foundation on reasoning only; your assumption being that because some arguments are seen to be devoid of foundation other arguments as belonging to the same class are likewise devoid of foundation. Moreover, if all reasoning were unfounded, the whole course of practical human life would have to come to an end. For we see that men act, with a view to obtaining pleasure and avoiding pain in the future time, on the assumption that the past, the present, and the future are uniform.—Further, in the case of passages of Scripture (apparently) contradicting each other, the ascertainment of the real sense, which depends on a preliminary refutation of the apparent sense, can be effected only by an accurate definition of the meaning of sentences, and that involves a process of reasoning. Thus Manu also expresses himself: 'Perception, inference, and the *s*âstra according to the various traditions, this triad is to be known well by one desiring clearness in regard to right.—He who applies reasoning not contradicted by the Veda to the Veda and the (Sm*ri*ti) doctrine of law, he, and no other, knows the law' (Manu Sm*ri*ti XII, 105, 106). And that 'want of foundation,' to which you object, really constitutes the beauty of reasoning, because it enables us to arrive at unobjectionable arguments by means of the previous refutation of objectionable arguments[1]. (No fear that because the

[1] The whole style of argumentation of the Mîmâ*m*sâ would be

pûrvapaksha is ill-founded the siddhânta should be ill-founded too;) for there is no valid reason to maintain that a man must be stupid because his elder brother was stupid.—For all these reasons the want of foundation cannot be used as an argument against reasoning.

Against this argumentation we remark that thus also there results 'want of release.' For although with regard to some things reasoning is observed to be well founded, with regard to the matter in hand there will result 'want of release,' viz. of the reasoning from this very fault of ill-foundedness. The true nature of the cause of the world on which final emancipation depends cannot, on account of its excessive abstruseness, even be thought of without the help of the holy texts; for, as already remarked, it cannot become the object of perception, because it does not possess qualities such as form and the like, and as it is devoid of characteristic signs, it does not lend itself to inference and the other means of right knowledge.—Or else (if we adopt another explanation of the word 'avimoksha') all those who teach the final release of the soul are agreed that it results from perfect knowledge. Perfect knowledge has the characteristic mark of uniformity, because it depends on accomplished actually existing things; for whatever thing is permanently of one and the same nature is acknowledged to be a true or real thing, and knowledge conversant about such is called perfect knowledge; as, for instance, the knowledge embodied in the proposition, 'fire is hot.' Now, it is clear that in the case of perfect knowledge a mutual conflict of men's opinions is impossible. But that cognitions founded on reasoning do conflict is generally known; for we continually observe that what one logician endeavours to establish as perfect knowledge is demolished by another, who, in his turn, is treated alike by a third. How therefore can knowledge, which is founded on reasoning, and whose object is not something permanently uniform, be perfect knowledge?—Nor can it be said that he who maintains the

impossible, if all reasoning were sound; for then no pûrvapaksha view could be maintained.

pradhâna to be the cause of the world (i. e. the Sâṅkhya) is the best of all reasoners, and accepted as such by all philosophers; which would enable us to accept his opinion as perfect knowledge.—Nor can we collect at a given moment and on a given spot all the logicians of the past, present, and future time, so as to settle (by their agreement) that their opinion regarding some uniform object is to be considered perfect knowledge. The Veda, on the other hand, which is eternal and the source of knowledge, may be allowed to have for its object firmly established things, and hence the perfection of that knowledge which is founded on the Veda cannot be denied by any of the logicians of the past, present, or future. We have thus established the perfection of this our knowledge which reposes on the Upanishads, and as apart from it perfect knowledge is impossible, its disregard would lead to 'absence of final release' of the transmigrating souls. Our final position therefore is, that on the ground of Scripture and of reasoning subordinate to Scripture, the intelligent Brahman is to be considered the cause and substance of the world.

12. Thereby those (theories) also which are not accepted by competent persons are explained.

Hitherto we have refuted those objections against the Vedânta-texts which, based on reasoning, take their stand on the doctrine of the pradhâna being the cause of the world; (which doctrine deserves to be refuted first), because it stands near to our Vedic system, is supported by somewhat weighty arguments, and has, to a certain extent, been adopted by some authorities who follow the Veda.—But now some dull-witted persons might think that another objection founded on reasoning might be raised against the Vedânta, viz. on the ground of the atomic doctrine. The Sûtrakâra, therefore, extends to the latter objection the refutation of the former, considering that by the conquest of the most dangerous adversary the conquest of the minor enemies is already virtually accomplished. Other doctrines, as, for instance, the atomic doctrine of which no part has been accepted by either Manu or Vyâsa or other authorities, are to be considered as 'explained,' i. e. refuted by the same reasons which enabled us to dispose of the pradhâna doctrine. As the reasons on which the refutation hinges are the same, there is no room for further doubt. Such common arguments are the impotence of reasoning to fathom the depth of the transcendental cause of the world, the ill-foundedness of mere Reasoning, the impossibility of final release, even in case of the conclusions being shaped 'otherwise' (see the preceding Sûtra), the conflict of Scripture and Reasoning, and so on.

13. If it be said that from the circumstance of (the objects of enjoyment) passing over into the enjoyer (and vice versâ) there would result non-distinction (of the two); we reply that (such distinction) may exist (nevertheless), as ordinary experience shows.

Another objection, based on reasoning, is raised against the doctrine of Brahman being the cause of the world.—Although Scripture is authoritative with regard to its own special subject-matter (as, for instance, the causality of Brahman), still it may have to be taken in a secondary sense in those cases where the subject-matter is taken out of its grasp by other means of right knowledge; just as mantras and arthavâdas have occasionally to be explained in a secondary sense (when the primary. literal sense is rendered impossible by other means of right knowledge[1]). Analogously reasoning is to be considered invalid outside its legitimate sphere; so, for instance, in the case of religious duty and its opposite[2].—Hence Scripture cannot be acknowledged to refute what is settled by other means of right knowledge. And if you ask, 'Where does Scripture oppose itself to what is thus established?' we give you the fol-

[1] The following arthavâda-passage, for instance, 'the sacrificial post is the sun,' is to be taken in a metaphorical sense; because perception renders it impossible for us to take it in its literal meaning.

[2] Which are to be known from the Veda only.

lowing instance. The distinction of enjoyers and objects of enjoyment is well known from ordinary experience, the enjoyers being intelligent, embodied souls, while sound and the like are the objects of enjoyment. Devadatta, for instance, is an enjoyer, the dish (which he eats) an object of enjoyment. The distinction of the two would be reduced to non-existence if the enjoyer passed over into the object of enjoyment, and vice versâ. Now this passing over of one thing into another would actually result from the doctrine of the world being non-different from Brahman. But the sublation of a well-established distinction is objectionable, not only with regard to the present time when that distinction is observed to exist, but also with regard to the past and the future, for which it is inferred. The doctrine of Brahman's causality must therefore be abandoned, as it would lead to the sublation of the well-established distinction of enjoyers and objects of enjoyment.

To the preceding objection we reply, 'It may exist as in ordinary experience.' Even on our philosophic view the distinction may exist, as ordinary experience furnishes us with analogous instances. We see, for instance, that waves, foam, bubbles, and other modifications of the sea, although they really are not different from the sea-water, exist, sometimes in the state of mutual separation, sometimes in the state of conjunction, &c. From the fact of their being non-different from the sea-water, it does not follow that they pass over into each other; and, again, although they do not pass over into each other, still they are not different from the sea. So it is in the case under discussion also. The enjoyers and the objects of enjoyment do not pass over into each other, and yet they are not different from the highest Brahman. And although the enjoyer is not really an effect of Brahman, since the unmodified creator himself, in so far as he enters into the effect, is called the enjoyer (according to the passage. 'Having created he entered into it,' Taitt. Up. II, 6), still after Brahman has entered into its effects it passes into a state of distinction, in consequence of the effect acting as a limiting adjunct; just as the universal ether is divided by its contact with jars and other limiting adjuncts. The conclusion is, that the distinction of enjoyers and objects of enjoyment is possible, although both are non-different from Brahman, their highest cause, as the analogous instance of the sea and its waves demonstrates.

14. The non-difference of them (i.e. of cause and effect) results from such terms as 'origin' and the like.

The[1] refutation contained in the preceding Sûtra was set forth on the condition of the practical distinction of enjoyers and objects of enjoyment being acknowledged. In reality, however, that distinction does not exist because there is understood to be non-difference (identity) of cause and effect. The effect is this manifold world consisting of ether and so on; the cause is the highest Brahman. Of the effect it is understood that in reality it is non-different from the cause, i. e. has no existence apart from the cause.—How so?—'On account of the scriptural word "origin" and others.' The word 'origin' is used in connexion with a simile, in a passage undertaking to show how through the knowledge of one thing everything is known; viz. *Kh*. Up. VI, 1, 4, 'As, my dear, by one clod of clay all that is made of clay is known, the modification (i. e. the effect; the thing made of clay) being a name merely which has its origin in speech, while the truth is that it is clay merely; thus,' &c.—The meaning of this passage is that, if there is known a lump of clay which really and truly is nothing but clay[2], there are known thereby likewise all things made of clay, such as jars, dishes, pails, and so on, all of which agree in having clay for their true nature. For these modifications or effects are names only, exist through or originate from speech only, while in reality there exists no such thing as a modification. In so far as they are names (individual effects distinguished by names) they are untrue; in so far

---

[1] Pari*n*âmavâdam avalambyâpâtato virodha*m* samâdhâya vivartavâdam âsritya paramasamâdhânam âha. Ân. Gi.

[2] Ânanda Giri construes differently: etad uktam iti, paramârthato vig*ñ*âtam iti sambandha*h*.

as they are clay they are true.—This parallel instance is given with reference to Brahman; applying the phrase 'having its origin in speech' to the case illustrated by the instance quoted we understand that the entire body of effects has no existence apart from Brahman.—Later on again the text, after having declared that fire, water, and earth are the effects of Brahman, maintains that the effects of these three elements have no existence apart from them, 'Thus has vanished the specific nature of burning fire, the modification being a mere name which has its origin in speech, while only the three colours are what is true' (*Kh*. Up. VI, 4, 1).—Other sacred texts also whose purport it is to intimate the unity of the Self are to be quoted here, in accordance with the 'and others' of the Sûtra. Such texts are, 'In that all this has its Self; it is the True, it is the Self, thou art that' (*Kh*. Up. VI, 8, 7); 'This everything, all is that Self' (B*ri*. Up. II, 4, 6); 'Brahman alone is all this' (Mu. Up. II, 2, 11); 'The Self is all this' (*Kh*. Up. VII, 25, 2); 'There is in it no diversity' (B*ri*. Up. IV, 4, 25).—On any other assumption it would not be possible to maintain that by the knowledge of one thing everything becomes known (as the text quoted above declares). We therefore must adopt the following view. In the same way as those parts of ethereal space which are limited by jars and waterpots are not really different from the universal ethereal space, and as the water of a mirage is not really different from the surface of the salty steppe—for the nature of that water is that it is seen in one moment and has vanished in the next, and moreover, it is not to be perceived by its own nature (i. e. apart from the surface of the desert[1])—; so this manifold world with its objects of enjoyment, enjoyers and so on has no existence apart from Brahman.—But—it might be objected—Brahman has in itself elements of manifoldness. As the tree has many branches, so Brahman possesses many powers

[1] D*r*ish*t*eti kadâ*k*id d*r*ish*t*a*m* punar nash*t*am anityam iti yâvat.—D*r*ish*t*agraha*n*asû*k*ita*m* pratîtikâle*pi sattârâhitya*m* tatraiva hetvantaram âha svarûpe*n*eti. Ân. Gi.

and energies dependent on those powers. Unity and manifoldness are therefore both true. Thus, a tree considered in itself is one, but it is manifold if viewed as having branches; so the sea in itself is one, but manifold as having waves and foam; so the clay in itself is one, but manifold if viewed with regard to the jars and dishes made of it. On this assumption the process of final release resulting from right knowledge may be established in connexion with the element of unity (in Brahman), while the two processes of common worldly activity and of activity according to the Veda—which depend on the karmakâ*nd*a—may be established in connexion with the element of manifoldness. And with this view the parallel instances of clay &c. agree very well.

This theory, we reply, is untenable because in the instance (quoted in the Upanishad) the phrase 'as clay they are true' asserts the cause only to be true while the phrase 'having its origin in speech' declares the unreality of all effects. And with reference to the matter illustrated by the instance given (viz. the highest cause, Brahman) we read, 'In that all this has its Self;' and, again, 'That is true;' whereby it is asserted that only the one highest cause is true. The following passage again, 'That is the Self; thou art that, O *S*vetaketu!' teaches that the embodied soul (the individual soul) also is Brahman. (And we must note that) the passage distinctly teaches that the fact of the embodied soul having its Self in Brahman is self-established, not to be accomplished by endeavour. This doctrine of the individual soul having its Self in Brahman, if once accepted as the doctrine of the Veda, does away with the independent existence of the individual soul, just as the idea of the rope does away with the idea of the snake (for which the rope had been mistaken). And if the doctrine of the independent existence of the individual soul has to be set aside, then the opinion of the entire phenomenal world—which is based on the individual soul—having an independent existence is likewise to be set aside. But only for the establishment of the latter an element of manifoldness would have to be assumed in Brahman, in addition to the element of unity.—Scriptural passages also (such as, 'When the Self only is all this, how should he see another?' B*ri*. Up. II, 4, 13) declare that for him who sees that everything has its Self in Brahman the whole phenomenal world with its actions, agents, and results of actions is non-existent. Nor can it be said that this non-existence of the phenomenal world is declared (by Scripture) to be limited to certain states; for the passage 'Thou art that' shows that the general fact of Brahman being the Self of all is not limited by any particular state. Moreover, Scripture, showing by the instance of the thief (*Kh*. VI, 16) that the false-minded is bound while the true-minded is released, declares thereby that unity is the one true existence while manifoldness is evolved out of wrong knowledge. For if both were true how could the man who acquiesces in the reality of this phenomenal world be called false-minded [1]? Another scriptural passage ('from death to death goes he who perceives therein any diversity,' B*ri*. Up. IV, 4, 19) declares the same, by blaming those who perceive any distinction.—Moreover, on the doctrine, which we are at present impugning, release cannot result from knowledge, because the doctrine does not acknowledge that some kind of wrong knowledge, to be removed by perfect knowledge, is the cause of the phenomenal world. For how can the cognition of unity remove the cognition of manifoldness if both are true?

Other objections are started.—If we acquiesce in the doctrine of absolute unity, the ordinary means of right knowledge, perception, &c., become invalid because the absence of manifoldness deprives them of their objects; just as the idea of a man becomes invalid after the right idea of the post (which at first had been mistaken for a man) has presented itself. Moreover, all the texts embodying injunctions and prohibitions will lose their purport if the distinction on which their validity depends

[1] In the passage alluded to he is called so by implication, being compared to the 'false-minded' thief who, knowing himself to be guilty, undergoes the ordeal of the heated hatchet.

does not really exist. And further, the entire body of doctrine which refers to final release will collapse, if the distinction of teacher and pupil on which it depends is not real. And if the doctrine of release is untrue, how can we maintain the truth of the absolute unity of the Self, which forms an item of that doctrine?

These objections, we reply, do not damage our position because the entire complex of phenomenal existence is considered as true as long as the knowledge of Brahman being the Self of all has not arisen; just as the phantoms of a dream are considered to be true until the sleeper wakes. For as long as a person has not reached the true knowledge of the unity of the Self, so long it does not enter his mind that the world of effects with its means and objects of right knowledge and its results of actions is untrue; he rather, in consequence of his ignorance, looks on mere effects (such as body, offspring, wealth, &c.) as forming part of and belonging to his Self, forgetful of Brahman being in reality the Self of all. Hence, as long as true knowledge does not present itself, there is no reason why the ordinary course of secular and religious activity should not hold on undisturbed. The case is analogous to that of a dreaming man who in his dream sees manifold things, and, up to the moment of waking, is convinced that his ideas are produced by real perception without suspecting the perception to be a merely apparent one.—But how (to restate an objection raised above) can the Vedânta-texts if untrue convey information about the true being of Brahman? We certainly do not observe that a man bitten by a rope-snake (i. e. a snake falsely imagined in a rope) dies, nor is the water appearing in a mirage used for drinking or bathing [1].—This objection, we reply, is without force (because as a matter of fact we do see real effects to result from unreal causes), for we observe that death sometimes takes place from imaginary venom, (when a man imagines himself to have been bitten by a venomous snake,)

[1] I.e. ordinary experience does not teach us that real effects spring from unreal causes.

and effects (of what is perceived in a dream) such as the bite of a snake or bathing in a river take place with regard to a dreaming person.—But, it will be said, these effects themselves are unreal!—These effects themselves, we reply, are unreal indeed; but not so the consciousness which the dreaming person has of them. This consciousness is a real result; for it is not sublated by the waking consciousness. The man who has risen from sleep does indeed consider the effects perceived by him in his dream such as being bitten by a snake, bathing in a river, &c. to be unreal, but he does not on that account consider the consciousness he had of them to be unreal likewise.—(We remark in passing that) by this fact of the consciousness of the dreaming person not being sublated (by the waking consciousness) the doctrine of the body being our true Self is to be considered as refuted[1].—Scripture also (in the passage, 'If a man who is engaged in some sacrifice undertaken for some special wish sees in his dream a woman, he is to infer therefrom success in his work') declares that by the unreal phantom of a dream a real result such as prosperity may be obtained. And, again, another scriptural passage, after having declared that from the observation of certain unfavourable omens a man is to conclude that he will not live long, continues 'if somebody sees in his dream a black man with black teeth and that man kills him,' intimating thereby that by the unreal dream-phantom a real fact, viz. death, is notified.—It is, moreover, known from the experience of persons who carefully observe positive and negative instances that such and such dreams are auspicious omens, others the reverse. And (to quote another example that something true can result from or be known through something untrue) we see that the knowledge of the real sounds A. &c. is reached by means of the unreal written letters. Moreover, the reasons which establish the unity of the

[1] Svapna*g*âgraddehayor vyabhi*k*âre*s*pi pratyabhi*gñ*ânât tadanugatâtmaikyasiddhe*s* *k*aitanyasya *k*a dehadharmatve rûpâdivat tadanupalabdhiprasaṅgâd avagate*s* *k*âbâdhât tadrûpasyâtmano dehadvayâtirekasiddher dehamâtrâtmavâdo na yukta ity artha*h*. Ân. Gi.

Self are altogether final, so that subsequently to them nothing more is required for full satisfaction[1]. An injunction as, for instance, 'He is to sacrifice' at once renders us desirous of knowing what is to be effected, and by what means and in what manner it is to be effected; but passages such as, 'Thou art that,' 'I am Brahman,' leave nothing to be desired because the state of consciousness produced by them has for its object the unity of the universal Self. For as long as something else remains a desire is possible; but there is nothing else which could be desired in addition to the absolute unity of Brahman. Nor can it be maintained that such states of consciousness do not actually arise; for scriptural passages such as, 'He understood what he said' (*Kh.* Up. VII, 18, 2), declare them to occur, and certain means are enjoined to bring them about, such as the hearing (of the Veda from a teacher) and the recital of the sacred texts. Nor, again, can such consciousness be objected to on the ground either of uselessness or of erroneousness, because, firstly, it is seen to have for its result the cessation of ignorance, and because, secondly, there is no other kind of knowledge by which it could be sublated. And that before the knowledge of the unity of the Self has been reached the whole real-unreal course of ordinary life, worldly as well as religious, goes on unimpeded, we have already explained. When, however, final authority having intimated the unity of the Self, the entire course of the world which was founded on the previous distinction is sublated, then there is no longer any opportunity for assuming a Brahman comprising in itself various elements.

But—it may be said—(that would not be a mere assumption, but) Scripture itself, by quoting the parallel instances of clay and so on, declares itself in favour of a Brahman

[1] As long as the 'vyavahâra' presents itself to our mind, we might feel inclined to assume in Brahman an element of manifoldness whereby to account for the vyavahâra; but as soon as we arrive at true knowledge, the vyavahâra vanishes, and there remains no longer any reason for qualifying in any way the absolute unity of Brahman.

capable of modification; for we know from experience that clay and similar things do undergo modifications.—This objection—we reply—is without force, because a number of scriptural passages, by denying all modification of Brahman, teach it to be absolutely changeless (kû*t*astha). Such passages are, 'This great unborn Self, undecaying, undying, immortal, fearless, is indeed Brahman' (B*ri*. Up. IV, 4, 25); 'That Self is to be described by No, no' (B*ri*. Up. III, 9, 26); 'It is neither coarse nor fine' (B*ri*. Up. III, 8, 8). For to the one Brahman the two qualities of being subject to modification and of being free from it cannot both be ascribed. And if you say, 'Why should they not be both predicated of Brahman (the former during the time of the subsistence of the world, the latter during the period of reabsorption) just as rest and motion may be predicated (of one body at different times)?' we remark that the qualification, 'absolutely changeless' (kû*t*astha), precludes this. For the changeless Brahman cannot be the substratum of varying attributes. And that, on account of the negation of all attributes, Brahman really is eternal and changeless has already been demonstrated.—Moreover, while the cognition of the unity of Brahman is the instrument of final release, there is nothing to show that any independent result is connected with the view of Brahman, by undergoing a modification, passing over into the form of this world. Scripture expressly declares that the knowledge of the changeless Brahman being the universal Self leads to a result; for in the passage which begins, 'That Self is to be described by No, no,' we read later on, 'O *G*anaka, you have indeed reached fearlessness' (B*ri*. Up. IV, 2, 4). We have then[1] to accept the following conclusion that, in the sections treating of Brahman, an independent result belongs only to the knowledge of Brahman as devoid of all attributes and distinctions, and that hence whatever is stated as having no special fruit of its own—as, for instance, the passages about Brahman modifying itself into the form of this

[1] Tatreti, s*ri*sh*t*yâdi*s*rutînâ*m* svârthe phalavaikalye satîti yâvat. Ân. Gi.

world—is merely to be applied as a means for the cognition of the absolute Brahman, but does not bring about an independent result; according to the principle that whatever has no result of its own, but is mentioned in connexion with something else which has such a result, is subordinate to the latter [1]. For to maintain that the result of the knowledge of Brahman undergoing modifications would be that the Self (of him who knows that) would undergo corresponding modifications [2] would be inappropriate, as the state of final release (which the soul obtains through the knowledge of Brahman) is eternally unchanging.

But, it is objected, he who maintains the nature of Brahman to be changeless thereby contradicts the fundamental tenet according to which the Lord is the cause of the world, since the doctrine of absolute unity leaves no room for the distinction of a Ruler and something ruled.—This objection we ward off by remarking that omniscience, &c. (i. e. those qualities which belong to Brahman only in so far as it is related to a world) depend on the evolution of the germinal principles called name and form, whose essence is Nescience. The fundamental tenet which we maintain (in accordance with such scriptural passages as, 'From that Self sprang ether,' &c.; Taitt. Up. II, 1) is that the creation, sustentation, and reabsorption of the world proceed from an omniscient, omnipotent Lord, not from a non-intelligent pradhâna or any other principle. That tenet we have stated in I, 1, 4, and here we do not teach anything contrary to it.—But how, the question may be asked, can you make this last assertion while all the while you maintain the absolute unity and non-duality of the Self?—Listen how. Belonging to the Self, as it were, of the omniscient Lord, there are name and form, the figments of Nescience, not to be defined either

[1] A Mîmâmsâ principle. A sacrificial act, for instance, is independent when a special result is assigned to it by the sacred texts; an act which is enjoined without such a specification is merely auxiliary to another act.

[2] According to the *S*ruti 'in whatever mode he worships him into that mode he passes himself.'

as being (i. e. Brahman), nor as different from it [1], the germs of the entire expanse of the phenomenal world, called in *S*ruti and Sm*ri*ti the illusion (mâyâ), power (*s*akti), or nature (prak*ri*ti) of the omniscient Lord. Different from them is the omniscient Lord himself, as we learn from scriptural passages such as the following, 'He who is called ether is the revealer of all forms and names; that within which these forms and names are contained is Brahman' (*Kh*. Up. VIII, 14, 1); 'Let me evolve names and forms' (*Kh*. Up. VI, 3, 2); 'He, the wise one, who having divided all forms and given all names, sits speaking (with those names)' (Taitt. Âr. III, 12, 7); 'He who makes the one seed manifold' (*S*ve. Up. VI, 12).—Thus the Lord depends (as Lord) upon the limiting adjuncts of name and form, the products of Nescience; just as the universal ether depends (as limited ether, such as the ether of a jar, &c.) upon the limiting adjuncts in the shape of jars, pots, &c. He (the Lord) stands in the realm of the phenomenal in the relation of a ruler to the so-called *g*îvas (individual souls) or cognitional Selfs (vi*gñ*ânâtman), which indeed are one with his own Self—just as the portions of ether enclosed in jars and the like are one with the universal ether—but are limited by aggregates of instruments of action (i. e. bodies) produced from name and form, the presentations of Nescience. Hence the Lord's being a Lord, his omniscience, his omnipotence, &c. all depend on the limitation due to the adjuncts whose Self is Nescience; while in reality none of these qualities belong to the Self whose true nature is cleared, by right knowledge, from all adjuncts whatever. Thus Scripture also says, 'Where one sees nothing else, hears nothing else, understands nothing else, that is the Infinite' (*Kh*. Up. VII, 24, 1); 'But when the Self only has become all this, how should he see another?' (B*ri*. Up. II, 4, 13.) In this manner the Vedânta-texts declare that for him who has reached the

[1] Tattvânyatvâbhyâm iti, na hî*s*varatvena te niru*k*yete *g*a*d*â*g*a*d*ayor abhedâyogât nâpi tato*-*nyatvena niruktim arhata*h* svâtantrye*n*a sattâsphûrtyasambhavât na hi *g*a*d*am a*g*a*d*ânapekshya*m* sattâsphûrtimad upalakshyate *g*a*d*atvabhaṅgaprasaṅgât tasmâd avidyâtmake nâmarûpe ity artha*h*. Ân. Gi.

state of truth and reality the whole apparent world does not exist. The Bhagavadgîtâ also ('The Lord is not the cause of actions, or of the capacity of performing actions, or of the connexion of action and fruit; all that proceeds according to its own nature. The Lord receives no one's sin or merit. Knowledge is enveloped by Ignorance; hence all creatures are deluded;' Bha. Gî. V, 14; 15) declares that in reality the relation of Ruler and ruled does not exist. That, on the other hand, all those distinctions are valid, as far as the phenomenal world is concerned, Scripture as well as the Bhagavadgîtâ states; compare B*ri*. Up. IV, 4, 22, 'He is the Lord of all, the king of all things, the protector of all things; he is a bank and boundary, so that these worlds may not be confounded;' and Bha. Gî. XVIII, 61, 'The Lord, O Arguna, is seated in the region of the heart of all beings, turning round all beings, (as though) mounted on a machine, by his delusion.' The Sûtrakâra also asserts the non-difference of cause and effect only with regard to the state of Reality; while he had, in the preceding Sûtra, where he looked to the phenomenal world, compared Brahman to the ocean, &c., that comparison resting on the assumption of the world of effects not yet having been refuted (i. e. seen to be unreal).—The view of Brahman as undergoing modifications will, moreover, be of use in the devout meditations on the qualified (sagu*n*a) Brahman.

15. And because only on the existence (of the cause) (the effect) is observed.

For the following reason also the effect is non-different from the cause, because only when the cause exists the effect is observed to exist, not when it does not exist. For instance, only when the clay exists the jar is observed to exist, and the cloth only when the threads exist. That it is not a general rule that when one thing exists another is also observed to exist, appears, for instance, from the fact, that a horse which is other (different) from a cow is not observed to exist only when a cow exists. Nor is the jar observed to exist only when the potter exists; for in that case non-difference does not exist, although the relation between the two is that of an operative cause and its effect [1].—But—it may be objected —even in the case of things other (i.e. non-identical) we find that the observation of one thing regularly depends on the existence of another; smoke, for instance, is observed only when fire exists.—We reply that this is untrue, because sometimes smoke is observed even after the fire has been extinguished; as, for instance, in the case of smoke being kept by herdsmen in jars.—Well, then—the objector will say—let us add to smoke a certain qualification enabling us to say that smoke of such and such a kind [2] does not exist unless fire exists.—Even thus, we reply, your objection is not valid, because we declare that the reason for assuming the non-difference of cause and effect is the fact of the internal organ (buddhi) being affected (impressed) by cause and effect jointly [3]. And that does not take place in the case of fire and smoke.—Or else we have to read (in the Sûtra) 'bhâvât,' and to translate, 'and on account of the existence or observation.' The non-difference of cause and effect results not only from Scripture but also from the existence of perception. For the non-difference of the two is perceived, for instance, in an aggregate of threads, where we do not perceive a thing called 'cloth,' in addition to the threads, but merely threads running lengthways and crossways. So again, in the threads we perceive finer threads (the aggre-

[1] So that from the instance of the potter and the jar we cannot conclude that the relation of clay and the jar is only that of nimitta and naimittika, not that of non-difference.

[2] For instance, smoke extending in a long line whose base is connected with some object on the surface of the earth.

[3] I.e. (as Ân. Gi. explains) because we assume the relation of cause and effect not merely on the ground of the actual existence of one thing depending on that upon another, but on the additional ground of the mental existence, the consciousness of the one not being possible without the consciousness of the other.—Tadbhâvânuvidhâyibhâvatvam tadbhânânuvidhâyibhânatva*m* *k*a kâryasya kâra*n*ânanyatve hetur dhûmavi*s*eshasya *k*âgnibhâvânuvidhâyibhâvatve*pi na tadbhânânuvidhâyibhânatvam agnibhânasya dhûmabhânâdhînatvât.

gate of which is identical with the grosser threads), in them again finer threads, and so on. On the ground of this our perception we conclude that the finest parts which we can perceive are ultimately identical with their causes, viz. red, white, and black (the colours of fire, water, and earth, according to *Kh*. Up. VI, 4); those, again, with air, the latter with ether, and ether with Brahman, which is one and without a second. That all means of proof lead back to Brahman (as the ultimate cause of the world; not to pradhâna, &c.), we have already explained.

16. And on account of that which is posterior (i. e. the effect) being that which is.

For the following reason also the effect is to be considered as non-different (from the cause). That which is posterior in time, i. e. the effect, is declared by Scripture to have, previous to its actual beginning, its Being in the cause, by the Self of the cause merely. For in passages like, 'In the beginning, my dear, this was that only which is' (*Kh*. Up. VI, 2, 1); and, 'Verily, in the beginning this was Self, one only' (Ait. Âr. II, 4, 1, 1), the effect which is denoted by the word 'this' appears in grammatical co-ordination with (the word denoting) the cause (from which it appears that both inhere in the same substratum). A thing, on the other hand, which does not exist in another thing by the Self of the latter is not produced from that other thing; for instance, oil is not produced from sand. Hence as there is non-difference before the production (of the effect), we understand that the effect even after having been produced continues to be non-different from the cause. As the cause, i. e. Brahman, is in all time neither more nor less than that which is, so the effect also, viz. the world, is in all time only that which is. But that which is is one only; therefore the effect is non-different from the cause.

17. If it be said that on account of being denoted as that which is not (the effect does) not (exist before it is actually produced); (we reply) not so, (because

the term 'that which is not' denotes) another quality (merely); (as appears) from the complementary sentence.

But, an objection will be raised, in some places Scripture speaks of the effect before its production as that which is not; so, for instance, 'In the beginning this was that only which is not' (*Kh.* Up. III, 19, 1); and 'Non-existent[1] indeed this was in the beginning' (Taitt. Up. II, 7). Hence Being (sattvam) cannot be ascribed to the effect before its production.

This we deny. For by the Non-existence of the effect previous to its production is not meant absolute Non-existence, but only a different quality or state, viz. the state of name and form being unevolved, which state is different from the state of name and form being evolved. With reference to the latter state the effect is called, previous to its production, non-existent although then also it existed identical with its cause. We conclude this from the complementary passage, according to the rule that the sense of a passage whose earlier part is of doubtful meaning is determined by its complementary part. With reference to the passage, 'In the beginning this was non-existent only,' we remark that what is there denoted by the word 'Non-existing' is—in the complementary passage, 'That became existent'—referred to by the word 'that,' and qualified as 'Existent.'

The word 'was' would, moreover, not apply to the (absolutely) Non-existing, which cannot be conceived as connected with prior or posterior time.—Hence with reference to the other passage also, 'Non-existing indeed,' &c., the complementary part, 'That made itself its Self,' shows, by the qualification which it contains, that absolute Non-existence is not meant.—It follows from all this that the designation of 'Non-existence' applied to the effect before its production has reference to a different state of being merely. And as those things which are distinguished

[1] For simplicity's sake, asat will be translated henceforth by non-existing.

by name and form are in ordinary language called 'existent,' the term 'non-existent' is figuratively applied to them to denote the state in which they were previously to their differentiation.

18. From reasoning and from another Vedic passage.

That the effect exists before its origination and is non-different from the cause, follows from reasoning as well as from a further scriptural passage.

We at first set forth the argumentation.—Ordinary experience teaches us that those who wish to produce certain effects, such as curds, or earthen jars, or golden ornaments, employ for their purpose certain determined causal substances such as milk, clay, and gold; those who wish to produce sour milk do not employ clay, nor do those who intend to make jars employ milk and so on. But, according to that doctrine which teaches that the effect is non-existent (before its actual production), all this should be possible. For if before their actual origination all effects are equally non-existent in any causal substance, why then should curds be produced from milk only and not from clay also, and jars from clay only and not from milk as well?—Let us then maintain, the asatkâryavâdin rejoins, that there is indeed an equal non-existence of any effect in any cause, but that at the same time each causal substance has a certain capacity reaching beyond itself (atisaya) for some particular effect only and not for other effects; that, for instance, milk only, and not clay, has a certain capacity for curds; and clay only, and not milk, an analogous capacity for jars.—What, we ask in return, do you understand by that 'atisaya?' If you understand by it the antecedent condition of the effect (before its actual origination), you abandon your doctrine that the effect does not exist in the cause, and prove our doctrine according to which it does so exist. If, on the other hand, you understand by the atisaya a certain power of the cause assumed to the end of accounting for the fact that only one determined effect springs from the cause, you must admit that the power can determine the particular effect only if it neither is other (than cause and effect) nor non-existent; for if it were either, it would not be different from anything else which is either non-existent or other than cause and effect, (and how then should it alone be able to produce the particular effect?) Hence it follows that that power is identical with the Self of the cause, and that the effect is identical with the Self of that power.—Moreover, as the ideas of cause and effect on the one hand and of substance and qualities on the other hand are not separate ones, as, for instance, the ideas of a horse and a buffalo, it follows that the identity of the cause and the effect as well as of the substance and its qualities has to be admitted. (Let it then be assumed, the opponent rejoins, that the cause and the effect, although really different, are not apprehended as such, because they are connected by the so-called samavâya connexion[1].)—If, we reply, you assume the samavâya connexion between cause and effect, you have either to admit that the samavâya itself is joined by a certain connexion to the two terms which are connected by samavâya, and then that connexion will again require a new connexion (joining it to the two terms which it binds together), and you will thus be compelled to postulate an infinite series of connexions; or else you will have to maintain that the samavâya is not joined by any connexion to the terms which it binds together, and from that will result the dissolution of the bond which connects the two terms of the samavâya relation[2].—Well then, the opponent rejoins, let us assume that the samavâya connexion as itself being a connexion may be connected with the terms which it joins without the help of any further connexion.—Then, we reply, conjunction (sa*m*yoga) also must be connected with the two terms which it joins without the help of the samavâya

[1] Samavâya, commonly translated by inherence or intimate relation, is, according to the Nyâya, the relation connecting a whole and its parts, substances, and qualities, &c.

[2] Samavâyasya svâtantryapaksha*m* dûshayati anabhyupagamyamânc*k*eti. Samavâyasya samavâyibhi*h* sambandho neshyate ki*m* tu svâtantryam evety atrâvayavâvayavinor dravyagu*n*âdînâ*m* *k*a viprakarsha*h* syât sa*m*nidhâyakâbhâvâd ity artha*h*. Ân. Gi.

connexion; for conjunction also is a kind of connexion [1].—Moreover, as substances, qualities, and so on are apprehended as standing in the relation of identity, the assumption of the samavâya relation has really no purport.

In what manner again do you—who maintain that the cause and the effect are joined by the samavâya relation—assume a substance consisting of parts which is an effect to abide in its causes, i.e. in the material parts of which it consists? Does it abide in all the parts taken together or in each particular part?—If you say that it abides in all parts together, it follows that the whole as such cannot be perceived, as it is impossible that all the parts should be in contact with the organs of perception. (And let it not be objected that the whole may be apprehended through some of the parts only), for manyness which abides in all its substrates together (i.e. in all the many things), is not apprehended so long as only some of those substrates are apprehended.—Let it then be assumed that the whole abides in all the parts by the mediation of intervening aggregates of parts [2].—In that case, we reply, we should have to assume other parts in addition to the primary originative parts of the whole, in order that by means of those other parts the whole could abide in the primary parts in the manner indicated by you. For we see (that one thing which abides in another abides there by means of parts different from those of that other thing), that the sword, for instance, pervades the sheath by means of parts different from the parts of the sheath. But an assumption of that kind would lead us into a regressus in infinitum, because in order to explain how the whole abides in certain

[1] A conclusion which is in conflict with the Nyâya tenet that sa*m*yoga, conjunction, as, for instance, of the jar and the ground on which it stands, is a quality (gu*n*a) inherent in the two conjoined substances by means of the samavâya relation.

[2] So that the whole can be apprehended by us as such if we apprehend a certain part only; analogously to our apprehending the whole thread on which a garland of flowers is strung as soon as we apprehend some few of the flowers.

given parts we should always have to assume further parts[1].—Well, then, let us maintain the second alternative, viz. that the whole abides in each particular part.—That also cannot be admitted; for if the whole is present in one part it cannot be present in other parts also; not any more than Devadatta can be present in *S*rughna and in Pâ*t*aliputra on one and the same day. If the whole were present in more than one part, several wholes would result, comparable to Devadatta and Yag*ñ*adatta, who, as being two different persons, may live one of them at *S*rughna and the other at Pâ*t*aliputra.—If the opponent should rejoin that the whole may be fully present in each part, just as the generic character of the cow is fully present in each individual cow; we point out that the generic attributes of the cow are visibly perceived in each individual cow, but that the whole is not thus perceived in each particular part. If the whole were fully present in each part, the consequence would be that the whole would produce its effects indifferently with any of its parts; a cow, for instance, would give milk from her horns or her tail. But such things are not seen to take place.

We proceed to consider some further arguments opposed to the doctrine that the effect does not exist in the cause.—That doctrine involves the conclusion that the actual origination of an effect is without an agent and thus devoid of substantial being. For origination is an action, and as such requires an agent[2], just as the action of walking does. To speak of an action without an agent would be a contradic-

---

[1] Kalpântaram utthâpayati atheti, tathâ *k*a yathâvayavai*h* sûtra*m* kusumâni vyâpnuvat katipayakusumagraha*n*e*pi g*ri*hyate tathâ katipayâvayavagraha*n*e*pi bhavaty avayavino graha*n*am ity artha*h*. Tatra kim ârambhakâvayavair eva teshv avayavî vartteta ki*m* vâ tadatiriktâvayavair iti vikalpyâdyam pratyâha tadâpîti. Yatra yad varttate tat tadatiriktâvayavair eva tatra vartamâna*m* d*r*ish*t*am iti d*r*ish*t*ântagarbha*m* hetum â*k*ash*t*e ko*s*eti. Dvitîyam dûshayati anavastheti. Kalpitânantâvayavavyavahitatayâ prak*ri*tâvayavino dûraviprakarshât tantunish*th*atvam pa*t*asya na syâd iti bhâva*h*. Ân. Gi.

[2] I.e. a something in which the action inheres; not a causal agent.

tion. But if you deny the pre-existence of the effect in the cause, it would have to be assumed that whenever the origination of a jar, for instance, is spoken of the agent is not the jar (which before its origination did not exist) but something else, and again that when the origination of the two halves of the jar is spoken of the agent is not the two halves but something else. From this it would follow that the sentence, 'the jar is originated,' means as much as 'the potter and the other (operative) causes are originated[1].' But as a matter of fact the former sentence is never understood to mean the latter; and it is, moreover, known that at the time when the jar originates, the potter, &c. are already in existence.—Let us then say, the opponent resumes, that origination is the connexion of the effect with the existence of its cause and its obtaining existence as a Self.—How, we ask in reply, can something which has not yet obtained existence enter into connexion with something else? A connexion is possible of two existing things only, not of one existing and one non-existing thing or of two non-existing things. To something non-existing which on that account is indefinable, it is moreover not possible to assign a limit as the opponent does when maintaining that the effect is non-existing before its origination; for experience teaches us that existing things only such as fields and houses have limits, but not non-existing things. If somebody should use, for instance, a phrase such as the following one, 'The son of a barren woman was king previously to the coronation of Pûr*n*avarman,' the declaration of a limit in time implied in that phrase does not in reality determine that the son of the barren woman, i.e. a mere non-entity, either was or is or will be king. If the son of a barren woman could become an existing thing subsequently to the activity of some causal

[1] Every action, *S*aṅkara says, requires an agent, i.e. a substrate in which the action takes place. If we deny that the jar exists in the clay even before it is actually originated, we lose the substrate for the action of origination, i.e. entering into existence (for the non-existing jar cannot be the substratum of any action), and have to assume, for that action, other substrates, such as the operative causes of the jar.

agent, in that case it would be possible also that the non-existing effect should be something existing, subsequently to the activity of some causal agent. But we know that the one thing can take place no more than the other thing; the non-existing effect and the son of the barren woman are both equally non-entities and can never be.—But, the asatkâryavâdin here objects, from your doctrine there follows the result that the activity of causal agents is altogether purposeless. For if the effect were lying already fully accomplished in the cause and were non-different from it, nobody would endeavour to bring it about, no more than anybody endeavours to bring about the cause which is already fully accomplished previously to all endeavour. But as a matter of fact causal agents do endeavour to bring about effects, and it is in order not to have to condemn their efforts as altogether useless that we assume the non-existence of the effect previously to its origination.—Your objection is refuted, we reply, by the consideration that the endeavour of the causal agent may be looked upon as having a purpose in so far as it arranges the causal substance in the form of the effect. That, however, even the form of the effect (is not something previously non-existing, but) belongs to the Self of the cause already because what is devoid of Selfhood cannot be begun at all, we have already shown above.—Nor does a substance become another substance merely by appearing under a different aspect. Devadatta may at one time be seen with his arms and legs closely drawn up to his body, and another time with his arms and legs stretched out, and yet he remains the same substantial being, for he is recognised as such. Thus the persons also by whom we are surrounded, such as fathers, mothers, brothers, &c., remain the same, although we see them in continually changing states and attitudes; for they are always recognised as fathers, mothers, brothers, and so on. If our opponent objects to this last illustrative example on the ground that fathers, mothers, and so on remain the same substantial beings, because the different states in which they appear are not separated from each other by birth or death, while the effect, for instance a jar, appears only after the cause, for instance the clay, has undergone destruction as it were (so that the effect may be looked upon as something altogether different from the cause); we rebut this objection by remarking that causal substances also such as milk, for instance, are perceived to exist even after they have entered into the condition of effects such as curds and the like (so that we have no right to say that the cause undergoes destruction). And even in those cases where the continued existence of the cause is not perceived, as, for instance, in the case of seeds of the fig-tree from which there spring sprouts and trees, the term 'birth' (when applied to the sprout) only means that the causal substance, viz. the seed, becomes visible by becoming a sprout through the continual accretion of similar particles of matter; and the term 'death' only means that, through the secession of those particles, the cause again passes beyond the sphere of visibility. Nor can it be said that from such separation by birth and death as described just now it follows that the non-existing becomes existing, and the existing non-existing; for if that were so, it would also follow that the unborn child in the mother's womb and the new-born babe stretched out on the bed are altogether different beings.

It would further follow that a man is not the same person in childhood, manhood, and old age, and that terms such as father and the like are illegitimately used.—The preceding arguments may also be used to refute the (Bauddha doctrine) of all existence being momentary only [1].

The doctrine that the effect is non-existent previously to its actual origination, moreover, leads to the conclusion that the activity of the causal agent has no object; for what does not exist cannot possibly be an object; not any more than the ether can be cleft by swords and other weapons for striking or cutting. The object can certainly not be the inherent cause; for that would lead to the erroneous conclusion that from the activity of the causal agent, which has for its object the inherent cause, there results something else

[1] Which doctrine will be fully discussed in the second pâda of this adhyâya.

(viz. the effect). And if (in order to preclude this erroneous conclusion) the opponent should say that the effect is (not something different from the cause, but) a certain relative power (atis*aya) of the inherent cause; he thereby would simply concede our doctrine, according to which the effect exists in the cause already.

We maintain, therefore, as our final conclusion, that milk and other substances are called effects when they are in the state of curds and so on, and that it is impossible, even within hundreds of years, ever to bring about an effect which is different from its cause. The fundamental cause of all appears in the form of this and that effect, up to the last effect of all, just as an actor appears in various robes and costumes, and thereby becomes the basis for all the current notions and terms concerning the phenomenal world.

The conclusion here established, on the ground of reasoning, viz. that the effect exists already before its origination, and is non-different from its cause, results also from a different scriptural passage. As under the preceding Sûtra a Vedic passage was instanced which speaks of the non-existing, the different passage referred to in the present Sûtra is the one (*Kh*. Up. VI, 2, 1) which refers to that which is. That passage begins, 'Being only was this in the beginning, one without a second,' refers, thereupon, to the doctrine of the Non-existent being the cause of the world ('Others say, Non-being was this in the beginning'), raises an objection against that doctrine ('How could that which is be born of that which is not?'), and, finally, reaffirms the view first set forth, 'Only Being was this in the beginning.' The circumstance that in this passage the effect, which is denoted by the word 'this,' is by Scripture, with reference to the time previous to its origination, coordinated with the cause denoted by the term 'Being,' proves that the effect exists in—and is non-different from—the cause. If it were before its origination non-existing and after it inhered in its cause by samavâya, it would be something different from the cause, and that would virtually imply an abandonment of the promise made in the passage, 'That instruction by which we hear what is not heard,' &c.

(VI, 1, 3). The latter assertion is ratified, on the other hand, through the comprehension that the effect exists in—and is not different from—the cause.

19. And like a piece of cloth.

As of a folded piece of cloth we do not know clearly whether it is a piece of cloth or some other thing, while on its being unfolded it becomes manifest that the folded thing was a piece of cloth; and as, so long as it is folded, we perhaps know that it is a piece of cloth but not of what definite length and width it is, while on its being unfolded we know these particulars, and at the same time that the cloth is not different from the folded object; in the same way an effect, such as a piece of cloth, is non-manifest as long as it exists in its causes, i. e. the threads, &c. merely, while it becomes manifest and is clearly apprehended in consequence of the operations of shuttle, loom, weaver, and so on.—Applying this instance of the piece of cloth, first folded and then unfolded, to the general case of cause and effect, we conclude that the latter is non-different from the former.

20. And as in the case of the different vital airs.

It is a matter of observation that when the operations of the different kinds of vital air—such as prâ*n*a the ascending vital air, apâna the descending vital air, &c.—are suspended, in consequence of the breath being held so that they exist in their causes merely, the only effect which continues to be accomplished is life, while all other effects, such as the bending and stretching of the limbs and so on, are stopped. When, thereupon, the vital airs again begin to act, those other effects also are brought about, in addition to mere life.—Nor must the vital airs, on account of their being divided into classes, be considered as something else than vital air; for wind (air) constitutes their common character. Thus (i. e. in the manner illustrated by the instance of the vital airs) the non-difference of the effect from the cause is to be conceived.—As, therefore, the whole world is an effect of Brahman and non-different from it, the promise held out in the scriptural passage that 'What is not heard is heard, what is not perceived is perceived, what is not known is known' (*Kh.* Up. VI, 1, 3) is fulfilled [1].

21. On account of the other (i.e. the individual soul) being designated (as non-different from Brahman) there would attach (to Brahman) various faults, as, for instance, not doing what is beneficial.

Another objection is raised against the doctrine of an intelligent cause of the world.—If that doctrine is accepted, certain faults, as, for instance, doing what is not beneficial, will attach (to the intelligent cause, i.e. Brahman), 'on account of the other being designated.' For Scripture declares the other, i.e. the embodied soul, to be one with Brahman, as is shown by the passage, 'That is the Self; that art thou, O *S*vetaketu!' (*Kh.* Up. VI, 8, 7.)—Or else (if we interpret 'the other' of the Sûtra in a different way) Scripture declares the other, i.e. Brahman, to be the Self of the embodied soul. For the passage, 'Having created that he entered into it,' declares the creator, i.e. the unmodified Brahman, to constitute the Self of the embodied soul, in consequence of his entering into his products. The following passage also, 'Entering (into them) with this living Self I will evolve names and forms' (*Kh.* Up. VI, 3, 2), in which the highest divinity designates the living (soul) by the word 'Self,' shows that the embodied Self is not different from Brahman. Therefore the creative power of Brahman belongs to the embodied Self also, and the latter, being thus an independent agent, might be expected to produce only what is beneficial to itself, and not things of a contrary nature, such as birth, death, old age, disease, and whatever may be the other meshes of the net of suffering. For we know that no free person will build a prison for himself, and take up his abode in it. Nor would a being, itself absolutely stainless,

[1] Because it has been shown that cause and effect are identical; hence if the cause is known, the effect is known also.

look on this altogether unclean body as forming part of its Self. It would, moreover, free itself, according to its liking, of the consequences of those of its former actions which result in pain, and would enjoy the consequences of those actions only which are rewarded by pleasure. Further, it would remember that it had created this manifold world; for every person who has produced some clearly appearing effect remembers that he has been the cause of it. And as the magician easily retracts, whenever he likes, the magical illusion which he had emitted, so the embodied soul also would be able to reabsorb this world into itself. The fact is, however, that the embodied soul cannot reabsorb its own body even. As we therefore see that 'what would be beneficial is not done,' the hypothesis of the world having proceeded from an intelligent cause is unacceptable.

22. But the separate (Brahman, i.e. the Brahman separate from the individual souls) (is the creator); (the existence of which separate Brahman we learn) from the declaration of difference.

The word 'but' discards the pûrvapaksha.—We rather declare that that omniscient, omnipotent Brahman, whose essence is eternal pure cognition and freedom, and which is additional to, i.e. different from the embodied Self, is the creative principle of the world. The faults specified above, such as doing what is not beneficial, and the like, do not attach to that Brahman; for as eternal freedom is its characteristic nature, there is nothing either beneficial to be done by it or non-beneficial to be avoided by it. Nor is there any impediment to its knowledge and power; for it is omniscient and omnipotent. The embodied Self, on the other hand, is of a different nature, and to it the mentioned faults adhere. But then we do not declare it to be the creator of the world, on account of 'the declaration of difference.' For scriptural passages (such as, 'Verily, the Self is to be seen, to be heard, to be perceived, to be marked,' B*ri*. Up. II, 4, 5; 'The Self we must search out, we must try to understand,' *Kh*. Up. VIII, 7, 1; 'Then he becomes united with the True,' *Kh*. Up. VI, 8, 1; 'This embodied Self mounted by the intelligent Self,' *Bri*. Up. IV, 3, 35) declare differences founded on the relations of agent, object, and so on, and thereby show Brahman to be different from the individual soul.—And if it be objected that there are other passages declaratory of non-difference (for instance, 'That art thou'), and that difference and non-difference cannot co-exist because contradictory, we reply that the possibility of the co-existence of the two is shown by the parallel instance of the universal ether and the ether limited by a jar.—Moreover, as soon as, in consequence of the declaration of non-difference contained in such passages as 'that art thou,' the consciousness of non-difference arises in us, the transmigratory state of the individual soul and the creative quality of Brahman vanish at once, the whole phenomenon of plurality, which springs from wrong knowledge, being sublated by perfect knowledge, and what becomes then of the creation and the faults of not doing what is beneficial, and the like? For that this entire apparent world, in which good and evil actions are done, &c., is a mere illusion, owing to the non-discrimination of (the Self's) limiting adjuncts, viz. a body, and so on, which spring from name and form the presentations of Nescience, and does in reality not exist at all, we have explained more than once. The illusion is analogous to the mistaken notion we entertain as to the dying, being born, being hurt, &c. of ourselves (our Selfs; while in reality the body only dies, is born, &c.). And with regard to the state in which the appearance of plurality is not yet sublated, it follows from passages declaratory of such difference (as, for instance, 'That we must search for,' &c.) that Brahman is superior to the individual soul; whereby the possibility of faults adhering to it is excluded.

23. And because the case is analogous to that of stones, &c. (the objections raised) cannot be established.

As among minerals, which are all mere modifications of earth, nevertheless great variety is observed, some being precious gems, such as diamonds, lapis lazuli, &c., others, such as crystals and the like, being of medium value, and others again stones only fit to be flung at dogs or crows; and as from seeds which are placed in one and the same ground various plants are seen to spring, such as sandal-wood and cucumbers, which show the greatest difference in their leaves, blossoms, fruits, fragrancy, juice, &c.; and as one and the same food produces various effects, such as blood and hair; so the one Brahman also may contain in itself the distinction of the individual Selfs and the highest Self, and may produce various effects. Hence the objections imagined by others (against the doctrine of Brahman being the cause of the world) cannot be maintained.—Further[1] arguments are furnished by the fact of all effects having, as Scripture declares, their origin in speech only, and by the analogous instance of the variety of dream phantoms (while the dreaming person remains one).

24. If you object on the ground of the observation of the employment (of instruments); (we say), No; because as milk (transforms itself, so Brahman does).

Your assertion that the intelligent Brahman alone, without a second, is the cause of the world cannot be maintained, on account of the observation of employment (of instruments). For in ordinary life we see that potters, weavers, and other handicraftsmen produce jars, cloth, and the like, after having put themselves in possession of the means thereto by providing themselves with various implements, such as clay, staffs, wheels, string, &c.; Brahman, on the other hand, you conceive to be without any help; how then can it act as a creator without providing itself with instruments to work with?—We therefore maintain that Brahman is not the cause of the world.

This objection is not valid, because causation is possible

[1] Which arguments, the commentators say, are hinted at by the 'and' of the Sûtra.

in consequence of a peculiar constitution of the causal substance, as in the case of milk. Just as milk and water turn into curds and ice respectively, without any extraneous means, so it is in the case of Brahman also. And if you object to this analogy for the reason that milk, in order to turn into curds, does require an extraneous agent, viz. heat, we reply that milk by itself also undergoes a certain amount of definite change, and that its turning is merely accelerated by heat. If milk did not possess that capability of itself, heat could not compel it to turn; for we see that air or ether, for instance, is not compelled by the action of heat to turn into sour milk. By the co-operation of auxiliary means the milk's capability of turning into sour milk is merely completed. The absolutely complete power of Brahman, on the other hand, does not require to be supplemented by any extraneous help. Thus Scripture also declares, 'There is no effect and no instrument known of him, no one is seen like unto him or better; his high power is revealed as manifold, as inherent, acting as force and knowledge' (*S*ve. Up. VI, 8). Therefore Brahman, although one only, is, owing to its manifold powers, able to transform itself into manifold effects; just as milk is.

25. And (the case of Brahman is) like that of gods and other beings in ordinary experience.

Well, let it be admitted that milk and other non-intelligent things have the power of turning themselves into sour milk, &c. without any extraneous means, since it is thus observed. But we observe, on the other hand, that intelligent agents, as, for instance, potters, proceed to their several work only after having provided themselves with a complete set of instruments. How then can it be supposed that Brahman, which is likewise of an intelligent nature, should proceed without any auxiliary?

We reply, 'Like gods and others.' As gods, fathers, *ri*shis, and other beings of great power, who are all of intelligent nature, are seen to create many and various objects, such as palaces, chariots, &c., without availing themselves of any.

extraneous means, by their mere intention, which is effective in consequence of those beings' peculiar power—a fact vouchsafed by mantras, arthavâdas, itihâsas, and purâ*n*as;—and as the spider emits out of itself the threads of its web; and as the female crane conceives without a male; and as the lotus wanders from one pond to another without any means of conveyance; so the intelligent Brahman also may be assumed to create the world by itself without extraneous means.

Perhaps our opponent will argue against all this in the following style.—The gods and other beings, whom you have quoted as parallel instances, are really of a nature different from that of Brahman. For the material causes operative in the production of palaces and other material things are the bodies of the gods, and not their intelligent Selfs. And the web of the spider is produced from its saliva which, owing to the spider's devouring small insects, acquires a certain degree of consistency. And the female crane conceives from hearing the sound of thunder. And the lotus flower indeed derives from its indwelling intelligent principle the impulse of movement, but is not able actually to move in so far as it is a merely intelligent being[1]; it rather wanders from pond to pond by means of its non-intelligent body, just as the creeper climbs up the tree.—Hence all these illustrative examples cannot be applied to the case of Brahman.

To this we reply, that we meant to show merely that the case of Brahman is different from that of potters and similar agents. For while potters, &c., on the one side, and gods, &c., on the other side, possess the common attribute of intelligence, potters require for their work extraneous means (i. e. means lying outside their bodies) and gods do not. Hence Brahman also, although intelligent, is assumed to require no extraneous means. So much only we wanted to show by the parallel instance of the gods, &c. Our intention is to point out that a peculiarly conditioned capability which

[1] The right reading appears to be 'svayam eva *k*etanâ' as found in some MSS. Other MSS. read *k*etana*h*.

is observed in some one case (as in that of the potter) is not necessarily to be assumed in all other cases also.

26. Either the consequence of the entire (Brahman undergoing change) has to be accepted, or else a violation of the texts declaring Brahman to be without parts.

Hitherto we have established so much that Brahman, intelligent, one, without a second, modifying itself without the employment of any extraneous means, is the cause of the world.—Now, another objection is raised for the purpose of throwing additional light on the point under discussion.—The consequence of the Vedânta doctrine, it is said, will be that we must assume the entire Brahman to undergo the change into its effects, because it is not composed of parts. If Brahman, like earth and other matter, consisted of parts, we might assume that a part of it undergoes the change, while the other part remains as it is. But Scripture distinctly declares Brahman to be devoid of parts. Compare, 'He who is without parts, without actions, tranquil, without fault, without taint' (*S*ve. Up. VI, 19); 'That heavenly person is without body, he is both without and within, not produced' (Mu. Up. II, 1, 2); 'That great Being is endless, unlimited, consisting of nothing but knowledge' (B*ri*. Up. II, 4, 12); 'He is to be described by No, no' (B*ri*. Up. III, 9, 26); 'It is neither coarse nor fine' (B*ri*. Up. III, 8, 8); all which passages deny the existence of any distinctions in Brahman.—As, therefore, a partial modification is impossible, a modification of the entire Brahman has to be assumed. But that involves a cutting off of Brahman from its very basis.—Another consequence of the Vedântic view is that the texts exhorting us to strive 'to see' Brahman become purposeless; for the effects of Brahman may be seen without any endeavour, and apart from them no Brahman exists.—And, finally, the texts declaring Brahman to be unborn are contradicted thereby.—If, on the other hand—in order to escape from these difficulties—we assume Brahman to consist of parts, we thereby do violence to those texts which declare Brahman not to be made up of parts.

Moreover, if Brahman is made up of parts, it follows that it is non-eternal.—Hence the Vedântic point of view cannot be maintained in any way.

27. But (this is not so), on account of scriptural passages, and on account of (Brahman) resting on Scripture (only).

The word 'but' discards the objection.—We deny this and maintain that our view is not open to any objections.—That the entire Brahman undergoes change, by no means follows from our doctrine, 'on account of sacred texts.' For in the same way as Scripture speaks of the origin of the world from Brahman, it also speaks of Brahman subsisting apart from its effects. This appears from the passages indicating the difference of cause and effect ('That divinity thought) let me enter into these three divinities with this living Self and evolve names and forms;' and, 'Such is the greatness of it, greater than it is the Person; one foot of him are all things, three feet are what is immortal in heaven' (*Kh.* Up. III, 12, 6); further, from the passages declaring the unmodified Brahman to have its abode in the heart, and from those teaching that (in dreamless sleep) the individual soul is united with the True. For if the entire Brahman had passed into its effects, the limitation (of the soul's union with Brahman) to the state of dreamless sleep which is declared in the passage, 'then it is united with the True, my dear,' would be out of place; since the individual soul is always united with the effects of Brahman, and since an unmodified Brahman does not exist (on that hypothesis). Moreover, the possibility of Brahman becoming the object of perception by means of the senses is denied while its effects may thus be perceived. For these reasons the existence of an unmodified Brahman has to be admitted.—Nor do we violate those texts which declare Brahman to be without parts; we rather admit Brahman to be without parts just because Scripture reveals it. For Brahman which rests exclusively on the holy texts, and regarding which the holy texts alone are authoritative—not the senses, and so on—must be accepted such as the texts proclaim it to be. Now those texts declare, on the one hand, that not the entire Brahman passes over into its effects, and, on the other hand, that Brahman is without parts. Even certain ordinary things such as gems, spells, herbs, and the like possess powers which, owing to difference of time, place, occasion, and so on, produce various opposite effects, and nobody unaided by instruction is able to find out by mere reflection the number of these powers, their favouring conditions, their objects, their purposes, &c.; how much more impossible is it to conceive without the aid of Scripture the true nature of Brahman with its powers unfathomable by thought! As the Purâ*n*a says: 'Do not apply reasoning to what is unthinkable! The mark of the unthinkable is that it is above all material causes[1].' Therefore the cognition of what is supersensuous is based on the holy texts only.

But—our opponent will say—even the holy texts cannot make us understand what is contradictory. Brahman, you say, which is without parts undergoes a change, but not the entire Brahman. If Brahman is without parts, it does either not change at all or it changes in its entirety. If, on the other hand, it be said that it changes partly and persists partly, a break is effected in its nature, and from that it follows that it consists of parts. It is true that in matters connected with action (as, for instance, in the case of the two Vedic injunctions 'at the atirâtra he is to take the sho*d*a*s*in-cup,' and 'at the atirâtra he is not to take the sho*d*a*s*in-cup') any contradiction which may present itself to the understanding is removed by the optional adoption of one of the two alternatives presented as action is dependent on man; but in the case under discussion the adoption of one of the alternatives does not remove the contradiction because an existent thing (like Brahman) does not (like an action which is to be accomplished) depend on man. We are therefore met here by a real difficulty.

[1] Prak*ri*tibhya iti, pratyakshad*ri*sh*t*apadârthasvabhâvebhyo yat para*m* vilaksha*n*am â*k*âryâdyupade*s*agamya*m* tad a*k*intyam ity artha*h*. Ân. Gi.

No, we reply, the difficulty is merely an apparent one; as we maintain that the (alleged) break in Brahman's nature is a mere figment of Nescience. By a break of that nature a thing is not really broken up into parts, not any more than the moon is really multiplied by appearing double to a person of defective vision. By that element of plurality which is the fiction of Nescience, which is characterised by name and form, which is evolved as well as non-evolved, which is not to be defined either as the Existing or the Non-existing, Brahman becomes the basis of this entire apparent world with its changes, and so on, while in its true and real nature it at the same time remains unchanged, lifted above the phenomenal universe. And as the distinction of names and forms, the fiction of Nescience, originates entirely from speech only, it does not militate against the fact of Brahman being without parts.—Nor have the scriptural passages which speak of Brahman as undergoing change the purpose of teaching the fact of change; for such instruction would have no fruit. They rather aim at imparting instruction about Brahman's Self as raised above this apparent world; that being an instruction which we know to have a result of its own. For in the scriptural passage beginning 'He can only be described by No, no' (which passage conveys instruction about the absolute Brahman) a result is stated at the end, in the words 'O *G*anaka, you have indeed reached fearlessness' (B*ri*. Up. IV, 2, 4).—Hence our view does not involve any real difficulties.

28. For thus it is in the (individual) Self also, and various (creations exist in gods[1], &c.).

Nor is there any reason to find fault with the doctrine that there can be a manifold creation in the one Self, without destroying its character. For Scripture teaches us that there exists a multiform creation in the one Self

[1] This is the way in which *S*ankara divides the Sûtra; Ân. Gi. remarks to 'loke*s*pi, &c.: âtmani *k*eti vyâkhyâya vi*k*itrâ*s* *k*a hîti vyâ*k*ash*t*e.'

of a dreaming person, 'There are no chariots in that state, no horses, no roads, but he himself creates chariots, horses, and roads' (B*ri*. Up. IV, 3, 10). In ordinary life too multiform creations, elephants, horses, and the like are seen to exist in gods, &c., and magicians without interfering with the unity of their being. Thus a multiform creation may exist in Brahman also, one as it is, without divesting it of its character of unity.

29. And because the objection (raised against our view) lies against his (the opponent's) view likewise.

Those also who maintain that the world has sprung from the pradhâna implicitly teach that something not made up of parts, unlimited, devoid of sound and other qualities—viz. the pradhâna—is the cause of an effect—viz. the world—which is made up of parts, is limited and is characterised by the named qualities. Hence it follows from that doctrine also either that the pradhâna as not consisting of parts has to undergo a change in its entirety, or else that the view of its not consisting of parts has to be abandoned.—But—it might be pleaded in favour of the Sâṅkhyas—they do not maintain their pradhâna to be without parts; for they define it as the state of equilibrium of the three gu*n*as, Goodness, Passion, and Darkness, so that the pradhâna forms a whole containing the three gu*n*as as its parts.—We reply that such a partiteness as is here proposed does not remove the objection in hand because still each of the three qualities is declared to be in itself without parts[1]. And each gu*n*a by itself assisted merely by the two other gu*n*as constitutes the material cause of that part of the world which resembles it in its nature[2].—So that the objection lies against the Sâṅkhya

[1] So that if it undergoes modifications it must either change in its entirety, or else—against the assumption—consist of parts.

[2] The last clause precludes the justificatory remark that the stated difficulties can be avoided if we assume the three gu*n*as in combination only to undergo modification; if this were so the inequality of the different effects could not be accounted for.

view likewise.—Well, then, as the reasoning (on which the doctrine of the impartiteness of the pradhâna rests) is not absolutely safe, let us assume that the pradhâna consists of parts.—If you do that, we reply, it follows that the pradhâna cannot be eternal, and so on.—Let it then be said that the various powers of the pradhâna to which the variety of its effects is pointing are its parts.—Well, we reply, those various powers are admitted by us also who see the cause of the world in Brahman.

The same objections lie against the doctrine of the world having originated from atoms. For on that doctrine one atom when combining with another must, as it is not made up of parts, enter into the combination with its whole extent, and as thus no increase of bulk takes place we do not get beyond the first atom[1]. If, on the other hand, you maintain that the atom enters into the combination with a part only, you offend against the assumption of the atoms having no parts.

As therefore all views are equally obnoxious to the objections raised, the latter cannot be urged against any one view in particular, and the advocate of Brahman has consequently cleared his doctrine.

30. And (the highest divinity is) endowed with all (powers) because that is seen (from Scripture).

We have stated that this multiform world of effects is possible to Brahman, because, although one only, it is endowed with various powers.—How then—it may be asked—do you know that the highest Brahman is endowed with various powers?—He is, we reply, endowed with all powers, 'because that is seen.' For various scriptural passages declare that the highest divinity possesses all powers, 'He to whom all actions, all desires, all odours, all tastes belong, he who embraces all this, who never speaks, and is

[1] As an atom has no parts it cannot enter into partial contact with another, and the only way in which the two can combine is entire interpenetration; in consequence of which the compound of two atoms would not occupy more space than one atom.

never surprised' (*Kh*. Up. III, 14, 4); 'He who desires what is true and imagines what is true' (*Kh*. Up. VIII, 7, 1); 'He who knows all (in its totality), and cognizes all (in its detail') (Mu. Up. I, 1, 9); 'By the command of that Imperishable, O Gârgî, sun and moon stand apart' (B*ri*. Up. III, 8, 9); and other similar passages.

31. If it be said that (Brahman is devoid of powers) on account of the absence of organs; (we reply that) this has been explained (before).

Let this be granted.—Scripture, however, declares the highest divinity to be without (bodily) organs of action[1]; so, for instance, in the passage, 'It is without eyes, without ears, without speech, without mind' (B*ri*. Up. III, 8, 8). Being such, how should it be able to produce effects. although it may be endowed with all powers? For we know (from mantras, arthavâdas, &c.) that the gods and other intelligent beings, though endowed with all powers, are capable of producing certain effects only because they are furnished with bodily instruments of action. And, moreover, how can the divinity, to whom the scriptural passage, 'No, no,' denies all attributes, be endowed with all powers?

The appropriate reply to this question has been already given above. The transcendent highest Brahman can be fathomed by means of Scripture only, not by mere reasoning. Nor are we obliged to assume that the capacity of one being is exactly like that which is observed in another. It has likewise been explained above that although all qualities are denied of Brahman we nevertheless may consider it to be endowed with powers, if we assume in its nature an element of plurality, which is the mere figment of Nescience. Moreover, a scriptural passage ('Grasping without hands, hastening without feet, he sees without eyes, he hears without ears,' *S*ve. Up. III, 19) declares that Brahman,

[1] The Sûtra is concerned with the body only as far as it is an instrument; the case of extraneous instruments having already been disposed of in Sûtra 24.

although devoid of bodily organs, possesses all possible capacities.

32. (Brahman is) not (the creator of the world), on account of (beings engaging in any action) having a motive.

Another objection is raised against the doctrine of an intelligent cause of the world.—The intelligent highest Self cannot be the creator of the sphere of this world, 'on account of actions having a purpose.'—We know from ordinary experience that man, who is an intelligent being, begins to act after due consideration only, and does not engage even in an unimportant undertaking unless it serves some purpose of his own; much less so in important business. There is also a scriptural passage confirming this result of common experience, 'Verily everything is not dear that you may love everything; but that you may love the Self therefore everything is dear' (B*ri*. Up. II, 4, 5). Now the undertaking of creating the sphere of this world, with all its various contents, is certainly a weighty one. If, then, on the one hand, you assume it to serve some purpose of the intelligent highest Self, you thereby sublate its self-sufficiency vouched for by Scripture; if, on the other hand, you affirm absence of motive on its part, you must affirm absence of activity also.—Let us then assume that just as sometimes an intelligent person when in a state of frenzy proceeds, owing to his mental aberration, to action without a motive, so the highest Self also created this world without any motive.—That, we reply, would contradict the omniscience of the highest Self, which is vouched for by Scripture.—Hence the doctrine of the creation proceeding from an intelligent Being is untenable.

33. But (Brahman's creative activity) is mere sport, such as we see in ordinary life.

The word 'but' discards the objection raised.—We see in every-day life that certain doings of princes or other men of high position who have no unfulfilled desires left have no reference to any extraneous purpose, but proceed from mere sportfulness, as. for instance, their recreations in places of amusement. We further see that the process of inhalation and exhalation is going on without reference to any extraneous purpose, merely following the law of its own nature. Analogously, the activity of the Lord also may be supposed to be mere sport, proceeding from his own nature [1], without reference to any purpose. For on the ground neither of reason nor of Scripture can we construe any other purpose of the Lord. Nor can his nature be questioned [2].—Although the creation of this world appears to us a weighty and difficult undertaking, it is mere play to the Lord, whose power is unlimited. And if in ordinary life we might possibly, by close scrutiny, detect some subtle motive, even for sportful action, we cannot do so with regard to the actions of the Lord, all whose wishes are fulfilled, as Scripture says. —Nor can it be said that he either does not act or acts like a senseless person; for Scripture affirms the fact of the creation on the one hand, and the Lord's omniscience on the other hand. And, finally, we must remember that the scriptural doctrine of creation does not refer to the highest reality; it refers to the apparent world only, which is characterised by name and form, the figments of Nescience, and it, moreover, aims at intimating that Brahman is the Self of everything.

34. Inequality (of dispensation) and cruelty (the Lord can)not (be reproached with), on account of

---

[1] The nature (svabhâva) of the Lord is, the commentators say, Mâyâ joined with time and karman.

[2] This clause is an answer to the objection that the Lord might remain at rest instead of creating a world useless to himself and the cause of pain to others. For in consequence of his conjunction with Mâyâ the creation is unavoidable. Go. Ân. Avidyâ naturally tends towards effects, without any purpose. Bhâ.

Ân. Gi. remarks: Nanu lîlâdâv asmadâdînâm akasmâd eva niv*ri*tter api dar*s*anâd î*s*varasyâpi mâyâmayyâ*m* lîlâyâ*m* tathâbhâve vinâpi sa*m*yag*gñ*âna*m* sa*m*sârasamu*kkh*ittir iti tatrâha na *k*eti. Anirvâ*k*yâ khalv avidyâ parasye*s*varasya *k*a svabhâvo lîleti *k*o*k*yate tatra na prâtîtikasvabhâvâyâm anupapattir avataratîty artha*h*.

his regarding (merit and demerit); for so (Scripture) declares.

In order to strengthen the tenet which we are at present defending, we follow the procedure of him who shakes a pole planted in the ground (in order to test whether it is firmly planted), and raise another objection against the doctrine of the Lord being the cause of the world.—The Lord, it is said, cannot be the cause of the world, because, on that hypothesis, the reproach of inequality of dispensation and cruelty would attach to him. Some beings, viz. the gods and others, he renders eminently happy; others, as for instance the animals, eminently unhappy; to some again, as for instance men, he allots an intermediate position. To a Lord bringing about such an unequal condition of things, passion and malice would have to be ascribed, just as to any common person acting similarly; which attributes would be contrary to the essential goodness of the Lord affirmed by *S*ruti and Sm*ri*ti. Moreover, as the infliction of pain and the final destruction of all creatures would form part of his dispensation, he would have to be taxed with great cruelty, a quality abhorred by low people even. For these two reasons Brahman cannot be the cause of the world.

The Lord, we reply, cannot be reproached with inequality of dispensation and cruelty, 'because he is bound by regards.' If the Lord on his own account, without any extraneous regards, produced this unequal creation, he would expose himself to blame; but the fact is, that in creating he is bound by certain regards, i. e. he has to look to merit and demerit. Hence the circumstance of the creation being unequal is due to the merit and demerit of the living creatures created, and is not a fault for which the Lord is to blame. The position of the Lord is to be looked on as analogous to that of Par*g*anya, the Giver of rain. For as Par*g*anya is the common cause of the production of rice, barley, and other plants, while the difference between the various species is due to the various potentialities lying hidden in the respective seeds, so the Lord is the common cause of the creation of gods, men, &c., while the differences between these classes of beings are due to the different merit belonging to the individual souls. Hence the Lord, being bound by regards, cannot be reproached with inequality of dispensation and cruelty.—And if we are asked how we come to know that the Lord, in creating this world with its various conditions, is bound by regards, we reply that Scripture declares that; compare, for instance, the two following passages, 'For he (the Lord) makes him, whom he wishes to lead up from these worlds, do a good deed; and the same makes him, whom he wishes to lead down from these worlds, do a bad deed' (Kaush. Up. III, 8)[1]; and, 'A man becomes good by good work, bad by bad work' (B*ri*. Up. III, 2, 13). Sm*ri*ti passages also declare the favour of the Lord and its opposite to depend on the different quality of the works of living beings; so, for instance, 'I serve men in the way in which they approach me' (Bha. Gî. IV, 11).

35. If it be objected that it (viz. the Lord's having regard to merit and demerit) is impossible on account of the non-distinction (of merit and demerit, previous to the first creation); we refute the objection on the ground of (the world) being without a beginning.

But—an objection is raised—the passage, 'Being only this was in the beginning, one, without a second,' affirms that before the creation there was no distinction and consequently no merit on account of which the creation might have become unequal. And if we assume the Lord to have been guided in his dispensations by the actions of living beings subsequent to the creation, we involve ourselves in the circular reasoning that work depends on diversity of

[1] From this passage we must not—the commentators say—infer injustice on the part of the Lord; for the previous merit or demerit of a being determines the specific quality of the actions which he performs in his present existence, the Lord acting as the common cause only (as Parganya does).

condition of life, and diversity of condition again on work. The Lord may be considered as acting with regard to religious merit after distinction had once arisen; but as before that the cause of inequality, viz. merit, did not exist, it follows that the first creation must have been free from inequalities.

This objection we meet by the remark, that the transmigratory world is without beginning.—The objection would be valid if the world had a beginning; but as it is without beginning, merit and inequality are, like seed and sprout, caused as well as causes, and there is therefore no logical objection to their operation.—To the question how we know that the world is without a beginning, the next Sûtra replies.

36. (The beginninglessness of the world) recommends itself to reason and is seen (from Scripture).

The beginninglessness of the world recommends itself to reason. For if it had a beginning it would follow that, the world springing into existence without a cause, the released souls also would again enter into the circle of transmigratory existence; and further, as then there would exist no determining cause of the unequal dispensation of pleasure and pain, we should have to acquiesce in the doctrine of rewards and punishments being allotted, without reference to previous good or bad actions. That the Lord is not the cause of the inequality, has already been remarked. Nor can Nescience by itself be the cause, as it is of a uniform nature. On the other hand, Nescience may be the cause of inequality, if it be considered as having regard to merit accruing from action produced by the mental impressions of wrath, hatred, and other afflicting passions[1]. Without merit and demerit nobody can enter into existence, and again, without a body merit and demerit cannot be formed; so that—on the doc-

[1] Râgadveshamohâ râgadayas te *k*a purusha*m* dukhâdibhi*h* kli*s*yantîti kle*s*âs teshâ*m* vâsanâ*h* karmapravr*i*ttyanugu*n*âs tâbhir âkshipta*m* dharmâdilaksha*n*a*m* karma tadapekshâvidyâ. Ân. Gi.

trine of the world having a beginning—we are led into a logical see-saw. The opposite doctrine, on the other hand, explains all matters in a manner analogous to the case of the seed and sprout, so that no difficulty remains.—Moreover, the fact of the world being without a beginning, is seen in *S*ruti and Sm*ri*ti. In the first place, we have the scriptural passage, 'Let me enter with this living Self (*g*îva),' &c. (*Kh*. Up. VI, 3, 2). Here the circumstance of the embodied Self (the individual soul) being called, previously to creation, 'the living Self'—a name applying to it in so far as it is the sustaining principle of the prâ*n*as—shows that this phenomenal world is without a beginning. For if it had a beginning, the prâ*n*as would not exist before that beginning, and how then could the embodied Self be denoted, with reference to the time of the world's beginning, by a name which depends on the existence of those prâ*n*as? Nor can it be said that it is so designated with a view to its future relation to the prâ*n*as; it being a settled principle that a past relation, as being already existing, is of greater force than a mere future relation.—Moreover, we have the mantra, 'As the creator formerly devised (akalpayat) sun and moon' (*Ri*. Sa*m*h. X, 190, 3), which intimates the existence of former Kalpas. Sm*ri*ti also declares the world to be without a beginning, 'Neither its form is known here, nor its end, nor its beginning, nor its support' (Bha. Gî. XV, 3). And the Purâ*n*a also declares that there is no measure of the past and the future Kalpas.

37. And because all the qualities (required in the cause of the world) are present (in Brahman).

The teacher has now refuted all the objections, such as difference of character, and the like, which other teachers have brought forward against what he had established as the real sense of the Veda, viz. that the intelligent Brahman is the cause and matter of this world.

Now, before entering on a new chapter, whose chief aim it will be to refute the (positive) opinions held by other teachers, he sums up the foregoing chapter, the purport of which it was to show why his view should be accepted.—Because, if that Brahman is acknowledged as the cause of the world, all attributes required in the cause (of the world) are seen to be present—Brahman being all-knowing, all-powerful, and possessing the great power of Mâyâ,—on that account this our system, founded on the Upanishads, is not open to any objections.

SECOND PÂDA.

REVERENCE TO THE HIGHEST SELF!

1. That which is inferred (by the Sâṅkhyas, viz. the pradhâna) cannot be the cause (of the world), on account of the orderly arrangement (of the world) being impossible (on that hypothesis).

Although it is the object of this system to define the true meaning of the Vedânta-texts and not, like the science of Logic, to establish or refute some tenet by mere ratiocination, still it is incumbent on thorough students of the Vedânta to refute the Sâṅkhya and other systems which are obstacles in the way of perfect knowledge. For this purpose a new chapter is begun. (Nor must it be said that the refutation of the other systems ought to have preceded the establishment of the Vedânta position; for) as the determination of the sense of the Vedânta-passages directly subserves perfect knowledge, we have at first, by means of such a determination, established our own position, since this is a task more important than the refutation of the views entertained by others.

Here an opponent might come forward and say that we are indeed entitled to establish our own position, so as to define perfect knowledge which is the means of release to those desirous of it, but that no use is apparent of a refutation of other opinions, a proceeding productive of nothing but hate and anger.—There is a use, we reply. For there is some danger of men of inferior intelligence looking upon the Sâṅkhya and similar systems as requisite for perfect knowledge, because those systems have a weighty appearance, have been adopted by authoritative persons, and profess to lead to perfect knowledge. Such people might therefore think that those systems with their abstruse arguments were propounded by omniscient sages, and might on that account have faith in them. For this reason we must endeavour to demonstrate their intrinsic worthlessness.

But, it might be said, the Sâṅkhya and similar systems have already been impugned in several Sûtras of the first adhyâya (I, 1, 5, 18; I, 4, 28); why, then, controvert them again?—The task—we reply—which we are now about to undertake differs from what we have already accomplished. As the Sâṅkhyas and other philosophers also quote, in order to establish their own positions, the Vedânta-passages and interpret them in such a manner as to make them agree with their own systems, we have hitherto endeavoured to show that their interpretations are altogether fallacious. Now, however, we are going to refute their arguments in an independent manner, without any reference to the Vedânta-texts.

The Sâṅkhyas, to make a beginning with them, argue as follows.—Just as jars, dishes, and other products which possess the common quality of consisting of clay are seen to have for their cause clay in general; so we must suppose that all the outward and inward (i.e. inanimate and animate) effects which are endowed with the characteristics of pleasure, pain, and dulness [1] have for their causes pleasure, pain, and dulness in general. Pleasure, pain, and dulness in their generality together constitute the threefold pradhâna. This pradhâna which is non-intelligent evolves itself spontaneously into multiform modifications [2], in order thus to effect the purposes (i.e. enjoyment, release, and so on) of the intelligent soul.—The existence of the pradhâna is to be inferred from other circumstances also, such as the limitation of all effects and the like [3].

Against this doctrine we argue as follows.—If you Sâṅkhyas base your theory on parallel instances merely, we point

---

[1] The characteristics of Goodness, Passion, and Darkness, the three constituent elements (guṇa) of the pradhâna. Sâ. Kâ. 12, 13.

[2] Viz. the great principle (mahat), ahaṅkâra, &c. Sâ. Kâ. 3.

[3] The arguments here referred to are enumerated in the Sâ. Kâ. 15; Sâ. Sûtras I, 129 ff.

out that a non-intelligent thing which, without being guided by an intelligent being, spontaneously produces effects capable of subserving the purposes of some particular person is nowhere observed in the world. We rather observe that houses, palaces, couches, pleasure-grounds, and the like—things which according to circumstances are conducive to the obtainment of pleasure or the avoidance of pain—are made by workmen endowed with intelligence. Now look at this entire world which appears, on the one hand, as external (i. e. inanimate) in the form of earth and the other elements enabling (the souls) to enjoy the fruits of their various actions, and, on the other hand, as animate, in the form of bodies which belong to the different classes of beings, possess a definite arrangement of organs, and are therefore capable of constituting the abodes of fruition; look, we say, at this world, of which the most ingenious workmen cannot even form a conception in their minds, and then say if a non-intelligent principle like the pradhâna is able to fashion it! Other non-intelligent things such as stones and clods of earth are certainly not seen to possess analogous powers. We rather must assume that just as clay and similar substances are seen to fashion themselves into various forms, if worked upon by potters and the like, so the pradhâna also (when modifying itself into its effects) is ruled by some intelligent principle. When endeavouring to determine the nature of the primal cause (of the world), there is no need for us to take our stand on those attributes only which form part of the nature of material causes such as clay, &c., and not on those also which belong to extraneous agents such as potters, &c. [1] Nor (if remembering this latter point) do we enter into conflict with any means of right knowledge; we, on the contrary, are in direct agreement with Scripture which teaches that an intelligent

[1] If we attempt to infer the nature of the universal cause from its effects on the ground of parallel instances, as, for instance, that of an earthen jar whose material cause is clay, we must remember that the jar has sprung from clay not without the co-operation of an intelligent being, viz. the potter.

cause exists.—For the reason detailed in the above, i. e. on account of the impossibility of the 'orderly arrangement' (of the world), a non-intelligent cause of the world is not to be inferred.—The word 'and' (in the Sûtra) adds other reasons on account of which the pradhâna cannot be inferred, viz. 'on account of the non-possibility of endowment,' &c. For it cannot be maintained[1] that all outward and inward effects are 'endowed' with the nature of pleasure, pain, and dulness, because pleasure, &c. are known as inward (mental) states, while sound, &c. (i. e. the sense-objects) are known as being of a different nature (i. e. as outward things), and moreover as being the operative causes of pleasure, &c.[2] And, further, although the sense-object such as sound and so on is one, yet we observe that owing to the difference of the mental impressions (produced by it) differences exist in the effects it produces, one person being affected by it pleasantly, another painfully, and so on[3].—(Turning to the next Sâṅkhya argument which infers the existence of the pradhâna from the limitation of all effects). we remark that he who concludes that all inward and outward effects depend on a conjunction of several things, because they are limited (a conclusion based on the observation that some limited effects such as root and sprout, &c. depend on the conjunction of several things), is driven to the conclusion that the three constituents of the pradhâna, viz. Goodness, Passion, and Darkness, likewise depend on the conjunction of several

---

[1] As had been asserted above for the purpose of inferring therefrom, according to the principle of the equality of cause and effect, the existence of the three constituents of the pradhâna.

[2] And a thing cannot consist of that of which it is the cause.

[3] Which differences cannot be reconciled with the Sâṅkhya hypothesis of the object itself consisting of either pleasure or pain, &c.—'If things consisted in themselves of pleasure, pain, &c., then sandal ointment (which is cooling, and on that account pleasant in summer) would be pleasant in winter also; for sandal never is anything but sandal.—And as thistles never are anything but thistles they ought, on the Sâṅkhya hypothesis, to be eaten with enjoyment not only by camels but by men also.' Bhâ.

antecedents[1]; for they also are limited[2].—Further[3], it is impossible to use the relation of cause and effect as a reason for assuming that all effects whatever have a non-intelligent principle for their antecedent; for we have shown already that that relation exists in the case of couches and chairs also, over whose production intelligence presides.

2. And on account of (the impossibility of) activity.

Leaving the arrangement of the world, we now pass on to the activity by which it is produced.—The three gu*n*as, passing out of the state of equipoise and entering into the condition of mutual subordination and superordination, originate activities tending towards the production of particular effects.—Now these activities also cannot be ascribed to a non-intelligent pradhâna left to itself, as no such activity is seen in clay and similar substances, or in chariots and the like. For we observe that clay and the like, and chariots—which are in their own nature non-intelligent—enter on activities tending towards particular effects only when they are acted upon by intelligent beings such as potters, &c. in the one case, and horses and the like in the other case. From what is seen we determine what is not seen. Hence a non-intelligent cause of the world is not to be inferred because, on that hypothesis, the activity without which the world cannot be produced would be impossible.

But, the Sâṅkhya rejoins, we do likewise not observe activity on the part of mere intelligent beings.—True; we however see activity on the part of non-intelligent things such as chariots and the like when they are in conjunction with intelligent beings.—But, the Sâṅkhya again objects, we never actually observe activity on the part of an intel-

[1] Sa*m*sargapûrvakatvaprasaṅga iti gu*n*ânâ*m* sa*m*s*ri*sh*t*ânekavastuprak*ri*tikatvaprasaktir ity artha*h*. Ân. Gi.

[2] For they limit one another.

[3] To proceed to the argument 'from the separateness of cause and effect' (Sâ. Kâ. 15).

ligent being even when in conjunction with a non-intelligent thing.—Very well; the question then arises: Does the activity belong to that in which it is actually observed (as the Sâṅkhya says), or to that on account of the conjunction with which it is observed (as the Vedântin avers)?—We must, the Sâṅkhya replies, attribute activity to that in which it is actually seen, since both (i.e. the activity and its abode) are matter of observation. A mere intelligent being, on the other hand, is never observed as the abode of activity while a chariot is. The[1] existence of an intelligent Self joined to a body and so on which are the abode of activity can be established (by inference) only; the inference being based on the difference observed between living bodies and mere non-intelligent things, such as chariots and the like. For this very reason, viz. that intelligence is observed only where a body is observed while it is never seen without a body, the Materialists consider intelligence to be a mere attribute of the body.—Hence activity belongs only to what is non-intelligent.

To all this we—the Vedântins—make the following reply.—We do not mean to say that activity does not belong to those non-intelligent things in which it is observed; it does indeed belong to them; but it results from an intelligent principle, because it exists when the latter is present and does not exist when the latter is absent. Just as the effects of burning and shining, which have their abode in wood and similar material, are indeed not observed when there is mere fire (i.e. are not due to mere fire; as mere fire, i.e. fire without wood, &c., does not exist), but at the same time result from fire only as they are seen when fire is present and are not seen when fire is absent; so, as the Materialists also admit, only intelligent bodies are observed

[1] The next sentences furnish the answer to the question how the intelligent Self is known at all if it is not the object of perception.—Pratyakshatvâbhâve katham âtmasiddhir ity âsaṅkya anumânâd ity âha, pravrittîti. Anumânasiddhasya *k*etanasya na pravrittyâsrayateti darsayitum evakâra*h*. Katham anumânam ity apekshâyâ*m* tatprakâra*m* sû*k*ayati kevaleti. Vailaksha*n*ya*m* prâ*n*âdimattvam. Ân. Gi.

to be the movers of chariots and other non-intelligent things. The motive power of intelligence is therefore incontrovertible.—But—an objection will be raised—your Self even if joined to a body is incapable of exercising moving power, for motion cannot be effected by that the nature of which is pure intelligence.—A thing, we reply, which is itself devoid of motion may nevertheless move other things. The magnet is itself devoid of motion, and yet it moves iron; and colours and the other objects of sense, although themselves devoid of motion, produce movements in the eyes and the other organs of sense. So the Lord also who is all-present, the Self of all, all-knowing and all-powerful may, although himself unmoving, move the universe.—If it finally be objected that (on the Vedânta doctrine) there is no room for a moving power as in consequence of the oneness (aduality) of Brahman no motion can take place; we reply that such objections have repeatedly been refuted by our pointing to the fact of the Lord being fictitiously connected with Mâyâ, which consists of name and form presented by Nescience.—Hence motion can be reconciled with the doctrine of an all-knowing first cause; but not with the doctrine of a non-intelligent first cause.

3. If it be said (that the pradhâna moves) like milk or water, (we reply that) there also (the motion is due to intelligence).

Well, the Sâṅkhya resumes, listen then to the following instances.—As non-sentient milk flows forth from its own nature merely for the nourishment of the young animal, and as non-sentient water, from its own nature, flows along for the benefit of mankind; so the pradhâna also, although non-intelligent, may be supposed to move from its own nature merely for the purpose of effecting the highest end of man.

This argumentation, we reply, is unsound again; for as the adherents of both doctrines admit that motion is not observed in the case of merely non-intelligent things such as chariots, &c., we infer that water and milk also move only because they are directed by intelligent powers. Scriptural passages, moreover (such as 'He who dwells in the water and within the water, who rules the water within,' Bri. Up. III, 7, 4; and, 'By the command of that Akshara, O Gârgî, some rivers flow to the East,' &c., Bri. Up. III, 8, 9), declare that everything in this world which flows is directed by the Lord. Hence the instances of milk and water as belonging themselves to that class of cases which prove our general principle[1] cannot be used to show that the latter is too wide.—Moreover, the cow, which is an intelligent being and loves her calf, makes her milk flow by her wish to do so, and the milk is in addition drawn forth by the sucking of the calf. Nor does water move either with absolute independence—for its flow depends on the declivity of the soil and similar circumstances—or independently of an intelligent principle, for we have shown that the latter is present in all cases.—If, finally, our opponent should point to Sûtra II, 1, 24 as contradicting the present Sûtra, we remark that there we have merely shown on the ground of ordinary experience that an effect may take place in itself independently of any external instrumental cause; a conclusion which does not contradict the doctrine, based on Scripture, that all effects depend on the Lord.

4. And because (the pradhâna), on account of there existing nothing beyond it, stands in no relation; (it cannot be active.)

The three gu*n*as of the Sâṅkhyas when in a state of equipoise form the pradhâna. Beyond the pradhâna there exists no external principle which could either impel the pradhâna to activity or restrain it from activity. The soul (purusha), as we know, is indifferent, neither moves to—nor restrains from—action. As therefore the pradhâna stands in no relation, it is impossible to see why it should sometimes modify itself into the great principle (mahat) and sometimes not. The activity and non-activity (by turns) of the Lord,

[1] Viz. that whatever moves or acts does so under the influence of intelligence.—Sâdhyapakshanikshiptatva*m* sâdhyavati pakshe pravish*t*atvam eva ta*k k*a sapakshanikshiptatvasyâpy upalaksha*n*am, anupanyâso na vyabhi*k*ârabhûmir ity artha*h*. Ân. Gi.

on the other hand, are not contrary to reason, on account of his omniscience and omnipotence, and his being connected with the power of illusion (mâyâ).

5. Nor (can it be said that the pradhâna modifies itself spontaneously) like grass, &c. (which turn into milk); for (milk) does not exist elsewhere (but in the female animal).

Let this be (the Sâṅkhya resumes). Just as grass, herbs, water, &c. independently of any other instrumental cause transform themselves, by their own nature, into milk; so, we assume, the pradhâna also transforms itself into the great principle, and so on. And, if you ask how we know that grass transforms itself independently of any instrumental cause; we reply, 'Because no such cause is observed.' For if we did perceive some such cause, we certainly should apply it to grass, &c. according to our liking, and thereby produce milk. But as a matter of fact we do no such thing. Hence the transformation of grass and the like must be considered to be due to its own nature merely; and we may infer therefrom that the transformation of the pradhâna is of the same kind.

To this we make the following reply.—The transformation of the pradhâna might be ascribed to its own nature merely if we really could admit that grass modifies itself in the manner stated by you; but we are unable to admit that, since another instrumental cause is observed. How? 'Because it does not exist elsewhere.' For grass becomes milk only when it is eaten by a cow or some other female animal, not if it is left either uneaten or is eaten by a bull. If the transformation had no special cause, grass would become milk even on other conditions than that of entering a cow's body. Nor would the circumstance of men not being able to produce milk according to their liking prove that there is no instrumental cause; for while some effects can be produced by men, others result from divine action only[1]. The fact, however, is that men also are able, by

[1] It might be held that for the transformation of grass into milk no other cause is required than the digestive heat of the cow's

applying a means in their power, to produce milk from grass and herbs; for when they wish to procure a more abundant supply of milk they feed the cow more plentifully and thus obtain more milk from her.—For these reasons the spontaneous modification of the pradhâna cannot be proved from the instance of grass and the like.

6. Even if we admit (the Sâṅkhya position refuted in what precedes, it is invalidated by other objections) on account of the absence of a purpose (on the part of the pradhâna).

Even if we, accommodating ourselves to your (the Sâṅkhya's) belief, should admit what has been disproved in the preceding Sûtra, viz. that the pradhâna is spontaneously active, still your opinion would lie open to an objection 'on account of the absence of a purpose.' For if the spontaneous activity of the pradhâna has, as you say, no reference to anything else, it will have no reference not only to any aiding principle, but also to any purpose or motive, and consequently your doctrine that the pradhâna is active in order to effect the purpose of man will become untenable. If you reply that the pradhâna does not indeed regard any aiding principle, but does regard a purpose, we remark that in that case we must distinguish between the different possible purposes, viz. either enjoyment (on the part of the soul), or final release, or both. If enjoyment, what enjoyment, we ask, can belong to the soul which is naturally incapable of any accretion (of pleasure or pain)[1]? Moreover, there would in that case be no opportunity for release[2].—If release, then the activity of the pradhâna would be purposeless, as even antecedently to it the soul is in the

body; but a reflecting person will acknowledge that there also the omniscient Lord is active. Bhâ.

[1] Anâdheyâtiśayasya sukhadukhaprâptiparihârarûpâtiśayaśûnyasyety arthaḥ. Ân. Gi.

[2] For the soul as being of an entirely inactive nature cannot of itself aim at release, and the pradhâna aims—ex hypothesi—only at the soul's undergoing varied experience.

state of release; moreover, there would then be no occasion for the perception of sounds, &c.[1]—If both, then, on account of the infinite number of the objects of pradhâna to be enjoyed (by the soul)[2], there would be no opportunity for final release. Nor can the satisfaction of a desire be considered as the purpose of the activity of the pradhâna; for neither the non-intelligent pradhâna nor the essentially pure soul can feel any desire.—If, finally, you should assume the pradhâna to be active, because otherwise the power of sight (belonging to the soul on account of its intelligent nature) and the creative power (belonging to the pradhâna) would be purposeless; it would follow that, as the creative power of the pradhâna does not cease at any time any more than the soul's power of sight does, the apparent world would never come to an end, so that no final release of the soul could take place[3].—It is, therefore, impossible to maintain that the pradhâna enters on its activity for the purposes of the soul.

7. And if you say (that the soul may move the pradhâna) as the (lame) man (moves the blind one) or as the magnet (moves the iron); thus also (the difficulty is not overcome).

Well then—the Sâṅkhya resumes, endeavouring to defend his position by parallel instances—let us say that, as some lame man devoid of the power of motion, but possessing the power of sight, having mounted the back of a blind man who is able to move but not to see, makes the latter move; or as the magnet not moving itself, moves the iron, so the soul moves the pradhâna.—Thus also, we reply, you do not free your doctrine from all shortcomings; for this your new position involves an abandonment of your old

[1] I. e. for the various items constituting enjoyment or experience.

[2] Tr*i*tîye *pi katipaya*s*abdâdyupalabdhir vâ samastatadupalabdhir vâ bhoga iti vikalpyâdye sarveshâm ekadaiva mukti*h* syâd iti manvâno dvitîya*m* pratyâha ubhayârthateti. Ân. Gi.

[3] The MSS. of Ânanda Giri omit sa*m*sârânu*kkh*edât; the Bhâmatî's reading is: Sarga*s*aktyanu*kkh*edavad d*ri*k*s*aktyanu*kkh*edât.

position, according to which the pradhâna is moving of itself, and the (indifferent, inactive) soul possesses no moving power. And how should the indifferent soul move the pradhâna? A man, although lame, may make a blind man move by means of words and the like; but the soul which is devoid of action and qualities cannot possibly put forth any moving energy. Nor can it be said that it moves the pradhâna by its mere proximity as the magnet moves the iron; for from the permanency of proximity (of soul and pradhâna) a permanency of motion would follow. The proximity of the magnet, on the other hand (to the iron), is not permanent, but depends on a certain activity and the adjustment of the magnet in a certain position; hence the (lame) man and the magnet do not supply really parallel instances.—The pradhâna then being non-intelligent and the soul indifferent, and there being no third principle to connect them, there can be no connexion of the two. If we attempted to establish a connexion on the ground of capability (of being seen on the part of the pradhâna, of seeing on the part of the soul), the permanency of such capability would imply the impossibility of final release.—Moreover, here as well as before (in the preceding Sûtra) the different alternatives connected with the absence of purpose (on the pradhâna's part) have to be considered [1].—The highest Self, on the other hand (which is the cause of the world, according to the Vedântins), is characterised by non-activity inherent in its own nature, and, at the same time, by moving power inherent in Mâyâ and is thus superior (to the soul of the Sâṅkhyas).

8. And, again, (the pradhâna cannot be active) because the relation of principal (and subordinate matter) is impossible (between the three gu*n*as).

For the following reason also activity on the part of the pradhâna is not possible.—The condition of the pradhâna

[1] On the theory that the soul is the cause of the pradhâna's activity we again have to ask whether the pradhâna acts for the soul's enjoyment or for its release, &c.

consists in the three gu*n*as, viz. goodness, passion, and darkness, abiding in themselves in a state of equipoise without standing to one another in the relation of mutual superiority or inferiority. In that state the gu*n*as cannot possibly enter into the relation of mutual subserviency because thereby they would forfeit their essential characteristic, viz. absolute independence. And as there exists no extraneous principle to stir up the gu*n*as, the production of the great principle and the other effects—which would require for its operative cause a non-balanced state of the gu*n*as—is impossible.

9. And although another inference be made, (the objections remain in force) on account of the (pradhâna) being devoid of the power of intelligence.

But—the Sâṅkhya resumes—we draw another inference, so as to leave no room for the objection just stated. We do not acknowledge the gu*n*as to be characterised by absolute irrelativity and unchangeableness, since there is no proof for such an assumption. We rather infer the characteristics of the gu*n*as from those of their effects, presuming that their nature must be such as to render the production of the effects possible. Now the gu*n*as are admitted to be of an unsteady nature; hence the gu*n*as themselves are able to enter into the relation of mutual inequality, even while they are in a state of equipoise.

Even in that case, we reply, the objections stated above which were founded on the impossibility of an orderly arrangement of the world, &c., remain in force on account of the pradhâna being devoid of the power of intelligence. And if (to escape those objections) the Sâṅkhya should infer (from the orderly arrangement of the world, &c.), that the primal cause is intelligent, he would cease to be an antagonist, since the doctrine that there is one intelligent cause of this multiform world would be nothing else but the Vedântic doctrine of Brahman.—Moreover, if the gu*n*as were capable of entering into the relation of mutual inequality even while in the state of equipoise, one of two things would happen; they would either not be in the condition of inequality on account of the absence of an operative cause; or else, if they were in that condition, they would always remain in it; the absence of an operative cause being a non-changing circumstance. And thus the doctrine would again be open to the objection stated before[1].

10. And moreover (the Sâṅkhya doctrine) is objectionable on account of its contradictions.

The doctrine of the Sâṅkhyas, moreover, is full of contradictions. Sometimes they enumerate seven senses, sometimes eleven[2]. In some places they teach that the subtle elements of material things proceed from the great principle, in other places again that they proceed from self-consciousness. Sometimes they speak of three internal organs, sometimes of one only[3]. That their doctrine, moreover, contradicts *S*ruti, which teaches that the Lord is the cause of the world, and Sm*ri*ti, based on *S*ruti, is well known.—For these reasons also the Sâṅkhya system is objectionable.

Here the Sâṅkhya again brings a countercharge.—The system of the Vedântins also, he says, must be declared to be objectionable; for it does not admit that that which suffers and that which causes suffering[4] are different classes of things (and thereby renders futile the well-established distinction of causes of suffering and suffering beings). For

[1] Anantaro dosho mahadâdikâryotpâdâyoga*h*. Ân. Gi.

[2] In the former case the five intellectual senses are looked upon as mere modifications of the sense of touch.

[3] Buddhi in the latter case being the generic name for buddhi, ahaṅkâra, and manas.

[4] Lit. that which burns and that which is burned, which literal rendering would perhaps be preferable throughout. As it is, the context has necessitated its retention in some places.—The sufferers are the individual souls, the cause of suffering the world in which the souls live.

those who admit the one Brahman to be the Self of everything and the cause of the whole world, have to admit also that the two attributes of being that which causes suffering and that which suffers belong to the one supreme Self (not to different classes of beings). If, then, these two attributes belong to one and the same Self, it never can divest itself of them, and thus Scripture, which teaches perfect knowledge for the purpose of the cessation of all suffering, loses all its meaning. For—to adduce a parallel case—a lamp as long as it subsists as such is never divested of the two qualities of giving heat and light. And if the Vedântin should adduce the case of water with its waves, ripples, foam, &c.[1], we remark that there also the waves, &c. constitute attributes of the water which remain permanently, although they by turns manifest themselves, and again enter into the state of non-manifestation; hence the water is never really destitute of waves, not any more than the lamp is ever destitute of heat and light.—That that which causes suffering, and that which suffers constitute different classes of things is, moreover, well known from ordinary experience. For (to consider the matter from a more general point of view) the person desiring and the thing desired[2] are understood to be separate existences. If the object of desire were not essentially different and separate from the person desiring, the state of being desirous could not be ascribed to the latter, because the object with reference to which alone he can be called desiring would already essentially be established in him (belong to him). The latter state of things exists in the case of a lamp and its light, for instance. Light essentially belongs to the lamp, and hence the latter never can stand in want of light; for want or desire can exist only if the thing wanted or desired is not yet obtained.

---

[1] In the case of the lamp, light and heat are admittedly essential; hence the Vedântin is supposed to bring forward the sea with its waves, and so on, as furnishing a case where attributes pass away while the substance remains.

[2] 'Artha,' a useful or beneficial thing, an object of desire.

(And just as there could be no desiring person, if the object of desire and the desiring person were not essentially separate), so the object of desire also would cease to be an object for the desiring person, and would be an object for itself only. As a matter of fact, however, this is not the case; for the two ideas (and terms), 'object of desire' and 'desiring person,' imply a relation (are correlative), and a relation exists in two things, not in one only. Hence the desiring person and the object of desire are separate.—The same holds good with regard to what is not desired (object of aversion; anartha) and the non-desiring person (anarthin). An object of desire is whatever is of advantage to the desiring person, an object of aversion whatever is of disadvantage; with both one person enters into relation by turns. On account of the comparative paucity of the objects of desire, and the comparative multitude of the objects of aversion, both may be comprised under the general term, 'object of aversion.' Now, these objects of aversion we mean when we use the term 'causes of suffering,' while by the term 'sufferer' we understand the soul which, being one, enters into successive relations with both (i.e. the objects of desire and the objects of aversion). If, then, the causes of suffering and the sufferer constitute one Self (as the Vedânta teaches), it follows that final release is impossible.—But if, on the other hand, the two are assumed to constitute separate classes, the possibility of release is not excluded, since the cause of the connexion of the two (viz. wrong knowledge) may be removed.

All this reasoning—we, the Vedântins, reply—is futile, because on account of the unity of the Self the relation, whose two terms are the causes of suffering, and the sufferer cannot exist (in the Self).—Our doctrine would be liable to your objection if that which causes suffering and that which suffers did, while belonging to one and the same Self, stand to each other in the relation of object and subject. But they do not stand in that relation just because they are one. If fire, although it possesses different attributes, such as heat and light, and is capable of change, does neither burn nor illumine itself since it is one only; how can the one unchangeable Brahman enter with reference to itself into the relation of cause of suffering and sufferer?—Where then, it may be asked, does the relation discussed (which after all cannot be denied altogether) exist?—That, we reply, is not difficult to see[1]. The living body which is the object of the action of burning is the sufferer; the sun, for instance, is a cause of suffering (burning).—But, the opponent rejoins, burning is a pain, and as such can affect an intelligent being only, not the non-intelligent body; for if it were an affection of the mere body, it would, on the destruction of the body, cease of itself, so that it would be needless to seek for means to make it cease.—But it is likewise not observed, we reply, that a mere intelligent being destitute of a body is burned and suffers pain.—Nor would you (the Sâṅkhya) also assume that the affection called burning belongs to a mere intelligent being. Nor can you admit[2] a real connexion of the soul and the body, because through such a connexion impurity and similar imperfections would attach to the soul[3]. Nor can suffering itself be said to suffer. And how then, we ask, can you explain the relation existing between a sufferer and the causes of suffering? If (as a last refuge) you should maintain that the sattva-guna is that which suffers, and the guna called passion that which causes suffering, we again object, because the intelligent principle (the soul) cannot be really connected with these two[4]. And if you should say that the soul suffers as it were because it leans towards[5] the sattva-guna, we point out that the employment of the phrase, 'as it were,' shows that the soul does not really suffer.

[1] In reality neither suffering nor sufferers exist, as the Vedântin had pointed out in the first sentences of his reply; but there can of course be no doubt as to who suffers and what causes suffering in the vyavahârika-state, i.e. the phenomenal world.

[2] In order to explain thereby how the soul can experience pain.

[3] And that would be against the Sâṅkhya dogma of the soul's essential purity.

[4] So that the fact of suffering which cannot take place apart from an intelligent principle again remains unexplained.

[5] Âtmanas tapte sattve pratibimitatvâd yuktâ taptir iti sankate sattveti. Ân. Gi.

If it is understood that its suffering is not real, we do not object to the phrase 'as it were [1].' For the amphisbena also does not become venomous because it is 'a serpent as it were' ('like a serpent'), nor does the serpent lose its venom because it is 'like an amphisbena.' You must therefore admit that the relation of causes of suffering and of sufferers is not real, but the effect of Nescience. And if you admit that, then my (the Vedântic) doctrine also is free from objections [2].

But perhaps you (the Sâṅkhya) will say that, after all, suffering (on the part of the soul) is real [3]. In that case, however, the impossibility of release is all the more undeniable [4], especially as the cause of suffering (viz. the pradhâna) is admitted to be eternal.—And if (to get out of this difficulty) you maintain that, although the potentialities of suffering (on the part of the soul) and of causing suffering (on the part of the pradhâna) are eternal, yet suffering, in order to become actual, requires the conjunction of the two —which conjunction in its turn depends on a special reason, viz. the non-discrimination of the pradhâna by the soul— and that hence, when that reason no longer exists, the conjunction of the two comes to an absolute termination, whereby the absolute release of the soul becomes possible; we are again unable to accept your explanation, because that on which the non-discrimination depends, viz. the guna, called Darkness, is acknowledged by you to be eternal.

[1] For it then indicates no more than a fictitious resemblance.

[2] The Sâṅkhya Pûrvapakshin had objected to the Vedânta doctrine that, on the latter, we cannot account for the fact known from ordinary experience that there are beings suffering pain and things causing suffering.—The Vedântin in his turn endeavours to show that on the Sâṅkhya doctrine also the fact of suffering remains inexplicable, and is therefore to be considered not real, but fictitious merely, the product of Nescience.

[3] Not only 'suffering as it were,' as it had been called above.

[4] For real suffering cannot be removed by mere distinctive knowledge on which—according to the Sâṅkhya also—release depends.

And as[1] there is no fixed rule for the (successive) rising and sinking of the influence of the particular gu*n*as, there is also no fixed rule for the termination of the cause which effects the conjunction of soul and pradhâna (i. e. non-discrimination); hence the disjunction of the two is uncertain, and so the Sâṅkhyas cannot escape the reproach of absence of final release resulting from their doctrine. To the Vedântin, on the other hand, the idea of final release being impossible cannot occur in his dreams even; for the Self he acknowledges to be one only, and one thing cannot enter into the relation of subject and object, and Scripture, moreover, declares that the plurality of effects originates from speech only. For the phenomenal world, on the other hand, we may admit the relation of sufferer and suffering just as it is observed, and need neither object to it nor refute it.

Herewith we have refuted the doctrine which holds the pradhâna to be the cause of the world. We have now to dispose of the atomic theory.

We begin by refuting an objection raised by the atomists against the upholders of Brahman.—The Vai*s*eshikas argue as follows: The qualities which inhere in the substance constituting the cause originate qualities of the same kind in the substance constituting the effect; we see, for instance, that from white threads white cloth is produced, but do not observe what is contrary (viz. white threads resulting in a piece of cloth of a different colour). Hence, if the intelligent Brahman is assumed as the cause of the world, we should expect to find intelligence inherent in the effect also, viz. the world. But this is not the case, and consequently the intelligent Brahman cannot be the cause of the world. —This reasoning the Sûtrakâra shows to be fallacious, on the ground of the system of the Vai*s*eshikas themselves.

11. Or (the world may originate from Brahman)

[1] This in answer to the remark that possibly the conjunction of soul and pradhâna may come to an end when the influence of Darkness declines, it being overpowered by the knowledge of Truth.

as the great and the long originate from the short and the atomic.

The system of the Vai*s*eshikas is the following:—The atoms which possess, according to their special kind[1], the qualities of colour, &c., and which are of spherical form[2], subsist during a certain period[3] without producing any effects[4]. After that, the unseen principle (ad*ri*sh*t*a), &c.[5], acting as operative causes and conjunction constituting the non-inherent cause[6], they produce the entire aggregate of effected things, beginning with binary atomic compounds. At the same time the qualities of the causes (i.e. of the simple atoms) produce corresponding qualities in the effects. Thus, when two atoms produce a binary atomic compound, the special qualities belonging to the simple atoms, such as white colour, &c., produce a corresponding white colour in the binary compound. One special quality, however, of the simple atoms, viz. atomic sphericity, does not produce corresponding sphericity in the binary compound; for the forms of extension belonging to the latter are said to be minuteness (a*n*utva) and shortness. And, again, when two binary compounds combining produce a quaternary atomic compound, the qualities, such as whiteness, &c., inherent in the binary compounds produce corresponding qualities in the quaternary compounds; with the exception, however, of the two qualities of minuteness and shortness. For it is

[1] I.e. according as they are atoms of earth, water, fire, or air.

[2] Parima*n*d*a*la, spherical is the technical term for the specific form of extension of the atoms, and, secondarily, for the atoms themselves. The latter must apparently be imagined as infinitely small spheres. Cp. Vai*s*. Sût. VII, 1, 20.

[3] Viz. during the period of each pralaya. At that time all the atoms are isolated and motionless.

[4] When the time for a new creation has come.

[5] The &c. implies the activity of the Lord.

[6] The inherent (material) cause of an atomic compound are the constituent atoms, the non-inherent cause the conjunction of those atoms, the operative causes the ad*ri*sh*t*a and the Lord's activity which make them enter into conjunction.

admitted that the forms of extension belonging to quaternary compounds are not minuteness and shortness, but bigness (mahattva) and length. The same happens[1] when many simple atoms or many binary compounds or a simple atom and a binary compound combine to produce new effects.

Well, then, we say, just as from spherical atoms binary compounds are produced, which are minute and short, and ternary compounds which are big and long, but not anything spherical; or as from binary compounds, which are minute and short, ternary compounds, &c., are produced which are big and long, not minute and short; so this non-intelligent world may spring from the intelligent Brahman. This is a doctrine to which you—the Vai*s*eshika—cannot, on your own principles, object.

Here the Vai*s*eshika will perhaps come forward with the following argumentation[2]. As effected substances, such as binary compounds and so on, are engrossed by forms of extension contrary to that of the causal substances, the forms of extension belonging to the latter, viz. sphericity and so on, cannot produce similar qualities in the effects. The world, on the other hand, is not engrossed by any quality contrary to intelligence owing to which the intelligence inherent in the cause should not be able to originate a new intelligence in the effect. For non-intelligence is not a quality contrary to intelligence, but merely its negation. As thus the case of sphericity is not an exactly parallel one, intelligence may very well produce an effect similar to itself.

This argumentation, we rejoin, is not sound. Just as the qualities of sphericity and so on, although existing in the cause, do not produce corresponding effects, so it is with

---

[1] I.e. in all cases the special form of extension of the effect depends not on the special extension of the cause, but on the number of atoms composing the cause (and thereby the effect).

[2] In order to escape the conclusion that the non-acceptance of the doctrine of Brahman involves the abandonment of a fundamental Vai*s*eshika principle.

intelligence also; so that the two cases are parallel so far. Nor can the circumstance of the effects being engrossed by a different form of extension be alleged as the reason of sphericity, &c. not originating qualities similar to themselves; for the power of originating effects belongs to sphericity, &c. before another form of extension begins to exist. For it is admitted that the substance produced remains for a moment devoid of qualities, and that thereupon only (i.e. after that moment) its qualities begin to exist. Nor, again, can it be said that sphericity, &c. concentrate their activity on originating other forms of extension [1], and therefore do not originate forms of extension belonging to the same class as their own; for it is admitted that the origin of other forms is due to other causes; as the Sûtras of Kanabhug (Kanâda) themselves declare (Vais. Sût. VII, 1, 9, 'Bigness is produced from plurality inherent in the causes, from bigness of the cause and from a kind of accumulation;' VII, 1, 10, 'The contrary of this (the big) is the minute;' VII, 1, 17, 'Thereby length and shortness are explained [2]').—Nor, again, can it be said that plurality, &c. inherent in the cause originate (like effects) in consequence of some peculiar proximity (in which they are supposed to stand to the effected substance), while sphericity, &c. (not standing in a like proximity) do not; for when a new substance or a new quality is origin-

[1] I.e. forms of extension different from sphericity, &c.

[2] The first of the three Sûtras quoted comprises, in the present text of the Vaiseshika-sûtras, only the following words, 'Kâranabahutvâk ka;' the ka of the Sûtra implying, according to the commentators, mahattva and prakaya.—According to the Vaiseshikas the form of extension called anu, minute, has for its cause the dvitva inherent in the material causes, i.e. the two atoms from which the minute binary atomic compound originates.—The form of extension called mahat, big, has different causes, among them bahutva, i.e. the plurality residing in the material causes of the resulting 'big' thing; the cause of the mahattva of a ternary atomic compound, for instance, is the tritva inherent in the three constituent atoms. In other cases mahattva is due to antecedent mahattva, in others to prakaya, i.e. accumulation. See the Upaskâra on Vais. Sût. VII, 1, 9; 10.

ated, all the qualities of the cause stand in the same relation of inherence to their abode (i.e. the causal substance in which they inhere). For these reasons the fact of sphericity, &c. not originating like effects can be explained from the essential nature of sphericity, &c. only, and the same may therefore be maintained with regard to intelligence [1]. Moreover, from that observed fact also, that from conjunction (saṃyoga) there originate substances, &c. belonging to a class different (from that to which conjunction itself belongs), it follows that the doctrine of effects belonging to the same class as the causes from which they spring is too wide. If you remark against this last argument that, as we have to do at present with a substance (viz. Brahman), it is inappropriate to instance a quality (viz. conjunction) as a parallel case; we point out that at present we only wish to explain the origination of effects belonging to a different class in general. Nor is there any reason for the restriction that substances only are to be adduced as examples for substances, and qualities only for qualities. Your own Sûtrakâra adduces a quality as furnishing a parallel case for a substance (Vais. Sût. IV, 2, 2, 'On account of the conjunction of things perceptible and things imperceptible being imperceptible the body is not composed of five elements'). Just as the conjunction which inheres in the perceptible earth and the imperceptible ether is not perceptible, the body also, if it had for its inherent cause the five elements which are part of them perceptible, part of them imperceptible, would itself be imperceptible; but, as a matter of fact, it is perceptible; hence it is not composed of the five elements. Here conjunction is a quality and the body a substance.—The origin of effects different in nature (from the cause) has, moreover, been already treated of under II, 1, 6.—Well then, this being so, the matter has been settled there already (why then is it again discussed here?)—Because, we reply, there we argued

[1] I.e. if the Vaiseshikas have to admit that it is the nature of sphericity, &c. not to produce like effects, the Vedântin also may maintain that Brahman produces an unlike effect, viz. the non-intelligent world.

against the Sâṅkhya, and at present we have to do with the Vaiseshika.—But, already once before (II, 1, 3) a line of argument equally applicable to a second case was simply declared to extend to the latter also; (why then do you not simply state now that the arguments used to defeat the Sâṅkhya are equally valid against the Vaiseshika?)—Because here, we reply, at the beginning of the examination of the Vaiseshika system we prefer to discuss the point with arguments specially adapted to the doctrine of the Vaiseshikas.

12. In both cases also (in the cases of the adrishta inhering either in the atoms or the soul) action (of the atoms) is not (possible); hence absence of that (viz. creation and pralaya).

The Sûtrakâra now proceeds to refute the doctrine of atoms being the cause of the world.—This doctrine arises in the following manner. We see that all ordinary substances which consist of parts as, for instance, pieces of cloth originate from the substances connected with them by the relation of inherence, as for instance threads, conjunction co-operating (with the parts to form the whole). We thence draw the general conclusion that whatever consists of parts has originated from those substances with which it is connected by the relation of inherence, conjunction co-operating. That thing now at which the distinction of whole and parts stops and which marks the limit of division into minuter parts is the atom.—This whole world, with its mountains, oceans, and so on, is composed of parts; because it is composed of parts it has a beginning and an end[1]; an effect may not be assumed without a cause; therefore the atoms are the cause of the world. Such is Kanâda's doctrine.—As we observe four elementary substances consisting of parts, viz. earth, water, fire, and air (wind), we have to assume four different kinds of atoms. These atoms marking the limit of subdivision into minuter parts can-

[1] Like other things, let us say a piece of cloth, which consists of parts.

not be divided themselves; hence when the elements are destroyed they can be divided down to atoms only; this state of atomic division of the elements constitutes the pralaya (the periodical destruction of the world). After that when the time for creation comes, motion (karman) springs up in the aerial atoms. This motion which is due to the unseen principle[1] joins the atom in which it resides to another atom; thus binary compounds, &c. are produced, and finally the element of air. In a like manner are produced fire, water, earth, the body with its organs. Thus the whole world originates from atoms. From the qualities inhering in the atoms the qualities belonging to the binary compounds are produced, just as the qualities of the cloth result from the qualities of the threads.—Such, in short, is the teaching of the followers of Ka*n*âda.

This doctrine we controvert in the following manner.—It must be admitted that the atoms when they are in a state of isolation require action (motion) to bring about their conjunction; for we observe that the conjunction of threads and the like is effected by action. Action again, which is itself an effect, requires some operative cause by which it is brought about; for unless some such cause exists, no original motion can take place in the atoms. If, then, some operative cause is assumed, we may, in the first place, assume some cause analogous to seen causes, such as endeavour or impact. But in that case original motion could not occur at all in the atoms, since causes of that kind are, at the time, impossible. For in the pralaya state endeavour, which is a quality of the soul, cannot take place because no body exists then. For the quality of the soul called endeavour originates when the soul is connected with the internal organ which abides in the body. The same reason precludes the assumption of other seen causes such as impact and the like. For they all are possible only after the creation of the world has taken place, and cannot therefore be the

[1] Or, more particularly, to the conjunction of the atoms with the souls to which merit and demerit belong.—Ad*ri*sh*t*âpeksham ad*ri*sh*t*avatkshetra*gñ*asa*m*yogâpeksham iti yâvat. Ân. Gi.

causes of the original action (by which the world is produced).—If, in the second place, the unseen principle is assumed as the cause of the original motion of the atoms, we ask: Is this unseen principle to be considered as inhering in the soul or in the atom? In both cases it cannot be the cause of motion in the atoms, because it is non-intelligent. For, as we have shown above in our examination of the Sâṅkhya system, a non-intelligent thing which is not directed by an intelligent principle cannot of itself either act or be the cause of action, and the soul cannot be the guiding principle of the ad*r*ish*t*a because at the time of pralaya its intelligence has not yet arisen[1]. If, on the other hand, the unseen principle is supposed to inhere in the soul, it cannot be the cause of motion in the atoms, because there exists no connexion of it with the latter. If you say that the soul in which the unseen principle inheres is connected with the atoms, then there would result, from the continuity of connexion[2], continuity of action, as there is no other restricting principle.—Hence, there being no definite cause of action, original action cannot take place in the atoms; there being no action, conjunction of the atoms which depends on action cannot take place; there being no conjunction, all the effects depending on it, viz. the formation of binary atomic compounds, &c., cannot originate.

How, moreover, is the conjunction of one atom with another to be imagined? Is it to be total interpenetration of the two or partial conjunction? If the former, then no increase of bulk could take place, and consequently atomic size only would exist; moreover, it would be contrary to what is observed, as we see that conjunction takes place between substances having parts (prade*s*a). If the latter, it would follow that the atoms are composed of parts.—Let then the atoms be imagined to consist of parts.—If so, imagined things being unreal, the conjunction also of the atoms would be unreal and thus could not be the non-

[1] According to the Vai*s*eshikas intelligence is not essential to the soul, but a mere adventitious quality arising only when the soul is joined to an internal organ.

[2] The soul being all-pervading.

inherent cause of real things. And without non-inherent causes effected substances such as binary compounds, &c. could not originate. And just as at the time of the first creation motion of the atoms leading to their conjunction could not take place, there being no cause of such motion; thus at the time of a general pralaya also no action could take place leading to their separation, since for that occurrence also no definite seen cause could be alleged. Nor could the unseen principle be adduced as the cause, since its purport is to effect enjoyment (of reward and punishment on the part of the soul), not to bring about the pralaya. There being then no possibility of action to effect either the conjunction or the separation of the atoms, neither conjunction nor separation would actually take place, and hence neither creation nor pralaya of the world.—For these reasons the doctrine of the atoms being the cause of the world must be rejected.

13. And because in consequence of samavâya being admitted a regressus in infinitum results from parity of reasoning.

You (the Vais*eshika) admit that a binary compound which originates from two atoms, while absolutely different from them, is connected with them by the relation of inherence; but on that assumption the doctrine of the atoms being the general cause cannot be established, 'because parity involves here a retrogressus ad infinitum.' For just as a binary compound which is absolutely different from the two constituent atoms is connected with them by means of the relation of inherence (samavâya), so the relation of inherence itself being absolutely different from the two things which it connects, requires another relation of inherence to connect it with them, there being absolute difference in both cases. For this second relation of inherence again, a third relation of inherence would have to be assumed and so on ad infinitum.—But—the Vais*eshika is supposed to reply—we are conscious of the so-called samavâya relation as eternally connected with the things between which it exists, not as either non-connected with them or as depending on another connexion; we are therefore not obliged to assume another connexion, and again another, and so on, and thus to allow ourselves to be driven into a regressus in infinitum.—Your defence is unavailing, we reply, for it would involve the admission that conjunction (sa*m*yoga) also as being eternally connected with the things which it joins does, like samavâya, not require another connexion[1]. If you say that conjunction does require another connexion because it is a different thing[2], we reply that then samavâya also requires another connexion because it is likewise a different thing. Nor can you say that conjunction does require another connexion because it is a quality (gu*n*a), and samavâya does not because it is not a quality; for (in spite of this difference) the reason for another connexion being required is the same in both cases[3], and not that which is technically called 'quality' is the cause (of another connexion being required)[4].—For these reasons those who acknowledge samavâya to be a separate existence are driven into a regressus in infinitum, in consequence of which, the impossibility of one term involving the impossibility of the entire series, not even the origination of a binary compound from two atoms can be accounted for.—For this reason also the atomic doctrine is inadmissible.

14. And on account of the permanent existence (of activity or non-activity).

Moreover, the atoms would have to be assumed as either

[1] Which is inadmissible on Vai*s*eshika principles, because sa*m*yoga as being a quality is connected with the things it joins by samavâya.

[2] Viz. from those things which are united by conjunction. The argument is that conjunction as an independent third entity requires another connexion to connect it with the two things related to each other in the way of conjunction.

[3] Viz. the absolute difference of samavâya and sa*m*yoga from the terms which they connect.

[4] Action (karman), &c. also standing in the samavâya relation to their substrates.

essentially active (moving) or essentially non-active, or both or neither; there being no fifth alternative. But none of the four alternatives stated is possible. If they were essentially active, their activity would be permanent so that no pralaya could take place. If they were essentially non-active, their non-activity would be permanent, and no creation could take place. Their being both is impossible because self-contradictory. If they were neither, their activity and non-activity would have to depend on an operative cause, and then the operative causes such as the ad*r*ish*t*a being in permanent proximity to the atoms, permanent activity would result; or else the ad*r*ish*t*a and so on not being taken as operative causes, the consequence would be permanent non-activity on the part of the atoms.—For this reason also the atomic doctrine is untenable.

15. And on account of the atoms having colour, &c., the reverse (of the Vai*s*eshika tenet would take place); as thus it is observed.

Let us suppose, the Vai*s*eshikas say, all substances composed of parts to be disintegrated into their parts; a limit will finally be reached beyond which the process of disintegration cannot be continued. What constitutes that limit are the atoms, which are eternal (permanent), belong to four different classes, possess the qualities of colour, &c., and are the originating principles of this whole material world with its colour, form, and other qualities.

This fundamental assumption of the Vai*s*eshikas we declare to be groundless because from the circumstance of the atoms having colour and other qualities there would follow the contrary of atomic minuteness and permanency, i.e. it would follow that, compared to the ultimate cause, they are gross and non-permanent. For ordinary experience teaches that whatever things possess colour and other qualities are, compared to their cause, gross and non-permanent. A piece of cloth, for instance, is gross compared to the threads of which it consists, and non-permanent; and the threads again are non-permanent and gross compared to the filaments of which they are made up. Therefore the atoms also which the Vaiseshikas admit to have colour, &c. must have causes compared to which they are gross and non-permanent. Hence that reason also which Kanâda gives for the permanence of the atoms (IV, 1, 1, 'that which exists without having a cause is permanent') does not apply at all to the atoms because, as we have shown just now, the atoms are to be considered as having a cause.—The second reason also which Kanâda brings forward for the permanency of the atoms, viz. in IV, 1, 4, 'the special negation implied in the term non-eternal would not be possible[1]' (if there did not exist something eternal, viz. the atoms), does not necessarily prove the permanency of the atoms; for supposing that there exists not any permanent thing, the formation of a negative compound such as 'non-eternal' is impossible. Nor does the existence of the word 'non-permanent' absolutely presuppose the permanency of atoms; for there exists (as we Vedântins maintain) another permanent ultimate Cause, viz. Brahman. Nor can the existence of anything be established merely on the ground of a word commonly being used in that sense, since there is room for common use only if word and matter are well-established by some other means of right knowledge.—The third reason also given in the Vais. Sûtras (IV, 1, 5) for the permanency of the atoms ('and Nescience') is unavailing. For if we explain that Sûtra to mean 'the non-perception of those actually existing causes whose effects are seen is Nescience,' it would follow that the binary atomic compounds also are permanent[2]. And if we tried to escape from that difficulty by including (in the explanation of the Sûtra as given above) the qualification 'there being absence of (originating) sub-

[1] Our Vaiseshika-sûtras read 'pratishedhabhâvah;' but as all MSS. of Sankara have 'pratishedhâbhâvah' I have kept the latter reading and translated according to Ânandagiri's explanation: Kâryam anityam iti kârye viseshato nityatvanishedho na syâd yadi kârane-py anityatvam ato-nûnâm kâranânâm nityateti sûtrârthah.

[2] Because they also are not perceptible; the ternary aggregates, the so-called trasarenus, constituting the minima perceptibilia.

stances,' then nothing else but the absence of a cause would furnish the reason for the permanency of the atoms, and as that reason had already been mentioned before (in IV, 1, 1) the Sûtra IV, 1, 5 would be a useless restatement.—Well, then (the Vaiseshika might say), let us understand by 'Nescience' (in the Sûtra) the impossibility of conceiving a third reason of the destruction (of effects), in addition to the division of the causal substance into its parts, and the destruction of the causal substance; which impossibility involves the permanency of the atoms[1].—There is no necessity, we reply, for assuming that a thing when perishing must perish on account of either of those two reasons. That assumption would indeed have to be made if it were generally admitted that a new substance is produced only by the conjunction of several causal substances. But if it is admitted that a causal substance may originate a new substance by passing over into a qualified state after having previously existed free from qualifications, in its pure generality, it follows that the effected substance may be destroyed by its solidity being dissolved, just as the hardness of ghee is dissolved by the action of fire[2].—Thus there would result, from the circumstance of the atoms having colour, &c., the opposite of what the Vaiseshikas mean. For this reason also the atomic doctrine cannot be maintained.

16. And as there are difficulties in both cases.

Earth has the qualities of smell, taste, colour, and touch, and is gross; water has colour, taste, and touch, and is fine; fire has colour and touch, and is finer yet; air is finest of all, and has the quality of touch only. The question now arises whether the atoms constituting the four elements are to be assumed to possess the same greater or smaller

[1] As they have no cause which could either be disintegrated or destroyed.

[2] This according to the Vedânta view. If atoms existed they might have originated from avidyâ by a mere parinâma and might again be dissolved into avidyâ, without either disintegration or destruction of their cause taking place.

number of qualities as the respective elements.—Either assumption leads to unacceptable consequences. For if we assume that some kinds of atoms have more numerous qualities, it follows that their solid size (mûrti) will be increased thereby, and that implies their being atoms no longer. That an increase of qualities cannot take place without a simultaneous increase of size we infer from our observations concerning effected material bodies.—If, on the other hand, we assume, in order to save the equality of atoms of all kinds, that there is no difference in the number of their qualities, we must either suppose that they have all one quality only; but in that case we should not perceive touch in fire nor colour and touch in water, nor taste, colour, and touch in earth, since the qualities of the effects have for their antecedents the qualities of the causes. Or else we must suppose all atoms to have all the four qualities; but in that case we should necessarily perceive what we actually do not perceive, viz. smell in water, smell and taste in fire, smell, taste, and colour in air.—Hence on this account also the atomic doctrine shows itself to be unacceptable.

17. And as the (atomic theory) is not accepted (by any authoritative persons) it is to be disregarded altogether.

While the theory of the pradhâna being the cause of the world has been accepted by some adherents of the Veda—as, for instance, Manu—with a view to the doctrines of the effect existing in the cause already, and so on, the atomic doctrine has not been accepted by any persons of authority in any of its parts, and therefore is to be disregarded entirely by all those who take their stand on the Veda.

There are, moreover, other objections to the Vaiseshika doctrine.—The Vaiseshikas assume six categories, which constitute the subject-matter of their system, viz. substance, quality, action, generality, particularity, and inherence. These six categories they maintain to be absolutely different from each other, and to have different characteristics;

just as a man, a horse, a hare differ from one another. Side by side with this assumption they make another which contradicts the former one, viz. that quality, action, &c. have the attribute of depending on substance. But that is altogether inappropriate; for just as ordinary things, such as animals, grass, trees, and the like, being absolutely different from each other do not depend on each other, so the qualities, &c. also being absolutely different from substance, cannot depend on the latter. Or else let the qualities, &c. depend on substance; then it follows that, as they are present where substance is present, and absent where it is absent, substance only exists, and, according to its various forms, becomes the object of different terms and conceptions (such as quality, action, &c.); just as Devadatta, for instance, according to the conditions in which he finds himself is the object of various conceptions and names. But this latter alternative would involve the acceptation of the Sâṅkhya doctrine[1] and the abandonment of the Vais*eshika standpoint.—But (the Vais*eshika may say) smoke also is different from fire and yet it is dependent on it.—True, we reply; but we ascertain the difference of smoke and fire from the fact of their being apperceived in separation. Substance and quality, on the other hand, are not so apperceived; for when we are conscious of a white blanket, or a red cow, or a blue lotus, the substance is in each case cognised by means of the quality; the latter therefore has its Self in the substance. The same reasoning applies to action, generality, particularity, and inherence.

If you (the Vais*eshika) say that qualities, actions, &c. (although not non-different from substances) may yet depend on the latter because substances and qualities stand in the relation of one not being able to exist without the other (ayutasiddhi[2]); we point out that things which are

[1] The Sâṅkhyas looking on everything (except the soul) as being the pradhâna in various forms.—There is no need of assuming with Govindânanda that by the Sâṅkhya of the text we have to understand the Vedânta.

[2] Yayor dvayor madhya ekam avinas*yad aparâs*ritam evâvatish*th*ate tâv ayutasiddhau yathâvayavâvayavinau.

ayutasiddha must either be non-separate in place, or non-separate in time, or non-separate in nature, and that none of these alternatives agrees with Vaiseshika principles. For the first alternative contradicts your own assumptions according to which the cloth originating from the threads occupies the place of the threads only, not that of the cloth, while the qualities of the cloth, such as its white colour, occupy the place of the cloth only, not that of the threads. So the Vaiseshika-sûtras say (I, 1, 10), 'Substances originate another substance and qualities another quality.' The threads which constitute the causal substance originate the effected substance, viz. the cloth, and the qualities of the threads, such as white colour, &c., produce in the cloth new corresponding qualities. But this doctrine is clearly contradicted by the assumption of substance and quality being non-separate in place.—If, in the second place, you explain ayutasiddhatva as non-separation in time, it follows also that, for instance, the right and the left horn of a cow would be ayutasiddha.—And if, finally, you explain it to mean 'non-separation in character,' it is impossible to make any further distinction between the substance and the quality, as then quality is conceived as being identical with substance.

Moreover, the distinction which the Vaiseshikas make between conjunction (sa*m*yoga) as being the connexion of things which can exist separately, and inherence (samavâya) as being the connexion of things which are incapable of separate existence is futile, since the cause which exists before the effect[1] cannot be said to be incapable of separate existence. Perhaps the Vaiseshika will say that his definition refers to one of the two terms only, so that samavâya is the connexion, with the cause, of the effect which is incapable of separate existence. But this also is of no avail; for as a connexion requires two terms, the effect as long as it has not yet entered into being cannot be connected with the cause. And it would be equally unavailing to say that the effect enters into the connexion after it has begun to exist; for if the Vaiseshika admits that the effect

[1] The connexion of cause and effect is of course samavâya.

may exist previous to its connexion with the cause, it is no longer ayutasiddha (incapable of separate existence), and thereby the principle that between effect and cause conjunction and disjunction do not take place is violated[1]. And[2] just as conjunction, and not samavâya, is the connexion in which every effected substance as soon as it has been produced stands with the all-pervading substances as ether, &c.—although no motion has taken place on the part of the effected substance—so also the connexion of the effect with the cause will be conjunction merely, not samavâya.

Nor is there any proof for the existence of any connexion, samavâya or sa*m*yoga, apart from the things which it connects. If it should be maintained that sa*m*yoga and samavâya have such an existence because we observe that there are names and ideas of them in addition to the names and ideas of the things connected, we point out that one and the same thing may be the subject of several names and ideas if it is considered in its relations to what lies without it. Devadatta although being one only forms the object of many different names and notions according as he is considered in himself or in his relations to others; thus he is thought and spoken of as man, Brâhma*n*a, learned in the Veda, generous, boy, young man, old man, father, son, grandson, brother, son-in-law, &c. So, again, one and the same stroke is, according to the place it is connected with, spoken of and conceived as meaning either ten, or hundred, or thousand, &c. Analogously, two connected things are not only conceived and denoted as connected things, but in addition constitute the object of the ideas and terms 'conjunction' or 'inherence,' which however do not prove

---

[1] If the effect can exist before having entered into connexion with the cause, the subsequent connexion of the two is no longer samavâya but sa*m*yoga; and that contradicts a fundamental Vai*s*eshika principle.

[2] This clause replies to the objection that only those connexions which have been produced by previous motion are to be considered conjunctions.

themselves to be separate entities.—Things standing thus, the non-existence of separate entities (conjunction, &c.), which entities would have to be established on the ground of perception, follows from the fact of their non-perception. —Nor, again[1], does the circumstance of the word and idea of connexion having for its object the things connected involve the connexion's permanent existence, since we have already shown above that one thing may, on account of its relations to other things, be conceived and denoted in different ways.

Further[2], conjunction cannot take place between the atoms, the soul, and the internal organ, because they have no parts; for we observe that conjunction takes place only of such substances as consist of parts. If the Vaiseshika should say that parts of the atoms, soul and mind may be assumed (in order to explain their alleged conjunction), we remark that the assumption of actually non-existing things would involve the result that anything might be established; for there is no restrictive rule that only such and such non-existing things—whether contradictory to reason or not—should be assumed and not any other, and assumptions depend on one's choice only and may be carried to any extent. If we once allow assumptions, there is no reason why there should not be assumed a further hundred or thousand things, in addition to the six categories assumed by the Vaiseshikas. Anybody might then assume anything, and we could neither stop a compassionate man from assuming that this transmigratory world which is the cause of so much misery to living beings is not to be, nor a malicious man from assuming that even the released souls are to enter on a new cycle of existences.

[1] A clause meant to preclude the assumption that the permanent existence of the things connected involves the permanent existence of the connexion.

[2] It having been shown above that atoms cannot enter into samyoga with each other, it is shown now that samyoga of the soul with the atoms cannot be the cause of the motion of the latter, and that samyoga of soul and manas cannot be the cause of cognition.

Further, it is not possible that a binary atomic compound, which consists of parts, should be connected with the simple indivisible atoms by an intimate connexion (sa*ms*lesha) any more than they can thus be connected with ether; for between ether and earth, &c. there does not exist that kind of intimate connexion which exists, for instance, between wood and varnish[1].

Let it then be said (the Vai*s*eshika resumes) that the samavâya relation must be assumed, because otherwise the relation of that which abides and that which forms the abode—which relation actually exists between the effected substance and the causal substance—is not possible.—That would, we reply, involve the vice of mutual dependence; for only when the separateness of cause and effect is established, the relation of the abode and that which abides can be established; and only when the latter relation is established, the relation of separateness can be established. For the Vedântins acknowledge neither the separateness of cause and effect, nor their standing to each other in the relation of abode and thing abiding, since according to their doctrine the effect is only a certain state of the cause[2].—Moreover, as the atoms are limited (not of infinite extension), they must in reality consist of as many parts as we acknowledge regions of space[3], whether those be six or eight or ten, and consequently they cannot be permanent; conclusions contrary to the Vai*s*eshika doctrine of the indivisibility and permanency of the atoms.—If the Vai*s*eshika replies that those very parts which are owing to the existence of the different regions of space are his (indestructible)

[1] Ekasambandhyâkarsha*n*e yatra sambandhyantarâkarsha*n*a*m* tatra sa*ms*lesha*h*, sa tu sâvayavânâ*m* *g*atukâsh*th*âdînâ*m* d*ri*sh*t*o na tu niravayavai*h* sâvayavânâm, ato dvya*n*ukasya sâvayavasya niravayavena paramâ*n*unâ sa nopapadyate. Brahmavidyâbh.

[2] In answer to the question how, in that case, the practically recognised relation of abode, &c. existing between the cause and the effect is accounted for.

[3] For they must in that case have a northern end, an eastern end, &c.

atoms; we deny that because all things whatever, forming a series of substances of ever-increasing minuteness, are capable of dissolution, until the highest cause (Brahman) is reached. Earth—which is, in comparison with a binary compound, the grossest thing of all—undergoes decomposition; so do the substances following next which belong to the same class as earth; so does the binary compound; and so does, finally, the atom which (although the minutest thing of all) still belongs to the same general class (i.e. matter) with earth, &c. The objection (which the Vai*s*eshika might possibly raise here again) that things can be decomposed only by the separation of their parts[1], we have already disposed of above, where we pointed out that decomposition may take place in a manner analogous to the melting of ghee. Just as the hardness of ghee, gold, and the like, is destroyed in consequence of those substances being rendered liquid by their contact with fire, no separation of the parts taking place all the while; so the solid shape of the atoms also may be decomposed by their passing back into the indifferenced condition of the highest cause. In the same way the origination of effects also is brought about not merely in the way of conjunction of parts; for we see that milk, for instance, and water originate effects such as sour milk and ice without there taking place any conjunction of parts.

It thus appears that the atomic doctrine is supported by very weak arguments only, is opposed to those scriptural passages which declare the Lord to be the general cause, and is not accepted by any of the authorities taking their stand on Scripture, such as Manu and others. Hence it is to be altogether disregarded by highminded men who have a regard for their own spiritual welfare.

18. (If there be assumed) the (dyad of) aggregates with its two causes, (there takes place) non-establishment of those (two aggregates).

The reasons on account of which the doctrine of the

[1] And that on that account the atoms which he considers as the ultimate simple constituents of matter cannot be decomposed.

Vai*s*eshikas cannot be accepted have been stated above. That doctrine may be called semi-destructive (or semi-nihilistic[1]). That the more thorough doctrine which teaches universal non-permanency is even less worthy of being taken into consideration, we now proceed to show.

That doctrine is presented in a variety of forms, due either to the difference of the views (maintained by Buddha at different times), or else to the difference of capacity on the part of the disciples (of Buddha). Three principal opinions may, however, be distinguished; the opinion of those who maintain the reality of everything (Realists, sarvâstitvavâdin); the opinion of those who maintain that thought only is real (Idealists, vi*g*ñânavâdin); and the opinion of those who maintain that everything is void (unreal; Nihilists, *s*ûnyavâdin[2]).—We first controvert those

---

[1] Because according to their opinion difference of size constitutes difference of substance, so that the continuous change of size in animal bodies, for instance, involves the continual perishing of old and the continual origination of new substances.

[2] The following notes on Bauddha doctrines are taken exclusively from the commentaries on the *S*aṅkarabhâshya, and no attempt has been made to contrast or reconcile the Brahminical accounts of Bauddha psychology with the teaching of genuine Bauddha books. Cp. on the chief sects of the Buddhistic philosophers the Bauddha chapter of the Sarvadar*s*a*n*asa*m*graha.—The Nihilists are the Mâdhyamikas; the Idealists are the Yogâ*k*âras; the Sautrântikas and the Vaibhâshikas together constitute the class of the Realists.—I subjoin the account given of those sects in the Brahmavidyâbhara*n*a.—Buddhasya hi mâdhyamika-yogâ*k*âra-sautrântika-vaibhâshikasam*g*ñakâ*s* *k*atvâra*h* *s*ishyâ*h*. Tatra buddhena prathama*m* yân prati sarva*m* *s*ûnyam ity upadish*t*a*m* te mâdhyamikâs te hi guru*n*â yathokta*m* tathaiva *s*raddhayâ *gri*hîtavanta iti k*ri*tvâ nâpak*ri*sh*t*â*h* punas *k*a taduktasyârthasya buddhyanusâre*n*âkshepasyâk*ri*tatvân notk*ri*sh*t*abuddhaya iti mâdhyamikâ*h*. Anyais tu *s*ishyair guru*n*â sarva*s*ûnyatva upadish*t*e *g*ñânâtiriktasya sarvasya *s*ûnyatvam astu nâmeti gurûktir yoga iti bauddai*h* paribhâshitopetâ*h* tad upari *k*a *g*ñânasya tu *s*ûnyatva*m* na sa*m*bhavati tathâtve *g*agadândhyaprasaṅgât *s*ûnyasiddher apy asa*m*bhavâ*k* *k*eti buddhamate â*k*âratvena paribhâshita âkshepo-pi k*ri*ta iti yogâ*k*âra*h*, vi*g*ñânamâtrâstitvavâdina*h*. Tadanantaram anyai*h* *s*ishyai*h*

who maintain that everything, external as well as internal, is real. What is external is either element (bhûta) or elementary (bhautika); what is internal is either mind (*k*itta) or mental (*k*aitta). The elements are earth, water, and so on; elemental are colour, &c. on the one hand, and the eye and the other sense-organs on the other hand. Earth and the other three elements arise from the aggregation of the four different kinds of atoms; the atoms of earth being hard, those of water viscid, those of fire hot, those of air mobile.—The inward world consists of the five so-called 'groups' (skandha), the group of sensation (rûpaskandha), the group of knowledge (vi*g*ñânaskandha), the group of feeling (vedanâskandha), the group of verbal knowledge (samg*ñ*âskandha), and the group of impressions (sa*m*skâraskandha)[1]; which

pratîtisiddhasya katha*m* *s*ûnyatva*m* vaktu*m* *s*akyam ato *g*ñânavad vâhyârtho*pi satya ity ukte tarhi tathaiva so*stu, para*m* tu so *numeyo na tu pratyaksha ity ukte tathâṅgîk*ri*tyaiva*m* *s*ishyamatim anus*ri*tya kiyatparyanta*m* sûtra*m* bhavishyatîti tai*h* p*ri*sh*t*am atas te sautrântikâ*h*. Anye punar yady aya*m* gha*t*a iti pratîtibalâd vâhyo*rtha upeyate tarhi tasyâ eva pratîter aparokshatvât sa katha*m* paroksho*to vâhyo*rtho na pratyaksha iti bhâshâ viruddhety âkshipann atas te vaibhâshikâ*h*.

[1] The rûpaskandha comprises the senses and their objects, colour, &c.; the sense-organs were above called bhautika, they here re-appear as *k*aittika on account of their connexion with thought. Their objects likewise are classed as *k*aittika in so far as they are perceived by the senses.—The vi*g*ñânaskandha comprises the series of self-cognitions (ahamaham ity âlayavi*g*ñânapravâha*h*), according to all commentators; and in addition, according to the Brahmavidyâbhara*n*a, the knowledge, determinate and indeterminate, of external things (savikalpaka*m* nirvikalpaka*m* *k*a pravr*i*ttivi*g*ñânasamg*ñ*itam).—The vedanâskandha comprises pleasure, pain, &c. —The samg*ñ*âskandha comprises the cognition of things by their names (gaur a*s*va ityâdi*s*abdasam*g*alpitapratyaya*h*, Ân. Gi.; gaur a*s*va ityeva*m* nâmavi*s*ish*t*asavikalpaka*h* pratyaya*h*, Go. Ân.; sa*m*g*ñ*â ya*g*ñadattâdipadatadullekhî savikalpapratyayo vâ, dvitîyapakshe vi*g*ñânapadena savikalpapratyayo na grâhya*h*, Brahmavidyâbh.). The sa*m*skâraskandha comprises passion, aversion, &c., dharma and adharma.—Compare also the Bhâmatî.—The vi*g*ñânaskandha is *k*itta, the other skandhas *k*aitta.

taken together constitute the basis of all personal existence[1].

With reference to this doctrine we make the following remarks.—Those two aggregates, constituting two different classes, and having two different causes which the Bauddhas assume, viz. the aggregate of the elements and elementary things whose cause the atoms are, and the aggregate of the five skandhas whose cause the skandhas are, cannot, on Bauddha principles, be established, i.e. it cannot be explained how the aggregates are brought about. For the parts constituting the (material) aggregates are devoid of intelligence, and the kindling (abhi*g*valana) of intelligence depends on an aggregate of atoms having been brought about previously[2]. And the Bauddhas do not admit any other permanent intelligent being, such as either an enjoying soul or a ruling Lord, which could effect the aggregation of the atoms. Nor can the atoms and skandhas be assumed to enter on activity on their own account; for that would imply their never ceasing to be active[3]. Nor can the cause of aggregation be looked for in the so-called abode (i.e. the âlayavi*gñ*âna-pravâha, the train of self-cognitions); for the latter must be described either as different from the single cognitions or as not different from them. (In the former case it is either permanent, and then it is nothing else but the permanent soul of the Vedântins; or non-permanent;) then being admitted to be momentary merely, it cannot exercise any influence and cannot therefore be the cause of the motion of the atoms[4].

[1] It has to be kept in view that the sarvâstitvavâdins as well as the other Bauddha sects teach the momentariness (ksha*n*ikatva), the eternal flux of everything that exists, and are on that ground controverted by the upholders of the permanent Brahman.

[2] Mind, on the Bauddha doctrine, presupposes the existence of an aggregate of atoms, viz. the body.

[3] In consequence of which no release could take place.

[4] The Brahmavidyâbhara*n*a explains the last clause—from ksha*n*ikatvâ*k* *k*a—somewhat differently: Api *k*a paramâ*n*ûnâm api ksha*n*ikatvâbhyupagamân melana*m* na sambhavati, paramâ*n*ûnâ*m* melana*m* paramâ*n*ukriyâdhînam, tathâ *k*a svakriyâ*m* prati paramâ*n*ûnâ*m* kâra*n*atvât kriyâpûrvaksha*n*e paramâ*n*ubhir bhâvyam, kriyâ

(And in the latter case we are not further advanced than before.)—For all these reasons the formation of aggregates cannot be accounted for. But without aggregates there would be an end of the stream of mundane existence which presupposes those aggregates.

19. If it be said that (the formation of aggregates may be explained) through (Nescience, &c.) standing in the relation of mutual causality; we say 'No,' because they merely are the efficient causes of the origin (of the immediately subsequent links).

Although there exists no permanent intelligent principle of the nature either of a ruling Lord or an enjoying soul, under whose influence the formation of aggregates could take place, yet the course of mundane existence is rendered possible through the mutual causality[1] of Nescience and so on, so that we need not look for any other combining principle.

The series beginning with Nescience comprises the following members: Nescience, impression, knowledge, name and form, the abode of the six, touch, feeling, desire, activity, birth, species, decay, death, grief, lamentation, pain, mental affliction, and the like[2]. All these terms con-

*s*rayatayâ kriyâksha*n*e*pi teshâm avasthânam apekshitam eva*m* melanakshane*pi, nahi melanâ*s*rayasyâbhâve melanarûpâ prav*ri*ttir upapadyate, tathâ *k*a sthiraparamâ*n*usâdhyâ melanarûpâ prav*ri*tti*h* katha*m* teshâm ksha*n*ikatve bhavet.—Ânanda Giri also divides and translates differently from the translation in the text.

[1] The kâra*n*atvât of *S*ankara explains the pratyayatvât of the Sûtra; kârya*m* praty ayate *g*anakatvena ga*kkh*ati.

[2] The commentators agree on the whole in their explanations of the terms of this series.—The following is the substance of the comment of the Brahmavidyâbhara*n*a: Nescience is the error of considering that which is momentary, impure, &c. to be permanent, pure, &c.—Impression (affection, sa*m*skâra) comprises desire, aversion, &c., and the activity caused by them.—Knowledge (vi*gñ*âna) is the self-consciousness (aham ity âlayavi*gñ*ânasya v*ri*ttilâbha*h*) springing up in the embryo.—Name and form is the rudimentary flake- or bubble-like condition of the embryo.—The

stitute a chain of causes and are as such spoken of in the Bauddha system, sometimes cursorily, sometimes at length. They are, moreover, all acknowledged as existing, not by the Bauddhas only, but by the followers of all systems. And as the cycles of Nescience, &c. forming uninterrupted chains of causes and effects revolve unceasingly like water-wheels, the existence of the aggregates (which constitute bodies and minds) must needs be assumed, as without such Nescience and so on could not take place.

This argumentation of the Bauddha we are unable to accept, because it merely assigns efficient causes for the origination of the members of the series, but does not intimate an efficient cause for the formation of the aggregates. If the Bauddha reminds us of the statement made above that the existence of aggregates must needs be inferred from the existence of Nescience and so on, we point out that, if he means thereby that Nescience and so on cannot exist without aggregates and hence require the existence of such, it remains to assign an efficient cause for the formation of the aggregates. But, as we have already shown—when examining the Vai*s*eshika doctrine—that the formation of aggregates cannot be accounted for even on the assumption of permanent atoms and individual souls in

---

abode of the six (sha*d*âyatana) is the further developed stage of the embryo in which the latter is the abode of the six senses.—Touch (spar*s*a) is the sensations of cold, warmth, &c. on the embryo's part.—Feeling (vedanâ) the sensations of pleasure and pain resulting therefrom.—Desire (t*r*ish*n*â) is the wish to enjoy the pleasurable sensations and to shun the painful ones.—Activity (upâdâna) is the effort resulting from desire.—Birth is the passing out from the uterus.—Species (*g*âti) is the class of beings to which the new-born creature belongs.—Decay (*g*arâ).—Death (mara*n*am) is explained as the condition of the creature when about to die (mumûrshâ).—Grief (*s*oka) the frustration of wishes connected therewith.—Lament (paridevanam) the lamentations on that account.—Pain (du*h*kha) is such pain as caused by the five senses.—Durmanas is mental affliction.—The 'and the like' implies death, the departure to another world and the subsequent return from there.

which the adrishta abides[1]; how much less then are aggregates possible if there exist only momentary atoms not connected with enjoying souls and devoid of abodes (i.e. souls), and that which abides in them (the adrishta).—Let us then assume (the Bauddha says) that Nescience, &c. themselves are the efficient cause of the aggregate.—But how—we ask—can they be the cause of that without which—as their abode—they themselves are not capable of existence? Perhaps you will say that in the eternal samsâra the aggregates succeed one another in an unbroken chain, and hence also Nescience, and so on, which abide in those aggregates. But in that case you will have to assume either that each aggregate necessarily produces another aggregate of the same kind, or that, without any settled rule, it may produce either a like or an unlike one. In the former case a human body could never pass over into that of a god or an animal or a being of the infernal regions; in the latter case a man might in an instant be turned into an elephant or a god and again become a man; either of which consequences would be contrary to your system.—Moreover, that for the purpose of whose enjoyment the aggregate is formed is, according to your doctrine, not a permanent enjoying soul, so that enjoyment subserves itself merely and cannot be desired by anything else; hence final release also must, according to you, be considered as subserving itself

[1] Ânanda Giri and Go. Ânanda explain: Âsrayâsrayibhûteshv iti bhoktrivisesha*n*am adrish*t*âsrayeshv ity artha*h*.—The Brahmavidyâbhara*n*a says: Nityeshv âsrayâsrayibhûteshv a*n*ushv abhyupagamyamâneshu bhoktrishu *k*a satsv ity anvaya*h*. Âsrayâsrayibhûteshv ity asyopakâryopakârakabhâvaprâpteshv ity artha*h*.—And with regard to the subsequent âsrayâsrayisûnyeshu: âsrayâsrayitvasûnyeshu, aya*m* bhâva*h*, sthireshu paramâ*n*ushu yadanvaye paramâ*n*ûnâ*m* sa*m*ghâtâpatti*h* yadvyatireke *k*a na tad upakârakam upakâryâ*h* paramâ*n*ava*h* yena tatkrito bhoga*h* prârthyate sa tatra karteti grahîtu*m* sakyate, ksha*n*ikeshu tu paramâ*n*ushu anvayavyatirekagrahasyânekaksha*n*asâdhyasyâsa*m*bhavân nopakâryopakârakabhâvo nirdhârayitu*m* sakya*h*.—Ânanda Giri remarks on the latter: Adrish*t*âsrayakartrirâhityam âhâsrayeti. Another reading appears to be âsayâsrayasûnyeshu.

only, and no being desirous of release can be assumed. If a being desirous of both were assumed, it would have to be conceived as permanently existing up to the time of enjoyment and release, and that would be contrary to your doctrine of general impermanency.—There may therefore exist a causal relation between the members of the series consisting of Nescience, &c., but, in the absence of a permanent enjoying soul, it is impossible to establish on that ground the existence of aggregates.

20. (Nor can there be a causal relation between Nescience, &c.), because on the origination of the subsequent (moment) the preceding one ceases to be.

We have hitherto argued that Nescience, and so on, stand in a causal relation to each other merely, so that they cannot be made to account for the existence of aggregates; we are now going to prove that they cannot even be considered as efficient causes of the subsequent members of the series to which they belong.

Those who maintain that everything has a momentary existence only admit that when the thing existing in the second moment[1] enters into being the thing existing in the first moment ceases to be. On this admission it is impossible to establish between the two things the relation of cause and effect, since the former momentary existence which ceases or has ceased to be, and so has entered into the state of non-existence, cannot be the cause of the later momentary existence.—Let it then be said that the former momentary existence when it has reached its full development becomes the cause of the later momentary existence.—That also is impossible; for the assumption that a fully developed existence exerts a further energy, involves the conclusion that it is connected with a second moment (which contradicts the doctrine of universal momentariness).—Then let the mere existence of the antecedent entity constitute its

[1] Bauddhânâ*m* ksha*n*apadena gha*t*âdir eva padârtho vyavahriyate na tu tadatirikta*h* kas*k*it ksha*n*o nâma kâlo*x*sti. Brahmâvidyâbh.

causal energy.—That assumption also is fruitless, because we cannot conceive the origination of an effect which is not imbued with the nature of the cause (i. e. in which the nature of the cause does not continue to exist). And to assume that the nature of the cause does continue to exist in the effect is impossible (on the Bauddha doctrine), as that would involve the permanency of the cause, and thus necessitate the abandonment of the doctrine of general non-permanency.—Nor can it be admitted that the relation of cause and effect holds good without the cause somehow giving its colouring to the effect; for that doctrine might unduly be extended to all cases[1].—Moreover, the origination and cessation of things of which the Bauddha speaks must either constitute a thing's own form or another state of it, or an altogether different thing. But none of these alternatives agrees with the general Bauddha principles. If, in the first place, origination and cessation constituted the form of a thing, it would follow that the word 'thing' and the words 'origination' and 'cessation' are interchangeable (which is not the case).—Let then, secondly, the Bauddha says, a certain difference be assumed, in consequence of which the terms 'origination' and 'cessation' may denote the initial and final states of that which in the intermediate state is called thing.—In that case, we reply, the thing will be connected with three moments, viz. the initial, the intermediate, and the final one, so that the doctrine of general momentariness will have to be abandoned. —Let then, as the third alternative, origination and cessation be altogether different from the thing, as much as a buffalo is from a horse.—That too cannot be, we reply; for it would lead to the conclusion that the thing, because altogether disconnected with origination and cessation, is everlasting. And the same conclusion would be led up to, if we understood by the origination and cessation of a thing merely its perception and non-perception; for the latter are attributes of the percipient mind only, not of the thing itself.—Hence

[1] And whereupon then could be established the difference of mere efficient causes such as the potter's staff, &c., and material causes such as clay, &c.?

we have again to declare the Bauddha doctrine to be untenable.

21. On the supposition of there being no (cause; while yet the effect takes place), there results contradiction of the admitted principle; otherwise simultaneousness (of cause and effect).

It has been shown that on the doctrine of general non-permanency, the former momentary existence, as having already been merged in non-existence, cannot be the cause of the later one.—Perhaps now the Bauddha will say that an effect may arise even when there is no cause.—That, we reply, implies the abandonment of a principle admitted by yourself, viz. that the mind and the mental modifications originate when in conjunction with four kinds of causes[1]. Moreover, if anything could originate without a cause, there would be nothing to prevent that anything might originate at any time.—If, on the other hand, you should say that we may assume the antecedent momentary existence to last until the succeeding one has been produced, we point out that that would imply the simultaneousness of cause and effect, and so run counter to an accepted Bauddha tenet, viz. that all things[2] are momentary merely.

---

[1] These four causes are the so-called defining cause (adhipati-pratyaya), the auxiliary cause (sahakâripratyaya), the immediate cause (samanantarapratyaya), and the substantial cause (âlambana-pratyaya).—I extract the explanation from the Brahmavidyâbhara*n*a: Adhipatir indriya*m* tad dhi *k*akshurâdirûpam utpannasya *g*ñânasya rûpâdivishayatâ*m* niya*kkh*ati niyâmakas *k*a loke*-*dhipatir ity u*k*yate. Sahakârî âloka*h*. Samanantarapratyaya*h* pûrva*g*ñânam, bauddhamate hi ksha*n*ika*g*ñânasa*m*tatau pûrva*g*ñânam uttara*g*ñânasya kârana*m* tad eva *k*a mana ity u*k*yate. Âlambana*m* gha*t*âdi*h*. Etân hetûn pratîya prâpya *k*akshurâdi*g*anyam ity âdi.

[2] Sa*m*skâra iti, tanmate pûrvaksha*n*a eva hetubhûta*h* sa*m*skâro vâsaneti *k*a vyavahriyate kârya*m* tu tadvishayatayâ karmavyutpattyâ sa*m*skâra*h*, tathâ *k*a kâryakâra*n*âtmaka*m* sarva*m* bhâvarûpa*m* ksha*n*ikam iti prati*g*ñârtha*h*. Brahmavidyâbhara*n*a.

22. Cessation dependent on a sublative act of the mind, and cessation not so dependent cannot be established, there being no (complete) interruption.

The Bauddhas who maintain that universal destruction is going on constantly, assume that 'whatever forms an object of knowledge and is different from the triad is produced (sa*m*skr*i*ta) and momentary.' To the triad there mentioned they give the names 'cessation dependent on a sublative act of the mind,' 'cessation not dependent on such an act,' and 'space.' This triad they hold to be non-substantial, of a merely negative character (abhâvamâtra), devoid of all positive characteristics. By 'cessation dependent on a sublative act of the mind,' we have to understand such destruction of entities as is preceded by an act of thought[1]; by 'cessation not so dependent' is meant destruction of the opposite kind[2]; by 'space' is meant absence in general of something covering (or occupying space). Out of these three non-existences 'space' will be refuted later on (Sûtra 24); the two other ones are refuted in the present Sûtra.

Cessation which is dependent on a sublative act of the mind, and cessation which is not so dependent are both impossible, 'on account of the absence of interruption.' For both kinds of cessation must have reference either to the series (of momentary existences) or to the single members constituting the series.—The former alternative is impossible, because in all series (of momentary existences) the members of the series stand in an unbroken relation of cause and effect so that the series cannot be interrupted[3].—The latter

[1] As when a man smashes a jar having previously formed the intention of doing so.

[2] I.e. the insensible continual decay of things.—Viparîta iti pratiksha*n*a*m* gha*t*âdînâ*m* yuktyâ sâdhyamâno*s* ku*s*alair avagantum a*s*akya*h* sûkshmo vinâ*s*o*x*pratisa*m*khyânirodha*h*. Brahmâv.

[3] A series of momentary existences constituting a chain of causes and effects can never be entirely stopped; for the last momentary existence must be supposed either to produce its effect or not to produce it. In the former case the series is continued; the latter alternative would imply that the last link does not really

alternative is likewise inadmissible, for it is impossible to maintain that any momentary existence should undergo complete annihilation entirely undefinable and disconnected (with the previous state of existence), since we observe that a thing is recognised in the various states through which it may pass and thus has a connected existence[1]. And in those cases also where a thing is not clearly recognised (after having undergone a change) we yet infer, on the ground of actual observations made in other cases, that one and the same thing continues to exist without any interruption.—For these reasons the two kinds of cessation which the Bauddhas assume cannot be proved.

23. And on account of the objections presenting themselves in either case.

The cessation of Nescience, &c. which, on the assumption of the Bauddhas, is included in the two kinds of cessation discussed hitherto, must take place either in consequence of perfect knowledge together with its auxiliaries, or else of its own accord. But the former alternative would imply the abandonment of the Bauddha doctrine that destruction takes place without a cause, and the latter alternative would involve the uselessness of the Bauddha instruction as to the 'path'[2]. As therefore both alternatives are open to objections, the Bauddha doctrine must be declared unsatisfactory.

---

exist, since the Bauddhas define the sattâ of a thing as its causal efficiency (cp. Sarvadar*s*a*n*asa*m*graha). And the non-existence of the last link would retrogressively lead to the non-existence of the whole series.

[1] Thus clay is recognised as such whether it appears in the form of a jar, or of the potsherds into which the jar is broken, or of the powder into which the potsherds are ground.—Analogously we infer that even things which seem to vanish altogether, such as a drop of water which has fallen on heated iron, yet continue to exist in some form.

[2] The knowledge that everything is transitory, pain, &c.

24. And in the case of space also (the doctrine of its being a non-entity is untenable) on account of its not differing (from the two other kinds of non-entity).

We have shown so far that of the triad declared by the Bauddhas to be devoid of all positive characteristics, and therefore non-definable, two (viz. prati-sa*m*khyâvirodha and aprati°) cannot be shown to be such; we now proceed to show the same with regard to space (ether, âkâ*s*a).

With regard to space also it cannot be maintained that it is non-definable, since substantiality can be established in the case of space no less than in the case of the two so-called non-entities treated of in the preceding Sûtras. That space is a real thing follows in the first place from certain scriptural passages, such as 'space sprang from the Self.'—To those, again, who (like the Bauddhas) disagree with us as to the authoritativeness of Scripture we point out that the real existence of space is to be inferred from the quality of sound, since we observe that earth and other real things are the abodes of smell and the other qualities.—Moreover, if you declare that space is nothing but the absence in general of any covering (occupying) body, it would follow that while one bird is flying—whereby space is occupied—there would be no room for a second bird wanting to fly at the same time. And if you should reply that the second bird may fly there where there is absence of a covering body, we point out that that something by which the absence of covering bodies is distinguished must be a positive entity, viz. space in our sense, and not the mere non-existence of covering bodies [1].—Moreover, the Bauddha places himself, by his view of space, in opposition to other parts of his system. For we find, in the Bauddha Scriptures, a series of questions and answers (beginning, 'On what, O reverend Sir, is the earth founded?'), in which the following

[1] What does enable us to declare that there is âvara*n*âbhâva in one place and not in another? Space; which therefore is something real.

question occurs, 'On what is the air founded?' to which it is replied that the air is founded on space (ether). Now it is clear that this statement is appropriate only on the supposition of space being a positive entity, not a mere negation.—Further, there is a self-contradiction in the Bauddha statements regarding all the three kinds of negative entities, it being said, on the one hand, that they are not positively definable, and, on the other hand, that they are eternal. Of what is not real neither eternity nor non-eternity can be predicated, since the distinction of subjects and predicates of attribution is founded entirely on real things. Anything with regard to which that distinction holds good we conclude to be a real thing, such as jars and the like are, not a mere undefinable negation.

25. And on account of remembrance.

The philosopher who maintains that all things are momentary only would have to extend that doctrine to the perceiving person (upalabdh*ri*) also; that is, however, not possible, on account of the remembrance which is consequent on the original perception. That remembrance can take place only if it belongs to the same person who previously made the perception; for we observe that what one man has experienced is not remembered by another man. How, indeed, could there arise the conscious state expressed in the sentences, 'I saw that thing, and now I see this thing,' if the seeing person were not in both cases the same? That the consciousness of recognition takes place only in the case of the observing and remembering subject being one, is a matter known to every one; for if there were, in the two cases, different subjects, the state of consciousness arising in the mind of the remembering person would be, '*I* remember; another person made the observation.' But no such state of consciousness does arise.—When, on the other hand, such a state of consciousness does arise, then everybody knows that the person who made the original observation, and the person who remembers, are different persons, and then the state of consciousness is expressed as follows, 'I remember that that other person saw that and that.'—

In the case under discussion, however, the Vainâsika himself—whose state of consciousness is, 'I saw that and that'—knows that there is one thinking subject only to which the original perception as well as the remembrance belongs, and does not think of denying that the past perception belonged to himself, not any more than he denies that fire is hot and gives light.

As thus one agent is connected with the two moments of perception and subsequent remembrance, the Vainâsika has necessarily to abandon the doctrine of universal momentariness. And if he further recognises all his subsequent successive cognitions, up to his last breath, to belong to one and the same subject, and in addition cannot but attribute all his past cognitions, from the moment of his birth, to the same Self, how can he maintain, without being ashamed of himself, that everything has a momentary existence only? Should he maintain that the recognition (of the subject as one and the same) takes place on account of the similarity (of the different self-cognitions; each, however, being momentary only), we reply that the cognition of similarity is based on two things, and that for that reason the advocate of universal momentariness who denies the existence of one (permanent) subject able mentally to grasp the two similar things simply talks deceitful nonsense when asserting that recognition is founded on similarity. Should he admit, on the other hand, that there is one mind grasping the similarity of two successive momentary existences, he would thereby admit that one entity endures for two moments and thus contradict the tenet of universal momentariness.—Should it be said that the cognition 'this is similar to that' is a different (new) cognition, not dependent on the apperception of the earlier and later momentary existences, we refute this by the remark that the fact of different terms—viz. 'this' and 'that'—being used points to the existence of different things (which the mind grasps in a judgment of similarity). If the mental act of which similarity is the object were an altogether new act (not concerned with the two separate similar entities), the expression 'this is similar to that' would be devoid of meaning; we should in that case rather speak of 'similarity' only.—Whenever (to add a general reflexion) something perfectly well known from ordinary experience is not admitted by philosophers, they may indeed establish their own view and demolish the contrary opinion by means of words, but they thereby neither convince others nor even themselves. Whatever has been ascertained to be such and such must also be represented as such and such; attempts to represent it as something else prove nothing but the vain talkativeness of those who make those attempts. Nor can the hypothesis of mere similarity being cognised account for ordinary empirical life and thought; for (in recognising a thing) we are conscious of it being that which we were formerly conscious of, not of it being merely similar to that. We admit that sometimes with regard to an external thing a doubt may arise whether it is that or merely is similar to that; for mistakes may be made concerning what lies outside our minds. But the conscious subject never has any doubt whether it is itself or only similar to itself; it rather is distinctly conscious that it is one and the same subject which yesterday had a certain sensation and to-day remembers that sensation.—For this reason also the doctrine of the Nihilists is to be rejected.

26. (Entity) does not spring from non-entity on account of that not being observed.

The system of the Vainâsikas is objectionable for this reason also that those who deny the existence of permanent stable causes are driven to maintain that entity springs from non-entity. This latter tenet is expressly enunciated by the Bauddhas where they say, 'On account of the manifestation (of effects) not without previous destruction (of the cause).' For, they say, from the decomposed seed only the young plant springs, spoilt milk only turns into curds, and the lump of clay has ceased to be a lump when it becomes a jar. If effects did spring from the unchanged causes, all effects would originate from all causes at once, as then no specification would be required[1]. Hence, as we see that young plants, &c. spring from seeds, &c. only after the latter have been merged in non-existence, we hold that entity springs from non-entity.

To this Bauddha tenet we reply, ('Entity does) not (spring) from non-entity, on account of that not being observed.' If entity did spring from non-entity, the assumption of special causes would be purportless, since non-entity is in all cases one and the same. For the non-existence of seeds and the like after they have been destroyed is of the same kind as the non-existence of horns of hares and the like, i. e. non-existence is in all cases nothing else but the absence of all character of reality, and hence there would be no sense (on the doctrine of origination from non-existence) in assuming that sprouts are produced from seeds only, curds from milk only, and so on. And if non-distinguished non-existence were admitted to have causal efficiency, we should also have to assume that sprouts, &c. originate from the horns of hares, &c.—a thing certainly not actually observed.—If, again, it should be assumed that there are different kinds of non-existence having special distinctions—just as, for instance, blueness and the like are special qualities of lotuses and so on—we point out that in that case the fact of there being such special distinctions would turn the non-entities into entities no less real than lotuses and the like. In no case non-existence would possess causal efficiency, simply because, like the horn of a hare, it is non-existence merely.—Further, if existence sprang from non-existence, all effects would be affected with non-existence; while as a matter of fact they are observed to be merely positive entities distinguished by their various special characteristics. Nor[2] does any one

[1] If the cause were able, without having undergone any change, to produce effects, it would at the same moment produce all the effects of which it is capable.—Cp. on this point the Sarvadar*s*a*n*a-sa*m*graha.

[2] This is added to obviate the remark that it is not a general rule that effects are of the same nature as their causes, and that therefore, after all, existent things may spring from non-existence.

think that things of the nature of clay, such as pots and the like, are the effects of threads and the like; but everybody knows that things of the nature of clay are the effects of clay only.—The Bauddha's tenet that nothing can become a cause as long as it remains unchanged, but has to that end to undergo destruction, and that thus existence springs from non-existence only is false; for it is observed that only things of permanent nature which are always recognised as what they are, such as gold, &c., are the causes of effects such as golden ornaments, and so on. In those cases where a destruction of the peculiar nature of the cause is observed to take place, as in the case of seeds, for instance, we have to acknowledge as the cause of the subsequent condition (i.e. the sprout) not the earlier condition in so far as it is destroyed, but rather those permanent particles of the seed which are not destroyed (when the seed as a whole undergoes decomposition).—Hence as we see on the one hand that no entities ever originate from non-entities such as the horns of a hare, and on the other hand that entities do originate from entities such as gold and the like, the whole Bauddha doctrine of existence springing from non-existence has to be rejected.—We finally point out that, according to the Bauddhas, all mind and all mental modifications spring from the four skandhas discussed above and all material aggregates from the atoms; why then do they stultify this their own doctrine by the fanciful assumption of entity springing from non-entity and thus needlessly perplex the mind of every one?

27. And thus (on that doctrine) there would be an accomplishment (of ends) in the case of non-active people also.

If it were admitted that entity issues from non-entity, lazy inactive people also would obtain their purposes, since 'non-existence' is a thing to be had without much trouble. Rice would grow for the husbandman even if he did not cultivate his field; vessels would shape themselves even if the potter did not fashion the clay; and the weaver too lazy to weave the threads into a whole, would nevertheless have in the end finished pieces of cloth just as if he had been weaving. And nobody would have to exert himself in the least either for going to the heavenly world or for obtaining final release. All which of course is absurd and not maintained by anybody.—Thus the doctrine of the origination of entity from non-entity again shows itself to be futile.

28. The non-existence (of external things) cannot be maintained, on account of (our) consciousness (of them).

There having been brought forward, in what precedes, the various objections which lie against the doctrine of the reality of the external world (in the Bauddha sense), such as the impossibility of accounting for the existence of aggregates, &c., we are now confronted by those Bauddhas who maintain that only cognitions (or ideas, vi*gñ*âna) exist.—The doctrine of the reality of the external world was indeed propounded by Buddha conforming himself to the mental state of some of his disciples whom he perceived to be attached to external things; but it does not represent his own true view according to which cognitions alone are real.

According to this latter doctrine the process, whose constituting members are the act of knowledge, the object of knowledge, and the result of knowledge[1], is an altogether internal one, existing in so far only as it is connected with the mind (buddhi). Even if external things existed, that process could not take place but in connexion with the mind. If, the Bauddhas say, you ask how it is known that that entire process is internal and that no outward things exist apart from consciousness, we reply that we base our

[1] According to the vi*gñ*ânavâdin the cognition specialised by its various contents, such as, for instance, the idea of blue colour is the object of knowledge; the cognition in so far as it is consciousness (avabhâsa) is the result of knowledge; the cognition in so far as it is power is mâna, knowledge; in so far as it is the abode of that power it is pramât*ri*, knowing subject.

doctrine on the impossibility of external things. For if external things are admitted, they must be either atoms or aggregates of atoms such as posts and the like. But atoms cannot be comprehended under the ideas of posts and the like, it being impossible for cognition to represent (things as minute as) atoms. Nor, again, can the outward things be aggregates of atoms such as pillars and the like, because those aggregates can neither be defined as different nor as non-different from the atoms[1].—In the same way we can show that the external things are not universals and so on[2].

Moreover, the cognitions—which are of a uniform nature only in so far as they are states of consciousness—undergo, according to their objects, successive modifications, so that there is presented to the mind now the idea of a post, now the idea of a wall, now the idea of a jar, and so on. Now this is not possible without some distinction on the part of the ideas themselves, and hence we must necessarily admit that the ideas have the same forms as their objects. But if we make this admission, from which it follows that the form of the objects is determined by the ideas, the hypothesis of the existence of external things becomes altogether gratuitous. From the fact, moreover, of our always being conscious of the act of knowledge and the object of knowledge simultaneously it follows that the two are in reality identical. When we are conscious of the one we are conscious of the other also; and that would not happen if the two were essentially distinct, as in that case there would be nothing to prevent our being conscious of one apart from the other. For this reason also we maintain that there are no outward things.—

---

[1] If they are said to be different from the atoms they can no longer be considered as composed of atoms; if they are non-different from atoms they cannot be the cause of the mental representations of gross non-atomic bodies.

[2] Avayavâvayavirûpo vâhyo-rtho nâsti *k*en mâ bhûd *g*âtivyaktyâdirûpas tu syâd ity âsa*n*kyâha evam iti. *G*âtyâdînâ*m* vyaktyâdinâm *k*âtyantabhinnatve svâtantryaprasaṅgâd atyantâbhinnatve tadvadevâtadbhâvâd bhinnâbhinnatvasya viruddhatvâd avayavâvayavibhedava*g* gâtivyaktyâdibhedo-pi nâstîty artha*h*.

Perception is to be considered as similar to a dream and the like. The ideas present to our minds during a dream, a magical illusion, a mirage and so on, appear in the twofold form of subject and object, although there is all the while no external object; hence we conclude that the ideas of posts and the like which occur in our waking state are likewise independent of external objects; for they also are simply ideas.—If we be asked how, in the absence of external things, we account for the actual variety of ideas, we reply that that variety is to be explained from the impressions left by previous ideas [1]. In the beginningless sa*m*sâra ideas and mental impressions succeed each other as causes and effects, just as the plant springs from the seed and seeds are again produced from the plant, and there exists therefore a sufficient reason for the variety of ideas actually experienced. That the variety of ideas is solely due to the impressions left on the mind by past ideas follows, moreover, from the following affirmative and negative judgments: we both (the Vedântins as well as the Bauddhas) admit that in dreams, &c. there presents itself a variety of ideas which arise from mental impressions, without any external object; we (the Bauddhas) do not admit that any variety of ideas can arise from external objects, without mental impressions.—Thus we are again led to conclude that no outward things exist.

To all this we (the Vedântins) make the following reply.—The non-existence of external things cannot be maintained because we are conscious of external things. In every act of perception we are conscious of some external thing corresponding to the idea, whether it be a post or a wall or a piece of cloth or a jar, and that of which we are conscious cannot but exist. Why should we pay attention to the words of a man who, while conscious of an outward thing through its approximation to his senses, affirms that he is conscious of no outward thing, and that no such thing exists,

[1] Vâsanâ, above translated by mental impression, strictly means any member of the infinite series of ideas which precedes the present actual idea.

any more than we listen to a man who while he is eating and experiencing the feeling of satisfaction avers that he does not eat and does not feel satisfied?—If the Bauddha should reply that he does not affirm that he is conscious of no object but only that he is conscious of no object apart from the act of consciousness, we answer that he may indeed make any arbitrary statement he likes, but that he has no arguments to prove what he says. That the outward thing exists apart from consciousness, has necessarily to be accepted on the ground of the nature of consciousness itself. Nobody when perceiving a post or a wall is conscious of his perception only, but all men are conscious of posts and walls and the like as objects of their perceptions. That such is the consciousness of all men, appears also from the fact that even those who contest the existence of external things bear witness to their existence when they say that what is an internal object of cognition appears like something external. For they practically accept the general consciousness which testifies to the existence of an external world, and being at the same time anxious to refute it they speak of the external things as 'like something external.' If they did not themselves at the bottom acknowledge the existence of the external world, how could they use the expression 'like something external?' No one says, 'Vishnumitra appears like the son of a barren mother.' If we accept the truth as it is given to us in our consciousness, we must admit that the object of perception appears to us as something external, not like something external.—But—the Bauddha may reply—we conclude that the object of perception is only like something external because external things are impossible.—This conclusion we rejoin is improper, since the possibility or impossibility of things is to be determined only on the ground of the operation or non-operation of the means of right knowledge; while, on the other hand, the operation and non-operation of the means of right knowledge are not to be made dependent on preconceived possibilities or impossibilities. Possible is whatever is apprehended by perception or some other means of proof; impossible is what is not so apprehended. Now the external things are, according to their nature, apprehended by all the instruments of knowledge; how then can you maintain that they are not possible, on the ground of such idle dilemmas as that about their difference or non-difference from atoms?—Nor, again, does the non-existence of objects follow from the fact of the ideas having the same form as the objects; for if there were no objects the ideas could not have the forms of the objects, and the objects are actually apprehended as external.—For the same reason (i. e. because the distinction of thing and idea is given in consciousness) the invariable concomitance of idea and thing has to be considered as proving only that the thing constitutes the means of the idea, not that the two are identical. Moreover, when we are conscious first of a pot and then of a piece of cloth, consciousness remains the same in the two acts while what varies are merely the distinctive attributes of consciousness; just as when we see at first a black and then a white cow, the distinction of the two perceptions is due to the varying blackness and whiteness while the generic character of the cow remains the same. The difference of the one permanent factor (from the two—or more—varying factors) is proved throughout by the two varying factors, and vice versâ the difference of the latter (from the permanent factor) by the presence of the one (permanent factor). Therefore thing and idea are distinct. The same view is to be held with regard to the perception and the remembrance of a jar; there also the perception and the remembrance only are distinct while the jar is one and the same; in the same way as when conscious of the smell of milk and the taste of milk we are conscious of the smell and taste as different things but of the milk itself as one only.

Further, two ideas which occupy different moments of time and pass away as soon as they have become objects of consciousness cannot apprehend—or be apprehended by—each other. From this it follows that certain doctrines forming part of the Bauddha system cannot be upheld; so the doctrine that ideas are different from each other; the doctrine that everything is momentary, void, &c.; the doctrine of the distinction of individuals and classes; the doctrine that a former idea leaves an impression giving rise to a later idea; the doctrine of the distinction, owing to the influence of Nescience, of the attributes of existence and non-existence; the doctrine of bondage and release (depending on absence and presence of right knowledge)[1].

Further, if you say that we are conscious of the idea, you must admit that we are also conscious of the external thing. And if you rejoin that we are conscious of the idea on its own account because it is of a luminous nature like a lamp, while the external thing is not so; we reply that by maintaining the idea to be illuminated by itself you make yourself guilty of an absurdity no less than if you said that fire burns itself. And at the same time you refuse to accept the common and altogether rational opinion that we are conscious of the external thing by means of the idea different from the thing! Indeed a proof of extraordinary philosophic insight!—It cannot, moreover, be asserted in any way that the idea apart from the thing is the object of our consciousness; for it is absurd to speak of a thing as the object of its own activity. Possibly you (the Bauddha) will rejoin that, if the idea is to be apprehended by something different from it, that something also must be apprehended by something different and so on ad infinitum. And, moreover, you will perhaps object that as each cognition is of an essentially illuminating nature like a lamp, the assumption of a further cognition is uncalled for; for as they are both equally illuminating the one cannot give light to the other.—But both these objections are unfounded. As the idea only is apprehended, and there is consequently no necessity to assume something to apprehend the Self which witnesses the idea (is conscious of the idea), there results no regressus ad infinitum. And the witnessing Self and the idea are of an essentially different nature, and may therefore stand to each other in the relation of knowing subject and object known. The existence of the witness-

[1] For all these doctrines depend on the comparison of ideas which is not possible unless there be a permanent knowing subject in addition to the transitory ideas.

ing Self is self-proved and cannot therefore be denied.—Moreover, if you maintain that the idea, lamplike, manifests itself without standing in need of a further principle to illuminate it, you maintain thereby that ideas exist which are not apprehended by any of the means of knowledge, and which are without a knowing being; which is no better than to assert that a thousand lamps burning inside some impenetrable mass of rocks manifest themselves. And if you should maintain that thereby we admit your doctrine, since it follows from what we have said that the idea itself implies consciousness; we reply that, as observation shows, the lamp in order to become manifest requires some other intellectual agent furnished with instruments such as the eye, and that therefore the idea also, as equally being a thing to be illuminated, becomes manifest only through an ulterior intelligent principle. And if you finally object that we, when advancing the witnessing Self as self-proved, merely express in other words the Bauddha tenet that the idea is self-manifested, we refute you by remarking that your ideas have the attributes of originating, passing away, being manifold, and so on (while our Self is one and permanent).—We thus have proved that an idea, like a lamp, requires an ulterior intelligent principle to render it manifest.

29. And on account of their difference of nature (the ideas of the waking state) are not like those of a dream.

We now apply ourselves to the refutation of the averment made by the Bauddha, that the ideas of posts, and so on, of which we are conscious in the waking state, may arise in the absence of external objects, just as the ideas of a dream, both being ideas alike.—The two sets of ideas, we maintain, cannot be treated on the same footing, on account of the difference of their character. They differ as follows.—The things of which we are conscious in a dream are negated by our waking consciousness. 'I wrongly thought that I had a meeting with a great man; no such meeting took place, but my mind was dulled by slumber, and so the false idea arose.' In an analogous manner the things of which we are conscious when under the influence of a magic illusion, and the like, are negated by our ordinary consciousness. Those things, on the other hand, of which we are conscious in our waking state, such as posts and the like, are never negated in any state.—Moreover, the visions of a dream are acts of remembrance, while the visions of the waking state are acts of immediate consciousness; and the distinction between remembrance and immediate consciousness is directly cognised by every one as being founded on the absence or presence of the object. When, for instance, a man remembers his absent son, he does not directly perceive him, but merely wishes so to perceive him. As thus the distinction between the two states is evident to every one, it is impossible to formulate the inference that waking consciousness is false because it is mere consciousness, such as dreaming consciousness; for we certainly cannot allow would-be philosophers to deny the truth of what is directly evident to themselves. Just because they feel the absurdity of denying what is evident to themselves, and are consequently unable to demonstrate the baselessness of the ideas of the waking state from those ideas themselves, they attempt to demonstrate it from their having certain attributes in common with the ideas of the dreaming state. But if some attribute cannot belong to a thing on account of the latter's own nature, it cannot belong to it on account of the thing having certain attributes in common with some other thing. Fire, which is felt to be hot, cannot be demonstrated to be cold, on the ground of its having attributes in common with water. And the difference of nature between the waking and the sleeping state we have already shown.

30. The existence (of mental impressions) is not possible (on the Bauddha view) on account of the absence of perception (of external things).

We now proceed to that theory of yours, according to which the variety of ideas can be explained from the variety of mental impressions, without any reference to external things, and remark that on your doctrine the existence of mental impressions is impossible, as you do not admit the perception of external things. For the variety of mental impressions is caused altogether by the variety of the things perceived. How, indeed, could various impressions originate if no external things were perceived? The hypothesis of a beginningless series of mental impressions would lead only to a baseless regressus ad infinitum, sublative of the entire phenomenal world, and would in no way establish your position.—The same argument, i. e. the one founded on the impossibility of mental impressions which are not caused by external things, refutes also the positive and negative judgments, on the ground of which the denier of an external world above attempted to show that ideas are caused by mental impressions, not by external things. We rather have on our side a positive and a negative judgment whereby to establish our doctrine of the existence of external things, viz. 'the perception of external things is admitted to take place also without mental impressions,' and 'mental impressions are not admitted to originate independently of the perception of external things.'—Moreover, an impression is a kind of modification, and modifications cannot, as experience teaches, take place unless there is some substratum which is modified. But, according to your doctrine, such a substratum of impressions does not exist, since you say that it cannot be cognised through any means of knowledge.

31. And on account of the momentariness (of the âlayavig*ñ*âna, it cannot be the abode of mental impressions).

If you maintain that the so-called internal cognition (âlayavig*ñ*âna[1]) assumed by you may constitute the abode

[1] The vig*ñ*ânaskandha comprises vig*ñ*ânas of two different kinds, the âlayavig*ñ*âna and the pravr*i*ttivig*ñ*âna. The âlayavig*ñ*âna comprises the series of cognitions or ideas which refer to the ego; the pravr*i*ttivig*ñ*âna comprises those ideas which refer to apparently external objects, such as colour and the like. The ideas of the

of the mental impressions, we deny that, because that cognition also being admittedly momentary, and hence non-permanent, cannot be the abode of impressions any more than the quasi-external cognitions (pravr*i*tti-vig*ñ*âna). For unless there exists one continuous principle equally connected with the past, the present, and the future[1], or an absolutely unchangeable (Self) which cognises everything, we are unable to account for remembrance, recognition, and so on, which are subject to mental impressions dependent on place, time, and cause. If, on the other hand, you declare your âlayavig*ñ*âna to be something permanent, you thereby abandon your tenet of the âlayavig*ñ*âna as well as everything else being momentary.—Or (to explain the Sûtra in a different way) as the tenet of general momentariness is characteristic of the systems of the idealistic as well as the realistic Bauddhas, we may bring forward against the doctrines of the former all those arguments dependent on the principle of general momentariness which we have above urged against the latter.

We have thus refuted both nihilistic doctrines, viz. the doctrine which maintains the (momentary) reality of the external world, and the doctrine which asserts that ideas only exist. The third variety of Bauddha doctrine, viz. that everything is empty (i. e. that absolutely nothing exists), is contradicted by all means of right knowledge, and therefore requires no special refutation. For this apparent world, whose existence is guaranteed by all the means of knowledge, cannot be denied, unless some one should find out some new truth (based on which he could impugn its existence)—for a general principle is proved by the absence of contrary instances.

32. And on account of its general deficiency in probability.

No further special discussion is in fact required. From

latter class are due to the mental impressions left by the antecedent ideas of the former class.

[1] Viz. in the present case the principle that what presents itself to consciousness is not non-existent.

whatever new points of view the Bauddha system is tested with reference to its probability, it gives way on all sides, like the walls of a well dug in sandy soil. It has, in fact, no foundation whatever to rest upon, and hence the attempts to use it as a guide in the practical concerns of life are mere folly. —Moreover, Buddha by propounding the three mutually contradictory systems, teaching respectively the reality of the external world, the reality of ideas only, and general nothingness, has himself made it clear either that he was a man given to make incoherent assertions, or else that hatred of all beings induced him to propound absurd doctrines by accepting which they would become thoroughly confused.—So that—and this the Sûtra means to indicate—Buddha's doctrine has to be entirely disregarded by all those who have a regard for their own happiness.

33. On account of the impossibility (of contradictory attributes) in one thing, (the *G*aina doctrine is) not (to be accepted).

Having disposed of the Bauddha doctrine we now turn to the system of the Gymnosophists (*G*ainas).

The *G*ainas acknowledge seven categories (tattvas), viz. soul (*g*îva), non-soul (a*g*îva), the issuing outward (âsrava), restraint (sa*m*vara), destruction (nir*g*ara), bondage (bandha), and release (moksha)[1]. Shortly it may be said that they acknowledge two categories, viz. soul and non-soul, since the five other categories may be subsumed under these two. —They also set forth a set of categories different from the two mentioned. They teach that there are five so-called

[1] Soul and non-soul are the enjoying souls and the objects of their enjoyment; âsrava is the forward movement of the senses towards their objects; sa*m*vara is the restraint of the activity of the senses; nir*g*ara is self-mortification by which sin is destroyed; the works constitute bondage; and release is the ascending of the soul, after bondage has ceased, to the highest regions.—For the details, see Professor Cowell's translation of the Ârhata chapter of the Sarvadarsa*n*asa*m*graha.

astikâyas ('existing bodies,' i.e. categories), viz. the categories of soul (*g*îva), body (pudgala), merit (dharma), demerit (adharma), and space (âkâ*s*a). All these categories they again subdivide in various fanciful ways[1].—To all things they apply the following method of reasoning, which they call the saptabhaṅgînaya: somehow it is; somehow it is not; somehow it is and is not; somehow it is indescribable; somehow it is and is indescribable; somehow it is not and is indescribable; somehow it is and is not and is indescribable.

To this unsettling style of reasoning they submit even such conceptions as that of unity and eternity[2].

This doctrine we meet as follows.—Your reasoning, we say, is inadmissible 'on account of the impossibility in one thing.' That is to say, it is impossible that contradictory attributes such as being and non-being should at the same time belong to one and the same thing; just as observation teaches us that a thing cannot be hot and cold at the same moment. The seven categories asserted by you must either be so many and such or not be so many and such; the third alternative expressed in the words 'they either are such or not such' results in a cognition of indefinite nature which is no more a source of true knowledge than doubt is. If you should plead that the cognition that a thing is of more than one nature is definite and therefore a source of true knowledge, we deny this. For the unlimited assertion that all things are of a non-exclusive nature is itself something, falls as such under the alternative predications 'somehow it is,' 'somehow it is not,' and so ceases to be a definite assertion. The same happens to the person making the assertion and to the result of the assertion; partly they are, partly they are not. As thus the means of knowledge, the object of knowledge, the knowing subject, and the act of knowledge are all alike indefinite, how can the Tîrthakara (*G*ina) teach with any claim to authority, and how can his followers act on a doctrine the matter of which is altogether

[1] Cp. translation of Sarvadar*s*a*n*asa*m*graha, p. 59.

[2] And so impugn the doctrine of the one eternal Brahman.

indeterminate? Observation shows that only when a course of action is known to have a definite result people set about it without hesitation. Hence a man who proclaims a doctrine of altogether indefinite contents does not deserve to be listened to any more than a drunken man or a madman.—Again, if we apply the *G*aina reasoning to their doctrine of the five categories, we have to say that on one view of the matter they are five and on another view they are not five; from which latter point of view it follows that they are either fewer or more than five. Nor is it logical to declare the categories to be indescribable. For if they are so, they cannot be described; but, as a matter of fact, they are described so that to call them indescribable involves a contradiction. And if you go on to say that the categories on being described are ascertained to be such and such, and at the same time are not ascertained to be such and such, and that the result of their being ascertained is perfect knowledge or is not perfect knowledge, and that imperfect knowledge is the opposite of perfect knowledge or is not the opposite; you certainly talk more like a drunken or insane man than like a sober, trustworthy person.—If you further maintain that the heavenly world and final release exist or do not exist and are eternal or non-eternal, the absence of all determinate knowledge which is implied in such statements will result in nobody's acting for the purpose of gaining the heavenly world and final release. And, moreover, it follows from your doctrine that soul, non-soul, and so on, whose nature you claim to have ascertained, and which you describe as having existed from all eternity, relapse all at once into the condition of absolute indetermination.—As therefore the two contradictory attributes of being and non-being cannot belong to any of the categories—being excluding non-being and vice versâ non-being excluding being—the doctrine of the Arhat must be rejected.—The above remarks dispose likewise of the assertions made by the *G*ainas as to the impossibility of deciding whether of one thing there is to be predicated oneness or plurality, permanency or non-permanency, separateness or non-separateness, and so on.—The *G*aina doctrine that aggregates are formed from the atoms—by them called pudgalas—we do not undertake to refute separately as its refutation is already comprised in that of the atomistic doctrine given in a previous part of this work.

34. And likewise (there results from the *G*aina doctrine) non-universality of the Self.

We have hitherto urged against the *G*aina doctrine an objection resulting from the syâdvâda, viz. that one thing cannot have contradictory attributes. We now turn to the objection that from their doctrine it would follow that the individual Self is not universal, i.e. not omnipresent.—The *G*ainas are of opinion that the soul has the same size as the body. From this it would follow that the soul is not of infinite extension, but limited, and hence non-eternal like jars and similar things. Further, as the bodies of different classes of creatures are of different size, it might happen that the soul of a man—which is of the size of the human body—when entering, in consequence of its former deeds, on a new state of existence in the body of an elephant would not be able to fill the whole of it; or else that a human soul being relegated to the body of an ant would not be able to find sufficient room in it. The same difficulty would, moreover, arise with regard to the successive stages of one state of existence, infancy, youth, and old age.—But why, the *G*aina may ask, should we not look upon the soul as consisting of an infinite number of parts capable of undergoing compression in a small body and dilatation in a big one?—Do you, we ask in return, admit or not admit that those countless particles of the soul may occupy the same place or not?—If you do not admit it, it follows that the infinite number of particles cannot be contained in a body of limited dimensions.—If you do admit it, it follows that, as then the space occupied by all the particles may be the space of one particle only, the extension of all the particles together will remain inconsiderable, and hence the soul be of minute size (not of the size of the body). You have, moreover, no right to assume that a body of limited size contains an infinite number of soul particles.

Well then, the *G*aina may reply, let us assume that by turns whenever the soul enters a big body some particles accede to it while some withdraw from it whenever it enters a small body.—To this hypothesis the next Sûtra furnishes a reply.

35. Nor is non-contradiction to be derived from the succession (of parts acceding to and departing from the soul), on account of the change, &c. (of the soul).

Nor can the doctrine of the soul having the same size as the body be satisfactorily established by means of the hypothesis of the successive accession and withdrawal of particles. For this hypothesis would involve the soul's undergoing changes and the like. If the soul is continually being repleted and depleted by the successive addition and withdrawal of parts, it of course follows that it undergoes change, and if it is liable to change it follows that it is non-permanent, like the skin and similar substances. From that, again, it follows that the *G*aina doctrine of bondage and release is untenable; according to which doctrine 'the soul, which in the state of bondage is encompassed by the ogdoad of works and sunk in the ocean of sa*m*sâra, rises when its bonds are sundered, as the gourd rises to the surface of the water when it is freed from the encumbering clay[1].'—Moreover, those particles which in turns come and depart have the attributes of coming and going, and cannot, on that account, be of the nature of the Self any more than the body is. And if it be said that the Self consists of some permanently remaining parts, we remark that it would be impossible to determine which are the permanent and which the temporary parts.—We have further to ask from whence those particles originate when they accede to the soul, and into what they are merged when they detach themselves from it. They cannot spring from the material elements

[1] Cp. Sarvadar*s*a*n*asa*m*graha translation, p. 58.

and re-enter the elements; for the soul is immaterial. Nor have we any means to prove the existence of some other, general or special, reservoir of soul-particles.—Moreover, on the hypothesis under discussion the soul would be of indefinite nature, as the size of the particles acceding and departing is itself indefinite.—On account of all these and similar difficulties it cannot be maintained that certain particles by turns attach themselves to, and detach themselves from, the soul.

The Sûtra may be taken in a different sense also. The preceding Sûtra has proved that the soul if of the same size as the body cannot be permanent, as its entering into bigger and smaller bodies involves its limitation. To this the Gymnosophist may be supposed to rejoin that although the soul's size successively changes it may yet be permanent, just as the stream of water is permanent (although the water continually changes). An analogous instance would be supplied by the permanency of the stream of ideas while the individual ideas, as that of a red cloth and so on, are non-permanent.—To this rejoinder our Sûtra replies that if the stream is not real we are led back to the doctrine of a general void, and that, if it is something real, the difficulties connected with the soul's changing, &c. present themselves and render the *G*aina view impossible.

36. And on account of the permanency of the final (size of the soul) and the resulting permanency of the two (preceding sizes) there is no difference (of size, at any time).

Moreover, the *G*ainas themselves admit the permanency of the final size of the soul which it has in the state of release. From this it follows also that its initial size and its intervening sizes must be permanent[1], and that hence

[1] The inference being that the initial and intervening sizes of the soul must be permanent because they are sizes of the soul, like its final size.

there is no difference between the three sizes. But this would involve the conclusion that the different bodies of the soul have one and the same size, and that the soul cannot enter into bigger and smaller bodies.—Or else (to explain the Sûtra in a somewhat different way) from the fact that the final size of the soul is permanent, it follows that its size in the two previous conditions also is permanent. Hence the soul must be considered as being always of the same size—whether minute or infinite—and not of the varying size of its bodies.—For this reason also the doctrine of the Arhat has to be set aside as not in any way more rational than the doctrine of Buddha.

37. The Lord (cannot be the cause of the world), on account of the inappropriateness (of that doctrine).

The Sûtrakâra now applies himself to the refutation of that doctrine, according to which the Lord is the cause of the world only in so far as he is the general ruler.—But how do you know that that is the purport of the Sûtra (which speaks of the Lord 'without any qualification')?—From the circumstance, we reply, that the teacher himself has proved, in the previous sections of the work, that the Lord is the material cause as well as the ruler of the world. Hence, if the present Sûtra were meant to impugn the doctrine of the Lord in general, the earlier and later parts of the work would be mutually contradictory, and the Sûtrakâra would thus be in conflict with himself. We therefore must assume that the purport of the present Sûtra is to make an energetic attack on the doctrine of those who maintain that the Lord is not the material cause, but merely the ruler, i.e. the operative cause of the world; a doctrine entirely opposed to the Vedântic tenet of the unity of Brahman.

The theories about the Lord which are independent of the Vedânta are of various nature. Some taking their stand on the Sâṅkhya and Yoga systems assume that the Lord acts as a mere operative cause, as the ruler of the pradhâna and of the souls, and that pradhâna, soul, and Lord are of mutually different nature.—The Mâhesvaras (Saivas) maintain that the five categories, viz. effect, cause, union, ritual, the end of pain, were taught by the Lord Pasupati (Siva) to the end of breaking the bonds of the animal (i.e. the soul); Pasupati is, according to them, the Lord, the operative cause.—Similarly, the Vaiseshikas and others also teach, according to their various systems, that the Lord is somehow the operative cause of the world.

Against all these opinions the Sûtra remarks 'the Lord. on account of the inappropriateness.' I.e. it is not possible that the Lord as the ruler of the pradhâna and the soul should be the cause of the world, on account of the inappropriateness of that doctrine. For if the Lord is supposed to assign to the various classes of animate creatures low, intermediate, and high positions, according to his liking, it follows that he is animated by hatred, passion, and so on, is hence like one of us, and is no real Lord. Nor can we get over this difficulty by assuming that he makes his dispositions with a view to the merit and demerit of the living beings; for that assumption would lead us to a logical see-saw, the Lord as well as the works of living beings having to be considered in turns both as acting and as acted upon. This difficulty is not removed by the consideration that the works of living beings and the resulting dispositions made by the Lord form a chain which has no beginning; for in past time as well as in the present mutual interdependence of the two took place, so that the beginningless series is like an endless chain of blind men leading other blind men. It is, moreover, a tenet set forth by the Naiyâyikas themselves that 'imperfections have the characteristic of being the causes of action' (Nyâya Sûtra I, 1, 18). Experience shows that all agents, whether they be active for their own purposes or for the purposes of something else, are impelled to action by some imperfection. And even if it is admitted that an agent even when acting for some extrinsic purpose is impelled by an intrinsic motive, your doctrine remains faulty all the same; for the

Lord is no longer a Lord, even if he is actuated by intrinsic motives only (such as the desire of removing the painful feeling connected with pity).—Your doctrine is finally inappropriate for that reason also that you maintain the Lord to be a special kind of soul; for from that it follows that he must be devoid of all activity.

38. And on account of the impossibility of the connexion (of the Lord with the souls and the pradhâna).

Against the doctrine which we are at present discussing there lies the further objection that a Lord distinct from the pradhâna and the souls cannot be the ruler of the latter without being connected with them in a certain way. But of what nature is that connexion to be? It cannot be conjunction (sa*m*yoga), because the Lord, as well as the pradhâna and the souls, is of infinite extent and devoid of parts. Nor can it be inherence, since it would be impossible to define who should be the abode and who the abiding thing. Nor is it possible to assume some other connexion, the special nature of which would have to be inferred from the effect, because the relation of cause and effect is just what is not settled as yet[1].—How, then, it may be asked, do you—the Vedântins—establish the relation of cause and effect (between the Lord and the world)?—There is, we reply, no difficulty in our case, as the connexion we assume is that of identity (tâdâtmya). The adherent of Brahman, moreover, defines the nature of the cause, and so on, on the basis of Scripture, and is therefore not obliged to render his tenets throughout conformable to observation. Our adversary, on the other hand, who defines the nature of the cause and the like according to instances furnished by experience,

[1] The special nature of the connexion between the Lord and the pradhâna and the souls cannot be ascertained from the world considered as the effect of the pradhâna acted upon by the Lord; for that the world is the effect of the pradhâna is a point which the Vedântins do not accept as proved.

may be expected to maintain only such doctrines as agree with experience. Nor can he put forward the claim that Scripture, because it is the production of the omniscient Lord, may be used to confirm his doctrine as well as that of the Vedântin; for that would involve him in a logical see-saw, the omniscience of the Lord being established on the doctrine of Scripture, and the authority of Scripture again being established on the omniscience of the Lord.—For all these reasons the Sâṅkhya-yoga hypothesis about the Lord is devoid of foundation. Other similar hypotheses which likewise are not based on the Veda are to be refuted by corresponding arguments.

39. And on account of the impossibility of rulership (on the part of the Lord).

The Lord of the argumentative philosophers is an untenable hypothesis, for the following reason also.—Those philosophers are obliged to assume that by his influence the Lord produces action in the pradhâna, &c. just as the potter produces motion in the clay, &c. But this cannot be admitted; for the pradhâna, which is devoid of colour and other qualities, and therefore not an object of perception, is on that account of an altogether different nature from clay and the like, and hence cannot be looked upon as the object of the Lord's action.

40. If you say that as the organs (are ruled by the soul so the pradhâna is ruled by the Lord), we deny that on account of the enjoyment, &c.

Well, the opponent might reply, let us suppose that the Lord rules the pradhâna in the same way as the soul rules the organ of sight and the other organs which are devoid of colour, and so on, and hence not objects of perception.

This analogy also, we reply, proves nothing. For we infer that the organs are ruled by the soul, from the observed fact that the soul feels pleasure, pain, and the like (which affect the soul through the organs). But we do not observe that the Lord experiences pleasure, pain, &c. caused by the pradhâna. If the analogy between the pradhâna and the bodily organs were a complete one, it would follow that the Lord is affected by pleasure and pain no less than the transmigrating souls are.

Or else the two preceding Sûtras may be explained in a different way. Ordinary experience teaches us that kings, who are the rulers of countries, are never without some material abode, i. e. a body; hence, if we wish to infer the existence of a general Lord from the analogy of earthly rulers, we must ascribe to him also some kind of body to serve as the substratum of his organs. But such a body cannot be ascribed to the Lord, since all bodies exist only subsequently to the creation, not previously to it. The Lord, therefore, is not able to act because devoid of a material substratum; for experience teaches us that action requires a material substrate.—Let us then arbitrarily assume that the Lord possesses some kind of body serving as a substratum for his organs (even previously to creation).—This assumption also will not do; for if the Lord has a body he is subject to the sensations of ordinary transmigratory souls, and thus no longer is the Lord.

41. And (there would follow from that doctrine) either finite duration or absence of omniscience (on the Lord's part).

The hypothesis of the argumentative philosophers is invalid, for the following reason also.—They teach that the Lord is omniscient and of infinite duration, and likewise that the pradhâna, as well as the individual souls, is of infinite duration. Now, the omniscient Lord either defines the measure of the pradhâna, the souls, and himself, or does not define it. Both alternatives subvert the doctrine under discussion. For, on the former alternative, the pradhâna, the souls, and the Lord, being all of them of definite measure, must necessarily be of finite duration; since ordinary experience teaches that all things of definite extent, such as jars and the like, at some time cease to exist. The numerical measure of pradhâna, souls, and Lord is defined by their constituting a triad, and the individual measure of each of them must likewise be considered as defined by the Lord (because he is omniscient). The number of the souls is a high one [1]. From among this limited number of souls some obtain release from the sa*m*sâra, that means their sa*m*sâra comes to an end, and their subjection to the sa*m*sâra comes to an end. Gradually all souls obtain release, and so there will finally be an end of the entire sa*m*sâra and the sa*m*sâra state of all souls. But the pradhâna which is ruled by the Lord and which modifies itself for the purposes of the soul is what is meant by sa*m*sâra. Hence, when the latter no longer exists, nothing is left for the Lord to rule, and his omniscience and ruling power have no longer any objects. But if the pradhâna, the souls, and the Lord, all have an end, it follows that they also have a beginning, and if they have a beginning as well as an end, we are driven to the doctrine of a general void.—Let us then, in order to avoid these untoward conclusions, maintain the second alternative, i. e. that the measure of the Lord himself, the pradhâna, and the souls, is not defined by the Lord.—But that also is impossible, because it would compel us to abandon a tenet granted at the outset, viz. that the Lord is omniscient.

For all these reasons the doctrine of the argumentative philosophers, according to which the Lord is the operative cause of the world, appears unacceptable.

42. On account of the impossibility of the origination (of the individual soul from the highest Lord, the doctrine of the Bhâgavatas cannot be accepted).

We have, in what precedes, refuted the opinion of those who think that the Lord is not the material cause but only the ruler, the operative cause of the world. We are now

[1] I.e. a high one, but not an indefinite one; since the omniscient Lord knows its measure.

going to refute the doctrine of those according to whom he is the material as well as the operative cause.—But, it may be objected, in the previous portions of the present work a Lord of exactly the same nature, i. e. a Lord who is the material, as well as the operative, cause of the world, has been ascertained on the basis of Scripture, and it is a recognised principle that Sm*ri*ti, in so far as it agrees with Scripture, is authoritative; why then should we aim at controverting the doctrine stated?—It is true, we reply, that a part of the system which we are going to discuss agrees with the Vedânta system, and hence affords no matter for controversy; another part of the system, however, is open to objection, and that part we intend to attack.

The so-called Bhâgavatas are of opinion that the one holy (bhagavat) Vâsudeva, whose nature is pure knowledge, is what really exists, and that he, dividing himself fourfold, appears in four forms (vyûha), as Vâsudeva, Sankarsha*n*a, Pradyumna, and Aniruddha. Vâsudeva denotes the highest Self, Sankarsha*n*a the individual soul, Pradyumna the mind (manas), Aniruddha the principle of egoity (ahankâra). Of these four Vâsudeva constitutes the ultimate causal essence, of which the three others are the effects.—The believer after having worshipped Vâsudeva for a hundred years by means of approach to the temple (abhigamana), procuring of things to be offered (upâdâna), oblation (îgyâ), recitation of prayers, &c. (svâdhyâya), and devout meditation (yoga), passes beyond all affliction and reaches the highest Being.

Concerning this system we remark that we do not intend to controvert the doctrine that Nârâya*n*a, who is higher than the Undeveloped, who is the highest Self, and the Self of all, reveals himself by dividing himself in multiple ways; for various scriptural passages, such as 'He is onefold, he is threefold' (*Kh*. Up. VII, 26, 2), teach us that the highest Self appears in manifold forms. Nor do we mean to object to the inculcation of unceasing concentration of mind on the highest Being which appears in the Bhâgavata doctrine under the forms of reverential approach,

&c.; for that we are to meditate on the Lord we know full well from Sm*ri*ti and Scripture. We, however, must take exception to the doctrine that Saṅkarsha*n*a springs from Vâsudeva, Pradyumna from Saṅkarsha*n*a, Aniruddha from Pradyumna. It is not possible that from Vâsudeva, i.e. the highest Self, there should originate Saṅkarsha*n*a, i.e. the individual soul; for if such were the case, there would attach to the soul non-permanency, and all the other imperfections which belong to things originated. And thence release, which consists in reaching the highest Being, could not take place; for the effect is absorbed only by entering into its cause.—That the soul is not an originated thing, the teacher will prove later on (II, 3, 17). For this reason the Bhâgavata hypothesis is unacceptable.

43. And (it is) not (observed that) the instrument is produced from the agent.

The Bhâgavata hypothesis is to be rejected for that reason also, that observation never shows us an instrument, such as a hatchet and the like, to spring from an agent such as Devadatta, or any other workman. But the Bhâgavatas teach that from an agent, viz. the individual soul termed Saṅkarsha*n*a, there springs its instrument, viz. the internal organ termed Pradyumna, and again from this offspring of the agent another instrument, viz. the ahaṅkâra termed Aniruddha. Such doctrines cannot be settled without observed instances. And we do not meet with any scriptural passage in their favour.

44. Or (if) in consequence of the existence of knowledge, &c. (Vâsudeva, &c. be taken as Lords), yet there is non-exclusion of that (i.e. the objection raised in Sûtra 42).

Let us then—the Bhâgavatas may say—understand by Saṅkarsha*n*a, and so on, not the individual soul, the mind, &c., but rather Lords, i.e. powerful beings distinguished by all the qualities characteristic of rulers, such as pre-eminence of knowledge and ruling capacity, strength, valour, glory.

All these are Vâsudevas free from faults, without a substratum (not sprung from pradhâna), without any imperfections. Hence the objection urged in Sûtra 42 does not apply.

Even on this interpretation of your doctrine, we reply, the 'non-exclusion of that,' i. e. the non-exclusion of the impossibility of origination, can be established.—Do you, in the first place, mean to say that the four individual Lords, Vâsudeva, and so on, have the same attributes, but do not constitute one and the same Self?—If so, you commit the fault of uselessly assuming more than one Lord, while all the work of the Lord can be done by one. Moreover, you offend thereby against your own principle, according to which there is only one real essence, viz. the holy Vâsudeva.—Or do you perhaps mean to say that from the one highest Being there spring those four forms possessing equal attributes?—In that case the objection urged in Sûtra 42 remains valid. For Saṅkarsha*n*a cannot be produced from Vâsudeva, nor Pradyumna from Saṅkarsha*n*a, nor Aniruddha from Pradyumna, since (the attributes of all of them being the same) there is no supereminence of any one of them. Observation shows that the relation of cause and effect requires some superiority on the part of the cause—as, for instance, in the case of the clay and the jar (where the cause is more extensive than the effect)—and that without such superiority the relation is simply impossible. But the followers of the Pâ*ñk*arâtra do not acknowledge any difference founded on superiority of knowledge, power, &c. between Vâsudeva and the other Lords, but simply say that they all are forms of Vâsudeva, without any special distinctions. The forms of Vâsudeva cannot properly be limited to four, as the whole world, from Brahman down to a blade of grass, is understood to be a manifestation of the supreme Being.

45. And on account of contradictions.

Moreover, manifold contradictions are met with in the Bhâgavata system, with reference to the assumption of qualities and their bearers. Eminence of knowledge and ruling capacity, strength, valour, and glory are enumerated as qualities, and then they are in some other place spoken of as Selfs, holy Vâsudevas, and so on.—Moreover, we meet with passages contradictory of the Veda. The following passage, for instance, blames the Veda, 'Not having found the highest bliss in the Vedas *S*â*nd*ilya studied this *s*âstra.'—For this reason also the Bhâgavata doctrine cannot be accepted.

TRANSLITERATION OF ORIENTAL ALPHABETS ADOPTED FOR THE TRANSLATIONS OF THE SACRED BOOKS OF THE EAST.

CONSONANTS.	MISSIONARY ALPHABET.			Sanskrit.	Zend.	Pehlevi.	Persian.	Arabic.	Hebrew.	Chinese.
	I Class.	II Class.	III Class.							
Gutturales.										
1 Tenuis	k	...	...	क	𐬐	[illegible]	ک	ك	כּ	k
2 " aspirata	kh	...	...	ख	𐬑	[illegible]	...	...	כ	kh
3 Media	g	...	...	ग	𐬔	[illegible]	گ	...	גּ	...
4 " aspirata	gh	...	...	घ	𐬖	[illegible]	...	...	ג	...
5 Gutturo-labialis	q	...	...	...	...	...	ق	ق	ק	...
6 Nasalis	ṅ (ng)	...	...	ङ	{ 𐬢 (ng) / 𐬣 (N) }	...	...	...	...	...
7 Spiritus asper	h	...	...	ह	𐬵 (𐬓 *hv*)	[illegible]	ه	ه	ה	h, hs
8 " lenis	'	...	...	...	...	...	ا	ا	א	...
9 " asper faucalis	ʻh	...	...	...	...	...	ح	ح	ח	...
10 " lenis faucalis	ʼh	...	...	...	...	...	ع	ع	ע	...
11 " asper fricatus	...	*ʻh*	...	...	...	...	خ	خ	ח	...
12 " lenis fricatus	...	*ʼh*	...	...	...	...	...	...	...	...
Gutturales modificatae (palatales, &c.)										
13 Tenuis	...	*k*	...	च	𐬗	[illegible]	چ	...	...	*k*
14 " aspirata	...	*kh*	...	छ	...	...	...	...	...	*kh*
15 Media	...	*g*	...	ज	𐬘	[illegible]	ج	ج	...	...
16 " aspirata	...	*gh*	...	झ	...	...	غ	غ	...	...
17 " Nasalis	...	*ñ*	...	ञ	...	...	...	...	...	...

CONSONANTS (continued).	MISSIONARY ALPHABET. I Class.	II Class.	III Class.	Sanskrit.	Zend.	Pehlevi.	Persian.	Arabic.	Hebrew.	Chinese.
18 Semivocalis	y	...	....	य	𐬫 (init. [illegible])	[illegible]	ي	ي	י	y
19 Spiritus asper	...	(y̔)	....	...	....	...	...	...	...	...
20 ,, lenis	...	(y̓)	....	...	....	...	...	...	...	...
21 ,, asper assibilatus	...	*ś*	....	श	𐬱	[illegible]	ش	ش	...	...
22 ,, lenis assibilatus	...	*ź*	....	...	𐬲	[illegible]	ژ	...	...	*ź*
Dentales.										
23 Tenuis	t	...	....	त	𐬙	[illegible]	ت	ت	תּ	t
24 ,, aspirata	th	...	....	थ	𐬚	...	...	...	ת	th
25 ,, assibilata	...	...	TH	...	....	...	ث	ث	...	...
26 Media	d	...	....	द	𐬛	[illegible]	د	د	דּ	...
27 ,, aspirata	dh	...	....	ध	𐬜	...	...	...	ד	...
28 ,, assibilata	...	...	DH	...	....	...	ذ	ذ	...	...
29 Nasalis	n	...	....	न	𐬥	[illegible]	ن	ن	נ	n
30 Semivocalis	l	...	....	ल	....	[illegible]	ل	ل	ל	l
31 ,, mollis 1	...	*l*	....	ळ	....	...	...	...	...	...
32 ,, mollis 2	...	...	L	...	....	...	...	...	...	...
33 Spiritus asper 1	s	...	....	स	𐬯	[illegible]	س (ث)	س	שׂ	s
34 ,, asper 2	...	...	s (ʃ)	...	....	...	...	...	ס	...
35 ,, lenis	z	...	....	...	𐬰	[illegible]	ز (ذ)	ز	ז	z
36 ,, asperrimus 1	...	...	z (ȥ)	...	....	...	ص	ص	צ	ȥ, ȥh
37 ,, asperrimus 2	...	...	ẓ (ʒ)	...	....	...	ض	...	...	...

Dentales modificatae (linguales, &c.)										
38 Tenuis	...	*t*	...	ट	...	...	ط	ط	ט	...
39 „ aspirata	...	*th*	...	ठ	...	...	ظ	ظ	...	...
40 Media	...	*d*	...	ड	[illegible]	[illegible]	...	...	...	...
41 „ aspirata	...	*dh*	...	ढ	...	...	...	ض	...	...
42 Nasalis	...	*n*	...	ण	[illegible]	...	...	...	...	...
43 Semivocalis	r	...	...	र	[illegible]	[illegible]	ر	ر	ר	...
44 „ fricata	...	*r*	...	...	...	...	...	...	...	*r*
45 „ diacritica	...	...	R	...	...	...	...	...	...	...
46 Spiritus asper	sh	...	...	ष	[illegible]	[illegible]	...	...	...	sh
47 „ lenis	zh	...	...	...	...	...	...	...	...	...
Labiales.										
48 Tenuis	p	...	...	प	[illegible]	[illegible]	پ	...	פּ	p
49 „ aspirata	ph	...	...	फ	...	...	...	...	פ	ph
50 Media	b	...	...	ब	[illegible]	[illegible]	ب	ب	בּ	...
51 „ aspirata	bh	...	...	भ	...	...	...	...	ב	...
52 Tenuissima	...	*p*	...	...	...	...	...	...	...	...
53 Nasalis	m	...	...	म	[illegible]	[illegible]	م	م	מ	m
54 Semivocalis	w	...	...	...	[illegible]	...	...	...	...	w
55 „ aspirata	hw	...	...	...	...	...	...	...	...	...
56 Spiritus asper	f	...	...	...	[illegible]	[illegible]	ف	ف	...	f
57 „ lenis	v	...	...	व	[illegible]	[illegible]	و	و	ו	...
58 Anusvâra	...	*m*	...	अं	[illegible] ã	...	...	...	...	...
59 Visarga	...	*h*	...	अः	...	...	...	...	...	...

VOWELS.	MISSIONARY ALPHABET. I Class.	II Class.	III Class.	Sanskrit.	Zend.	Pehlevi.	Persian.	Arabic.	Hebrew.	Chinese.
1 Neutralis	o	. . .	. . . .	. . .	. . . .	. . .	. . .	. . .	ֲ	ă
2 Laryngo-palatalis	ĕ	. . .	. . . .	. . .	. . . .	. . .	. . .	. . .	. . .	. . .
3 ,, labialis	ŏ	. . .	. . . .	. . .	. . . .	𐭠 fin.	. . .	. . .	. . .	. . .
4 Gutturalis brevis	a	. . .	. . . .	अ	𐬀	𐭠 init.	َ	َ	ַ	a
5 ,, longa	â	(*a*)	. . . .	आ	𐬁	𐭠	ـَا	ـَا	ָ	â
6 Palatalis brevis	i	. . .	. . . .	इ	𐬌	. . .	ِ	ِ	ִ	i
7 ,, longa	î	(*i*)	. . . .	ई	𐬍	𐭩	ـِي	ـِي	ִי	î
8 Dentalis brevis	*li*	. . .	. . . .	ऌ	. . . .	. . .	. . .	. . .	. . .	. . .
9 ,, longa	*lî*	. . .	. . . .	ॡ	. . . .	. . .	. . .	. . .	. . .	. . .
10 Lingualis brevis	*ri*	. . .	. . . .	ऋ	. . . .	. . .	. . .	. . .	. . .	. . .
11 ,, longa	*rî*	. . .	. . . .	ॠ	. . . .	. . .	. . .	. . .	. . .	. . .
12 Labialis brevis	u	. . .	. . . .	उ	𐬎	. . .	ُ	ُ	ֻ	u
13 ,, longa	û	(*u*)	. . . .	ऊ	𐬏	𐭠	ـُو	ـُو	וּ	û
14 Gutturo-palatalis brevis . . .	e	. . .	. . . .	. . .	𐬈 (e) 𐬆 (*e*)	. . .	. . .	. . .	ֶ	e
15 ,, longa . . .	ê (ai)	(*e*)	. . . .	ए	𐬉, 𐬇	𐭩	. . .	. . .	ֵ	ê
16 Diphthongus gutturo-palatalis	âi	(*ai*)	. . . .	ऐ	. . . .	. . .	ـَیْ	ـَیْ	. . .	âi
17 ,, ,,	ei (ĕi)	. . .	. . . .	. . .	. . . .	. . .	. . .	. . .	. . .	ei, êi
18 ,, ,,	oi (ŏu)	. . .	. . . .	. . .	. . . .	. . .	. . .	. . .	. . .	. . .
19 Gutturo-labialis brevis	o	. . .	. . . .	. . .	𐬊	. . .	. . .	. . .	ָ	o
20 ,, longa	ô (au)	(*o*)	. . . .	ओ	𐬋	𐭠	. . .	. . .	וֹ	. . .
21 Diphthongus gutturo-labialis	âu	(*au*)	. . . .	औ	𐬈𐬎 (*au*)	. . .	ـَوْ	ـَوْ	. . .	âu
22 ,, ,,	eu (ĕu)	. . .	. . . .	. . .	. . . .	. . .	. . .	. . .	. . .	. . .
23 ,, ,,	ou (ŏu)	. . .	. . . .	. . .	. . . .	. . .	. . .	. . .	. . .	. . .
24 Gutturalis fracta	ä	. . .	. . . .	. . .	. . . .	. . .	. . .	. . .	. . .	. . .
25 Palatalis fracta	ï	. . .	. . . .	. . .	. . . .	. . .	. . .	. . .	. . .	. . .
26 Labialis fracta	ü	. . .	. . . .	. . .	. . . .	. . .	. . .	. . .	. . .	ü
27 Gutturo-labialis fracta	ö	. . .	. . . .	. . .	. . . .	. . .	. . .	. . .	. . .	. . .

SACRED BOOKS OF THE EAST

TRANSLATED BY

VARIOUS ORIENTAL SCHOLARS

AND EDITED BY

F. MAX MÜLLER

*** *This Series is published with the sanction and co-operation of the Secretary of State for India in Council.*

REPORT presented to the ACADÉMIE DES INSCRIPTIONS, May 11, 1883, by M. ERNEST RENAN.

'M. Renan présente trois nouveaux volumes de la grande collection des "Livres sacrés de l'Orient" (Sacred Books of the East), que dirige à Oxford, avec une si vaste érudition et une critique si sûre, le savant associé de l'Académie des Inscriptions, M. Max Müller. . . . La première série de ce beau recueil, composée de 24 volumes, est presque achevée. M. Max Müller se propose d'en publier une seconde, dont l'intérêt historique et religieux ne sera pas moindre. M. Max Müller a su se procurer la collaboration des savans les plus éminens d'Europe et d'Asie. L'Université d'Oxford, que cette grande publication honore au plus haut degré, doit tenir à continuer dans les plus larges proportions une œuvre aussi philosophiquement conçue que savamment exécutée.'

EXTRACT from the QUARTERLY REVIEW.

'We rejoice to notice that a second series of these translations has been announced and has actually begun to appear. The stones, at least, out of which a stately edifice may hereafter arise, are here being brought together. Prof. Max Müller has deserved well of scientific history. Not a few minds owe to his enticing words their first attraction to this branch of study. But no work of his, not even the great edition of the Rig-Veda, can compare in importance or in usefulness with this English translation of the Sacred Books of the East, which has been devised by his foresight, successfully brought so far by his persuasive and organising power, and will, we trust, by the assistance of the distinguished scholars he has gathered round him, be carried in due time to a happy completion.'

Professor E. HARDY, Inaugural Lecture in the University of Freiburg, 1887.

'Die allgemeine vergleichende Religionswissenschaft datirt von jenem grossartigen, in seiner Art einzig dastehenden Unternehmen, zu welchem auf Anregung Max Müllers im Jahre 1874 auf dem internationalen Orientalistencongress in London der Grundstein gelegt worden war, die Übersetzung der heiligen Bücher des Ostens' (*the Sacred Books of the East*).

Oxford

AT THE CLARENDON PRESS

LONDON: HENRY FROWDE

OXFORD UNIVERSITY PRESS WAREHOUSE, AMEN CORNER, E.C.

FIRST SERIES.

VOL. I. The Upanishads.

Translated by F. MAX MÜLLER. Part I. The *Kh*ândogya-upanishad, The Talavakâra-upanishad, The Aitareya-âra*n*yaka, The Kaushîtaki-brâhma*n*a-upanishad, and The Vâgasaneyi-sa*m*hitâ-upanishad. 8vo., cloth, 10*s*. 6*d*.

The Upanishads contain the philosophy of the Veda. They have become the foundation of the later Vedânta doctrines, and indirectly of Buddhism. Schopenhauer, speaking of the Upanishads, says: 'In the whole world there is no study so beneficial and so elevating as that of the Upanishads. It has been the solace of my life, it will be the solace of my death.'

[See also Vol. XV.]

VOL. II. The Sacred Laws of the Âryas,

As taught in the Schools of Âpastamba, Gautama, Vâsish*th*a, and Baudhâyana. Translated by GEORG BÜHLER. Part I. Âpastamba and Gautama. 8vo., cloth, 10*s*. 6*d*.

The Sacred Laws of the Âryas contain the original treatises on which the Laws of Manu and other lawgivers were founded.

[See also Vol. XIV.]

VOL. III. The Sacred Books of China.

The Texts of Confucianism. Translated by JAMES LEGGE. Part I. The Shû King, The Religious Portions of the Shih King, and The Hsiâo King. 8vo., cloth, 12*s*. 6*d*.

Confucius was a collector of ancient traditions, not the founder of a new religion. As he lived in the sixth and fifth centuries B.C. his works are of unique interest for the study of Ethology.

[See also Vols. XVI, XXVII, and XXVIII.]

VOL. IV. The Zend-Avesta.

Translated by JAMES DARMESTETER. Part I. The Vendîdâd. 8vo., cloth, 10*s*. 6*d*.

The Zend-Avesta contains the relics of what was the religion of Cyrus, Darius, and Xerxes, and, but for the battle of Marathon, might have become the religion of Europe. It forms to the present day the sacred book of the Parsis, the so-called fire-worshippers. Two more volumes will complete the translation of all that is left us of Zoroaster's religion.

[See also Vols. XXIII and XXXI.]

VOL. V. Pahlavi Texts.

Translated by E. W. WEST. Part I. The Bundahis, Bahman Yast, and Shâyast lâ-shâyast. 8vo., cloth, 12s. 6d.

The Pahlavi Texts comprise the theological literature of the revival of Zoroaster's religion, beginning with the Sassanian dynasty. They are important for a study of Gnosticism.

VOLS. VI AND IX. The Qur'ân.

Parts I and II. Translated by E. H. PALMER. 8vo., cloth, 21s.

This translation, carried out according to his own peculiar views of the origin of the Qur'ân, was the last great work of E. H. Palmer, before he was murdered in Egypt.

VOL. VII. The Institutes of Vish*n*u.

Translated by JULIUS JOLLY. 8vo., cloth, 10s. 6d.

A collection of legal aphorisms, closely connected with one of the oldest Vedic schools, the Kathas, *but considerably added to in later time. Of importance for a critical study of the Laws of Manu.*

VOL. VIII. The Bhagavadgîtâ, with The Sanatsugâtîya, and The Anugîtâ.

Translated by KÂSHINÂTH TRIMBAK TELANG. 8vo., cloth, 10s. 6d.

The earliest philosophical and religious poem of India. It has been paraphrased in Arnold's 'Song Celestial.'

VOL. X. The Dhammapada,

Translated from Pâli by F. MAX MÜLLER; and

The Sutta-Nipâta,

Translated from Pâli by V. FAUSBÖLL; being Canonical Books of the Buddhists. 8vo., cloth, 10s. 6d.

The Dhammapada contains the quintessence of Buddhist morality The Sutta-Nipâta gives the authentic teaching of Buddha on some of the fundamental principles of religion.

VOL. XI. Buddhist Suttas.

Translated from Pâli by T. W. RHYS DAVIDS. 1. The Mahâparinibbâna Suttanta; 2. The Dhamma-*k*akka-ppavattana Sutta. 3. The Tevigga Suttanta; 4. The Âkaṅkheyya Sutta; 5. The *K*etokhila Sutta; 6. The Mahâ-sudassana Suttanta; 7. The Sabbâsava Sutta. 8vo., cloth, 10*s*. 6*d*.

A collection of the most important religious, moral, and philosophical discourses taken from the sacred canon of the Buddhists.

VOL. XII. The *S*atapatha-Brâhma*n*a, according to the Text of the Mâdhyandina School.

Translated by JULIUS EGGELING. Part I. Books I and II. 8vo., cloth, 12*s*. 6*d*.

A minute account of the sacrificial ceremonies of the Vedic age. It contains the earliest account of the Deluge in India.

[See also Vol. XXVI.]

VOL. XIII. Vinaya Texts.

Translated from the Pâli by T. W. RHYS DAVIDS and HERMANN OLDENBERG. Part I. The Pâtimokkha. The Mahâvagga, I–IV. 8vo., cloth, 10*s*. 6*d*.

The Vinaya Texts give for the first time a translation of the moral code of the Buddhist religion as settled in the third century B.C.

[See also Vols. XVII and XX.]

VOL. XIV. The Sacred Laws of the Âryas,

As taught in the Schools of Âpastamba, Gautama, Vâsish*th*a, and Baudhâyana. Translated by GEORG BÜHLER. Part II. Vasish*th*a and Baudhâyana. 8vo., cloth, 10*s*. 6*d*.

VOL. XV. The Upanishads.

Translated by F. MAX MÜLLER. Part II. The Ka*th*a-upanishad, The Mu*nd*aka-upanishad, The Taittirîyaka-upanishad, The B*ri*hadâra*n*yaka-upanishad, The *S*vetâ*s*vatara-upanishad, The Pra*s*ña-upanishad, and The Maitrâya*n*a-brâhma*n*a-upanishad. 8vo., cloth, 10*s*. 6*d*.

VOL. XVI. The Sacred Books of China.

The Texts of Confucianism. Translated by JAMES LEGGE. Part II. The Yî King. 8vo., cloth, 10*s*. 6*d*.

VOL. XVII. Vinaya Texts.

Translated from the Pâli by T. W. RHYS DAVIDS and HERMANN OLDENBERG. Part II. The Mahâvagga, V–X. The *K*ullavagga, I–III. 8vo., cloth, 10*s*. 6*d*.

VOL. XVIII. Pahlavi Texts.

Translated by E. W. WEST. Part II. The Dâ*d*istân-î Dînîk and The Epistles of Mânû*sk*îhar. 8vo., cloth, 12*s.* 6*d.*

VOL. XIX. The Fo-sho-hing-tsan-king.

A Life of Buddha by A*s*vaghosha Bodhisattva, translated from Sanskrit into Chinese by Dharmaraksha, A.D. 420, and from Chinese into English by SAMUEL BEAL. 8vo., cloth, 10*s.* 6*d.*

This life of Buddha was translated from Sanskrit into Chinese, A.D. 420. It contains many legends, some of which show a certain similarity to the Evangelium infantiae, etc.

VOL. XX. Vinaya Texts.

Translated from the Pâli by T. W. RHYS DAVIDS and HERMANN OLDENBERG. Part III. The *K*ullavagga, IV–XII. 8vo., cloth, 10*s.* 6*d.*

VOL. XXI. The Saddharma-pu*nd*arîka; or, The Lotus of the True Law.

Translated by H. KERN. 8vo., cloth, 12*s.* 6*d.*

'The Lotus of the true Law,' a canonical book of the Northern Buddhists, translated from Sanskrit. There is a Chinese translation of this book which was finished as early as the year 286 A.D.

VOL. XXII. *G*aina-Sûtras.

Translated from Prâkrit by HERMANN JACOBI. Part I. The Â*k*ârâṅga-Sûtra and The Kalpa-Sûtra. 8vo., cloth, 10*s.* 6*d.*

The religion of the Gainas was founded by a contemporary of Buddha. It still counts numerous adherents in India, while there are no Buddhists left in India proper.

VOL. XXIII. The Zend-Avesta.

Translated by JAMES DARMESTETER. Part II. The Sîrôzahs, Ya*s*ts, and Nyâyi*s*. 8vo., cloth, 10*s.* 6*d.*

VOL. XXIV. Pahlavi Texts.

Translated by E. W. WEST. Part III. Dînâ-î Maînôg-î Khira*d*, *S*ikand-gûmânîk Vigâr, and Sad Dar. 8vo., cloth, 10*s.* 6*d.*

SECOND SERIES.

VOL. XXV. Manu.

Translated by GEORG BÜHLER. 8vo., cloth, 21*s*.

This translation is founded on that of Sir William Jones, which has been carefully revised and corrected with the help of seven native Commentaries. An Appendix contains all the quotations from Manu which are found in the Hindu Law-books, translated for the use of the Law Courts in India. Another Appendix gives a synopsis of parallel passages from the six Dharma-sûtras, the other Sm*ri*tis, the Upanishads, the Mahâbhârata, etc.

VOL. XXVI. The *S*atapatha-Brâhma*n*a.

Translated by JULIUS EGGELING. Part II. Books III and IV. 8vo., cloth, 12*s*. 6*d*.

VOLS. XXVII AND XXVIII. The Sacred Books of China.

The Texts of Confucianism. Translated by JAMES LEGGE. Parts III and IV. The Lî *K*î, or Collection of Treatises on the Rules of Propriety, or Ceremonial Usages. 8vo., cloth, 12*s*. 6*d*. each.

VOL. XXIX. The G*ri*hya-Sûtras, Rules of Vedic Domestic Ceremonies.

Part I. *S*âṅkhâyana, Â*s*valâyana, Pâraskara, Khâdira. Translated by HERMANN OLDENBERG. 8vo., cloth, 12*s*. 6*d*.

These rules of Domestic Ceremonies describe the home life of the ancient Âryas with a completeness and accuracy unmatched in any other literature. Some of these rules have been incorporated in the ancient Law-books.

VOL. XXX. The G*ri*hya-Sûtras. Part II. [*In the Press.*]

VOL. XXXI. The Zend-Avesta.

Part III. The Yasna, Visparad, Âfrînagân, Gâhs, and Miscellaneous Fragments. Translated by L. H. MILLS. 8vo. cloth, 12*s*. 6*d*.

VOL. XXXII. Vedic Hymns.

Translated by F. MAX MÜLLER. Part I. [*In the Press.*]

VOL. XXXIII. The Minor Law-books.

Translated by JULIUS JOLLY. Part I. Nârada, B*ri*haspati. 8vo. cloth, 10*s*. 6*d*.

VOL. XXXIV. The Vedânta-Sûtras, with *S*ankara's Commentary.

Translated by G. THIBAUT. [*Immediately.*]

VOL. XXXV. Milinda. Translated by T. W. RHYS DAVIDS. [*In the Press.*]

VOL. XXXIX. The Sacred Books of China.

Tâo Teh King. Translated by JAMES LEGGE. [*In the Press.*]

VOL. XL. The Contents of the Nasks, as stated in the Eighth and Ninth Books of the Dînka*r*d. Translated by E. W. WEST.

***** The Second Series will consist of Twenty-four Volumes in all.**

SOME ORIENTAL WORKS

RECENTLY PUBLISHED BY THE CLARENDON PRESS.

A Catalogue of the Chinese Translation of the Buddhist Tripi*t*aka, *the Sacred Canon of the Buddhists in China and Japan.*

Compiled by order of the Secretary of State for India by BUNYIU NANJIO, Priest of the Temple, Eastern Hongwanzi, Japan; Member of the Royal Asiatic Society. 4to., 32*s.* 6*d.*

'An immense service rendered to Oriental scholarship.'—*Saturday Review.*

Record of Buddhistic Kingdoms; being an Account by the Chinese Monk FÂ-HIEN of his Travels in India and Ceylon (A.D. 399–414) in search of the Buddhist Books of Discipline. Translated and annotated, with a Corean recension of the Chinese Text, by JAMES LEGGE, M.A., LL.D. Crown 4to., boards, 10*s.* 6*d.*

Catalogue of the Hebrew Manuscripts in the Bodleian Library and in the College Libraries of Oxford.

Compiled by AD. NEUBAUER, M.A. *With* 40 *Facsimiles.* cloth, 5*l.* 5*s.*

Also separately:

The Catalogue. 3*l.* 13*s.* 6*d.*
The Facsimiles. 2*l.* 12*s.* 6*d.*

Anecdota Oxoniensia.

ARYAN SERIES.

Buddhist Texts from Japan. I. Vagra*kkh*edikâ; *The Diamond-Cutter.*

Edited by F. MAX MÜLLER, M.A. Small 4to., 3*s.* 6*d.*

One of the most famous metaphysical treatises of the Mahâyâna Buddhists.

Buddhist Texts from Japan. II. Sukhâvatî-Vyûha: *Description of Sukhâvatî, the Land of Bliss.*

Edited by F. MAX MÜLLER, M.A., and BUNYIU NANJIO. With two Appendices: (1) Text and Translation of Saṅghavarman's Chinese Version of the Poetical Portions of the Sukhâvatî-Vyûha; (2) Sanskrit Text of the Smaller Sukhâvatî-Vyûha. Small 4to., 7*s.* 6*d.*

The *editio princeps* of the Sacred Book of one of the largest and most influential sects of Buddhism, numbering more than ten millions of followers in Japan alone.

Buddhist Texts from Japan. III. *The Ancient Palm-Leaves containing the* Pragñâ-Pâramitâ-H*ri*daya-Sûtra *and the* Ushnîsha-Vigaya-Dhâra*n*î.

Edited by F. MAX MÜLLER, M.A., and BUNYIU NANJIO, M.A. With an Appendix by G. BÜHLER, C.I.E. With many Plates. Small 4to., 10*s.*

Contains facsimiles of the oldest Sanskrit MS. at present known.

Dharma-Sa*m*graha, *an Ancient Collection of Buddhist Technical Terms.*

Prepared for publication by KENJIU KASAWARA, a Buddhist Priest from Japan, and, after his death, edited by F. MAX MÜLLER and H. WENZEL. Small 4to., 7*s.* 6*d.*

Kâtâyana's Sarvânukrama*n*î of the *Ri*gveda.

With Extracts from Sha*d*guru*s*ishya's Commentary entitled Vedârthadîpikâ. Edited by A. A. MACDONELL, M.A., Ph.D. 16*s.*

Oxford

AT THE CLARENDON PRESS

LONDON: HENRY FROWDE

OXFORD UNIVERSITY PRESS WAREHOUSE, AMEN CORNER, E.C.